IN LETTERS OF FIRE

Thirteenth Regiment
West Virginia Infantry Volunteers

HEIDI C. EADS JONES, M.A.
EDITOR AND COMPILER

ISBN: 978-1-955622-02-8 (hardcover)
978-1-955622-01-1 (paperback)

Contact the author by mailing coorespondence to:

Heidi C. Eads Jones
heidi.eads.jones@gmail.com
10375 Paradise Boulevard
Treasure Island, FL 33706

Published by

Fideli Publishing, Inc.
119 W. Morgan St.
Martinsville, IN 46151

www.FideliPublishing.com

Some Opening Words
and Acknowledgments

Well 'Comp,' you and I quit business at Lynchburg, but the boys got into it in the valley under Sheridan. I have seen but very little said in the papers about the 13th Regt. But it is often said, and it has been my experience, that the bravest and those who did the most, say the least. This may be the case with the 13th W.Va.

—Fred Ohlinger,
Private Company D 13th West Virginia Volunteer Infantry Regiment to the "Editor of the Pomeroy, Ohio *Leader*", dated "Haines City, Florida, March 9, 1913", "Fred and 'Comp' Get in Touch After Almost 50 Years," Pomeroy, Ohio *Leader* No. 342, pp. 127-128, courtesy of Terry Lowery.

How much can be told 150 years later about a regiment of men that "say the least"? Apparently, quite a bit. Were they among the bravest as supposed by Fred Ohlinger? Here follows the story of a regiment with tremendous grit and resilience — "the gamest set of fellows"— who looked to themselves and time and again stood their ground with unflinching courage; who sacrificed, loved freedom and their country. It is a "simple story" that perhaps now more than ever, needs telling and bears re-telling, that it may "be engraved upon the hearts of the American people in letters of fire."

Many people generously shared their time, talent, research, expertise, enthusiasm and encouragement for this project, and without them it would never have come to be. Finding out about the "Bloody 13th," who they were and what they did, became pretext for adventure, travel through beautiful country and meeting marvelous people and I would not have missed a moment of it. I am humbled and supremely grateful for the opportunity and for all of the help, received over a period of some 20 years in pressing forward this project. I would like to thank all of my family (many now 'beyond the veil'), most especially my husband, Bruce, and son, Donald, for going with me to hunt up old camps and battlegrounds in East and West Virginia—rollicking trips in the heat and dust of Virginia summers armed with maps (old and new); James E. Taylor's drawings; and various verbal descriptions of battles and fields and for, as a general rule, affording me, 'lo, these many years, time and opportunity to collect research and to write. Heartfelt thanks to my husband for his encouragement and invaluable input. Librarians and archivists from Kansas to the eastern seaboard made available important materials and my gratitude goes out to them, each and all. Special thanks to Terry Lowery with the Charleston Archives and History Library for all of his help; to Mike Musick at the National Archives; Michael Greenburg at the Bethesda Medical History Library; Darl Stephenson; Larry Strayer; Dr. Richard Summers at Carlisle Barracks Army History Library; Richard Hunt; Elijah Myers and to Robin Surface for her creative work, candor and expertise in guiding the publication of this volume.

Table of Contents

In Letters of Fire

A number of contemporary speakers and writers commented upon the particular and often precarious position of Union volunteers in Western Virginia, of the extreme nature of their service, their devotion and the extraordinary sacrifices made by them in the early months of the Rebellion. Here are two examples. W.H.H. Flick, Department Commander of the Department of West Virginia, G.A.R. speaking at the Department's 2nd Annual Encampment held at Parkersburg, West Virginia, March 20, 1884 noted the following:

> In the North how easy it was for a young man to enter the service of his country! He was born along on the wave of popular excitement. Public sentiment made the raw recruit a hero. — The rostrum, the bench, the bar and the pulpit praised and applauded him. The smiles of youth and beauty, and the blessings of the aged and venerable were showered upon him like rain. How well I remember the departure of my own regiment for the front — the crowded streets, the cheering multitudes, the streaming banners and the waving hankerchiefs! How proudly we stepped! What heroes we were in our own estimation! And how all this changed when we crossed Mason and Dixon's line. [...]
>
> The silent and gloomy streets through which we then marched, the closed shutters, the sullen looks of the few remaining men and the open and bitter hostility of the women! Then for the first time did we fully realize that we had entered upon a struggle which would be long, fierce and bloody. With you it was different. From the first you knew all this and more, you were citizens of the section which was to be the theater of the war. In opposition to you was arrayed the wealth of your State, a violent public sentiment and your State officials, the threats of the bench, the eloquence of the bar, and thunders of the pulpit, and even in many instances you were threatened by the hands of your nearest relatives. Yet with [a pure and true devotion] you took your muskets, and in behalf

of the Union of these States, dashed into the thickest of the fight. There is a courage vastly superior to the courage which enables a soldier to die bravely on the field of battle, and that is courage to stand by ones convictions of right upon all circumstances and in spite of all danger. That courage was exhibited by you and your Comrades from the Southland.

—W.H.H. Flick,
Department Commander, "Address of Department Commander" in *Proceedings of the 2nd Annual Encampment of the Department of West Virginia G.A.R. held at Parkersburg, West Virginia March 20, 1884*, Goulden & Reilly, 1884, p. 4.

Major General George Crook addressing a re-union of the Army of West Virginia in 1884 spoke the following:

It is good that we should revive the feelings of devotion to our great country, its laws, its integrity, its grandeur, which strengthened us in the darkest hour of our terrific struggle, and made us face unflinchingly and without murmur,—cold and hunger, sickness, danger and death, that the Union—One and Indivisible, should not perish from the face of the Earth. [...] You men of West Va., [...] I know your sacrifices, I know of the homes, the wives and children whom the call of your country compelled you to leave. Few soldiers in other armies had the same experiences to endure, or the same sacrifices to make. The Mountains of West Virginia furnished as a class the purest patriots in the army. They fought for love of freedom, for love of country.

The Mountaineer is always free.

The time will come when your simple story of love of country and devotion to principle shall be engraved upon the hearts of the American people in letters of fire [...].

—Maj. Gen. George Crook,
U.S. Army, Address at the re-union of the Army of West Virginia, at Cumberland, Maryland, September 1884, pp. 1-2.

Heidi C. Eads-Jones, M.A.
Martinsville, Indiana, in the 157th year since the regiment was mustered in.

Abbreviations

A.C. or C.	Army Corps
A.G.O.	Adjutant General's Office
A.N.V. or A.N. Va.	Army of Northern Virginia
Adj. or Adj. Gen.	Adjutant General
anon.	anonymous
Apr.	April
Arch.	Archives
Art.	Artillery
Asst. Adj. Gen.	Assistant Adjutant General
b.	born
Brig. Gen.	Brigadier General
C.H.	Court House
C.S.A.	Confederate States of America (the Confederacy)
ca.	circa or about
Capt.	Captain
Cav.	Cavalry
cmdg.	commanding
Co.	company or county
Col.	Colonel
Coll.	Collection
Comm.	commissioned
comp.	compiler
Corpl.	Corporal
cos.	companies
Dept. of W. Va.	Department of West Virginia
Dist.	District
Div.	Division
ed.	editor
Fr.	French language

Gen.	General field officer or General Orders
Gov.	Governor
HdQtrs. or Hdqtrs.	Head Quarters or Headquarters
i.e. or id.est.	that is
IHS	Indiana Historical Society, Indianapolis
illeg.	illegible
Inf. or Inftry.	Infantry
infra.	below
Lieut. Col.	Lieutenant Colonel
Maj. Gen.	Major General
Pub. Lib.	Public Library
M.E.	Methodist Episcopal Church
micro.	microfilm
Misc.	Miscellaneous
Mtn. Dept.	Mountain Department
n.d.	no date
n.p or n.pp.	no page number[s]
NARA	National Archives and Records Administration, Washington D.C.
No.	Number
O.C.	o'clock
O.R.	Official Records of the War of the Rebellion
OHS	Ohio Historical Society, Ohio Historical Center, Columbus
orig. manu./orig. pub.	original manuscript or publication
O.V.I.	Ohio Volunteer Infantry
p. or pp.	page or pages
pseud.	pseudonym, nom de plum or pen name
Pt.	Part
Pt. Pleasant	Point Pleasant
Reg. or Regt.	Regiment
Rev.	Reverend
RG	Record Group
Sec.	Secretary
Ser.	Series
Sergt.	Sergeant
Spec.	Special (as in Special Orders)
Supp. O.R.	Supplement to the Official Records of the War of the Rebellion
trans.	transcription
U.S. or U.S.A	United States of America (the Union)
Unpub.	Unpublished

Uncat.	Uncatalogued
V.V.I.	Virginia Volunteer Infantry
Va.	Virginia
Vet.	Veteran
Vol.	Volume
Vols.	Volunteers
W.Va.	West Virginia
WVSA	West Virginia State Archives, Charleston
WVU	West Virginia University, Morgantown

IN LETTERS OF FIRE

Thirteenth Regiment
West Virginia Infantry Volunteers

"... the gamest set of fellows ..."

HEIDI C. EADS JONES, M.A.
EDITOR AND COMPILER

Before the War and Including 1862

"Before the war the principal amusement[s] for the boys were fighting, pitching quoits [tossing horseshoes at a spike in the ground] and footracing."

—John L. Mason
to the *State Gazette*, "A Reminiscence. West Columbia of a Half Century Ago Contrasted With the West Columbia of Today. Second Letter," *State Gazette*, Point Pleasant, W.Va., June 24, 1909 in *History of Mason County, W.Va.* Accession # 203668, Cabell County Public Library, Huntington, West Virginia.

The "ordeal [...] as it is to solve, in no small degree,
[is] man's *capacity fort self-government!*
[...] 'Who would be a traitor knave?
Who would fill a coward's grave?
Who so base as be a slave?
Let HIM — turn and flee!'"

—"WEST VIRGINIA"
to the Ironton *Register*, Oct. 6, 1863, p. 2.

"[...] if the Federal army attempted to invade the Kanawha Valley, they would have to march over the dead body of every Union man in the Kanawha Valley before they reached Charleston."

—*Kanawha Republican*, 1861
as quoted in the Point Pleasant *Weekly Register*,
Nov. 3, 1864, p.3.

The overwhelming majority of people in the 1860s, in both North and South, were conservatives: fiscal and social conservatives. The 1830s, '40s and '50s had been a period of westward expansion and the issue of whether to permit the extension of slavery into new States compelled a largely conservative population to deal with questions of sovereignty and national identity; how broad the individual's right of self-determination and what of the individual's relationship to the government both Federal and State? The institution of American slavery, a tainted thing that had really nothing but the property rights argument to support it, was a can that had long been kicked down the road by politicians but an impasse was reached, and the struggle to deal with questions of sovereignty rent the nation and the fabric of American society.

The Atlantic trade in slaves hit a peak in the 1780s but after the turn of the century began to decline. Britain and the United States had abolished the slave trade in 1807 and in 1833, Britain passed an act directing the gradual abolishing of slavery in all her territories and colonies. Other European nations followed suit. The transition effected by passage of anti-slavery laws abroad was hardly a blip on the United States radar. That on this side of the Atlantic, terrible Civil War had to be fought to the utter exhaustion of one side to settle the matter, when elsewhere slavery had been ended under the weight of its own economic inefficiency, if not for moral reasons, is a strange thing for a nation founded upon the principles that "[a]ll men are born equally free and independent and have certain inherent natural rights" of which they cannot be "deprived nor divested of," namely "the enjoyment of liberty," the means of earning a livelihood, acquisition and ownership of property, "and happiness."[1]

In the Virginia counties west of the Alleghenies and in areas of the "Old Dominion" where the Quaker Church had exerted an influence, it had long been recognized that the institution of slavery was counter-productive to efficient utilization of resources, economic prosperity and community development. It was especially ruinous to the white trade and laboring class trying to eke out a living in competition with slave labor, which could be had for hire more cheaply and according to one view, required far less supervision. Neither were immigrants keen to settle where slave labor was widely used.[2] In addition, slavery was protected by the laws of the land, by the arbitrary "three-fifths person" standard for purposes of taxation and voting. The Great Compromise setting a slave at just three-fifths of a person was passed at the 1787 United States Constitutional Convention. It established how slaves would be counted for apportionment purposes, that is, for representation in Congress, but it also cut in favor of slave owners for purposes of taxation. The Compromise was not only critical to ratification of the new national Constitution for the loose confederation of independent States then comprising the United States of America, but it allowed the slave-holding interest to largely dominate the U.S. government until Lincoln took office in 1861. In Western Virginia, the State "born of the storm," the slave-holding interest controlled until the northwestern counties seceded from Virginia. Just as the Virginia Treason Act was being read in court houses in the western counties making it treasonable to speak in favor of the Union,[3] a new state government was set up by an audacious group of individuals over a two week period in June 1861, at what is known as the 2ⁿᵈ Wheeling Convention. This reorganization of the western counties upon a basis loyal to the Northern Union flew in the face of both the mother state and in the face of the entire Southern Confederacy. It was a terrible embarrassment to Eastern Virginia and Richmond sought by hook or crook to bring the wayward West to heel. Former governor of Virginia, then Confederate Brigadier General Henry A. Wise at once pronounced the resolutions of the 2nd Wheeling Convention of June 13ᵗʰ as outright treason, the people of the counties supporting it to be put down and a considerable number of troops were promptly marshalled and advanced into the Kanawha Valley.⁴ Again, in Spring of 1862, another concerted attempt was made to coerce the loyal counties in the form of the "Partisan Ranger Acts."

In the West it was a dangerous business to be *for* formation of the new State in any public capacity. All civil and military service that was not pro-South invited severe reprisal. This posture made targets not only of those who attended and spoke at community meetings, who served on committees of safety, as county delegates, as court justices, sheriffs, tax collectors, militiamen and volunteers in the Union army regiments being recruited, but their families and property became targets as well. William W. Harper, a Minister of the Methodist Evangelical Church and officer in the 13ᵗʰ Virginia/West Virginia Infantry Regiment writing in favor of the New State movement had this to say about "Eastern despotism:"

> If you want the world to know that you are at heart a rebel and deeply in sympathy with treason. If you want to do a kind act for the Southern Confederacy, if you want to please such men as Jeff Davis, Rhett, Yancey, Cobb, Keit, Wise, Letcher, Toombs, Pryor. Wigfall, &c., if you want to fill all rebeldom with shouts of joy over the defeat of this great and noble project, and one vote alone will do it. Then sir, you had better cast your vote against the new State.
>
> If you want to worse than throw away the vast sums of money already expended by the loyal people of West Virginia, in their honest struggles to shake off the yoke, that Eastern despotism has placed upon them. Then vote against a new State.
>
> If you want to thwart and render null and void all our efforts hitherto to build up for ourselves and our children, a government at once, grand and glorious and which will secure to all the rights of freemen. Then vote against the new State.
>
> If you want to heap upon the people of West Virginia a burthen of taxation to help pay the expenses of this Southern rebellion, that will grind you and them down for twenty generations to come,

and perhaps not one single dollar [go] in the benefit of those from whom it has been extorted. Then vote against a new State.

If you want to establish a government under which no man can exercise the right of suffrage, unless he is worth $5,000 or has a few negroes, and where all the power is in the hands of an aristocracy.[5] Then vote against a new State.

If you want to establish permanently and forever the system of human slavery. If you want to set up a slave market where human beings are sold like horses and mules and where fathers will sell their own offspring, and under the cover of which is perpetrated crimes so heinous and revolting, that even a devil might shudder to commit them, and which ignores and puts to blush, every sentiment and principle of the christian religion. Then we say vote against the new State.[6]

While many Southern Democrats viewed the conflict as merely a political one, an opportunity for "Black abolitionist Republicans" to reduce the political dominance of the Democratic South, and indeed it was that as well, it is probably no stretch to say that all realized that slavery was at bottom the cause of the differences between Northerners, Southerners, Eastern and Western Virginians, in families and between the sexes. Virginia churches such as the Methodist Episcopal Churches North and South divided over the morality and legality of enslaving a people and the so-called "mulattoes" that populated many if not all Southern plantations served as evidence to wives, sisters, daughters and neighbors that their menfolk had a yen for their black slave-women. For the conservative and by-and-large religious population as then comprised the United States, slavery, though tolerated, was uncomfortable. It was a tainted thing that had to be dressed up under names such as "our peculiar institution," sanitized and politicized under the argument of "States' rights." To quote Barbara Holland from her excellent article on the 18th and 19th century penchant for dueling: "Indeed the Civil War itself, and the Southern response to it, sometimes seems more an affair of honor than a war, involving what might be called collective personal pride more than common sense or public advantage."[7] Certainly, those who fought bravely for the Southern Confederacy deserved a better cause than to keep enslavement of a race on the table as an option; and it would have been far better for all of us, if the cause had never been argued under the rubric of "States' rights". All of this of course is moot but for the shudder of consequences still felt today as a result of it and for the necessity of laying some historical groundwork as we take up consideration of how the 13th West Virginia came to be needed, recruited and organized.

On April 13ᵗʰ, 1861, Fort Sumter fell. April 17ᵗʰ, the Virginia State legislature convened at Richmond in irregular session and voted to secede from the Union. On May 23ʳᵈ, 1861, voters in the State of Virginia voted on two issues: secession and an amendment to the State Constitution that would lift the State limitation on slaves held as property for purposes of taxation. 13ᵗʰ West Virginia companies were recruited predominantly from the northwestern Virginia counties of Mason, Cabell, Wayne, Jackson, Putnam, and Kanawha. Results for these two referenda from these counties where voting records survive (taking also into account the very real possibility of tampering and destruction of records) indicate a solid majority against secession: Mason County, 119 for secession 1841 against; Cabell County, 232 for secession 882 against; Wayne County, 204 for secession and 427 against; Kanawha County, 520 for secession and 1697 against; Putnam County, 216 for and 695 against; and records of the Jackson County vote not found.[8]

Dan Rice, from Erie County, Pennsylvania, an ardent advocate for preservation of the Union had been hard at work for "the last six months" speaking out against secession and he was at the time of May 23ʳᵈ referendum in Western Virginia "giving full scope to his patriotism and eloquence." On Election Day, he visited several of his old friends in Mason City,[9] decried secession and commended Mason City and Mason County "citizens and Volunteers" for voting against secession.[10] Rice spoke passionately to citizens and soldiers and a description of the occasion and transcription of his speech was recorded in Gibbs' history of Mason City:

> The soldiers and citizens of [Mason City] aware of the fact, [that Rice was in town] called all hands to muster, waited on Dan, and through a committee, requested him to address them on the political aspect of the present crisis. He, though somewhat reluctant, acquiesced, mounted the rostrum rudely and hurriedly prepared amid the rolling of the drum, the shrieking of the fife, the waving of the National Emblem, the cheers of the men, and the smiles of ladies, and then proceeded to grant their request. [A synopsis of a part of his speech is the following:]
>
> Fellow-citizens and Volunteers of Mason City:
>
> During the past few weeks my ears have been shocked by the cries of secession, uttered by those whom I had always loved with heartfelt tenderness—men who were my friends in the dark days of tribulation—men who but a year or two ago would have struck to earth as a dastard he who would have dared to sow in this happy land the seed of discord. I believe that in the seceding States already the throes of the fetus of monarchy, the coming shadow of discord, the approaching footsteps of the dragon dissolution, have completely

paralyzed them.[11] Surely Satan has been loosed for a season, and his fiery breath is drying up the wells of loyalty. Would there were more men in the forum and tripod South like Parson Brownlow and Andrew Johnson, of Tennessee, who dare write their thoughts and are not afraid to speak them.[12] But exclusive power and coercion rule, and well-meaning men have bowed their necks to receive the yoke of oppression, and unlike you, have lacked the moral courage to step forth and in a proud tone exclaim to the leaders of the rebellion, This far shalt thou go and no farther. Yes, my fellow citizens, whether to the manor born, or children of the United States by adoption, you have nobly done your work to-day and indelibly stamped upon the historical pages of this country acts that will not cause your posterity to blush when future time shall point them to the record. This evening as the sun hies him to his golden couch, and your cannon proclaims the Union men's triumph, the hills and valleys of your sister State, Ohio, will reverberate with joy, and before old Sol shall have risen, the lightning conductor, that fleet courier, the telegraph will make the whole country aware, that the fires of liberty have not resolved themselves into ashes, nor have the favored altars set up by our patriotic sires of '76 been overturned. (Cheers) [...]

I assure you, men in arms, that you are not to meet ordinary men in the coming conflict. The Southern soldiers are not cowards, although their leaders are demagogues and speculators. [...] You wish the banner of independence to stand where our forefathers planted it, they wish to flaunt a foreign rag in its stead. Never let this be done, and although the field of carnage may be more deeply reddened by your blood, remember the escutcheon of your country must never be stained by the rapacious hand of speculation. [...].[13]

Ultimately of course, while Mason County voted against secession in the referendum of May 23rd, the ordinance was in short order pronounced carried and ratified by a majority of Virginians. This placed the pro-Union people of Western Virginia in a "peculiar position" to quote language from a speech made by (then "Mr.") Arthur Boreman to the convention of pro-Union delegates assembled at Wheeling in the critical days after the results of the Statewide vote became known. Boreman simply and elegantly explained their "peculiar position:"

[W]e are awakened by the astounding announcement in one section of our country that we have no government worthy of our support, and the announcement is at once accompanied by a rebellion to throw off this government under which we have been so long happy and prosperous, and the inauguration of a system such as never would have been countenanced by our fathers. We of Western Virginia are asked to concur in this action. We are placed in a peculiar position. The Convention at Richmond, so far as they have power, have by the passage of an Ordinance of Secession withdrawn us from the Union of our fathers. They submitted their action to a vote of the people, as they proclaimed it, but in a way that made that vote a mockery. The vote in form has ratified the Ordinance of Secession—thus in the estimation of that Convention withdrawing us from the United States of America. Under these circumstances Western Virginia is placed in a peculiar position.

—Arthur [I.] Boreman,
to the assembly of delegates gathered at the Wheeling Convention,
[West] Virginia, June 1861. In Virgil A. Lewis, *History of West
Virginia. In Two Parts*, Philadelphia: Hubbard Brothers, Publishers,
1889, p. 409.

Seizing the Reins

"We were thrown into the vortex of rebellion by the passage of the ordinance of secession by force of arms, and against the wishes of an overwhelming majority of the legal voters. Troops were sent from East Virginia to excite the people to arms and overawe the patriotic masses. Sensation tales were related,—how the Northern vandals were advancing, burning and plundering private property, and driving innocent women and children to the mountains, when the tread of the federal foot had not been heard east of the Ohio. By glaring and unsurpassed falsities a rebel force was organized. Business was suspended—in fact, the whole region was in a *furor* of excitement. Projects of vital importance to the public were necessarily abandoned, and private enterprises fearfully crippled. As soon as Federal protection was given, the work of formation of a new State commenced."

—A VETERAN,
"West Virginia," Wheeling *Daily Intelligencer,*
January 7, 1865, p. 1.

"Speaking of duels, I think I could wipe out dishonor by crippling the other man, but I don't see how I could do it by letting him cripple me."
—Mark Twain

"The fighting in Western Virginia was vigorous from the start in 1861 and the fighting continued there until the closing months of the war in 1865. More than 500 military events at over 250 different places, gives some idea of the extent of the war in West Virginia."

—Allen Jones,
"Military Events in West Virginia During the Civil War, 1861-
1865," *West Va. History,* pp. 39-52.

Virginia's secession from the Union the previous year had thrown the Northwestern part of the State into chaos. At first there was shock and disbelief as the State joined the Southern confederation. Many offices civic and military were held by Secessionists and they lost no time in seizing the initiative in the name of defending "The Old Dominion" and bringing the rest of the State to heel.[14] Immediately upon learning that the Richmond legislature had by vote adopted the secession ordinance, Governor John Letcher mobilized the Virginia militia (the standing army of the State comprised of all able-bodied men whose service was mandated and directed pursuant to the Militia Acts of 1791 and '92). Letcher ordered seizure of State arsenals and Virginia State militia companies were called up and committed to service in the army of the Confederate States. Harper's Ferry and Norfolk arsenals were seized and one presumes that county arsenals were also subject to seizure, however outmoded or deficient these caches may have been. Little is known about what happened to county arsenals in Western Virginia. We know only that there *should* have been arms, powder and lead. The Federal Militia Act of 1792 directed that militiamen east of the mountains be armed with muskets and that militia west of the mountains were required to be armed with rifles. Further, in 1798 the Virginia General Assembly enacted supplementary laws directing "that each militiaman in the counties on the western waters should always keep ready in addition to his musket or rifle, a half pound of powder and one pound of lead" (*Hening's Virginia "Statutes at Large"*). What happened to weapons in the western part of the State is perhaps best expressed in the verse of "A Song" which appeared in the Morgantown *Post*:

> *We too, have felt the tyrants tread*
> *Indeed we were alarmed*
> *When usurped power, in Richmond halls,*
> *Had left us without arms.*[15]

More is known about the militia companies. When the war broke out in 1861, the Virginia militia consisted of 198 regiments of the line, 92 troops of cavalry, 26 companies of artillery, 111 companies of light infantry and 113 companies of riflemen. This army was called upon for short terms of duty in 1861 by Governor Letcher and by President Lincoln (under the act of March 6th, 1861) but events set in motion by the Virginia Legislature's adoption of the Secession Ordinance in April of 1861 and Richmond's adoption of an ordinance on July 1st, 1861 authorizing Governor Letcher to draft men from the militia to fill any insufficiency in the Virginia quota required by the Confederate States, brought about a dissolution of the Virginia Militia in the West as it had been known under the militia acts of the 1790s.[16] Instead, the militia reorganized by county, based on loyalty to the Union. These companies in turn formed a nucleus for Union regiments recruited in 1861 and '62, such as the 13th West Virginia.[17]

In the Northwestern part of the state, civil disintegration was the order of the day, business ground to a halt. Private citizens opposed to secession and not wishing to be dragged off into the Confederacy set about restoring the civil and military framework upon a basis loyal to the Northern Union. It took no small amount of courage and nerve to fly in the face of the rising tide. Pro-Southern recruiters, "terror men" and bushwhackers sought to enforce military service in Southern armies and bring the loyal population to heel by undermining and disrupting anti-secessionist/pro-Union efforts to regroup and re-establish local government and military on a loyal footing.

Immediately, Unionists came to understand that fighting would be necessary and many took to the field singly and in squads to defend their families, property, and neighborhoods.[18] Then, a call went out from loyal Western Virginia counties to Washington to send arms and troops. May 13th, 1861, General George B. McClellan assumed command of the military district (the Department of the Ohio) and national troops crossed into Virginia. McClellan was effective on the field and Southern troops and agitators were driven beyond the mountains or into submission.

Captain R.B. Wilson, a soldier from Ohio, who served with what became the Kanawha Division was among those first troops in blue sent in with McClellan to answer Western Virginia's first call for help in fighting "the Rebels." After the war, he set down his war experiences and perceptions of it. In the following excerpt, he outlined the problems of conducting a campaign in the "great natural fortress" that was West Virginia and described operations of the 1861 campaign which quieted the country there to such an extent that it was believed that Western Virginia had been effectively taken out of the military theater, a misapprehension which allowed a slacking off in recruitment and a lull in organization of Western Virginia regiments for the Union (and thus retarded military preparedness) which resulted in fresh alarms when Secessionists re-doubled efforts to retake the State in 1862. Wilson wrote:

> It is difficult to convey to the mind of the reader who is not familiar with it a comprehensive idea of the vast maze of mountains, without range or system or apparent trend, that occupies the entire territory embraced within it. From the headwaters of the Kanawha, diverging eastward to the points of the compass, a few main roads lead out over the intervening mountains to and across the Alleghany and Blue Ridge ranges through seemingly interminable ascents and descents and intricate windings that box the compass and bewilder the traveler. From these main roads by-roads lead off into the mountains, and from these again bridle-paths that penetrate the deep glens and profound solitudes only the mountaineers know where. Out of these latter came the guerrilla and bushwhacker, whose depredations required the sleepless vigilance of the soldiers, and into

them they disappeared beyond hope of discovery when hunted to their haunts and homes.

Into this great natural fortress, then occupied and held by the Confederate forces of Lee, Garnett, Floyd, and Wise, in the early Summer of 1861 entered the little armies of Gens. McClellan and Cox—the former by the Little Kanawha in June, and the latter by the Great Kanawha early in July,—composed chiefly of the first organized Ohio reg[imen]ts. They at once began active hostilities, and each had successful engagements with the enemy before the first battle of Bull Run was fought in the East. Before the 1st of August Wise had been driven back to Sewell Mountain by Cox, and Garnett and Lee to Cheat Mountain by McClellan; only Floyd was left on the Gauley. The successful issue of this campaign led to McClellan being called to the command of the Army of the Potomac, and Rosecrans succeeded him in command of the department.

Reinforced by a part of Cox's command, about the 1st of Sept., Rosecrans moved southeastward from Weston, and attacked Floyd in his fortified camp at Carnifax Ferry. Floyd hastily retreated in the night to Sewell M[oun]t[ai]n, where he joined Wise, Garnett, and Lee. Rosecrans followed and Cox advanced from Gauley Bridge, and the combined forces of both armies were confronting each other on Sewell Mountain. Floyd crossed over New River to Cotton Mountain and attacked the camp at Gauley Bridge. A brigade sent to his rear caused him to make a precipitate retreat to Princeton, leaving the road strewn with his wagons and camp equipage. Lee's forces then retreated to Lewisburg, and the first campaign in West Virginia was ended with practically the whole of its territory west of the Alleghenies in possession of the Union forces.[19]

"Frank H." Adjutant of the 1st West Virginia Veteran Infantry also wrote a retrospective recalling the hazards of organizing themselves in the early days of the conflict. Veterans of the 5th and 9th West Virginia Infantry Regiments who re-enlisted when their terms of service had expired were consolidated on November 9th, 1864, to form the 1st Veteran Regiment. In recalling the military record of both regiments he began:

> The former old regiments were organized seven miles from each other [both in 1861, the 5th at Ceredo and the 9th at Guyandotte, now a part of Huntington]—about the time Jenkins' and Clarkson's

notorious raid on Guyandotte; in the days when Jeff. Davis said Beauregard should in a few weeks, take Washington, sack and burn Philadelphia and winter in New York.

Those who know the trials of the loyal people of Virginia, alone can realize the difficulties in the progress of the organization of Union regiments on that then hostile territory. For the humble Union man or simple hearted boy then to resist the blandishments and threats of powerful, informed and wealthy neighbors, and be 'a Union man' and a 'U.S. Soldier,' was to bring down on themselves and families derision, abuse and insult, and not seldom, robbing, plundering and murder.

Posterity, and the soldiers whose homes are in peaceful States, will call to mind that the West Virginia soldier often dared not accept a furlough to visit his home, for fear of being waylaid and shot or captured by his old neighbors.

Though dispersed, captured and murdered, and with their loyal fellow-citizens made to taste 'the sweets' of Libby whenever they were found organizing–they with other Virginia soldiers have, in spite of these discouragements at home and abroad, clung to the old flag with a simplicity and tenacity that has called forth the admiration of their various commanding Generals.

Before learning the manual of arms they were inducted into the war in West Virginia, under Generals Rosecrans and Cox.[20]

On the upside, the successful 1861 campaign in Western Virginia and the small number of regiments left to occupy at key posts (such as Point Pleasant, Charleston and Gauley Bridge) bought time for the loyal population to find their footing, their voice and steadied the Union cause in the Western part of the State. The reins of power had been seized and held by delegates sent from the Western counties to the Wheeling Conventions of summer 1861. They successfully set up what was termed the "Restored" or "Provisional State Government" which pledged loyalty to the Union. This was done without funds or military might to back it up. Virginia had seceded from the Union and the West would secede, not from the Union but from Virginia and form its own State. Organization of the New State comprised of the counties west of the Alleghenies proceeded apace and West Virginia militia companies were to some extent re-organized on a loyal footing.

Having failed to secure Western Virginia for the Confederacy with her armies, rebel guerrilla bands were being organized with "all the men that could be spared" for the purpose of targeting loyal citizens over the winter (usually the off season for military campaigning). "Accounts from different parts of Western Virginia indicate that the infamous guerrilla warfare, instead of being at an end, is just commencing. There is no doubt that the rebels are organizing these bands daily, and sending them out to plunder and murder loyal citizens," began an article in the *Wheeling Intelligencer*.

> In some of the counties where there are no military forces, there is hardly a good horse left. Harrison county alone has lost at least one hundred horses within the past five weeks, and when the bands which are now organizing within the rebel lines are turned loose upon us, there will be no end to the plundering and killing which will follow. A prominent gentleman, with whom we conversed on Saturday, is of the opinion that the rebels, having failed to make any headway in the West with their armies, have decided to organize into guerrillas bands all the men they can spare, with a view of spending the winter in ravaging the country.[21]

Governor Pierpont was also not idle in issuing commissions to get up small companies of independent scouts to counter new depredations in the West. Consider the following notice placed by one "Capt. Bill Turner" appealing to Union men on both sides of the Ohio.

SNAKE HUNTERS!"

Capt. Bill Turner wants One Hundred Snake Hunters!

> GOVERNOR PIERPONT COMMISSIONED me, December 1, 1861, as Captain of Independent Scouts, in the service and pay of the United States, for three years—to Scout in Western Virginia, or where needed. I want persons who have been exiled by the rebels from their homes. If you refuse, you are not worthy of the name or home of a Virginian. I know a number of Ohioans who are just the kind of men I want—brave, energetic men. Fall in! I want men who are *men*; who will fight to the death; who hate rebels worse than snakes; who have "to do and dare to" in them. Every man whether private or Captain, will be expected to do his duty. [...][22]

The above notwithstanding, some quiet prevailed during the winter of '61—a function of the proximity of military presence. With the new year, however, came a new series of calamitous and catalyzing events to the Union cause and to denizens of the border counties of Western Virginia. Virginia and the Confederate States both passed Partisan Ranger Acts. A war of predation, plunder, detention and murder of private citizens again sparked and spiked in the West after passage of the Ranger acts.[23]

Western Virginians rallied and rose to the occasion. In the midst of this new threat a new sense of purpose and commitment to winning a struggle that bore every earmark of being a war of extermination emerged. That remarkable American will to be free, self-determine and self-govern according to one's own conscience asserted itself and with it a cautious optimism floated to the surface and conjoined to bring about a new force and focus. Public confidence in the Provisional State government rose; the courts re-opened and saw much business conducted; public meetings were held and resolutions of the meetings were published in local papers; election of county and state officers and public referenda on conditions for admittance as a new State in the National Union; organization of militia, Home Guard companies, and opening of recruiting stations complete with pomp and ceremony were set up at what had once been commercial hubs along the rivers; recruiting officers set off for the interior to enlist volunteers unwilling or unable to enroll at stations; and public levies to provide bounties for volunteers, also collection of state taxes ... all this and more was realized. On April 17th, 1862, the following invocation was published in the columns of the *Weekly Register:*

> The Government of Virginia as vindicated and restored by the loyal people of the State, is rapidly gaining strength in the hearts and minds of the people.—When Eastern traitors attempted to disrupt the Union and transfer our State Government to [a] bastard Confederacy, the Western patriots wrested it from their hands and restored it to the people in the Union as it always was—thereby preserving to us—our rights and liberties—under the laws of the land.
>
> Under it we have Courts and officers elected by the people to render justice and execute the laws.
>
> And it is a harbinger of better days to see such men as John Laidiley of Cabell, Andrew Parks and George W. Summers of Kanawha, and Jas. W. Hoge of Putnam; not only taking part but as counsel and attorneys taking the oath to uphold and defend the reorganized Government.
>
> The Circuit Court sat in Wayne on the 20th of March; in Cabell on the 27th of March, in Putnam on the 8th of April. And we are informed that upwards of a hundred indictments were found at the first, nearly as many at the second, and more than half as many at the third.
>
> The grand juries are thus showing to the outlaws—the fallacy of the Secessionists—that 'there is no law in the country'—and reb-

els who rob houses, steal horses, and kidnap quiet citizens because they love the Union, will learn by experience, that the Government of Virginia, restored as it was in the Union is no humbug.[24]

The Virginia Partisan Ranger Act had been issued to foil Western Virginia's bid for Statehood in hopes that the errant western counties might yet be retaken for the Confederacy but the act went too far and people took a stand. Also on the national stage, a threshold had been passed. The Union cause appeared to teeter upon the edge of a knife. McClellan's disastrous campaign of summer 1862 across the Virginia peninsula and on the Chickahominy; his retreat North; and President Lincoln's calls for 300,000 more volunteers to fill the shattered and depleted ranks of the army seemed to signal that the Union cause was faltering. This dire aspect served to awaken the people of the North generally to the nature and magnitude of the conflict. In loyal western counties, these recent reverses to the Union arms served to catalyze the new force and focus driving the militarization of loyal Western Virginia with a heightened sense of urgency. The Union had to be saved, their very lives, the future of their children depended on it. Extreme measures had to be taken. Spring and summer, the largely conservative Democratic population of the Northwest, who did not cast their votes for Lincoln and the Republican party, came out from the shadows and were now openly pro-Union. Men from the border, from Western Virginia and Southern Ohio volunteered with a will to fill Western Virginia regiments. As result of this new force and focus, the immediacy and urgency of the local and national threat, the 13th West Virginia Volunteers was recruited, organized and came to take its place on the "Union line" in the "vast maze of mountains without range or system" and in history.

The Partisan Acts.
Intended and Unintended Consequences

Union advantage at Philippi, Scary and in the Kanawha, Tygarts and New River Valleys in 1861, seemed to have pushed the border of the Confederacy back from the Ohio River to beyond the Allegheny mountains. General McClellan had even made so bold as to announce that all guerrillas had been driven from Western Virginia. Efforts to organize and equip West Virginia troops slacked off over the winter of 1861-'62 but guerrillas, always an unknown quantity, were quietly gathering and arming. Soon, Virginia secessionists began to clamor that guerrilla type warfare be conducted to subdue and secure the rebellious northwestern part of the State. Virginia Governor John Letcher responded with a Proclamation to the People of Virginia on March 10th, 1862, in which he earnestly invoked '[t]he loyal citizens of the west and northwest in counties not herein named [...] to form guerilla compan[ie]s and strike when least expected once more for the state that gave them birth.' John Booth of the 36th Ohio Volunteer Infantry added in comment upon Letcher's invocation, that by this, "the chivalrous Governor of the Old Dominion gives [his] approval to all the crimes committed by the bands of robbers infesting wilds of western Virginia and calls for more banditti; whose chief delight is to perpetrate atrocities that would bring the blush of shame to the cheek of a savage."[25]

The timing of Governor Letcher's proclamation and the Virginia Ranger Act passed by the Virginia legislature at Richmond two weeks later was by design. These aired just prior to elections to be held in the Western counties on Thursday April 3rd, 1862, this referendum to ratify or defeat the newly revised West Virginia State Constitution. The original State Constitution which had been submitted to Federal Congress as a requirement for admission as a new State, had been rejected by the House of Representatives because it called for gradual rather than immediate manumission of slaves. The Constitution thus had to be rewritten and again voted upon in a general referendum. Letcher's proclamation was issued to intimidate voters and deter them from going to the polls. Indeed, voters were intimidated and although the revised State Constitution was carried, voter turnout was low. In Mason County, for one, the vote was taken at Point

Pleasant at the Court House, where through foresight or failure, were stockpiled some weapons. The people who voted there were unanimously for the new Constitution, but less than one third of those entitled to vote (free men) did. Only about 600 voted. By contrast, at the election of May 1861 when the referendum on the Ordinance of Secession was held, the vote in Mason county had been about 1,900. Only about a quarter of the male population of Mason was absent at this time in Union and Rebel armies, and thus, the reduction in votes should in theory at least, have been down also by only about a quarter.

Having lost their foothold in Western Virginia, the Confederacy adopted a new strategy, the Partisan Ranger Acts, by which light mobile units of cavalry would be authorized to attack Federal military and local pro-Union militia companies thus undermining newly established civil organization and support for the Union and the new State movement. The Virginia Partisan Ranger Act was passed on March 27th, 1862. This statute established ranger companies as a legal part of the State military forces. At least ten and not more than twenty companies of rangers could form. These companies were to be made up of men who had their homes in the western portions of the State (those parts held by the Federals). The Rangers were to operate in detachments of one or more companies "on the northern, western and northwestern frontiers of the State." Their chief purpose was outlined as being "to operate against enemy marauding and foraging parties"[26] in conformity with the 'usage of civilized warfare,' provided that the enemy also conducted themselves within such usages.[27] Partisan troops were subject only to the orders of the commanding officer of regular Confederate States troops, and they were expected to co-operate with regulars only when in close proximity to them. If the purpose of the law was to target Union military troops and supply depots, this happened only incidentally as there were few regulars and depots in the Northwestern counties at this time. In practice, the Ranger Act essentially authorized operatives to be a "law-unto themselves." In other words, in granting such wide latitude, Letcher had given license to roving bands of partisans to prey upon the general population.

On April 21st, 1862, the Confederate States Congress followed suit, passing their own Partisan Rangers Act. This version of the Ranger Act gave the Confederate States military more control over the rangers (*i.e.*, after acceptance into the Confederate States service, Partisan Rangers were subject to Confederate States Army Regulations and rangers were entitled to the same pay and rations as other troops in Confederate service) on the one hand, but on the other hand, "the enemy" was more broadly defined. The "enemy" was not limited to "marauding and foraging parties" as in the Virginia Partisan act. The Confederate States act offered incentive money (which Virginia's act did not)— monetary compensation for captured arms and munitions; and gave flexibility as to how partisan ranger "companies, battalions, or regiments" might serve (*i.e.*, either as infantry or cavalry). In reality, all Confederate States Army Partisan Ranger units were mounted.

Almost immediately after passage of the Ranger Acts, it was obvious to denizens of the Kanawha Valley that the Rebellion had gained impetus and momentum. Commentary of the time suggests that even to the most casual Kanawha Valley observer, it was obvious that Secessionists and their sympathizers were organizing. Not only had they been organizing but they seemed quite thoroughly and completely organized and, "even the poorest" secessionists suddenly had "means." Indeed, with passage of the Ranger Acts, secessionists who had fled the northwestern counties during the campaigns of 1861, returned with commissions in hand to recruit mounted forces for "detached" (partisan) service.

In practice, the civilian population and Union military were all fair game for partisan operatives. Union mail routes were disrupted and citizens could not receive national news, nor the acts of the new legislature at Wheeling. The graves of soldiers were desecrated, and water wells and food were poisoned. Typically, in the dead of night, a band[s] would surround the house of a Union man supposed to have cash or other valuables on hand and demand a ransom or threaten to burn the house down over the family's heads. For the Unionists, it was in many ways the story of the previous year in replay: not enough arms, not enough ammunition, and neither could be procured in time and quantity to quash the new mischief. The 'trap and release' policy of Union military authority (termed 'the milk and water' or 'rosewater policy' by frustrated citizens, by which arrested partisans were released back into the community upon swearing an oath of allegiance) betrayed a reluctance on the part of the War Department in Washington to act for fear of alienating pro-Southern citizens of border states. For the loyal population the situation was provoking in the extreme.[28]

Already as early as April 1862, complaints of the conduct of new Virginia State Rangers reached Governor Letcher. Nothing about them could be overseen. Recruitment and organization of companies proceeded in an unregulated way without keeping records of enlistment or service in the field. It was not then, nor today possible to tally up the actual number of companies raised. Some bands operated effectively against legitimate military targets by gathering intelligence, disrupting communications, capturing horses and supplies, but many bands were made up of men who had been outlaws before the war and they used the conflict as a pretext for unbridled lawlessness.[29] So troublesome had they become, that in February 1863, the Virginia State Rangers were transferred to the Confederate States Regular Army and on February 17th, 1864, they were abolished altogether by the Confederate States Congress.

As a result of the Ranger Acts, Northwest Virginia came to have many partisan bands. Some were made up of locals and some came over considerable distances to harass Union citizens and military. One journalist writing for the Gallipolis, Ohio *Journal* (issue of February 18th, 1864) remarked that "[t]he State of W[est] V[irgini]a is not so intensely loyal as some persons wish it to be considered. The fact is, that region of the country is just as well stocked with rebels, both armed and unarmed as any other portion of the South."[30] To name a few, there was the Tom Holly squad that operated in Mason County; and a "nest of guerrillas" from Tazewell County "at the waters of Big Hurricane."[31] There was Jim Mitchell of Point Pleasant; the "notorious Bill Smith" who operated with his band in Wayne County (with a preference for Ceredo and vicinity) and Cabell Counties. There was 'Nounings gang;' the "notorious" Bill Harper;[32] Doc Bledsoe who was determined to hold Western Virginia for the Confederacy; and one Lieutenant Keaton operating along Guyan River. There was also one Captain Downs, a "noted guerrilla" who operated with a small band on the Little Kanawha.[33] There was a Captain [Hurston ?] Spurlock of Wayne County [of Co. E 16th Va. Cavalry?] who operated around Guyandotte and another Spurlock [Burwell?[34]] ranged in Mason and in adjacent counties. There was Ferguson's gang; William and Phil Thurmond; Albert G. Jenkins of "Green Bottom," Cabell County;[35] and Colonel John N. Clarkson who operated in Cabell and Wayne Counties with his Border Rangers. Colonel Clarkson commanded troops in the Virginia State Line. It was a partisan organization (according to the *Weekly Register*) that been recruited from counties in West Virginia and Eastern Kentucky.[36] Clarkson had been responsible for the attack on the 5th and 9th West Virginia Volunteer Infantry Regiments at Guyandotte on November 10th of 1861 (called the "Guyandotte Massacre"), a murderous affair involving citizens of the town who attacked both military and Union citizens. Among Clarkson's command this day were the Petersburg Rangers, Missouri State Militia, commanded by Captain Henry Clay Pate, who on June 2, 1856 had been defeated and captured at the battle of Black Jack by abolitionist John Brown and his band.[37] "Hammerclaw" or "Claw-Hammer" Witcher, "a living skeleton of a man" operated with a band of over 200 against Union citizens and Federal forces in the Kanawha Valley and on both sides of the Ohio River, in Kentucky and Western Virginia. At Beech Creek, 45 miles south of Chapmansville, on August 6th, 1862, he attacked a detachment of the 4th Virginia Infantry Regiment routing the Federals, killing three and wounding eight.[38] Among those killed, was Major John T. Hall in command of the detachment. He was younger brother to James R. Hall, future Lieutenant-Colonel of the 13th Virginia. Some contemporaries who knew the Hall brothers as cadets at Virginia Military Institute, have pointed out that while James had thus far avoided enlisting in the army—presumably due to his responsibilities as deputy sheriff—but perhaps, as has been suggested, because his sympathies lay with the South, it was his brother's death and the brutality shown him while for two hours he lay mortally wounded, a prisoner in Witcher's hands, that changed James' mind and compelled him join the Union army and to go at the business of raising men for the 13th Regiment with such energy and devotion.

Major General John Fremont
Stirs Things Up

On March 11th, 1862, there was a re-organization of the Federal military districts[39] and a new commander appointed which brought a glimmer of hope to pro-Union men. The Mountain Department was created from the Department of West Virginia and Eastern Kentucky and Major-General John Charles Fremont assumed command of it on March 29th, 1862. Fremont could hardly be called a great military mind but he was a man of action, goal-oriented, with an extraordinary reputation of accomplishment. Importantly, he was an anti-slavery man who had no little tolerance for guerillas which for West Virginians could well have been enough in itself to recommend him. His appointment signaled to Unionists in the Kanawha Valley, civilians and soldiers, that a sterner policy in dealing with rebel partisans might at last be implemented.[40]

John C. Fremont (1813-1890) also known as "The Pathfinder," had been many things: an explorer and expedition leader, navy and army officer, topographical engineer for the U.S. Army, who conducted important surveys of rivers west of the Mississippi facilitating the westward expansion of the 1830s, '40s and '50s. He settled in the Sierra Foothills of California, entered politics as a Republican and anti-slavery candidate and was elected as one of the first two senators from California to Congress in Washington. He made a run for U.S. President against James Buchanan in 1851 but was defeated. After the outbreak of the Civil War in 1861, Major General Fremont was put in command of the Western Department with headquarters in St. Louis, Missouri. Just a few thousand men were available to him but he made of them an effective fighting force despite chronic problems supplying his men and the fact that pro-South Missourans were in rebellion. His methods of dealing with the latter which included emancipation of slaves, however, were considered extreme at that early stage in the conflict when loyalties of slave-owning border States still hung in the balance, and he was relieved of command by President Lincoln.[41] Fremont's methods were however, exactly what recommended him to pro-Union West Virginians.

Fremont's reputation was saved, so the story goes, by influential Republican friends who secured his appointment to the newly created Mountain Department. Be that as it may, editors of pro-Union West Virginia newspapers indicate that Fremont's fame had preceded him and Unionists in the Kanawha Valley were favorably disposed to his appointment, anticipating that he would make practical and prompt, a more stringent policy toward secessionists and partisan rangers in particular. Relief from guerrilla depredations seemed at hand in the person Fremont. Fremont might well have been that man for the job, but his attention was immediately diverted by orders to retake Chattanooga, Tennessee and by the uproar caused by General Stonewall Jackson's operations in Eastern Virginia. As a result, although Fremont broadened the scope of how to handle the partisan element (that is, "to fight them in their own style, and by rapid marches, vigorous attacks and severe measures, annihilate them") the matter of containing guerrillas remained still a matter for the unmounted infantry and local militia.

One need only consider the small number of troops as compared to the wide area of wild country west of the Alleghenies and in the Kanawha Valley to be scouted and policed to appreciate the enormity of the task of keeping guerillas in check. Note particularly the small number of cavalry—exactly the kind of troops needed in force, to go after partisans rangers who were all mounted, struck suddenly without warning and then melted into the rough Virginia terrain. The total Union force reported present in the Kanawha District by General William Rosecrans on March 24th, 1862, was "twelve and three-tenths Regiments of Infantry numbering 10,780 men; [a mere] fifteen companies Cavalry numbering 1,086 men; and two Batteries Artillery with two hundred and five men."[42] The District of the Kanawha, along with the other forces of the Mountain Department (these being the Cheat Mountain District; the Railroad District; the District of Big Sandy Valley and District of the Gap numbering *in toto* some "35 and two tenths Regiments of Infantry: 30,434 men; 36 companies Cavalry: 2,741 men and 9 Batteries Artillery: 1,096 men") guarded "a frontier 350 miles long approached by roads more or less perpendicular to that line of frontier, with few cross communications. They also guard[ed] the depots, bridges + tunnels on 300 miles of rail-road + 200 miles of water communication."[43] Insufficient numbers of cavalry and insufficient numbers of infantry to garrison and support cavalry operations (as was later done later by detachments of 13th West Virginia troops by companies, who worked effectively together with the 3rd West Virginia Cavalry) could do little to counteract the rising number of guerrilla incursions and depredations which occurred with renewed vigor in consequence of the Partisan Act.

As indicated above, Maj. Gen. Fremont urged individual initiative and that all troops operate against guerrillas in kind, employing guerrilla counter-measures of ambush, shock attack etc., as evidenced by Orders No. 11, issued by him on April

7th, 1862, a week after assuming command of the Mountain Department. Fremont's orders indicate both his resolve and experience with irregular warfare as fought in the far West:

> I. Commanders of Posts, and all troops not moving in the field, are directed to use their utmost exertions to destroy the various bands of guerrillas now beginning to infest the Department. The activity of the rebels must be met by corresponding watchfulness. While it is impossible to guard all the points liable to be attacked by these bands, it is easy to fight them in their own style, and by rapid marches, vigorous attacks and severe measures, annihilate them. To this end, therefore, sudden and frequent movements must be made, both by night and day. Commanders will obtain from scouts, and every other source of information, the earliest and best intelligence with regard to the movements and haunts of the marauders, and surprise and attack them whenever possible. It is desirable that all the reliable information of any such guerrilla movements shall be also transmitted directly to the Headquarters of this Department, By command of Major General Fremont. Albert Tracy, Captain and Assistant Adjutant General.[44]

A public forum convened at Point Pleasant, Mason County, coincidentally on the same day (Monday April 7th, 1862) that Fremont issued "Orders No. 11." The meeting as reported in the Point Pleasant *Weekly Register* suggests that Fremont was both stirring things up and having a positive effect along the line of the Kanawha River. Large numbers of farmers had taken the boat down the river to lay in seed for a new crop—their entire stock having been either taken away or destroyed by "rebels under Jenkins and Clarkson."[45] On April 16th, 1862, J.B. Baumgardner (a future recruiting officer for the 13th) wrote to State Adjutant General H. J. Samuels[46] from Ceredo regarding guerrilla depredations in Cabell County and the need for ammunition for two new companies of militia:

> Please forward to me at this place one thousand (1000) rounds 'Enfield cartridges' for the use of two 'Home Guards' now in this county commanded by Capts Wm. Shannon[47] and Wm. Battram. These Capts want commissions they are willing to take their commissions under the 'Militia' or as 'Home Guards' Rebels again have made their appearance in the county and are committing depredations of the vilest kind they are taking and confiscating all property belonging

to Union men that they can lay their hands 'Clawhammer' is now in Cabell (true to his instinct) stealing and plundering everything that comes in his way. You will please send if possible 20 Guns if you cannot get Riffles send muskets for they are badly needed.[48]

While Western Virginia contended with its "plague of guerrillas," the Union army there opened its spring campaign. During the first weeks of May, Federal troops were typically moved from positions behind "the lines" and moved forward towards the enemy. This left communities in their rear open to guerrilla depredation. To offset the withdrawal of forces and complement these movements, on May 1st, Francis Pierpont, Governor of the Restored Government at Wheeling called out all Western Virginia volunteer forces. On May 3rd, he issued a call for additional forces to all commanding officers of the State militia.[49]

Partisans in the Northwest counties kept pace with the escalation of activity attending the opening of the campaign season. Anna Starr, living in Mason City, Mason County, wrote to her mother on May 5th regarding the current onslaught of guerrilla incursions, her fears regarding her husband William Starr then serving with the 9th Regiment West Virginia Infantry at Guyandotte and that Fremont was "stirring" things up militarily:

> The guerrillas have commenced operations here already four hundred of the moccasin rangers came into Spencer a town in Roane Co northeast of our county, and took three companies (what was left of them after the fight) prisoners of the 11th Virginia (Union) according to report they now have possession of the town but I heard this morning that a detachment of Union soldiers from Parkersburg Va had been sent out there to fight them. [...] I feel very uneasy about William's being left at Guyandotte with <u>so small</u> a force I think he is in <u>great</u> danger of just such another raid from Clarkson's Cavalry as <u>was</u> enacted there last summer, when the <u>whole</u> regiment was there I felt easier, but with only <u>half</u> of it, I think his position a very <u>important</u>, <u>responsible</u> and <u>dangerous</u> one. [... T]here is little doubt they will have fighting to do before long Gen. Fremont is stirring the mountain department up War prospects as far as our <u>armies</u> are concerned look <u>very bright</u>, but these dreadful guerrillas when, where, or <u>how</u>, will they <u>ever</u> be put down it is thought <u>here</u>, that they will dev[a]state Western Virginia <u>worse</u> this summer than last, keeping our border towns in constant <u>fear</u>.[50]

Just prior to May 10[th], Governor of the Provisional Government, Francis H. Pierpont received intelligence deemed reliable that Albert G. Jenkins Cavalry were "on the headwaters of the Guyandotte and the rivers that interlock therewith, and that guerrilla parties are forming within 50 miles of the Ohio River, who have already shot and killed peaceable citizens in Wayne and other border counties."[51] Inhabitants of the tri-State area: of Point Pleasant, Virginia; Gallispolis and Ironton, Ohio and "other border towns" anticipating "the long-threatened vengeance of Jenkins and Clarkson" moved away "in considerable numbers." Pierpont appealed to Gen. Fremont (cmdg. the Mountain District) for military support requesting that Colonel J.A.J. Lightburn (4th Virginia Infantry, comdg. forces in the Kanawha Valley) spare no effort and

> by frequent and sudden attacks, by rapid marches without transportation, by surprises and severity, to destroy all bands forming and organized in your district, and by terrorizing these marauders finally to uproot the whole system.[52]

May 14th (1862), J.B. Baumgardner wrote from Ceredo on behalf of himself and concerned citizens of Ceredo (namely Thomas J. Merritt, J.B. Bowen, Randolph Reeding, Abraham Ludy, P. Edmonds, Eli Porter, W.L. Hall, A.F. Morse, and O.W. Griswold, future 1st Lieutenant of Company H 13th Virginia Infantry Regiment) to Adjutant General H.J. Samuels. Bumgardner and the above named men, who signed his petition, requested authority to organize a "Patrol Company" to drive out a band of guerrillas who were prowling through the county. Wrote Bumgardner in his addenda: "All are willing to join. All the men desire are arms and encouragement."[53] Together with the petition was a separate letter written by Bumgardner referencing his own efforts to organize and arm volunteers in Wayne County. Bumgardner supplied Samuels with ample detail of the precarious nature of the current situation. He petitioned for a "patrol company" to be "continually on the scout" and noted that while many came forward to sign the petition, fear prevented more than just a few to actually volunteer for duty:

> Enclosed you will find a petition to raise a 'Patrol Company' for this county the purpose of this company is to be continually on the scout. I could have got three times as many names to this petition but have not been 15 minutes getting it up. I and Thomas J Merritt, Prestinon, Edmons, Oliver Griswel, Wright, Wash Stewart, and A.F. Morse have been standing guard evry night since the 4th Va Reg left.[54] We are the only ones that have taken any interest in it the rest seem to be afraid to do anything. I want you to write to me as soon as you get this and let me know the particulars as regards this

Company also let me know what pay they are to receive. There must
something be done or wayne county will suffer. Sergeant Hall has
been left here in charge of the fort, there is a great deal of Government property here which would be sacrificed should they burn this
place. I intend to go to making up a company right away and will
come to Wheeling as soon as I here from you. I give the 20 Riffles
you sent and part of the ammunition to Capt Bartram and took
his receipt I will send you his list of officers and men in a few days.
The Enfield Riffles that was sent to Capt Damron Col Lightburn
got and took them on to Charleston with him These companies I
intend to get up will be of great service in assisting the commissioner
and collector[55] I have not organized the Militia yet The citizens in
the upper end of the county thought it best not to organize yet as
it would drive the most of them the southern sympathizers into the
Southern Army. Please do all you can as regards these companies.
Your obt sevt J B Baumgardner[56]

Nor did Western Virginia's problem with rebel guerrillas go unnoticed nationally
as evidenced in the following (dating to probably the second half of April 1862 and
reprinted from the columns of the *New York Times*):

Rebel marauders and guerillas are making their appearance, with the
green leaves, in quite a number of counties of Western Virginia. We
hear of some of them suddenly springing up in some unexpected
quarter, attacking a hamlet, or a Union camp, or a supply train, or
executing vengeance upon some loyal citizen, or in some other way
disturbing the peace of the country. Gen. Fremont is doing his best
to put these gangs down; but the work, is one which, in the thinly
peopled mountain regions of Western Virginia can neither be done
easily nor quickly and the consequence is civil turmoil and social
insecurity.[57]

Virginia terrain was particularly suited to be a theater for guerrilla warfare, and
partisans who were at home in the area were without doubt well-acquainted with their
ground. Guerrilla or 'irregular' type warfare was also, as has often been pointed out,
particularly well-suited to 'frontier mentality' and Southern temperament, where men
tended to prefer to fight not in the conventional European style of grand movements
of troops under a chain of commanding officers but more in squads and on their own
hook. They employed methods of the shock attack: stealth; ambush; thunder and
lightning strike and just as suddenly disappearance into the landscape. There was no

way to predict or anticipate a single strike or coordinated attack. As indicated by Fremont in his orders, Baumgardner in his petition and Pierpont in request for effective counter-guerilla operations, the only remedy for the deplorable state of affairs was to fight fire with fire: to undertake a systematic program of constant scouting; intelligence gathering from a civilian population with whom a relationship of trust had been established; close attention to terrain that vulnerable points might be anticipated in camp and on the march; and by "terrorizing the marauders" "to uproot the whole system." Larger scouting expeditions made it possible to sweep the country for a time, but it was scouting by companies that made possible the 'micro-surgical' offensives that were most effective in the short and long term. These required that Union soldiers and militia think as the partisans, and that they hatch counter-strategies (also called "jayhawking") of their own.[58] The difficult terrain which cut in favor of the guerrillas in the first instance could also cut in favor of locals willing to fight them. Many things were needed to make practical such a program, arms for one and more soldiers but first and last nerve, steadiness, and a sure aim. Men of Western Virginia and Ohio responded.

The Gamest Set of Fellows

The 13th Virginia (West Virginia) Infantry Regiment consisted solely of volunteers. No drafted soldiers were ever added to the 13th.

> *"[F]or they must remember that this is the blody 13 Regment and can capture more chickens than you ever saw [...]."*

—Jesse Hart,
Private Co. B 13th Virginia Infantry Regiment to his father,
manuscript dated "herican brig Putnam county Virginia February
24, 1863," Jesse Hart Military Pension file, National Archives,
Washington D.C.

The 13th Regiment would spend the better part of two years garrisoning areas infested with partisan rangers and bushwhackers. They were or became (to say the least and not get ahead of myself) *very steady* in combat situations. It might even be said they did not know when they were whipped. Moreover, the cumulative effect of doing this kind of hard duty for so long made of the 13th and other troops stationed in this part of the Union line something of what we might call today "special forces." These troops learned that they not only *had* to rely upon each other to make it through but that they could. They became good on the sneak and ambush (and adept it seems at stealing chickens). They were capable of astonishing mobility, stamina and like the partisan rangers with whom they had to deal (even though unlike rangers, they were *not* mounted), they became most adept at the shock attack. The hardships of their duty inured them to hardship. They became tough and tough-minded; adapted without orders to fluid combat situations; and demonstrated repeatedly tremendous capacity for standing their ground in the most extreme situations—a capacity for which they gained renown and respect.

Irresistible on the charge and the meteoric strike, they came to excel in a tactic that had previously been the prerogative of the cavalry. George Crook, who commanded these troops for the greater part of the Civil War, once let loose that the two brigade sized divisions which constituted his Army of West Virginia (to which the 13th West Virginia belonged) were more like a large raiding party than an army. Not a few of them came to feel that there could be no half-way measures.

Colonel George Crook (cmdg. 36th Ohio Infantry Vols.; promoted brigadier-general Sept. 7, 1862) was popular among the officers and men of the Kanawha Valley military district. His men were not just cogs in the military machine but his 'fellow man.' They trusted him and carried out his strategies with controlled abandon. They performed 'secret marches' and set up flanking maneuvers at great personal hardship but with the confidence that Crook's strategies saved lives and gun powder. Because of his effective service in quieting guerrillas in West Virginia, he was also a favorite with the Restored State Government and with the loyal civilian population at large. When he was called to command outside of the district, guerrillas became more brazen and troublesome and the public clamored for his return. He had a sharp mind and was a strict disciplinarian but he was no elitist. There was no bombast nor swagger to him. He was a plain man of medium height and build, unostentatious, given to reticence and self-possessed under the most trying circumstances, especially so in the presence of the enemy. On the battlefield he blazed. He was habitually found to be where the fighting was hottest, so much so that couriers with orders to deliver to him, complained of it. He was a younger son in a large family; had grown up on a farm near Dayton, Ohio, with all that entails—hard work, self-sufficiency and practicality. He became a career military man and a West Point graduate. He was a superb tracker and huntsman with extraordinary skills in comprehending and utilizing terrain to advantage when hunting for game or outsmarting an enemy on the battlefield. He came into the Civil War from service in the Indian Wars fought out west. Because of his natural abilities and the skills he had developed in fighting Indians in the western military theater, he was highly effective in rooting out and neutralizing the militant bands of secessionist guerrillas, who prowled the Kanawha Valley and preyed upon pro-Union citizens and U.S. military.

Raising a Regiment:
Mason County, Virginia.
A Case Study

Mason County claimed the 13th Volunteers as "their regiment" for a number of reasons. Many denizens of Mason stepped up to fill her ranks and she was organized and mustered into the U.S. Service at Point Pleasant, the county seat. For other reasons it is useful to take a look at Mason as a case study of how a small community of individuals stubbornly and against great odds seized the initiative with other like-minded individuals *and* the reins of power that they might be free from tyranny and oppression. They did this at great personal risk in midst of civil war. In the course of making practical their belief in the right and duty of Americans to govern and determine for themselves what star they hitched their wagon to, they reinstated civil authority despite deteriorating circumstances and raised a volunteer army of militia, home guards and regulars. That the 13th Virginia was organized to put iron behind the enterprise justifies a look at the mosaic of particulars that together give a sense of what it was to organize a Union regiment in the South at this time.

The Court convenes. On March 3rd, 1862, the regular March term of the Mason County Circuit Court convened. Attendance was not large, but considering the inclement weather, turnout was respectable. A considerable amount of business was transacted, including qualification of the new magistrates elected to fill vacancies occasioned by the resignation or refusal of the late incumbents to take the oath of loyalty to the national Union, as prescribed by the Wheeling Convention. The reorganization of the Court in "old Mason" was almost complete and speedy re-establishment of civil authority was underway. Restoration of law and order was anticipated.

Public Union meetings are held. The new pro-Union newspaper, the Point Pleasant Weekly Register, in its March 6, 1862, issue, called to the Union people of the county to rally and for the first time to have a public meeting. This idea was so well received that a meeting was proposed for the first Monday in April (the 7th). Policy would be decided as to what should be done regarding rebels returning that summer to their homes in the county from the "rebel army" or from otherwise being absent aiding the rebellion. The issue to be decided being whether or not they should they be permitted to resume their places in the community.

The meeting took place at the Point Pleasant Court House on April 7th, just days after the vote on the revised State Constitution had taken place. (The Mason County election had tallied 639 for the Constitution and 22 against.) The weather was unfavorable but the capacious courtroom was nonetheless, densely crowded with citizens. It was reported to be the largest public meeting ever assembled in Mason County and was described in the *Register* as giving "full and fair expression of the sentiment of the Union element of the county." The "familiar faces of many of the oldest and most prominent men" in the community lent weight and prestige to the deliberations of the assembly. Business was conducted with the utmost decorum. "Good order" was the order of the day and nothing occurred to interfere in the least with the "harmonious feelings" of all present.[59]

Officers were elected to conduct the meeting. On motion of John Hall, Esquire, Colonel Charles B. Waggener (veteran and a local hero of the War of 1812) was elected president and Lewis Wetzel (President of the Mason County Court Justices) elected secretary of the meeting. Judge Daniel Polsley, the incumbent Lieutenant Governor (to Francis Pierpont, Governor of the Restored State Government, Wheeling) addressed the meeting at length. He discussed the purpose of the gathering and explained the principles upon which the recent reorganization of the State was based. Polsey concluded by submitting to the meeting a preamble with resolutions which were deliberated and unanimously adopted. The rest of the meeting seems to have been concerned with safety and military defense. While the assembly fell short of *utterly* condemning what it termed the "milk and water policy" pursued by Federal government and military authority as to the treatment of rebels, it was obvious that as a group, those in attendance were resolved to protect their own interests and take the defense of their rights into their own hands, when the laws failed to do the one or the other. This sentiment included and extended to known secessionists in their midst and to those who had left to get the Rebellion on firm footing (civilians, soldiers and politicians) who could be expected to return to their homes in Mason and adjacent counties.

The problem with the current policy (the "milk and water policy") was how off-hand it was. To return home, rebels were required only to take what the Union folk called the "rattlesnake" oath. Having sworn the oath, secessionists were permitted back into their neighborhoods with all their former rights and privileges. They enjoyed protection of both military and civil authority and were free to prey again upon the community at their own convenience and opportunity. This policy was entirely unacceptable and would no longer be tolerated by the April 7th assembly.

The group unanimously voiced their protest "against releasing on bail or otherwise prominent rebels, who [had] been indicted for treason or conspiracy against the Government of the United States as unwise, impolitic and dangerous to the peace and public safety of the community." Moreover, those rebel fugitives of Mason county who were expected home by their friends that Spring and Summer should be immediately arrested, imprisoned, or expelled from the State until the Rebellion was suppressed. The assembly maintained that they had become convinced by the conduct of "released traitors" now among them that the object of their return was to encourage the "insurrectionary party in the country," to effect a more thorough organization among them, and to obtain and communicate to the rebel leaders information that would enable them to commit depredations on peaceable citizens "with impunity." In accordance with these perceptions, the citizens at the meeting resolved to take extreme measures to protect themselves in the absence of a strong position coming down from the Federal government. The assembly wanted all active rebels including those "leading county or district politicians" to be arrested without bail; that no loyal person directly or indirectly post bail with exception of loyal attorneys; that the Federal army not issue passes to permit rebels to return to their homes but issue instead only passes beyond Federal lines and that practice to remain in place until peace be restored; that persons of Mason County, who, within the County have been writing, speaking or otherwise been aiding in establishing the rebel government, should be indicted in the Mason County Circuit Court at its next term under Chapter 190 of the Virginia Code (irrespective of whether they had been indicted or not in Federal Court) and jailed without bail.

Chapter CXC (190) of the 1860 Virginia Code defined treason, its elements and outlined its punishments. The sovereignty of the State (whether of East or West Virginia) is evident in the following language from Chapter 190:

1. Treason shall consist only in levying war against the state, or adhering to its enemies, giving them aid and comfort, or establishing, without authority of the legislature, any government within its limits, separate from the existing government, or holding or executing, in such usurped government, any office, or professing allegiance or fidelity to it, or resisting the execution of the laws, under color of its authority; and such treason, if proved by the testimony of two witnesses to the same overt act, or by confession in court, shall be punished with death.

2. If a free person, knowing of any such treason, shall not, as soon as may be, give information thereof to the governor, or some conser-

vator of the peace, he shall be punished by fine not exceeding one thousand dollars, or by confinement in the penitentiary not less than three nor more than five years.

3. If a free person attempt to establish any such usurped government, and commit any overt act therefor, or by writing or speaking, endeavor to instigate others to establish such government, he shall be confined in jail not exceeding twelve months, and fined not exceeding one thousand dollars. [...][60]

The assembly of April 7 further resolved that

Joseph Sly, Benjamin Lemaster, J.D. Thompson, William Smith, S. Comstock [future Regimental Quartermaster for the 13th], Spencer H. Aumiller, Morgan Greenlee, Green Beard and Jno. O. Butler, be appointed a committee of safety for the county, whose duty it shall be to communicate to the Governor the names of such suspicious persons as are described in the ordinance of June 19, 1861, together with the evidence of their guilt, and request him to have them dealt with according to the provisions of said ordinance.[61]

Further, "Resolution 7" enjoined "Justices, Sheriffs and all other conservators of the peace" to be vigilant and watchful and arrest all persons engaging in treasonable practices," the public now expecting a "faithful and prompt performance of this duty." Notice was also given by John Hall, Esquire[62] of the upcoming election of State officers (Governor, Lieutenant Governor and Attorney General) to be held on May 4th (1862). Hall recommended that the incumbents be re-elected.[63]

The escalating problem with roving bands of partisan rangers in combination with the removal of Federal troops for use in the spring military campaign soon made necessary another call to assemble a public meeting. On May 20th, another Town Meeting was held at the Point Pleasant Court House. A number of issues were addressed and policy decided. Insofar as all Union troops had been removed from Point Pleasant (except one company of the 9th Virginia Infantry Regiment) leaving loyal citizens there

to some extent exposed to the depredations of the infamous rebels and Secesh cut-throats who are now prowling through our mountain districts; and whereas our own safety requires that we should be organized and united, to the end that we may afford mutual aid and protection to each other against those in armed rebellion as well as those sneaking traitors in our midst [...].[64]

At this meeting it was resolved that:

1) the loyal people of Point Pleasant should enroll themselves as members of a Home Guard and pledge themselves to do whatever service necessary to protect their homes and their firesides

2) those professional Union men, who up to that moment had refused or failed to aid in guarding the lives of Union families other than their own were henceforth considered more dangerous than open and avowed Secessionists

3) if the peace and property of Union folk was disturbed or destroyed by roving rebel thieves and murderers, the traitors living yet in the midst of the Union people would be held personally responsible because it would be assumption that they were invited in, to do their misdeeds

4) all midnight meetings convened by home traitors will hereafter be dispersed in the most summary manner possible.[65]

Editor of the Point Pleasant *Weekly Register,* Lewis Wetzel,[66] chastised the local pro-Union citizenry (in his column of May 20th) for their failure thus far, to put "organization and equipment on a war footing." He then went on to set out his own ideas as how to put an end to guerrilla warfare along the border:

It is amazing that during the winter the loyal men of Western Virginia have not taken measures to organize themselves for home protection. Their experience last summer must certainly have suggested its value. They knew with what sort of an enemy they had to deal and that nothing but organization and equipment on a war footing would secure immunity from incursions and outrages of the most fearful character. Every precinct should have been organized. Minute men, ready to punish aggressions at once, and expel any of Letcher's bands of out-laws, are far more effective, and would be much more feared and respected than bodies of U.S. troops, necessarily occup[ying] forts at some distance from each other, and subject to be withdrawn at any time, to support military movements having no reference to the inhabitants of any locality in particular.

The Government has been very generous in its course toward the people of Western Virginia, has done all in its power to protect them from the vindictiveness of their evil minded neighbors and the prowling bands of guerrillas sent west of the mountains to harass and distress them. It behooves the people of Western Virginia to bestir themselves. Don't wait for Federal or State assistance. That is not the best reliance.— A good rifle or musket, with a determined spirit to use it on any marauder who disturbs the peace of the citizens, is the best guarantee the citizens can have that their peace will not be disturbed. Organization should be so well perfected in every neighborhood, that when it is threatened by numbers, numbers can be immediately summoned and so direct[ed] as to make collective strength of some value. The guerrillas who roam about the country stealing horses, robbing stores, and shooting citizens engaged in their peaceful pursuits, should if caught, be hung without formality of trial. A few prompt punishment[s] of this sort by the citizens themselves, would soon put an end to guerrilla warfare along the border.[67]

The week following, this was published:

It seems that we are to have no peace however much we may desire and plead for it and if the loyal people and the traitors have become so far separated that it is not possible for them again to live together under the same government, the sooner the shooting commences the better.[68]

Toward the end of May, there was a "good deal of dissatisfaction" prevailing in Kanawha County "on account of the rebels that are permitted to return from the rebel army and enjoy the protection of the Government they would have destroyed but for their inability to do so there evidently has been much Leniency displayed toward Treason."[69]

By end of May, "Unionism [wa]s on the gain" in the Kanawha Valley" indicated one Greenbury Slack.[70] Elections were over and a pro-Union State government was firmly in place in West Virginia. New State officers had been chosen all over the loyal counties. On June 11th, delegates had been sent to Wheeling. The assembly elected new officers: Governor, Lieutenant Governor, Auditor, Treasurer and Secretary to replace "the deposed defaulters" who had gone South. By taking these steps, the loyal people of Western Virginia showed to the Confederate States and Washington that they were in earnest in their secession from the mother State. By July 10th, 1862, the 37th Federal Congress at Washington, in its second session, was considering Western Virginia's request to be admitted to the Union. (The measure granting secession from Virginia and creating a new State had passed the previous session of Congress in the U.S. Senate on July 14th.) Despite discouraging news from the Virginia military theater, July 4th, Independence Day, was greeted by Unionists with more than usual enthusiasm. The day held more than ordinary meaning. A great deal had happened in one year. Festivities held to commemorate the day strengthened Union solidarity and sense of purpose. People came from all precincts to their county seat to commemorate the day. Patriotic speeches were made. West Virginia army volunteers and militia, in which many future soldiers of the 13th Regiment served, would have paraded, perhaps with bands playing patriotic tunes. Some repast would have been brought.

Just one year ago, representatives in convention had restored the State government without State treasury funds or an organized militia to back it up. Wheeling had declared Western Virginia a separate State (done on May 6th, 1862); set a new State Constitution before the people and Congress at Washington; and was in process of petitioning the government at Washington for admittance to the Union. State government officials were "Collecting Taxes as fast as we Can."[71] In counties and districts, elections had been held to replace officials "gone South" and civic government resumed. Courts were again in session. Citizens who had suffered at the hands of local Confederate regulars and irregulars brought suit: suits for assault, unlawful confinement, property damage and theft. Efforts were made to restore postal routes, so that the people again had opportunity to receive news of current developments and receive copies of the laws and acts of their legislature. Union newspapers were making every effort to provide a forum for local issues, to focus and promote Union sentiment and to publish news of military movements and developments in the Provisional State and Federal government. Along the Ohio and in the Kanawha Valley re-organization, militarization, meetings and more public meetings were the order of the day. On June 16th, in Kanawha County, a mass meeting so large gathered, that it had to be held on the shady lawn of the Courthouse because the building would not accommodate the crowd. John D. Carter, soon to be commissioned Captain of Company E (13th West Virginia Regiment), was named Secretary of the meeting. Speeches were given and resolutions were passed affirming the resolve of those present to stand firm with the Federal government.[72]

Those who had assumed roles of civic leadership continued calling public meetings throughout the summer. Word of meetings was widely circulated and the meetings were well-attended. Discussion continued to concentrate upon the same concerns: how best to secure public safety; enforcement of the laws; eradication of the guerrilla element; and how to promote their best interests and the Union cause in general in their counties. Developments on progress and issues connected to status for admittance to the Union as a new State were heard, discussed and voted on. Commitment to the Union was continually confirmed and policy in regards to mischief done by local secessionists and by partisan rangers was invariably a topic at meetings.

Loyal citizens continued to express profound dissatisfaction with Federal military authorities for their failure to subdue the rebellious population and ranger operations.

The problem was clearly too widespread for the Federal military to effectively control, and border counties looked to one another to find systematic local counter-measures to best deal with what was essentially *their* local problem. D.R. King's orders of June 7 to his post at Ravenswood, Jackson County, were regarded as so much of the "right thing" in dealing with the "bogus war" then being waged by many members of the pre-war militia which remained loyal to Virginia under the guise of Moccasin Rangers, Mountain Rangers, etc., that his orders were published in the *Weekly Register* of June 19 and the Gallispolis, Ohio, *Journal* of June 26, 1862. "D[ixon]. R. King, commanding Federal forces at Post Camp Ravenswood, Va." (Jackson County) issued the following orders concerning guerrillas and the Moccasin or Mountain Rangers. The order was dated Camp Ravenswood, June 7, 1862. King wrote:

> 1) All armed persons, known as Moccasin or Mountain Rangers found in Jackson county, will be shot. It will avail them nothing to claim to have or to have authority from John Letcher or Jefferson Davis or any other person to band together for the purpose of doing unlawful acts.
>
> 2) If the person or property of person holding Federal office or office in the Wheeling government is molested, by the marauders, the penalty is death and all the old officers and other persons who voted for the Ordinance of Secession will be arrested too.
>
> 3) If the persons or property of any Union man, woman or child is molested or otherwise injured by the Moccasin Marauders or anyone sympathizing with the Confederacy, 5 times the number of Union persons so injured will be seized and made to respond for all damages, life for life and by 5 times the amount of property seized or stolen.
>
> 4) All persons harboring, sympathizing with, concealing or giving information to any Moccasin or Mountain Ranger within Jackson Co. or knowing of their presence within this co. and not giving this information to the commander of this Post will be treated like a Moccasin Ranger themselves and anyone giving information to aid the Rebellion or engaging in it will be treated as spies. No one will be allowed to advocate the doctrine of Secession, or to speak offensively either of the Restored Govt. at Wheeling or the U. S. Govt.
>
> 5) The Commander at the Post will hold the known Secessionists responsible for the killing, maiming or wounding of any Union soldier, man, woman or child or destruction of property public or

private in Jackson Co. It is within the power of the restored Govt.
of Va. to vindicate the laws and protect the lives and property of
the people. All who would see law and order restored be vigilant in
reporting to his Hd. Qtrs. at Ravenswood any infractions of law or
of this order.[73]

This issue of partisans more than any other fueled the local militarization which
came to be everywhere in evidence. Indeed, organization of local militia groups and
"Home Guards" was after a year finally progressing under capable hands, and the
Kanawha Valley was taking steps to recruit Union army regiments of their own. West
Virginians had done well to simply "hold their own" while Ohioans across the river
had enjoyed increased prosperity. The topic of what constituted prosperity compared
and contrasted in a back and forth in the Point Pleasant *Weekly Register* and the Gallipolis *Journal*. An editorial appeared in the *Journal* on June 26, 1862, claiming that
Gallipolis had not been in the least set back by the war, on the contrary, had expe-
rienced "an increase of wealth in both town and country." The editor of the *Journal*
asked "Can our Point Pleasant neighbors say as much ?" The editor of the *Weekly
Register* responded on June 3rd, that:

> The people of Point Pleasant can't boast of any remarkable degree of
> prosperity just at this time. In fact, a large majority of our people are
> content that, under the circumstances, they have been able to hold
> their own, and some again are glad that they are alive, when they
> consider the many trials and tribulations through which they have
> been called to pass during the last twelve months. For our own part,
> we do not anticipate any marked improvement in the condition of
> our affairs until we are received into the Union as a new State, and
> then we expect to start upon a career of prosperity unsurpassed in
> the history of any other portion of our wide extended country.[74]

There were however, across the river telltale signs of improvement. On Monday
May 12th, 1862, the Point Pleasant Academy, a secondary or high-school (funded by
private subscription) was reopened. Also in May, the Kanawha County salt industry
which had been failing (from 35 to 40 salt furnaces down to 6 or 7 in the past year)
was reviving. Crops also looked promising. In Mason County, farmers from various
parts of the county expressed their satisfaction: wheat looked good, corn was mostly
planted and apples, peaches, plums, grapes and blackberries—every species of fruit
was setting on in great abundance. Only the wheat crop looked to be poor, as by June
it was suffering greatly from the weevil, the result said farmers, of late sowing. As the
summer progressed (end of July and beginning of August) the prospects looked good

for an excellent harvest. On the economic front there was promise as well. The price of gold had fallen and Government stocks had risen correspondingly.

In the larger military theater, however, prospects were less promising. It appeared, in fact, as though the Union cause was faltering. In the space of a month the war had changed sharply in favor of the Confederates. In June and July Federal armed forces had suffered serious setbacks in Virginia. A great number of men and treasure had been expended by the North and the results across the board had been disappointing. General George B. McClellan and the magnificent Army of the Potomac had commenced a lackluster campaign across the Peninsula. In an abortive attempt to take Richmond (since May 1861, the capital of the United Confederate States), McClellan was attacked in his position east of Richmond by Lee and driven back in a series of engagements. By June 30th, it was clear that Richmond was safe. McClellan withdrew northward with shattered columns. In the Southwest, results to Union arms were also dismal. Morale in the Union Armies was at a low ebb. Union forces East and West suffered from widespread demoralization due to the very severe casualties taken (totaling in all some 75,000 men killed, wounded and missing). To replenish the armies two more calls for more volunteers went out that summer, the first on July 2nd and the next on August 4th.

Local Secessionists, living in Kanawha Valley neighborhoods, were jubilant upon hearing of the Federal reverses and for other reasons, overall, the Rebellion was encouraged. By mid-Summer 1862, the States in Rebellion—the entire South, extending far and wide— were well organized and unified in opposition to the United States. They had elected President and Vice-President to serve for a term of six years. Southern statesmen for their part, made necessary enactments that the Rebellion might be legalized, and large armies had been collected in different parts of the South to enforce Southern independence and sovereignty. A universal conscription act was passed by the Confederate States Congress in anticipation of spring campaigning on April 16th, 1862, which both relieved the Confederacy of dependence on volunteers and permitted that the entire fighting population be called out.

At Washington, President Lincoln and his cabinet were gravely concerned over the military situation in general and realized that a new call for men had to be made. All being in agreement, on July 2nd, 1862, the War Department published an order calling for 300,000 more volunteers. Suffice it to say, it took a good deal of nerve for men to volunteer at this call, as it was known that Union armies had been sorely depleted by battles and by disease, and those discharged on account of wounds and impaired health were returning home to their neighborhoods and towns—living testimony to the grim realities of a soldier's life. Then a second call for volunteers came. State quotas were set and if these were not met with volunteers, a draft would commence, until quotas were met.

Lincoln's second call for volunteers followed closely upon the heels of the first. On August 4th, the second call—an order—was issued by the War Department for the draft of 300,000 more Federal Militia to serve for nine months (the order to go into effect September 1st). This second call also stipulated that if the State quota failed to be met by August 15th, that deficiency would be made up by drafting from the permanent militia. There had until now been no such thing in the North as an actual draft. The "draft" as imposed at this time had no legal force, no means of enforcement to back it and thus was not considered as a real source of manpower, but the *idea* of it was intended as a "whip" to boost volunteering. On August 9th, another general order issued from the War Department listing those who would be automatically exempted.[75] On August 21st, the *Ironton Register* published a list of orders (six in all from Secretary of War Edwin Stanton, by order of President Lincoln) that were to regulate the upcoming conscription. "Fourth" among these orders stipulated that the draft called for by the President would begin on "Monday, the 5th day of September, between the hours of 8 an 9 A.M. and 4 and 5 P.M., and continue from day to day, between the same hours, until completed."[76] Inducements in the form of government bounties were offered to volunteers but only those who enlisted for three years were eligible to receive the $100 bounty offered by the Federal government.

Any action taken to boost the Federal military that the rebellion might be speedily quashed found whole-hearted support in the Kanawha Valley. In Mason County, Virginia, where Unionists felt that Secessionists had enjoyed the upper hand for all too long, even the draft was viewed with favor, as any measure that fell on Secessionist and Unionists alike was welcomed. The draft, wrote Lewis Wetzel in his weekly editorial (published July 31st) "would compel some of the infamous scoundrels who are throwing obstacles in the way of the recruiting service now, to share some of the privations, dangers and labors of a soldier's life" and give them a sense of the "dreadful state of affairs they have helped to bring about."[77]

Increased militarization was welcomed and eagerly anticipated by Union citizens for other reasons as well. Since the six days battle before Richmond, in which the Confederates claimed a victory, guerrillas were boldly showing themselves all along the border States. Heartened by recent victories to the Southern arms, they operated against Union civilians with renewed energy. Stealing, "midnight murder" and assassination were again on the menu. As the Governor of Western Virginia stated in his Proclamation of July 16th:

> Thousands of good loyal and law abiding citizens have been, and are to be murdered and destroyed for no other cause or offence, than their loyalty to the Government under which they have ever lived. There is not nor can there be any security to life or property while

> this state of things shall exist amongst us. [...] To crush the rebellion, the President has called for 300,000 more volunteers.[78]

Of this number two thousand and eighty were required of Virginia.

In the Kanawha Valley, insufficient number of men, arms and horses had been at bottom the problem in maintaining sovereignty and safety. Lincoln's calls for more men fueled momentum there with the distinct hope that the rebellion would at last be quenched, take what it will. It was in response to these calls that the 13th was organized and mustered into service. A contributing factor to the good response to calls for new volunteers was the fact that business was at a low ebb due to the war and the agricultural season (by-and-large the majority of men who volunteered for the 13th were farmers) had passed, and many enlisted to provide for themselves and their families. There was however, a counter current. A political movement afoot at the national level calling into question the constitutionality of the war may have retarded recruitment of the 13th Regiment. Governor Pierpont referenced this new attempt by northern politicians to thwart Lincoln and "the fight for restoration of the Union as it had been before the Rebellion," when he spoke to the State Senate and House of Representatives at years end saying:

> At one point during the past season, our cause looked dark, and it seemed as if victory would perch upon the banners of treason and rebellion. Contemporaneous with the call for 600,000 troops to replenish our army, a school of politicians sprang up throughout the country, advising the people to wait and see whether, the war was conducted constitutionally before they enlisted. This advice prevented thousands from enlisting, and for a season our cause looked gloomy, but, with patriotic ardor, the people came to the rescue and our ranks were rapidly filled with fresh troops.[79]

All representatives of county and State government were authorized to recruit in their own districts. To aid and facilitate enlistments, the Governor at Wheeling charged Senators and members of the House of Delegates returning to their home counties to cast a wide net, and they were given broad latitude in determining how best to raise volunteers. Senators were appointed to act as agents to procure volunteers and "to associate themselves with such other men as shall be deemed advisable and expedient to accomplish and obtain the number of men required with as little delay as practicable."[80] Specifically, delegates and senators were to organize themselves and co-ordinate with members of their magisterial district to form recruiting committees and to recommend "active, intelligent and brave men" to be commissioned 2nd Lieutenants of the companies raised. In the 45th Senatorial District (which embraced

Mason, Wayne, Cabell, Jackson, Wirt and part of Roane—all counties from which 13th recruits hailed), until committees could be formed, the following named gentlemen were to be considered committees to receive the names of volunteers who desired to enlist:

> W.W. Branfield, Jno. B. Bowen and Wm. Dixen of Wayne county; Grenville Parker, George T. Miller and John Everett of Cabell county; John Hall, John D. Thompson and George W. Murdock [all] of Mason county; James F. Scott, U.W. Flesher and George Leonard of Jackson county; B.T Stewart, Robert S. Brown and _____ Grayham of Wirt county; and H.D. Chapman of Roane county.

These men were to confer with their respective county delegates and together as agents of the Governor, to make such arrangements as they deemed best for obtaining volunteers.[81] Those volunteers who came forward from this section of the State were to rendezvous at Charleston, Guyandotte, Parkersburg and Clarksburg as might be most convenient.[82]

After Lincoln's calls for volunteers became publicized, meetings were held across Western Virginia counties. Stirring addresses were made urging men to support the government by volunteering. County magistrates convened as "Recruiting Committees" and, as encouraged by Governor Pierpont, they established an amount raised by levy to provide for volunteers and their families. Men of the embattled border country along the Ohio River responded with "patriotic ardor" to Lincoln's call of volunteers. The 91st Ohio Volunteer Infantry Regiment was raised in Southern Ohio in July 1862, and the 13th Virginia was raised from both Virginia and Ohio. Not only in Ohio and Western Virginia was there a sense of exigency and vigorous impulse to arm and militarize, the entire North at last began to awaken to the desperate nature and the magnitude of the contest. If the country was to be saved it would be only by concerted action. The officer responsible for recording "Annual Return of Alterations and Casualties" for the 13th Virginia Regiment noted for 1862 that the 13th "was raised under Gen. Order No. 75 from War Dept. Washington D. C. Series 1862" (superceded in 1864), regarding all aspects of recruitment, assignment and pay.[83]

The Point Pleasant *Weekly Register* and the 13ᵗʰ Regiment

The Point Pleasant *Register* was highly supportive of the men of 13ᵗʰ Regiment throughout the war and contributed in no small degree to promoting recruitment and keeping the regiment connected with family and friends in the Valley and across the border. The importance of town meetings and the nerve it took to hold such meetings in midst of a "barbarous and disgraceful system of guerilla warfare" urged on at the recommendation of the "rebel pretended Governor of Virginia, at Richmond" and carried on with "the aid and convenience of resident sympathizers and abettors in the neighborhoods where it is practiced"[84] cannot be readily understood today. The same could be said for pro-Union town and county newspaper proprietors and editors who needed no small amount of courage to generate their papers week after week. Death threats came with the job. Prior to this time newspapers were either "American,"[85] Whig (or Republican), or Democratic—touting a particular political agenda and candidates, much as today. Before the outbreak of the Rebellion—as it was then termed—there had been twenty-seven daily newspapers published in Virginia. Within a year after the outbreak of hostilities, most of these papers had been "very much curtailed in size" and the rest had ceased publication altogether.[86] Some of these papers, such as the Point Pleasant *Weekly Register* were pro-Union and pro-Republican during the war then Democratic once the war was over.

The importance of the newspaper in those days to Unionists in Western Virginia cannot be overemphasized. The counties west of the Alleghenies had long been subjected to a kind of cultural isolation—kept as a kind of back-water adjunct to Eastern Virginia, with few roads, no railroads, no public school system, university or public welfare projects, facilities or services of any real impact. Newspapers in general worked to counter such backward tendencies, providing in their columns the chief means of disseminating local and national developments. After the outbreak of hostilities, the more "radical" Union papers promoted Union solidarity and the Union cause generally. They supported the militarization of county life by promoting recruitment in new regiments (such as the 13ᵗʰ) and enrollment in militia regiments and home guard groups.

Local newspapers also provided a chief means of communication as local post offices were raided, mail was captured and mail routes were subsequently closed. Local papers enabled inhabitants to stay connected with other loyal Virginia counties and the nation. Newspapers announced the date and time of public meetings and issues to be discussed; the opening of recruiting stations;[87] and of recruiting season for the new 13ᵗʰ Regiment in various towns such as Point Pleasant, Charleston and Mason City. Pro-Union newspapers also proved highly effective in pummeling the Confederacy, a function of how effective can be inferred from the statements of newspaper editors and proprietors who claimed to be on the receiving end of threats constantly.

One such newspaperman was George Ways Tippett,[88] a pro-Union Democrat who started the *Weekly Register* at Point Pleasant sometime during the month of February 1862 (the enterprise commenced about Feb. 27ᵗʰ, 1862, with a first issue appearing on March 6ᵗʰ, 1862). There is some discrepancy as to when the *Register* actually began publication, but its importance particularly as a conduit for news about the soldiers of the 13ᵗʰ West Virginia Regiment both during and after the war can scarcely be appreciated in the linked in world of today.

What spare references to the beginnings of the paper were made in the columns of the paper itself, suggest that Tippet purchased the newspaper office from attorney and Secessionist Henry J. Fisher,[89] who had published a paper in Point Pleasant before leaving town for the more "congenial South" to support the Confederate cause at Richmond, sometime before the arrival of the Union troops (specifically the 11ᵗʰ Ohio Volunteer Infantry which occupied the town beginning July 10ᵗʰ, 1861, and into winter 1861). Fisher seems to have left his residence and other property in the care of his "Negro servants," "Aunt Violet and her daughter Abbey, who were among the lady residents of the 'Point' kindly held in remembrance by the boys of the 11ᵗʰ."[90]

The 11ᵗʰ Ohio apparently appropriated Fisher's printing office to publish their own Union paper which they called *The Eleventh Ohio*. Horton and Teverbaugh, compilers of an 11ᵗʰ Regiment history noted that the "former proprietor" of the newspaper office "had left all materials: type, presses etc. and soon after the 11ᵗʰ became established in the town, several 'typo' members of the Regiment, opened up the office and started a Union paper [...]."[91]

Decades later Tippett stated that he had started his paper on February 27ᵗʰ, 1862. The Wheeling *Daily Intelligencer,* of March 3, 1862, announced the start-up of a new weekly Union paper adding (surely in some error) that they (the editors of the *Intelligencer*) had already received "[t]he fourth issue of this new weekly" and "[i]t is an unusually good paper considering the disadvantages under which it starts. [...] Subscription for the *Register* is $1.00 per year."[92] The *Intelligencer* notice if accurate, would indicate that the *Register* had begun printing about the first week of February 1862. Be that as it may, the first issue of the *Weekly Register* (Volume 1, Number 1) appeared on March 6th, 1862. It was modestly priced at ten cents a copy or one dollar per year. It was "first housed in a twenty by thirty-two foot frame building on Fifth Street."[93] It was to quote Tippett a "doubtful enterprise" at the onset.[94]

> At first the *Register* was printed on a ram-shackle of a hand-press, of undoubted antiquity, and the same press was used for all kinds and sorts of job work, from the full sheet poster down to the one line visiting card, while the types, which [had] seen their best days years before, were of antediluvian style, and the variety limited to an exceedingly small number of fonts.[95]

At that time (1862) continued Tippett, Point Pleasant

> contained a population of about three hundred people, with few business houses, and no manufacturing interests, and only one or two fine residences, the others being small frame buildings, while here and there the early settler's log cabin could be seen. The town had dirt streets and no pavements worthy of the name.[96]

The stated purpose of the new paper *(Tippett's Register)* was to offer "a strictly Union" viewpoint "identified with the best interests of Western Virginia," "warmly supporting the Provisional Government established at Wheeling and pledged to the prosperity of Western Virginia and the nation."[97] Tippett was sole proprietor. He was "his own local and business manager and principal type setter, then a creative art, unknown to machinery."[98] All type set by hand and in all a very slow method. Certainly he did some writing but the editorial chair was 'hired out.' Tippett's first editor was the Honorable Lewis Wetzel. Wetzel served in many capacities. He was at this time in his second term as Justice of the Peace. He first term of service as Justice began on August 1st, 1856. During this term, he was also elected "presiding justice," also called "President of Justices of the Mason County Circuit Court." He was again chosen President in 1860, during his second term. He was appointed to serve on the Committee on Division of the State. Wetzel serve as House Delegate for the fledgling State government, (at convention and on the Committee on Division of the State. together with J. P. R. B. Smith and George W. Tippett, all of Point Pleasant) and as recruiter for the 13th Regiment.[99]

One cannot overstate the importance of Tippett's undertaking in focusing Union sentiment in Mason and adjoining counties and in promoting and concentrating efforts to organize what would become the 13th Regiment West Virginia Volunteers. There was a need for newspapers in this part of the country. Papers had made little showing in that section of the State and particularly pro-Union newspapers were needed at that time to provide a forum for the discussion of local and national public matters and issues, to report on the New State question, and on military matters and the progress of the war. Indeed, in this, to put it mildly, the *Register* was more than a "strictly Union paper."

It was emphatically, unconditionally, and unabashedly devoted to promoting the cause of the Union, Western Virginia and the National Government. That Tippett's efforts had the desired effect; got people's attention and stirred things up is evident by the fact that local "insurgents" marked the paper and the editor "as one to be ostraci[z]ed" and some "cut-throat guerrillas" declared they would "yet come here and cut our heart out," wrote editor Wetzel.[100] Wetzel and Tippett were, however, unwavering and adamant that under no condition would they consent to dismemberment of the country. Division of the State, however, was another matter altogether. With its first issue, the *Weekly Register* deplored the bloody civil war then desolating the land and flung out a call to arms with the following justification: the time for argument had passed and inasmuch as the South had been the first to appeal to arms, the Union should persuade in like manner that it was still powerful enough to punish treason at home. The first issue also provided each subscriber—"at considerable expense to the paper"—with a copy of the Constitution of the proposed new State of Western Virginia, so that voters could become acquainted with its provisions before voting on it, the vote to be held on the first Thursday in April, 1862.

In the months that followed, with florid language and dramatic imagery, the paper promoted Federal Army enlistment and published soldiers letters, poems and other news items about Western Virginia Regiments serving both at home and farther afield. It also provided detailed reports about the Conventions at Wheeling and meetings conducted by members of the Provisional Government and published the dates and times of local Union meetings and their resolutions. Recruitment of the Thirteenth was strongly supported and encouraged in the most vehement language, Tippett's columns making place for anything of note (however small) regarding "our Regiment." W.W. Harper was especially supportive of the new paper. Letters penned by Methodist Minister William W. Harper (enlisted in the 13th Regiment October 4th, 1862, and promoted Chaplain of the Regiment in February 1864) frequently appeared in its columns.[101] His letters provided an all-important link between the regiment and their families at home. This kind of hard news from the front also boosted the *Register's* circulation.

On page two, of the August 28th (1862) issue, there appeared "Who Will Take Responsibility," in which Harper called on men to take positive action to crush the rebellion. In a letter to the *Register* dated "Hartford City, Va., Sept.22, 1862,"[102] "W.W.H." (as he signed his letters to the paper) extolled his reason for supporting the *Register:* newspapers were the only means of conveying the "light and truth" to the great masses and that as regards this paper in particular, "[w]e know that the secessionists don't like it, and that they are doing all they can against it. This fact is notorious."[103] One hand washed the other, the editor announcing that their "esteemed friend," W. W. Harper, was appointed Sergeant-Major of the 13th and that he will bring to his new and arduous duties "ready penmanship, a business tact and unexceptionable habits."[104]

In response to threats from some of the more cut-throat Southern sympathizers among the readership, Wetzel and Tippett took the low ground: Pro-Southern voices in the community were not to be heard and loyal citizens were urged to wage guerrilla warfare against the Southern raiders and bushwhackers which plagued the area. On an entirely different and more positive note, the paper also promoted development of Western Virginia's mineral resources, supported local business, and education. It held issues of the moment before its readers, encouraged voting and published numerous notices regarding the activities of the local State Militia, Committee of Safety[105] and reports of Union meetings held at the Point Pleasant Courthouse and in private homes. In these groups, many men, who later joined the ranks of the 13th, took prominent rolls.

Once recruitment for the 13th had begun in earnest, it proceeded with momentum. A number of factors fueled the brisk pace. While avoidance of the stigma of being drafted played a part in such small communities, where everyone knew everyone else, the economic necessity of earning a living at a time when the U.S. Service offered the best opportunity, was no doubt another compelling inducement to volunteering. Other conditions also played a role as well.

There was a scarcity of currency. Coins, especially silver ones were hoarded and various means were resorted to, to remedy the inconvenience. One of the ways people coped with the situation was to pay with postage stamps of various denominations. Tokens were also issued by merchants for exchange in their businesses. Moreover, prospects for earning a living in such business and industry as there was along the Ohio and Kanawha Rivers had ground to a halt with the commencement of hostilities. People's reserves in cash, stock and other property became exhausted. People avoided going out unless they had to and this, at night, when under the proverbial "cover of dark" they enjoyed somewhat greater safety. At night, people ventured out for necessary errands, such as buying provisions, taking their grain to mill to grind, etc. Business and to a lesser extent farm work had been curtailed due to enlistments in both Southern and Northern armies and because of guerrilla raids. Many farmers had hidden their horses or had no animals to farm with, as they had secreted them off (typically to Ohio) so that they might not be stolen by partisans "recruiting" their mounts. Those farmers who had sown or re-sown destroyed crops were now (in August and September 1862 when the 13th was being recruited) finished and they needed another way to get money until harvest time. Army pay and other promised benefits in the shape of bounties, land and pensions were compelling inducements and certainly steadier work at this juncture than work in the field.

To make matters worse, while the 1862 harvest looked to be excellent in mid-summer, it began to be effected by what would become a severe drought — the worst in decades. By harvest time, the drought in that area had made the ground so hard that farmers could not even set out seed for a replacement crop. It had parched all kinds of vegetation and rendered whole fields of corn unworthy of harvest labor.[106] No significant rain fell in Mason County during summer until Saturday, October 4th,[107] just days before those companies then comprising the 13th Regiment would be mustered into the U.S. Service. Not only was harvest effected by the lack of rain. The Ohio and Kanawha rivers were lower at this time than they had been for years. Navigation of the rivers, the best means of conveyance and communication, like trade, industry, and farming wound down.

The inducement of county and federal bounties and prospect of a monthly salary—though none could have anticipated how sporadically the 13th would be paid—compelled men of all ages, predominantly farmers by occupation, to join the Government service as a way to provide for themselves and their families. Another attractive inducement to enlist came on July 14th, 1862, when an act was signed into law by the U.S. Congress, providing a system of pensions for veterans and for next of kin in case of death.[108] Aside from this, there was the weight of opinion from without and the weight of conscience from within. Public opinion was shrill, that the war be taken to secessionists in their neighborhoods and behind Southern lines. The need for armed forces — especially mounted — in Western Virginia had been and continued to be keenly felt. Secessionists were actively promoting their cause, from merely passing mail to and from Confederate lines,[109] to stealing laundry, horses, and supplies, to arrest, abduction, confinement, to robbery, mayhem and murder. They needed only to look about them to see that action was imperative.

The focusing of public opinion and appearance of recruiting stations headed up by local men brought pressure to bear on the individual conscience. The view that the men of the previous generations had already done their part for their country and the belief that the rebellion could be crushed by joining the national forces came (*i.e.,* by the concerted effort of many and ready access to regulation arms and ordnance) into focus in the hearts of those eligible for enlistment. Their communities had been the battleground since the beginning of the conflict, and many, by their own admission, felt the weight of obligation to step forward to protect hearth and home against secessionists in their neighborhoods, as well as from invasion from without. Not surprisingly, for all of the above, the young and not so young of Mason and adjacent counties, stepped up and joined the army.

June and July 1862:
"Will we be driven out of the Kanawha Valley?"

With the end of June came such widespread concern that Confederate strength in the Kanawha Valley was building toward another invasion and re-occupation of region, that on July 2nd, Gen. George B. McClellan ordered Brigadier General Jacob Dolson Cox to Gallipolis, Ohio, to prepare an invasion of the Kanawha Valley with a command of 3,000 men.[110] Plans were quickly made. J.B. McGinnis, member of the Mason County Committee for Public Safety, likewise fearing that another perhaps even more destructive return raid than heretofore lay on the horizon, wrote to Judge H.J. Samuels (State Adjutant General from Cabell County) on June 27th (1862). McGinnis relayed that Mason County citizens had requested permission to arm to prepare for the contingency, and he recommended that fellow Committee member, Major John O. Butler (of Mason County) be authorized to raise a company of 200 armed men to protect property and person.[111] McGinnis described the gloom that hung in the air in these graphic terms:

> The spoiler has been in our land and our once smiling villages look
> like fragments sown by the hand of destruction and that is but half,
> for we dayly look for greater, or worse things. The loyal citizens
> of our country are bowed down with fear, and they go about like
> mourners [...].[112]

By end of July, the Gallipolis *Journal* observed in "What is the Prospect?" that the question "revolving in more than one mind" was "Will we be driven out of the Kanawha Valley?" "The bitter unrelenting secesh," continued the author "have lately become jubilant, and many of them publicly say that the Yankees will have to 'ske-daddle' out of this before long and couple the name of Stonewall Jackson with such an event."[113] A soldier-correspondent (*pseud.* "S.P.C.") wrote to the Cincinnati *Gazette* reporting on the discovery and seizure of a packet of letters at Lewisburg, written by soldiers from the 22nd Virginia. All letters indicated that the soldiers soon expected to drive back the Union army and regain the Kanawha Valley.[114] The 22nd Virginia was a Confederate regiment that had been recruited in the Kanawha Valley and the letters were written to the soldiers' families there. This regiment was in fact at this time present with Confederate Gen. W.W. Loring—Loring to command troops which in fact did invade and occupy Charleston that autumn.

Despite greater commitment and activity on the part of Federal military and the general populace to curb partisan activities, Confederates continued to successfully target weak points in Mason County and adjacent counties of the Valley. The more beleaguered points of Summer 1862, would become stations for the various detachments of the 13th until the regiment's departure for the Shenandoah Valley in 1864. Meanwhile, at end of July, editor Lewis Wetzel (at that point in time recruiting men for the 13th Regiment at Point Pleasant) posed the following remedy which he hoped might be utilized by State authorities. The tenor of his column conveys the sense of urgency prevailing in this and other Kanawha Valley counties. He wrote:

> There is in the Kanawha Valley and in the counties adjacent thereto able bodied men now in the State militia organization sufficient to protect this whole region of country. Why could not the entire military force of the counties of Mason, Putnam, Kanawha, Cabell &c., be called out and employed in garrison duty in the Valley and the various regiments now distributed around in this section, be moved on to join Cox or engage in active service wherever they may be most needed. [...] Let us wake up in Heavens name to the importance of some kind of prompt vigorous and energetic action [on the part of those eligible to serve and on the part of the State authorities].[115]

Concern for this area went all the way to the Executive office at Washington City. President Lincoln telegraphed Governor Pierpont on July 28th, asking for information as to when the Western Virginia regiments could move so that calculations could be made at Washington.[116]

Cabell County (where detachments of the 13th Regiment would spend over a year doing service, beginning in 1863) had been and continued to be a hive of Secessionist activity.[117] On Monday, July 4th, Sheriff of Cabell County, John Alford brought suit against local Confederates (William A. Jenkins, Thomas J. Jenkins, George W. Holderby, Robert Holderby by Peter Buffington, John Chapman, Hurston Spurlock, Milton J. Ferguson, Warren R. Reece, John N. Clarkson, Calwellsy Simmons, Joseph W. Morris, Wilson B. Moore, Henry Buffington, Leander Gilkerson, James Ferguson, Burwell Spurlock, Vincent A. Witcher, James R. Morris, John Plymale, Henry Everett, John S. Everett, James Everett, Henry C. Poteet, V. R. Moss, Charles K.

Morris, Charles L. Roffe, Charles Shelton, Henry H. Miller and Asa L. Wilson) for "falsely & wrongfully arresting the person of plaintiff [Alford] & wrongfully & falsely imprisoning him for the space of six months" and for a suit of 'trespass on the case' with damages in the amount of 30,000 dollars.[118] A few days later, on July 10th, 1862, Sheriff Alford wrote to H.J. Samuels from the Cabell Court House requesting that "one co[mpany]" be sent to them there until Superior Court was over as

> there is some little danger here at present. Dr. Jennius was killed up mud some days Ago Charly Hanles + William Jefferson was the men engaged and it can be proven when he was found his hed and hand was cut off: he was A Union man they got A very fine horse and the reports is that there is 10 of Jenkins men here now and 25 of Conuses men in wain County and what their business is I can't tell [...].[119]

On July 12th, 1862, Samuel A. Childers wrote from Barboursville, Cabell County, that the countryside was in awful condition. The "Secesh" who had taken the oath were letting it be known that they would not "regard it." When the commissioner made rounds taking names for tax purposes, they would not give their names "as they say there is no law." The horse thief held in jail at Barboursville had to be safeguarded "day and night" that he would not be broken out. Continued Childers:

> [T]here is a quantity of the border rangers now in Cabell they are lurking in the woods and about their homes [...] unless something is done soon this country will not be worth staying in any longer. I know only one Union man now that is I Laidly and it is very disheartening to him.[120]

On July 18th, Alford wrote again to Samuels from the Cabell County Court House, saying that he was "under grate embarresment as to the future of our country." He remarked further that he had been "very creditably informed" that on about July 24[th], there would be "about 4,000 cavelry in the county under Jenkins' command." Alford's informant telling him "as a Friend and that the intention was to take all men who had taken office under the Provisional Gov[ernmen]t and as a Grand Military skeme showing [...] that the Confeds can invade the border and hold it as long as the[y] pleas [...]." Alford asked Samuels "what can be done" for them in Cabell?[121]

West Columbia, Mason County, was another focal point for secessionist activity in what would become the bailiwick of the 13th Regiment. On July 21st (1862), A.C. Mason (soon to be 1st Sergeant of Company F) wrote to William E. Wetzel (Marshal of Mason County), from West Columbia, proposing the removal of a store of United States arms, then at a "Company Store" in Mason City. Mason's letter written on patriotic paper — Washington on a rearing charger and "Strike for the memory of Washington!" printed underneath, contained the following:

> Wm E. Wetzel Sir the object of this Note is to inform you that it is the wish of a Goodly number of the best Loyal Citizens of this place that you adopt some measures to remove the US arms from its present place in the town of Mason City Va to a More Secure place and Distribute them among those Known to be Loyal in the town + vicinities along the border for the following Reasons Viz — we are creditably informed that 50 of them is in the Company Store of Mason Cty + that the Clerks are not Sound and further Lately there has been Several Meetings held in the S[ai]d Store by those known to be Secesh — Lasting till Mid night and as it is well known here that there is a majority of Secesh in that town (Mason C[i]ty) it is thought best to have the arms Distributed as you think best or removed to Some More Secure place for Safe keeping, it is Evident that Something Should be done to put them where they cannot be brought to bear against us. As you are the Marshal we Look for you to attend to it, or authorize Some one to do it, — You should investigate the Matter.

A.C. Mason's letter to Wetzel was forwarded to H.J. Samuels by John Hall, I think, as Hall penned a post script to Samuels recommending: "would it not be well to order Mr [R.C.M.] Lovell to ship Those arms fourthwith to Point Pleasant or Gallipolis for safekeeping?"[122]

R.C.M. Lovell was a prominent Union man resident in Mason City. He promoted the Union cause during the war in a number of ways. He owned of a fleet of steamers and as business was down and wagons in short supply, he used his steamers to transport supplies and men for the U.S. Government. He wrote passes for people to travel through the country and seems to have been a major player in stockpiling arms for the loyal members of the Mason County militia before hostilities officially opened with the firing on Fort Sumter. Evidence to support this is a communication sent by Lovell to Wheeling, on February 31st, 1862. In this telegraph, Lovell spoke regarding "a lot of muskets in his possession" and that upon orders, he would "turn them over to Captain McCowen or to Lieut. Neal. Out of the lot, there are 80 muskets belonging to the State of Ohio, which were obtained about one year ago." These 80, Lovell advised to be returned.[123] Captain McCowen is likely Captain Albert F. McCowen of the 106th Mason County Militia (and future Captain, cmdg. Co. F, 13th Virginia Regiment).

Then, more alarming news came. On July 25th, 1862, the Moccasin Rangers attacked the 9th Virginia Infantry stationed at Summerville, Virginia. Unfortunately for the 9th, this was the second time they were surprised and over-run. The previous year on November 10th and 11th (called the "Guyandotte Massacre"), they were being recruited when they were caught in a trap laid at Guyandotte. They had lost heavily in men. Now, again, in the surprise attack at Summerville, the 9th lost about sixty prisoners—captured by the Rangers.[124]

Then came more alarms. In Cabell County, on July 27th, Union officer Colonel J.A.J. Lightburn commanding 4th Brigade, Kanawha Valley military district (headquarters at Charleston) received a report that Albert G. Jenkins and his brother Jeff were at Jenkins' home at Greenbottom, Cabell County. The presence of the two officers seemed to catalyze Secessionists in the Cabell area. The Gallipolis *Journal* reported that the return of the Jenkins brothers—both officers in the Confederate army and the return of several other pro-South men not seen since the beginning of the war, who had recently returned to their homes and were reportedly "threatening the neighborhood," had "much excited" local Rebels resident in Cabell. These were threatening that "now" was the time for action.[125] Cox sent a company of cavalry to Lightburn with advice to keep his detachments busy scouting, gathering intelligence, and staying on top of any secessionist activity within a 30 mile radius.

On August 1st, Lightburn implemented a strict regimen for managing threats posed by the Secessionist element in his district. He began with language. Orders were issued from Charleston that all men in the vicinity of Buffalo, Putnam County,[126] who had *certainly* engaged in using treasonable language, had engaged in treasonable conduct or had incited others to do so, were to be arrested and brought to 4th Brigade Headquarters at Charleston. J.W. Davis was to depart from Charleston by steamboat with twenty men for Buffalo, Putnam County,

> and having made enquiries of Union men at that place as to the condition of the country will proceed to scout the country and arrest all male persons who it can be proven are using treasonable language or engaged in treasonable conduct or in any way inducing others to do so. Such persons are to be arrested and brought to these Head Qtrs. By order of J.A.J. Lightburn Col. Comdg. 4 Brig.[127]

Recruitment in the Valley

In June 1862, officers commissions were being issued to men who had been or who wished to recruit for the Federal army in the Kanawha Valley. Whether due to recruiters efforts or to the fact that a number of 13th soldiers were already in the field as members of re-organized State militia regiments, it is clear that a number of 13th soldiers (or men who would soon become members of the 13th as privates, non-commissioned and commissioned officers) were already in the field doing military duty — probably without pay and certainly without adequate equipment and supplies. (See Martin and Shannon letters *infra.*)

Many of the men who volunteered for the 13th Regiment in a wave of enlistment were farmers from Southern Ohio and Virginia. Those few from overseas worked as miners—a tough lot. They were in all, used to the rigors of the outdoors, were self-reliant, independent types. Extant orders indicate that Colonel William R. Brown (late of the 4th Regiment loyal Virginia Infantry), who commanded the regiment from its first to last day in service, had no easy task conforming the men to the life of military discipline. Dr. F.H. Patton referred to this independent streak in West Virginia soldiers at a reunion held at Wheeling in 1886. Dr. Patton, formerly Surgeon of the 12th West Virginia Volunteer Infantry and after the war in charge of the Soldiers' Home at Dayton, Ohio, related that he was often asked why there were so few West Virginia soldiers to be found residing at the Soldiers' Home at Dayton. Patton replied that there were in general, few West Virginia soldiers to be found in Soldiers' Homes. He explained. West Virginia soldiers "were a self-reliant class of men, used to and feeling themselves fully capable of looking after and taking care of themselves during the war," and that this feature of looking out for themselves characterized them yet and accounted for the fact that so few West Virginians resided in soldiers' homes.[128]

Two early letters from 13th soldiers—Moses Martins and William Shannon— describe life in the regiment before muster in. Martin, probably recruited by Lieutenant W.N. Hawkins (later 1st Lieutenant Co. E, 13th Regiment), wrote to his father on June 7th, from Charleston (Martin was mustered in with the rank of Private, Co. K, 13th Regiment). Captain Shannon, (future 2nd Lieutenant of Co. I, 13th Regiment) on duty with Wayne County Militia on recruiting duty wrote to H.J. Samuels from Wayne on June 24th.

> Camp Simmons
> Charlestown Va
> June 7th/62
>
> Dear Father this pleasant morning affords Me the pleasure of writing you afew lines to let You no that I am stil on the land and among The living I am well and truley hope that this may find you all enjoying the same blesings I arrived here yesterday abot 4 o clock and was on guard last night I am at an invalid Camp camd [commanded] by Lt Hawkens out back of Charlestewn there is severl of our boys here Polk and Charley hill is up at gaulley they air [illeg. word or two] well and doing guard duty up there [illeg. words] dave harris and thomas Harris air here I cant tell you when We will leave here or whether we will leave Here atol or not we got the word yesterday That the 1st Briggade was coming back. If that is so the 13th will be back but I don't Bileave they will come nor wonte until I see them Comeing and I am afeard it will be sometime Before I see them if I wait for them
>
> To come back here they air now beyen Stenton And what of us is here is expecting orders To go their but if it is so about them coming Back her we wont go out their atol tell will That Tom wants him to come up and if we Stay here you must come also I don't know When we will be paid off and when you come up bring some monney with you So that you can let me have two or 3 dollars I have no news so I will close hoping To here from you all son write soon and Beleave this to be from you Affectionate son.
>
> Until Death
> M Martin
> Address: Mr Moses Martin
> Co K 13 Va
> Camp Simmons Charleston
> Ka. Co W. Va.
> In care of Lt Hawkens[129]

June 24, 1862, Capt. William Shannon wrote to Samuels from Wayne County, saying, "I have not received eny guns yet though I have been looking for them for some time ples foured them on as soon as you can I need them bad." Shannon also sent along requesting a commission for John R. Gilkerson for 2nd Lieutenant of Shannon's company, also for cartridges and powder to be sent along with guns and bullet molds. He added: "there is som out rages committed in this country I have mad some arrests and some of the Rebels have left the County. I [have] also gotten some volunteers since I last saw you."[130]

Organization of the Regiment
Moves Forward

By end of July (1862), good progress was being made organizing the 13th Virginia and a suitable point of rendezvous for the 13th was contemplated. On July 29th, 1st Lieutenant and Adjutant of the 13th Regiment, William I. Mathews wrote to Adj. Gen. H.J. Samuels reporting on the best place to establish Head Quarters for the 13th. Mathews suggested that

> Some town in the Kanawha country must be selected as a regimental rendezvous and Parkersburg in my opinion will suit better for that purpose than others in the section of Western Virginia in which the Reg. is to be raised. It affords fine camping grounds, ample storage for clothing camp and garrison equipage + c. is easy of access by rail or river from all the counties of the state in which the recruiting officers of the Reg will operate and is moreover connected by rail, river + telegraph with the Department at Wheeling.
>
> The advantages which it possesses over either Charleston, Guyandotte or the other towns in the Kanawha region seem to me most worthy of consideration in selecting a place for Regimental Head Quarters.[131]

Point Pleasant, Mason County, was chosen for 13th Headquarters and point of rendezvous and shortly before August 19th, companies being recruited for the 13th were ordered by State Adj. Gen. H.J. Samuels to report there. On August 19th, 1862, 1st Lieutenant, W.I. Mathews wrote to Samuels from Point Pleasant informing that he had received Samuels' order by way of Colonel Norton, and pursuant to that order, Head Quarters for the 13th was established immediately, at Point Pleasant. Mathews continued:

> Today Lieut. G.W. Gist reported with 52 men from Hartford City, Mason Co. Va. He + Simon Williams were chiefly instrumen-

tal in getting them + Lieut Gov. Polsley assures me they can raise a
full company. To satisfy the men I organized them into a company +
allowed them to choose a 1ˢᵗ Lieut whereupon Simon Williams was
elected unanimously.

Upon representations made to me by Lieut Gov Polsley + other
prominent men here I allowed them to return to Hartford City for
the purpose of filling up the Company, to report next Monday.[132]

George W. Gist, of Letart Falls, Mason County, was Lieutenant Governor Daniel
Polsley's son-in-law.[133] Miscellaneous records at the West Virginia State Archives indicate that he recruited many men for the Union with and without appointment or special authority of any kind. In the foregoing reference, the company of men recruited
at Hartford City, became Company D of the 13ᵗʰ Regiment (Capt. Simon Williams
commanding). In regard to this company, 2ⁿᵈ Lieut. Gist wrote to Samuels on August
30ᵗʰ, from Letart, informing that he had

reported to Adj Mathews at Pt Pleasant on the 18 inst with 53 men
and wish his consent to organize the co. by electing Simon Williams
first Lt. [...] I have now 68 men and hope to be able to get enough to
fill up to the minimum (83) for a general organization on Saturday
(30ᵗʰ).[134]

T[heophilus] Maher, also recruiting for the 13ᵗʰ, wrote to H.J. Samuels, from
Point Pleasant, on September 1ˢᵗ, informing that ninety-three articles of enlistment
had been sent to Samuels at Wheeling, and that the men for this company (Co. A,
13ᵗʰ) all enlisted at and around Charleston from August 11ᵗʰ to the 19ᵗʰ. The company,
continued Maher, was organized by election of James W. Johnson as Captain and
Greenbury Slack Jr.[135] as 1ˢᵗ Lieutenant. Maher retained his position as 2ⁿᵈ Lieutenant.
He added: "In obedience to the instructions brought to Charleston by Col[onel] Norton we left for this rendezvous [Point Pleasant] on [Aug. 24ᵗʰ]."[136]

Twenty-five year old James M. Johnson was elected captain on August 19ᵗʰ, 1862.
His commission was dated September 9ᵗʰ, 1862, and he was mustered in as Captain
of Co. A on October 7ᵗʰ, at Point Pleasant. On July 20ᵗʰ, 1863, he transferred for
promotion to the 3ʳᵈ Regiment U.S. Colored troops by order of the War Department
Order No. 335.[137] Greenbury Slack Jr. was commissioned in the Kanawha County
153ʳᵈ Militia State Troops, on May 14ᵗʰ, 1862, to rank from April 30ᵗʰ, 1862.[138] He
was elected 1ˢᵗ Lieutenant by the recruits comprising Co. A, on August 19ᵗʰ. He was
promoted from 1ˢᵗ Lieutenant to Captain (Co. A), succeeding J.W. Johnson on or
about August 14ᵗʰ, 1863 (the date of Slack's commission).

Appointment of Officers
and Recruitment of the 13th Continues

Efforts to appoint suitable officers to recruit for the 13th began late in 1861 and continued for almost another year. Recruiting for the Union army got off to a slower start in Western Virginia for obvious reasons, but that recruitment of the 13th Regiment dragged out over a year after Lincoln issued his first call for 75,000 troops to aid in suppressing the rebellion after the fall of Fort Sumter strains for an explanation. Would be officers from a variety of counties were recommended and applied for appointments as lieutenants to recruit for the 13th. That other men without proper authority also went recruiting on their own initiative is faintly but certainly indicated by extant correspondence to the State Government at Wheeling.

On February 24th, 1862, at Wheeling, Lieutenant H. Atkinson, "13th Va. Vols." was examined by a Board of Examination consisting of Brigadier General R.C. Schenk, President of the Board; Major D.H. McPhail, U.S. Paymaster and Captain E.C. Bainbridge, Assistant G[eneral] of Muster, U.S.A. Atkinson was examined as to his fitness for the Colonelcy. Atkinson testified that he was 22 years of age, and that he had entered the service as Captain of Scouts under General McClellen in the Department of Western Virginia. He stated further that he received his present commission as 1st Lieutenant of the 13th Virginia Volunteers on September 16th, 1861. His past service consisted of about one month's duty as Captain of Mounted Scouts; then as Captain of Foot Scouts until September 15th, 1861, "during which time he was also assigned to the command of a piece of artillery and was with the expedition in command of a piece from Oakland, Maryland to Hardy County, Virginia." Beginning September 16th, 1861, he had served as aide-de-camp to General Henry W. Benham. After careful examination the examining board reached the opinion that Lieut. Atkinson was fully competent to perform the duties of Field and Company officers and a fit appointee to the rank of Colonel for the 13th Virginia.[139] This appointment seems to have gone nowhere.

Well in advance of the 13th Regiment's organization in October 1862, was the appointment of two other men to the colonelcy of the regiment. These were Kellian Van Rensalear Whaley, West Virginia politician and Charles R. Dorone/Doran, a well-educated, well-connected fraud. Whaley (born in New York in 1821), was a Republican and before the war earned a living in the lumber business in Mason County. With the opening of hostilities between North and South, he served as a delegate to the conventions which effectively restored Western Virginia's loyal State government. He was a recruiter for the Union army and instrumental in pushing forward the New State movement. At the time of his appointment to the rank of Colonel of the 13ᵗʰ Virginia, he was serving as a Representative from Virginia to the 37ᵗʰ Congress (March 4, 1861-March 3, 1863) at Washington. Under his watch as colonel and recruiting officer for the 13ᵗʰ, the regiment also failed to organize. The appointment of suitable officers was impeded by disorganization, petty politics and in at least one instance, by fraud. (There is no paper evidence that Whaley ever recruited anyone, and one wonders if his appointment as colonel was purely some sort of honor conferred for his political activism, or payment for some political debt.) Following the failed attempt to organize the 13ᵗʰ Regiment in early in 1862, Whaley devoted himself to serving the Union cause in West Virginia and the New State cause in Congress. He would be elected to serve for two more terms: as "Unconditional Unionist" from West Virginia to the 38ᵗʰ Congress and as U.S. Representative to the succeeding Congress (December 7ᵗʰ, 1863 to March 3ʳᵈ, 1867).[140]

"How Many Soldiers Have We Got!"
(Point Pleasant *Weekly* Register, March 20, 1862, [p. 2].)
Charles R. Dorone and his attempt to recruit the 13ᵗʰ Virginia

The case of Charles R. Dorone (also written or known as Doron or Doran) is of particular interest. Among other things, it indicates that in their zeal to raise troops, the War Department at Washington and Gov. Pierpont were not overly discriminating and that considerable fraud, even to the selling of commissions and bamboozling on grand scale went on as self-serving men with "delusions of grandeur," finagled to acquire positions of command in the Federal army. That the door stood open in Washington to such opportunists is easily attributable to the loose practice there in delegating authority to recruit. The President granted authority to raise troops to men who came to Washington requesting this favor; so too did the Secretary of War give authority; and clerks in the War office were also conferred with authority to raise regiments and transact business in the name of the Secretary of War. As a result, neither the War Office nor the President, nor anyone in Government had any real idea about how many recruiters, nor how many volunteer soldiers there were in the field.[141]

Charles R. Dorone was born in Philadelphia, Pennsylvania, and in his adult life was a resident of that city. In those days, when the title of "medical physician" was elastic (*i.e.*, could be precise and indicative of advanced study and skill, or broad and loosely applicable to a wide range of "expertise") Dorone was reportedly "a medical physician." He began his military career as a Private of Company D, 27th Pennsylvania Volunteer Infantry. He was enrolled in Philadelphia, on May 5th, 1861, and served as "Nurse" or "Assistant Hospital Steward." He was discharged from the United States service on September 29th, 1861, at Roach Mills, Virginia, on a "Surgeon's Certificate of Disability." His disability was attributed to "Disease of the heart, or Pericarditis" and "frequent attacks of Rush of Blood to the Head."[142]

Kilian V. Whaley, endorsed Dorone and requested Gov. Pierpont to order Dorone's appointment and send the commission on, in Whaley's care. The following is Congressman Whaley's endorsement of Dorone:

> Since my arrival here I have renewed an acquaintance with Col Chas R. Doran, and Major Bosler of the Eastern Va Brigade. You will see by the enclosed papers that Col Doran has been appointed Col of the second Regt and his regiment accepted as a part of said Brigade. Major Bosler has also been selected by Hon John C. Underwood as the Brigade Quartermaster. Col Doran requests of me that Major John Bosler [illeg. abbreviated word] receive his commission from your Excellency as the Regimental Quartermaster of his regiment until the Brigade is formed he having held that position previous to his appointment as Brigade Quartermaster by Hon John C. Underwood. It appears to be necessary for the formation of the Brigade as well as the welfare of the Regiment that Col Doran receive his commission as Colonel of said Regiment as soon as your Excellency can conveniently forward it.
>
> Colonel Doran has shown me letters of recommendation as to his capability as an officer, he has more than his compliment of men, his regiment numbers nearly twelve hundred men. He was an officer at the battle of Bull's Run and Falls Church.
>
> Mr. John F. Cowan of Georgetown has written to your Excellency upon the same subject.
>
> P.S. You will please have the commission addressed to my care.[143]

Pierpont commissioned Dorone Colonel of the 13th Virginia Regiment on January 30th, 1862, to rank from January 15th, 1862.[144] On January 13th, 1862, John F. Cowan wrote the following to Pierpont regarding Dorone's commission:

> Previous to John C. Underwood's getting sick, he appointed Charles R. Doran Colonel of the 13th Regiment, in his Brigade. The Colonel

is desirous of having his commission forwarded to Washington. You will please send it to me care of F.E. Spinner Esq. U.S. Treasurer.[145]

Charles Dorone wrote to Pierpont from "Head Quarters 13ᵗʰ Regiment Co A Eastern Virginia Brigade, Philadelphia, Pennsylvania, February 18, 1862 No. 344 and 347, North 3ʳᵈ Street" regarding a captain's commission in the 13ᵗʰ Virginia, for one "Captain John H. Rehren," who had "raised a company for this regiment." Rehren, continued Dorone, had "served 18 years in the regular army and was on Gen. Mansfield's staff for a long time." He had also served in Mexico and was "a thorough soldier, in every respect." "He has recruited his Co[mpany], in the neighborhood of Pittsburg, Penn[sylvania], where I have obtained the most of my men." "It is my wish [...] that you will attach my Reg[imen]t, to a Brigade, in Western Va, [...] to see active service." "With many thanks to your Excellency, for the kindness you have shown towards me, through my friend Major-Whaley." Pierpont wrote on the back of Dorone's letter: "Answer letter informing him that the Eastern Va Brigade is under the direction of the War Dept. at Washington. I can only commission officers—not order the regt.—if he has 83 men his capt[ain] can be comm."[146]

There seems however, to have been some shadiness about the Dorone appointment suggesting that commissions may have been bought and sold. Consider in tandem the following two cryptic letters, both written by Auditor, John C. Underwood. The first dated "Fifth Auditor's Office Feby 10, 1862," was addressed to Gov. Pierpont. The second letter was dated "Fifth Auditors Office Feby 28, 1862" and was addressed (I presume) to H.J. Samuels, Adjutant General of the Restored State Government, at Wheeling.

> His Excellency Gov Pierpoint
> Dear Sir
> I am informed that certain persons or at least a certain person during my sickness, pretending to act by authority from me has been offering to give commissions to be obtained from your Excellency + in one case has sold such a commission + received a valuable consideration in money therefor — I hope you are well enough acquainted with me to know I entirely scorn + detest such conduct being unalterably opposed to corruption + bribery in all their forms — No earthly power can induce me either to accept for myself any such consideration or countenance it in others + I drop this note to put you on guard against any who have acted or may assume to act under my authority.
> I remain Your Obt Servt John C. Underwood[147]

Dear Sir

Your favor of the 25th is just received. The person to whom I referred + whom I did not name because, although I believed as I now believe him guilty, I had not positive proof, is Charles R. Doran of Philadelphia. He is a plausible man + so far imposed upon me as to obtain a favorable letter from me to the War Department. As soon however as I learned his true character I wrote to the Dept cancelling any former recommendation, of which I duly informed W.D. I did not think proper to name him to Gov Pierpoint for another reason to wit I had not recommended W.D. to him

Since your note of enquiry however lest others might be suspected I feel constrained to name the person of whom I have the strongest grounds of suspicion — I found him under the fairest pretensions to be guilty of the grossest falsehood + deception + of course repudiated him immediately.

Very Respectfully
Your Obt Servt
John C. Underwood[148]

Dorone, "Col. 13th Regt. Va. Vols." wrote to "General Lorenzo W. Thomas, Adjutant Genl. U.S. Army", on February 19th, 1862. The letter was penned on "13th Regiment" stationary and designated "Official Business." Dorone stated that

> he had been authorized, and Commissioned, by Governor Pierpoint, the Governor of Virginia, to raise the 13th Regiment Virginia Volunteers, and have recruited some 300 men, in the City of Philadelphia, and Pittsburg, I desire to draw Clothing for them [...].[149]

Dorone complained that he had been given the run around in this regard. First, he tried to draw clothing for his recruits in "Philadelphia and Pittsburg, from Colonel Crossman, Deputy Quartermaster General at Philadelphia." On February 5th, Dorone wrote to Secretary of War Stanton of the failed attempt to obtain clothing from Crossman. Dorone received reply from Stanton by the Assistant Secretary of War, John Tucker, in a communication dated February 10th. Tucker explained that Doran's letter had been referred to Quartermaster General Montgomery Meigs. Dorone immediately fired off a letter to Meigs explaining his case. Dorone received no reply from Meigs and Colonel Crossman telegraphed Meigs that Dorone was waiting for a reply. Meigs wired back on February 17th, that Dorone's papers had been referred to General (Lorenzo W.) Thomas (Adjutant General of the U. S. Army), the addressee of

Dorone's current letter. In a rather exasperated tone, Dorone asked where he might draw clothing for his recruits. He wrote:

> My men are very anxious to be clothed, and to get into Service, and, it is with difficulty that I can keep them together without being clothed. I think my Case, is a very urgent one, and having recruited the men, at a considerable expense, I do not think, that the United States Government, desires me to loose all my men, that I have recruited in the State of Pennsylvania, or elsewhere, I there-fore appeal to you for advice as to how I shall proceed in the mat-ter. [...] The 12th Regt. Virginia Volunteers under the Command of <u>Colonel Wm. Wall</u> draws Clothing of Quartermaster General Meigs in Washington, and if it is necessary, for me to draw my Clothing also, in Washington, and no where else, will you please be kind enough to let me know immediately [...].[150]

The crux of Col. Doran's clothing dilemma is indicated in his telegraph to Gov. Pierpont, sent from Washington, on February 27th, 1862. Doran states he is awaiting the order from the Secretary of War furnishing him with clothing, rations and transportation, but the War Department will not recognize Doran without an order from Pierpont.[151]

On February 28th, 1862, a most cryptic letter was sent by Auditor John C. Underwood from Washington City (to Governor Pierpont, presumably). Underwood stated that he writes in reply to a letter from "addressee" dated February 25th which presumably made inquiry regarding Charles Dorone. Underwood wrote that "the person formerly referred to is Charles R. Doran of Philadelphia." Underwood "believed and still believes that Doran is guilty, although he (Underwood) has no positive proof. Underwood names Doran now that others may not be under suspicion."[152] On March 1st, 1862, K.V. Whaley telegraphed Pierpont from Washington saying that "the 13th Va. Regt. is a failure. Commissions for the regiment are still in my possession. Doran is an imposter. I will send the details by letter."[153]

Not to be deterred, Dorone, pursuant to Lincoln's July call for more volunteers, again wrote to Washington. Signing himself "Late Colonel Command'g 13th; Regiment Virginia Volunteers," Dorone wrote to Secretary of War Stanton on July 10th, 1862, "again" offering his services to the War Department and requesting authority "to re-organize the 13th Regiment Virginia Vols." or be authorized "to Organize a Regiment in Pennsylvania, my native State" or "any other [State]." Dorone claimed that he "was an officer in the 27th Penn[sylvania] Regiment (late Colonel Einstein's) at the Battle of Bull's Run, and also, at the Battles of Fall's Church, and Cheat Mountain"and that he was "very anxious again, to go into the Field."[154] Dorone had not been an officer in the 27th Pennsylvania Infantry Regiment in the sense he suggests but rather he had served as Hospital Steward. Dorone continued:

> I was authorized on the 16[th] Day of December, 1861, to raise the 2[nd] Regiment, Eastern Virginia Brigade, by the War Department, through Hon: Thomas A. Scott, the Assistant Secr[etar]y of War (Said Brigade under the authority of Hon: John C. Underwood, 5[th]: auditor of the Treasury) and I was Commissioned by his Excellency Govr. Pierpoint, the Colonel of the 13[th]: Regiment Virginia Vols: — After recruiting nearly 600 men, I received orders to stop further enlistments, and was compelled to disband my men, having suffered a great loss, and Expense by so doing.
>
> I am certain now, (having competent officers, who will work with me) of being able to Recruit a full Regiment of men in the State of Pennsylvania, in from 30, to 50 days, after authority has been furnished me to do so. The most of the men I Recruited before, were from Seuzerne [or Suzerne], Schuylkill & Northumberland Cos. in this State, strong, active men, who would again come with me, to fight the battles of our Country.
>
> Therefore, I respectfully request of you, the authority to organize a Regiment in this State, (or any other) and I am certain I can do it, in the time specified by you. Please let me hear from you, as soon as possible, so that I can go to Recruiting again, and by so doing, oblige

Your Obedient Servant
Charles R. Doron
(Late Colonel Command'g 13th; Regiment Virginia Volunteers.)

P. S. — Please address your Reply to me, South West Corner of Richmond & Schachamaxon Street & 18th Ward, Philadelphia.

P.S. — I would respectfully refer you to the following named persons, for information, as to my ability, & services. Viz.

Major J.B. Way, Paymaster U.S. Army
Major Truman, Paymaster U.S. Army
Hon. Thos. B. Florence. Ex ch. C. from Penna
Hon: John P. Verree. M.C. from Penna
Hon. Edgar Cowan Senator from Penna
Mr. Moore, formerly Private Sec. of Genl Cameron
Mr: John T. Wolff, Record Clerk War Dept.
Mr. Lewis Baker Librarian War Dept.[155]

Doron wrote substantially the same letter to Abraham Lincoln on July 19th, as he had to Stanton on July 10th, but with fuller explanation relating to his recruiting activities:

> I was authorized on the 16th Day of December, 1861, to raise the 2d Regiment Eastern Virginia Brigade, by the War Department, through Hon. John C. Underwood, present 5th Auditor of the Treasury, then authorized by your Excellency, and by Governor Pierpoint, to raise an Eastern Virginia Brigade to serve for 3 years, or during the War.
>
> I also received my Commission from his Excellency Governor Pierpoint, as the Colonel of the 13th Virginia Volunteers. After recruiting nearly 600 men, I received orders to stop further enlistments, as the authority granted to Mr. Underwood for to raise an Eastern Virginia Brigade had been countermanded. I was compelled therefore to disband my men, *Secretary Cameron* informing me that it was not in the power of the War Department to accept any more troops, although earnestly urged to do so by my Friends, Genl. Robinson of Pittsburg, Penna, and Hon: John F. Cowan of Georgetown, Hon: John P. Verree, and others. Therefor, I have suffered a great loss of time and money by so doing.
>
> I am certain now, (having competent Officers, who will work with me) of being able to recruit a full Regiment of men in the State of Pennsylvania, or Virginia, in from 30, to 50 days, after authority has been furnished me to do so. I have done it once before, and can do it again.
>
> I was an Officer in the 27th: Penna Regiment (late Col: Einstein's) [Army of the Potomac] at Camp Lincoln, Halorama Heights, at the time of your Excellency's visit to our Camp; and was with the Regiment at the Battle of Bull's Run. I also, was in the engagements of Falls Church and Cheat Mountain, being wounded in the shoulder at the latter place.
>
> [...] will not your Excellency either grant me the privilege of Re-Organizing the 13th: Virginia Vols, or furnish me with authority to Recruit an Independent Regiment, or a Regiment in the State of Pennsylvania. [...]
>
> Charles R. Doron.
Late Colonel Commad'g 13th Regiment Virginia Vols.
Eastern Virginia Brigade.
No. 164. Richmond Street,
Philadelphia, Penna.[156]

Dorone never did received authority to recruit for the 13th. Of far less questionable nature was the appointment and recommendation of many other men who became connected with the 13th Virginia Volunteers. These are the following.

Early in the year 1862, Christopher L. Grafflin of Sir John's Run, Morgan County, Virginia was recommended for and subsequently commissioned Lieutenant-Colonel of the 13th. His recommendation came from "General A.J. Williams, *et.al.*," who wrote to Secretary Edwin M. Stanton for this purpose on February 26th, 1862. Petitioners noted that to help the Union cause, Grafflin had totally sacrificed his business and "from his extensive influence throughout the northwestern part of Virginia [...] procured accurate and valuable information of movements of the enemy," information that was acquired at great personal risk to himself. Grafflin subsequently received a commission with permission to raise a regiment in Morgan, Berkley and Hampshire Counties.[157] Christopher L. Grafflin was commission Lieutenant-Colonel, 13th Regiment on March 12th, 1862, to rank from that date. His oath of office was dated March 28[th], 1862.[158]

On August 2[nd], 1862, Lewis Wetzel, W.H. Tomlinson. Charles B. Waggoner, James H. Holloway and W.E. Wetzel, all of Mason County, wrote to Adjutant General Samuels from Point Pleasant requesting the appointment of Samuel S. Mathe[r]s for Major of the 13[th] Regiment of Virginia Volunteers.[159] Samuel S. Mathers did not receive the requested appointment but was mustered in with the rank of Private in Co. A, 13[th] Regiment, on August 12[th], 1862, at Wheeling. He was eventually promoted to 2[nd] Lieutenant on February 4[th], 1863, and promoted to 1st Lieutenant October 31st, 1864.[160]

After Lincoln's call for more volunteers, recruiting officers went out in all directions to gather up volunteers for the 13th Virginia. Among these recruiters was Lieutenant William E. Feazel, native of Gallipolis, Ohio, and member of the 1st Virginia Cavalry Regiment. There is no preliminary paper record documenting Feazel's appointment to recruit specifically for the 13th except his muster-in showing that the thirty-eight year old resident of Gallispolis was mustered into the 13th Virginia Volunteer Infantry, on July 19th, 1862, as 2nd Lieutenant and Recruiting Officer. Extant paperwork of the Mountain Department at the National Archives, however, indicates that Feazel had been detailed for a six month tour of recruiting service sometime before January 24th, 1862, while he was yet a member of 1st Virginia Cavalry.[161] Whether Feazel was already recruiting for the 13th on that assignment or for other units, he would recruit extensively for the 13th and served in other positions of command with the regiment. On July 19th, 1862, Gov. Pierpont wrote to Adj. Samuels stating that all requisition made by 2nd Lieutenant W.E. Feazel (recruiting for the 13th) for clothing and subsistence of recruits would be approved.[162] Just before the first companies of the regiment were organized, Feazel was assigned to duty in Company C—commissioned

2ⁿᵈ Lieutenant of Co. C, 13ᵗʰ Virginia on September 12ᵗʰ, 1862. He was shortly there-after detached on recruiting service beginning October 1862 by Special Order from General Robert H. Milroy.[163]

Others who wished to recruit for the 13ᵗʰ or who were recommended to the State Government at Wheeling to recruit for the 13ᵗʰ were:

> George A. Palmer recommended for a lieutenancy to recruit on July 19ᵗʰ, 1862.[164]
>
> David W. Brown recommended to be commissioned to raise an additional number of volunteers for the 13ᵗʰ in Cabell county. E.D. Wright wrote recommending Brown in a letter to H.J. Samuels dated July 19ᵗʰ, 1862.[165]
>
> Lieutenant I.W. (or I.N.) Neale, resident of Mason City, desired to obtain a commission for 2ⁿᵈ Lieutenant to recruit a company for the 13ᵗʰ. Neale was recommended by R.C.M. Lovell (of Mason City) in a letter to H.J. Samuels dated July 22ⁿᵈ, 1862.[166]

On July 23ʳᵈ, 1862, Lewis Wetzel wrote on behalf of himself and the Mason County Committee of Safety members Joseph Sly, S. Comstock, Benjamin Lemaster and William Smith, to Governor F.H. Pierpont. Wetzel indicated that upon consulta-tion they had all concurred in recommending that "James R. Hall, Charles T. Latham & Van. D. McDaniel"[167] were "suitable gentlemen to be commissioned Second Lieu-tenants to raise Companies of Infantry for the Thirteenth Regiment Va Vols." Wetzel added that he and the Committee of Safety members "are of the opinion that Mason County will furnish two and possibly three Companies of Volunteers." Wetzel and Committee members were eager to get the 13ᵗʰ recruited, hence they asked for three appointments to facilitate the process.[168]

In July of 1862, Cornelius Mercer of Clarksburg and R.W. Blue of Taylor County wished to recruit for the 13ᵗʰ.[169] Greenberry Slack (Greenberry Slack Sr. or Jr.) wrote to H.J. Samuels from Charleston on July 24ᵗʰ, informing that Edward H. Mayo and William N. Hawkins (mustered in as 1ˢᵗ Lieutenant Company E, 13ᵗʰ Regiment, on October 9ᵗʰ, 1862) wished to engage in recruiting for the 13ᵗʰ.[170] W.N. Hawkins did, in fact, recruit a company for the 13ᵗʰ. John Hall, Esq., in a letter dated "Point Pleasant July 25ᵗʰ [1862]" wrote to Adj. Gen. Samuels at Wheeling, recommending "E. Maloney" to the command of "some company." Endorsing him, Hall wrote that Maloney "is young and has served about 3 y[ea]rs recruiting companies for the gov-[ernmen]t."[171]

Jacob W. Heavens was trying to recruit a company for the 13[th] in Buckhannon. J.P. Muller was trying to recruit a company in Preston county around July 28[th], 1862. J.W. Dunnington was recruiting around Pruntytown, Virginia, pursuant to Pierpont's call to raise troops under his late proclamation. Lieutenant John W. Neale received a commission authorizing him to recruit in Mason County for the 13th Regiment. Lewis Wetzel had recommended Neale in a letter to H.J. Samuels dated "Point Pleasant, Virginia, July 29th, 1862."[172]

George W. Story of the 4th (West) Virginia wrote to Pierpont on August 1st, 1862, from Charleston, Virginia, expressing his desire to be a recruiting officer for the 13th and further to receive an appointment in the 13th "now in process of formation in this part of the State."[173] On the same day, August 1st, John Slack wrote a letter from Charleston, Virginia, to Governor Pierpont, recommending George W. Story for Adjutant of the 13th Virginia Volunteers.[174]

On August 1st, John Hall Jr., Major of the 4th (West) Virginia wrote to his father, John Hall, from Charleston regarding recruitment of the 13th and of his desire to be transferred into it, his brother James' regiment:

> Dear Father
>
> I wrote to you last night but did not get off as I expected and concluded to write you again ———
>
> I think that the 13 Reg will be recruited very soon — and I wish that you would request Gov Peirpont to transfer me to that regiment immediately I think in a week from this time that this regiment will be entitled to a field officer — Several persons are recruiting here — and they are filling up rapidly — I will leave for Chapmansville tomorrow — I understand that Copl Dayton has built a block house at that place — I wish that you would write or have Ja[me]s write immediately — and write to me frequently untill I can tell what I am to do — the prospect for this new regiment is good Serg [Milton] Stewart is recruiting for James — I got Judge Brown + Col Smith to recommend him He expects the 1[st] lieutenancy [paper crumbling and illeg.] nite here — I saw Jas [B]oye of Putnam and he tells me that a company can be recruited in Putnam and that no one is recruiting there —
>
> Give my love to the family
>
> I am your
> aff son
> John Hall[175]

John's older brother, James, soon sought to obtain commissions for recruiting officers that Putnam County might be recruited. He wrote to Adj. Gen. Samuels requesting recruiting commissions for Cicero Bowyer of Putnam County and Henry C. Crawford of Mason County. The two men, related Hall, had been recruiting in Putnam and Mason Counties and had so far "succeeded well but it is impossible for them to recruit as fast as could be wished without having the authority to muster in recruits while they are in the humor."[176] Hall requested that Bowyer and Crawford be given recruiting commissions as he believed that "a company can soon be raised by these men."[177] Hall asked that if approved, the commissions be sent to him, as he could give them to the men immediately. Recruiting in Putnam may have been a harder task than it appeared from a distance. At the beginning of August 1862, Union men in Putnam County were considering putting together a military force to do garrison duty in the Kanawha Valley. A writer to the *Weekly Register,* who signed his name "Putnam" commented skeptically as to the feasibility of doing this, inasmuch as already "three Federal and three rebel companies ha[d] been made up in this small county — will make volunteering an up-hill business — as most of those remaining, that could go in for the war are of the secesh persuasion."[178]

Mason County Provides for Its Volunteers

Under Lincoln's first call for 300,000 men, Virginia's obligation (*i.e.,* quota of men to be supplied for the Federal army) had been 2,080 men. Following Lincoln's second call, for an additional 300,000, Virginia's quota was raised to 4,650. To promote recruiting and fulfill Virginia's obligation, the Recruiting Committee for Mason County (also called the Mason County Committee of Safety) convened on Monday, July 28th, 1862. The Recruiting Committee, included members Joseph Sly, Stephen Comstock, William Smith, B. Lemaster, J.D. Thompson and Lieutenant James R. Hall. The Committee unanimously resolved that,

> recognizing the urgent necessity for the prompt enlistment of our quota of the volunteers recently called for by the Governor of our State, and believing that the example set to us by other States and communities, of voting additional bounty to all accepted recruits within their limits, has the effect of materially stimulating the cause, as well as showing our appreciation of the patriotism of those who leave their homes at their country's call, and with the view that the burden may be equally borne by all classes of persons.
>
> That it be, and is hereby, recommended [to the Mayor and Council of the town of Point Pleasant, Virginia], to vote an appropriation of *twenty-five dollars* to each accepted recruit, residing within the limits of your corporation; and to the County Court, an appropriation of a like amount to those who reside out of the corporation, and who shall enlist in the county.
>
> Believing that such action will meet the approval of all loyal men, we commend it to your earnest consideration. [Signed by] Joseph Sly, S. Comstock, Wm. Smith, B. LeMaster, J.D. Thompson.[179]

In addition to the Federal bounty of $100.00 either the city bounty or the county bounty would be given. The patriotic citizens of Point Pleasant and immediate vicinity voluntarily subscribed liberally to meet the expense of obtaining and bringing in volunteers. To fund the county bounty, the Committee requested the court and authorities of the incorporated towns of the county to lay levy and direct payment to each volunteer. The money for the extra bounty was to be raised by a levy on the incorporated towns and the taxable persons and property of the county. The levy for the Mason County bounty was much favored by local Union folk, because it would fall on Union and Secessionists alike. Local county rebels were thus also compelled to contribute a proportion of their means towards the support of Union volunteers. The Committee also determined that arrangements would be made that each volunteer, who had a family or relatives dependent upon him, would be provided for out of a fund of money appropriated and paid out monthly according to the circumstances and needs of the family or relatives. A competent person was to be appointed to render this service.[180] On Tuesday, July 29th, the Mayor and Town Council of Point Pleasant convened, and on a motion of Stephen Comstock (member of both the Point Pleasant Town Council and Committee for Public Safety), the Council ordered that the sum of $25.00 be given to each volunteer mustered into the United States Army within the incorporated limits of the town.[181] Each volunteer who qualified to receive the county bounty (*i.e.,* was not a resident of Point Pleasant nor a citizen of another county) received $30.00 upon being sworn into the United States Service.

The Mason County Court likewise sought to stimulate enlistment and during its first day in session (Monday, August 4th, 1862) ordered that a county bounty of $30.00 be offered to each of the first 125 men to volunteer. The quarterly term of court went into session at the Point Pleasant Court and adjourned on Wednesday. These were busy days for the town of Point Pleasant. A large number of people were in attendance at court particularly on Monday, when court convened and an unusual amount of business was transacted on that day. The Grand Jury made twenty or more indictments, principally for assault and battery and violations of the revenue laws, and several members of the Grand Jury seem to have become volunteers along with a number of others, who were enrolled by Lieutenant W. E. Feazel for Co. B.

For his part, Lieut. Feazel, encouraged, perhaps, by the number of enlistments taken at Point Pleasant, thought to expand his recruiting operations and change his base. He wrote on August 5th, he wrote from his recruiting station at Point Pleasant to Adj. Gen. H.J. Samuels at Wheeling requesting an appointment for Samuel A. Childress to organize a company in Cabell County. Feazel added that recruiting could be jump-started there by calling a meeting of the militia and that he planned to move his headquarters soon from Charleston to Barboursville.[182]

It comes as no surprise that for the time being no more reference was made to recruiting for the 13th in Cabell County. Guerrillas and Confederate recruiting parties continued to operate under the noses of civil and military authorities in this area. Potential volunteers for the Union were likely as not "laying low." In September of 1862, the number of men recruited in Cabell County for the Confederate army "increased dramatically" with "at least 58 men" joining the 36th Battalion Virginia Cavalry on September 17th.[183] The larger portion of Cabell Countians who volunteered for the 13th Regiment did so at the end of 1863 and the early months of 1864, joining Companies G, H and I of the 13th.

Provision for the $30.00 County Bounty came about in this wise. Present in court at Point Pleasant, on that Monday (August 4, 1862) were Justices Lewis Wetzel, Lewis Bumgardner, Richard Bush,[184] George Stephenson, E.B. Davis, D. George, John McCulloch, Jacob B. Kester, S.W. Somerville, and F.J. Daffer. The Clerk, W.W. Harper took down proceedings. A majority of acting Mason County Justices being present, the Court ordered that a levy of $1.00 be made on each "tithable" and 25% be laid on the amount of State revenue on the taxable property of Mason county for its defense. Mason County bonds had been sold, or were about to be sold and these levies had been laid to make payment on the bonds. The levy was to be used as collateral for the taxing power of the county. The newly available funds were to be used to promote recruitment in Mason County by offering a county bounty; to support the families of Mason County volunteers in needy circumstances; and to defray expenses incurred in the defense of the County. The funds raised were to be applied as follows: "Thirty dollars to each of the first one hundred and twenty-five volunteers, who may join a company or companies raised in this county, the same to be paid as soon as the volunteer may be mustered into service." This did not apply to volunteers residing in Point Pleasant, because Point Pleasant had already provided for its volunteers. The residue of the fund raised by the levy would be applied to the support of volunteers' families in Mason county in needy circumstances, as directed by the County Commissioners. If there should be any balance after so providing for volunteers and needy families, it was to be used to defray other expenses as might be necessary for the defense of the County. John Hall, J.D. Thompson and Lewis Wetzel were to be appointed Commissioners

> with authority to negotiate a loan and to execute the bonds of the county, therefore equal to such amount, as may be necessary to carry out the provisions of the foregoing order, and to do and perform such other and further acts as may be necessary to effect the purpose of this order, provided they do not contract to pay more than six per cent per annum.[185]

Sheriff Samuel Windon was ordered by the Court to proceed to collect the levy "by distress or otherwise" and pay the same to the Commissioners to be applied to the payment of the bonds.[186] John Hall seeking to fulfill the obligation laid upon him and the other commissioners, not only to provide for the paying of a county bounty to volunteers but also to look to the defense of Mason County,

> went to Wheeling and obtained of Gov. Pierpont one hundred choice rifled muskets for that purpose and gave [his] individual receipt for them, but after he got them here [to Point Pleasant] Col. Lightburn, (whose regiment [the 4th Virginia Infantry] was without effective arms) seized them and gave [Hall] a receipt and certificate of such seizure.[187]

The condition limiting the payment of the $30.00 county bounty to the first one hundred and twenty-five men was extended just a week or so later to all qualified volunteers who enlisted before September 1st. When the Mason County Court again convened on Monday September 1st (1862), the qualifications for county bounty were again extended. A majority of acting justices again being present (Lewis Wetzel, George Stephenson, F.J. Duffer, John L. Jordan, Jacob P. Kester, E.B. Davis, S.W. Somerville, John McCullock, E.M. Rollins, and John J. Wees) and in agreement, it was ordered that the sum of thirty dollars be paid to every "bona fide citizen" of the county "for the defence thereof, in the service of the United States, up to the tenth day of [September]." After September 10th, the county bounty would "positively cease."[188] Commissioners John Hall, Lewis Wetzel and J.D. Thompson were authorized by the court to borrow on the County's credit, whatever amount of money was considered necessary to pay volunteers when they had been mustered into the U.S. Service. The Commissioners were also ordered by the Mason County Board of Supervisors to report their proceedings "at the next meeting of the Board" scheduled for November 8th, 1862.[189]

Would-be recruiting officers continued to come forward. James J. Fulton of Parkersburg desired a lieutenancy to recruit.[190] J.B. Bumgardner, who did in fact recruit a number of men for the 13th, wrote to Adj. Gen. Samuels on August 3rd, saying that he was out recruiting "this company, this week and in all [his] route out and back [he] did not see 10 men they all heard that I was recruiting offiser and that I was drafting every person as I went a long and they ware all out in the woulds waiting to hear the musician going out tomorrow to stay all week and do all I can." Bumgardner also wrote: "I have some recruits that wants some shoes and clothing I went and saw Capt. Shannon whether or not he would go in to the Company or not [J.B.B. desired Shannon to join with the company he was recruiting and be Captain of the Company. Shannon would agree to be Captain.] Harvey Dunkell wants the same situation. He says he can get 20 men." J.B.B. asked Samuels to write to Shannon and Dunkel, presumably to encourage them.[191] F.M. Loury of Randolph County obtained a commission for 2nd Lieutenant, 13th Regiment to recruit for the 13th, "one of two new regiments in need of recruiting and filling up at this time."[192] Supplying volunteers now being raised in Western Virginia was also on the minds of those in Washington. On August 4th, 1862, J.F. Taylor, Officer of the Commissary General of Subsistence (at Washington City) wrote to Gov. Pierpont conveying the information that the Adjutant General in Washington sent Major Bennett H. Hill, 2nd Artillery to Wheeling, Virginia, with funds for the purpose of supplying the volunteers now being raised in Western Virginia.[193]

There was of course, a certain amount of jockeying to be commissioned 2nd Lieutenant and recruiting officer. A man with such a commission in hand, had received official authority (and commensurate pay) to recruit for a particular regiment, with opportunity to command it when it reached the minimum number to satisfy the Federal requirement. James P[oindexter] Elkins (probably James P. Elkins, later Corporal of Co. H, 13th Regiment), writing from Coalsmouth, Kanawha, County, Virginia, on August 5th, complained to Adjutant General Samuels that he understood that one "Mr. Cunningham" was trying to obtain an appointment as 2nd Lieutenant with Elkins' company. Cunningham, explained Elkins, was "an outsider, who would not join and take his chances when the company [wa]s full but wanted the position beforehand." Elkins did not think this a justice to the other men and a move which would be bad for the men's morale as the men of this company did not favor Cunningham. The majority of the members of the company had "given all they own to the cause" and insisted that Cunningham not be appointed.[194]

John S. Cunningham, formerly of the 1st Virginia Cavalry and then with Company G, 11th Virginia, who in August of 1862, was recruiting men for the 13th which went into Captain J.V. Young's Company (G, 11th and 13th Virginia Infantry Regiments). Cunningham wrote to Samuels to report on the success of his recruiting. On August 28th, Cunningham wrote from Coalsmouth informing that Capt. Young's Company numbered 88 men and that "[s]ince July 23d I have been instrumental in bringing into the co[mpany] 17 men, and if we are not interrupted by removal I have the assurance of having the number (101) within two weeks from this date."[195]

Doctors were also up for recommendation at this time.[196] S.S. Slack at Charleston, Virginia, telegraphed Governor Pierpont on August 20th, 1862, recommending Dr. William Mavis, (a Virginian by birth) for the position of 1st or 2nd Surgeon of 13th Virginia Regiment. Mavis was also endorsed by Drs. Patrick Slacke, Whittaker, Newton Hindeman and others.[197]

James R. Hall Recruits a Company

On the face of the record of the recruitment of the 13th, it would appear that one of the most successful recruiting officers was James R. Hall, son of John Hall Sr., of Point Pleasant. The elder Hall wrote to H.J. Samuels from Point Pleasant on July 25th, 1862, that "My son, James R. Hall is busily engaged hunting up recruits, with a fair prospect of good success and is very anxious to secure 'Co A' if possible in the Regt."[198] James was born in Mason County in1838, one of nine children born to John Hall and Olivia Hogg. He had entered the Virginia Military Institute at Lexington in 1855, when he was about 17 years old and in the words of his father had spent "between two and three years [as] a military student [at the Virginia Military Institute, at Lexington] and had to leave on account of ill health of course he did not graduate but stood high in his school and was pirty much through with infantry tactics" when he left the Institute.[199] When James entered the Union army in 1862, he was engaged as a clerk, in the firm of Beale, Hall & Co. and also served as Deputy Sheriff of Mason County. He issued his spirited call for troops under Lincoln's call for 300,000 more men. His advertisement for volunteers in the local paper (reprinted below) was accompanied by a passionate appeal, calling the men to do their duty and come to the aid of their brothers already in the field.

Volunteers Wanted!

Fellow citizens of Mason county:— You are well aware that we are in the midst of war — a cruel, wicked and unnecessary war brought upon our country by ambitious designing demagogues and wicked and bad men, to destroy the best Government the world ever knew. Many of our friends and friends of the Union, are already in this field, nobly battling for the country and the perpetuity of their liberties; but they are outnumbered by the traitors, they having more men in the field than we have. Shall we stand by as idle spectators in this unjust and unholy contest in which your existence as a nation is concerned. For me, I say no, never ! I propose to go to the rescue, won't you go with me ! Our cause is the cause of our country, and the cause of human rights. I appeal to you as freemen worthy of that noble heritage, to come to the rescue of your brethren in arms — to the rescue of your country from the grasp of tyrants. Let us strike for our liberties, our altars and our fires.

James R. Hall.
2d Lieutenant, 13th Reg., V.V.I.

P.S. The pay of a private soldier is over two hundred ($200) dollars per year,[200] besides subsistence, medical attention, and probably a bounty of 160 acres of land, one hundred ($100) dollars in money, $25 of which is to be paid down, also one month's pay in advance, and two dollars for the enlistment, making in all forty dollars, which the soldier receives when mustered into service, in case he is not *drafted*. I am prepared to furnish arms, subsistence and quarters from the date of enlistment. Pay will commence from the same date. J.R.H. Point Pleasant, Va.[201]

Ever ready to promote the Union cause, the Point Pleasant *Weekly Register* commented upon Hall's advertisement:

It will be seen by today's paper that Lieut. J.R. Hall is recruiting a company for the 13th Va. Reg[iment]. Mr. Hall is a young man of excellent habits and having attended the Military Academy at Lexington, Va. is fully competent for any command that may be assigned him. Those desiring to enlist can have no better opportunity afforded.[202]

The columns of the *Weekly Register* offered stout support to recruiters at this juncture. Editor and Justice Lewis Wetzel explained the "liberal pension laws" then in place which provided for soldiers and their dependents; encouraged those too old or incapacitated to serve to hire substitutes; chastised those slow to enlist and stigmatized draftees in print; argued for the economic benefits of volunteering and argued against being drafted. The hiring of substitutes by those "too old for military service or otherwise incapacitated" might, offered the *Register,* induce someone "whose patriotism was not extinct, to step into the ranks."[203] The "sluggish spirit of enlistments," continued Wetzel, "on the part of those who desire to sustain the Union [as compared with] with the active and determined spirit of those who desire to destroy the Government [...] is truly humiliating."[204]

Many there were who thought there was little difference between volunteering and drafting and their position was, that they didn't intend to volunteer but if drafted they would serve. The differences, as pointed out by the *Register* were these. The volunteer received upon muster in the first month's pay in advance ($13.00); a recruiting fee ($2.00) and a quarter of the federal government bounty ($25.00). Upon discharge the volunteer received the balance of the government bounty ($75.00) and would be eligible for a land bounty (not mineral lands) of 160 acres. Mason County and the town of Point Pleasant had also, by subscription, raised money to offer their own bounties, although one local bounty was offered to the exclusion of the other. Volunteers living in Point Pleasant town did not also receive the Mason County bounty. In addition, local commissioners promised that any money over and above that needed to pay the soldiers bounties, would go to provide for the more destitute of the soldiers' families, in their absence. The draftee, on the other hand, received only the regular militia pay ($11.00) a month and no land bounty.[205]

Would-be draftees were put in the "hot-seat." Draftees, continued the *Register,* would be "dragged away and forced to the front of the army;" it was a disgrace to be drafted; drafted men had to furnish their own clothes. "No sympathizing tear would be shed for the draftee, on leaving friends and neighbors, no friendly hand would be extended, no 'God be with you' would ever reach the ear of one who remained deaf to the cries of his country." In addition, a list of all subject to the "war call" indicating who had not volunteered was then in the process of being compiled by the Commissioners of Revenue, the list to be completed during the month of August 1862. With this list, the government needing men, would direct the different governors to send their proportion *nolen volens.*[206]

"Within a week" James R. Hall had recruited a company. So busy was James with his civic duties as Deputy Sheriff and with recruiting that he had to delay a trip east to meet with the Governor and Adj. Gen. Samuels, presumably regarding the 13th Regiment. John Hall Sr. wrote to Samuels from Point Pleasant on July 30th, concerning his son James' recent responsibilities:

> Will you please say to the Gov that when Maj. J.T. Hall got down that James R. Hall had much process to serve for court and some recruits to see which would take him full 3 days until this evening and that now the Committee of Public Safety insist he must not leave until after court. That he can do more in getting Vols than any of us can do for him under these circumstances he may not reach your place before this day week.[207]

August 4th, Hall again wrote to Samuels from Point Pleasant regarding enlistment of the 13th and requested that his sons, James R. and John T. be given the ranks of Lieutenant-Colonel and Major in the new regiment.

My son James has been laboring very hard to get up a Company for the last ten or twelve Days and will Resign his Sheriffing Business tomorrow with the view of giving it his entire attention of course to quit his business and go to work as a Lieutenant is a sacrifice to him — but the Friends here thought that he could get more volunteers that any one else ever had (and the indications so far are that they were right) He is willing to make any sacrifice in his power to promote the cause — I hope he will be able to get up a Company in the next ten or twelve Days and he is very anxious if possible to secure Company A would you please let us know what infermation you have from other companies in this Regiment — My boys both James + John have their hearts set upon drilling up this regiment and they would like to be together they say they think that from the oppertunaties they have had that they think if placed in position to do so that they could give this Regiment a proficientcy of Drill that few in the United States have had before entering into service. This would suggest the idea of giving them the Lt Col + Majors place that is giving James one and transferring John to the other If this could be effected consistent with the Governor and your own opinion of the promotion of the best interest of the service I should feel very gratefull to the Governor + and yourself to effect it this would leave the office of Col — at your disposal hereafter. I however only suggest this for your consideration — If well enough it is likely I will be in Wheeling the last of this week — In speaking of the appointment of Field Officers I had not expected any of them to be made untill the filling up of the Regiment will warrent it

James is pledged to the men he has recruited and would be unwilling to go in any Regiment than the one they are assigned to — Give my kind regards to your lady and Governor Peirpoint and except for yourself my best wishes

Very Truly John Hall

P. S. please lay this befor the Governor

John Hall[208]

The two Hall brothers' hopes of serving together in the 13th were dashed when on August 6th, a band of guerrilla cavalry under the command of Col. Stratton, Major Witcher of Wayne County and Captain Herndon[209] attacked two companies from the 4th Virginia Infantry (a force of about 48 men[210] on recruiting service) at Kennedy's farm on Beech Creek in Logan County. The Confederates killed and wounded some and plundered the bodies but took no prisoners. Among the mortally wounded was Major John T. Hall, in command of the detachment. Sergeant M[ilton] Stewart of Co. K, 4th Virginia Regiment, who was with Hall in the fight and who remained with him until he was buried, wrote a detailed account of the fight, for his brother, Robert L. Stewart's paper, the Gallipolis *Journal* (Stewart, was at this time editor of the Gallipolis *Journal.*)[211] Stewart's letter contained a description of Witcher and his "crew of brigands" giving some idea of what Union troops were up against at this time in the war. Stewart observed:

> This man Witcher is certainly the most infuriated madman I ever saw.—He is a lean-faced hungry villain—a mere anatomy, a living dead man, but at the same time the most savage and demoniac in his conduct you can conceive of. [...] His crew of brigands looked to me like the 'cankers of a calm world after a long peace,' or like tattered prodigals lately come from swine-keeping, 'having but about a shirt and a half in the whole company, and the half shirt two napkins tacked together and thrown over the shoulders,' and the whole shirt stolen off the wash line of some poor Unionist. Even Witcher cursed them as a troop of cut-throats and thieves.[212]

James R. Hall was elected Captain of Co. A (13th V.V.I.) in August 1862. He was commissioned on August 19th, 1862 (to rank from August 5th, 1862), and took the Oath of Office as Captain on the same day (the 19th). Upon reporting at the State capital at Wheeling for his captain's commission, he was commissioned Lieutenant-Colonel of the new regiment, the 13th Virginia Infantry, then being raised in not only Point Pleasant but in a number of places in the Kanawha Valley. He was commissioned Lieutenant-Colonel of the 13th, on August 21st, 1862, to rank from this date. He was 25 years of age. He was mustered in October 10th, 1862 (when the 13th underwent its first formal stage of organization), at Point Pleasant, to serve for a period of 3 years.

James Hall was remembered as highly solicitous of those in his command, many of whom had been his school-mates and life-long acquaintances and his sense of duty kept him constantly in camp.[213] The training of volunteer units was not as a general thing entrusted to Regular Army officers. In point of fact, neither the States nor the War Department for that matter, had a true training program for volunteers. General preparedness for battle was on the whole a function of the efficiency of officers. Any regiment which happened to be officered by someone who had studied at a military academy, as James Hall had done, was very lucky indeed. Regiments in the field made more progress and held their own better in a fight than those whose drill masters were volunteers without benefit of professional military training. Such was the case with the 4th West Virginia Volunteers which had, albeit briefly, Major John T. Hall (James' brother); with the 36th Ohio which had then Colonel George Crook, a graduate of West Point for its colonel;[214] and such was also the case for the 13th Regiment which had James R. Hall. Although not a graduate, Hall had the benefit of over a year at the Virginia Military Institute, a period of study which sufficed to cover all or nearly all infantry drill and tactic. The advantage of having such men as Crook and the two Hall brothers was extra-ordinary for this military district. Officers with experience in drill and military protocol could train subordinate officers and men faster, thus increasing effectiveness and preserving the lives of their men.

On the military fronts, late summer continued to be a disappointment for the North. They were defeated a second time at Bull Run (fought August 28th–30th, 1862). Lee crossed the Potomac into Maryland creating great alarm in Washington and Philadelphia. McClellan met him at Sharpsburg on September 12th and defeated him but at great cost. Certain that Kentucky would rally to the Confederate cause if Confederate forces were in their midst, the combined forces of Braxton Bragg and Kirby Smith invaded Kentucky. Albert G. Jenkins raided through Western Virginia. As in the towns of Northwestern Virginia, many Northern cities held war meetings to promote enlistments. Reports filtered back to West Virginia that while recruiting in the North proceeded apace some individuals were mutilating themselves to avoid the militia draft and others had attempted to flee to Canada.

With the latest call for volunteers, the War Department at Washington had issued orders regarding the organization of new regiments, a summary of which was published in the Point Pleasant paper of July 31st.

1) Governors of States were authorized to appoint in addition to staff officers, a 2nd Lieutenant for each company, "who shall be mustered into the service at the commencement of the organization with authority to muster in recruits as are enlisted."

2) If a recruit was enlisted who obviously was unfit for service, at the time of enlistment and not able to pass the medical inspection, all expenses caused thereby were to be paid by the mustering-in officer and taken out of his salary.

3) Recruits were to be sent to the regimental rendezvous at least as often as once a week, where they were to immediately be examined by the regimental surgeon and if found unfit for duty, by reason of permanent disability, they were to be discharged from the service "forthwith" by the surgeon, whose duty it would be to report such discharges to the Adjutant General of the State, and also the Adjutant of the regiment, noting particularly those cases where the disability was obvious at the time of enlistment.

4) As soon as the organization of a regiment was completed, the regiment was to be carefully inspected by the mustering officer for the State, who would see to it that at least the minimum number for each company was present. No absentees except the sick in hospital were to be counted. The State mustering officer would also compare muster-in rolls and certify to the muster of each man at the date of enlistment.

5) Officers were to be mustered into the service only upon authority of the Governor of the State to which their regiments belonged.

6) Until regiments are organized and their muster rolls completed, they will be under the exclusive control of the [illegible] State [illegible] requisitions for quartermaster, medical and ordnance stores and contracts for subsistence will if approved by them, be allowed and not otherwise.[215]

On August 8th, the War Department at Washington issued more orders relating to recruitment. Those liable for the draft, under the latest call for 600,000 men, who absented themselves from their county or State before the draft was made, would be arrested by the Provost Marshal. Anyone discouraging enlistment in any way would also be arrested.[216]

All over Western Virginia public war meetings were held. Citizens of Monongalia County held a rousing war meeting around August 10th, at Morgantown. Speeches were made by Auditor Crane and Senator Willey.[217] On "Court day" (the day court convened) at Point Pleasant (August 4th), a public meeting was held at the Point Pleasant Court House. Justice Lewis Wetzel was called to the chair and E.M. Fitzgerald was appointed secretary. A number of issues were discussed. Major General Pope's new orders to the Army of Virginia were approved by the assembly at the courthouse. It was believed that the "prompt and rigid enforcement" of these orders would strengthen and consolidate the Union sentiment of the South and lead to a swift suppression of the rebellion in Virginia and elsewhere. General Pope had issued orders ending the "milk and water treatment," the "rosewater policy" of dealing with captured Secessionists. In its place would be a much more stringent policy. This pleased Union people in Western Virginia everywhere. It was upon the faith of that promise that people came to again rally to the country's defense.[218] The assembly also approved the President's recent call for 300,000 more volunteers and thanks were tendered to the county court for levying a bounty for volunteers and providing a fund for the support of the volunteers' families. The assembly also tendered thanks to the Representatives in Congress from Virginia who voted for the confiscation law. It was resolved that "the militia of the State ought to be thoroughly organized, and drilled once a month" and that a "military Post ought to be established at once, in each of the counties on the Ohio river, garrisoned by the militia of the county: The several companies in a county alternating [duty], so that none should be required to serve longer than a week at a time, except in emergencies."[219]

In the meantime recruitment for the 13th was going along very well. On August 11th, 2nd Lieut. William E. Feazel wrote to Adj. Gen. H.J. Samuels that:

> [W]e have already mustered in More than one Company all of which I have charge of at this time and by the last of this week I am inclined to believe we will have men enough to organize two companies I understand from Mr. Hall that Col. Waggoner had gone to make arrangements from arms and clothing for recruits at this Station I have drawn some clothing enough to raise an excitement and if he does not draw I will draw all we need at Charleston you will please instruct me whether I shall hold an election for company officers before I return the papers to you or not and whether I will be authorized to employ a private physician as an inspecting Surgeon or not
>
> Please answer on receipt of this Genl. Orders was received from your office I wish to call your attention to one thing that is that there is a physician in this county by the name of Griffith that is able to give a good recommendation that wants to be Assistant Surgeon of the 13th Va Regt. Dr. Griffith and has done a great deal for the Service he is now out recruiting for this place please give him a chance before those that has done nothing
>
> I wish to inform you that I could not go to Nicholas county on account of the rebel forces being to[o] many for our troops at the time I was on my way there.

> Your Obt. Svt.
> Wm E Feazel 2nd Lieut.
> 13th Regt. vol. Inft
> Rect. officer

> P.S. I would like to be Regl. Q. M. [Quarter Master][220]

By August 12th (1862), Brigadier General W.S. Rosecrans at Clarksburg, Virginia, telegraphed Gov. Pierpont that there were ten "Companies: two Virginia companies in Kanawha, seven in Mason City and Point Pleasant and one at Grafton will make a regiment." Rosecrans asked if field officers had already been appointed for these companies, if not he suggested consulting with Major Oakes and R.C.M. Lovell, of Mason City. Rosecrans wanted to "embody" these troops.[221]

August 13th, 1862, the 106th Regiment Virginia Militia, Colonel J.P R.B. Smith[222] commanding, assembled at Point Pleasant, at the Mason County Court-House, at 10 o'clock A.M., for a regimental muster. Muster of the 106th as well as of the "various Regiments of this Brigade" had been ordered "with a view to thoroughly organize the militia and to facilitate volunteering."[223]

Extant State Militia records, though of course fragmentary, indicate that County Militia and Home Guard units probably formed the nuclei around which the first 13th Regiment Companies were formed. Militia law provided that battalion and regimental courts would convene in October and November each year but the reorganization of "many" militia regiments in Western Virginia "disintegrated by our civil conventions was not perfected within the time" to permit the holding of battalion and regimental courts in October and November of 1861.[224] Records do support the impression that the 106th Virginia Militia of Mason County (to which Mason and Putnam County militia members belonged) was reorganizing, at least by November 1861, and that its re-organization was completed at the latest by early March 1862 with the election of new officers J.P.R.B. Smith, Colonel; Junius Kincade, Lieutenant Colonel; and Van. D. McDaniel, Major.[225] (Note that this March date coincides with Gov. Letcher's Proclamation and passage of the Virginia Ranger Act.) Smith authorized the newspaper to quote him as saying that he would hold his officers "to strict observance of the laws regulating the militia and especially the requirements in regard to uniform &c."[226] to which the editor appended this parting shot: "With the inauguration of a new order of things generally, let us, for Heaven's sake, have some improvement, if we can upon these non-sensical farces known as militia musters."[227] As the 13th was recruited mainly of men from Mason and Kanawha Counties in 1862, a look at records for the 106th Mason County Militia Regiment (for the years 1861 and 1862) is helpful as a model to understand the connection between the membership of re-organized county militias and volunteer regiments such as the 13th. What one discovers, is that a considerable number of men serving in the ranks of the 106th went on to serve as officers and enlisted men in the 13th Volunteers.

John McDaniel was commissioned Captain in the Mason County 106th Militia on December 10th, 1861, to rank from November 25th, 1861. Upon organization of the 13th Virginia Volunteers, he would be mustered in as Third Sergeant for Co. B. John Plants was commissioned Captain of the 106th on December 10th, 1861, to rank from November 26th, 1861. Upon organization of the 13th, Plants was mustered in as Orderly Sergeant in Co. C. Timothy Russell was commissioned Captain in the 106th on December 10th, 1861, to rank from November 20th, 1861. He was mustered into the 13th Regiment as 1st Lieutenant of Co. F and was promoted and commissioned Captain of Co. F on December 14th, 1864. Joseph Bromley/Brumley was commissioned 1st Lieutenant in the Mason County 106th on December 10th, 1861, to rank from November 20th, 1861. He was mustered into the 13th Infantry Volunteers as 1st Lieutenant Co. F on October 9th, 1862, and promoted to 1st Lieutenant, Co. F on

December 14th, 1864. Lovell C. Rayburn was commissioned 1st Lieutenant of the 106th on December 10th, 1861, to rank from November 26th, 1861. He was mustered in as 1st Lieutenant, Co. B upon organization of the 13th. Francis (Frank) W. Sisson was commissioned 1st Lieutenant in the 106th on December 10th, 1861, to rank from November 16th, 1861. Sisson was mustered into the 13th on October 8th, 1862, as Quarter Master Sergeant, Co. A. During the course of the war he was promoted to 2nd Lieutenant, Co. F and commissioned 1st Lieutenant and Adjutant of the 13th. Marshall Smith was commissioned 1st Lieutenant in the 106th on December 10th, 1861, to rank from November 23rd, 1861. Smith was mustered into Co. D as Private and then detached to serve with the Blazer Scouts (in which only the best woodsmen and soldiers from Crook's troops served in a "special forces" counter-guerrilla capacity) on May 30th, 1864. James H. Gaskins was commissioned 2nd Lieutenant in the 106th on December 10th, 1861, to rank from November 18th, 1861, and then mustered as Private into Co. B when the 13th was organized. Adam Wigand/Wiggand was commissioned 2nd Lieutenant in the 106th on December 10th, 1861, to rank from November 25th, 1861. Wigand was mustered in as Corporal of Co. D, upon organization of the 13th Virginia. Peter Yeager was commissioned 2nd Lieutenant of the 106th on December 10th, 1861, to rank from November 20th, 1861. Forty-one year old Yeager was enlisted by Justice Lewis Wetzel on September 9th, 1862, and mustered in as Corporal Co. F on October 9th, 1862.[228]

Men commissioned as officers in the 106th Militia in 1862 would likewise leave its ranks for a better opportunity to render effective service as members of the volunteer army later that year. Van D. McDaniel was commissioned Major of the reorganized 106th on February 26th, 1862, to rank from February 22, 1862. He would raise Co. "C" for the 13th Regiment and be mustered in as its Captain. Albert McCown was commissioned Captain of the 106th on May 27th, 1862, to rank from April 19th, 1862. McCown would also raise a company for the 13th ("F") and command it as Captain. Elijah M. Roseberry was commissioned Captain of the 106th on May 27th, 1862, to rank from April 29th, 1862. He was mustered in as Private of Co. C and promoted to 2nd Orderly Sergeant on October 15th, 1863. William Harris was commissioned 2nd Lieutenant in the 106th, by order of December 27th, 1862, to rank from December 1st, 1862. Harris recruited men for Co. G and was mustered into this company when it was mustered into the Regiment in early 1864. James B. Swan/Swain was commissioned 2nd Lieutenant in the 106th by order of November 4th, 1862, to rank from September 8th, 1862. Swain would serve as Sergeant for Co. D in the 13th Regiment.[229]

Another document offers a similar story. An old ledger book belonging to Captain John Thomas Greer (son of John Greer, the pioneer), cmdg. Co. A, 116th Virginia Militia of Mason County, lists the members of Greer's Company, for the date March 10th, 1861. His company numbered 104 soldiers and 7 officers. From this Company alone, of these one hundred and eleven men, about twenty went into the 13th Virginia. One went into Co. A; about eleven went into Co. B; and eight went into Co. C.[230] The following named soldiers—listed under "Solgers"—Greer's company, were numbered (probably in order of appearance at muster or enrollment). On the original document is notation indicating that the men enlisted "probably after March 10th, 1861." The following from that list, appear to have gone on to serve in the 13th Volunteer Infantry.

"Solger" number:

"78 Glover, William." William Morton Glover subsequently enlisted August 16th, 1862, at Charleston, Virginia, in the 13th Regiment and was mustered into Co. A, at Point Pleasant, Virginia on October 7th, 1862.

"100 Samples, Griff." Agrippa Samples subsequently served as Private in Co. A, of the 13th Regiment. He enlisted August 12th, 1862 at Charleston, Virginia and was mustered into the United States Service on October 7th, 1862, at Point Pleasant.

"63 Adkins, Spencer." Engineer, Spencer Adkins, enlisted on August 9th, 1862, at Point Pleasant and joined Co. B, serving as Private, Corporal and Sergeant.

"66 Chapman, Oscar." Chapman enlisted at Point Pleasant, on August 9th, 1862 and served as Private in Co. D.

"80 Gaskins, John." John Gaskins of the 116th, was probably John R. Gaskins, of Mercer's Bottom, Mason County, who was enlisted by Capt. Milton Stewart, for Co. B, of the 13th Regiment, on July 15th, 1863, at Point Pleasant.

"83 Harris, Silas." Silas Harris of the 116th Militia, was probably the same Silas Harris, who was enlisted on August 11th, 1862, at Point Pleasant, Virginia, by Lieut. W.E. Feazel and who served in Milton Stewart's Co. B.

"70 McDaniel, Ellick." "Solger 70" may have been Alex McDaniel, one of two Alex McDaniels residing near Point Pleasant, in the 1860s. Alex McDaniel the younger, enlisted August 9th, 1862, in the 13th Regiment, becoming a member of Co. B.

"72 McDaniel, Ruben." Ruben/Reuban McDaniel, enlisted on August 4th, 1862, becoming a member of Co. B.

"90 Meeks, Henry." Militiaman Henry Meeks may well have been Henry A. Meek, born in Allegheny County, Pennsylvania, who enlisted August 4th, 1862, at Point Pleasant, in the 13th Regiment, becoming a member of Co. B.

"94 Piller, William." This militiaman is probably William J. Pillow, one of a set of male twins, who enlisted August 9th, 1862, at Point Pleasant, and who served in Co. B.

"101 Schools, Pal." Irishman Paul Schools, became a member of Co. B, enlisting in the 13th Regiment, on August 6th, 1862, at Point Pleasant.

"99 Sinclair, Alfred." This militiaman was likely the same Alfred Sinclair/St. Clair, who enlisted in the 13th Regiment on August 8th, 1862, at Point Pleasant, becoming a member of Co. B.

"65 Burris, John T." Burris subsequently joined the 13th Regiment on August 3rd, 1863, at Point Pleasant and was mustered into Capt. Van D. McDaniel's Co. C, as Private.

"75 Eads, Charles." Charles Eads was likely Charles H. Eads, son of John and Nancy Eads, who all lived in the vicinity of Point Pleasant. On August 11th, 1862, Charles enrolled for duty in the new 13th Regiment. He would serve as Private, together with his cousins, William A. and David Eads as members of Co. C.

"85 Johnson, Asey." Asa S. Johnson, son of Ariel Johnson, of Point Pleasant was enlisted on December 8th, 1862 at Point Pleasant, by Colonel W.R. Brown. He was mustered in with the rank of Private, on December 11th, 1862 at Point Pleasant and served with Co. C.

"Private Cullough, John Mc." John McCullough who had enrolled with the 116th Militia, was perhaps the same as John S. Mucolloch (son of John McCulloch) who enlisted in the 13th Regiment, on August 14th, 1862 and was mustered in as Private Co. C, at Point Pleasant, on October 8th, 1862.

"71 McDaniel, George." It is possible but not certain, that George McDaniel of the 116th Militia, was the same George McDaniel who enlisted September 29th, 1863, at Barboursville, for service in Co. C.

"91 Meeks, Bazel." Bezalleel or Bazallee Meek enlisted at Point Pleasant on August 21ˢᵗ, 1862 and served as Private with Van D. McDaniel's Co. C.

"87 Mornen, Andy." Andrew J. Mourning was enlisted August 20ᵗʰ, 1863 at Coals Mouth, Virginia, by Lieutenant L[emuel] Harpold and was mustered in as Private Co. C, on August 20ᵗʰ, 1863 at Barboursville.

"86 Mornen, George." George Mourning was enrolled August 8ᵗʰ, 1862, at Point Pleasant by Lewis Wetzel to serve for a term of three years. He became a member of Co. C and was mustered in on October 8ᵗʰ, 1862 at Point Pleasant.[231]

For further information regarding how militarization (by reorganization and muster of local militia, etc.) proceeded at this time and how this informed recruitment of the 13ᵗʰ Regiment we must look to neighboring counties. While not a terribly fruitful search, the results are worthy of some small mention in this context. Kanawha County records include a letter from Greenbury Slack [Sr.?] of Kanawha County to his friend, Gov. Pierpont that underscores the level of commitment at this time in the newly organized militia companies (Kanawha County State troops were reorganized between March and June 1862):

> [O]ur adjutants have nearly completed the organization, of the Militia of this County [Kanawha County]. [T]he people take hold of the thing with an enthusiasm that is truly astonishing nearly the entire force of the county, attend the musters promptly and seem only to wish for something to do.[232]

Officers' commissions for new militia companies in the process of being raised and reorganized in Kanawha County had been issued by Governor Pierpont and were being given out. Some commissioned persons refused to take the oath of office and were replaced by others who would; some did "not like the reduced Compensation of 2$ instead of 4$ per day" some didn't care and only wanted the opportunity to serve.[233] The Kanawha County 80ᵗʰ Militia in which John S Cunningham (future adjutant of the 13ᵗʰ Volunteers) mustered and was commissioned Captain on June 20ᵗʰ, 1862, was organized during this period. Likewise, the 153ʳᵈ Kanawha County Militia in which Greenbury Slack Jr. (future 1ˢᵗ Lieutenant and later Captain of Co. A, 13ᵗʰ Regiment) was commissioned May 14ᵗʰ, 1862, to rank from April 30ᵗʰ, 1862, and Captain David Wilson's Co. A in which Daniel Childress enrolled as Private, on April 10ᵗʰ, 1862 at

Davis Creek, Kanawha County, and mustered June 10th, 1862, were militia groups from which other 13th volunteers, of summer 1862, were also drawn.[234]

The Militia of Jackson County (soldiers of the Jackson County Home Guard) became members of Companies A, D, E, F, and K of the 13th Regiment. Capt. Joseph E. McCoy's Co. K was largely composed of Jackson County men.[235] The militia of Putnam County (reorganized about November 1861), Cabell County (reorganizing by October 28, 1861) and Wayne County (167th Wayne County Militia reorganized and mustered by May 7, 1862[236]), all contributed soldiers who formed a nuclei for 13th Companies mustered in autumn of 1862, 1863, and in time for spring campaigning in 1864.

Volunteers from "the Bend"

West Columbia was located at the mouth of Ice Creek in Waggoner District, Mason County, just 12 miles above Point Pleasant. It was the oldest town in the district. Though a small town (about 3,000 inhabitants), West Columbia was before the war a flourishing commercial center, its people eager to ride the waves of developing industry as far as it might take them. It should come as no surprise that West Columbia was also one of the towns (together with the town of Point Pleasant, Hartford City and Mason City) where in 1862 public meetings took place on the issue of the New State. According to the local papers, meetings were "well-attended as the majority of the sentiment in the [West Columbia] area was for separation from Virginia, and the establishment of a new State."[237]

The bald facts in history books indicate that West Columbia's pre-war prosperity began when the first salt well was bored there in 1847. The same year the first salt furnace on the Ohio River was built. Coal was also mined and conveniently, salt and coal were shipped to market on the Ohio River. Salt and coal company stores provided supplies and necessaries, and a market for country produce also came to thrive here. There was much more, however, to the story of West Columbia's success. Old timer, John L. Mason (born in West Columbia shortly before 1859), recalled that before the war, the town was on her way to becoming the "commercial mistress of the Ohio Valley." "[T]here was no better place on the face of the map to make money *legitimately* [my italics] than was offered at West Columbia." West Columbia was "the best town between Pittsburg and Cincinnati on the Ohio river." At West Columbia, "[e]very line of business was in action, and money turned rapidly." "[A]stute financiers" came to town and "doubled their income by judicious investments." "Commerce, finance, manufacture and official and professional distinction" flourished there and West Columbia looked the part. She had "beautiful roadways, laced with velvet lawns, tree embossed walkways, gemmed with numerous lovely homes."[238]

Before the war coal mining at what was known as "the high bank" was going full throttle. Coal diggers employed here were making what for the time was considered good wages: "from $3 to $5 per hundred bushels." The coal was then shipped out on the waterways. When operating at full capacity, the town's salt furnaces and coal works required three tow-boats to transport salt and coal "to the lower markets." The three tow boats recalled John L. Mason, were "the *Dutchess,* the *Sam Snowden* and the *Hamburg.*" The "*Hamburg* and *Dutchess* were fine side-wheel tow-boats while the *Sam Snowden* was of the stern-wheel type."[239]

Before hostilities put a freeze on commerce and industry, West Columbia also had a flourishing, and from the descriptions of it, a sophisticated dry docks business. The docking lot was located at "a point a few hundred yards above the Methodist Church." Here barges and steamboats were parked for storage and repair. The docks were equipped with "[p]owerful machinery" which pulled barges and steamboats up "on the ways" for repair and "[a] large force of workmen were kept busy" operating equipment, repairing and maintaining the barges and steamboats docked here.[240]

West Columbia had its own newspaper (no small thing for a Virginia town west of the mountains): the *Virginia Messenger.*[241] The town had a hotel, the Van Matre House, owned and operated by O.H.P. Vanmatre who kept a "fleet of carriages and horses" on hand for the use of his guests. Prominent among the town's mercantile establishments was the firm of A. D. Strinback and John Mason (Strinback & Mason) and that of W.H. Linslow, Peter Hogg and Isaac Williams. Strinback & Mason "carried a general line of groceries and dry goods, boots, shoes, hats, caps, bonnets and tinware," and the "general merchandizing" firm of Linslow, Hogg and Williams sold salt "at 25 cents per bushel by the barrel."[242] Several other stores, company stores perhaps, connected with the salt works and mines also sold salt. Matthew Cohen had a tailoring and clothing store. Hogg's flour mill (an old water mill) was in operation about six or seven miles below West Columbia on the Point Pleasant road. Lemuel Harpold (who rose through the ranks of the 13th Regiment to become Major in March of 1865) owned and operated a tan yard. Harpold kept all kinds of leather in stock for sale. West Columbia was also home to a construction company. Carpenter and contractor, William P. Shank headed up the business and employed a large force of carpenters for his building jobs. Many of these went into the 13th Regiment. There were of course, town officers. Among these was millwright Peter Darnell, who served as town mayor before the war and also enlisted.

When the war broke out, the salt works and coal mines around West Columbia closed down. No one had any idea as to when the mines might re-open and need workers. In addition, there was a general breakdown in civic organization and town officers such as there were turned their attention to public safety issues and defense. Town offices were closed and the annual election of new officers were abandoned as the exigencies of the moment seemed to justify. All that seemed left for the men to do was join the service. Male residents joined the Northern and Southern militia and armies. Former mayor, 45 year old Peter Darnell, enlisted in the 13th Virginia (West

Virginia) Regiment. He was mustered in as Sergeant of Co. F and later served as 1st Lieutenant and then Captain of Co. I. Peter's son Arthur W. or "Wick" Darnell was about 17 years at the time of his enlistment August 23rd, 1862, in the 13th Virginia, first as Sergeant of Co. D, then as 2nd Lieutenant of Allen C. Mason's (a school teacher at West Columbia before the war[243]) Co. G, upon organization of that Company in early 1864.

During those stirring days, noted John L. Mason, West Columbia became a desolate place.

> The able bodied men had gone into service leaving a few old men the women and children to hold the fort and do the best they could. When the corn meal bin began to run low, there was nothing to do but buy a sack of corn shell it and take the corn to Hogg's old water mill and either exchange the corn for meal or wait until your grist was ground before returning home. [...T]he trip down to the mill for meal was generally made by the women. It was a common sight in those days to see a woman on a horse with a sack of corn on her way to mill and I often think that the horses did not all go to the front in battle. Much of the success of the Federal arms belong to the brave women who were left at home unprotected to battle singlehanded and alone against the pangs of hunger and privation [...].[244]

Among those of West Columbia who answered the first call for volunteers in summer 1862, and joined the13th Regiment were the following (Woodrum through Van Matre):

> Richard "Dick" Woodrum, an engineer, enlisted September 9th, 1862 at Point Pleasant by Lewis Wetzel, Justice.

> Joseph Bromley, 1st Lieutenant of Mason County 106th Militia, farmer and farmer manager, mustered in as 2nd Lieutenant of Co F 13th W.V.V.I. on October 8th, 1862.

> Lemuel Harpold, a tanner and carpenter, was about 38 years old, enrolled August 9th, 1862, commissioned 1st Lieutenant of Co. C on September 12th, 1862.

> Hamilton Johnson (J. Hamilton Johnson born about 1836 died September 8, 1917), a farmer, enlisted September 9th, 1862, mustered in as Corporal on October 9th, 1862.

> Hamilton Johnson was taken prisoner and sent to Andersonville Prison where he remained for several months. He was finally

exchanged and returned to his home—a mere shadow of his former self—broken in health and nearly starved to death but still in full possession of that proud, brave spirit of the true soldier.[245]

High (Hiram) Russel, a laborer, enlisted, on September 9th, 1862 at Point Pleasant, mustered in as Private in Co. F.

David Forbes, a blacksmith, enlisted on August 14th, 1862 at Point Pleasant, mustered in as Corporal Co. F.

Allen C. Mason, a clerk and school teacher at West Columbia, enlisted September 9th, 1862 at Point Pleasant, mustered in as 1st Sergeant Co. F.

Thomas McMaster, a native of Down County, Ireland, a miner, enlisted September 21st, 1862 at Point Pleasant, mustered in as Private in Co. F.

Albert F. McKown, a merchant and Captain of the 106th Militia (West) Virginia State Troops, commissioned Captain Co. F 13th Regiment V.V.I. on October 8th, 1862.

Two men named "James Wilson from West Columbia answered the call and were mustered into Co. F on October 9th, 1862. One was James V. Wilson and the other James B. Wilson. The elder James (aged about 40 years at the time of enrollment) was a miner and a native of Scotland, enlisted September 10th, 1862 at Point Pleasant, mustered in as Private. The younger James (about 31 years of age), an engineer, enlisted on September 9th, 1862 at Point Pleasant, was promoted to Company Sergeant October 1st, 1862.

John McSherry age about 36 years old, a native of Scotland and a miner, enlisted August 18th, 1862 at Hartford City, mustered in as Private in Co. D.

Francis M. Van Matre, farmer, enlisted September 10, 1862 at Point Pleasant, mustered in as Private in Co. F.

Gwin Van Matre, a laborer, enlisted September 9th, 1862, mustered in as Private in Co. F.

Leonard Van Matre, a boatman, enlisted at Point Pleasant, mustered in as Private in Co.F.

"Jack" Van Matre (William J. Vanmatre), farmer, enlisted on September 9th, 1862 at Point Pleasant, mustered in as Private in Co. F.

The 4 brothers (Francis, Gwin, Leonard and Jack) and their father, Rezin Van Matre all served in the Federal army during the war.[246]

August 1862

In August and September Rebels in Northwestern Virginia were very active in their efforts to disrupt and retake. Their purposes were multifarious: to disrupt the operation of civil government and recruitment of Union regiments; to gain access to abundant military supplies at Point Pleasant and Gallipolis; and ultimately, to gain access to Kanawha and Ohio River waterways, railroads, resources and the Northern States.

The second week of August Confederate troops again became troublesome. W.H.H. Russell, Lieutenant Colonel of the 4th Virginia (West Virginia) Volunteer Infantry Regiment, with a detachment of just 150 men, reported that his "pickets had been driven in from Chapmansville, Logan County, by a force of 600 Rebels."[247] Confederates also operated in vicinity of Point Pleasant. To settle them, Co. A of the 4th Virginia (Lieutenant Davis commanding) was sent to Point Pleasant the week of August 14th. "They came down to see that all things are right, and to put the troubling Secesh where they will cease from troubling. We welcome him [Davis] and wish him and his little band success and that speedily" appeared in the *Register*. In Wayne County, "prowling bands of armed rebels and the close proximity of the public enemy" had made it "extremely hazardous" to hold the Court at the Wayne County Courthouse. To side step this exigency, Gov. Pierpont authorized a change of venue issuing a proclamation making Ceredo where the Courts of Wayne County would sit.[248]

Volunteering in August was active and in Mason County, exceeded expectations; the community buoyed up by the hope that with 600,000 more volunteers the rebellion would soon be quashed. The turnout of "patriotic and loyal men of old Mason" at the time of General Muster of the militia (held on August 13th) was overwhelming. It was noted in the *Weekly Register* for August 14th that:

As we go to press the patriotic and loyal men of old Mason, are pouring into town in obedience to the call, directing the assembling of the 106th Regiment Virginia Militia, for the purpose of a General Muster. The indications are that, the turn out will be much larger than was anticipated, and the war spirit seems to be at its highest pitch. Volunteering we understand is progressing very satisfactorily.[249]

The General Muster of the 106th Regiment Virginia Militia, indeed the entire gathering (military and non-military assembled at Point Pleasant on August 13th) was quite large, all things considered. The *Register* reported that at General Muster:

there were eight hundred and ninety men in the ranks, besides a vast concourse of persons who seemed to be, though not participants in the exercises of the day, quite interested in the proceedings. [...] full as many men were in attendance on that day as on the occasion of former General Musters, notwithstanding the fact, that the county had furnished five or six hundred men for the Union army during the past year.[250]

Col. J.P.R.B. "Alphabet" Smith commanding the militia, took the opportunity to announce to the assembly the news of Major John T. Hall's death at the hands of Confederate guerrillas. Maj. Hall while serving with the 4th West Virginia Infantry Regiment at the time of his death, had been pressing to be transferred to command in the 13th Regiment, that he and his brother James might serve together. Resolutions regarding the Major's passing were read and unanimously adopted by the members of the 106th as expressive of the feelings of the militiamen upon this loss. In addition to the 106th, townsfolk of Point Pleasant and the new volunteers of Co. A and what would become Company B (both 13th West Virginia) were likely also in attendance, as also very possibly James R. Hall and his family.

Resolutions comprising a "tribute of respect" for Major Hall, designed also to incite a sense of outrage, "War spirit" and bolster volunteerism were passed and reported as follows:

Resolved, That we deeply deplore the loss of our gallant young friend, and in cherishing his manly virtues, we hereby pledge ourselves anew to make every effort in our power to promptly suppress this horrid rebellion which has caused this and similar sacrifices.

Resolved, That while he has been suddenly torn, in early manhood from his doting family and admiring friends; we have the satisfaction of knowing, that he lost his life in the discharge of his duty as a soldier and patriot.

Resolved, That while his untimely death is a public calamity and an unreparable loss to his bereaved family and afflicted friends; it is a source of great consolation to believe that his chivalric character and [example] remain a rich legacy to us, his former comrades, which we now promise to emulate.

Resolved, That while the manner in which he fell elicits our unqualified admiration — that when a surrender to his traitor foe, was insolently demanded, he not only enjoined his comrades *'never to surrender'* but spurning himself the demand died as he would have wished to die — in mortal combat with his country's foe's — and his death *shall be avenged.*

Resolved, That our heartfelt sympathies are hereby tendered to the [parents and relatives] of the diseased [their spelling].

Resolved, That we desire also to testify our appreciation of the faithfulness and heroism of the brave men who sacrificed their lives in the effort to rescue their intrepid young commander from the ruthless foe, — we cherish their memories and offer our sincere condolence to their respective families and friends.

Resolved, That a copy of these resolutions be forwarded to the Colonel of the 4th Va. Regt. and published in the *Weekly Register* and other loyal papers.[251]

The week of August 14th and prior to, marked a watershed in other respects as well, much to the approval of the editor of the *Weekly Register* who wrote the following:

Mason county is at last fully aroused. The people now realize their actual position, and are coming forward from all parts of the county and volunteering. — If they continue for the next ten days to rally as they have done for the past week, Mason county will fill her quota under both of the last calls. The Government needs men and is determined to have them, to crush this hell-born conspiracy during the coming fall and winter. [...] It has been determined that every man that enlists before the last day of grace, shall fare, as to the extra bounty, equally though private purses have to be drawn on to do so. When the county levy was laid the last call for 300,000 had not been made, and was not then expected, but the patriotism and liberality of the people of our county is equal to the emergency and every man immediately volunteering in this county, will fare alike in every respect. In some Secession counties scarcely any will volunteer and the Government will draft their full quota for each Secession locality [...] that the burden of war will fall on all alike.[252]

As for the volunteers of the 13th Virginia Volunteers, they were being outfitted. On August 15th, the enlisted men of Co. A were issued their clothing.[253] On the same day, 1st Lieutenant and Adjutant of the 13th, William I. Mathews wrote to Adj. Gen. Samuels from Ravenswood, Virginia, concerning the progress of the companies being raised for the 13th:

I hav[e] just returned from a business trip to Mason County + am able to give a cheering report of the recruiting business there.

At Point Pleasant I found Lieuts Feazel Hall and Latham (this one is commissioned in the 4th) by whose l[i]mited exertions one hundred and twenty nine men hav been mustered into service.

Lieut Feazel himself has mustered most if not all of the recruits into service while Latham + Hall hav[e] been mainly instrumental in getting them

An election was held by the men, who desired Lieut. Hall for Captain + he was accordingly elected. He will proceed to Wheeling, lay the report before you, + claim his commission.

I do not know whether it is in accordance with your policy in organizing the new regiments for company officers to be elected by a body of recruits amounting to either the minimum or maximum of a company without first having been sent to Depot, or indeed to be elected at all. Please instruct me in regard thereto.

At Mason City Lieut Neal is recruiting but has not succeeded well.

At Hartford City there is one Simon Williams recruiting for the 13th, but has no commission I told him to go on + get forty men, have them mustered in, take proper evidence of the fact + that he had recruited them, lay it before you + apply for a 1st Lieuts commission.

Lieut Bumgardner from Guyandotte told me he had mustered in 33 men. Other Lieuts recruiting for the 13th in this part of Va I have heard nothing from.

Information, unofficial though reached me the other day that there were 200 recruits for the 13th in Ritchie County, + I intend starting to see about it on first boat.

I reported to you, at least two weeks ago in relation to establishing Regimental Head Quarters [...] no reply as yet. Hoping you will give me orders at Parkersburg soon.[254]

On August 16th, Justice Lewis Wetzel wrote to H.J. Samuels from Point Pleasant. He discussed the death of Major John T. Hall, Captain James Hall, recruitment of the 13th and the effect that Major Hall's death had upon the County. Wetzel wrote:

Just as my young friend, Capt Jas R Hall was starting for Wheeling for the purpose of arranging some business connected with his company, it occurred to me that it would not be inappropriate for me to say a word to you in regard to the sad death of his brother, the lamented Major John T Hall of the 4th Va Reg.

The Major was several years the junior of Capt Hall, being in his twentieth year at the time of his death. I had known him intimately from his infancy, and never in my life have I known a man, young or old, as entirely insensible to fear — as perfectly courageous and brave, at all times, as he was and we all predicted for him such a brilliant future! You may imagine the sadness and gloom his death has caused, far and near. Mason County has ever been loyal but if any doubt had heretofore existed of that fact, that doubt is now removed. If you had heard the many solemn oaths both loud and deep, that I have to avenge the death of the murdered young officer, you would conclude with me that treason hereafter will find no apologist in Mason County.

The circumstances attending the death of Major Hall will reach you through the public press. You will see that he died like a young hero, — fighting gallantly and gloriously, until he fell pierced by <u>ten bullets</u>. — The Regimental muster which was largely attended passed resolutions on the death of the Major, deploring his loss and pledging that his death shall be avenged.

Our whole community seems overwhelmed and the aged father of the young soldier is like one bereft of all. Any expression of sympathy with him from your office, would be most gratefully received I know.

The Captain can advise you more particularly concerning the recruiting business in our County than I can write and therefore refer you to him for any information you desire concerning our affairs. Hoping you will excuse me for troubling you, I am

Respectfully Yours Lewis Wetzel

P.S. If you should think proper to consider the claims of Capt Hall to a field appointment in the 13th Va Regiment, I am very certain that it would gratify his numerous friends in his own and adjoining Counties. Although, he is not a military graduate, he has had considerably military teaching at the Lexington Institute.[255]

On August 17th, John Hall Sr., wrote from Point Pleasant to his friend, Adjutant General H. J. Samuels (at Wheeling) about the loss of John and that his other son, James, would soon visit Samuels regarding his company and to confer with the Governor as to the state of affairs in and around Point Pleasant generally. Hall wrote with unmistakable pride:

My son James [...] raised in a few days one hundred and thirty men and if he could have commanded them could have got more then 200 his company will have many of the best young men in the County and we have a prospect of a Very fine Regiment I hope you will see that it has the Right kind of officers temperate and business men and if you should be at a loss for such men I am sattisfied I can name them to you of the 4th Virginia Regiment and will name them for your consideration They will embrace the very best men in that regiment you know I have been with them and heard enough of them to know something of them Capt William R Brown would make a good Col[256] and Lieut Shephard Blake and Russel would fill any lower commission with credit to themselves and profit to the government my son is not very able to walk and I think he might fill well the office of Leut Col or maj[or] and if you could secure to him the office Leut Col I would be thankfull. [...].[257]

On August 19th, John Hall telegraphed Gov. Pierpont at Wheeling, with the message that Mason County now had 217 recruits. "Gist labored hard," wrote Hall.[258] George M. Gist had "reported to Adjutant Mathews at Point Pleasant with 53 men on the 18th and with his consent made Simon Williams 1st Lieutenant."[259] Hall informed Pierpont that Gist's recruits desired and he seconded with recommendation and request that Gist receive a field appointment.[260] By August 30th, Gist, then recruiting at Letart (Mason County) would report to Adj. Gen. Samuels that he "now had 68 men and expected to have 83 by Saturday, the 30th."[261] Lieut. Mathews at Point Pleasant, also telegraphed Pierpont on the 19th with news of the 13th, relating that there "are 30 recruits in Jackson County and there will be 50." Mathews asked whether the 11th Virginia Regiment is entitled to all the recruits raised there in Jackson County or if these may be credited to the 13th.[262] Also this day, James R. Hall took his oath of office as Captain in the 13th Regiment Virginia Volunteer Infantry in Ohio County (probably at Wheeling), before L.A. Hagans, Secretary of the Commonwealth of Virginia. He swore the following oaths. First, that he would

> support the Constitution of the United States and the laws made in pursuance thereof, as the supreme law of the land, anything in the Constitution and laws of the State of Virginia, or the Ordinances of the Convention which assembled at Richmond on the 13th day of February, 1861, to the contrary notwithstanding.

Further, he swore to "uphold and defend the government of Virginia as vindicated and restored by the Convention which assembled in Wheeling on the 11th day of June, 1861" and that he had not fought nor been directly or indirectly involved in a duel since January 10, 1860, nor would he engage directly or indirectly in a duel while continuing in his military office.[263]

On August 21st, 1862, W.N. Hawkins, Adjutant, telegraphed Gov. Pierpont from Charleston, Virginia, informing that he had received one full company of recruits and organized them. Hawkins stated further that he had twenty-five men for a second company and further, asked: "Can you furnish some pants and socks?"[264] Until "sufficiently drilled for active service," the "13th Va. Regt. now being raised in [Mason] and other counties" was to rendezvous at Point Pleasant. As for the pace of recruitment at this time, the Point Pleasant *Weekly Register* (dated August 21st) reported that while recruiting was still underway in Mason County, it was "not with the same spirit and enthusiasm that it was a few days ago." The editor offered as explanation that there were still eligible men, who wish to stay neutral and take their chances with the draft.[265] Also on August 21st, Jacob Hornbrook was empowered to act as government agent on behalf of Virginia volunteers: to see to their needs and comfort. Specifically, Hornbrook was authorized to aid soldiers in getting their pay and to carry it to their families at home. He also had authority to acquire descriptive lists and necessary papers to discharge sick soldiers.[266] Soldiers customarily sent money home with pay agents, such as Hornbrook. With so much guerrilla activity—burning of trains, etc. which carried the mails—it was a safer way to get badly needed salaries home to loved ones. When he had occasion to visit the army on business, Col. J.P.R.B. Smith also conveyed money home for 13th soldiers.[267]

By August 21st, 1862, the water in the rivers had become so low that to a considerable extant navigation had become suspended. On August 22[nd], 1862, Col. J.A.J.

Lightburn (cmdg. District of Kanawha, at Gauley, Virginia) telegraphed Gov. Pierpont, at Wheeling, requesting that Headquarters of the 13th Virginia Regiment be located at Charleston to enable him (Lightburn) "to use the 4th Reg[imen]t. in front." At Charleston, added Lightburn, he could cloth and arm the regiment at any time it reported for duty.[268]

On August 23rd, the first company of the 13th elected its commissioned officers. These were James R. Hall, elected Captain; Lovell C. Rayburn, 1st Lieutenant; and Charles T. Latham, 2nd Lieutenant. Inasmuch as James Hall had in the meantime been appointed Lieutenant Colonel of the Regiment, Milton Stewart, Sergeant of the 4th Regiment Virginia Volunteer Infantry "whose commission is already here" was chosen in Hall's place. James Hall telegraphed Samuels on August 24th, 1862, from Point Pleasant with direction to appoint Milton Stewart as Captain in Hall's stead, as Stewart was also the choice of the men.[269]

Toward the end of August it looked as though the northwestern counties would be caught in the crossfire of offensives played out on grand scale. On August 25th, Kirby Smith advanced toward Kentucky with no less than 10,000 men. Colonel Jonathan Craynor at Catlettsburg, Kentucky, learned that Rebel leaders Menifee, Witcher and Jenkins had a plan afoot. First, Ceredo, Virginia, which was within sight of Catlettsburg would be attacked and plundered. Then, the raiders would cross the Sandy River to rob and plunder Catlettsburg. Next, they would proceed to Ashland, Kentucky, to plunder the bank there, and then move across to plunder Ironton, Ohio.

There were no Union forces to protect this area but Craynor's force which consisted of infantry and cavalry amounting to only about 1,100 men. Then on August 28th, it was reported that Rebel troops without tents, clothes or transportation were pouring into Kentucky. On the same day (August 25th), General Lee began his Virginia offensive in earnest. The Confederate armies were indeed stirring. Stonewall Jackson marched north again followed by Longstreet's Corps from below the Rappahannock. On August 26th, the Second Battle of Bull Run began and Col. J.A.J. Lightburn (cmdg. the Kanawha District) wrote to Captain C.W. Moulton requesting a boat to transport troops belonging to the 13th Regiment from Point Pleasant and Mason City to Charleston. "How soon can a boat be gotten ?" Lightburn asked.[270]

Recruiting took on renewed urgency in States caught in the cross-hairs of these movements, and attention continued to focus on its progress (or lack thereof) in the local press. The August 28th issue of the Gallipolis *Journal* reported on recruiting in Mason County:

> Recruiting goes on briskly in Mason county, V[irgini]a the 13th
> Regiment is nearly full. James Hall of Point Pleasant holds the commission of Lieutenant Colonel. He had raised a fine company of
> which he was Captain, but on the death of his brother, Major John

Hall of the 4th V[irginia], he was promoted to the position he now holds.—Our friend Comstock will act as Quartermaster.[271]

On August 28th, John [S.] Cunningham, future Adjutant of the 13th, wrote State Adjutant General Samuels from Coalsmouth (now St. Albans, Kanawha County, West Virginia) that the recruitment of Capt. John V. Young's Company had been progressing well since July, having 88 men at that date and "if not interrupted for two weeks will have 101 men. Of the total [Cunningham claims to have] recruited seventeen men."[272] On August 30th, Confederates were victorious for a second time at Bull Run. With General John Pope defeated, Lee invaded Maryland.

The 13th Regiment for its part was to be concentrated and provided for at Wheeling. This, reportedly came down as a decision from none other than the Secretary of War at Washington. Pursuant to this order, Lieutenant-Colonel J.R. Hall was directed by Adj. Gen. Samuels (letter dated August 29th) to "be prepared for embarkation on steamer Science that leaves this place [Wheeling] today for Point Pleasant."[273] There is no evidence that the 13th Companies were transported to Charleston, to Wheeling or anywhere else but remained in place at Point Pleasant. Alarms floated that the Confederacy was planning to invade the Kanawha Valley and wrest control of that valuable area from the Union.[274] Amidst alarms, pro-Union meetings and public rallies were also held to drum up volunteers for the 13th. Herbert L. Roush, writing about his grandfather, David Burrows (who enlisted in the 13th Regiment at Hartford City becoming a member of Co. F), in a book entitled *If Thou Wilt Remember,*[275] noted that in preparation for a war rally held at this time, stacks of posters publicizing Lincoln's recent call and the urgent need for more troops to end the rebellion had been left at a store and at the Post Office at Hartford City—these to be given out to patrons and post-box holders. Word then was also spread that a rally to further enlistments in the "new Regiment" being formed at Point Pleasant would be held on September 1st (1862) at the Hartford City Methodist Episcopal Church.

As was customary for the time, officers were appointed to speak, present and record resolutions to be voted upon at meetings, and generally to conduct the business of the meeting and see to it that protocols were respected that the conduct of the things might not fall below a *certain level* of urbanity (*i.e.,* that the meeting might not degenerate into a free for all). These posts were usually filled by local worthies. Reverend J.M. Phelps, Chaplain of the 9th Virginia spoke and George Wilding and the 13th's own W. W. Harper having been appointed to the Committee on Resolutions introduced the preamble and resolutions encouraging all loyal citizens of Hartford City and vicinity to do all in their power to bring to a speedy close the civil war that was spreading desolation and ruin throughout almost every section.[276]

Roush related with great detail that "Abe Barringer, Tom Roush, Frank Van Meter and David Burrows" attended the meeting together while their wives waited at David's house. The men returned from the rally in an animated state and in short order had told their wives what had gone down at the meeting. Reverend J. M. Phelps had been first to address the crowd. He gave notice of the new Regiment being formed at Point Pleasant, and he urged the men to step up and do their patriotic duty and join in the fight to squelch the rebellion and preserve the Union. George W. Moredock, founder of Hartford City and one of its "most respected citizen[s]" also spoke and

> made a passionate appeal, accenting his speech with stirring patri-
> otic phrases. W.W. Harper and Joe Pounds had already signed up
> and came forward, as examples of those who stood ready to do their
> duty. Their words made a deep impression on the young men; espe-
> cially when emotional pleas were made for them to help in this time
> of trouble.[277]

"Joining up," continued the speakers was the way to stand on the cross-boards and take part in the action playing out—to make a difference, to make a reputation, to be able to say one stood shoulder to shoulder on the battlefield in the great strug-gle of their time—with friends and family for hearth and home and for the future. Expressed in not-so-many words, was that joining the army offered a new adventure: opportunities for travel and glory. Also explained at the Hartford City gathering were the important compensations for volunteer service (as opposed to drafted service): bounty monies, salary, bounty land, etc., as set out by the War Department at Wash-ington. Another persuasive argument for volunteering as opposed to taking chances with the draft which may well have been made was the notion that enrolling now would enhance chances of getting choice duty. The great need for cavalry to curb guerrillas (who were invariably all mounted) may have found expression in the idea which floated for a time that the 13th might eventually be mounted as cavalry. This idea persisted into spring of 1863 when the idea was dashed and instead, Company G of the 3rd West Virginia Cavalry was attached to Col. W.R. Brown's command of 13th infantry. Inevitably, the realization came, that volunteer or draftee, there was for West Virginia troops no "choice duty."

Alarms become real:
invasion of the Kanawha Valley

Washington, it was feared, was in imminent danger from Confederate attack. One consequence was that on August 11th, Gen. John Pope (commanding Federal forces in Virginia) directed Gen. Jacob D. Cox (then commanding the Kanawha District) that all but 5,000 men were to be sent from Western Virginia to defend Washington. This left just five thousand men in the district to defend the Kanawha line should the Confederates advance upon it in force. Federal forces under Gen. Cox had occupied the Kanawha Valley since Gen. Henry Wise's evacuation of the Kanawha Valley in July of 1861. After having been in camp for fifteen months, from "Point Pleasant to Flat Top Mountain," Cox's brigade was ordered out of the Valley to join Pope's Army.[278]

Col. J.A.J. Lightburn was left in charge of the Kanawha District and assumed command on August 17th. Lightburn's command at this time was reported as comprised of "7 regiments of infantry, 1 regiment of cavalry, and 14 pieces of artillery."[279] The 34th and 37th Ohio Volunteer Infantry were stationed at Raleigh Court House; the 44th and 47th Ohio, together with two companies of the 2nd Virginia Cavalry were stationed at Gauley Bridge at Camp Ewing; and two companies of the 2nd Virginia were at Summersville. The 8th, 9th and 4th Virginia Infantries and remainder of the 2nd Virginia Cavalry were stationed at various points along the Kanawha River between Gauley Bridge and Charleston, including an out-post at Coal River in Boone County. Army Headquarters were at Gauley Bridge.[280] Lightburn's flanks were left unprotected. The only forces posted around Point Pleasant to hold the countryside in the event of a Confederate attack here were the 106th State Militia and the 13th Regiment companies, and perhaps, two companies of Paxton's 2nd Virginia Cavalry and two companies of 4th Virginia Infantry. The 13th Infantry, still in the process of recruiting, outfitting and organizing, was at Point Pleasant, their point of rendez-vous.

On August 17th, Halleck requested Indiana Governor Morton[281] and Governor Tod of Ohio to send troops as rapidly as possible into Kentucky. Confederates were concentrating in Tennessee and an invasion of Kentucky was feared. The War Department created the Department of the Ohio on August 19th, with Major General Horatio G. Wright assigned to command. The Department was composed of the States of Ohio, Michigan, Indiana, Illinois, Wisconsin and Kentucky east of the Tennessee River, including the Cumberland Gap and troops there. On August 22nd, the news from Louisville was that the country west of Tennessee was overrun by Rebel guerrillas, and the Union people had been subjugated. Upon taking command of the Department of the Ohio (headquarters at Cincinnati), Wright reported to Washington that everything there was disjointed and working badly. Wright confirmed that Kentucky, like Western Virginia had suffered a general deterioration and break down in civil power and had not yet sufficient military strength to exercise control over what had become a crisis.

The reduction of Federal forces in the Kanawha district began on August 14th. This reduction of strength was not lost on the Confederacy. Their scouts observed and reported in the days that followed of the movement of men, horses, artillery and wagons away from the Kanawha Valley. The *Pomeroy Telegraph* (Pomeroy, Ohio, located across the river from Point Pleasant on the Ohio River) noted that

> [a] lively scene was exhibited [...] all along shore [...] on Monday night and Tuesday, as the fleet of boats passed up with Gen. Cox's Division of the army on their way from the Kanawha Valley to join Gen. Pope. The cheering as they passed was continual and hearty. The boys looked in fine health and were in the best possible spirits.[282]

To make matters worse, in addition to the intelligence obtained by the Confederacy from their spies, Gen. Pope's letter-book was captured, revealing the fact that only five thousand men had been retained for the defense of Western Virginia. Consequently, on August 29th, Confederate Secretary of War, George W. Randolph, wired General W.W. Loring.[283] Loring was informed of this weakening of strength on the Kanawha line and directed to clear the Kanawha Valley entirely of what remained of the Federal army. He was then to "operate northwardly" to form a junction with Confederate forces in the Shenandoah Valley.[284]

The campaign now being launched—to recover the Kanawha Valley—was of very great consequence to the Confederacy because of the salines there. In Virginia and North Carolina the want of salt (formerly satisfied by shipments of salt from the Kanawha salines up river from Charleston[285] and King Saltworks in southern West Virginia) was acutely felt. With this new campaign, the Confederate Government hoped to take and hold the Kanawha Valley with its vast salt works. The removal of troops to the East, resulted in Western Virginia being overrun for a second time, Cumberland Gap being evacuated and Kentucky being invaded by Braxton Bragg and Kirby Smith.

Confederate General William W. Loring was already contemplating an invasion of the Valley before Randolph's missive. Aware of the Federal movement of troops eastward, he had begun planning to invade the Kanawha Valley as early as August 18th. He planned to regain the Valley not only for its resources but to gain control of the Weston and Gauley Bridge turnpike—the conduit that connected the military posts of the Kanawha Union line. The pike connected the Federal posts in Northwestern Virginia and the head of the Kanawha Valley, connecting Northwestern Virginia to Gauley Bridge (the most advanced post).[286]

To scope out the situation in the Kanawha Valley, Loring sent Brig.-Gen. Albert Gallatin Jenkins to raid and scout the country lying to the north of it. Meanwhile, he (Loring) concentrated his main force (or the greater part of it) just above "the narrows" of New River. From Friday, August 22nd to September 19th, Confederates made a lengthy expedition into Western Virginia and Ohio. Small fights flared along the entire Western Virginia war front. Jenkins set out upon his expedition with 500 to 550 men of the 8th Virginia Cavalry on August 22nd, from Salt Sulphur Springs, Monroe County and raided through Western Virginia and Ohio. Col. Lightburn, at Gauley, was inescapably aware of Jenkins' thrust into the area but was prevented from catching Jenkins, as the Confederate force in his own front precluded any detachment of troops westward.[287] It was up to local militia and the companies of 13th recruits stationed at Point Pleasant to take care of their own bailiwick and Jenkins.

Jenkins' troops skirmished with Union forces in Randolph, Upshur, Lewis, Roane and Jackson Counties.[288] When he struck the Ohio River, Union people in the border counties along the Ohio flocked to assist in repelling the raiders.[289] On September 3rd, Jenkins reached Ravenswood, skirmished there and briefly occupied the town. Jenkins' command destroyed all the stores and printing office.[290] On September 4th, Jenkins crossed the Ohio River (at Ravenswood) with his force, stole horses in the night and continued the march.

What happened next is open to interpretation. Col. Daniel Frost (cmdg. 11th Virginia/West Virginia Infantry Regiment) at Parkersburg, whose printing office had been burned at Ravenswood, informed Governor Pierpont that from Ravenswood, Jenkins marched for Pomeroy.[291] An unofficial account which appeared in the *Ironton Register* stated that Jenkins crossed into Ohio at Buffington Island and divided his force at the Ohio River (at Buffington? at Ravenswood?). His main force, of about 350 men went overland to capture Racine, Ohio, while the remainder (550 minus 350 leaves us with about 200 to take the river road) continued west along the river on the Virginia side toward Point Pleasant.[292] Still another account which appeared in the Pomeroy *Telegraph* informed that after recruiting some horses at Racine, Jenkins troops continued down the river road and about 5 miles from Pomeroy, crossed into

Virginia. Be that as it may, Jenkins' troops (in part or in force) made for Point Pleasant. The *Telegraph* supplied some particulars. At Racine,

> the rangers swore terrible vengeance on Point Pleasant and Galli-polis declaring that they would not leave a stone or brick of either standing, but the prompt turnout of the people of Mason and Gallia Counties, [the County Militias et. al.] made the raid too dangerous and the band passed on for the present. Militias thwarted this purpose. The Rangers were at Racine to secure horses and arms and threatened to burn the town, if they were molested. Having taken a dozen of the best horses, they left town about midnight and continued down river to Wolfs Bar, about 5 miles above Pomeroy, and crossed into Virginia. Friday, Sept. 5th, Jenkins was reportedly only a few miles above Point Pleasant. He did not attempt to make an advance upon the town since there was an equal force there to oppose him.[293]

As noted in the Pomeroy *Telegraph,* "[a] brief skirmish" occurred in the vicinity of Point Pleasant, on September 5th.[294] Lewis Wetzel at Point Pleasant, wrote to Adj. Samuels regarding these events that: "Jenkins has robbed our people of many fine horses but he did give Point Pleasant a wide berth for we had a strong force to await him."[295] In his editorial column, Wetzel described in graphic detail what was going on for border folk such as themselves, and he made specific mention of the part played by the 400 men of the 13th Regiment:

> We live in the midst of alarms. — Ever since the reverse of the Federal arms in front of Washington, the border has been in danger. This was not unexpected. Armed hordes of rebels rendered audacious by success, now hover at each exposed point from the Potomac to the Missouri River. They are resolved to push their advantage while they can. Raids are the order of the day. Talk of the 'northern hive!' We have heard that phrase mouthed over a thousand times, but now we are of the opinion that there is a 'Southern hive' and at present, it seems to be sending out swarms of modern Goths, Vandals, Suevi, Franks, Huns, Secesh and Guerrillas. They are moving everywhere — in Virginia, in Ky., in Md., in Missouri and in Kansas. Beat them back this week and they are on hand again next week. Morgan made an irruption into K[entuck]y got as far as Cynthiana, then wheeled and left as suddenly as he had appeared. The folks had not fairly left off gaping at him before

Kirby Smith came in sight and astonished them still more. Strange, very strange — is it not — that somehow, the Federal forces are never ready for these bravos, but need let them come and go just as they please! On Thursday, [September 4th], Jenkins, at the head of about 600 rebel cavalry came into the town of Ravenswood at 10 o'clock A.M. and crossing the Ohio River at that point came down to Racine, where they recrossed the river and camped that night about 6 miles above Mason City. On Friday, [September 5th], they marched across the country to Thirteen Mile on the Kanawha River, passing within about 6 miles of Point Pleasant, which place he doubtless intended to take but learning that about 400 of 13th Regt. Va. Vols. under the command of Lieut. Col. James R. Hall and about [illegible three digit number] of the 106th Reg. Va. Militia under command of Col. J.P.R.B. Smith were ready to receive them, concluded to give that place a wide berth, which they did by passing around it as above stated. We are informed that the citizens of that portion of the county through which the d—d villains passed were robbed of about one hundred and twenty-five of their most valuable horses, besides destroying large quantities of their grain and hay. From 13 Mile Creek, the half starved hounds passed up to the town of Buffalo, where they crossed the Kanawha river, a portion of them dividing into squads, and the balance going in the direction of Hurricane Bridge — or h—ll—we hope the latter place.[296]

An interesting story relevant to this juncture is related by Austin Butler about his grandfather, Joseph Martin Butler. J. M. Butler was a sawyer and an ardent supporter of Abraham Lincoln before the war. Austin Butler was about 11 years old at the time these events took place. He recalled that about the time Lincoln was elected President, his father moved his family from Point Pleasant to Glenwood. They named their new place "Lincoln Hill" to commemorate the move and Lincoln's victory. Then, the war began and his father received a 2nd Lieutenancy to recruit for the 13th Regiment (and perhaps other regiments) and that in fact, he joined 13th Regiment.[297]

[T]hen the Bushwhackers and rebel sympathizers began to make it hot for us, (there being a lot of them). The rebels offered a thousand dollars for Grandfather's head, dead or alive. I couldn't tell you half that happened. [...] Sam and I [Sam and Austin, J.M. Butler's sons] slept upstairs on Lincoln Hill. Father was home and one morning right early, there was a column of soldiers passing by. [The brothers Sam and Austin] went to the window and commenced howling for Abe Lincoln. The soldiers shouted for Jeff Davis and come to find out they were rebel soldiers, Gen. Jenkins command. Jenkins stopped at the gate and asked father if he would give him a drink of water. Father took a pitcher of water out to him. He asked father if he knew Gen. Jenkins. Father told him yes. Well, he says, I'm Gen. Jenkins. Father told him he wouldn't have known him in uniform. They [Jenkins' men] had robbed a store at Ravenswood of Government uniforms and the head of the marchers had on Union uniforms and that is what fooled us. [...] father didn't hang around there very long. He skipped back to Point Pleasant to his regiment. But in a day or two mother and us children were on our way to Alton [Illinois].[298]

Writers of accounts a bit farther removed in place and time also found occasion to remark on the resolute stand taken by the defenders who came out to meet the enemy on the Point Pleasant road.[299] In the Washington, Ohio, *Register* (reprinted in the Cincinnati *Enquirer*), it was reported that Jenkins was met by a small force of "raw militia" (the untrained men of the 13th were indeed scarcely more than "raw militia") in position about seven miles from Point Pleasant and that these resisted Jenkins' men in a "determined" way.[300] Horton and Teverbaugh in the regimental history of the 11th Ohio (published 1866) also referred to the events of the 5th, noting that a few troops at Point Pleasant were attacked by a "small force" of Jenkins' which appeared as far down the river as that point, but "the defenders fought vigorously and drove the rebels away."[301]

After Jenkins' men were deflected from the Point (on September 5th), the 13th companies were scattered in hopes of arresting Jenkins and his men. 2nd Lieut. William E. Feazel, recruiting officer for the 13th wrote on September 7th from 13th Headquarters at Point Pleasant: "We have been hunting for Jenkins for two days and we expect to start again to night in pursuit of him he has done much mischief and if he is not captured Soon he will do much more."[302]

Jenkins meanwhile had reassembled his troops about six miles from Point Pleasant, then fell back from there and encamped first at Buffalo in Putnam County, and then near Jenkins' home at Greenbottom opposite Swann Creek.[303] On September 7th, Jenkins marched for Guyandotte. Fire-bells were rung to spread the alarm that Jenkins was on the move and volunteer companies reported to their respective court houses (the 13th Regiment Companies to Point Pleasant?) to await orders. Jenkins took Guyandotte on the 7th. Two days later (September 9th), the 2nd Virginia Cavalry drove him out of Guyandotte, then attacked and routed him out of Barboursville and remained in pursuit of him up the Guyandotte River on September 10th.[304]

Jenkins' expedition continued until September 19th, when by a route south of the Kanawha he returned to his main command. His success[305] and the threat of an even larger invasion (W.W. Loring's troops) on the way had put the Kanawha Valley on the *que vive* (Fr. meaning on the look out). Local secessionists were jubilant and active.[306]

Pressure from without and within

Not surprisingly, in the midst of these alarms and rumors of invasion, the 13th Regiment, now consisting of about four hundred untrained recruits, was being called upon on a "daily" basis for service by Col. Lightburn. Lieut. Col. Hall was attempting to drill the men but his time was so taken up with other duties that he was afraid his men would be detached and scattered before they were adequately drilled. The need for efficient officers to take over training the recruits became imperative. As if the current Confederate threat was not enough, the question of who would be appointed as officers sparked tensions within the regiment and among civilian 'movers and shakers,' who looked upon the 13th as 'their' regiment. The following correspondences shed light upon this prevailing personal dynamic. J.R. Hall, explained his predicament in a letter to Adj. Gen. Samuels dated "Pt Pleasant Va August 30th 1862."

> We are collecting in recruits as fast as we can and now have about Four hundred men expect three Companys in this comeing week perhaps Four — I have been doing the very best I could towards our organization — But permit me to say a word to you which I hope will be kept strictly confidential There is not in the Troops thus far except myself one single man who has ever been Drilled or do they know anything about Guard or Picket duty (I certainly mean nothing unkind of the officers many or all of them will I think make excellent officers when they have an opportunity of Drilling but you know that will take more time than we are likely to have to spare Nor do I know of any Drilled officers that are to come in with the Companies that are now being raised for the Regiment (I omited to mention Stewart who I regard as an excellent man and his Services have been of great value to me) from this you will see the importance of getting some well Drilled and efficient officers the Early Efficiency and value of the Regiment will in a great measure depend upon it

I certainly have no disposition to attempt to dictate to you or request you to depart from your own wishes in the matter but if you should be at a loss in the selection of a Major — I hope you will pardon me in recomending several person who I regard as well drilled Men of good practical sense of industrious Moral and Temperate Habits to wit

2nd Lieut B F Thomas of the 1st Va Light Artillery Lieut Shephard Lieut Blake Lt Rollins & Lt Russel of the 4th Va Regt I am satisfyed that any one of those Gentlemen would discharge the duties of the office with profit to the Government and credit to themselves But it is only my purpose to request the favor of you to give us for Major some good practical Soldier of Temperate Habits Courage and Moral worth with such assistance soon and a good Colonel at your own time I think we could soon shew you a Regiment fit for Service and if we do not work fast we neaver will be well drilled as Col Lightburn is already calling daily on us for service and we may soon be scattered but I trouble you over much My thanks to you for past favors

Very Respectfully & Truly
James R Hall

P.S. Enclosed please find Col Lightburns order clipped from the Kanawha Paper which you will please hand my Friend Foster JRH[307]

As the 13th approached the time of its organization (with election and appointment of officers, mustering-in, etc.) concerns were aired regarding undo influences being brought to bear on the appointment of field officers. It was the desire of citizens and soldiers that *Virginians* be appointed to lead the regiment and not men from out-of-State. So broad-based was this concern it seems that a public meeting was called to discuss it. On September 1st, at a public meeting convened at the Mason County Courthouse, the issue was presented and several resolutions were passed expressing the community sentiment. It was the intention also to send a copy of these resolutions to Governor Pierpont and to other loyal papers in Virginia for publication:

Whereas it was the desire of the 13th Virginia Regiment, now recruiting at Point Pleasant to be led by Virginians it was resolved that the wishes of the Regiment be respected and the field officers of the Regiment should be citizens of Virginia and should not be appointed from other States. This resolution was not intended to disparage or reflect poorly upon citizens of other States but to encourage citizens of their own State. The assembly also resolved to censure and denounce all undue influences brought to bear upon the appointing power, for the appointment of all such officers, whether by citizens of this or other States, and that in all appointments, the object should be, to select those most competent irrespective of favoritism.[308]

The following two letters, both penned to State Adjutant General Samuels on September 1st, suggest that there was considerable foment in the community as to the appointment of officers for the 13th. At the center of the conflict was apparently one trouble-making individual—probably John Hall Sr.—who wished to have Ohio-born officers taken from the 4th Virginia Infantry, his son John's old command. Chief Justice, Lewis Wetzel wrote on behalf of "concerned citizens of Mason County" (*i.e.,* Charles B. Waggener, W.H. Tomlinson, John Hoits, C.C. Miller, James H. Holloway, Lewis Wetzel, J.P.R.B. Smith and S.M. Campbell) to Samuels conveying the following:

> The undersigned citizens of Mason County, having a deep interest in the Welfare of the men composing the Thirteenth Virginia Regiment, claim the right to be heard in regard to the appointment of the field officers for said regiment as well as <u>one</u> individual who seems to have the disposing of all the offices to be filled.
>
> We here enter our protest against the appointment of any person to said offices not a resident of this State, but if that rule is to be departed from, we must urge that Major Lodine be appointed to the Colonelcy in said Regiment, according to the recommendation of Gen Mclellan.[309]

William H. Tomlinson, an attorney who had offices at Point Pleasant, wrote more pointedly to Samuels in his plea that it was unnecessary to go out of State to furnish the 13th Regiment with officers:

> [...] we have men competent in Virginia for officers for the 13th Va. Regt. and expect to hear of no more going out of the State to get officers for Va. regts. and hope that you will speak to the Gov. upon this subject every officer in the 4th but Col. Lightburn are from Ohio and it is the desire of all the Union men here but one that you will look to our interest he has been the dictator for this part of the State long enough and if his friends are to receive all the offices we here wish to know it you are aware who I allude to as being dictator

we can raise the 13th below little Kanawha and expect officers from the same section of the State.[310]

On September 2nd, four more 13th Companies were organized. On September 3rd, W.I. Matthews reported to Adj. Gen. Samuels that in obedience to Samuels' orders, he had organized five companies for the 13th Regiment and officers had been elected. The first company (Company B), had already elected its commissioned officers August 23rd. September 1st, the second company (Company C) selected their commissioned officers: Van D. McDaniel was elected Captain; and Captain Lemuel Harpold, 1st Lieutenant. No election was held for 2nd Lieutenant, as that position was claimed by Lieutenant William E. Feazel "who has mustered most of the recruits volunteering in Mason County."[311] September 2nd, the third company (Company A) selected James W. Johnson, Captain; and Greenbury Slack Jr., 1st Lieutenant. The position of 2nd Lieutenant was claimed by Lieutenant Theophilus Maher, officer mustering for the company. Also on September 2nd, the fourth company (Company D) organized by electing Simon Williams, Captain; James W. Hanna, 1st Lieutenant and John W. Neal received a recruiting commission

> but he has not been very successful in getting recruits. [Matthews] threw his men together with Williams', there being enough of both to organize a minimum company. [Mathews] allowed [Williams] to act as 2nd Lieutenant of the company pending your [Samuels] action in the premise as to confirmation or rejection.

Mathews added that "There is part of another company here [probably Company H] enough to elect a 1st Lieutenant and in order to have some officer in command of the men I allowed them to elect a 1st Lieutenant. Oliver W. Griswold was chosen for the position."[312]

By September 7th, 2nd Lieutenant and Recruiting officer, William E. Feazel reported the status of the 13th Regiment to Samuels. What followed was a line of haggling for rank in the regiment which would extend over months. Feazel wrote from 13th Headquarters at Point Pleasant:

> [T]here is four full companies here and one with 41 men they have elected a first Lieut. I have mustered the men for two companies and have made myself as useful as I possibly could when I left Wheeling I understood from you that there would none commissioned in this Regt. except 2nd Lieuts. other than those elected by the respective companies but since I left there I understand that you commissioned one M. Stewart a Sergeant from the 4 Va as Captain of the 1st company and upon hearing this I did not try to be elected

in the 2nd company as I had confidence to believe that if you would commission him that had done nothing for the Regt. you would certainly commission me knowing as you do that I have done all that I could for the Service from the beginning it is not because I want to be called Captain but because I believe that I am capable of doing justice to the Service as commander of a company

Since if it is your purpose to do justice as I believe it is to the Service you would do well to know something of the qualifications of the officers elected in this Regt. There has been a captain and first Lieut. elected over the 2nd company that I mustered without opposition because I would not be a candidate

I feel that it is due to me to command the 2nd company for two Reasons first because I mustered all the men for two and they divided into two companies and 2nd because I have done more for the Service than any Virginian below little Kanawha this is a matter you can arrange quite easy for if you would commission me as Capt. and the one elected as first Lieut and the one elected 1st Lieut as 2nd it would all be for the best [...]313

Jenkins' raid caused a "right smart" (to use a contemporary colloquialism) bit of excitement in the Kanawha Valley and brought into relief just how much more was needed militarily that the people here might avoid being "constantly liable" to such raids.314 The obvious vulnerability of the Kanawha Valley in view of the recent reduction of Federal troops, together with the late raid and rumors of more of the same to come boosted militarization and enlistment as can be seen in following letter written by Justice Lewis Wetzel. In the midst of active duty, organization of the 13th continued in a determined way. On September 9th, Wetzel wrote from Point Pleasant to Adj. Gen. Samuels reporting on enlistment, requesting a captain's commission for Albert McCown and describing how the 400 volunteers of the 13th Regiment (about 100 men to a company) and militia sallied forth to meet Jenkins on the Point Pleasant road.

Mr McCown has already 43 men, all of which volunteered to-day, and as he is one of the nicest young men in Mason, I would like to see him placed in a position to forward as much as possible, his claims to the Captaincy of the new Company. This Company of McCowns makes the 4th that Mason has turned out under the late calls.315

We have had most exciting times here during the last five days. The expected raid of Jenkins alarmed the whole section of country, but he concluded that he would give Point Pleasant a wide berth when he heard that five hundred Militiamen and four hundred volunteers, were so glad to hear of his approach that they advanced to meet him. — Jenkins robbed our people of many fine horses, but farther than that done no injury. He evidently was not on a fighting expedition.

Very Respectfully
Lewis Wetzel[316]

Meanwhile, in wake of the current state of affairs Governor Pierpont sought to boost numbers and the proficiency of the Virginia Militia. On September 9th, Pierpont called out the Militia and urged each man "able to handle a gun" regardless of age "to enroll himself in some militia or volunteer company, arm himself, turn out frequently for drill until he acquires the necessary knowledge [to defend his home] and more than this he should see that all his neighbors do the same too." Pierpont continued:

> I do therefore request the Commander of every Brigade and Regiment within the loyal counties, now organized, immediately on receipt of this order to order regimental musters and proceed to organize by companies, battalions, and regiments the militia in their respective districts.
>
> Whenever any companies should have been reduced by the members having gone into the service of the United States, to order such companies to be consolidated, so as to form companies of not less than fifty nor more than one hundred members.
>
> All persons having arms belonging to the State are required to produce them at the Regimental muster and the commanders of the [regiments] take possession of any [arms] known to be in their district in the hands of any person not enrolled, and use them for arming such [militia] and volunteer companies as may be formed.
>
> [... P]ersons in the State military [...] service without regard of age will form themselves into volunteer companies without delay; and should there not be State arms enough in the county to supply such volunteers, let them supply themselves with such guns as can be procured from private persons. No person not in service, having a firearm will object to giving up his gun to be used for the common defense.

The commandants of each regiment is required immediately on the organization of the militia in his district to report to the Adj. Gen. of this State, the number of men enrolled in his regiment, the volunteer companies formed within his district with the number of men in each, and the number, kind, and condition of the arms with which they are [equipped] distinguishing those belonging to the State from those belonging to private persons.

Until further orders, the commandant of each regiment will muster his regiment for inspection and drill at least [once a week and the commandant] of each militia and volunteer company will muster in company for inspection and drill at least once every week.

At each regimental and company muster, the roll will be called absentees marked and returned to the Court of Inquiry held at the time required by law.[317]

On September 11th, officers of the 13th Regiment met for the

purpose of recommending certain persons to be colonels, major, and quartermaster of [the] regiment, it was unanimously resolved that Capt. W.T. Brown [William Rufus Brown] of the 4th Va. Regt. be recommended to receive appointment of Colonel, Lieutenant Comstock that of Major, and Lt. T. Maher, quartermaster.[318]

Meanwhile, General William W. Loring ...

On September 6[319], Loring left his camp at the Narrows, Virginia, with the intention of clearing Federal military from the Kanawha Valley. This accomplished he planned to use the Valley as a base of operations from which to launch north. From the Narrows he proceeded by forced march down the south side of the Kanawha River. It was the largest Confederate force ever sent into the region.[319] Federal forces in Western Virginia had few options. On September 9th, Col. J.A.J. Lightburn, commanding Kanawha troops (a skeleton crew of an occupying force) wrote to General H.W. Halleck at Washington, from Gauley Bridge (the most remote Federal outpost on the Kanawha line) that it had become necessary for him to fall back from his previous positions to protect his flanks and rear. Lightburn would fall back to "take position on the Kanawha River, 12 miles above Charleston, embracing the Kanawha Salt-Works and at the head of low-water navigation."[320]

Lightburn called in all the troops under his command, not to concentrate for a stand up fight but to protect the exposed flanks of the army and to protect the retreat. Clearly, Lightburn felt a great weight of responsibility for the immense store of army supplies with which he was entrusted, nor had he the heart to risk his troops against so formidable a force as Loring's was rumored to be and indeed was. To J.R. Hall, commanding the 13th Regiment at Buffalo, Lightburn wrote on September 9th, directing that he (Hall) should proceed with his command to Point Pleasant.[321] John Hall wrote to the Governor, from Gauley on September 10th, that there were then "750 troops at Gauley and Gallipolis."[322] The troops at Gallipolis (and Point Pleasant) were troops of last resort.

Loring continued by forced march by way of Flat Top Mountain and Raleigh Courthouse to Fayetteville. On September 10th, he attacked Lightburn's troops in two columns. At Fayetteville, he attacked in front and at Gauley Bridge, he attacked in flank. Lightburn's forces were driven out of their position at Fayetteville on September 10th and from Cotton Hill on the 11th. The Federals fell back rapidly back from Cotton Hill (near Gauley Bridge) on several roads to follow the Kanawha River westward. The Confederates pursued closely, and there was a great deal of firing all along the route of retreat.

Up until this point in time there had been rumors, yes, that the Confederates were planning a major offensive. There were what was called the "usual rumors" and "usual threats of hostile demonstration" but up to this point these referred only to cavalry movements involving Jenkins' troops. There had been no information of a reliable character, no direct creditable testimony whatever that the Kanawha Valley would be invaded. It was only when Loring suddenly appeared before Fayetteville that it was surmised that "he was moving on the valley with a view of contesting [Federal] supremacy."[323] The effect was electric.

The general unpreparedness of the Kanawha troops to fend off a large-scale invasion was brought out in relief. Neighbors to the North were worried as well. In southern Ohio, the alarm raised by Loring's sudden attack and defeat of Lightburn's forces at Fayetteville taken together with another report that General John B. Floyd was advancing by way of Wyoming County to cut off Federal forces at Coalsmouth (it was supposed),[324] brought militia flocking to Gallipolis and Point Pleasant from Gallia, Mason and other adjacent counties. It was feared that these border towns were in great danger.

At Point Pleasant the entire available force was called out. The 13th had arrived from Buffalo where they had been scouring for Jenkins' troops.[325] On Saturday evening September 13th, General George C. Bowyer commanding the a brigade of militia was directed (in a dispatch from Gov. Pierpont) to call out his command. Pursuant to this order, Col. J.P.R.B. Smith ordered all able-bodied men of the 106th Regiment to assemble immediately at the Mason County Court House. They were to report "with all arms in their possession to render Col. Lightburn, commander of the Federal forces in the Kanawha Valley any and all aid, that it may be their power to give."[326]

All along the Ohio River excitement and tension ran high. No one seemed to know anything for certain. Confederate troops were thought to be invading from west and east and no one was sure how far it all would go. Lincoln and the North watched and wondered just how events in Virginia were unfolding. It was not precisely known where General R.E. Lee was with the Army of Northern Virginia; it was known that General John Pope's army had been beaten but not how badly. On September 2nd, Pope ordered his army back to the Washington area for reinforcements. Lincoln restored McClellan to full command in Virginia and left Pope without a command. The victorious Confederates gathered at Chantilly, Virginia, to plan new operations and the Federal army evacuated Winchester in the Shenandoah Valley. On September 4th, Lee's army crossed the Potomac at fords in the Leesburg area on its way into Maryland. This unsettled Maryland, Pennsylvania and the entire East. The derogatory label for those against the war: "Copperhead" was becoming known as synonymous with anti-war feeling and abolitionists called increasingly for a public posture against slavery. Western Virginians took a particularly hostile view of Copperheads who constantly denounced and criticized the U.S. government's efforts to suppress the Rebellion but never breathed a word against "Rebels" who were daily "murdering our people."

Gen. Halleck was concerned for Western Virginia and pressed to send more troops there. Gen. H.G. Wright, cmdg. the Department of Ohio was concerned mainly for Kentucky which he viewed as on the brink of disaster and he braced for it. John Hunt Morgan and his men joined Kirby Smith at Lexington, Kentucky, and A.G. Jenkins culminated his raiding in Western Virginia and Ohio near Point Pleasant. On September 5th and 6th, Indiana Governor Oliver P. Morton called upon citizens in areas along the Ohio River believed to be threatened by E. Kirby Smith and Braxton Bragg to form military companies. On September 4th, Smith's forces occupied Fort Maysville, Kentucky. September 7th, Braxton Bragg in Tennessee moved steadily north toward Kentucky. Then on the 10th, he pushed to within about 7 miles of Cincinnati with considerable skirmishing. A thousand "squirrel hunters" from the Ohio Valley volunteered their services in Cincinnati as home guards and forestalled Smith. In the east, R.E. Lee continued moving toward Frederick, Maryland on September 5th, then he fell back from Frederick across the Monocacy River. McClellan followed cautiously and the two armies skirmished. On September 11th, Confederate forces entered Hagerstown, Maryland.

In Mason County, many militiamen felt the rebels would be upon them while they were yet organizing. Brig. Gen. George C. Bruyer's [Browyer] Militia Company was at last "ready" on about September 14th but they still needed arms and supplies issued to them. Col. J.P.R.B. Smith's 106th Regiment Virginia Militia was at the "ready" at Point Pleasant but was likewise not equipped. Evidence of this lack of preparedness is Smith's letter to Pierpont on September 15th (1862) requesting the Governor to instruct the quartermaster at Point Pleasant to furnish Smith's regiment with rations, tents and blankets. Not that the border counties of the northwest corner held a monopoly on this state of affairs. Colonel Samuel B. Burnett commanding the 19th Regiment of Virginia Militia at Weston (Weston recently hit by Jenkins) found himself in a perplexing position. To sort it out he wired to Gov. Pierpont on September 15th, stating that he had about 400 men in his regiment but a large number of these were secessionist. Burnett queried "shall I arm them or shall I call out only the loyal part?"[327]

Abandoning the Kanawha

Lightburn made a stand at Charleston on September 12th, to allow time to load and remove military supplies stored there and to destroy anything that might be of use to the enemy and on September 13th, when he "had all the transportation at hand, transports and wagons loaded with the most valuable Government stores" he ordered them to move off "in the direction of Point Pleasant."[328] The evacuation began about 1 o'clock in the afternoon of the 13th. The entire army with a train "about 5 miles long"[329] in tow (about 700 wagons) crossed over the suspension bridge at Elk River. Buildings containing government stores which could not be removed were fired. As a last measure, the suspension bridge across Elk was cut down. The Kanawha Valley thus abandoned, Loring took possession and established headquarters at Charleston.

Wild rumors flew fast and furiously in the towns and countryside west of Charleston. Both armies were reported victorious. Both were reported defeated and slaughtered. It was widely believed that without a larger Federal force to repel the Confederates, they would retake possession of the entire Kanawha Valley.

Lightburn meanwhile followed the Kanawha river westward until the night of September 13th. Then, to avoid encountering Jenkins' command posted on the south side of the Kanawha below, he took the road north to the Ohio River through Ripley and Ravenswood. The night of September 14th, the Federals camped at Ripley, the Jackson County seat. On September 15th, the army crossed the Ohio River at Ravenswood, a little below Buffington Island. The road on the retreat "was dusty"[330] and on the river, it was hot. All were glad to have made it through to the Ohio shore.

Federal troops had arrived at Ravenswood at about 11 o'clock A.M. on the 15th and subsequently crossed the Ohio at what was known as Sand Creek Riffle ford (reportedly the same ford used by Jenkins' raiders to cross into Ohio, just a few days before).[331] Steamers were sent to Lightburn's assistance and some troops, such as the 4th Virginia were taken by steamer to Racine, Ohio, at about 3 o'clock p.m. From Racine they again traveled by boat, this time bound for Pomeroy. They were then ordered by Lightburn to proceed to Point Pleasant. The 4th arrived at Point Pleasant "at about 8 P.M. on the 1[6th]."[332]

The 13th companies may have marched up the river road to Ravenswood with the 34th, 37th, and 44th Ohio and the 4th and 9th West Virginia Regiments to meet Lightburn at Ravenswood while militia such as Smith's and Browyer's Mason County Militia held at the Point (Point Pleasant). Ultimately the entire force together with the large train brought from Charleston marched down to Point Pleasant on the Ohio side of the river. Point Pleasant was reached on September 16th, the army marching just beyond to occupy "a strong position on the Kanawha, about 4 miles above [Point Pleasant]."[333]

At Point Pleasant, the broken portions of the Army of the District of the Kanawha were brought together and other troops were brought in to augment the force.[334] By Wednesday, September 17th, wrote Sarah Frances Young (daughter of John Valley Young, Captain of Co. G of the 11th Virginia Volunteer Infantry, a company soon to be attached to the 13th Regiment when the latter was mustered into service—October 7th, 8th, and 9th— a month hence) there was collected at Point Pleasant "a very large force of Federal troops."[335] Lightburn still faced the enemy and now more "pleasantly situated" at Point Pleasant on the banks of the Ohio, the men of his command were reported as in generally good spirits.[336]

Point Pleasant had until now been without fortifications but this was rectified immediately. By Wednesday, September 17th, Mason County resident and Lieu-tenant-Governor Daniel Polsley reported that when he left Point Pleasant, that day (Sept. 17th), "Col Lightburn was at [Point Pleasant] throwing up some fortifications, and felt comparatively secure."[337] "MAC" writing from Gallipolis on September 18th, on the other hand, remarked that the lack of fortifications, breastworks and trenches at Point Pleasant was the reason escaped Negro slaves did not rally at Point Pleasant as Lightburn had hoped they would to swell the ranks of defenders. Instead, they appar-ently did not "linger long at Point Pleasant" but kept on moving, past the river and into the interior of Ohio towards Chillicothe and Marietta to find employment with farmers there.[338] It would be no stretch to suppose that some did not stop at all until they had reached Canada and freedom.

On September 18th, Lightburn looking for reinforcements to re-establish his for-ward position at Gauley, wrote to Pierpont inquiring at to "Gen. Kelley's whereabouts" and "Col. Mulligan's position" in hopes that one or the other could "make a feint or advance towards Gauley."[339] Near Sharpsburg, Maryland, the Battle of Antietam was fought between McClellan's Army of the Potomac and Lee's Army of Northern Vir-ginia. It was a Union victory but won at great price and not followed up. Lee fell back with his army into Virginia.

On September 18th, a powerful call to arms was published in the Point Pleasant *Weekly Register* urging all Union men to be at the ready and fight as they might, to turn back the enemy. Some sense of the life and times is expressed in the following:

TO ARMS!! TO ARMS!!"

Union men of Mason county the safety of your homes and your families is threatened by a ruthless invader. A horde of miserable half-starved wretches, led on by desperadoes without character or honesty, would overrun your land, destroy your substance, and deprive you of the rights of freemen. We call upon you to rally now before all is lost. We will have assistance as soon as it can be rendered; but let us show ourselves worthy of receiving it, by doing the best we can to protect ourselves, until it comes. Rally every man who is worthy of the name. Let mean dastards and white-livered cowards skulk from their share of the danger if they will but do your duty to yourselves and your government and if necessary die in its defence.

Fight any way you can. Fire from behind trees, rocks and logs, and from hedges, but be sure and take deliberate aim and save a Secessionist every fire.[340]

The existence of two State governments within a single State was a powder keg for all manner of chaos. Now that the Kanawha Valley was in the hands of the Confederacy, Secessionists rejoiced and announced that they were living in the Southern Confederacy. Levels of chaos and uncertainty reached new heights. Refugees from Western Virginia lined the Ohio border. Union men from various counties fled their homes. Those who stayed hid their horses. Some slept in the woods. "We are in worse condition that we were a year ago,"[341] wrote Arthur I. Boreman (elected Governor of West Va. in 1863) to Francis Pierpont on Sept 20th. Indeed, it was estimated that after the fight at Fayette Court House on September 10th, "[n]ot less, than three or four thousand people" (mostly Union families and slaves) were driven from their homes in the Kanawha Valley.[342] A correspondent to the Cincinnati *Commercial* wrote that during the week of September 10th through the 18th, the Kanawha and Ohio Rivers between Cincinnati and Gauley were

full of flatboats, bateaux, skiffs, rafts, and all manner of bouyant conveyance laden with the families of Unionists, who find themselves compelled to flee on the approach of the Confederate army, fearing the rebel General will carry into execution his recently made threat to hang every citizen 'Yankee' he found in the Kanawha Valley. Hundreds of people who two years ago, were the quiet possessors of large farms, are now driven away from home in a condition bordering on destitution. Unable to remove their farm stock, they are obliged to leave behind them what they depended on for subsistence during the coming winter. Arriving at Gallipolis, or elsewhere, most of them have to seek a charitable home among strangers—a few only, comparatively, have relatives or friends to live with. It is a pitiable sight to see families sent adrift, with their little lots of household furniture, to find a home, they know not where [... because of their loyalty to the] Government of [their] fathers. The rebels in Western Virginia have declared themselves unsatisfied with anything less than armed resistance to the Federal [presence and] citizens whom they meet in their raids. It will not do to say you have not taken sides either way, or that your sympathies only are with one side or the other. They demand active participation in their cause, and 'confiscation,' robbery and outrage are the punishments for Federalism. The whites are not the only emigrants from the Kanawha Valley. The negroes have absconded in hundreds, and few less than a thousand have left their disloyal masters to inquire as to their whereabouts and wonder at the answer. The darkies have constructed the most ingenious kind of sailing craft, and in the efforts to elude the rebel advent, which they have learned to dread greatly, have entrusted themselves to the most fragile of home-made vessels. I heard an escaped contraband say, today, that he came down the Kanawha fifty miles on a log, but that he would rather drown than remain with his master, who is in Loring's army and is expected home in a few days.[343]

The Meigs County (Ohio) newspaper noted that for Kanawha Valley dwellers, now long used to raids, Lightburn's retreat was attended with "some apprehension of danger but no great alarm," in fact "[t]his retreat was more remarkable for the general exodus of the colored population of the Kanawha Valley than any other result." Slaves gathered together their household goods and movable goods and employing any kind of "improvised conveyance" man might conceive of, they followed Lightburn's retreating troops all moving by "easy marches."[344]

Gen. Loring, now in headquarters in Charleston, went about the business of burrowing in. Thinking to reclaim the western part of the State, Loring made Charleston his base of operations.[345] Charleston was an excellent choice. Many lateral roads converged at Charleston, roads which led to the Ohio River through Guyandotte, Point Pleasant and Ravenswood. Charleston and the Kanawha were fortified at several points. On September 14th, he had a broadside published addressed to his troops and "To the People of Western Virginia." He congratulated his men on their victories at Fayette Court House, Cotton Hill and Charleston and declared to the people that the Army of the Confederate States had "come among them to expel the enemy, to rescue the people from the despotism of the counterfeit State Government imposed on [them] by Northern bayonets, and to restore the country once more to its natural allegiance to State." A new periodical also began publication in Charleston in September called *The Guerrilla. Devoted to Southern Rights and Institutions.*

Loring remained at Charleston until October 8th. In that time he put garrisons in place at Fayetteville and at Gauley and occupied Charleston with about 4,000 men. Lightburn's army had been too hard pressed in their retreat to destroy either the Charleston salt furnaces or the great accumulation of salt there. After Loring's take over, salt production was a priority, salt being a much-needed article for food preservation for the armies and civilian population of the South and it was processed as quickly as possible. "[T]here was" noted one Confederate officer "a constant train of Wagons hauling salt away from the Kanawha Valley on roads leading eastward"[346] through Fayetteville to the Virginia and Tennessee Railroad and to supply the Confederate armies and the Southern States. Loring remained at Charleston, however, for only six weeks. Recruiting for the Confederacy had proven disappointing and his request to the Confederate War Department for outside reinforcements to drive off Union troops collecting at the mouth of the Kanawha River was denied. The drought and low levels of water in the rivers likely also made supplying the army problematical. He contented himself with having carted off large quantities of salt and withdrew from Charleston. He was relieved of command. There would be no more invasions on grand scale of the Kanawha Valley.

Gov. Pierpont stated in his year-end speech to the State legislature that during Loring's six week long occupation of Charleston, about "2,500 barrels of salt" were sent off and the rebels "completely robbed the people of everything they had of a moveable character." A number of men were reportedly killed for their pro-Union sentiments and many people were left without any means of subsistence. Some of these went to Ohio, others were not able to get away. "How the poor of this district" concluded Pierpont, were to "get through winter and spring, is anybody's guess."[347]

During this crisis no decisive action was taken by 'upper management' to alleviate the situation in the Kanawha Valley. While the people living along the Ohio River and in the Kanawha Valley volunteered, armed organized, drilled and set out to meet the emergency, confusion and inertia at the War Department in Washington as to what to do about the state of affairs in Western Virginia exacerbated the situation in the Kanawha Valley. Halleck, who was most apprehensive about the Valley, urged that more troops be sent there but for the following lame reasons this was not done.

There was "a want of authority" to send Ohio troops (the nearest reinforcements at hand) to Point Pleasant to assist Lightburn. The Department of the Ohio was under the jurisdiction of Maj. Gen. H.G. Wright and those troops sent by Ohio Governor

David Tod to Western Virginia could not be ordered in by Tod over Wright.[348] Nor was this the extent of the problem. No general officer with both fighting experience and knowledge of the Kanawha Valley could be located or spared from the field. On September 12th, as Loring's forces advanced down the Kanawha, Gov. Pierpont wrote to Halleck suggesting that George Crook be sent to assist Lightburn in the command of this section but Halleck supposing Crook was already in Western Virginia wrote in response: "As soon as I can find where Crook now is, I will give him orders."[349] Halleck commanded Crook to report immediately to Wright at Cincinnati (Special Order No. 227) but Crook could not be located.

Closer to the truth, perhaps, was that every available man was needed in Kentucky and Maryland. Loring's was just one prong of a multi-pronged advance into the North. Clearly the Confederate strategy was keeping the Federal army busy and guessing. Kirby Smith and Gen. Humphrey Marshall were both in H.G. Wright's front and Wright had learned from Major-General D.C. Buell that Gen. Braxton Bragg had thrown his whole force into Kentucky, where he might join with Smith and Marshall for a joint undertaking. Likewise, the War Department at Washington was anxiously watching McClellan's Army of the Potomac and Lee's Army of Northern Virginia near Sharpsburg, Maryland, then skirmishing and in short order to be locked in fierce fighting in one of the bloodiest battles of the war: the battle of Antietam.

Wright, of course, did not wish to weaken himself by sending troops to the Kanawha with the possibility of a Rebel invasion of Kentucky looming on the horizon. He searched elsewhere for troops to send to Gallipolis and Point Pleasant. On September 13th, he contacted Ohio Gov. David Tod, who, it will be remembered, had initially proffered troops to aid his Virginia neighbors at the beginning of Loring's occupation of the Kanawha. Wright asked if Tod could furnish a force for Gallipolis, since Wright had not only no troops to spare but no arms to issue to militia there either. Gov. Pierpont, urgently seeking to reinforce Lightburn before Federal troops were entirely driven from that section (with the consequences of that scenario still all too vivid in people's minds from the previous year), visited Tod on September 14th, at Columbus. Together, Pierpont and Tod recommended to Secretary of War E.M. Stanton that Western Virginia be attached to the Department of the Ohio so that someone, anyone, might have authority to send troops into Western Virginia. At last, on September 19th, Western Virginia was attached to the Department of the Ohio, Headquarters at Cincinnati.[350] Halleck conveyed this information to Pierpont adding "Consult Gen. Wright about officers and troops to be sent to Col. Lightburn."[351]

On Saturday evening September 19th, Captain John D. Carter (commanding Co. E, 13th Regiment W.Va. Volunteers) addressed the soldiers and citizens of Point Pleasant at the Mason County Court House. The issue up for discussion was a political one: the recent voting record of Senator Kellian V. Whaley (former Colonel of the 13th

Regiment) during the 87th Congress at Washington. An anonymous convalescent at the Point Pleasant army hospital attended the meeting and noted that "[t]he Captain started off on facts, as he introduced the record to prove his assertions—asking no one to believe him but to take the [record] and examine for themselves."[352] Capt. Carter continued, wrote "Convalescent."

> He reviewed the history of Mr. Whaley—ex Congressman from Wayne District—now before the people for their suffrages, from the beginning of his political career up, to this time. [Carter] scrutinized and sifted the acts of Mr. Whaley, in the last Congress very close, and introduced some stubborn facts, which we, as friends of Mr. Whaley's ask him to prove or explain to our satisfaction, if he expects our support in this election. They are as follows:
>
> Voting against the Resolution, 'That it is no part of the duty of the Army of the United States, to catch and return fugitive slaves.' Dodging the Revenue Bill; Voting against the Conscription Bill; dodging Confiscation Bill &c. These bills we consider of vital importance, and we demand an explanation of your actions in regard to them, Mr. Whaley, for at this crisis in the affairs of our country, we need men of nerve and backbone—men who will show their hand—men who have the moral courage to stand up in the face of a thousand Vallandighams[353] and vote men and money to put down this unholy rebellion. These are the kind of men we want in the 88th Congress. Let us hear from you.[354]

Exciting times continued at Point Pleasant. On September 20th, a skirmish flared there, probably the result of the considerable scouting detachments being sent out by both Lightburn and Loring to see what the other was about. Loring kept his cavalry especially active. They scouted both to the northwest and to the northeast to the Baltimore and Ohio railroad. These movements were probably connected to the Point Pleasant skirmish of the 20th and raids on Barboursville and Guyandotte on the 21st.

The night of September 20th, Lightburn sent a dispatch to Wheeling informing that he had that day been "threatened with an attack from the rebels."[355] On September 21st, at about 10:30 p.m., a force of between 20 and 40 Confederates under Vincent ("Clawhammer") Witcher raided both Guyandotte and Barboursville. Capture of the Cabell County Sheriff was attempted but all they made off with was his hat, some cash and about $500.00 in goods looted from a couple of Guyandotte merchants.[356] Nor was this the end of mischief. On or about September 23rd, with no available force to hold this point, Federal military transportation on the Ohio River

was interrupted at Guyandotte.[357] Extant correspondence between Loring and Secretary of War Randolph confirms that these reconnaissances were preface to a larger
movement. On September 22nd, Loring was planning to advance to the "mouth of the
Kanawha" (*i.e.,* Point Pleasant) with a part of his army, presumably to clear the place
of Federal troops, albeit his cavalry had reported Federals "in position and strength
at Point Pleasant."[358] Lightburn for his part, suspected that something was up and
on the 22nd notified Pierpont that fortification of Point Pleasant continued and he
recommended that the same be done all along the B&O Railroad as well, to protect
this conduit.[359]

There is no doubt that Lightburn had his hands full. In addition to fortifying the
town, Lightburn turned to the business of reorganizing his command and disciplining
his troops.[360] Lightburn issued a series of general orders which are yet preserved in 13th
regimental papers. These suggest that he had to some extent, a rowdy crew to contend
with. On September 20th, came General Order No. 10, to end the "firing at will" of
some of his troops. General Orders No. 10, provided that:

> Hereafter no firing will be allowed within reach of this command
> under any circumstance whatever except upon the approach of the
> enemy, or upon the regular day for practice which will be designated
> by an order from these Head Quarters. Any neglect or disobedience
> of the above order, will be severely punished.[361]

General Order No. 12 directed that "Until further orders the troops of this command
will be kept with two days uncooked rations in their haversacks."[362] General Order
No. 13 directed that the troops of the district would hereinafter perform picket duty
by regiment. "One field officer on duty will perform the duties of field officer of the
day, and will report with his Regiment at Gen'l Hd. Qtrs. at 8 o'clock A. M. for orders
and instructions."[363] On September 21st, Lightburn had again to admonish undisci-
plined behavior by his troops in General Orders No. 14:

> Whereas numerous complaints have been made to these Head
> Quarters by loyal citizens residing near the various Camps of this
> Command of many depredations being committed by the soldiers
> upon the property of citizens; it is hereby ordered that no officer or
> Soldier upon any condition shall molest any private property what-
> ever unless so ordered by the Officers in command.
>
> Commanders of Regiments + Companies will be held strictly
> responsible for the enforcement of this order.[364]

On September 21st, with General Order No. 15, Lightburn addressed absenteeism
among officers directing that: "No officer or soldier will be permitted to be absent

from his command except upon a written permission from his Brig[ade] Commander, and in no case for a longer period than 12 hrs."[365]

While recruiting was curtailed in those areas occupied by the Confederates, at Point Pleasant and vicinity, recruiting for the 13th continued unabated. The skirmish at Point Pleasant on September 20th and raids on the 21st, spurred recruiting efforts and volunteering alike. The Point Pleasant *Weekly Register* of Thursday October 2nd,[366] reported that Lieutenant John A. Martin was in the process of raising a "crack"company of sharp-shooters and that he had, at this date, half his company recruited. Martin had some military service under his belt. He had served in the Mexican War and been a member of the 4th Virginia Infantry Volunteers. On July 14th (1862), he had written to Lieut. Gov. Daniel Polsey requesting a Lieutenant's commission, with authority to recruit a company at Charleston, Virginia. July 25th, Lightburn weighing in for Martin wrote to H.J. Samuels recommending Martin as fit to raise a regiment and described Martin as "industrious and energetic."[367] Martin subsequently received his commission and was sworn in as 2nd Lieutenant "to Recruit for the 13th Virginia Regiment Volunteers" on August 21st, 1862, in Kanawha County before Justice of the Peace Watson Eastwood, just hours before Jenkins commenced his raid on the Kanawha Valley.[368]

George Rucker (mustered in as Private in Company E, 13th Regiment, on October 9th, 1862) had been recruited for Martin's company. After the war, Rucker wrote an itinerary and synopsis of his time in service. He related that he volunteered September 19th, 1862, for

> a company that was got up by Lt. Martin as he claimed for Sharp
> Shooters. The company, however, was never finished, and the men
> Martin had enlisted were mustered into the 13th W. Va. Vol. Inf'try
> then at Point Pleasant Mason Co. at the old Fair Ground, then at the
> Court House in town Point Pleasant thence across the Kan[awha]
> River to Camp Sherman [...].[369]

On September 19th, the Kanawha District was officially attached to the Department of Ohio. Together with the Ohio counties bordering on it, Western Virginia was designated as the District of Western Virginia, the District of the Kanawha becoming a sub-district of the District of Western Virginia. Lightburn's troops comprised the District of the Kanawha. These units were: First Brigade commanded by Edward Siber (34th Ohio, John T. Toland and 37th Ohio, Louis Von Blessingh); Second Brigade commanded by Samuel A. Gilbert (44th Ohio, Ackber O. Mitchell; 47th Ohio, Lyman S. Elliot; 4th Virginia, William H.H. Russell and Unbrigaded Regiments of the 8th Virginia, John H. Oley; 9th Virginia, Leonard Skinner). Since Loring's takeover of the

Valley, headquarters for the District of the Kanawha were at Point Pleasant (prior to that, headquarters had been at Gauley Bridge).

The District of Western Virginia would remain a part of the Department of the Ohio until March 16th, 1863. The transfer to the Department of the Ohio had been a necessary one in light of recent problems as to authority and "pecking order," and Gov. Pierpont also urged that the change go through. As one editor put it, Western Virginia had been under the command of 78 year old General Wool,[370] "but when the rebels recently commenced making raids upon the borders, it was found that there was a cloud" between the departments (*i.e.,* between that of Wool's command and the Department of Ohio under command of Gen. Wright). "Hence the change."[371]

Western Virginia did indeed begin to emerge from "the cloud" with this shift. Now that it was attached to the Department of the Ohio, troops from that department could be sent to reinforce Lightburn at Point Pleasant. Troops from Washington were also sent westward, as Halleck in particular, was anxious to increase the force on the Kanawha and to appoint an officer to command the whole and alleviate the situation. As Gen. Crook, Halleck's first choice, had still not reported, Gen. Thomas A. Morris was ordered for duty there but he also did not report. On September 20th, Halleck directed Wright to increase the force on the Kanawha as soon as possible[372] and Gov. Pierpont was also requesting troops. Wright, however, had already sent one regiment of infantry and some cavalry under Col. Jonathan Craynor to reinforce Lightburn and felt he could spare no more troops in view of Confederate operations in Kentucky. Halleck promised Pierpont that he would send troops to Western Virginia from Washington. In October, Samuel A. Gilbert's 2nd Brigade was transferred from the District of Western Virginia to the Army of Kentucky and Colonel John T. Toland (in civilian life a dentist now commander of the 34th Ohio Volunteer Infantry Regiment) was assigned to the command of a new brigade in the Kanawha District. To Toland's new brigade the 13th was attached.

On September 22nd, Lincoln issued the Emancipation Proclamation. On September 23rd, word of the proclamation freeing the slaves spread over the North. It appeared on the front page of the Point Pleasant *Weekly Register* on October 9, 1862 (Vol. I, No. 29). What effect this news had on the soldiers of the 13th is not known as there is a complete absence of reference to it in extant contemporary private correspondences. Known only, is what in general seemed to be true, gleaned from West Virginian newspapers. The loyal West Virginian would have protested to have their motivation to war called abolitionist which it frequently was by secessionist Virginians wishing to insult their loyal neighbors (their individual and collective pride).[373] Even taking into account the widespread influence of the Methodist Evangelical Church in the northwest and contemporary statements on the subject made by Methodist minister W.W. Harper (soon to be Sergeant-Major Harper of Albert McCown's Company F), slavery was not often cast in humanitarian terms but viewed as a degenerative influence on the general public welfare, in terms economic and moral. Undoubtedly there were a number of men serving in the 13th, like George Washington Smith of Company K, who after the war, recounted his utter aversion to slavery because he had been saved from drowning by a family slave. Generally, however, in the absence of other evidence, it is to be presumed generally, that for the West Virginian: (1) the war was never one to free the slave but to end the rebellion that law and order might be restored; that life might continue in safety; and (2) to free themselves from Virginia (which had done little to develop the West *i.e.,* that part of the State west of the Alleghenies) and that by hitching their hope of future prosperity to the rising star of the national Union rather to the State (which had done little for them) that they might have better prospects for themselves and their children. Another reaction to the Proclamation which may have had held some broad currency for the loyal populace was that expressed by Governor Francis H. Pierpont in his address to the Restored Senate and House given in December (1862). In his view, the Proclamation was a peace offering, a request to Southern States to return to the Union *with* slavery before January 1st, 1863. As for "abolitionism," Pierpont stated that the war was most emphatically not to abolish slavery but was a "necessity," forced upon the President by the "pertinacity with which they [the secessionists] waged the war for the destruction of the government."[374]

By September 23rd, the 13th was attached to the 3rd Brigade, District of Kanawha, Colonel John A. Turley commanding. That day, Col. Turley, ordered Colonel Brown, commanding the 13th Virginia to designate men for guard duty as follows:

> furnish for Guard duty tomorrow from the Regiment under your command two (2) Sergeants two (2) Corporals and thirty (30) men for Post Guards, and two (2) Sergts, two (2) Corporals and sixteen (16) men for Patrol Guards. Also one (1) Captain as Officer of the Day, and one (1) Lieutenant as officer of the Guard.[375]

William Starr, an officer serving with the 9th Virginia, wrote to his wife, Anna, from Point Pleasant on September 25th (1862), describing the lay of Lightburn's encampment, fortifications and making mention of new regiments:

> Our Regiment [the 9th Virginia] is Brigaded with the 34th and 37th Ohio under command of Col. E. Siber [...] the 44th and 47th Ohio and 4th Va are brigaded under Col. Gilbert — There are four or five other new regiments here encamped on both sides of the river — All but three regiments are on the Ohio side where we are [...] We have fortified the hill on the Va. side — I took my regiments over last Tuesday and built a fort or rather a large battery large enough to mount six pieces. [It was named Fort 9th Va.][376]

Jockeying continued among 13th recruiting officers for commissions. James R Hall wrote a letter to Adj. Gen. Samuels, dated "Pt Pleasant Virginia September 25th 1862," referencing some difficulty over the election of captain for Company C. William Feazel (an able recruiter but not one to be popular with the rank and file) had thought he would receive the captaincy of Co. C and suspecting that the vote had been swayed by a liberal application of "Sperits," preferred charges against Van D. McDaniel, who in fact won the vote. Hall's letter reveals some of the tensions within the regiment and the manner in which the officers dealt with them. Hall wrote:

> Sir
>
> I have the honor to acknowledge the Receipt of yours of September 19th in which you order an investigation of the charges made against Captain Van D McDaniel by his second Lieutenant William E Feazel I immediately gave the parties notice and ordered the investigation and from the best information I could get — Lt Feazel was informed (by enemies of Capt McDaniel that he Capt McDaniel was useing ardent Sperits to secure his election. But from the evidence nothing of the kind could be proven — That Lieut Feazel did believe that Capt McDaniel was useing unfair means I do not doubt —but that he was mistaken I am eaquelly certain — I think Lieut Feazel was expecting the Captaincy of the company and being Defeated and hearing these Reports felt mortified and appealed to the Governor without giving it the investigation he should I think the matter as it now stands is perfectly satisfactory to both parties and no feeling exist between them — Lieut Feazel is not with his company at present but (with my advice and consent)[377] is out recruiting for the Regiment Hopeing that the above will be satisfactory to Governor Peirpoint and Yourself I am
>
> Very Respectfully
> Your Obt Servant
> James R Hall[378]

As for outfitting the soldiers, Company B had been issued their clothing for "August to November 1862," on some date that went unrecorded and Company C was issued clothing for the first time on September 25th. William A. Eads, a Private of Co. C, drew clothing in the amount of $31.52 and Private David Eads, also of Co. C, drew $36.97 worth of clothing. This had to do them as Co. C would not draw clothing again until January 20th, 1863.[379]

Confederate movements erupted in fighting in other areas of the Department of Ohio. On September 24th, an attack was expected at Louisville, Kentucky, and every able-bodied man was impressed there to defend the city or work in the entrenchments. September 25th, D.C. Buell's Federal army arrived at Louisville and beat back Bragg's advancing Confederates. Alarms sparked anew on the Kanawha. From Point Pleasant, Lightburn reported on the 25th to Wheeling that Rebels were advancing on Point Pleasant, in force.[380] This time immediate action was taken. That same day (September 25th), at Lincoln's direction, Brigadier General Robert H. Milroy's brigade of infantry with the artillery of his command was ordered to proceed to Point Pleasant;[381] Milroy to report to Gen. Wright for orders.[382] As the transfer of Milroy's troops could not be effected with requisite speed to meet the new crisis, Wright ordered General Quincy Gillmore to Point Pleasant from Cincinnati (for temporary duty) with two regiments on September 27th.

Lightburn for his part, sent out a detachment of troops (comprised of the 40th or 44th and 91st Ohio Infantry Regiments and the 2nd Virginia Cavalry) from Point Pleasant on September 26th bound for Buffalo (expedition returned the 27th). The 91st Ohio left camp at Point Pleasant at 6 p.m. on the 26th. As it turned out only the 91st was engaged. The 2nd Virginia and the 40th (or 44th) Ohio were to have met the 91st to co-operate with it, but only the 91st was first to come upon the Confederates and consequently only they engaged the enemy. Within a mile of Eighteen-Mile Creek, the 91st encountered Jenkins' vedettes. The 91st skirmished with Jenkins' cavalry up 18 Mile Creek and forced them back through the town of Buffalo to the river. Jenkins' men split and dispersed at the river. The 91st captured tents, camp equipage and brought away 13 head of horses, 17 head of cattle, and a number of Enfield rifles.[383]

In retaliation for "Rebels stripping Union men of Mason of horses," Federal cavalry (probably the 2nd Virginia Cavalry) took "25 horses." These were turned over to the 13th Regiment "to be disposed of" as Gov. Pierpont might direct. Col. William R. Brown wrote to Pierpont from Point Pleasant on September 27th, requesting "immediate reply as these horses are much needed by the 2d Va. Cavalry."[384]

October 1862

Military affairs continued much as they had since the Confederate take-over of the region. Likewise, organization of the 13th went on with a will. On October 1st, Private James Wilson of Company F was promoted to Commissary Sergeant[385] and Lieut. Hall allowed the company recruited by Albert C. McCown (Co. F) to hold an election to choose their officers.[386] On October 3rd, Private William W. Harper of Co. F was promoted to Sergeant Major.[387] The same day (October 3rd), pursuant to a rumored threat that another attempt to raid Point Pleasant was in the chute, the 3rd Virginia Infantry Regiment was ordered from Clarksburg to the Point. The raid did not materialize, however, and the 3rd Virginia was ordered back to Clarksburg.[388] What did materialize on the 3rd, however, was that the pickets on the Point Pleasant side of the Kanawha River discovered a white flag of truce waving on the other side of the river. It was carried by a squad of cavalry. As the correspondent narrating this event (George K. Jenvy) rode up to where the cavalry was "by the water's edge," he "found them all well armed and mounted." What their business was he never learned but "[s]ome have since said it was to demand the surrender of [Point Pleasant], or remove all the women and children within three days; but of course, we can see on the face of things that this could not be so."[389]

The arrival of Brigadier General Quincy A. Gillmore was also anticipated. Wright had ordered Gillmore to take temporary command of the District of Western Virginia until Gen. Milroy could arrive with his command. It had been no easy task to find someone to take command here. Brig. Gen. T.A. Morris had declined the command and Gen. J.J. Reynolds (who had suffered a reduction in rank) based his acceptance on the condition that his original rank be restored to him. (Wright determined that Reynolds did not deserve to have this request granted and withdrew the offer of appointment.) Then Gillmore was to be sent but Wright countermanded the order upon notice that Milroy and his brigade had been sent, but Halleck reconsidered and sent Gillmore anyway.

For all the concern in Washington for the Kanawha Valley, particularly on Halleck's behalf, reinforcements came slowly into Western Virginia. Gillmore was sent to Point Pleasant with two regiments from Cincinnati: the 40th (or 44th) Ohio and 84th Indiana and a detachment of cavalry. His troops seem to have arrived ahead of the General. Gillmore himself arrived in Western Virginia about October 1st, first however, he went to Wheeling to consult with government officials there regarding "at what points and in what numbers Federal troops [we]re stationed on the river between Point Pleasant and Wheeling."[390]

General George W. Morgan's army from Cumberland Gap was also slowly making their way to join the concentration of Union forces at Point Pleasant.[391] On the morning of October 4th, at Halleck's insistence, Wright ordered Morgan and his command from Cincinnati to the Point. The summer drought had made water levels in the river too shallow for the larger transport boats and limited access by rail allowed the transport of just one regiment per day.[392] At last on October 19th, Morgan joined Lightburn's army at Point Pleasant. Soon after their arrival however, they were withdrawn; Morgan's brigade of troops from Eastern Tennessee, apparently not wishing to spend another winter "freezing and starving" in the hills of Western Virginia.

After the battle of Antietam (fought September 17, 1862), Jacob D. Cox was appointed major general (to rank from October 6th, 1862) and returned to his old command in the west. The Kanawha Division was likewise returned to Western Virginia. On October 7th, Gillmore was relieved and returned to Cincinnati. Reports to Wright as to the total force gathered at Point Pleasant, at this time, placed strength at nearly 9,000. This number did not include State troops of which Wright had no report.[393] This number corresponds closely with Confederate Gen. Loring's estimate of strength at Point Pleasant which he placed at about 10,000 men.

For his part, Loring had reduced his force at Charleston to about 4,000 that he might detach troops to guard Gauley Bridge, Fayette Court House and other prominent points in his rear. The summer drought worked in his favor as low water in the river channel impeded concentration of Union forces with which to launch an offensive but should it rain and the river rise, he could expect an attack from Point Pleasant and Clarksburg where troops waited for their opportunity. Loring had hoped to recruit men for the Confederacy during his occupation of the Valley but recruitment had proved to be a disappointment.[394] This Loring attributed to two things: to the wide circulation of Cincinnati newspapers and to doubts raised in their columns as to the likelihood of continued Southern success in adjacent areas such as Maryland and in front of Cincinnati and to the poor conduct of the troops of the Virginia State Line under General J.B. Floyd. Disappointing enlistment led Loring to the conclusion that he could not continue to hold the Kanawha region without reinforcements from outside.[395] He requested of Secretary of War

Randolph that "5,000 infantry and a corresponding force of artillery" be sent that he might retain "the magnificent advantages to the public of the acquisition of this country" and be enabled to drive away the National force around the mouth of the Kanawha river, and get at "[t]he most abundant supplies" lying there.[396]

Muster-in of the
13th Virginia Volunteer Infantry Regiment

"The sounds that greet the ear from every side at this place,
now, may be said to be:

And far from over the distance

The faltering echoes come,

Of the flying blast of trumpet,

And the rattling roll of drum."

—George K. Jenvy,
Letter from the 2nd Virginia Cavalry to the *Marietta, Ohio Register,*
dated "Point Pleasant, Oct. 5, 1862"

On Saturday, October 4th, Point Pleasant and vicinity was at last "refreshed by a glorious shower of rain" which settled the dust and cleared the atmosphere. The "protracted and severe drouth" which had "parched all vegetation and so hardened the earth that farmers could not seed" was broken at last.[397] On October 5th, Corporal J. Hamilton Johnson of Company F (13th Virginia Regiment) was appointed Company Commissary.[398] The same day, (October 5th), George K. Jenvy, a soldier correspondent with the 2nd Virginia Cavalry stationed at Point Pleasant reported that there were at the Point between "10,000 and 15,000 men" and "'still they come.' [...] Rebel pickets will not long be able to stand within 15 miles of the Ohio, as they have been doing of late." The entire morning of October 5th was taken up with the movement of Federal troops at Point Pleasant. They were "moving down the road to take up their new camp on the other side of the Kanawha."[399] Jenvy painted a lively picture of camp life at Point Pleasant:

Sunday in Camp. — Long before daybreak the cavalry bugles awake the weary trooper, while the drum does the same for the infantry. Breakfast and then comes the hasty rubs for inspection; swords are drawn to see that no rust has gathered on them during the night, guns touched up anew; and at last out marches the band, with shining instruments making melody to the answering echoes of the soldiers' feet. Next come the friends of those who live in this part of the country for a Sunday visit. Their gay dresses and sweet faces are quite a charm to those who have been in the mountains of Western Virginia during the last spring and summer.

Dust. — If anyone wants to know what dust is, let him come here and ride behind the 2d Va. Cavalry, while on its way to water the horses, trees, everything; no matter what color your clothes are, it is all the same here.[...]

Troops. — There are here, 1st Ohio Squadron of Cavalry, and the 2d Virginia; 4th, 9th, 11th and 13th Virginia Infantry, and the 34th, 37th, 44th, 47th, 89th and 91st Ohio Infantry.[400]

On October 6th, the 13th was also moved to the south side of the Kanawha River away from the main town. Col. John T. Toland commanding the brigade (1st Provisional Brigade) to which the 13th was attached issued General Order No. 4, providing that:

It is hereby ordered that the several Regiments comprising this Brigade strike tents at 2 O.C. P.M. of this day and remove their camps to the South Bank of the Kanawha River, where the Brigade will be encamped.

The Signal for striking tents will be given by the Bugler from Brig. Hd. Quarters.

The Regiments will be encamped as follows.

The 34th Ohio on the right. The 4th Va. on the left. The 91st Ohio on the right center. The 13th Va. on the left center.[401]

Brigadier General Gillmore issued orders to ascertain the health of his new command and on October 6th, Special Order No. 6 provided that:

Assistant Surgeon A. Hoeltge 47th Ohio Infantry is appointed Medical Inspector of the Division of the Kanawha. He will make an immediate inspection of the command under the instruction of the Medical Director and report upon the same. The Senior Surgeon in each Brigade will act as Brigade Surgeon and report to the Medical Director.[402]

Col. Lightburn for his part, issued orders to assure that all under his command were fully supplied. His orders directed: "Commandants of Brigades and Detached Regts. will require their Quarter Masters Commissaries to keep their respective commands supplied if possible with everything to which they are entitled by regulations."[403]

On October 6th (or 7th) companies of the 13th Virginia began to be mustered into the United States service. The regiment whose soldiers had to some extent been on the *que vive* since the beginning of hostilities but whose regimental organization itself was marked by fraud, delay and petty politics, was at last becoming officially organized and mustered, with benefit of supplies, equipment, salary and bounty. The 13th companies were it seems, mustered in at their station at Camp Lightburn (on the Point Pleasant side of the Kanawha) and then transferred to the new encampment located on the south-side of the Kanawha River, called Camp Toland.[404] Richard Ross Crawford, Second Lieutenant, Seventh Infantry and Mustering Officer of the United States Army, mustered in all men of the 13th "for a term of three years, unless sooner discharged." In mid-October, some or all companies were moved back to Camp Lightburn. The people of the Point were naturally proud of "their regiment." The muster-in of its companies coincided with completion of fortifications around the town, and now with these defenses in place, the question in the minds of people and soldiers alike seems to have been: "when would the army of the Kanawha make a forward movement?"[405] Would the Confederates or the Unionists be driven out of the Valley?

Company A which had been organized by Captain James W. Johnson at Charleston, Virginia, in August of 1862, was mustered at Point Pleasant on October 7th and continued to be stationed at the Point Pleasant after muster-in until October 31st, 1862.[406] A Federal bounty of $27.00 was paid to each recruit.[407] On October 7th, Colonel Toland issued orders to his brigade regarding camp discipline, directing that:

> I. Commandants of Regiments and companies comprising the 1st Prov[isional] Brig[ade] are hereby ordered to see to it that no depredations are committed upon private property. No rails or fences will be disturbed except by orders from the Commanding officers. Plundering and marauding will in no case be permitted. It is alike disgraceful to the Service and Subversive of discipline, and will meet with the Severest punishment.
>
> II. No firing of guns will be permitted. Attention of Commanding officers is called to general orders upon this subject, from Div[ision] H[ea]d Quar[ters].[408]

On October 8[409], Company B (J. R. Hall's Company) which had been organized upon the election of recruiting officer, Milton Stewart as Captain, in August of 1862, was mustered into service. They were mustered-in at their station, at Point Pleasant but were it seems transferred straightway on October 9th to Camp Toland.[409] Co. B remained encamped near Point Pleasant through October 31st.

David Bailey of Leon,[410] Mason County, was among those mustered-in on October 8th, a member of Company B. It had been a hard decision for forty year old Bailey to leave his wife and children but he nonetheless, decided to throw in his lot with his friends and neighbors, who had also volunteered for service in the 13th. Among these, also mustered into Co. B were Alfred Sullivan, William Clark Greenlee, John H. Ferguson, William Edwards, Perry Smith and William Riley Hill. Bailey's eldest son also volunteered and served with his father in Co. B. In time, the son became a bugler for the company.[411]

Company C was mustered in on October 8th and 9th at Point Pleasant. The Company had been recruited by Lieut. William Feazel and Van McDaniel and had been organized at Point Pleasant with the election of Van D. McDaniel to the rank of Captain.[412] Upon muster-in, the company numbered 83 men total.[413] A note appended to the Muster-in Roll of Co. C by Mustering Officer Crawford informs that premiums and bounties were paid to all men on the roll and "parents and guardians of all minors here enrolled [...] freely g[ave] their consent to the enlistment of said minors."[414] John Spenser (Spencer) of Co. C, was detailed for teamster on October 8th.[415] Co. C was stationed at Point Pleasant on October 9th (1862)[416] but October 10th, its location was changed to Camp Toland. As reinforcements arrived at Point Pleasant the military camp had to be divided. There were two main encampments: Camp Lightburn outside Point Pleasant on the north (also referred to as east side of the Kanawha) and Camp Toland across the Kanawha on the south (or west side).[417] Captain Simon Williams' Company D was likewise mustered in on October 8th at Point Pleasant.[418] Co. D was transferred on October 9th to Camp Toland, was moved back to Camp Lightburn in mid-October and remained there through October 31st.[419] William Starr (9th Virginia Inf.) wrote to his wife, Anna, from Camp Lightburn, Point Pleasant, on October 8th that:

> We have now 12 Regiments sleeping around Pt. Pleasant Our Brigade (the 2nd composed of the 37th 89th Ohio and 9th Va. under Col. Siber) is encamped on Kanawha River about a mile above the Pt. The 1st Brigade (34th Ohio 4th and 13th Va.) on the southside of Ka The 3rd Brigade is encamped on the Ohio above the town and the 4th Brig. near Gallipolis — we have the hills fortified and are ready to see the enemy two to one — we have a pontoon bridge across the Ka

and will throw another across the Ohio in a day or so — Gen. Milroys Brigade is at Pomeroy this evening on its way to this place — Gen. Cox is coming — Gen Morgan is coming — Gen. Crook is said to be coming altogether will mass some 30,000 to 40,000 troops at this point and when we move you make look out for breakers. [...] The rebel cavalry came down to our pickets frequently and get shot at and run away again [...]

Mr. Woodhull the Chaplain of the 4th Va, was captured by the rebs while marrying a couple 6 miles up Ka[nawha]. last week. [...].[420]

On October 9th, camp accommodations for the southside camp (Camp Toland) were ordered and five men from Co. A of the 13th Regiment were detailed to dig three sinks (sewer basins) for camp.[421] Also on the 9th, Captain John Deriah Carter's Co. E had its general rendezvous and was mustered in at the Point. Co. E had been recruited by Carter at Point Pleasant during the month of September 1862, and was stationed at Point Pleasant through October 31st.[422] Some of Lieut. John A. Martin's company of sharpshooters went into Co. E and F. The Company was first issued clothing on October 14, 1862.[423]

Company F had been organized by Albert F. McCown at Point Pleasant during September and October 1862.[424] McCown was elected Captain. Co. F had its general rendezvous on October 9th and was mustered in for the requisite term on that date at Point Pleasant by Lieut. Crawford with a total of 83 men.[425] The Company was stationed at Point Pleasant from October 10th through the 31st.

Entirely in keeping with the chaotic nature of things was the muster in (a partial muster at best) of Captain John V. Young's Company G into the 13th Regiment. Capt. Young himself had served with a number of units since voluntarily taking to the field early in 1861, well before the reorganization of the Putnam County Militia (reorganized *ca.* mid November, 1861). He had served with the 3rd Virginia Cavalry, 8th and 11th Virginia Infantry and now he attached his Company to the 13th Virginia. He and his men had been mustered in with the 11th Virginia Infantry, but they had mostly (or entirely) freelanced "on their own hook" in a wild west sort of way. So perhaps, it is not surprising that Young was not overly particular that about half of his command (including himself) was already mustered into the 11th Virginia Infantry while the rest were mustered in with the 13th. Clearly his own preference was to serve with the 13th under Col. Brown and not under Col. Daniel Frost, commander of the 11th, whom he seemed to hold in some contempt.

Despite what had gone before, Young considered his company's place in the 13th settled, and in the fullness of time—as questions began to surface—he was able to cite to authority for believing this. Young stated in a letter to Gov. Pierpont (written August 12th, 1863) that his Company (though formerly with 11th Virginia Infantry) had been doing duty with the 13th Virginia Infantry Regiment since October of 1862. He stated that he was in October "ordered to report to the 13th Regt Vol Inft with some 40 or 59 more Recruits" (these were in addition to the forty-four men already in his company), and that these recruits were mustered into the 13th by Mustering Officer Crawford "under instructions from Adj Genl Samuels with the understanding that the company should be consolidated and permanently attached to the 13th."[426]

The time line which brought Young into connection with the 13th was this. He and his company had been doing duty in the area (first at Coals Mouth and then Buffalo) since March of 1862.[427] On the night of September 7th, he was back at Coals Mouth, where, reinforced by cavalry and infantry (13th companies scouring for Jenkins men ?), Young stood his ground on Coal Mountain against a force of advancing Rebels (Jenkins' men, probably). The Confederates opposing Young retreated but by September 14th, Loring's advance down the Kanawha Valley forced Young from Coals Mouth back down the river. He fell back to Point Pleasant as did Lightburn with all of his troops and wagon train. At Point Pleasant, Young and his men encamped with the 13th and thus began the connection. There was collaboration and collegiality between the two commands. Young expressed to Lightburn his desire "to go into the 13th if it can be arranged." Lightburn concurred and thought this would "be the best" and conveyed as much to Pierpont in a telegraph dated September 19th.[428] What began as a loose collection of companies became, in the exigencies of the time and place, a single command.

The 13th needed men and Young needed to be connected, legitimized as it were, as he had apparently received no salary up to this point in time and was likely in dire straits that way. Young's company was also at a similar stage in its organization as the other 13th companies: it needed officers (at the very least a lieutenant), equipment and probably medical attention (there is indication that Young had been paying for such necessities as equipment, rations, etc., out of his own pocket). Young reported to Pierpont on September 30th, 1862, that he had 86 men present for duty and 97 men present and absent. Further, he needed a 2nd Lieutenant and requested of Pierpont that Clark Elkins be commissioned for that position. Young recommended Elkins as suitable to fill the office and said further that "[h]e has been of more service to my Co. than any man in it or outside of it. And Co wishes to give him the best office they can."[429] By October 20th, 1862, Young was receiving mail as Company G, 13th Regiment. Young received a letter from E.B. Linch, the Second Auditor of the Treasury Department as follows:

> Your return of clothing Camp + Equipage appertaining to Co.
> 'G' 13th Reg. W. Va. Vol. Inftry for [...] part of the 4 [quarter] 1862

has been received, examined and found correct. Except as follows issues to men who have not signed R.[egimental] Roll must be verified by 'affidavit' Return <u>subsequent</u> to the above are required to show what disposition was made of stores remaining on hand. Please state the periods for which you made returns, for each organization. Ordnance of enclosed.[430]

That Young felt at home with the 13ᵗʰ Regiment is not surprising. These men lived in adjacent counties and shared a commonality of experience as civilians and soldiers that went deep. Belonging to this or that regiment probably did not mean much against the backdrop of living literally in the midst of civil war. John S. Cunningham, for example, 1ˢᵗ Lieutenant and Adjutant of the 13ᵗʰ Regiment, had first belonged to the 1ˢᵗ Virginia Cavalry and then to Young's Co. G. In August of 1862, he (Cunningham) was recruiting men for the 13ᵗʰ Regiment who went into Young's Co. Cunningham himself, was transferred from Co. G to be promoted to 1ˢᵗ Lieutenant and Adjutant of the 13ᵗʰ Regiment on June 6ᵗʰ, 1863, when it became clear that the 11ᵗʰ would win in the tug of war over Young's command. Cunningham filled the position of adjutant until he resigned from the regiment on January 10ᵗʰ, 1865.[431]

Captain Young

John Valley Young, resident of Putnam County, a devoted family man and adherent of the Methodist Episcopal church, was something of a wild card in more ways than one. He took to the field, early in 1861. His daughter Sarah wrote in her diary for February 11th, 1861, that

> Pa has gone into camp at Coals Mouth today. He has only a few men yet. Oh, what shall we do without him? But we would much rather he was there, or on the battlefield, fighting bravely for his country, than to be a coward and run to the Federal troops for protection unless he was not able to fight. And we know if he remains at home the Rebels will take him to Richmond as Prisoner.[432]

Nor as we have seen, did he stand upon military protocol. Muster Rolls for the 11th and 13th Virginia Infantries indicate that Young's Co. G: was mustered with the 11th Regiment on April 16th, 1861; also on May 23rd, 1862 (at Coals Mouth, Virginia) and about half of his men (new recruits) were mustered with the 13th Regiment in October 1862.

Young started his company on November 5th, 1861.[433] We must rely on Young's own statements as to his early military service as he seems to have never once furnished a monthly return to the 11th nor to the 13th regimental headquarters until 1863. In October of that year he apparently submitted his first monthly return to 11th Regiment headquarters at Parkersburg. It seems that all duty rendered prior to the Co. G's attachment to the 13th Regiment was done in the Kanawha Valley at Coals Mouth and then at Winfield, the county seat of Putnam County, a thriving town with a ferry, merchants, hotel, tradesmen, etc.

Young also served with 3rd Cavalry and 8th Virginia Infantry. He was first commissioned as 1st Lieutenant, 3rd Regiment Virginia Cavalry on November 15th, 1861. He was mustered in at Charleston and directed to report to Gen. W.I. Rosecrans.[434] Since his appointment as 1st Lieutenant he had been

Industersly engaged ever since in recruiting my Company and arresting and takeing prisoners to Wheeling and in Feb 1862 was put under the Command of Col Losier of the 8th Va Regiment and on the 10th day of Feb was ordered into Camp at Coals Mouth under the Command [of] Capt R H Lee of the 8th Va regiment and there received clothing for my men and since that time we have been actively engaged in Scouting the Country and Capturing and keeping the bushwhackers + horsethieves in check and I have been to considerable expense in the company and have not myself received any pay neither directly or indirectly and am in great need of my pay.[435]

On May 6th, 1862, Young's Company was "[c]hanged from Cavalry into Infantry service" and apparently became Company G of the 11th Virginia Infantry Regiment.[436]

It goes without saying that Young and his men did considerable scouting in the interior counties and that as cavalry they could indeed have rendered the State valuable service. Consider the following excerpt from a letter he wrote to Adj. Gen. H.J. Samuels on May 24th, 1862, in which he gives a brief synopsis of his services to the Union since he received his first commission on November 15th, 1861:

Shortly after my commission was received I arrested Major John McAllister + William H Morris + brought them to Wheeling — on my return I arrested Col Jos R Hill + others as hostages for the safe Return of Fredericks — I took prisoners Lieut Morn Kirtly of the Rebel Cavalry[437] + private Miller + some fourteen horses arms +c and delivered them at Charleston, from which place Lieut Kirtly afterwards escaped —

We afterwards took C U Swayne Jackson Smit[h] and a number of other Bushwhackers who are now at Columbus — During all this while my personal expenses were considerable I had two horses stolen from me by Lieut Kirtly after he escaped from Charleston — I had vouched for my men when they were procuring provisions for their families or medicines for themselves — My Company number 45 effictive men. I obtained all the recruits except two. I received the commission of Captain on the 6th day of May inst— [1862...]

All the time Lieut Brooks obtained arms + his + my commissions, from the Governor in the beginning of this month I could not leave the Post as we were threatened to be attacked by Guerillas [...]

I now respectfully ask you to grant a special order for the payment of my services as commissioned officer from the 15th day of November last, as I have not received any pay from the government directly or indirectly to the present time. —

Yours Respectfully
John V Young
Capt 11th Va Regt

P S Tomorrow I start on a scouting expedition to Cabal + Boone Counties on my Return you will hear from me again J. V. Y.[438]

Capt. Young was something of a 'jayhawker,' a loose cannon, who had adopted for his own, the "shock and awe" tactics of the guerrillas he so loathed. One correspondent—"Peg"— referred to him and his little Company of "Regulators" in a short piece which appeared in the *Weekly Register* of July 1862. Young and his men, wrote "Peg," would storm into town or a neighborhood to surprise the inhabitants. They would then proceed to confiscate contraband whiskey belonging to a Secessionist or Secessionists, retrieve stolen livestock, or arrest bushwhackers or Confederate soldiers.[439]

Young was passionately devoted to his family and their welfare was uppermost in his mind when he had to be away from them scouting in areas other than his home county of Putnam. It was likely in their behalf that he took to the field in 1861. He was almost as passionately devoted to his men as to his wife and children. He had a strong personality and a novel approach to spelling, a good sense of humor and a short fuse. A dispute arose between Young and his subordinate officer, Lieut. Robert Brooks as to who was in charge. Brooks reported to Adj. Samuels in May 1862, that he "returned from Wheeling" to obtain arms and commissions for himself and Young and found upon his return

the Co was sadly demoralized and when Major Weed [the mustering officer] was here Capt Young had 16 of the men in the guard house. We did not muster and Some depends upon who the officer will be mustered with them whether they will Muster [i.e., whether that officer will be Brooks or Young].[440]

The above suggests that there was some dispute as to who was in command of the company (Brooks or Young) and one can well imagine that Young "became afflicted" to have his authority questioned in this way. To settle the question, Lieut. Brook's wrote to Pierpont on May 24th. Brooks asked:

Is Capt <u>Young</u> now the commanding officer of this Co. or am I the officer till we have a Co Proper, or 83 men. Major Weed when he came to muster us told Capt Young that he could not Recognize but one officer <u>viz</u>.a 1st <u>Lieut</u>. But Capt Young Became afflicted and in the presents of the men gave me abusive language charging me with the violation of eve[r]y pricinipal of honor. Supplanting him [...] Young claiming that [he has] command and, has appointed a <u>lieut</u>, and last knight put me out with a Guard over some Refractory men relieving <u>Sergents</u> and <u>Corporals</u> to take rest every duty that is calculated to secure the <u>prejudice</u> of the men he imposes on me, the <u>object</u> is to Secure my removal and promote another [...]⁴⁴¹

That Young was removed from command of his company as a result of the above dispute is clear from a letter fired off by Clark E. Elkins, one of Young's men. Elkins addressed Pierpont requesting for the good of the company that Young be reinstated to command as the men were unwilling to be under the command of Lieut. Robert Brooks.⁴⁴²

After muster into the 13th, Young's Company was transferred from Point Pleasant when the 13th Companies were also dispersed for garrison duty in areas which needed watching. Co. G was stationed at Winfield until December 31st, 1862; then at Coals Mouth to April 30th, 1863; and during May and June 1863, they were stationed at Camp White in Kanawha County. July and August of 1863, Young was again stationed "Near Coalsmouth." September and October, they were at Barboursville. November and December 1863, they were stationed at Hurricane Bridge.⁴⁴³

While the attachment of Young's Company to the 13th Regiment helped the 13th initially, it also hurt the regiment on down the road. When the War Department directed that Co. G was to be returned to the 11th and was to be taken off 13th rolls, it had to be replaced. Another Company G had to be recruited for the 13th from a countryside which was fairly exhausted of men by winter 1863/1864. The recruiting of a replacement company was no small feat at this juncture. Nonetheless, by February 1864, the 13th had at length the requisite numbers to qualify as "organized" and thus be entitled to its full complement of officers, something it had not had up to this point in time.

The last soldiers to be mustered into the 13th Virginia in October of 1862 was a detachment of recruits not sufficient to comprise a full company. They were mustered-in on October 9th "to serve under command of Colonel William R. Brown." They had been recruited by Taylor W. Hampton at Point Pleasant in August and September of 1862.⁴⁴⁴ These recruits were mustered-in for the requisite term of duty by 2nd Lieut. Richard R. Crawford and were likewise stationed at Point Pleasant, October 1st through 31st.⁴⁴⁵ This detachment became Company H.⁴⁴⁶ On October 11th, Company H began its status as a full-fledged company with one Lieutenant and forty-eight Privates reported present.⁴⁴⁷

Some summary remarks about the process of muster in and what was termed "the point of rendez-vous" (Fr., meaning meeting at an agreed upon time and place) are useful. The military camp at Point Pleasant (Camp Lightburn) was outside of town. Recruits arrived to report at a field tent, perhaps. Here the men were checked in, paper work was done, they were assigned to their units and physical exams such as they were, were conducted. Martial spirit (*esprit de corps*) was strong. The mustering-in ceremony would have been conducted on the "parade ground." "Old Glory" was set up, uniformed men and an army musician—a drummer, bugler or fifer or a corps of these, were typically in attendance at such ceremonies. Recruits were assembled on the parade ground. As martial music began, men in uniform snapped to attention and their commanding officer, Colonel William R. Brown stepped forward to address the recruits. The men would have been instructed to remove hats, raise their right hands and repeat the solemn oath of service and devotion before the mustering officer.[448] The men swore to defend the flag, the Constitution and laws of the United States for 3 years or to the end of the war. Then, all who had sworn were paid their bounties and records of payment would have been set down. Such records are preserved as part of West Virginia University's Civil War Manuscript Collection. In the case of the 13th, officers had no forms and had to glue on a side sheets of what appears to be two pieces of butcher's paper to create the large sheets required for muster-in. Full headings were written in and the paper lined by hand. Thus began army life. The new soldiers were then taken to the Quartermaster to receive what part of their equipments were on hand. Extant correspondences reveal that there was consensus: the new young soldiers had good times at Point Pleasant.

As for the soldiers' pay, the following notice appeared in the Point Pleasant *Register* of October 9, 1862. The writer had learned with the "greatest satisfaction" that the unofficial word was that "our own new regiment" the 13th Virginia was "in the course of 'receiving their pay' so long and so cruelly withheld." So far, added the writer, "it is only a rumor."[449] Unfortunately for the men of the 13th, at this point in time, all Federal funds went to pay bounty for new regiments and almost nothing was left to pay soldiers' salaries with. "General [G.W.] Morgan's command got about all the money in the department [of the Ohio]." Other troops in the Department of the Ohio, besides the 13th, were leaving for the field without having been paid, and a certain portion of the Army of the Potomac was in similar straits.[450]

October 9th, the Gallipolis *Journal* noted the military aspect "on the Kanawha" remarking that since Gen. Gilmore had assumed command of the forces in the Kanawha Valley:

> Order is already coming out of the chaos into which matters were thrown by the retreat from Gauley. It is quite apparent that a military head is now at work We see fewer drunken, disorderly soldiers,

roving about town, officers riding furiously in pursuit of nothing, no longer render our public thoroughfares dangerous to footmen.— Interminable trains of wagons, pass without any longer blocking up the roads, and in short everything begins to wear the appearance of war, not in Gallipolis but on the Kanawha. Forces are coming in daily, and are quietly taking up their positions.[451]

W.W. Harper, of Hartford, "esteemed friend" of the management of the Point Pleasant *Weekly Register,* had been appointed Sergeant-Major in the new regiment, the 13th Virginia. "He will bring to the discharge of his new and arduous duties, ready penmanship, a business tact, and also unexceptionable habits," appeared in the columns of the *Register.* Harper was wished all the best in his "new field of labor for the glorious old Union so dear to him."[452]

Confederate Occupation of the Kanawha Valley Is Concluded

General Jacob D. Cox was called back to Kanawha Valley with the Kanawha Division from the Army of the Potomac and returned to his old command in Western Virginia. The Kanawha Division had been attached to the 9th Corps, Army of the Potomac during Major General McClellan's Maryland Campaign but on October 4th, McClellan ordered Cox and his command to immediately go to Point Pleasant to take command of operations on the Kanawha River and end Confederate occupation in that portion of the country.[453] Cox left Washington for Point Pleasant the night of October 6, 1862. Before his departure, Cox wired Pierpont from Washington, informing him that he would make a brief stop at Wheeling on his way to Point Pleasant (probably on October 8th) to confer and pick up "a statement of the present position and force of all Federal troops in Western Virginia infantry, cavalry, and artillery with their condition in all respects." Cox requested Pierpont to compile this and have it ready for him to pick up when he stopped at Wheeling.[454]

Before Cox left for Point Pleasant he was advised by Gen. H.G Wright "of the importance of pushing operations as rapidly as possible;" to determine what minimum of troops he required to hold the Valley; and to send the surplus to Wright, to reinforce the Army of Kentucky.[455] Cox assumed command of the Federal District of Western Virginia on October 13th, with headquarters at Gallipolis, Ohio. After an absence of less than two months, Cox found that the district had been enlarged to include the whole of Western Virginia and the Ohio Counties bordering on the river.

October 10th was an eventful day. Rain fell again on the heretofore parched countryside and the 13th Virginia Regiment field and staff officers were mustered in at Point Pleasant by Mustering Officer Richard Crawford.[456] Thus, the first phase of 13th Regiment's organization was concluded. Field officers were William R. Brown (formerly Captain of Company E, 4th Virginia Infantry Volunteers) mustered in as Colonel[457] and James R. Hall mustered in as Lieutenant-Colonel. 13th companies, field officers and staff were all stationed at Point Pleasant at this point in time.[458] The regiment tallied 657 men.[459] Such as it was, the regiment, eight companies — still two companies short — was now attached to the District of Kanawha, Western Virginia, Department of the Ohio.[460]

On the 10th, Gen. Robert H. Milroy's Brigade arrived from Washington and camped on the shore "opposite" from the 13th.[461] Known as "the fighting General," the grey-haired Milroy, instilled awe in those who had not seen him before. Judging from his appearance while at Point Pleasant, he had indeed seen some service and did "not appear as one who had just emerged from a bandbox."[462] Milroy's stay at the Point was short-lived however, as he left for Clarksburg already on Monday, October 13th.[463] Once troops, such as Milroy's began to arrive, a number of operations were launched. Upon his arrival, Milroy sent a brigade to Guyandotte to 'look after' Jenkins cavalry. October 12th, a scouting party was sent up the Kanawha river to get information[464] and then on October 15th, Gen. J.D. Cox sent a brigade up the Kanawha to build bridges on the road at Ten Mile Creek.[465]

Government Issue

Exactly what was issued, if anything, to the 13th upon its organization is any-one's guess as quartermaster records are missing. In 1862, a standard kit of equipment issued to any infantryman consisted of a knapsack, haversack, canteen, cartridge box (capable of carrying 40 rounds of ammunition) cap box, belt and bayonet scabbard. The very practical rubber blanket was also dispensed in 1862. These were about 6-1/2 feet long and 3-1/2 feet wide. In the ends and sides were eyelet holes so that two or more might be laced together at the sides to form a tent. The regiment itself should have been furnished with tents: 3 hospital tents to the regiment and Sibley tents to the soldiers.[466] Flags should also have been issued. Virgil A. Lewis (1848-1912), a revered Mason County historian, wrote that all West Virginia Civil War military organizations were supplied with three types of flags. These were "the National Flag, State Flag and Guidons." The United States flag had thirty-four stars (West Virginia the 35th State, the "child of the storm" had not yet been admitted to the Union), representing the States admitted to the Union up to that time. The 13th Regiment was perhaps, issued its National flag upon its organization (*ca.,* October 10th, 1862). State Flags were not issued to regiments until after 1862.[467] Guidons were battle flags (small swallow-tailed United States flags) whose purpose it was to convey orders in the heat and roar of bat-tle when the bugle (an instrument which sounded out the rhythm of the soldier's day and orders in battle) could not be heard. Whether or not guidons were issued to the 13th is likewise a matter of conjecture. In the vaults of the West Virginia State Archives are what remains of the flags carried by the 13th. Wrote Lewis, "little remains" of the 13th Regiment's 'Stars and Stripes.'

> The blue Canton with its thirty four stars is entirely gone, save a small remnant around the staff. Not a fourth part of the stripes remain and the part left of them is badly rent. Members of this Reg-iment now surviving say this Flag was torn to pieces by the bursting of a shell in battle. The staff of ash is ten feet in length and on it is roughly carved the number '13.'[468]

At the time the 13th was mustered in the War Department had not yet assigned a regular ordnance officer for duty in Western Virginia. All outfitting and arming of new Western Virginia regiments had been done by Governor Pierpont from supplies at Wheeling.[469] Supplies came slowly. There were plenty of steamboats but the river was too low to be used due to the drought. Overland transport was another problem. Transportation by rail was inefficient as that part of the railroad which ran through Western Virginia was very deficient in rolling stock and wagon transportation was no option at all as wagons were entirely lacking.[470]

Sutlers could be counted upon to provide items for sale in camp to regiments. Sutlers carried anything a soldier might need in camp (*i.e.,* canned food, cheese, tobacco, sewing kits, etc.) Military law required that sutlers be appointed and each regiment was permitted to have one sutler. Brigade commanders occasionally appointed sutlers on recommendation of a regiment's commissioned officers, but as a general thing the appointment of sutlers fell to State Governors.

After receiving his appointment, a sutler purchased a stock of wholesale goods and had these goods shipped to his regimental camp. Once his order arrived in camp, the sutler took up residence with his wares. He set up his goods in a large tent and secured them. During the day, for display and custom, he opened the tent on one side. The other three sides of the tent extended well down and were secured in place. In the tent's open side he displayed wares on a wide board, table or shelves, whatever came to hand. This served as display area and counter. To protect his investment, the sutler slept in his tent in the midst of his stock. Sutlers incurred considerable risk and inconvenience to bring their wares to the field particularly when the army lay in proximity to an active enemy and they charged high retail prices.

The 13th was naturally, also serviced by sutlers. Late in1862, a soldier of the 7th Virginia Cavalry named Kenan (probably Lieutenant Samuel Kenan) was serving as sutler to the 13th.[471] Another sutler to service the 13th was W.W. Sherwood. The starting date of his trade relation with the 13th is not known. What is known is that he had brass trade tokens cut and stamped in denominations of five and twenty-five cents by John Stanton of Cincinnati.[472] Tokens were cut by sutlers for issue in lieu of currency which had grown exceedingly scarce at this time as people hoarded coins.

While the 13th would wait some time before they caught sight of that ever elusive figure of the paymaster, the soldiers were payed one quarter of their Government bounty ($25.00), county bounty and premium upon muster-in. This was remarked upon in the Point Pleasant *Register* in a notice published October 16th:

> This Regiment now in camp at this point, under the command of
> Col. Brown, has eight companies, raised in this and adjoining coun-
> ties. Although a new Regiment, the 'boys' are rapidly learning the
> drill, and will when called into action give a good account of them-

selves. The members of the Regiment received their Government bounty of twenty-five dollars, county bounty of thirty dollars and two dollars premium last week.[473]

A report regarding the financial obligation assumed by the county and the generous contribution of time, talent and money on the part of certain Mason County citizens that a county bounty might be offered to 13th recruits warrants inclusion here. On Wednesday, November 8th, 1862, the Board of Supervisors for Mason County met at the Mason County Court House. A second set of Commissioners, which included John Hall, J.D. Thompson, W.H. Tomlinson, C.B. Waggener and William Smith, appeared as ordered by the last county court (in session September 1st, 1862) before the Board of Supervisors and reported on how the payment of local bounties to volunteers had proceeded.[474]

John Hall, one of the commissioners, presented payrolls to the Board, showing (1) who had been paid the $30 bounties and (2) the checks given by the commissioners in payment. There remained yet a balance of $25.13 in the Merchants National Bank of Point Pleasant, and it was decided that this sum was to be paid over to the Mason County Treasurer.[475] The Commissioners had paid $30 bounties to 288 men (for a total $8,640).[476]

The commissioners were given no compensation. The original commission—John Hall, Wetzel and Thompson—had executed two bonds on behalf of the county amounting to $9,000. The three commissioners endorsed them and had them discounted at the bank in Point Pleasant. "The discount taken off the balance was placed to our credit in the bank and afterwards checked out as we paid the bounty." That is, the money amounts represented by the bonds were borrowed against the county's credit, and drawn upon as each qualifying volunteer was paid his county bounty. The payrolls, checks and other evidence of disbursement was laid before the Board of Supervisors by Hall, together with the statement that there remained in the bank a balance of $25.13 which was afterwards credited by the bank cashier to the county on one of the bonds. This closed the accounts as to bonds and bounties. Hall went on to say that his responsibilities as ordered by the court were, however, not over. The court order, wrote Hall after the war,

> imposed duties on us [the first set of commissioners—Hall, Wetzel, and Thompson] which were not imposed on any other set of commissioners. We were required to look after the defence of the county, and I went and obtained of Gov. Pierpont one hundred choice rifled muskets for that purpose and gave my individual receipt for them, but after I got them here Col. Lightburn, (whose regiment was without effective arms) seized them and gave me a

receipt and certificate of such seizure. As to compensation for nego-
tiating county bounties or for paying bounties, I never charged
or received one cent, and do not think my associates did. I know
Mssrs. Thompson and Wetzel did not. My expenses to Wheeling
and telegraphing were not charged to the county nor paid by the
county, nor by any other means. I claim no credit for liberality.
There were others who were just as *Conservative* as myself, who gave
equally as freely of their labor and money for the cause. But I do
not wish to be understood as making a complaint against Mr. Fitz
Gerald or Mason for presenting their claims. If they ought not to
have been paid, the fault lays with the Radical Board of Supervisors
who ordered their payment. As to the motive which influenced the
board I know nothing. They may have regarded them as right or
they may have felt that they owed them for party services and took
this way to pay the debt.[477]

The 13th Regiment commenced its tour of duty doing mostly guard duty and
scouting in the Kanawha Valley by detachments of companies.[478] On October 10th,
Colonel J.T. Toland (cmdg. 1st Provisional Brigade at Point Pleasant to which the 13th
still belonged) wrote to Col. W.R. Brown, ordering him to detail from his Regiment
"for Guard Duty" on October 11th: "one 1st Lieutenant; one 2nd Lieutenant; one Sergeant; two Corporals; fifteen men and one orderly for Head Quarters 1st Provisional
Brigade." This detachment to be "provided with one days rations" and to "report on
the parade ground in front of the right of the Brigade at 7 o. c. A. M."[479] On October
11th, it rained a little but not enough to raise the Kanawha and the Ohio Rivers, and
Sergeant Hovey of the 4th Regiment Virginia Infantry drilled Company A. The 13th
practiced drill twice during the day: from eight to eleven in the morning and from
two to four o'clock in the afternoon.[480] Fifteen year old, native of Ireland, Private Peter
Douneely (Donnelly) of Company F, deserted.[481] In Kentucky, on this day, the battle
of Perryville raged.

On October 12th, the 1st Provisional Brigade was inspected on dress parade. The
following description appeared in the columns of the *Register:*

> On the last Sabbath morning [Oct. 12] we witnessed one of the
> most magnificent military displays it was ever our lot to witness.—
> The regiments on parade were the 4th Virginia, 13th Virginia, [3]4th
> Ohio , and 91st Ohio. The inspection took place in a large field on
> the other side of the Kanawha river, owned by J.G. Henderson Esq.
> The regiments were inspected by Col. J.A.J. Lightburn, assisted by
> Lieutenant-Col. Russell, of the 4th Virginia; Col. Brown, of the 13th

Virginia; Col. Toland, of the 34th Ohio; and Col. Turley of the 91st Ohio.

We do not wish to make distinctions as to the proficiency of drill in these Regiments, but must say, in our judgement the 4th Virginia is decidedly the best drilled Regiment, but the other three, although they have not had the advantages of the 4th, are very well drilled. We particularly noticed the 91st under the command of Colonel Turley; this is a new Regiment but moves off like an old one. Col. T. is very popular with his men, and receives all their plaudits for his kind and courageous treatment to them.

In rear was a battery consisting of four pieces. Taking the display all in all, it was a beautiful sight.— There were probably three thousand men, who seemed to be well disciplined and ready for the contest.[...]

While we write we hear the soul stirring martial music emanating from the different camps in this vicinity. The tocsin is sounding, and soon we expect to hear of West Virginia, and it is hoped the entire State, being snatched from the grasp of the infernal rebels, who are eating out our substance and spreading desolation, want and misery wherever they go.[482]

At least one correspondent from the Gallipolis *Journal* had also taken the opportunity to observe the October 12th dress parade of the 1st Provisional Brigade at Camp Toland. The writer(s) offered remarks as to the exemplary behavior and conduct of the soldiers at Camp Toland as compared to another unnamed military camp (at Point Pleasant or Gallispolis) "on the Ohio side" of the river. The following appeared in the columns of the *Journal*:

Camp Toland is located on the Virginia side of the Ohio River, on a farm belonging to Mrs. Smith, whose son has been an active member of Jenkins' cavalry since the outset of this rebellion.[483] The old lady herself makes little or no concealments of her secesh sentiments. In this camp are found the 'Piatt Zouaves,' whose reputation for 'foraging' is widely known. There are also three other regiments [the 91st O.V.I., the 4th and 13th Virginia Regiments] and two sections of a battery in the same camp. We were struck with the good order which pervaded it, at every point. No lounging no straggling soldiers passing in and out at will, loaded with plunder from the neighboring farms. No visible destruction of fences, fruit trees, &c. Not a board, rail, or even paling displaced. And this, too, with four thousand men in camp, and the 'Zouaves' amongst them. The camp located on the farm of a secesh too well known to admit of a doubt.

On Sunday last we paid a visit to Camp Toland, on the South side of the Kanawha, opposite Point Pleasant. We had the pleasure of witnessing a grand inspection and review of the Brigade under command of Col. Lightburn, composed of the 34th, (Zouaves), 91st O.V.I, 4th and 13th Va. Vols., and two sections of a battery. It was a sight worth going that distance to see. The Zouaves and 4th Va., being old regiments and well drilled, moved with great precision and skill. The 91st O. and 13th Va., although newly formed, and part of the 13th not yet equip[p]ed, gave evidence that the material for good soldiers was on hand, needing only time and practice to make them equal to their brethren of the older regiments.[484]

On October 12[th], Col. William R. Brown received orders from Colonel Toland, to detail from his regiment one 1[st] Lieutenant; one Second Lieutenant; one Sergeant; two Corporals, nineteen Privates and one orderly for Head Quarters 1st Provisional Brigade "for Guard Duty tomorrow, Oct. 13th, 1862."[485]

On October 14th, Brigadier General Milroy informed Col. Brown, that 2nd Lieutenant William. E. Feazel and 2nd Lieutenant John B. Baumgardner both belonging to the 13th Virginia Volunteers had been "temporarily detached from their Regt. on recruiting service" but would nonetheless, "be subject to the orders of Col. Brown Comdg. 13th Va. V.I."[486] On October 15th, the 13th Regiment received from Wheeling, by way of Gallipolis, a new supply of clothing: first overcoats, knapsacks and haversacks.[487] On October 16th, Company A received new Austrian guns (Lorenz guns?) from Gallipolis and returned the rifled muskets they had received from Gauley.[488]

A note regarding foreign weapons which were purchased by the Federal government and which then passed into the hands of American volunteers is relevant here. The burning of the United States arsenal at Harper's Ferry in April of 1861 left the government with only the Springfield, Massachusetts armory. The output of this armory was so small at this point in time that the government had to arm her volunteers of 1861 and 1862 with older models of United States weapons (mostly percussion weapons). In addition, the Government and various States purchased considerable numbers of foreign weapons. European governments taking advantage of the United States' need, sought to rid themselves of obsolete and unreliable muskets and thus sold to the U. S. their refuse weapons. There was a myriad of problems with such guns. Defective sights and barrels made them inaccurate; they were slow to fire, heavy and hard to handle. Possibly, from this stock of debris, came the Austrian guns issued to volunteers in Company A. The Austrian guns were probably dispensed with as soon as possible and replaced, as records also bear out. By 1863 and 1864, 13th soldiers were armed with Enfield and Springfield rifled muskets. These were better guns. They did not require heavy charges, were lighter and easier to load and handle. With these, soldiers could make a better record.

October 16th, George Barnet (or Barret) of Company C, was detailed to serve as nurse in the military hospital at Point Pleasant[489] and Maj. Gen. Wright notified Cox that Quartermaster's supplies for 30,000 men were on their way to Western Virginia.[490] "The Medical Purveyor at Cincinnati had also been directed "to furnish medical supplies on requisition to the new regiments forming in Western Virginia" and Medical Inspector George H. Lyman (inspector for the 2nd District) was charged with the immense task of "supervision of the sanitary condition of hospitals, camps and garrisons etc." in Western Virginia (also in Wisconsin, Michigan, Ohio, Indiana, Kentucky and "east of the Cumberland River."[491] Ever one to support a comrade-in-arms, W.W. Harper wrote to the Point Pleasant *Register* in vivid style, notifying the readership that A.F. McCown, Captain of Company F, 13th Regiment, had in the preceding days, been presented

> with a splendid new sword from Mr. L.H. Sargent, of Cincinnati as a reward for his gallantry and loyalty to his country, in this her time of deep affliction, in taking up arms to defend her flag from the encroachments of its implacable foes, and to preserve the government in its purity, that generations yet to come may be permitted to enjoy in all their heights, and depth and breadths, the blessings of civil and religious liberty. May his life be preserved to his country and he be permitted to gather many laurels on the battlefield, and afterward to enjoy the rich boon of a peace honorably conquered. And we assure the man who presented this emblem of power, will never have it to say that it was bestowed upon an unworthy person. Capt. McCown is a man who is in every respect and will preserve its blade, untarnished from disgrace.[492]

Swords tended to be one of the most expensive items of an officer's equipment and newly commissioned officers appreciated the thoughtfulness of such gifts.

Mid-October the leaves were yellow, and it was evident that winter was at hand. There had been quite a change in the temperature; the market price for everything had become exorbitant; and the atmosphere was "clear and bracing giving vigor to the frame."[493] On October 17th, the 13th Regiment moved camp from the west side to the east side of the Kanawha River to the Point Pleasant Fairgrounds.[494]

The question as to where these fairgrounds were located is a devilishly tricky business. One reason for this is that in the 150 years since the 13th mustered, drilled and camped there, the grounds may have in part or entirely eroded away into the confluence of rivers. Another factor is the fairgrounds seems to have moved about a good deal in that time. Printed references to it and local lore suggest that this open common ground, where the Virginia Militia mustered, where Camp Lightburn was likely set up and where in peacetime agricultural fairs, baseball was played and picnics were had was on the east side of the Kanawha River adjacent to the town which at that time "was built in the neighborhood of the Kanawha."[495]

Colonel G.B. Thomas remembered that on "Muster day" at Point Pleasant in the 1850s the Virginia Militia would gather

> in front of what is now Tu-Endie-Wei Park on the plot of ground ranging 60 to 150 feet in breadth, which has long since gone over the bank, and marched from there onto the commons adjacent to town, which was most any place now included in the main part of town. [...] The main part of town was at that time built in the neighborhood of the mouth of the Kanawha river.[496]

October 19th and 20th, 1886, on the anniversary of the battle of Cedar Creek in which the 13th bore "a conspicuous part" and where Lieutenant Colonel James Hall was mortally wounded, the fairgrounds were the final destination of the parade.

> Reveille and the reception of guests, together with music in the Court House yard came off early in the morning, after which a procession was formed on Sixth street, the footmen being headed by Major McCown and H.R. Howard, and the horsemen by Capt. Joseph Hein. They marched east to Viand, down Viand to First, thence up Main to the Fair Grounds, and recalled to the minds of many of us the dark days of our internecine strife. Arriving at the Fair Grounds, the procession disbanded, and seated themselves comfortably in front of the music stand. [Major A. F. McCown, Major of 13th gave a speech] in fine style [followed by Col. J.L. Vance of Gallipolis, Col. of the 4th W.Va.[497]

Another reference was made in 1909. Former Point Pleasant resident Mr. John Dasher started at what had been his old home on North Viand and walked down Viand towards the River. As he passed Old Central School (built in 1890 on the site where the Mason County Public Library now stands on 6th and Viand), Dasher commented that the grounds upon which Central School was built "were the old muster grounds, not only for the state militia but later for the soldiers of the Civil War."[498]

Now, Point Pleasant was not large by any means, but if one consults an old map of the town (for example the 1877-78 map) one finds that these descriptions are so difficult to reconcile, that one is left with the impression that they refer to entirely different sites. In the absence of something more concrete—like a definitive archaeological layer—one really cannot say anything more useful than that the 13th encampment was located at the fairgrounds "on the east side of the Kanawha," and that army supplies, guard house, parade ground, stables, the 13th hospital(s), etc.,[499] were spread out in between and around town as they might find place.

A correspondent (*nom de plum* "WEST VIRGINIA") to the Wheeling *Intelligencer* wrote the following favorable review of the 13th Virginia in process of organizing:

Point Pleasant, Va. Oct. 17, 1862.

Editors Intelligencer:

The 13th regiment in process of formation at this place, is nearly completed, and when completed will be one of the best regiments in the service. It would have been complete before now had not the recruiting officers been driven from their fields of operation by the rebel troops in their raid into this part of the State. It will be composed of men that will fight, not because endowed with more natural courage than other men, but because they fully realize the importance of fighting. Many of them are 'as a lion robbed of its whelps,' having been driven out from home and friends by the rebel army—and will fight for their families and property. But they will fight for higher considerations than these: They love their country and their government as dearly as ever Jew loved Jerusalem, have endured much for their sake—more than they will ever get credit for—are willing to endure more, nay to see their last hope expire and sink amid the darkness that would necessarily gather over the ruins of this government, should rebellion succeed in its overthrow.

The officers are such men as are necessary to make the regiment complete. The Colonel, Mr. Brown, formerly Capt. Brown, of the 4th Regiment of Va. Volunteers, is a good officer and a perfect gentleman. He is none of your kid-glove gentry from the hot-house of politics, afraid to take hold of the work of crushing out this rebellion in good earnest lest he should offend the tender conscience of some of his weak brethren, but he has the ring of the clear metal in him, and is ready and willing to take the rebel bull by the horns whenever he shall choose to venture across his path. He has seen service in the camp, in the field, in handling rebel sympathizers, and in every respect has met the most sanguine expectations of his friends. By universal consent he is regarded as the 'right man for the right place.'

The Lieut. Colonel, Mr. Hall, is a young man of good reputation, excellent family, pleasant address, mingles freely with the regiment, and with experience and practice will make a popular and useful officer. He is a brother to Major Hall, (late of the 4th Reg't, Va. Vols.) who was killed near Logan Court House in a skirmish a few months ago, and who died as the soldier dieth, upholding the flag of his country.

The company officers are an intelligent and fine looking set of men, but with few exceptions have their reputations as military men to make, but have the will and the energy to make it, or else all signs deceive. Perfect harmony as a general thing exists between them and their companies, and also between them and their superiors. And now, sir, if the 'back-bone of this ungodly rebellion is not broken,' and the rebels 'driven to the wall' before the Thirteenth is ready for the field, you may depend upon it, it will make for itself a record of which its friends will not be ashamed.

Many of the men are immediate and actual sufferers of secession, and whenever occasion shall offer, they will handle it and its sympathizers without gloves. They are not the men to strain at a gnat and swallow a secession camel. Their position upon the putting down of the rebellion is about the same as that of a certain young lady on the subject of religion. Said she, 'Father, I have made up my mind to be religious,' 'Ah!' said he, 'my daughter, that's a very serious business; have you counted the cost?' 'Yes, father, I have counted the cost, and am resolved to be religious, let it cost what it may.' The 13th have counted the cost of their position and are determined that this rebellion shall be put down, let it cost what it may.

There is not much news here that can be communicated. There is considerable shuffling among regiments, and there may be news of importance in a few days from this department.

A citizen from Charleston, Va., who came down the other evening, reports no rebel forces in the Valley except Jenkins' cavalry, who are scouring the country hunting down Union men, and stealing horses and property. Their main army retreated towards Lewisburg, taking their sick, wounded and everything with them. Prominent rebel citizens left with them also. This is reliable.[500]

On October 18th, Colonel William R. Brown issued General Order No. 1 from 13th Regiment Headquarters at Point Pleasant, Virginia. The order was read at parade that day and established for Brown's men the day to day rhythm of camp life and certain aspects of military procedure. The order directed that

> Hereafter company drill will be from 8 to 10 o'clock A.M. and Battalion drill from 2 to 4 o'clock P.M. Dress Parade will be at 5 P.M. [and] any soldier missing roll call unaccounted for will be kept on extra guard duty of from three (3) to ten days (10) days. [In addition, p]apers to enlisted men must be signed first by the company commander, then by the commanding officer in the Regiment.[501]

Also on the 18th, Arthur Edwards of Co. F, entered upon his duties as teamster.[502]

As Gen. W.W. Loring now occupied almost the entire Kanawha Valley and the Federal Army was pushed into the area at the mouth of the Kanawha River, the town of Point Pleasant gained in strategic importance and security became a priority for military authorities there. "Things look brisk and war-like here" began "D" writing from Point Pleasant on October 18th. Point Pleasant had not only its own small population of citizens but it was "full of refugees," who were anxiously awaiting what the movements up the river would be.[503] It was a time of arrest and parole provided the oath of allegiance was sworn.[504]

One parole of more than passing interest was that of A.M. McCausland, whose parole is preserved today in a box of unbound, miscellaneous papers, once belonging to the 13th Regiment. Alexander McCausland of West Columbia was a native of Ireland; a friend of John Hall Sr.; and a successful merchant. By May of 1862, however, it was required by law that any person who took out a license to do any kind of business also take the oath of allegiance. This law applied to merchants of all kinds, doctors, lawyers, ministers, grand and petit jurors, bank directors, officers of banks, officers and clerks of corporations, and clerks or agents of any person required to take out license. Failure to do so resulted in a fine of from $10 to $500. Why McCausland's parole is preserved with 13th regimental papers is something of a mystery. One possibility is that the oath may have been administered by a 13th officer and kept with other papers at 13th headquarters. The document provides an example of the purposes of such an exercise at this particular time and place. The parole is dated October 18th, 1862 and reads as follows:

> I A.M. McCauslin in accepting this my parole of honor do solemnly promise that I will remain within the lines of the town of Point Pleasant Mason County Virginia. Untill further orders from the commanding officer of the Federal Troops at this Post and that I will hold no conversation whatever with any person or person[s] regarding the numbers position movement or conditions of troops

of this command or any other whear I have been so long as this my parole may exist. [Signed] A.M. McCausland[505]

The fortunes of war had again shifted in the Valley (and for the last time). On October 8th, Major General Loring pulled back from Charleston. On the 15th, Loring was relieved of his command in Western Virginia. Brigadier General John Echols was now assigned to command the Department of Western Virginia. Echols was ordered to march his forces back into the Kanawha Valley and make its defense his first objective.[506] Jenkins' cavalry, still in the Kanawha Valley, was ordered to remain there. By October 18th, reports of Rebels evacuating Charleston and the Kanawha Valley were confirmed by Federal military authorities. While it was impossible to be sure what might happen next "[i]t now look[ed]," wrote Gen. J.D. Cox, "as if the country as high as the Gauley [c]ould be occupied [by the Union army] without a contest."[507] Cox resolved to retake the Valley and move troops under Lightburn up the Kanawha on "Monday morning, without waiting longer for [reinforcements under] General Morgan."[508] Concerned that Confederates might concentrate in areas between himself and other Union forces in Western Virginia, he ordered that the country and passes be watched closely.[509]

As the Union army retook the Kanawha Valley, guerrillas again became active. On the 19th, Gen. H.G. Wright wrote to Col. Jonathan Craynor (cmdg. 40th Ohio Vols.) at Guyandotte that small guerrilla groups of Rebels, from 500 to 600 at most and another force said to belong to Floyd's command, were reported to be in possession of the Northeastern Kentucky counties of Greenup (just across the Ohio from Mason County), Carter and Lawrence and other counties as far south as Pike. They were "committing depredations upon the property and outrages upon the persons of loyal citizens which call for prompt repression." Craynor was instructed to suppress such mischief and operate on both sides of the Big Sandy River; the operations in Western Virginia were to be conducted under instructions from Gen. Cox. Operations on the Kentucky side were to be undertaken without delay.[510] Thanks to Craynor and his command, by October 19th, there were no rebels in the immediate vicinity of Guyandotte. Cabell County had been "cleaned-up" to such an extent that it was "now safe to open a recruiting office in that county."[511] Despite such progress, rebels still persisted in being a problem in Wayne and Logan Counties.[512] On October 19th, the 13th Regiment was reviewed by Gen. Cox "at one thirty P.M."[513] Also on this date, John A. Winkleblack, Co. F, was detailed for carpenter in the Regimental Quartermasters Department.[514]

On October 20th, Lightburn moved with part of his division up the Kanawha. He was to remove obstructions in the river at Red House, 25 miles up-river and push on, putting this waterway in a state of good repair, repairing roads, etc., as might be needed. Lightburn's division moved slowly up the Kanawha making a thorough job of it as, in the event the Rebels retook Charleston, the water ways would be of "critical importance" to Union forces.[515] The 13th remained in camp and watched while her sister regiments, the 4th Virginia and 34th and 91st Ohio Infantry regiments moved out about ten o'clock in the morning on October 20th. One "MILES," a member of the 91st Zouaves wrote with graphic detail about the anticipation in camp regarding the forward movement and preparations in camp for the departure:

> At last the tedium of inaction has been broken. Something new, something long desired, seems to have been inaugurated. Can it be a forward movement? We shall see. All is life and animation now. Tents are being struck, and already the work of destroying such property as cannot be removed has commenced. But we are not to move till morning, so the ground with nothing to shelter us from the chilly frost, must be our resting place tonight. But we are going to move, and all is good cheer. Many are the conjectures as to where we are about to go; some suppose to Kentucky, others up the Ohio, and others up the Kanawha, all having good reasons for their beliefs. We settle down upon the conclusion that it matters not, we are in for it now, and we must learn to wait as well as conjecture. Little is the sleep that many of us enjoy on account of the many more who are too jubilant to rest.

> Oct. 20th

> Morning comes. Its earliest streaks have scarcely appeared till the order comes to be ready to move. 'Tis a welcome mandate. The humming of 3000 voices mingled with the crackling of burning barrels and boxes, and the glare of the conflagration, produces on the spectator not accustomed to such scenes, a sensation of something wild and fantastic. 'Fall in,' is the cry, and now we have slung knapsacks, shouldered arms, and are in line of battle. Now we are doomed to wait under our heavy burdens, suffering not only from the pains of the body, but from an excruciating suspense till the whole brigade is ready to move.— The sun is getting higher and higher, still we are on a stand march, as the boys say when we don't march at all.— We move a short distance and we are stopped. Suspense continues. At length we are permitted to move without interruption, and that suspense is relieved. We turn up the Kanawha.[516]

Lightburn's movement up the Kanawha Valley left Col. W.R. Brown, cmdg. 13th Virginia, in command of the military post at Point Pleasant.[517] A wagon, a rare item indeed, was received for Cos. A and F on October 20[th518] and John J. Chancey of Company F, was detailed to assist the regimental carpenter[519] (John A. Winkleblack, also Co. F). By October 20th, Gen. Morgan's Tennessee troops still had not arrived but other movements in the district were underway in cooperative effort to drive the Confederates out. Milroy's force was to move toward Beverly from Clarksburg and Crook, also at Clarksburg, was to advance in the direction of Summerville. The two commands to co-operate until they reached Beverly and quieted that part of the country. October 20th, Cox issued the following unusual order regarding military clothing:

> Commandants of Posts, Provost Marshals, and officers in Command of Separate Detachments, &c., are ordered to correct the practice of the wearing of U.S. soldiers' uniform by citizens not in Army employ. Such abuse of the uniform is strictly prohibited, and the prohibition must be enforced. The uniform must indicate that the wearer is a soldier, and the person wearing it without authority is *prima facie* a soldier absent without leave, or a deserter. If Government clothing has been sold to citizens by any officer, such cases will be immediately investigated and reported to these Head-Quarters. By Command of Major-General J. D. Cox. G. M. Bascom, Major and A.A.G. Official Theo. Cox Lieut. & A.D.C.[520]

"... the greatest political feud in [Mason] County."

— Livia Simpson-Poffenbarger,
"Battle of Point Pleasant" in *Poffenbarger Papers* Vol. 9, pp. 17-18,
Mason County Public Library, Point Pleasant.

The war effort, like any human endeavor, was both helped and hindered by various personal perceptions of the individuals involved, even when they were working towards the same goal. Illustrative is the case of Lewis Wetzel and John Hall Sr., which had as its nexus, a series of appointments (and non-appointments) of officers of the 13th Virginia Regiment. Both Wetzel and Hall had been political activists for the Union cause. Hall, the older of the two men (aged fifty-five years in October of 1862), was at the time of the shooting, one of the county elders: an attorney with an office on Main Street in downtown Point Pleasant; a prominent representative from Mason County in the new State government at Wheeling; and longtime entrepreneur and developer of industry in the county.

Lewis Wetzel, although nearly twenty years Hall's junior, was hardly less accomplished and a man of good character and reputation. At the time of his death at the hands of Hall, on October 23rd, 1862, Wetzel was in the prime of life, about 37 years old (born about 1825). He was born and raised in "old Mason" County, reputedly a descendant of the famed Indian scout and fighter, Lewis Wetzel of Marshall County, Western Virginia. The young man had been a life-long resident of Point Pleasant, "a highly respected citizen, a staunch Union man, and a polished gentleman."[521] He was longtime Presiding Justice and President of the Mason County Circuit Court and member of the House of Delegates at the State Legislature. He was a merchant, member of the firm of Setzser, Beale and Company (in Point Pleasant) and "acting editor" of the Point Pleasant *Weekly Register,* "for some time," a paper "ardently devoted to the Union cause, and with marked effect in Mason county."[522] He had since the beginning of hostilities, been keenly devoted to the Union cause and was a champion of the interests of Western Virginians and the New State question. He had served as chairman of Mason County public meetings held during the precarious times of 1861 and 1862.

On the morning of October 23rd, while he stood in the counting room of his mercantile business, Setzser, Beale & Company, Wetzel was shot to death by Hall, who had shot Wetzel in the left breast with a pistol. In a moment, Wetzel was dead. Hall was arrested and confined in the Mason County jail.[523] The "difficulty arose from an article which had appeared in that morning's paper."[524] The murder rocked the county and some feared that because of the prominent standing of the two parties, the Union cause in Western Virginia might also be compromised. Ohio and Virginia papers reported at length on this grievous and confounding affair. Both men had since the outbreak of the rebellion,

> taken a most active part on behalf of the Union. Both seemed to be aiming at the same end. They differed somewhat as to the mode of operations, and it seem[ed] that influence had been exerted with a military commandant for the suppression of the *Register*. This induced Mr. Wetzel to comment through the columns of his paper, upon the motives of the individual, in a manner deemed by Mr. Hall as highly slanderous and unwarranted. He called on Mr. Wetzel, at his store, immediately on reading the article, and denounced him. Mr. W. immediately retreated to the counting room, closing the door in which was a glazed sash, through which nearly one-half his body in a perpendicular line was visible. Hall fired, the ball taking effect in the region of the heart and causing almost instant death. The affair has caused considerable excitement in the vicinity and it is difficult to tell where it may end.[525]

The inciting article penned by Wetzel appeared in the Point Pleasant *Weekly Register*, on Thursday October 23rd (the day of publication for this weekly), under the title "Suppression." One correspondent reported that the article was written in "bold and sarcastic tone but it [was] general and indefinite, and more remarkable for what it promise[d] to do and say, than for what it actually disclose[d]."[526] Writers for the Wheeling *Daily Intelligencer* also covered the story and offered up their view of the events and strong animosities which culminated in the shooting of Wetzel:

> We published yesterday a dispatch announcing the death of Lewis Wetzel on the morning of the 23d, at the hands of John Hall, Mr. Wetzel was acting as the editor of the Point Pleasant *Register*, and, as it appears had for some time back alluded offensively to the Governor here on account of some appointments made in the military service, as well as on account of some that were not made. It

appears also, that Mr. Hall called the attention of the Commander of the post (at Point Pleasant) to these articles, on the ground that they were doing much to impair the confidence of the people in the existing order of things in Western Virginia, and gave it as his opinion, that either the editor of the paper, or the paper itself, ought to be suppressed.

These statements we make on general rumor. We have seen nothing reliable concerning the origin of the quarrel between Mr. Wetzel and Mr. Hall. We know that the *Register* is a loyal sheet, a truly one, and that Mr. Wetzel was a sound Union man. We have seen two or three allusions in his paper to the appointing powers here at Wheeling, critici[z]ing harshly and unjustly their actions in some cases.— But we looked upon the criticisms as the natural mistakes of a man remote from the source of explanations and justifications, and not as prompted by any other motive than a zeal and anxiety in the good cause. Certainly no more devoted patriot than Lewis Wetzel lived in Western Va.

The suggestions which it appears Mr. Hall made to the commandant at Point Pleasant irritated Mr. Wetzel to a high degree and in his paper (the *Register)* coming to hand yesterday, we find the violent editorial that no doubt lead to the deplorable collision between himself and Mr. Hall.— We most deeply regret this terrible affair, inasmuch as it has cost the Union cause in Western Va, so needy at the best, the services of one patriotic man and the influence of another. Mr. Wetzel is dead and Mr. Hall's remaining days will count for nothing. Bitterness and feud will reign between the friends of each party, and their efforts in the great cause of the Government will, we fear, now be subordinated to their personal feelings.

One of the strongest and most decided articles that we have seen on the late elections appears in the number of the *Register* to which we refer. It grieves us to think that the hand that penned it is now stilled in death and will no more be moved in aid of the cause which the writer loved so well. We devoutly hope that the true friends of the Union cause and of each of the unfortunate parties to the terrible tragedy, will exert themselves to see that the county of Mason is not lit up with the burning passions of personal animosity on account of this misfortune, Let the matter be investigated and tried by the proper authorities, and all necessary feeling held in subjection to the pressing necessities of the common cause. All patriotic men in Western Va will deplore this unfortunate affair between two of our prominent Union men, and all will hope to see it confined to the legitimate circle of the law.[527]

I also studied the article at length and found nothing on the surface of it which might have provoked such violent reaction.[528] Conversation with a descendant of John Hall suggested that something of a much more personal nature between the two men was operating, something that can only be conjectured today. Certainly, Hall was in poor health and something of a manipulator in the community. He had pushed for and succeeded to some degree in having the government at Wheeling appoint out-of-state soldiers to fill officers' positions in the 13th rather than countenance the election and appointment of West Virginians to high command (*id est.,* other than his two sons). Appointments attributable to pressure from Hall Sr. were the commissioning of William R. Brown formerly a manufacturer at Pomeroy, Ohio, Captain Co. E, 4th Virginia Infantry for colonel and Milton Stewart's appointment (also of the 4th Virginia) to Captain of Co. B in place of James R. Hall, who had been commissioned lieutenant-colonel. Not that these men did not warrant these appointments but this impulse to appoint 'outsiders' naturally ran counter to what the West Virginians in the 13th and the county wanted. That is, they wanted West Virginias to lead the regiment.

Leading Western Virginians, such as Lewis Wetzel, had written to Wheeling conveying their objections to the way Hall was railroading the proceedings. Wetzel also voiced his dissatisfaction over Wheeling's appointments and non-appointments to the regiment in his editorial columns which prompted Hall to suggest to Col. Brown that the *Register* be suppressed (*i.e.,* shut down). This in turn prompted Wetzel to respond with an article that so incensed the older man that without warning, he shot Wetzel down in the counting room of his store "like a dog."[529] Hall was jailed.

On November 3rd, 1862, Hall's attorney moved to quash the indictment of felony, but the Mason County Court overruled. Evidence was heard from both sides, and the Court concluded that there was probable cause to charge Hall with felony, and Hall was remanded to the Mason County jail to await trial in the Circuit Court. Bail was denied.[530] A curious development in the Court proceedings of this day (November 3rd, 4th or 5th) was that a warrant was also issued for Col. William R. Brown (commanding the military post at Point Pleasant). He was arrested and arraigned on what was probably a charge of conspiracy to commit murder or accessory to murder. Brown appeared and moved for the Court to quash the warrant. This was overruled and thereupon, the Court examined all witnesses offered by the Defense and the State and the Court concluded (Justice E.B. Davis, presiding) that no felony had been committed by the defendant (Brown) and he was discharged from further prosecution.[531]

On November 13th, attorney for the Commonwealth, William H. Tomlinson, of Point Pleasant and Hall's attorneys, B.H. Smith, A. Parks and B.J. Redmond (Hall's son-in-law) all appeared at Circuit Court held at Charleston in Kanawha County before Judge James H. Brown presiding. Hall was on this day admitted to bail for $30,000 pleading that he had a dangerous and painful disease—cancer—of the left eye. For securities he offered himself, John McCulloch, A[lexander] McCausland and Benjamin J. Redmond.[532] Hall's attorneys persuaded the Court that confinement in the Mason County jail would hasten Hall's death insofar as

> the jail has long been and still is used as a guard house by the U.S. Troops occupying the post at Point Pleasant [which included at this time half of the 13th Regiment under Brown which was encamped in close proximity to the jail] often confining great numbers of them day and night, and is surrounded by wagons, teams and teamsters connected with the army by whom great noise, disorder and confusion have been and is kept up day and night to the great disgust and annoyance of the prisoner and those visiting him in jail — that the room in which he was confined, being one of the best in the jail has the plaster fallen off half across the whole room with an open garret above admitting the cold air and wind [...].[533]

Hostilities continued between the *Register* and the Hall family. George W. Tippett, editor-owner of the *Register* stated that Col. J.R. Hall made an "armed assault" upon him (Tippett) in wake of the killing of Wetzel. See Tippett's letter to Adjutant General Samuels as follows:

> I have an account against the Commonwealth of Virginia, for printing 'Volunteer Enlistment' blanks, which were ordered to be done by Lieut. Col. James R. Hall of 13th Va., and Lieut. Wm. E. Feazel Recruiting officer, also some Volunteer Posters for Lieut. Feazel — amounting in all to about $31.00. Now I write to you for information as to how I shall proceed to get the above amount due me. Col. Hall told me that he was authorized to certify my account but since the killing of Lewis Wetzel by his father and his armed assault upon myself, he has obstinately refused to do so, I have written him twice but have received no answer in return. Lieut. Feazel is here. He says he will certify the account if you authorize him to do so.[534]

Hall's trial was begun March 2nd, 1864. His eldest son, James and Milton Stewart (Capt. Co. B 13th V.V.I.) received furloughs to testify at Hall's trial. A jury of 12 men was sworn to uphold the U.S. Constitution and the Constitution of the State of West Virginia. After 6 days of presentation of evidence and two days of argument the case was given to the jury. Evidence was presented on March 3rd, 4th, 5th, 7th, (the 6th was a Sunday). On March 8th, arguments by counsel began to be heard. Arguments continued to be presented until the 11th. On the 11th, the jury deliberated for about five hours and then returned with a verdict of 'involuntary manslaughter.' This was a lenient verdict given that the original indictment was for murder; likely rendered in light of Hall's considerable efforts to promote Western Virginia interests and the Union cause there. Hall was assessed a fine of four thousand dollars plus costs.[535]

General Cox Retakes the Kanawha Valley

When Gen. J.D. Cox returned to his old command and arrived at his head-quarters at Gallipolis, he assessed his district. Insufficient overland conveyance would embarrass efforts to supply the army as it advanced to re-take and occupy the Kanawha Valley. Cox determined that 400 wagons and 2,000 mules were needed to supply the immediate necessities of the district. One hundred wagons were promised from Cincinnati. One hundred more were contracted to be built at Wheeling. The need for wagons was great as there was "no navigation on the Ohio or Kanawha".[536] This lack of transport by river was due to low water —at its lowest level since the summer of 1838[537]—caused by the recent drought. The Confederate occupation of northwestern Virginia also disrupted communication by water. Unfortunately, Cox would have difficulty in getting enough wagons for logistics. By October 20th, the problem of obtaining stores, even by railroad, was still embarrassing Cox's operations.[538] Not only was Cox's command lacking in transportation, his artillery was in bad condition and due to "great mismanagement in the Quartermaster's Department," "the wants great in all parts of the quartermaster's department, both stores and transportation."[539] Cox nonetheless resolved to push toward the interior and the Confederate army with what he had at his disposal.[540]

Cox first reorganized his command. This was accomplished between October 24th and 30th. Then, with select forces from Point Pleasant, he planned to advance up the Kanawha River and converge at the mouth of the Pocataligo. From the mouth of the Pocataligo, his united forces would advance on Charleston. On October 24th, Cox wrote to his commanders Col. Jonathan Craynor, Gen. R.H. Milroy, Brig. Gen. George Crook and Col. J.A.J. Lightburn (at the mouth of Pocotaligo) setting them in motion to dislodge the "concentration of rebels" reported to be at or near Charleston. Cox directed Craynor, commanding a brigade at Guyandotte, to reconnaissance the "country above" him and if possible, to open and stay in communication with Federal forces at Red House (Lightburn's advance) and Winfield, on the Kanawha River. "If everything is quiet between you and the Sandy," wrote Cox, he (Craynor) was to scout "carefully toward the mouth of Coal River,"and gather intelligence and clear that area of guerrillas.[541] Milroy at Buckhannon was to operate toward Monterey protecting Crook's line of communication in rear while Crook at Clarksburg was to move toward Summerville. Crook was to threaten rebel communications at Gauley, which movement in conjunction with Lightburn's, it was anticipated, would dislodge the enemy concentrated in the Kanawha Valley. Gen. G.W. Morgan's force, fearfully slow in getting forward, would join Lightburn above Red House in a day or two. This latter junction effected, Cox intended to push all forward against the Rebels in Charleston as fast as transportation and low water would permit.[542] To be taken into account in these movements was that Confederate officer John B. Floyd had reportedly a small force of 1,500 men at Logan Court House and from the Kentucky side of the Ohio the news was bleak. The Sandy Valley and adjacent counties were still overrun by large bands of "marauding and guerrilla parties" under Witcher among others and Humphrey Marshall. These were reported to be infesting that country and preying upon the persons and property of the loyal people of Northeastern Kentucky.[543]

Col. Lightburn with Col. Siber's Brigade and Col. Toland's new brigade (Col. Lightburn's Division) but without the 13th Regiment was ordered forward immediately on October 29th, to Tyler's Creek at the mouth of the Pocataligo. Certain 13th men, detailed to drive cattle for the army accompanied the advance but the new regiment seems otherwise to have remained in their encampment near Point Pleasant. Cox joined Lightburn at the Pocataligo with that part of Morgan's division which had finally reported to Cox for duty. Cox had pushed the whole force forward, one column on the left bank of the Kanawha (Siber's brigade of Lightburn's division, with one four gun battery of mountain howitzers) and on the right bank traveled two columns. One column (Toland's brigade of Lightburn's division; Foster's six-gun rifled battery; a battalion of 2nd Virginia Cavalry supported by De Courcy's brigade, of Morgan's division, with a section of 20-pounder Parrott guns) traveled by the river road. The second column (Carter's brigade of Morgan's division and Lamphere's six-gun rifled battery) proceeded on the turnpike over Tyler Mountain. Charleston was reached on October 29th.

The Confederates fell back as soon as Cox's advance was known. Wrote Clarkson Fogg (Corporal 4th Virginia Infantry Regiment, Toland's brigade), on October 30th:

> The rebels, about 8000 strong, evacuated their position here yesterday morning, crossed to the west side of the Kanawha River at Camp Piatt and took a southwesterly direction. [...] Morgan's force, close below us, with Lightburn's division, numbers about 13,000 with 35 pieces of artillery.[544]

Gen. Echols wrote to Richmond on October 28th, informing authorities there, that a force of 12,000 Nationals was in front of him at Charleston and there was a "considerable force under Milroy" advancing from Clarksburg in the direction of Montgomery's Ferry, probably to intercept his (Echols') retreat. Echols lost no time and with his troops made a forced march of 31 miles beginning at 2:00 A.M. Jenkins and his cavalry were positioned in rear to hold the Federals in check. No stores and other army property were left behind. Echols added that judging from the strength of the advancing Federal force and the size of its trains on the morning of October 28th, he thought it probable that their objective went beyond just the recovery of the Kanawha Valley but that they might endeavor to penetrate to the Virginia and Tennessee Railroad.[545]

By October 31st, the Kanawha Valley was re-occupied from Point Pleasant to Gauley and Fayetteville "and the authority of the Government restored."[546] The late rains had caused a slight rise in the river (the Kanawha had risen three feet) which was of material advantage in getting supplies forward to supply the army. Steam navigation could be gotten forward as far as Camp Piatt located about "10 miles above" Charleston.[547] If the rise in water level held, steamboats could be more widely used which would have been of help to the entire district. In the meantime, the Quartermaster's department was concentrating their efforts to supply Lightburn and Crook in the immediate vicinity of Gauley Bridge.

By October 31st, Cox turned his immediate attention to the eradication of guerrilla bands targeting specifically those groups striking and making their escape in the hilly and mountainous country between the Kanawha and Sandy Rivers. Reinforcements sent to Cox had been likewise detailed to tend to the guerrillas, but difficulty in supplying troops in advanced positions bogged down operations. Gen. Morgan's division (with the exception of Speare's Tennessee brigade which had not been moved from Gallipolis because Cox could not have supplied them with rations *vis-à-vis* the lack of overland transport) was divided and posted as follows: Carter's brigade at Malden on the Kanawha, with instructions to clear the country of guerillas from the Salines south through Boone and Logan counties and De Courcy's brigade was at Charleston on like duty up Elk river and in the vicinity of the town of Kanawha.[548] On November 1st, the War Department expressed its dissatisfaction with the slow movement of troops in Western Virginia.[549]

Now that the Confederates were pushed out of the Kanawha beyond the mountains and into the Shenandoah Valley, Cox proceeded to establish a succession of defensive posts to hold the most vital areas of country. In the northern section of the district, two divisions guarded the B & O Railroad and the Cheat Mountain region. In the south, the Kanawha Valley was protected by two divisions of approximately 6,000 men each. The First Division (Kanawha Division) was under command of Gen. George Crook, who had assumed command of it in October 1862.[550] The Kanawha Division was organized as follows: 1st Brigade Eliakim Parker Scammon, commanding; 2ⁿᵈ Brigade, Ebenezer B. Andrews, commanding; and Third Brigade, Jonathan Cranor/Craynor commanding. In December 1862, the designation of the division was changed to First Kanawha Division.

With Confederate occupation of the Kanawha Valley at an end efforts to recruit more men for the 13th were again attempted in the interior of the country. These drives to enlist men continued as a complement of two more companies (I and K) were still needed, and companies already mustered were under-sized. Joseph Kneff was to recruit 13th volunteers around Point Pleasant beginning November 11th, 1862.[551]

In camp with the 13th

Morning Reports for the 13th Regiment suggest that the recruits were settling into the new rhythm of things. Peter Yeager of Co. F was detailed for butcher on October 23rd. On October 25th, William P. White, B.N. Tilden and John Twaddle, all from Co. F, were detailed to go to Charleston with the "Train as Teamsters." On October 26th, John P. Harmon of Co. C was detailed for nurse in the hospital at Point Pleasant, and John M. Young, Russell B. Shrewsberry and Samuel P. Robinson, all of Co. F, were detailed to go to Charleston as teamsters.[552]

On October 27th, Company A received ten bushels of coal "from the Quarter Master, from the coal bank" and Thomas Williamson of Co. F, was detailed to go to Charleston as blacksmith.[553] Also the 27th, Greenbury Slack, 1st Lieutenant, Company A, wrote a letter to Governor Pierpont requesting that "Rev[eren]d Henry Stevens of the M[ethodist] Episcopal] Church" be commissioned Chaplain of the 13th Virginia Regiment. Slack remarked that it was his belief that Stevens "has been recommended to [Pierpoint] as the Choice of the officers of said Regiment"and so far as he has been advised, it was the "unanimous wish of both officers and men that he be appointed at once." "Mr Stevens" wrote Lieut. Slack, "is a man of unexceptionable Character and undoubted piety and possessing Talents far above mediocrity." Slack's post script gives some indication of what was known and surmised by those yet in camp at Point Pleasant: "Our troops are advancing up the Kana[wha] valley. [T]he rebels are said be in Large force in the neighborhood of the 'Saltworks' but I have some doubt of the fact Genl Coxs headquarters is still at this place."[554]

In the days following the departure of Cox's troops up the Kanawha Valley to their new positions. A correspondent from Point Pleasant, calling themselves "WEST VIRGINIA," writing from his boardinghouse within sight of the military camp at Point Pleasant, represented:

> There is not much of importance going on in this valley at present. The 13th Va. regiment is still encamped at this point, and Gen. Spear's brigade, of the Cumberland Gap army, is encamped across

the river just below. The most interesting thing in progress here at present is the catching and breaking of mules, of which there is a fine lot in respectable distance of my boarding house. [Then follows a humorous discussion in which the breaking of mules is likened to the breaking of the rebellion.] However be this as it may, the process puts a good many mules into the trains of the army of the Kanawha, which is a very important arm of the service, and will soon be more so if the good Being does not soon see proper to send rains to raise the river.[555]

On the morning of October 28th, Capt. James W. Johnson and ten men of Co. A, were ordered on detached service to guard trains and scout up the right bank of the Kanawha. They were to accompany a larger detachment from the 13th (110 men), the whole under the command of Lieutenant-Colonel Hall. A wagon was ordered to carry enough rations for four days.[556] Hall wrote to Col. Brown on November 2nd (1862) reporting as follows regarding this expedition:

> Sir:
>
> Agreeable to orders I left this place for Ripley and vicinity on Tuesday morning the 28th October with 125 men, marched up the Kanawha 15 miles. Remained ther until 9 o clock P.M. reaching Ripley early on Wednesday morning found no enemy except some 5 or 6 Cavalry who left in great haste. We were afterward within sight of 30 or 40 Cavalry, but not within gunshot. From the best information I could gain in the country, there are two Companies or parts of Companies of Cavalry in Jackson County and one Company of Infantry at or near Spencer 28 miles east of Ripley. We found it impossible to do anything with the Cavalry. They are recruiting stealing Horses and subsisting on the County in Jackson and Roane. We were in Jackson 36 hours and reached this place Nov. 1st.
>
> I am Sir, Very Respectfully
> Your Obt Servt
> James R. Hall
> Lt. Col. Comdg Detachment
> Official Copy:
> W. I. Mathews
> Adjutant[557]

Captain J.V. Young wrote to his wife, Paulina, from Point Pleasant, on October 28th (1862), revealing not only certain aspects of camp life but the anxiety soldiers felt on behalf of their loved ones at home and vulnerable to abuse by secessionists.

I again will attempt to write to you to let you know how we are getting along. I am tolerable well and the most of my men are well. We are here laying at Pt. Pleasant doing nothing but cooking and eating, and I am really tired of staying here. I want to hear from home so much. I have been wishing and listening for some news from home but I can't hear any. [...I]f you can come down I can get you such things as you need without the money. I can get groceries from the Quartermaster Dept. at govt. prices.

Lt. Col. Hall started this morning with 200 men and towards Teays Valley. 40 of my men are with him. I hope he will avenge the death of his brother bef[ore] he returns. I just now hear, while I am writing, that our men are fighting at the mouth of Coal, and if this is true you will soon be delivered from the rebels. There are now about 25,000 troops in the Kanawha Valley. Gen. Milroy is on his way to Gauley with 15 or 20 thousand, and you may guess what will become of Jeff & his vandals.

Dear wife, I am afraid you and my children are suffering for the necessities of life. I hear so much about what the rebels have done up there. I don't know how you can get along without a horse, [Young has sent her his horse Alex by James Elkins] but I told Col. Lightburn if any woman who lived in the Valley could, you would. Oh Paulina, I want to see you and the children so bad. I dream of you at night and think of you by day. I think of the happy hours and years we have enjoyed at home at our hard labor. The happy hours! When will they return? But our consolation — those who have disturbed our peaceful home will be disturbed in return, and that right speedily. I love to think of 'home sweet home' indeed to me; and those fort[une]s that bind us more closely together.

Col. Frost had ordered me and my command to Parkersburg, but Gen. C[ox?] says he has use for Capt. Young's company in the Kanawha Valley.

Mrs. Higginbotham has just gotten here and has been telling me your troubles when I had to retreat and when the Reb[e]ls were taking horses. It makes me indignant but I intend to retaliate fourfold on their heads. Mrs. Higginbotham is in a destitute condition, has no house to go into. I feel very uneasy about James Elkins and my horse.

Paulina, do come as soon as you can. I repeat it. [...] My troubles since I came down here have reduced me considerably, but I try to bear it as well as I can under the circumstances. But I assure you it is hard to do when I know my dear family is insulted and abused by thieves and traitors and have their living taken from them when I know they have worked hard for it. Well, I must quit writing and go on dress parade. The drum is now beating, the Captains are shouting 'fall in, fall in.' I must go. Colonel Brown has his uniform on already, so goodbye at present. I will say more sometime shortly.

Dress parade is over now and I will finish my letter. Brooks & J.S. Cunningham are my Lieuts. [...]

Yours in love until death
J.V. Young, Capt. Comd. Co. G
13th Reg. Va. Vol. Infty.

Dear Paulina:

As Ferdinand Cash is going up to drive some cattle to Gen. C[ox] and has promised to go to see you, if he comes you must try to come with him. Tell Sarah, Emma, Ben, and Jacob that their Pa wants to see them very badly indeed. [...] My prayer is, and shall be, that you all may be preserved and kept from evil, and that you may soon be delivered from them who have stripped you and insulted you on account of your loyalty to the best Government in the world and our holy religion. May the Lord bless you all and cause you to remember that this is a world of trouble and disappointment. But may the Lord grant that we may meet again and have peace at home once more. [...] J.V. Young.[558]

To his daughters Sallie and Emma, Young wrote from camp at Point Pleasant on October 29th:

I am tented out in the field and just have a little stove in my tent, and it makes it very comfortable; and if I knew you all had plenty I would be very well satisfied [...]

I read your letters to Colonel Brown and he said he wanted to see you for he knew you were the right stripe. I was proud of your letters. Nearly everybody in Point Pleasant read them and praised you for your valor. Some said 'they are heroes,' others said 'they had the ring of their Pa.'

These military men here think I made a most glorious retreat from Coals Mouth. They think very few men would have conducted the retreat better, and I got great praise for it. Some had said Captain Young would never get out; others that Captain Young would report at Point Pleasant. When Colonel Lightburn came to Point Pleasant he inquired at once if Captain Young had gotten out.

I don't know but I shall come up in eight or ten days with my men. If Ferd Cash comes out to see you write everything you know and give me a straight account of what the Rebels and neighbors have been doing, and especially what they have said to you and your Ma. It is nearly midnight and I am cold.

We drill twice a day, have Battalion drill once a day; dress parade once. We have eight companies in the 13th Regiment all full.[559] Three companies from Kanawha. They are fine looking men and I believe will fight. At least they want to come up the Kanawha Valley very much. Most of their families are up there. Your Uncle Cy is here, and if it had not been for me he would have gone to Columbus, but I got him paroled and he will be at home soon as our troops get to Charleston. Wes'es horse is here and your grandpa's filly is also here, but I can't get her back. They took her from Cy and they say he and Wes were bushwhacking. They found bullets in Wes'es saddle bags.[560]

As of October 30th, the 13th was for the most part still at Point Pleasant with the exception of some details of men on detached duty.[561] Privates Henry Sands and John T. Newell (both of Company A) were out on detached duty on the 30th, to conduct cattle to army headquarters near the mouth of the "Pocatolus" (Pocataligo). On October 31st, two Privates of Company A (Milton Wilson? and Samuel V. Fluck or Flake) were detached to drive wagons for General Cox's staff.[562]

A look at extant Morning Reports is useful to gain a sense of the strength and health of the various 13th companies. All information and quotations as to specific duty are taken from Regimental Books (Record Group 94 Morning Reports and accompanying Remarks for October 1862, National Archives and Records Administration, Washington D.C.) As of October 31st, Co. A had a total of 3 commissioned officers and 81 enlisted men present and absent. Co. B had total present and absent of 3 commissioned officers and 93 enlisted men and in addition to its captain and 2nd lieutenant: one drummer, one fifer; five sergeants, eight corporals and 70 privates.

There were no "Buglers; Farriers; Blacksmiths; nor Artificiers" (skilled laborers such as mechanics, engineers, wheelwrights, etc.) present. Two enlisted men were reported absent without leave October 23rd through 25th. As for the health of the company, already on October 9th, eight privates were "present sick." One private was "absent sick" at the end of the month. On October 17th, one private was reported and October 26th through 28th, two privates were reported in camp "in arrest and confinement."

Co. C had 3 commissioned officers and 80 enlisted men total, present and absent and these numbers held to the end of the month. Co. D began its term of duty on October 9th with 3 commissioned officers and 82 enlisted men, present and absent. At the end of the month, Thomas Oliver enlisted in Company D, bringing the number of enlisted men to 83. Co. F mustered in with 3 commissioned officers and 80 enlisted men. At the end of the month there was a gain of one recruit enlisted October 12th and two enlisted men deserted on October 25th, bringing the company to 3 commissioned and 79 enlisted men. Co. H had a total of 2 commissioned officers and 66 enlisted men.

While the 13th Regiment was not ordered down the Kanawha with the main body of troops, it was for the time being kept busy taking care of the rear of the army. Larger and smaller squads were being detailed from the regiment for detached duty from October 23rd to the 31st. This duty included scouting expeditions and duty guarding supply trains: all part of the next tier of Cox's concerns (guerrillas and supplying the army). Co. B reports provide examples of orders to the regiment directing such detachments. From October 23rd to 24th, one commissioned officer and ten enlisted men; on October 25th one commissioned officer and thirteen enlisted; October 26th through 28th, four enlisted; October 29th through 31st, one commissioned and fifty-seven enlisted men were on detached service. These details left a total number of Co. B in camp at the end of the month at forty-one enlisted men and two commissioned officers.

Company C had among its non-commissioned staff one drummer present from October 10th through the 31st and one fifer present only from October 10th through 11th. There were no farriers, no blacksmiths, no artificiers present. No one was absent with or without leave and none were in "arrest or confinement". The company had its full complement of officers: 3 commissioned, 5 sergeants and 8 corporals and except for one commissioned officer on detached service (probably Lieut. William Feazel recruiting for the regiment) from October 16th through the 31st, it appears that the company was settling in, assuming the day to day duties of army life. None had "special duty" during the month but from four to nine Privates had "extra duty," with more detailed for this duty at the end month of October. On October 10th, 4 privates had "daily duty." As to the overall health of Co. C, already on October 11th there were 2 non-commissioned officers and 6 privates sick. From October 12th through to the end of the month, there were seven to thirteen privates "present sick" in camp with numbers increasing as the month progressed.

Company D had one drummer and one fifer present from October 9th through 31st. No farriers, blacksmiths, no skilled workers were present during the month and none were present or absent in arrest or confinement. One commissioned officer and one enlisted man were absent with leave from October 25th through 27th. On October 30th, one commissioned officer and two enlisted men were absent with leave. None were absent without leave. Co. D had its full complement of officers with 3 commissioned, 5 sergeants, and 8 corporals. As to duty, only one to three privates had extra duty. On October 9th, already 2 but no more than 4 were sick at any one time during the month. October 11th, 2nd Lieutenant (Michael Roseberry) was also present sick. Only about 1-3 men sick were reported for each day from October 9th (when the company was mustered in) to October 31st.

Company F had present for the month, one drummer and one fifer. No buglers, farriers, blacksmiths, nor artificiers were reported present. The company had its full complement of officers with captain, 1st and 2nd lieutenants, 5 sergeants and 8 corporals. On October 10th, there were 61 privates in camp. Co. F had some minor problems with absenteeism: October 11th through 15th, one enlisted man was reported absent without leave; October 16th — 24th, two enlisted men were reported; and October 31st, two enlisted were again reported absent without leave. On October 25th, 2 enlisted men were reported "deserted." None were present in arrest or confinement. No one had special or detached duty; one non-commissioned officer had extra duty October 11th; one Private had extra duty October 19th — 24th; four Privates had extra duty October 25th — 27th; 6 Privates had extra duty October 28th — 31st; and 2 to 5 Privates had daily duty October 10th — 31st. On October 10th, two but no more than four men were sick at any one time during the month in Co. F.

On October 11th, the first morning reports for Company H were written up. 1st Lieutenant and 48 Privates were reported present. On October 28th, one bugler was reported present and on October 31st, captain, drummer and 56 privates were reported present. Entry for October 29th through 30th records that six enlisted men were absent with leave (men were at this juncture permitted leave to make arrangements for their families and attend to personal business, etc.), and on October 31st, three enlisted men were reported absent with leave. During the month, Co. H gained 18 recruits and a commissioned officer. At the end of the month, the company numbered 2 commissioned officers and 66 enlisted men. As to company duty, one commissioned officer had detached duty (perhaps recruiting) from October 11th through 31st and four to six Privates had daily duty for the four day period of October 28th through 31st. Four men were reported "present sick" on October 11th. For the remainder of the month from one to seven men were present sick with the company. No one was present or absent in arrest or confinement.

Companies A, B, D, E, F and H were all stationed at Point Pleasant for the month of October 1862.[563] On October 31st, Col. Brown reported to Adj. Gen. H.J. Samuels from Point Pleasant regarding recruiting and progress in training the men. Among other news came a request for a commission for Taylor W. Hampton of Ohio:

> I have become convinced that the 13 Va. Regt cannot be filled by recruiting in these parts. The <u>Refugees</u>, who were our only hope now that the Army are moving up the Kanawha, are returning to their homes and will not enlist under any circumstances. What recruits that we are getting are from Ohio.
>
> Mr. Hampton from that State is filling up the Co. commanded by Lieut Griswold, and I have the honor to request that you commission him as Captain in said Company, as he will have enough recruits to entitle him to that position.
>
> By his request, 2d Lieut Wm E Feazel will start to Wheeling in the morning, and if there is any chance to get any recruits for the 13th he will make the necessary arrangements with you.
>
> The Regiment is progressing finely in drill and Garisson duty and I am very anxious to have it filled up.[564]

One D. Hallsty also wrote with some urgency to Wheeling on October 31st from Point Pleasant. Hallsty wired Pierpont that: "The Regiment is furnished with old condemned guns; it is a regiment of superior men and if possible should have good guns immediately."[565]

Monthly Returns for the Department of the Ohio, "Troops of the District of Western Virginia serving in West Virginia, October 31st, 1862," indicate the 13th's position in the District of Western Virginia as a whole. As part of the forces of the District of the Kanawha, the regiment was under of commanded Col. J.A.J. Lightburn. The district had 271 officers and 6,452 men present for duty (not counting the post at Ceredo, which did not return a report).[566] These troops were stationed at three places. The bulk of Lightburn's troops (including the 13th Virginia) were stationed at Point Pleasant. Also at Point Pleasant was the 4th (West) Virginia, Lieut. Col. William H.H. Russel cmdg.; the 8th (West) Virginia, Lieut. Col. John H. Oley cmdg.; the 2nd (West) Virginia Cavalry, Lieut. Col. Rollin S. Curtis cmdg.; the 34th Ohio, Lieut. Col. F.E. Franklin cmdg.; the 89th Ohio Col. John G. Marshall cmdg.; the 91st Ohio, Col. John A. Turley cmdg.; the 92nd Ohio, Col. Nelson H. Van Vorhes cmdg. and a Battery, commanded by one Lieut. De Lille. At Ten-Mile Creek was the 37th Ohio, Lieut. Col. Louis Von Blessingh cmdg.; the 47th Ohio, Major Frederick Heser cmdg. and a

Howitzer Battery, Lieut. James Shiels cmdg. At Ceredo was the 5th West Virginia, Col. John L. Zeigler cmdg.[567]

The District of Western Virginia was divided into three commands. Besides Lightburn, there was the Kanawha Division commanded by Brigadier General George Crook and the Railroad Division commanded by Brigadier General Benjamin F. Kelley. The Kanawha Division was divided into three brigades: First Brigade, at this time commanded by West Point Graduate Colonel Eliakim P. Scammon; Second Brigade commanded by Col. Ebenezer B. Andrews, and Third Brigade by Col. Jonathan Cranor (Craynor). The Kanawha Division also had some cavalry troops under command of Captain G.W. Gilmore.[568]

November and December 1862

The problem of supplying the army had only grown more acute as Gen. Cox advanced his troops and sought to establish posts in the West Virginian interior. Cox complained time and again to Cincinnati of his continuing transportation problems and inability to adequately supply his men stating repeatedly that he had too few wagons and mules. Overland conveyance was the only viable option as the long spell of dry weather had made the Kanawha so low that although smaller craft might be used, steamboats which could convey everything in quantity could not be used. Upon his return to the Kanawha Valley, Cox and his quartermaster had estimated that four hundred wagons and two thousand mules were needed to supply old and new posts. The mules had never been ordered. One hundred wagons promised to Cox's command during the second week of October by Department Headquarters at Cincinnati had never arrived. Another one hundred wagons were contracted to be built at Wheeling. By the start of November seventy of these had been finished but they came slowly: these were at or near Portland, Ohio on their way to Gallipolis. Additional wagons were to be procured from Wheeling as fast as they could be built. Not only was the river low and still falling, but with onset of winter and freezing temperatures if the river froze at this low level, troops posted along the entire length of the Kanawha would be entirely dependent on overland transport for their supplies. Exacerbating the situation was the fact that during the Confederate occupation the Valley had been stripped of subsistence. The Confederates had also obstructed roads and destroyed bridges, ferries, flat-boats, lumber-mills, storehouses and buildings which could have been used for purposes of transport and storage. These had all been cut up and burned.[569] Once winter weather set in roads would soon be rendered impassable. Operations and occupation of Western Virginia could not be pushed farther than occupation of the country west of Flat Top Mountain.

For the foregoing reasons, Cox issued orders to his troops which put them into a kind of holding-mode for the season. This did not imply that there was a lessening of vigilance or perilous duty. One of the trickiest tasks to have in such a locale of forests, hills, mountains and ravines with few roads was the task of scouring the countryside thoroughly for partisan irregulars and to perform this dangerous duty time and time again. To make matters worse, the few roads in Western Virginia became very poor—even impassable—in late fall and winter. Even main roads were bad between major cities such as Grafton, Clarksburg and Charleston making progress difficult at best. Consequently, Gen. Cox charged his field officers to (1) give attention to the most economical organization of their transportation so that as much as possible could be done without outside help (2) to assess the tenability of their posts (3) to move forward into hostile sections disturbed by irregular forces but if they could not advance, to employ smaller groups with great energy to scour the country moving toward the front or into areas disturbed by irregular forces; open communication with every reliable Union citizen and punish and eradicate the guerrilla parties which were found to infest the country. And (4) to assess the condition of buildings etc., for storing quartermaster's and commissary stores and to procure materials to build new buildings and ferry boats. For the time being, troops would follow this plan of operations and prepare for future subsequent duties. Troops in Western Virginia were moved into positions to take possession of the district following the new guidelines.

With the re-allocation of troops came time to settle up accounts for subsistence and lodging. Lieut.-Col. James R. Hall wrote to Adj. Gen. Samuels on November 1st from Point Pleasant forwarding outstanding accounts for the boarding of recruits for the 13th Virginia. Hall explained:

> When the Recruiting Officers for this Regiment commenced bringing in their men the Quartermasters were not willing to issue Rations on the Requisitions of Recruits Officers. consequently it was some days before any arrangements could be made to get subsistence from the commissary department. I have, since my connection with the Regiment been careful, as to the interests of the State by having as fair, and reasonable accounts, as could be had under the circumstances.
>
> I am Sir Very
> Resptly
> James R Hall
> Lt Col 13th Va V Infty[570]

During the months of November and December 1862, 13th Headquarters, Companies C, E, F, and H were stationed at Point Pleasant. Companies A, B, D and G were stationed at Winfield.[571] November 2nd, Capt. J.V. Young's men were all paid.[572]

The transfer of half of the 13th Companies to Winfield on November 10th was part of Cox's strategy to clean out the guerrillas on the lower Kanawha to ensure safe navigation and to keep them from other mischief. This transfer was one of a number of shifts of forces to "hotspots." Cox wished to post "some infantry and cavalry at Hurricane Bridge with instructions to scour the country on both Mud and Hurricane Creeks, and to scour over to Winfield, on the Kanawha." Col. Jonathan Cranor, at Guyandotte, was to drive beyond the mountains a concentration of irregular forces. These were reported at "something less" than 1,000 men located in vicinity of Logan Court House. They were causing "a good deal"of trouble along the Kentucky-Virginia border. Cox, for his part, hoped to reach Floyd on the upper Kanawha, from Charleston.[573] November 3rd, Cranor left with his command moving in the direction of Barboursville taking "Jack Conner with them as a Prisoner."[574] November 4th, Gen. E.P. Scammon (commanding 1st Brigade Kanawha Division) at Gauley Bridge, wrote to Col. W.R. Brown, cmdg. 13th Virginia directing him: "You will at once send these Hd. Qtrs. a monthly report of your Regt."[575] About the same time, Brown also received a similar directive from Major General Wright, commanding the department: "You will direct to forward to this office without delay, the return of your Regt for the month of Oct. You will report the reason why it was not sent at the proper time. By order of Maj. Gen. Wright."[576] 13th Reports were apparently "hindered by Rebel Guerillas."[577]

The Point Pleasant *Register* of November 6th reported on the condition of the Federal armies. The army of the Kanawha was at Charleston. Its advance was beyond Gauley with reinforcements constantly going forward. In Kentucky, Rosecrans was in command in place of Buell. Rosecrans had driven out Braxton Bragg and was now postured to occupy central Tennessee. Ulysses S. Grant at Chattanooga, Tennessee, was being strongly reinforced by convalescent soldiers and new regiments. On November 5th, Lincoln ordered McClellan to be replaced by Burnside to command the Army of the Potomac. The immense Army of the Potomac had been recently paid off, newly clothed and armed and was making advances. Federal operations were underway in Augusta, Bath and Highland Counties, Virginia, and in Pendleton and Pocahontas Counties, Western Virginia. Rosecrans and Grant in Tennessee were actively pressing the enemy. From the frontier department the news was that the Indian war was finished. "The people," noted the *Register* were anxious that after copious promises to the effect that at last the "rebels" in Western Virginia "would be bagged."[578]

On November 8th, Gov. Pierpont proclaimed Thursday November 27th, a day of prayer and Thanksgiving. The purpose of the day being "to give thanks to God for blessings and to pray that the people may be delivered from their afflictions, that victory be granted the Union arms, and that there will be a speedy suppression of the rebellion and restoration of peace." Pierpont recommended that all secular business be suspended and that people attend church. Commanders of Virginia Regiments were requested "wherever they may be stationed to give the soldiers under their command, on that day, the facilities for its proper observation."[579]

On the 10th of November, Companies A, B, D and G, of the 13th Regiment under the command of Lieutenant Colonel J. R. Hall were ordered from Point Pleasant to Winfield, Putnam County. They would stay at that post on garrison duty into 1863. Only Company G under command of Captain Young was ordered away from there on January 28th (1863) to Coals Mouth (also "Coalsmouth") in Kanawha County.[580]

13th soldiers were granted short furloughs, during the month of November. When the soldiers came home, Unionists in their neighborhoods felt more secure. The furloughs, however, were apparently of too short duration for some soldiers whose homes were father away from camp. Some wives and family members came to visit them in the field renting rooms in the nearby town when possible.

The November 13th issue of the Point Pleasant *Register* announced that Reverend Henry Stevens was appointed Chaplain of the 13th Virginia Regiment. The same day, J. Drummond, S.R. Brokmer, L. Barnes, R.S. Woodyard and James L. Clark, clergymen of the Methodist Episcopal Church wrote to Pierpont certifying that "Henry Stephens elected chaplain, 13th Virginia Volunteers is duly authorized to preach the Gospel by the authority of the church."[581]

Jackson's Movements Have Repercussions in the West

On November 13th, General Thomas Jackson ("Stonewall") moved with a large force. He left Winchester heading toward of Romney in Northwestern Virginia. It was feared that a heavy movement into Western Virginia to recapture it and against the B&O Railroad at Grafton and eastward from there was underway. Gen. Cox, at Charleston disposed his troops as best he could to meet such a contingency. He sent Milroy east to Gen. B.F. Kelley at Cumberland, Maryland, that their combined forces might better prevent Jackson from entering Western Virginia. Gen. George W. Morgan's troops at Gallipolis had been ordered to Tennessee to reinforce Rosecrans but Wright counter-ordered. He directed that Morgan's forces be held at Point Pleasant. These orders, however, failed to reach Morgan in time and instead Morgan was sent to Rosecrans. Cox for his part, was pressed to send troops to protect the B&O Railroad but he was reluctant to detach any more troops from the Kanawha Valley. He was vulnerable at the advance post at Gauley. If Gauley were turned, communications would be cut off at Charleston unless Charleston was held in considerable force. In addition, no significant stock piling of supplies had been done at Gauley due to the low state of the river and troops holding at that point could not hold out long as communications with Charleston were interrupted. The necessity of retaining force enough in West Virginia to prevent another occupation of the Valley and to keep communications open were brought especially into focus in lieu of rumors then flying that Marshall and Floyd were "coming that way." "Withdrawing Crook," wrote Cox to Department of Ohio Head Quarters was also not an option and "would leave the valley in a critical position."582 And, argued Cox to further reduce the Union military presence in the Kanawha Valley would have demoralizing effect on the civilian population which had in the meantime "been resuming manufactures and trade." Such reduction could invite a new raid as well. "Until at least the full rigor of winter has set in," contended Cox, the force in the district "ought not, in my opinion, to be further diminished."583

189

For the present, Cox was permitted to keep his troops. Halleck at Washington and Wright, at Department Head Quarters in Cincinnati, however, urged Cox to have sufficient troops posted to hold "the access to the Kanawha Valley" and to be prepared to send a force—perhaps Crook's command numbering about 4,500 at last return—into the valley should protection of the B&O Railroad become urgent.[584] Cox disposed his troops and instructed his field officers accordingly. Cox had his hands full to supply the army, clear the district of guerrillas and prepare an offensive, all the while knowing that enemy movements in progress in the east would "change all the conditions of the problem here."[585]

For the time being, the new threat occasioned by Jackson's movements seems to have brought no change to the 13th Regiment's daily regimen, save perhaps, fueling-up camp rumors and the sense of "living among war's alarms." The regiment—divided half at Point Pleasant, half up the Kanawha River at Winfield across the river from Red Shoals—continued to scout, recruit and render guard and garrison duty. The latest alarm finally settled when within a few days, it became apparent that Jackson would not attempt a movement into Western Virginia and should he advance with a force sufficient to drive Kelley back, he would not be able to subsist his army.[586]

Loyal Western Virginians keeping abreast of the new State issue also had cause for concern. Recent national elections had gone adversely to the Lincoln administration and in Western Virginia it was feared that if the sitting Congress did not admit them as a separate State they would never be admitted to the Union when the new Congress convened. The prevailing feeling among Union citizens was that Western Virginia would never be a prosperous nor a contented population except as an independent State. This was the critical moment. Just one one month remained until the 37th Congress re-convened (the 37th U.S. Congress served from March 1861 to March 1863) to consider new bills, and proponents of the new State movement in eastern counties redoubled their efforts circulating petitions extensively and collecting signatures in the panhandle and in the whole country east of the Little Kanawha. It is worth noting in this context that Mason County and counties to the west "were slow to bestir themselves" on this issue.[587]

During mid-November administrative issues in the army were tended to. F.H. Pierpont's letter of November 6th to Col. Brown and Lieut. Col. Hall suggests that obtaining more recruits to fill the last two companies of the 13th would be no easy task and that there had been more problems designating which men to be commissioned. Pierpont wrote:

> I have made enquiries in all the Counties in the N.W. part of the states about recruits and I fear I shall not be able to raise any more. The old regts are working hard for new recruits. They can get a few of their friends But none for New regiments — I would advise

you to get good energetic men for your officers — Each to raise his quota — and let the officers head their lists with the names of the officers and then there can be no dispute about an election.[588]

Then on November 14th, Maj. Gen. Cox issued Special Order No. 41, providing that

I. The Brigade at present commanded by Col. E. Siber consisting of the 37th + 47th Ohio the 8th + 13th Va. Regts. Infantry and Fishers Mountain Howitzer Battery will report to Brig. Genl Geo. Crook and hereafter form part of the 1st Kanawha Division.

II. The Brigade at present commanded by Col. Hugh Ewing consisting of 30th 23rd +12th Ohio Regiments of Infantry McMullins Battery + Harrisons + Gilmores troops of Cavalry will report to Brig Genl E. P. Scammon and hereafter form part of the 2d Kanawha Division.

III. Major Hoffman with Companies C + B 2d Va. Cavalry will report to Genl Scammon and the remainder of that Regiment report to Genl Crook.

IV. Genl Crook will have command of the Kanawha Valley below and including Camp Piatt and the right bank of Kanawha and New River above including the Gauley Valley.

V. Genl Scammon will have command of the left bank of New River and of the Kanawha to Camp Piatt and the Country South of that boundary within the District.

VI. The above named Commandants of Divisions will put their troops in posts for the most advantageous occupation and quitting of the territory assigned them subject to the approval of the General Commanding the District. If active military operations of the whole force shall become necessary in the absence of the Comdg General from the Kanawha Valley the command of both Divisions will devolve upon Genl Crook as ranking Officer who will be obeyed and respected accordingly; but reports etc. in the Staff Departments will be made to these Head Quarters by Divisions.[589]

November 14[th], Col. Edward Siber commanding 2[nd] Brigade at Charleston, Virginia, wrote to Col. W.R. Brown commanding the 13[th] Regiment at Point Pleasant regarding the insufficiency of his latest reports:

I have rec[eive]d your Morning report of 12 inst. You will send consolidated reports to these Hd. Qrs. on the 7 — 17 — + 27 days of each Month. The detached companies will report to you as often as you may deem necessary and at least four times a month.

In your reports you will include all the companies stating their stations and commanding officer.

You will also include the report of Public horses + mules. Serviceable + unserviceable Present + absent. Horses and Mules reported in a separate column.[590]

On November 15th, Colonel Crook was promoted to the rank of Brigadier General U.S. Volunteers and returned to the Kanawha Valley with his brigade to relieve Cox and take command of the Kanawha Division. On the 15th, Brigadier-General George Crook took command of the 1st Kanawha Division and issued General Order No. 1 regarding the disposition of his troops. The forces in his command were the

I. [...] 37th + 47th Regts O.V.I. and the 8th + 13th Regts Va V. I. the 2d Regt. Va. Cavalry excepting Cos B + C.

II. The 1st Brigade will be composed of the 11th, 37th + 49th Regts O.V.I. and Simmonds Battery of Light Artillery to be commanded by Col E Siber and will be stationed as follows the 11th Regt O V I at Summerville Va, the 37th Regt O V I at Gauley Bridge and the 47th O V I at Gauley Mount.

III The Regiments composing the remainder of the Division will be stationed as follows, the 28th Regt O V I and 2d Va Cavalry at Camp Piatt, the 36th Regt O V I at Charleston the 8th Regt Va V. I. at the Mouth of Cole, one half of the 13th Va. Regt (5 Cos. of the 13th) at Red House and one half (5 Companies) at Point Pleasant. Until further orders they will make their reports direct to these Head Quarters. All Companies belonging to the 2d Va Regt Cavalry will report to their Regimental Commanders at Camp Piatt immediately except Cos B + C. These movements will be commenced without delay.[591]

The above order indicated no change for the 13th Regiment. The regiment was still divided. Lieut.-Col. J.R. Hall was in command of the post at Winfield and Col. W.R. Brown in command at 13th Regiment headquarters at Point Pleasant. In addition to the five 13th Companies stationed at Point Pleasant, the 106th Virginia Militia, J.P.R.B. Smith commanding, had its headquarters at Point Pleasant and was tending to business there.[592] On November 15th, there was action on the Guyandotte River and Captain Milton J. Ferguson (commanding 16th Virginia Cavalry Regiment, C.S.A.) of Jenkins' band was captured at Buchhannon. Also on the 15th, J.V. Young wrote to J.R. Hall, reporting on the results of a scout his Company made in the vicinity of the Middle Fork of Mud River:

> [... O]ur progress to this place has been quite successful having cap-tured this far. Sixteen contraband horses, two yoke of cattle, and two prisoners, and have a fair prospect of having all our company mounted on our return. Yesterday morning we sent a despatch to Col. Oley at Coals' Mouth giving him information and asking cooperation. He had the Kindness to send us a despatch in answer informing us he would send us fifty men to operate with us and they will form a junction with us tomorrow evening. There has been a party of jayhawkers here within the past three days, and we think we will be on their heels by tomorrow or the next day at farthest Capt Williams had gone wild, and is now a perfect jayhawker[593]

On November 23rd, Brig. Gen. Crook issued General Orders No. 3, pertaining to the organization and the administrative regimen expected of his field officers:

> I. Commandants of Brigades, Regts. & Detachments will make regular Monthly and tri-monthly reports to these Head Qtrs.: the tri-monthly reports will be promptly made on the 10th, 20th and last days of Each month respectively.

> II. All persons employed on Extra or daily duty in this Div. belong-ing to Brigades, Regts, or Detachments not connected with this Div. are hereby relieved from duty and will report to their Regtl + Co. Commanders.[594]

When the men of the 13th joined the old Kanawha Division, they found them-selves brigaded with veterans who had won success in their previous campaigns. They had an *esprit de corps*. Active duty in the face of the enemy had given them discipline, confidence and "the long and arduous marches of hundreds of miles over difficult mountain roads had inured them to its hardships."[595] Moreover, with George Crook at the helm, the bar had been raised. On November 24th, Col. W.R. Brown issued General Order No. 2 from 13th Regiment Headquarters at Point Pleasant, directing his men to conduct themselves professionally as becoming a soldier:

> The Colonel commanding has seen with regret many practices indulged in by the men of his command prejudicial to good order

and military discipline and therefore orders that the officers suppress among the non-commissioned and privates under their control, all immoral and vulgar conduct, such as card playing profane swearing, loud and indecent conversation etc. All violations of this order will be severely punished.[596]

Thursday, November 27th, the 13th Regiment and all troops constituting the Virginia Regiments observed Thanksgiving Day. In accord with Governor Pierpont's Proclamation, all were enjoined to strictly observe the day. James R. Hall issued orders to his detachment of companies at Winfield that all duty, except Guard duty, be suspended, and the day was to "be in every respect duly reverenced and all the soldiers to attend divine service." The day was to be set aside for Thanksgiving and prayer, to thank the "Almighty God for his many blessings, and that this unholy Rebellion may be brought to a speedy close, and that peace and prosperity may again be restored to our once happy country."[597]

Extant regimental records for Cos. A, B, C, D, F and H provide some indication of day-to-day military life for the soldiers at this time. Some discrepancies exist and are indicated. Company A was stationed at Camp Samuels, at Point Pleasant from November 1st to November 10th. On Monday, November 10th, Co. A with Companies A, B and G were ordered to Winfield Putnam County; six men of Co. A—Michael Baxter and Joseph Scott among these—were left sick at the Hospital at Point Pleasant.[598] On the 10th of November, Co. A with Cos. B, D and G was detached from 13th regimental Head Quarters at Point Pleasant to occupy and guard the Post at Winfield.[599] On November 11th, Co A moved to "Camp Siber" at Winfield. It remained at Camp Siber through November 30th, 1862.[600] Cos. A and B were detached on scouting duty at a time coincident with a threatened attack on Sommerville around November 22nd, by "McCausland's regiment of infantry and about 1,000 cavalry."[601] On November 27th, Benjamin F. High, Private in Company E, died of "congestion of brain" in Hospital at Point Pleasant and his "Corpse [was] sent home."[602]

Morning Reports for Company A indicate that present and absent for the month totaled three commissioned officers and eighty-one enlisted men. Commissioned and non-commissioned officers consisted of: one captain, one 1st lieutenant, one 2nd lieutenant, 3 sergeants, 6 corporals, one drummer and one fifer. November 13th, two more sergeants were added. On November 14th, a recruit was received and the drummer lost his position and went back into the rank and file. November 15th, another recruit was received, raising the number of enlisted men to 83. November 24th, however, one enlisted man was discharged for disability and November 29th, one enlisted man died of disease, thus, by the end month the company again numbered 81 enlisted men.

Co. A had detached duty every day during the month of November. On Saturday, November 1st, 2nd Lieutenant Theophilus Maher and 11 men were detached to conduct 124 head of cattle to Charleston. Maher returned on Tuesday, November 11th, to Point Pleasant but with just 9 men. On November 1st, Captain Johnson and 10 men returned by way of Ripley to camp. On Monday, November 3rd, Corporals (Robert H. or Andrew J.) Davis and William H. Hoffman were detached to drill 11 privates to drive wagons to Charleston laden with corn. Wednesday, November 12th, Lieutenants Greenbury Slack and Theophilus Maher with 9 men and baggage left Point Pleasant on the steamboat *Glenwood*" to join the balance of the company at Winfield. On November 14th, 1st Lieut. Slack was ordered with 20 men from Co. A to escort Lieutenant Feazel and Sergeant Hovey of the 4th Virginia on a recruiting tour up Coal and Elk Rivers. On the 28th, Privates Milton Wilson and Samuel Flake, Lieutenant Slack and 38 enlisted men reported back from recruiting expedition. November 15th to 21st, 1st Lieutenant Slack and 38 enlisted men were on detached duty. On Friday, November 21st, James Hudson Tully was relieved at Charleston from "waggoning" and reported to his company (A) on his return from Charleston. November 21st, Captain J.W. Johnson was ordered out with 22 men from Co. A to go on a scout to Mud Bridge (modern day Milton, Cabell County) 22 miles southwest of the Winfield post. On Monday, November 24th, Captain J.W. Johnson and his 22 men returned from their scout of the Mud Bridge area. Also on the 24th, three of the thirteen men detailed for "wagon service" returned to camp. Friday, November 28th, four more men detailed on wagon service reported for duty on their return from Charleston.[603]

The health of Co. A declined during the month of November. For the first two weeks of the month, the number of sick hovered around five but beginning November 15th and continuing through to the end of the month, with the onset of cold winter weather, sickness was on the rise. By November 30th, the number of sick had reached as high as nineteen. November 28th, one enlisted man (Private Frederick Frame) had "died of disease."

On Saturday, November 15th, Michael Baxter, one of the men left sick at Point Pleasant on November 11th, when Company A left Point Pleasant for Winfield, reported back to the company for duty. Thursday, November 20th, Baxter was ordered to the regimental surgeon at Point Pleasant to procure trusses (for hernia?). On Sunday, November 23rd, Baxter returned from Point Pleasant with trusses. Though a young man in his early twenties, Private Michael Baxter was subject to chronic health problems. In less than a year, on August 12th, 1863, he would be dead of consumption.

On November 15th, William C., G., or A.. Hodges, who had been enlisted in August by Lieutenant William Hawkins, but who had not yet been mustered, was entered on the Roll Book of Company A as a "Recruit." On November 15th or 20th, Hodges was ordered to the regimental surgeon at Point Pleasant to receive his initial medical examination. On November 23rd, Hodges was rejected by surgeon for disability and returned to Charleston.[604]

Monday, November 17th: forty-eight-year-old Jo[seph] Scott, another of the men left sick at Point Pleasant Hospital when Company A moved to Winfield on November 11th, reported again for duty. In the afternoon of Friday, November 28th, Private Frederick Frame died from "congestive fever" (cause of death also recorded as "brain fever") after "a severe illness of four days" at Winfield. Saturday, November 29th, Lieutenant Colonel James R. Hall, commander of the Post at Winfield, permitted Frederick's brother Christopher C. Frame and Corporal John Baxter to escort the body home. On Sunday, November 30th, Corporal Baxter and C.C. Frame detached to escort the body of Frederick home by steamboat. C.C. Frame returned from Charleston to Co. A on Sunday, December 4th.[605]

Company B Morning Reports show that the company was stationed at Point Pleasant from November 1st to the 11th. It left Point Pleasant on November 11th, and "[a]fter a fatiguing march" arrived at Camp Brown in Putnam County on November 12th. From November 12th through the 30th, Co. B was stationed at Camp Brown in Putnam County. The Company had one drummer present for the entire month. One fifer was present from November 1st through the 8th; the company had no fifer from November 9th through the 18th; when from November 19th to the 31st, again a fifer was recorded present. On November 8th, a new recruit, Isiah McCoy, enlisted and was sworn into the U.S. Service the same day. November 16th, one enlisted man, Private Nelson O. Rice, died in Hospital at Point Pleasant "of disease." The number of present and absent held steady for the month at 3 commissioned officers and 93 enlisted men. One enlisted man was absent without leave November 14th through 21st.

As in Co. A, members of Co. B were on detached service each day of November. From November 1st through the 21st, five to ten enlisted men were on detached duty; November 22nd through the 24th, one to two commissioned officers and thirty-one enlisted men were detached; and November 25th through 30th, eight to nine enlisted were serving on detached duty. On November 21st, Lieutenant L.C. Rayburn with 16 Privates, 4 Corporals and 2 Sergeants, the whole under command of Capt. Johnson of Co. A, was ordered on a scout with 5 days rations. Overall, Co. B had seven to seventeen of its members present sick during the month of November, with two absent sick from November 2nd to the 30th. November 4th, one musician was present in arrest or confinement.[606]

Company C Morning Reports indicate that the command was stationed at Point Pleasant from November 1st to the 30th. One drummer was noted as present for the entire month and that the company had no fifer, farrier and blacksmith, nor artificiers present. No one was absent with leave, and one enlisted man was absent without leave from November 20th through the 30th. At the end of the month the company had present and absent three commissioned officers and eighty enlisted men. While Cos. A and B had detached duty every day of the month, few soldiers of Co. C had detached service. Co. C had a larger proportion of privates on extra duty than had Cos. A and B. Co. C had six to thirteen privates on extra duty with the numbers declining during the second half of the month. One commissioned officer of Co. C was on detached service from November 1st through the 30th, and November 14th to November 30th, three enlisted men had detached duty. The company had no absent sick but reported twelve to fifteen present sick for the month.[607]

Company D Morning Reports show it was stationed at Camp Samuels, Point Pleasant from November 1st through the 30th. The company was fortunate in its music corps, as it had one drummer and one fifer present for the entire month. Co. D reported no farriers and blacksmiths, nor artificiers present. The company had a significant number of soldiers on short leave of absence during the month. One commissioned officer was absent with leave from November 4th through the 6th; five enlisted men were absent with leave November 6th to 7th; one enlisted man was absent with leave November 9th and 10th; and four enlisted were absent with leave November 11th through the 13th. Two enlisted men were absent without leave November 14th to 30th. One enlisted man was reported deserted November 21st through the 25th. At the end of the month Co. D had present and absent a total of three commissioned officers and eighty-three enlisted men.

As for the nature of duties performed by Co. D: no one had special duty. Five privates had extra duty for the entire month; November 1st, four non-commissioned officers and seven privates had daily duty. November 11th through the 13th, five enlisted men had detached duty; November 14th through 20th, two commissioned officers and twenty-two enlisted men had detached service; November 23rd through 24th, ten enlisted men were on detached and November 29th through 30th, one enlisted man had detached duty.

Co. D enjoyed good health for the month of November. There were just one to four men present sick, a number which included Captain Simon Williams, sick on November 8th and then 1st Lieutenant James Hanna, sick on November 9th and 10th. Four enlisted men were reported absent sick November 29th and 30th. The company had no one in arrest or in confinement during the month.[608]

Morning Reports for Company F indicate that the company was stationed at Point Pleasant. It had one drummer present for the entire month and from November 1st through 19th and November 26th through 28th, one fifer was present. No buglers, farriers, blacksmiths, and no artificiers were present with the company.

November 4th through the 6th and 10th and 11th, one commissioned officer had leave of absence. Two enlisted men were reported absent without leave on November 1st, and one enlisted man was noted as absent without leave on November 2nd to 3rd and 8th. One new recruit, Private Jarret C. W. Hackworth, joined the Company on November 9th or 11th, and two enlisted men, William W. Harper and James Wilson, were promoted on November 22nd, and "were dropped from the reports." At the end of the month the company numbered a total of three commissioned officers and seventy-eight enlisted men. Two to three non-commissioned officers had extra duty for most of the month (November 3rd through the 30th). Four to thirteen privates had extra duty each day of the month. Among these was Private B.N. Tilden detailed for "Extra Duty" on November 21st, in the Quartermasters Department at Charleston "by order of Gen'l. Crook." From three to six privates had daily duty each day and no one had detached duty. November 24th, John M. Young, R.B. Shrewsberry and Samuel P. Robinson returned from Charleston. November 28th, Private John Lewis was detailed for "Ambulance Driver."

The health of Co. F was fair for the month of November. There were present sick in camp from two to ten men. From November 20th to the 25th and again November 29th and 30th, the company fifer was sick. No one was absent sick. One private was in arrest or confinement November 3rd through the 5th. No one was absent in confinement.[609]

Company H Morning Reports for the same period show that the company was stationed at Point Pleasant, Virginia, for the entire month of November. Reports for those present and absent indicate that Captain J.W. Hampton returned to the Company on November 12th. A drummer was noted as present November 1st through the 30th. Two to seven enlisted men were granted leave of absence between November 1st through 25th. One enlisted man was reported absent without leave November 1st to 6th; 8th to 11th; 14th; 19th and 24th to 30th. Two enlisted men were reported absent without leave on November 7th. Co. H gained at least four new recruits, who joined on dates variously given as November 1st; the 12th (Oliver Taylor enlisted November 12th, 1862); the 13th (William Reynolds enlisted November 13, 1862); the 15th (Jacob Shoemaker enlisted November 15th, 1862); the 19th (John Snyder enlisted November 19th, 1862); the 25th (Francis M. Crofoot and James M. Drake enlisted November 25th, 1862); and the sixty-five-year-old, Charles F. Hoy, professional musician, enlisted as musician November 30th, 1862 at Point Pleasant. He was discharged for disability before being mustered into service. The company lost two enlisted men during the month. Albert Jamison was discharged on November 8th, by "Civil Authority" and another enlisted man, Monterville Perdue, formerly a resident of Wayne County, "died of disease &c." in Regimental Hospital at Point Pleasant on November 28th, 1862. At the end of the month, Co. H had a total, present and absent of three commissioned officers and seventy-four enlisted men. No soldier had special duty or extra duty. Three to six Privates had daily duty each day and one commissioned officer had detached duty each day. As the month progressed the health of the company worsened. There were from four to twenty men present sick with the lower numbers during the first three days of November. None were absent sick, nor was any one present or absent in confinement.[610]

Rumors of Rebels in Logan County

On November 14th, Gen. Floyd, commanding the Virginia State Line, sent out a strong cavalry force under Col. John N. Clarkson (cmdg. First Brigade, Virginia State Line Cavalry) to operate against "the enemy in Wayne, Cabell &c. Counties," "to prevent Yankee forces from occupying the country between the Kanawha Valley and the Kentucky border and to destroy the military organization of the country under the traitor Wheeling government." Clarkson set out from Chapmanville on the 14th, and proceeded down the Guyandotte River in the direction of Cabell. On the 15th, Clarkson "fell in with a detachment of the enemy, which he quickly routed and dispersed" and continued the march until he was within a few miles of the Ohio River. Clarkson, according to Floyd, succeeded in "breaking up the Home Guard organizations of the enemy, which are very numerous in all that country, and taking prisoners every day." "A strong guard of Yankee troops" protecting a Wayne County assessor (representative of the Restored Government of Virginia) "was attacked and dispersed after a short skirmish," in which some Union soldiers were killed and wounded and a few were taken prisoner. Clarkson then proceeded to the Sandy River "to attack a large and formidable organization" of Yankees there "composed mainly of the native population" who had posted themselves strongly "amid the cliffs and forests upon the precipitous banks of that river." These according to Floyd, Clarkson took by complete surprise, killing and wounding a number of them and taking a large number of prisoners. After that, Clarkson formed a junction with Floyd at the mouth of Pidgeon Creek in Logan County on the Kentucky border. "The military organizations," wrote Floyd which were "very numerous and well appointed in every particular, were almost entirely destroyed, and the attempts to set up the spurious government were entirely foiled."[611]

On November 28th, Maj. Gen. Cox wrote to Crook at Gauley concerning "numerous" rumors coming from "different quarters" that the enemy was in Logan County "with some force, both of cavalry and infantry." Cox referred Crook to the reports (not found) of Lt.-Col. Hall and Major Schache which Captain Kennedy would be sending on to Crook that evening. Cox advised Crook that it was desirous that whatever their force, "that country should be thoroughly secured" and for this purpose Crook was to proceed to Brownstown on the 29th, with all or part of the Thirtieth Regiment to unite there with whatever was available to be taken of the Twenty-eighth Regiment and to "send them, with some cavalry, out through Logan County to, if possible catch or destroy part of the enemy"— Crook's force going on the expedition to be "about 1,000 men strong, and [...] prepared to move rapidly." Mills and "such other property at Logan Court House" were to be burned "to effectually prevent the place being used as a rendezvous in the future."[612] Brigadier General George Crook wrote to Lieutenant Colonel James Hall with the following orders:

> Charleston, Va. November 28, 1862
> Lieut. Col. J. R. Hall,
> Thirteenth Virginia, Red House:
>
> Put yourself in communication with Lieutenant-Colonel Oley, at Coalsmouth immediately. If your forces united, after leaving a sufficient camp guard, can be at the intersection of the road ten miles in front of Winfield tomorrow, sufficiently strong without risks to engage the enemy, do so. If not, keep your scouts well out on that side of the river and report anything of importance to the headquarters.
>
> By command of Brigadier. Gen. George Crook.
> R.P. Kennedy,
> Captain and Assistant Adjutant-General.[613]

On the same day (Nov. 28th), Cox had his Adjutant G.M. Bascom write to Colonel J.L. Zeigler, commanding the 5th Virginia Infantry, then at Ceredo, engaged in exchanging 'hostile compliments' (to use a colloquialism) with Captain Clawhammer Witcher's bands which infested Wayne County. Bascom advised Ziegler that "Floyd with some 700 or 800 men, principally cavalry, had been sighted on the Upper Guyandotte" and that Ziegler was to send out "scouting parties well out in that direction" and to "report promptly" all information obtained. If Floyd were to show himself, Ziegler was to communicate with Colonel Cranor, then at Guyandotte, and together "take the most effectual measures to drive the enemy back."[614]

The Confederate activity reported in Logan County and on the Guyandotte River involved all military posts and the 13th Regiment at Winfield was on the alert as the following letter from Patrick H. Caldwell of Company B, suggests. Caldwell wrote to his father on November 29th, on a fine example of patriotic paper:

Company B
13th Va reg
In care of capt Stewart
Winfield Putnam County Va November the 29th 1862.

Dear father I have taken my pen in hand to let you know that I am well at this time and hope that these lines ma find you all well I wrote a letter home some two weeks ago and recieved no awnser we have been looking for the rebels to come in for some time but I guess the darn fools are afraid to come I guess it is another Jenkins I have seen that great herican bridge and that awful mud river and what a place it is nothing more at present so I will bring my letter to a close write soon and let me no how you are all geting along

P. H. Caldwell to mr Robert Caldwell
direct your letter to Winfield Putnam County
Virginia Company B
13th Va reg In care of capt Stewart[615]

End of November and early December, William E. Feazel was still about the business of recruiting and reminding Wheeling to settle accounts regarding, presumably, expenses incurred by private citizens in connection with the boarding of recruits. Feazel wrote to Adj. Gen. Samuels on November 30th and December 7th, as follows, respectively:

Sir
I have this day made application to Col. Wm R Brown to ask you for a 1st Lt.'s com[mmission] for me and for a 2nd Lt.'s com for William Hovey I am filling a Company fast and there is an officer of the regular Army at Charleston that will muster me and my men into the Service as soon as I get 42 men William Hovey is helping me to Raise my Company with a Special Understanding that he is to have a Lieutenants com. Gov Pierpoint wrote to Col. Brown to have the Rolls of the next Companies headed with the officers names that are to be commissioned and not have anymore elections

Your Respect Wm E Feazel[616]

Sir
I have the honor to request you if you have not attended to those accounts I sent to you that you do so and Send the checks to me by Lt. John D Young and also Send Henry Snyder's check by him for

his account Sent by mail Mr Young is al [...]right and Mr Snyder and all others are in need of their money

Sir I am your Obt Set.
Wm E Feazel
2nd Lt. 13th va vol inf
Rect officer[617]

On December 16th (1862), Lieutenant Colonel Hall, at Camp Piatt, sent a telegraph to Governor Pierpont informing him that in the 13th Virginia, there were "7 full companies, not counting Captain Young's company and 20 men were recruited on Dec. 8th." Hall added that "no more recruits can be gotten in this valley [the Kanawha Valley]."[618]

December 1862

Early in December, the designation of Crook's Kanawha Division was changed to "First Kanawha Division." Lightburn's Division was designated Second Kanawha Division and placed under the command of Eliakim P. Scammon.[619] Scammon made his headquarters at Fayette Court House; Fayette at this time— a barren wasteland. Crook had command of the Kanawha Valley with headquarters at Charleston. On December 11th, Major General Cox issued General Order No.7 establishing Head Quarters for the District of Western Virginia "for the present" at Marietta, Ohio, due to the "lowness of the rivers."[620] All Official Communications were for the time-being to be addressed to Marietta.[621] The removal of Headquarters to Marietta, on the north side of the Ohio River, made communication with the commanding General "a little troublesome," as that point was "somewhat difficult of access," due to the low stage of water. Freezing over of either the Ohio or Kanawha would only make access to district headquarters more problematic.[622]

National forces in Western Virginia continued to pursue Confederate forces reported to be operating within their districts. Even with the close of the season for active campaigning, Rebels were still actively engaged in guerrilla warfare. Guerrillas in the northwestern counties, already in the business for nearly two years, had become very cunning. They knew every mud path, stream bed and hiding place inland from the Ohio River for seventy-five miles. When Federal troops pulled out of an area, raids upon loyal citizens could be expected as retribution.

To combat regular troops, guerrillas would hover unseen "skulking" around Federal troops or squads of men detached on reconnaissance or guard duty and then, when the Federal men halted for a rest, the guerrillas would attack and "run." During the ensuing confusion of attending to wounded, etc., the guerrillas perfected their escape. In mountainous areas, this system of warfare was carried on "wholesale." Robbery, murder, stripping of "Union citizens of horses, cattle and every other kind of property," seizure and taking "away captive the people themselves" including "many of the foremost and worthy Western Virginian citizens" who ended up "suffering in Southern prisons and d[ying] of starvation."[623]

Scouring the country and engaging these partisans, regardless of the winter weather and exceedingly rough terrain, was continued by Western Virginia forces unabated. The soldiers all suffered to greater and lesser extent from exposure. Frost bite and illness induced by living in the field was an ever-present possibility. Detachments from the 13th had their share of exposure: marching, picketing, foraging, scouting for Rebels and truant Federal soldiers, and guard duty conducting wagon trains. Correspondence of 13th soldiers suggests that there was no murmur of complaint made by the men under their hardships, as they were protecting their homes and friends.

The disposition of the 13th companies—half at Point Pleasant, half at Winfield—continued during the month of December. Regimental Headquarters continued at Point Pleasant. 13th Companies continued scouting duty as weather would permit. On December 9th, Capt. J.W. Johnson was ordered with 19 men from his command (Co, A) to scout to Mud Bridge "and beyond." They returned on December 15th, with "2 wounded Rebel prisoners and 2 Union prisoners released by this capture."[624] This scout south into Cabell County, to Mud Bridge on the Kanawha, "and beyond" may well have been ordered in response to raiding being done by Colonel Clarkson through Logan into Cabell County. (See *infra*.)

Scouring of the countryside for Rebels did not always proceed according to "lex militaire," but according to the notion of "just deserts."[625] This was the case for Charles T. Hedges, formerly of Liberty but at that time, a resident of near Spencer, Roane County. He reportedly met with a terrible end sometime during the first week of December. Since the outbreak of the Rebellion, Hedges had apparently been a very active leader of a gang of guerrillas. The outrages perpetrated by the gang had at last become unbearable, and Union dragoons rode up to Hedges' house, called him out and shot him dead in the presence of his wife and two small children. They then dismounted and set fire to his clothes and "burned them to a crisp on the body."[626]

Meanwhile, outsiders criticized the lack of effort in Western Virginia. The December 4th issue of the Gallipolis *Journal* took a critical tone in two small articles reporting about the army of West Virginia. The Kanawha correspondent[s] reported that Cox's army was sent up the Kanawha merely to hold it, with no intention of doing anything else but go into winter quarters. The army was scattered "up and down the Valley of the Kanawha, as safe from rebel attacks as though north of the Ohio river." There was no news to publish, continued correspondent and as far as could be gleaned from appearances

the programme of last winter is literally repeated, only a little more so. Government steamers are leaving daily, loaded with forage and supplies, and returning with 'old horses.' Every energy of our A.Q[uarter] M[asters] and C.S. at this point is taxed to the utmost to keep up with supplies, and the country is being exhausted of forage for an immense army doing—what? We pause for a reply. [...] The secesh are most outrageously let alone, and my short experience satisfies me that on the whole, it is a 'leetle' safer to be secesh than Union in this region. Some of the boys have had to return a lot of horses, hogs, cattle &c., taken from the secesh, by order of the Commanding officer —which don't go down very well with many from whom the secesh stole everything. [... W]e have done nothing as yet, toward crushing the rebels, and for all practical results, might as well have staid at Point Pleasant.[627]

In December, "[a] deplorable state of things" existed in Cabell County and at Guyandotte due to "the presence of rebel cavalry and horse thieves." Colonels Clarkson, [Henry M.] Beckley and Gen. Floyd were operating in the Logan-Chapmanville area. Floyd's troops, some 1500 men, used Logan Court House as a base and "form[ed] the nucleus"[628] to which Colonels Clarkson and Beckley attached their cavalry commands. Chapmanville (also called Chapmansville) was a small town on the Guyan River in Logan where secessionists of the surrounding country tended to meet. Governor Pierpont requested General Cox to give attention to this section of country and stated:

> There can be no safety to the people in Cabell and Wayne as long as these rebel troops have a headquarters on the heads of those Streams which empty into the Ohio in those Counties. I am in great hopes that some move may be made in that direction before the season becomes so far advanced that nothing can be done. Those people who are left behind are becoming clamorous for some protection. They have sent nearly all their able bodied Union men into the field. The section has done its whole duty in that respect. And they have a right to ask for protection.[629]

During about the second week of December, U.S Marshall Bumgardner of Cabell County reported at Point Pleasant that Colonel Clarkson, who had come down through Tazewell and Logan counties with a large cavalry force, had been scouring Cabell County and the country between Big Sandy and Kanawha rivers for several days capturing prisoners and driving off cattle, horses and hogs. On Wednesday, Thursday and Friday, December 10th, 11th and 12th, Clarkson was in Cabell County and approached within 12 miles of Guyandotte. With no Federal troops near enough to deter him, Clarkson captured about 40 Union men and took them away with him, besides also taking a large number of hogs and cattle. Clarkson came down through Tazewell and Logan Counties and returned by the same route. Col. Ziegler with the 5th Virginia Infantry at Ceredo could not go after Clarkson because, according to reports, he was too busy fighting Captain "Clawhammer" Witcher's bands, then actively operating in Wayne county.[630]

Alarms continued to plague the area. On December 19th, Thomas Hayslip, postal worker at Guyandotte wrote to H.J. Samuels at Wheeling regarding a letter he had found in his post office desk indicating that a raid at Guyandotte could soon be expected. Hayslip requested help for himself and the town. Federal troops, continued Hayslip, had left Guyandotte that morning (December 19th) and that as a matter of course when troops were withdrawn, Guyandotte was threatened. Hayslip continued at length observing that he thought it strange that a point like Guyandotte should be so neglected in general, and particularly as no "less than 4 steamers" were aground opposite Guyandotte since "day before yesterday" (December 17th). Hayslip asked for Samuels to use his influence to have other troops stationed at Guyandotte. Until "now," Hayslip wrote, he had "to flee to Ohio every time the Federal troops leave Guyandotte"and that in the last 8 months he expended "nearly $100 in expenses just to leave the town, and if the rebels ever get me I shall have to pull hemp."[631]

Why the 13th was not detached to tend to Confederate operations in Logan and Cabell Counties is anyone's guess. Certainly the time of year was not conducive to any kind of field duty for infantry and Clarkson and Beckley were mounted. Perhaps it was thought, "if the Rebels want to operate in this winter weather, let them." In any event, the 13th had no horses to scout as mounted infantry and would have to take their provender with them, as they could not be supplied overland in Logan County, nor even at Guyandotte due to the impassable state of the rivers. Col. Brown and the 13th Virginia would soon have cavalry support in the shape of a company being formed at Ceredo in December 1862 by Lieutenant John S. Witcher. These troops would become Company G, 3rd Virginia Cavalry Regiment. For the next year and half, Witcher's Co. G would be attached to and often operate in conjunction with the 5th and 13th Virginia Regiments during their period of garrison duty in Cabell, Putnam and Wayne Counties.

The second or third week of December, Brig. Gen. George Crook visited Point Pleasant with his staff. Just a year or so before, while as Colonel of the 36th Ohio, he had stood on a porch near Camp Sunday Road almost unnoticed except by some soldiers of the 11th Ohio Volunteer Infantry (the 11th stationed at Point Pleasant during fall and winter of 1861) who recalled his appearance:

> His costume was half civil, half military, and as he had probably been taking it rough and tumble his appearance was not very prepossessing. We judged him to be Captain or Lieutenant of a company of Union bushwhackers and we intend this in no disparaging sense, for it required a smart man to fill such a position at that time.[632]

Crook arrived at the Point enjoying fame and in high command. His training in Indian methods of tracking game in warfare in Oregon and California in the decade between his graduation from West Point in 1852 and his commission as Colonel of the 36th Ohio, prepared him well for mountain warfare in Virginia. He had rendered highly effective service fighting both Confederate regulars and partisan irregulars in interior counties that had been despaired of. The mountainous and rolling Virginia landscape leant itself to the effective use of maneuvers designed to deceive and surprise an enemy with a sudden lightning strike as employed by the highly mobile Native warrior tribes of the West, and he drew on this training to quiet the mountain counties west of the Alleghenies. Certainly, he had not learned this at West Point which at that time still offered an education based squarely on principles of Napoleonic warfare and the grand movement armies. His unostentatious appearance, plainspoken, quiet manner ingratiated him to strangers and this together with keen powers of observation made possible effective intelligence gathering without which counter-guerrilla operations were unlikely to succeed. Crook became "one of the shrewdest generals in the world for tricking an enemy."[633] Indeed, some biographers have suggested that Crook learned to fight Indians in West Virginia as his successful campaigns against great Indian war chiefs such Geronimo and Red Cloud (who called Crook "Grey Fox") seem to suggest.

When General Cox reorganized his army for the campaign of 1862 he put Crook, then Colonel of the 36th Ohio, in command of a brigade composed of the 11th, 36th, and 44th Ohio Infantry Volunteers and a portion of the 2nd Virginia Cavalry. In action at Lewisburg on May 23rd, 1862, Crook defeated a superior force under General Henry Heath with just two regiments. This victory earned Crook standing, vaulted his reputation and renown as being a highly skilled, resourceful commander and determined opponent. His brigade took prominent part in the battles fought on the Potomac in 1862. He distinguished himself in action at Antietam and for these services was promoted to Brigadier General of Volunteers and given command of the Kanawha Division. His men said of him that his headquarters were "on the skirmish line." He issued orders in the moment and on the ground being contested. Indeed, there is probably no officer of equal rank (he finished the Civil War as a Major General of Volunteers) who issued fewer paper orders or left so little behind in the way of a paper trail.

Gen. Crook was a principled man as well, something that did not always sit well with his subordinates who felt that all secessionists (in and out of uniform) should get their "just desserts." Nonetheless, Crook insisted that his men treat all civilians justly, secessionist or not. He was honest and disapproved of some of the practices of his citizens soldiers. Fence rails, pigs, chickens and the like, were considered public property by some of his men and when ordered by Crook to pay for or replace anything of that kind consumed, or return what had been taken, Crook was not the most popular and the men "complained of him."[634] On December 11th, Lieut. Col. Hall wrote to Col. W.R. Brown reporting on his compliance with an order received from Brown which had come down from Crook "for the return of a certain Pony, the property of Mrs. E.T. Thompson —which was taken by Capt. J.V. Young while he was Commanding Post at Coals mouth, and also in regard to other property which was alleged as being in his possession."[635] Hall "immediately investigated the matter as directed" and found and reported that

> the Pony spoken of was in possession of Captain Young. I ordered him to return it to the proper owner, and enclosed, please find receipt for delivery of said property. He had at his residence — as I understand and am satisfied is true — one other horse which I ordered should be returned. The pony was taken before Capt Young's connection with this Regiment. All the property taken since his connection with this Regiment has been reported to Division Head Quarters.[636]

This did not sit well with Young who had suffered at the hands of marauders at the onset of hostilities, and his rancor found vent in his letters home to his wife.

Crook's visit to Point Pleasant in December was followed in the local newspapers. The Gallipolis *Journal* (reprinted in the Point Pleasant *Register*) described Crook in glowing terms. He was "[m]odest and unassuming in his manner" winning for himself scores of friends during his stay. He was "a gentleman in every sense of the word," a "brave and gallant commander."

> The love and respect his men bear him, shows how highly they esti-mate these qualities. If anything can be done in the Kanawha Valley this winter, we feel assured Gen. Crook will do it. He is now in com-mand of the forces in the Valley, Gen. Cox and staff having removed their Headquarters to Marietta, on the north side of the River, a point somewhat difficult of access in the present low stage of water. A freezing up of either the Ohio or Kanawha, might render com-munication with the commanding General a little troublesome.[637]

While visiting Point Pleasant, Crook saw to a complaint that had been made con-cerning the use of the county Court House and jail as barracks for soldiers garrisoning the town *i.e.,* the 13[th] Virginia Regiment. On December 4[th], Governor Pierpont had written to General Cox regarding these complaints received from "[t]he people of Mason County" who stated that their county "Court house + jail" was "oc[c]upied as a barracks for the Soldiers." "It is a fine Court house," wrote Pierpont and is becoming very much abused and defaced by the soldiers and will become much more so. They are anxious to preserve the house and think it is a very expensive bar[r]acks. I am in hopes you will cause it to be vacated and other bar[r]acks provided.[638]

The matter was referred to Gen. Crook with instructions to have the Court House vacated and returned to its legitimate civil uses. Crook obliging responded on December 19[th], that "the Court House is not, nor has [illeg.] been used by the 1[st] K[anawha] Division]. The jail is now in use as a Guard House and there are now confined in it some 60 Rebel prisoners. This can be vacated if necessary."[639]

Morning Reports submitted for the 13th Virginia Volunteers for December 1862

Company A had a total present and absent of three commissioned officers and eighty-two enlisted men. A drummer was reported present beginning Sunday, December 11th. Co. A had many details made upon it for detached duty to obtain fuel (wood and coal). On Saturday, December 3rd, Corporal John W. Baxter reported in on his return from Charleston and Saturday, December 10th, Private John M. Naylor returned from Elk River and reported back. Thursday, December 8th, Sergeant George W. King and Privates John Green, Sam Teel, Lewis D. Humphrey, Samuel Commack/McCormick were detached under command of Capt. Milton Stewart, commanding Co. B, to escort five prisoners up to Charleston. December 13th, Private Lewis D. Humphrey returned from Charleston. December 9th, Captain J.W. Johnson was detached on a scout with 1st Sergeant Miletus Grinstead, 2nd Corporal Robert H. Davis, Corporal Elijah Hemmings and sixteen Privates: James Light, Calvin Vance, Agrippa Samples, Alfred Jones, Richard George, Daniel Snodgrass, John Tully, James H. Tully, Woodson B. Hall, Andrew Snodgrass, William P. Copen, Christopher C. Frame, John G. Moore, William Henry George, Jobe Hall and Abner Nanley. On December 15th, Captain Johnson and men returned "from Mud" with "1 prisoner wounded and 2 Union prisoners released." Also on the 15th, John (or Thomas) Moore, Robert Gray, William Gray, one D. Cool and 2nd Lieutenant Theophilus Maher were ordered to Charleston with Irdell Hurel and John Hunter to "conduct 5 yolk of cattle, 4 horses and 2 mules." On December 16th, Samuel McCormick and Irdell Hurel returned from Charleston. Saturday December 17th, 2nd Lieutenant Maher, John Green/Grin, Samuel Teel/Trel and John Hunter "returned from Charleston."

A considerable number of men were detached this month for extra duty chopping wood and digging coal for fuel. December 4th, Privates John Thomas, William A. Cobb and William P. Compton were detailed for extra duty wood chopping. Monday, December 5th, Privates James R. Spradling, William H. George, and Jesse J[o]b[ling] had wood chopping duty. December 8th, Private James A. Means, Andrew J. Cobb,

William W. Riley, Christopher C. Frame, Francis M. Cobb and William P. Copen had extra duty wood chopping. December 9th, Privates Martin Snodgrass, William Glover and Elijah Newell chopped wood. December 12th, four Privates— Aaron V. Facemires, Martin Snodgrass, Elijah Newell and John T. Newell had wood chopping duty. December 13th, Elijah or Preston Newell, John T. Newell, Robert H. Snodgrass and W. Wiens [Wintz?] were detailed for wood chopping. Thursday, December 15th, Nathan Snodgrass, Job Hall, John T. Newels, Robert H. Snodgrass were detailed "for wood chopping." Friday, December 16th, John (or Thomas) Moor, Robert Gray, William Gray, D. Cool, James Light, Alfred Jones, Richard George and Daniel Snodgrass were detailed for wood chopping. December 17th, John Moor, Robert Gray (prior to enlistment a miner by occupation), William Gray, Abner Nanley and Baron Wintz were detailed for "Co[a]l Di[gg]er." Sunday, December 18th, Samuel Snodgrass, John T. Moor, Robert Gray and William Gray were detached for coal digging. December 19th and 20th, S. Thomas Moor, Robert Gray, and William Gray dug coal and on December 20th, James Light, Alfred Jones, Richard George and Daniel Snodgrass were detached for wood chopping. Thursday, December 22nd through Saturday the 24th, Thomas Moor, Robert Gray and William Gray were detached for coal digging. December 25th through Saturday the 31st, Thomas Moor, Robert Gray and William Gray were detached digging coal. "Remarks" following Company Morning Reports indicate that as of Saturday, December 31st, Richard George had "been chopping 2 days."

December 23rd and 24th, Martin Snodgrass was reported absent without leave. No one from Co. A was in arrest or confinement. On December 1st, Co. A had a total of fifteen reported sick. The number of sick hovered around fifteen for the month—a few more or a few less. On Friday, December 2nd, Private John F. Teel reported from Regimental Hospital at Point Pleasant fit for duty. December 12th, George Walter Fitzwater returned from Regimental Hospital at Point Pleasant and reported for duty with his company.

For the month of December, Company B was still stationed at Camp Brown, in Putnam County. From December 1st through 26th, the company had one drummer present and one fifer present December 1st and 2nd. Two enlisted men were absent without leave December 3rd through 7th, and one enlisted man was absent without leave December 27th through 29th. Vincent O. Rice was discharged from hospital December 15th or December 19th.[640] Co. B finished the month with three commissioned officers and ninety-two enlisted men present and absent. Four to nine privates had daily duty during the month. December 1st, there were two commissioned officers and twenty-four enlisted men on detached duty. Again December 9th to 11th, one to two commissioned officers and ten enlisted men were on detached duty.

On December 15th, various shifts in rank and new appointments were made in Co. B. Nehemiah Shin, 1st Corporal, was reduced to the ranks for disability. Samuel

C. Love was promoted to 8ᵗʰ Corporal. Charles Carrol was assigned to teamster duty in place of Harrison Frost who was returned to the ranks for disability. Co. B had 10 to 21 present sick in camp and one to two absent sick. One private was reported present in arrest or confinement on December 8ᵗʰ.

Company C continued to be stationed at Point Pleasant for the month of December. The company had one drummer present December 1ˢᵗ through 31ˢᵗ. No one was absent with leave. One enlisted man was absent without leave December 1ˢᵗ through 31ˢᵗ. December 8ᵗʰ, Asa S. Johnson enlisted in the regiment and joined Co. C on December 10ᵗʰ. December 20ᵗʰ, John Gillespie deserted the company. At the end of the month, the company numbered present and absent three commissioned officers and eighty enlisted men. No one had special or daily duty and five to six privates had extra duty. One commissioned officer had detached duty each day. As for the health of Co. C, ten to eighteen men were present sick for the month including Captain Van McDaniel who was sick from December 17ᵗʰ through 31ˢᵗ. No one was absent sick and no one was present or absent in arrest or confinement.

Company D, stationed at Camp Samuels, Winfield, for the duration of December had present and absent at the end of the month, three commissioned officers and eighty-two enlisted men. One drummer and one fifer were present for the entire month. No one was absent with leave, however, one enlisted man was reported absent without leave on December 1ˢᵗ. Two enlisted men were absent without leave December 2ⁿᵈ through the 4ᵗʰ. Then, between December 23ʳᵈ and 31ˢᵗ, four to five enlisted were absent without leave.

Co. D had no loss or gain and no one had special duty during the month. December 1ˢᵗ through 3ʳᵈ, five privates had extra duty. December 5ᵗʰ through 31ˢᵗ, one private had daily duty. This could perhaps have been Leonard Oliver who was appointed ambulance driver by Lieut. Col. J.R. Hall on December 5ᵗʰ. One to ten enlisted men were on detached service each day of the month. On December 10ᵗʰ, seven men were detailed to scout with Capt. J.W. Johnson. December 30ᵗʰ, John Blackburn was appointed "Hospital nurse in Regimental Hospital." Co. D had from two to six men present sick and four to five men absent sick each day of December. From December 5ᵗʰ through 16ᵗʰ, one commissioned officer was absent in arrest.

For the month of December 1862, Company F was stationed at Point Pleasant. It had one drummer present for the entire month and one fifer present December 13ᵗʰ through 31ˢᵗ. The company fifer had been sick from December 1ˢᵗ to the 12ᵗʰ. No one was absent with leave. One enlisted men was reported absent without leave December 5ᵗʰ through 7ᵗʰ or 8ᵗʰ and December 8ᵗʰ, there may have been six enlisted men absent without leave. December 9ᵗʰ, four enlisted men were reported absent without leave. The company had neither loss nor gain during the month and at the end of the month, it numbered three commissioned officers and seventy-eight enlisted men. None had detached duty nor special duty but one to two (mostly two) non-commissioned officers had extra duty December 1ˢᵗ through 31ˢᵗ. Three to fifteen privates had extra duty each day. December 13ᵗʰ, Private Thomas Williamson was relieved from extra duty at Charleston and returned to the company. From four to five privates were detailed for daily duty each day of December. There were seven to eleven men present sick for the month and none absent sick. Co. F was first issued clothing on December 31ˢᵗ. On October 28ᵗʰ, 13ᵗʰ Regiment Drummer Hazard Farley, Co. F, was promoted to "Drum Major" and his clothing allotment was transferred to the non-commissioned staff.[641]

Company H was stationed at Point Pleasant for the entire month of December. The company had no 2ⁿᵈ lieutenant, no sergeants, corporals, buglers, farriers, blacksmiths nor artificiers present. A drummer and fifer were present each day of December. No one had leave of absence during the month. One enlisted man was reported absent without leave for the period of December 1ˢᵗ through the 6ᵗʰ and one enlisted man, Doliver Workman, just enlisted on December 1ˢᵗ, deserted on December 13ᵗʰ. New recruits joined on December 1ˢᵗ, 3ʳᵈ, 26ᵗʰ, 30ᵗʰ and 31ˢᵗ. Gideon Searls enlisted December 1ˢᵗ. William T. Shaver enlisted December 23ʳᵈ and on December 29ᵗʰ, Winfield Scott Hobbs enlisted. December 30ᵗʰ, Alexander Eves who had been enlisted August 9ᵗʰ, 1862, at Guyandotte by J.B. Bumgardner joined the Co. H. One enlisted man, sixty-five year old musician, Charles F. Hoy was discharged for disability on December 11ᵗʰ or 12ᵗʰ. At the end of December, the company had present and absent three commissioned officers and seventy-seven enlisted men.

No one in Company H had special duty. Between one and six privates had extra duty from December 9ᵗʰ to the 31ˢᵗ. Between one to seven privates had daily duty each day of December and one commissioned officer had detached duty each day of December. No one had been arrested or confined during the month. Co. H had between 9 to 14 privates present sick for the month. Around December 16ᵗʰ, 1862, while on picket post at Point Pleasant, Private Albert Ray came down with mumps. He was treated at Point Pleasant by Dr. Samuel G. Shaw in early spring 1863.[642] Co. H first drew clothing "from time of enlistment to Dec. 31, 1862." Company I drew clothing for the first time, probably on December 3ʳᵈ.[643]

Every unit in the 1ˢᵗ Kanawha Division (Simmonds Battery; Schambeck's Cavalry; 2ⁿᵈ Regiment Virginia Cavalry; 11ᵗʰ Regiment Ohio Volunteer Infantry; 37ᵗʰ Regiment Ohio Volunteer Infantry; 47ᵗʰ Regiment Ohio Volunteer Infantry; 28ᵗʰ Regiment Ohio Volunteer Infantry; 36ᵗʰ Regiment Ohio Volunteer Infantry; 8ᵗʰ Regiment Virginia Volunteer Infantry; and 5ᵗʰ Regiment Virginia Volunteer Infantry) had been paid up to August 31ˢᵗ of 1862, with the exception of the 13ᵗʰ Regiment Virginia Volunteers. As of beginning December, the 13ᵗʰ was the only unit which had not been paid at all (not counting the county bounties), except two dollars for enlistment and a partial payment of the government bounty ($25.00), paid by Mustering Officer Richard R. Crawford.[644]

A Muster-In Roll of a Detachment of Recruits (for the 13ᵗʰ Regiment Virginia Infantry Volunteers dated "Point Pleasant, December 11, 1862") indicates that the 13ᵗʰ had gained twenty-nine new recruits for Companies H, F and C. Company H got the lion's share of these rejecting just two men—Charles F. Hoy aged 65 and William Raynolds—but in all gaining 25 men. The men recruited for Company H were recruited between August 20ᵗʰ and December 1ˢᵗ at the following places. At Point Pleasant, five men were enlisted by what seems to have been the joint efforts of O.W. Griswold, A.F. McCown, T.W. Hampton, J.B. Bumgardner. At Kygerville, Hampton and Bumgardner enlisted seventeen men. At Pomeroy, Hampton recruited two men. At Guyandotte, Hampton recruited one man. John A. Martin recruited one man at "Browns Town." At Glenwood, J.B. Bumgardner recruited one. One man was recruited for Company F — Jarret C. Hackworth — was enlisted by A.F. McCown at Point Pleasant on November 9ᵗʰ, 1862. A recruit for Co. C was enlisted by Lieut. Lemuel Harpold at Point Pleasant on December 8ᵗʰ, 1862. Recruits of minor age: Francis M. Crofoot aged 17; Albert Jamison 16; and Doliver Workman 17, all recruited for Co. H, were reported as "enlisted with the consent of their parents or guardians." All these new recruits were sworn in by Mustering Officer, R.R. Crawford.[645]

On December 8ᵗʰ, Col. William R. Brown issued from 13ᵗʰ Regiment Headquarters at Point Pleasant, General Order No. 3. The order indicates the challenges of maintaining military discipline in garrison close to the soldiers' homes. Brown's order indicated in no uncertain terms his annoyance with men absenting themselves without leave and provided that:

> II The Col[o]n[el] Commanding this Regiment being extremely desirous of preserving good order and discipline among the men under his command that he may thereby have his Regiment at all times in such a condition as to enable it to render efficiant service to the Government whenever called upon.
>
> And being exceeding annoyed of late by men absenting themselves without permission from their respective companies which is in violation of all military Law issues the following Order with the penalties hereunto annexed.
>
> II No Soldier or Soldiers shall be permitted to absent themselves beyound the Picket Lines of the Regiment without a written permit from the Officer commanding the company countersigned by the commanding officer of the Regiment.

II II No Soldier or Soldiers will be permitted to take or use any of the Horses belonging to the Government within this command without first obtaining permission to do so from the Regimental Q[uarter] Master

II II II And any Soldier or Soldiers within this command violating Order No. II will be tried by a Regimental Court Marshall and shall suffer for the first offense a reduction of not less than Thirteen Dollars or one months wages or whatever other punishment deemed necessary by said Court Marshall and for the second violation shall be tried for desertion the penalty of which is death.

And any Soldier or Soldiers violating the second Order will be tried before a General court Marshall for a Felony and shall suffer whatever the decisions of said Court Marshall shall be.[646]

Major General H.G. Wright commanding the Dept. of the Ohio also took advantage of the winter months to review his subordinate officers' fitness to command and on December 13th, issued Special Order No. 70. Part IV provided that: "Division commandants are hereby ordered to have made out and sent to the President of the Board, a list of such officers of their command as may be deemed inefficient in order that they may be examined." Pursuant to Wright's order, Maj. Gen. Cox issued Special Orders No. 162, directing that a military board be appointed

to meet at 10 o'clock A. M. on the 18th instant, or as soon thereafter as practicable, at such point or points as may be designated by the commanding officer of the district of Western Va. to examine and report the capacity, qualifications propriety of conduct and efficiency of such commissioned officers of Volunteers as may be ordered before it by the commanding officer of the District of Western Virginia." [Detail for the Board were] Col. E. Siber 37th Regt. O.V.I; Lt. Col. J.M. Comly 23d O.V.I. and Maj. E.M. Carey 12th O.V.I. Field officers will be required to understand in addition to what is required of Captains the school of the battalion, at least as far as to the part 5th United States Infantry Tactics, the manner of keeping the Regimental Books, the Adjutants and Quartermaster duties complete, also the duties of Field officer of the day the mode of encamping a regiment and the mode of conducting a march.[647]

VI. Every Captain and Lt. who shall appear before the Board will submit to it a sealed letter from his Regimental commander giving his statement on honor, as to his conduct, and qualifications in every respect and also the time he has been absent from duty, either from sickness or on leave of absence, Lieutenants will in addition bring a similar statement from their Captains.

VII. The Board will examine officers 1ˢᵗ on the knowledge of the tactics 2ⁿᵈ The rules and regulations pertaining to the duties of their command 3ʳᵈ Their character and moral and physical fitness to discharge the duties of their grade.

VIII. Lieutenants will be required to understand the school of the soldier, school of the squad, and the school of the company, the organization of the company, its messing camp and garrison duties, the keeping of company books, and the making of company papers. Captains, will be required in addition to understand the first and second part of the battalion.

The Board will report each case with its opinion thereon without waiting for the close of its proceedings. Should the Departmental commander confirm their decision the officer will be notified that his resignation will be accepted to take effect at a date to be designated in the notice. [...]

IX. On recommendation of the Board a re-examination at the end of a limited time will be granted to officers who have failed to come up to the required standard, and who may be deemed worthy of it. Gross immorality, habitual drunkenness, keeping low company, shirking duties, under familiarity with subordinates, or incapacity to govern men will be considered as disqualifications.[648]

The 13ᵗʰ Regiment seems to have been employed in a provost capacity at this time bringing in what were probably truant soldiers belonging to other regiments. December 19ᵗʰ, Col. Brown was receipted for the following prisoners received at the Provost Marshal's Office, Charleston, by Sergeant H. Scott: Alvin Chaise 23ʳᵈ Ohio Volunteer Infantry; William S. Homes 34ᵗʰ Ohio Volunteer Infantry; Valentine Shaulis 37ᵗʰ Ohio Volunteer Infantry; Frederick Bictelor 37ᵗʰ Ohio Volunteer Infantry; John W. Kay 34ᵗʰ Ohio Volunteer Infantry; Frank K. Streets 123ʳᵈ Ohio Volunteer Infantry; J. Muiss 11ᵗʰ Ohio Volunteer Infantry.[649] December 25ᵗʰ, Sergeant J. [or W.] R. Walkup of Co. F delivered up the following named prisoners to Head Quarters District of Western Virginia: Alfred Hampton 2ⁿᵈ Indiana Infantry, C.D. Lawrence 114ᵗʰ Ohio Volunteer Infantry, J.D. Craig 114ᵗʰ Ohio Volunteer Infantry, James M. Clemens 2ⁿᵈ U.S. Cavalry.[650]

On December 23rd or Tuesday, December 30th, J.E.T. Mitchell, a returned Rebel, used disrespectful language in speaking to a Private of the 13th Regiment, who "knocked Mitchell down for his trouble."[651] The December 25th issue of the Point Pleasant *Register* reported that the generous people of "the Point" had furnished the soldiers a turkey dinner and a note of thanks was sent to the *Register,* particularly thanking "the fair ones" for "the highly satisfactory Turkey dinner."[652]

The lamentable lack of medical treatment and medical supplies with the 13th Regiment is preserved for history in a letter written by G.S. Guthrie to H.J. Samuels on December 12th, 1862. Guthrie began: "I know something about the wants of the regt. — one part of it at Red house [Lieut. Col. J.R. Hall's detachment] with about 20 sick and without medical aid and some other things necessary for the sick this I learned last week from a reliable source in the Sutler dept."[653] On December 28th, Lieut. Col. Hall wrote to his mother from Winfield, regarding his inability to take furlough for the holidays, because of sickness among his men.

> Dear Mother
>   I had expected to have come Home between Christmas and New Year but it was absolutely impossible for me to leave there is a good deal of sickness in Camp here the men all Have the Typhoid Pneumonia Meazeals + Mumps — Robert Boggess has been quite sick but is now better he has the Aresepalis I think he will be able to move to Pt Pleasant in a day or two — There is no news here — I will try and come home about the 7th of Jany Give my love to all
>
> Your affectionate son
> James R Hall
> Lt Col 13th Va Vol Infty[654]

On December 30th, Gen. Crook ordered Col. W.R. Brown "to forward at once to these Hd. Qtrs. a monthly Return for Dec. of all Ordnance and Ordnance stores on hand in your command."[655]

In December, as Federal Congress reassembled, Union men of Western Virginia and Representatives to the Restored State Legislature urged immediate admission of West Virginia as a new State.[656] Friends of Western Virginia, who had been canvassing the House on December the 8th, expressed confidence that the bill would get through.[657] All alterations having been made to the new West Virginia State Constitution as requested by the U.S. Congress (chief among these, provisions for the immediate manumission of slaves and abolishment of slavery), the U.S. House of Representatives passed the act admitting West Virginia as a new State, on December 10th, and it was approved by President Lincoln. West Virginia would not be admitted on the President's proclamation until after ratification by general vote on the altered State Constitution could be made by the West Virginia people. Elections on this issue, would be held in Spring of 1863, at the usual time for holding elections.

On a darker note, many suits for forfeiture and confiscation were also being brought at this time by State and Federal Government against individuals' real property on grounds that they had aided the Rebellion.[658] Also during this term of Congress, provisions were decided upon at Washington directly effecting soldiers and their families. Congress had passed a law providing that no soldier should collect their $100 federal bounty before the war had ended and he forfeited his bounty entirely if he was discharged before he had served two whole years, or before the end of the war, if sooner ended. Upon discharge he was entitled to back dues for wages and "50 cents for each 20 miles traveled from the place of discharge to the place of enrollment from his nearest paymaster." Under the law, a soldier was deemed to have served to the end of the war if he was killed or died of disease before the end of 2 years. At the end of the war, the bounty would be immediately paid as soon as audited. An order and rule made by the War Department further provided that the wives of prisoners of war could collect the monthly wages of their husbands. If there was no wife, the minor children by their guardian were entitled. If the soldier was unmarried, his widowed mother could collect his wages. In addition, an important decision made by the Secretary of War and the Paymaster General resulted in an order providing that a soldier was entitled to pay from the day he enlisted and that he need not wait until his company was full or for the formal muster of the regiment into the Government service.[659]

Proponents of the New State movement had much to be glad about. At the end of 1862, though guerrillas continued to commit depredations, indeed as Governor Pierpont stated in his 'state of the State' speech, Western Virginia had successfully "resisted the tide of secession" and much of the State had been preserved from "the rebels." While about 173 Rebel regiments had been supplied by the State of Virginia to the Confederacy, nearly 19 regiments of infantry and cavalry and batteries of artillery have been furnished for the Union. The new State was fiscally also in pretty fair condition notwithstanding that revenues could only be collected in a very few counties and a large portion of expenditures had been for extraordinary purposes. For the fiscal year ending September 30th, 1862, the State had $205,251.80. Expenditures were $165,450.17 leaving in the treasury $120,157.47.[660]

While the army in Western Virginia and the fledgling State Government were holding their own, to the east, a fearful disaster befell the Army of the Potomac on Saturday, December 13th, at the battle at Fredericksburg, Virginia. Here, Union forces under Burnside received a punishing repulse with heavy loss. The battle begun on December 11th ended on December 15th. It was a terrific set-back to Union arms.

On December 12th, Gen. H.W. Halleck, believing that no Rebel movement of force could be made across the mountains during the winter, ordered that all of Cox's troops not necessary for the defense of the Kanawha Valley be sent to join Gen. B.F. Kelley's command at Romney and Martinsburg, to concentrate at Harper's Ferry and operate in the Shenandoah Valley. Wright asked Cox specifically if Crook's force could be spared and sent. Cox responded next day writing that he had no report yet from Crook, but his division was scattered in a long line "along the north bank of the Kanawha"[661] deterring the enemy from cutting off supplies, which could not be "accumulated much in advance until the Kanawha River rose."[662] Continued Cox: Scammon's division was "enough to hold the front of the valley, but the long stretch of country to the Kentucky line has required Crook's command to be active to prevent raids into the river." Cox also thought it advisable to keep a heavy force in Western Virginia until the new State question was settled by the final vote, to take place in the spring of 1863. "If the rebels by extraordinary effort, can prevent the election on that question, they will doubtless do so," reasoned Cox. Western Virginia's "leading men predict a new flight of the loyal citizens on the appearance of removing our troops," and from Cox's own knowledge of the people, he believed this to be accurate unless the feeling of security could be maintained with continued heavy military presence.[663]

Crook reporting to Cox on December 13th on this issue, concurred with Cox and added that with the onset of bad weather, his command could be removed without danger and would of necessity need to be removed as "[t]he present arrangements for getting supplies up for the troops in this river is very defective. Should there come a freeze within the next ten days, the greater portion of the troops would have to leave, for want of provisions. Day warm."[664] Gen. H.G. Wright, commanding a large military department that spanned a number of States (Dept. of the Ohio) and perhaps not understanding the need to concentrate troops at Harper's Ferry preferred to wait "awhile, if permissible, before sending any of the troops out of the Kanawha."[665] Halleck agreed to leave the withdrawal of troops from the Kanawha to Wright's judgement for the moment.[666]

Before leaving the Kanawha Valley for Marietta, Ohio, Cox considered "the feasibility of putting a force at Hurricane Bridge, but the lack of wagon transportation had so far deterred" him from doing this. Cox referred this matter to Crook. The problem of giving the people of this area sufficient protection was at last addressed in January of 1863, when a detachment of the 13th Regiment was sent there.[667]

Complaints were being lodged by Lieutenant-Colonel Daniel Frost (cmdg. 11th Virginia Volunteers) in reference to Captain Young's company which had been acting in conjunction with the 13th and into which part of its men were mustered, when the 13th was mustered in. The organization of the 11th Virginia Infantry, begun in December 1861, was completed in December 1862 and Frost no doubt wanted his Company G (Young's) returned. Cox wrote to Pierpont asking for information as to how best to settle this issue. Cox added as if to punctuate the urgency of resolving this matter: "The tone of Lieut. Col. Frost's letter is unmilitary and improper in its reference to yourself and Adj.-Gen. Samuels, and he will be reprimanded for it."[668]

On December 23rd, Gen. Cox wrote a rather cryptic letter to a A.G. Leonard, United States Collector of Taxes, Parkersburg, W[estern] Virginia, in response to Leonard's letter regarding a missive from a Mr. D.S. Montague, dated December 11th, 1862. Cox's references to Montague's letter suggest that Montague made complaint against the 13th Virginia Volunteers stationed at Winfield and against "the general officers in command in the valley."[669] For his part, Cox referred the matter to Brig.-Gen. Crook, commanding in the Kanawha Valley but wrote Leonard:

> Mr. Montague's wholesale assertion that Union men in the valley have 'no more favors shown them than the meanest dogs,' deprives the rest of his communication of reliability, as, if he knows anything of the matter, he knows he is making a misstatement, and it is quite probable that he is trying to cover up his neglect of duty in his dept. by such abuse of the military officers.
>
> Any specific complaints will meet with prompt investigation. The troops stationed at Winfield are part of the Thirteenth Virginia Volunteers, and I desire that you will require Mr. Montague to report at once whether he complains of them or of the general officers in command in the valley, giving full and specific details of the ground of his complaint, informing him that he will be expected to make good the charges, or be held responsible for a malicious effort to make trouble between the civil and military authorities in West Virginia.[670]

On December 27th, "two stragglers and one deserter" held at Cincinnati were ordered to be delivered to the Commanding Officer (Colonel William R. Brown) at Point Pleasant, to be "forwarded to their Regiments." Upon reaching Point Pleasant, Brown detailed Corporal James H. Gunter and Privates Mark E. Robinson and Daniel Childers, all of Co. E, to deliver the prisoners to the Provost Marshall at Charleston.[671] Also on December 27th, Brown wrote to Capt. Kennedy, A.A.G. 1st Kanawha Division requesting that certain 13th soldiers be granted furloughs. (Crook granted these furloughs.) Brown wrote:

> There are several men belonging to my Regiment who were formerly members of the Home Guard in the Counties of Cabell

and Wayne and they desire permission to go to Ceredo the last of this month for the purpose of getting the pay due them as members of that organization.

Their names are Francis Rigg, John Hazlett, Harrison Thacker, Joel Canterbury, George Lemaster, James Johnson + William Shannon.

If permitted to go their absence will not be necessarily be longer than two or three days + I would respectfully ask authority from your Head Quarters to grant them the [illeg.] leave of absence.[672]

December 30th, 1862, 13th soldier, Demarcus Ward wrote to his parents and Jacob Plybon (another 13th soldier) added a note. The double letter written from Point Pleasant is the following:

December 30th /62
Pt. Pleasant Mason County Va

Dear father and Mother I take this oppertunity to rite you a few in ansur to your leter Which I Received this Morning by W Crook[673] It found me well and harty as I ever was and I hope those few lines will find you injoying the same like Blessing Well I hav nothing of importance to rite this time More the we had a fine dinner here at chrismas Given by the sitisans of this town it was the finest dinner I suppose that ever was set for a Regiment of men it appears that we are much respeted by both officers and sitisans all so we will muster for pay tomorrow so tha say and I suppose that we will Be paid off between the 1st and 10th of January and after we are musterd then the Col says that we shal have furlows so I Shal Come home some time this winter you said in your leter that you was coming up in a few days Come on as soon as you can for we are Glad to see any body from old Wayne so I must Bring my leter to a close so fare well for this time Give my love to all my friends

Rite Soon
Demarcus Ward

To Wm R Ward
And Anna Ward

Jacob Plybon I wish to Be Rememberd by you both Well I red your leter that you sent to your son told him to obey his officers so he does that Shure Demarcus is a funny boy Some of those Swell heads say some times tha are going to whip him tho you know I am here and I don't think tha will hurt any Body when tha whip him thare will be some Body elce Get it next So no more Come up and see us all as soon as you can

J Plybon
To Wm Ward
And family[674]

By the end 1862, the District of Western Virginia was the largest in terms of man and firepower of all other districts in the Department of the Ohio. Western Virginia had 1,061 officers; 24,368 men and 51 pieces of field artillery and was divided into four commands. First Kanawha Division commanded by Gen. George Crook; Second Kanawha Division commanded by Gen. E.P. Scammon; Cheat Mountain Division, commanded by Brig. Gen. R.H. Milroy; and the Railroad Division was commanded by Brig. Gen. B.F. Kelley.[675] Both First and Second Kanawha Divisions had 10 pieces of field artillery[676] and the following manpower in raw numbers: First Kanawha Division (Crook) had 232 officers and 5, 031 men. It had an aggregate present of 5, 983 and an aggregate present and absent of 7, 382. The division had 10 pieces of field artillery. Second Kanawha Division (Scammon) had 217 officers and 5,134 men. It tallied an aggregate present of 6,281 and an aggregate present and absent of 7,562 and 10 pieces of field artillery.[677] On December 28ᵗʰ, the 30ᵗʰ, 37ᵗʰ, and 47ᵗʰ Ohio and 4ᵗʰ Virginia Regiments of Infantry were ordered out of the district and sent to General U.S. Grant's command on the Mississippi River. They were attached to the 15ᵗʰ Army Corps commanded by General William T. Sherman.

"Annual Return of Alterations and Casualties" in Unbound Regimental Papers at the National Archives gives in stark form a brief history of changes in regimental personnel during the brief time since the 13ᵗʰ Regiment's organization:

List of Alterations and Casualties Incident to the 13ᵗʰ Va. for the Year 1862

Nelson O. Rice Co B. died at Point Pleasant Post, Va.

Benjamin F. High Co. E died at Point Pleasant Post, Va.

John H. Cyrus Co. G died at Point Pleasant Post, Va.

Monterville Perdue Co. H died at Post Point Pleasant, Va.

Frederick Fraim Co. A died at Post Winfield, Va.

Lewis Midkiff Co. C deserted at Post Point Pleasant, Va.

Peter Donelly Co. F deserted at Post Point Pleasant, Va.

Harry F. Sherman Co. D deserted at Post Winfield, Va.

John L. Gillespie Co. C deserted at Post Point Pleasant, Va.

No name Co. G deserted

5 deaths

5 desertions

Remarks. This Regt. was raised under Gen. Order No. 75 from War Dept. Washington D.C. and has been in service only 3 or 4 months. The Regt. consists principally of recruits raised in the counties of Mason and Kanawha, W.Va. The Head Qrs. have been at Point Pleasant ever since its formation. Four cos. under Lt. Col. Hall marched to Winfield Putnam Co. and now garrison that Post. The Regt. had at this time 1 subaltern resign (Comm. officer); 3 Non-comm. Officers discharged for disability; 1 minor discharged by civil authority; 5 ordinary deaths; 2 accidental woundings; 5 desertions.[678]

End of December, the Confederates in the 1ˢᵗ Kanawha Division's front numbered between 3,000 and 5,000. They were posted as follows: Gen. Echols' command was at Princeton and at the Narrows of New River; Gen. Williams' command was at and near Union; and some 250 infantry and two companies of cavalry were stationed at Lewisburg. Gen. Floyd was in Kentucky.[679] Union troops, militia and home guards in Northwestern Virginia gained ground against guerrillas by striking ruthlessly at their leaders and the last Pro-Secessionist newspapers were suppressed by military authorities.

During the winter of 1862-63 the regiments of the Kanawha Division were separated and stationed at different posts, on the several roads leading out from Charleston, where army headquarters were, to outposts beyond Gauley Bridge to the southeast and posts along the Kanawha to the northwest. The most important of these posts were fortified by the regiments occupying them.[680] The winter of 1862-63 was as one cavalry officer put it, "a dark and fruitless time." Forces in Western Virginia

without either railroad or water transportation (the river being frozen a good part of the time), found plenty to do in moving around to keep from starving to death. Thus passed the winter [...]. Scouting by day and picketing by night through the winter and spring, grew monotonous and we all longed for an opportunity to do something—something that would count.[681]

An officer of infantry wrote that the winter of 1862-63 in the Kanawha Valley, would pass "with no active military operations beyond numerous mountain expeditions against the enemy by detachments of our troops."[682] It was cold and unpleasant work.

For its part, the 13th Virginia troops continued to be divided between Point Pleasant and Winfield. In addition to their various garrison duties, they doubtless spent considerable time in drill preparing for the "opening of the ball," to commence with the arrival of warmer weather in 1863. Military discipline on and off duty became the challenge. The monotony of garrison duty, the proximity of their home neighborhoods, the hardship of living in the field in severe weather and sickness, with no major movements kept pressure on Colonel Brown and his subordinate officers to maintain discipline and morale. No doubt considerable time was scheduled with drill. The 13th had gone into active operations without benefit of much training in infantry drill and movements in formation and now was their time to catch up. Daily practice would have been devoted to perfect the essence of drill and tactics: coordination, rhythm, and economy of movement. With time on their hands for practice, the winter of 1862-63 with its hardships and mountainous terrain gave the 13th opportunity to hone their skills and inure to hardship; to make of themselves what they came to be, what we might call today a kind of "special forces unit," superb on the sneak, masters of the mountain march and the lightning charge; and steady... very steady, in the face of the enemy. But that is a story for another year.

Appendix

"Who Are Exempt From the Draft"
(Point Pleasant *Weekly Register,* November 6, 1862, Vol. 1 No. 33, [n.p.])

The following is supposed to be the list which the war department intends to make out, embracing all persons that are not subject to draft. If any class of citizens are omitted in this list, that ought not to be drafted, they are requested to give notice without delay. Those not subject to draft are:

All females under 18. All females over 45. All negroes, mulattoes, and ministers of the gospel. Quadroons and Quakers. Octoroons and idiots. All colored females. Lunatics and custom house officers. Exempt firemen. Men with wooden legs. Men without legs. Cripples. Blind men. Seamen and habitual drunkards. Telegraph operators. Public printers. Mariners. Teachers in the public schools. Old maids. Bachelors over 45. Married men over 45, whose wives won't let them go. News boys under 18. Bootblacks under 18. Organ grinders who have not been naturalized, including their monkeys. British subjects. Shakers. Young ladies at boarding schools. Young ladies not at boarding schools. Wet nurses. Veterans of the revolution. Veterans of the war of 1812. The oldest inhabitant.

John Hall Sr., James R. Hall; John T. Hall and John McCausland

The involvement of the Hall family with the raising of the 13th West Virginia Regiment merits inclusion of a short family history here. The story of the Hall family is one typical for West Virginia. Hall Sr. was born in Tyrone County, Ireland in 1807, the son of John and Margaret Houston Hall. The family emigrated to America in 1813 and settled in Rockingham County, Virginia. About 1829, the family moved to Mason County. Two years later, the parents returned to Rockingham County. John the son, remained in Mason and lived at Point Pleasant with the family of Robert McDonough, who was related to him through his grandmother, Jane Kyle. John began farming "lands adjacent to those of the Hendersons below the Kanawha"[683] (lands upon which later the town of Henderson stood). During the years 1833-34, Hall rode as Deputy Sheriff for Mason County, serving under Sheriffs Major John Cantrell (1833) and John McCulloch (1834) and he served as jailor. A widely circulated story recounts that it was when Hall was serving as jailor that he became acquainted with a prisoner who taught Hall how to read, write and cipher. The prisoner was being held on a charge of kidnaping slaves. This prisoner was in time released through the efforts of no less than the Governor of Ohio, William Allen. Hall married well. In 1834, Hall he was joined in marriage to Olivia Hogg, the grand-daughter of Scottish emigrant Peter Hogg. Hogg was by profession a surveyor and lawyer and he served as captain of militia in the French and Indian War. Family lore holds that he was a friend of George Washington. For his military service he received a land patent for 8,000 acres in Mason County and here he settled, becoming one of the early settlers in the county.

John Hall, Sr. and his wife, Olivia, were Presbyterians. Eight or nine children were born to them but only four survived into adulthood. These were James Robert born 1838, John T. born 1842, and two daughters, Diane and Mary. John Hall the father prospered. As one observer put it, he "owned everything from Point Pleasant to Hartford [City]." Hall was a professional man: an attorney, business man, entrepreneur and he became heavily involved in politics first as a Whig then as a Republican. He served as delegate to the Virginia Assembly from 1844 to '46; as commissioner of revenue in 1847; he was re-elected to the General Assembly on the Whig ticket to serve as "a presidential elector on the Whig ticket"[684] in 1852; and he represented his district (consisting of Mason, Jackson, Cabell, Wayne and Wirt Counties) in the Virginia State Senate at the January to June and November to April sessions of 1852 and 1853 and in the December to March session of 1854.

At the outbreak of the Rebellion, Hall lived with his family in the house that is located at what is now 707 North Main Street, Point Pleasant, on the north end of town. Built in *ca* 1837, Hall bought the house in 1860 from John Hale (Hall sold it again in 1865). It was a typical four room over four room frame house, at that time considered "far up" on the edge of town. It was reputedly a "safe house" for escaping slaves—the wood ball on the downstairs landing of the stairway (which was still there at the time of my visit) was removable and was used to signal to escaped slave[s] whether it was safe to enter. Hall maintained a law office down near the river at the south end of town, on Main Street.

At the time of the outbreak of the Rebellion, John Hall, now in his fifties, was contending with issues of health. He was diagnosed and operated for "cancer of the left eye" and by March of 1861, he had undergone four operations.[685] This notwithstanding, he became not only a prominent leader in reorganization of the Provisional State government at Wheeling but he was instrumental in recruiting West Virginia regiments from his section (the 4th and 13th West Virginia Infantry Regiments to name two); secured arms at his own expense; and secured funds that bounties might be offered to volunteers. In 1861, Hall was chosen to represent Mason County at the first Constitutional Convention at Wheeling. He was elected President of the Convention by that assemblage but stepped down due to his indictment and imprisonment (awaiting trial) for the shooting of Lewis Wetzel in October of 1862.

Both of his sons, James Robert and John T., studied at the Virginia Military Institute at Lexington. They were not graduates having failed to complete the course of study—a four to five year course of study modeled after the curriculum required at the United States Military Academy at West Point. James was permitted to drop out due to "severe family affliction" (the death of a much younger brother) and John T. did not return because of the outbreak of the war. It has been suggested that John was one of the corps of cadets manning guns and instructing green Confederate army artillerists at the first battle of Bull Run. John served with the rank of Major with the 4th Virginia (West Virginia) Volunteer Infantry. He was one of the officers assigned to the organization of the 4th Virginia along with Col. Joseph A. Lightburn and Lieut. Col. Wm. H.H. Russell. Maj. Hall died as a result of wounds received at the fight at Kennedy's Hill (Chapmanville) on August 6th, 1862. James was a driving force in raising volunteers for the 13th Virginia and served with the rank of Lieutenant-Colonel in the 13th West Virginia and was killed at the battle of Cedar Creek, October 19th, 1864.

There has been considerable interest in the brothers over the years as they were two of a very small number of V.M.I. cadets to don Union blue. Student files at the Institute provide absorbing reading. The seventeen-year-old James Robert Hall reported for duty at the Institute on August 1st, 1855, a member of the "class of 1859." There were no public schools in Western Virginia at this time and James as well as John T. had been students at the Point Pleasant Academy, a subscription school.[686] This education had sufficed to permit James to by-pass the first year of school (the 5th class) and enter the next class (the 4th class). As a member of the 4th class, James studied the following courses (names of textbooks used at this time follow the course title):

> Algebra Completed (textbook: Smith's Algebra); Geometry Completed (Davies' Legendre's Geometry); Plane and Spherical Trigonometry (Davies' Legendre's Geometry); Geography (Mitchell's Geography); French (Bolmar's Levizac's Grammer); and English Studies with Composition and Declamation (Picot, Nos. 5 and 6).[687]

The West Point "Merit of Conduct" (a demerit system) was also in place at V.M.I. and it functioned this way. If a student had more than 100 demerits in half a year (by January 1st, or 200 in one school year), there was sufficient cause for dismissal. This could be appealed as was necessary in the case of John T. At the end of James' first year (ending July 1st, 1856), he was ranked academically in 20th place out of 59 cadets in the 4th class and he had 98 demerits for the year. All cadets were counted and ranked together as to conduct and thus his number of demerits put him in 45th place in the school.

Before the end of his first year, father, John Hall wrote to V.M.I. School Superintendent Colonel Francis H. Smith on May 15th, 1856. Hall acknowledged receipt of Smith's letter and that he was "pleased to hear that James has connected himself with the church and I do most sincerely hope he may make a good and consistent member."[688] Hall proceeded to describe his sons to Smith. "James is young warmharted and impulsive." Fourteen-year-old John, whom Hall Sr. also hoped to send to V.M.I., on the other hand, he described in a curious way which suggests that the younger son was a rather hard-boiled character. As my Schwaebian mother would say: "Perhaps the apple doesn't fall very far from the tree." John T., wrote his father, is "of a wholy different temperment he will give you less trouble and he never will love you half so well he is cold calculating and safe but has never been half so affectionate or kind a son but then he kneeds much less looking after."[689]

In the next academic year, on October 24th (1856), father, John Hall again wrote to Superintendent Smith. His youngest son, a boy of "about 5 years, the fifth of eight children" to die in childhood, had recently died. Hall's letter to Smith clearly conveys concern that James may also not be well. "When last visiting James at Lexington," wrote Hall

> on the 3d and 4th instant I thought my son James Robert had the appearance bad health and since the death of his brother I thought I would ask the favour of you to procure for him ef in your powr the privilege to resign and come home having lost most of my children and with great doubts as to James' health. I shall as will as his Mother for a while be very unhappy if he is not whare we can see him often please procure his resignation.[690]

On October 31st, 1856, James was permitted to drop out of school. The reason given was "severe family affliction." It was further noted in James' file that the cadet was "a brave soldier; [who] gave every promise of a brilliant future."[691]

James returned home. Three years later his younger brother, John, also received an appointment to V.M.I. His father wrote to Superintendent Smith on July 12th, 1859. He thanked Smith for the appointment tendered to John and added a word about James: "James has been at home with me ever since he left the Institute he has been constantly employed in the Store his habits are fine but his constitution still continues delicate."[692]

James' brother, John Taylor Hall was sixteen years old when he reported for school at V.M.I. on August 29th, 1859 (class of 1863). John also bypassed the 1st year of school and was admitted directly to the 4ᵗʰ class. At the end of his first year (1860), he was ranked academically 20ᵗʰ place out of a class of 59 cadets. In terms of "Merit in Conduct," he was in 148ᵗʰ position. His talent for accumulating demerits continued and he was dismissed from the institute for an excess of demerits during his second year, on March 9ᵗʰ, 1861.[693]

As the Hall brothers were among a very small minority of cadets to join the Union army, there persists to this day a question as to whether the brothers were forced by their father into Federal service. The young men had many friends in the cadet corps and their sympathies were known to be with their school comrades and the South.[694] James, of course managed to stay clear of the conflict until summer of 1862. Some apocryphal stories have it that James remarked early on to a friend that he would rather see his right arm paralyzed than raise it against the South. By strange coincidence, his right arm was shattered by a ball in 1864. There are also indications that the brutal death of his brother, John, decided the issue for him. The conflict became personal. Motive aside, James fulfilled the promise shown at V.M.I.: he became an outstanding field officer. This is documented by an extraordinary letter written by Colonel Rutherford B. Hayes, commanding 2ⁿᵈ Division at the great battle of the morning at Cedar Creek, Virginia, where James lost his life. James was killed while in command of the regiment that morning, Col. W.R. Brown being absent from the regiment on duty as officer of the day, on this day of battles. This was hardly the first time Hayes had opportunity to observe the soldier. James served continuously under Hayes, first, when Hayes had command of 1ˢᵗ Brigade (of the Kanawha Division, 2nd Division, Dept. W. Va.) and then during the Shenandoah Valley Campaign of 1864, when Hayes commanded a division (2ⁿᵈ Infantry Division, Army of West Virginia). Hayes wrote the following to John Hall:

> *My Dear Sir:* — Although personally a stranger to you, I feel that I ought to write you a few words in regard to the death of your gallant and noble son — Lieut.-Colonel James R. Hall, of the 13ᵗʰ Va. Vol. Infantry. He had not yet recovered from the wounds received at Winchester on the 24ᵗʰ of July, and in the opinion of all of us, might well have been excused from doing any further duty during the present campaign. But his heroic and patriotic spirit would not allow him to be absent from the stirring scenes of the Valley campaign. — With his arm in a sling, still weak and suffering on the morning of the 19ᵗʰ, when our prospects were gloomiest and the bravest were beginning to feel discouraged, Col. Hall, with a reckless disregard of self, was everywhere conspicuous rallying and encouraging his men — crowding to the extreme front where the fire was the hottest, affording to all of us, an example which it would

be an honor, even faintly to imitate. I need not attempt to tell you how much we admired him — how generally we lament his loss. Among the multitude of brave and generous men who have given their lives to their country in this great struggle, your son will be remembered as one of the bravest of the brave. Sincerely, R.B. Hay[e]s. Col. Commanding.[695]

A large double portrait of James and John T. was engraved and printed posthumously. This was hired done by father, John Hall. These were drawn from existing photographs of the soldiers wearing the uniforms of their rank (Lieutenant-Colonel and Major). Beneath the likenesses was printed "Young, patriotic, brave, and generous they gallantly fell in defence of their country, with their faces to the foe." The large prints were distributed to family and friends of the Hall family. One hangs today, unless it has been removed, in the Tu-Endi-Wei Mansion House Museum at Point Pleasant. Another copy was said to hang in the home of General John McCausland, C.S.A., former professor of mathematics and artillery practice at V.M.I. and relative of the Hall brothers. (McCausland's mother and the brothers' grandmother were half-sisters; daughters of grandmother, Jane Kyle.) McCausland had the boys in class at V.M.I. and was reported to have stated that they were "the two best soldiers he ever had." Certainly, theirs was the *only* picture of soldiers he permitted in his house. His house (once called "Grape Hill") stands yet today, although entirely shut up, off Route 35, near the Kanawha River at Fraziers Bottom in Mason County, West Virginia.

A great deal of information was shared with me by William B. Matthews of Huntington, West Virginia, when I quite unexpectedly made his acquaintance about twenty years ago. Matthews was a descendant of John Hall through one of his daughters. He and his wife graciously welcomed me and my youngster into their home. He shared memories of the Hall family and she, of Charlotte, McCausland's daughter. Charlotte had resided in the house at Fraziers Bottom. Like her father, she didn't care for visitors and was perfectly "satisfied to shoot first and ask questions later."

13th Regiment Infantry Volunteers Officers and Men

bounties, premiums, duty and an opportunity to stand up together for the ancient American commitment to freedom from tyranny and oppression

The following is a roster of the men who volunteered for military service in the 13th Regiment Virginia Infantry Volunteers, Union Army. To compile this list, I took my cue from extant data drawn from a variety of sources. It would be a stretch to claim that this roster is somehow complete and definitive. Too much has been lost regarding the early militarization of this section of the North-South border and the 13th Regiment in particular for this to be so. Still, a few summary remarks by way of introduction can be made as to this particular set of men, recruitment history of the Regiment and Companies comprising it.

Enlistments for the 13th Virginia Volunteers (later "West Virginia" Volunteers to distinguish Union army regiments raised in Virginia from Confederate units) began in July and August 1862 and continued intermittently until February 1865. All recruits were enrolled and mustered into the United States Service (the Union Army) in the northwestern counties of Virginia that became West Virginia. It was claimed that the 13th was made up entirely of volunteers and this seems to have been the case. There seems not to have been a draftee, not a substitute, nor, for that matter, a female combatant in the mix.[696]

I have arranged soldiers alphabetically by surname. Entries include some personal information and particulars pertaining to the soldiers' enlistment and early service. When known, dates of enlistment; dates of muster into the United States Service; Company to which recruits were appointed; the soldier's age and identification as to place of birth (by country); and occupation at the time of enlistment are provided. Service with other Union or Confederate States units (militia and regular army) when plausible are also indicated. Rank is indicated with dates of promotion, even if there was a later reduction due to disability or misbehavior. Death dates and cause of death for soldiers who died within months of their muster into Service are also included. At the end of this chapter is a separate list of soldiers who have at one time or another been attributed to the 13ᵗʰ Regiment. Included here are names of recruits (almost certainly a partial list) enrolled by Captain John V. Young for his Company (Co. G, 11ᵗʰ Regiment Virginia/West Virginia) while it was attached to the 13ᵗʰ Regiment and mistakenly mustered into service with the 13ᵗʰ when it was mustered in October 1862.

Source materials include importantly, all things "Record Group 94". RG94 is a registry of records maintained by the Adjutant General's Office, National Archives and Records Administration (NARA), Washington D.C. It contains an enormous wealth of information.[697] That is, 13ᵗʰ West Virginia "Regimental Books" containing descriptive rolls, morning reports and "Remarks," also registers of death, desertion, promotion, reduction and transfer. Also in RG 94 are court martial records; "Carded Medical" files; "Compiled Service Records;" casualty lists; "Telegrams Sent and Received;" "Orders;" "Carded Applications for Military Pension;" "Military Pension Files;" "Applications for Headstones;" correspondence to and from the Adjutant General's Office, War Department Washington; and miscellaneous files and documents to be found in the diverse collection of materials archived under heading "Record Group 94". U. S. Civil War Draft Registration Records; Tax Assessment Lists; and university catalogs now available digitally through databases such as Ancestry.com provided some interesting details as to regimental sutlers and surgeons. Early militia and enlistment rolls preserved in Records of the West Virginia State Adjutant General's Office held at the West Virginia State Library, Charleston and at Colson Hall, West Virginia University at Morgantown, as well as published lists of casualties, county histories, and cemetery records were also useful in creating this roster.

Information in Regimental Books (Descriptive Rolls; Morning Reports and accompanying "Remarks") provide *the* official record of enlistments over the life of the Regiment and were used as a primary source in compiling this roster. These books traveled with the Regiment and whatever the conditions of the field, it is obvious upon examining the entries that great care was taken in entering the various types of information. For accuracy, they are given primary weight here as to name, rank, enlistment and dates of promotion.

Descriptive Rolls for Company A, one of the first companies recruited, contained not one but two lists, a "First" and "Second" list of soldiers. The "Second List" included beyond the usual information taken down at enlistment (age, occupation, place of birth and brief personal description as height, color of hair, eyes and skin) the soldiers' full middle name(s). The dizzying knot-ball of James Johnsons of Company A, however, resisted all my efforts to disentangle: there may have been one recruit by that name or a dozen scattered throughout the Regiment.

As always, when dealing with old manuscripts there were problems of legibility. This was due to the age and condition of the documents as well as to the elaborately ornamented style of script, *i.e.,* capitalization and numerals then used by the more (and less) practiced hands at work here (examples of problem characters being "I" and "J;" "H" and "K;" "C" and "L;" and "13;" "15" and "18"). Officers also it seems, found a myriad ways to spell and record a man's name. On the upside, these creative spellings may be an indication of how names were both pronounced and spelled. Nick names and creative spellings are included here. Spellings of names as found in federal and state records have been indicated. Spellings as they appear in what seem to be true signatures (that is, where the soldier could, or did sign for himself) are also included and identified. Lastly, for purposes here, West Virginia towns, counties and districts are sometimes designated "Virginia" (*i.e.,* Mason County, Virginia) when accompanied by a date earlier than June 20, 1863, that is, when Western Virginia became the 35th State to enter the Union.

Now, to provide a bit more historical context for the reader using this index ... Volunteers resident in Mason County, Virginia, received a county bounty of $30.00 and a $2.00 Premium upon being mustered in to the United States Service when companies of the Regiment were first organized at the place of rendez-vous, that is, Point Pleasant, Mason County, October 6th, 7th, 8th, 9th and 10th, 1862. Upon muster in recruits swore an oath of allegiance to the United States administered by Lieutenant C. S. Roberts. They were mustered into the United States Service by mustering officer, Lieutenant Richard R. Crawford. The Regiment did not have a full complement of companies when it was first organized and mustered and was consequently, considerably undersized. Colonel William R. Brown commanding, reporting on the strength of the regiment at the end of 1863 recorded that the

> Regiment was mustered into the U. S Service on the 10th of October 1862. At that time it consisted of 8 companies making an aggregate of 657 men. Since that time we have recruited enough to raise the aggregate to over a thousand men provided there had been no deaths nor desertions.[698]

Indeed, subtracting out Young's Company (about 80 men in October 1862, by my calculations) which had to be returned to the 11th Virginia, (being mistakenly mustered in with the 13th in October 1862) there remained only about 577 men mustered in on October 10, when Company H, the last to be mustered, was sworn in. Companies I and K were of course, not yet recruited and could not be mustered until 1863 (Company I was mustered with 45 men on July 26th, 1863, at Charleston; Company K was mustered with 34 men October 3rd, 1863, at Charleston). This left about 85 men for Company A (mustered October 7th, 1862, at Point Pleasant); 102 men for

Company B (also known as James R. Hall's Company, presumably consisting of first recruits raised for the "new regiment" and mustered October 8ᵗʰ, 1862, at Point Pleasant; 83 men for Company C (mustered October 8ᵗʰ, 1862, at Point Pleasant); 87 men for Company D (mustered in October 8ᵗʰ, 1862); 82 men for Company E (mustered in October 9ᵗʰ, 1862, at Point Pleasant); 85 men for Company F (mustered in October 9ᵗʰ, 1862, at Point Pleasant); and 53 men for Company H (mustered in October 10ᵗʰ, 1862, at Point Pleasant).

Federal and County bounties were offered to promote enlistment. Enrollment sheets such as those preserved in the Civil War Collection at Morgantown (non-regulation sheets, improvised in the moment, consisting of two blank sheets of paper glued together on a side) do not today exist for all companies mustered in time to qualify for the Mason County Bounty, but one can safely assume, I think that all citizens of the county who enrolled before the deadline passed received bounty monies. Thirty dollars plus was at that time, no small amount and that pains were taken to offer it gives some fair idea of the gravity of the situation at this juncture of the war and commitment of county officials to both raise "their regiment" and provide some immediate means of relief for soldiers and their dependents. Mason County far exceeded other counties from which 13ᵗʰ Regiment soldiers were recruited, levying and paying out in local bounties for volunteers a whopping $40,110 (not all of this to qualifying 13ᵗʰ Regiment Volunteers, of course), as opposed to $14,000 paid out by Jackson County; $9,400 by Kanawha County; and $3,600 by Cabell County.[699]

The first deadline for receipt of the Mason County Bounty seems to have been September 10, 1862, with another extension and new cut-off date set for September 20, 1862. September 20, seems to have been the last extension of the deadline under the current call for volunteers and the date on which this inducement to volunteer was allowed to expire.[700] Federal bounties, however, continued to be offered and increased as the war dragged on. All recruits mustered in when the Regiment was first organized received Federal bounty of $25 bounty paid down with $75 yet due. By comparison, recruits enrolled in the 13ᵗʰ Regiment in time for the spring campaign of 1864 received Federal bounty of $60 paid up front with $240 due at muster out.[701] The following fragment of a telegraph message from "Miscellaneous unbound regimental papers" (telegrams mostly) indicated how men were to be categorized for purposes of payment and receipt of bounties:

> All men enlisted prior to Jan 1, 1864 place upon Muster for Pay Rolls 1ˢᵗ or 2ⁿᵈ installments + Premium bounty due all men enlisted between Oct. 24, '63 + Jan 1, 64 inclusive are entitled to premium $2, + 300 $ bounty between Oct. 24, 63 + Mch 1, 1864 All men enlisted since Jan. 1 64 place upon Muster for Pay roll 1ˢᵗ installment of Bounty due Premium before Jan. [illeg.][702]

Discharged soldiers were only entitled to bounty if they served two years or were wounded in battle.[703]

By and large, recruits for the 13th Regiment were enlisted at towns lying upon the Ohio and Kanawha River, in Virginia/West Virginia at stations such as Charleston, Point Pleasant, Coals Mouth, Hurricane Bridge, Guyandotte, Walton, to name a few. Recruiters did not, it seems, venture into the hill country back of the rivers, and that for very good reason. River towns were hubs for news, commerce and communication—likely places to advertise and recruit. Neighborhoods to the "interior" were more remote and more dangerous for both recruiters and recruits as partisans and guerrillas roamed this country to greater and lesser extent for the duration of the war: to greater extent when Confederate military fortunes were on the wane and to lesser extent when their fortunes waxed.

In the early stages of recruiting the 13th Regiment, recruiting stations were set up with all the military pomp and ceremony that could be brought to bear. In the columns of the *Point Pleasant Weekly Register* (George W. Tippett, proprietor) we learn that in late summer 1862, recruiting officer Lieutenant James R. Hall published stirring calls to enlist, had printed and posted banners, made speeches, paraded militia and played martial music at the Point Pleasant station. After the Regiment was organized in October 1862, recruiting stations were kept open at Point Pleasant, Wheeling and Mason City and recruits for the 13th continued to be enrolled there during the war.[704] As long as the Regiment remained in its home neighborhood, that is in 1862, 1863 and early 1864, men also came forward to join up where Companies of the 13th were posted, garrisoned or encamped. All recruits were enlisted for a term of three years or until the end of the war. Recruits enrolled in early 1865 when the Confederacy was on its last legs (and the 13th in winter quarters at Cumberland, Maryland), were mustered in (by one "James Smith, Captain" enlisting at Point Pleasant) to serve for just one year.

13th Regiment recruits hailed from all over Virginia (east and west of the Alleghenies), from Ohio, Pennsylvania, Maryland, from as far west as Indiana and as far east as New York and the New England States, the British Isles and from Northern Europe. Occupations and trades ran in families and, as many 13th Regiment volunteers were related by blood and/or marriage, it is surprising that we find represented the variety of occupations that we do. They were largely farmers but also teamsters and wagon-makers, boatmen and steam-boatmen and day laborers. There were skilled laborers such as carpenters, caulkers and plasterers, blacksmiths, stonemasons, coopers, coppersmiths, shoemakers, sawyers and lumbermen, millers and millwrights, and also clerks and merchants. There was a printer and a "master painter," a butcher, a tanner, a geologist and teachers. There was one Irish tailor, a couple of lawyers, several physicians (allopaths: medical school graduates and non-graduates) and engineers. Immigrants from the British Isles were largely miners. Colonel W.R. Brown, who commanded the Regiment for its entire tour of duty, was a machine shop foreman before the war and Lieutenant-Colonel James R. Hall was a clerk and deputy sheriff.

More than a dozen men had sufficient musical ability to warrant being appointed regimental musicians. These made up the regimental drum and fife corps. The corps was led by the Drum Major Hazard Farley of Company F in September 1862, and Samuel D. Hanna Company D in July 1863.[705] Other 13th army musicians were John W. Bailey bugler, James Edwards fifer, Isaac M. Glaze, William A. Hurel fifer, Albert C. Jamison, Marcus L. Jones drummer, James King drummer, Levi Hemmons drummer, Mathew Hanna, Jasper M. Hill, James McDermitt, Calvin C. Shanks drummer, James H. Tully, George E. Warner and possibly Samuel Stineman, a professional musician. Typically, musicians in volunteer regiments had no formal training as army musicians. They may have had some training as members of militia under guidance of a militia musician but more likely they had to learn on the job, and a job it was too. All aspects of military life, in camp and field, on dress parade, in battle, all were signaled and directed by company and regimental fifers and drummers by means of some fifty different sound pieces. These pieces were both melodic and rhythmic and all had to be played from memory. Nor was this all. Sometimes army musicians 'serenaded,' that is, played simply for the soldiers' entertainment and they served in other capacities as well. During a battle they often worked as hospital staff as stretcher bearers, nurses and with army surgeons aiding with emergency treatment, operations and amputations.

Enlistment in the army also provided opportunity for men to obtain money for their families at a time when farming, commerce, manufacture, mining and shipping of resources (salt and coal) had all but ground to halt in the northwestern part of Virginia. They were also patriotic in a way that many today cannot even remotely relate to. For those who were descendants of early settlers who fought in the Indian Wars and in the American wars for independence in 1776 and 1812, enlistment was a way of re-affirming an ancient commitment to freedom from tyranny and oppression (*i.e.,* freedom from the tyranny of Virginia, the Confederate States and their partisans and armies). For immigrants, who joined the American Civil War, their enlistment affirmed their solidarity with neighbors and loyalty to their adopted homeland. For those recruits who had never left their homes, many of whom had at best a rudimentary schooling, who could scarcely write and knew little of the world outside of their own neighborhoods, enlistment in the army provided a way of seeing "the world."

The War Department at Washington had issued guidelines for taking enlistments which included minimum height and age requirements. These were at best loosely followed as a general matter and such also was the case with 13th Virginia in which the minimum age requirement (no younger than 18 nor more than 45) was implemented by recruiting officers with casual elasticity of conscience. Records suggest that with few exceptions, every man and boy that came forward to volunteer was taken. Brutal evidence of civil war was not on some distant field but in their midst and had been for over a year. Historians today agree, about half the male population of northwestern Virginia had joined Confederate forces. Being first to organize when Virginia seceded, these units had also been first to appropriate local arms caches, enforce conscription, confiscate foodstuffs, horses, and etc. This left the other portion of the male population—ill-equipped but of necessity already in the field, in need of proper arms and eager to join in the larger effort to strike at the Confederacy and end the state of constant alarm—of raids, kidnappings and other depredations to person and property—under which they had been living. Notwithstanding the casual disregard of enlistment requirements, West Virginia regiments such as the 13th tended to be undersized as compared to other regiments raised in North. This seems not to have been due to lack of patriotism but may have been due to the lower population density in that part of the State.

Just as many recruiting officers signed up boys whom they must have known were under the minimum age requirement, so too did many young men who joined the 13th understate their ages. The discrepancy is evident by comparison of soldiers' ages as given on regimental descriptive rolls with census records. Men and especially boys under 18 years of age lied about their ages to recruiting officers. The minimum age requirement could be sidestepped in the event that a minor's parent(s) gave their consent. Underage soldiers could enlist with a parent's permission and the regimental record as it survives today, preserves mention of underage young men, who came into the Regiment under this exception to the rule.

As indicated above, there were also economic reasons why in late summer 1862, so many youths were eager to join the army. For one thing business had ground to a halt with the war and farming such of it as there may have been, was at an end for the year. Western Virginia had at this time no public school system and many young men under the age of 18 were typically already a part of the work force as opportunity presented, working as day laborers and farmers and they attended school sporadically if at all. Bottom line, volunteering for army service was simply a better way of earning money at this time. As hardy as these young men seem to have been, accustomed as they were to the rigors of life out-of-doors as farm hands and trade labor, many underage soldiers in the 13th Regiment succumbed to the extreme rigors of the raid on Lynchburg in June 1864: many upon their return were hospitalized at Gallipolis Army Hospital and pronounced unfit for any further service. As for men exceeding the age limit, recall that a man at this time was considered old in his forties. Indeed, few in their forties survived life in the field as lived by the 13th. For the white-haired elder in his forties or the downy-cheeked youth in his teens, volunteering for army service at this point in time was a better way of earning money, and the Union cause, needed men. Few were turned away. As to the minimum height requirement ("five feet" as fixed by the War Department), regimental descriptive rolls with their precise entries recorded in feet and inches, suggest that the minimum standard for height was strictly implemented with rare exception. The volunteers who filled the ranks of regiment were by-and-large a fairly tall set.

The raising of the 13th Virginia was a culmination of efforts that had as much to do with defending West Virginia's secession from Virginia as it had to do with ending the Rebellion of the South. Extant materials indicate that some of the men who volunteered for the 13th had already seen service as militia and in local and State government as spokesmen and delegates at a time when it was to risk life and limb to do so. Such was the case for two officers: Methodist minister and man of letters, William W. Harper and tanner, Lemuel Harpold. Both had served in the political arena as Delegates to the 1st Wheeling Convention, where representatives from twenty-seven Western Virginia Counties responded to Virginia's adoption of the Ordinance of Secession with a united posture of opposition and intention to make practical their determination not to be dragged into the Southern Confederacy but to remain with "the Union." It is worthwhile to note that such determination to serve and self-determine was hardly extraordinary in this population. It is known that in October 1861, when Secession forces hemmed in those opposed to Virginia's secession from the Union, Virginians of the northwestern counties and the interior, encountering difficulty in getting past secessionist forces to join the Union army, attached themselves where they might, many taking to the field on their own hoof individually, in squads or as militia, with and without commanding officers. The necessity of every Union man, woman and child taking up arms to defend themselves against the intense hatred and scorn of Secessionists rings out from the stanzas of the following poem, or song, taken from the pages of the Rockingham, Virginia, *Register*. It is an anonymous offering, anonymous now as then, written in the early weeks of 1861, as indicated by reference to the various States (Alabama declared secession January 11, 1861, with Georgia not far behind). It was entitled "Call All" and is included here for several reasons: to provide perspective on the utter calamity of civil war in 1861-62, the utter necessity of militarization of the Union population which informed recruitment of West Virginia Regiments such as the 13th and to show in relief some of the causes and conditions which "put the iron in the hearts" of her soldiers.

> *Whoop! The Doodles have broken loose,*
> *Roaring round like the very deuce!*
> *Roaring round like the very deuce!*
> *Lice of Egypt, a hungry pack,*
> *After 'em, boys, and drive 'em back.*

Bull-dog, terrier, cur and lice;
Worry 'em, bite 'em, scratch and tear
Everybody and everywhere.

Old Kentucky's caved from under,
Tennessee is split asunder,
Alabama awaits attack,
And Georgia bristles at her back.

Old John Brown is dead and gone!
Still his spirit is marching on,
Lantern-jawed, and legs, my boys
Long as Apes from Illinois!

Want a weapon? Gather a brick!
Club or cudgel, or stone or stick;
Anything with blade or butt,
Anything that can cleave or cut.

Anything heavy, or hard, or keen!
Any sort of slaying machine!
Anything with a willing mind,
And the steady arm of a man behind.

Want a weapon? Why capture one!
Every Doodle has got a gun,
Belt and bayonet, bright and new,
Kill a Doodle, and capture two!

Shoulder to shoulder, son and sire!
All! Call all! To the feast of fire!
Mother and maiden, and child and slave,
A common triumph, or a single grave.[706]

The intense emotion of this poem also suggests that there are parallels between 1861-62 to our own time. These parallels are so pronounced that they can scarcely be passed over without comment. Again, the American people are compelled to tackle questions of sovereignty. Now again, we watch astounded the ratcheting up of emotions and worse: that increasingly, there seems less common purpose, less common ground upon which to stand together as Americans.

Returning to the militarization of Western Virginia in 1861–62 and how this relates to recruitment of the 13th Regiment, few original muster rolls enumerating Virginia militia survive from the early months of the conflict. One does, however, for Company A of the 116th Regiment. If the muster roll of one company of militia is any indication of when soldiers who eventually joined the 13th Regiment first saw service, indeed how many of one company of militiamen joined the 13th, of interest is Captain John A. Greer's Muster Roll of Company A 116th Regiment Virginia Militia dated "March 10, 1861," (with a supplementary list of soldiers "Solgers" appended, who seem to have joined the 116th after March 10, 1861) a record torn from "an old Ledger," given by Greer to Mason County newspaper woman Livia Simpson-Poffen-barger, who donated it to Virgil A. Lewis' archives at Charleston, where it is preserved in microfilm at the West Virginia Department of Archives and History.[707] Accepting for the sake of argument that I have correctly identified the soldiers named on Greer's list as also volunteers in the 13th Virginia, of the 7 officers and 104 soldiers recorded on Greer's list, roughly 21% joined the 13th Regiment. Of these, most (11) were assigned to Company B; 8 were assigned to Company C; 2 to Company A; 1 to Company D; and 1 perhaps, went into Mason's Company G (Mason's recruited to replace Captain J. V. Young's Company G).

The reader may notice that a handful of soldiers listed below were transferred to the Veteran Reserve Corps. The Veteran Reserve Corps ("V.R.C.") or Invalid Corps was organized in 1863 pursuant to Adjutant General's Office ("AGO") General Order 105, April 28, 1863. The Invalid Corps consisted of companies or of battalions as seemed most appropriate. Companies were to be made up of

(1) Officers and enlisted men of commands then in the field who because of wounds or service-connected disease were unfit for field service but were capable of effective garrison or other light duty;

(2) Officers and enlisted men still in service and on the rolls who were absent from duty in hospitals or convalescent camps or who were otherwise under the control of medical officers; and

(3) Officers and enlisted men who had been honorably discharged because of wounds or disease and who wanted to reenter the service.[708]

The Companies

Company A was almost entirely recruited in Charleston, Kanawha County, in the second and third week of August 1862 by Lieutenant Theophilus Maher. Maher also enrolled recruits at Point Pleasant in August 1862, and at Winfield in December 1862. Other officers who enrolled recruits appointed to Company A were Lieutenant William E. Feazel at Point Pleasant in August 1862; Lieutenant John B. Bumgarner at Glenwood in September 1862; Lieutenant William N. Hawkins in August, 1862; and Greenbury Slack, at Coals Mouth in August 1863, at Barboursville in October and December 1863, and at Hurricane Bridge in March and May 1864.

Lieutenant George Danner enrolled at Barboursville in October 1863, and at Charleston in December of 1863; James R. Hall, first Major then Lieutenant-Colonel of the 13th Regiment, took recruits for Company A at Barboursville in October 1863; James W. Johnson, Captain Company A enrolled at Hurricane Bridge in March of 1863; and James C. Wheeler (a civil officer?) enlisted at Charleston in March 1864. Company A was mustered into the United State Service at Point Pleasant on October 7th, 1862, with about 85 men.

Recruitment of Company B was largely credited to Lieutenant William E. Feazel who enrolled volunteers at Point Pleasant in August of 1862. Feazel enlisted recruits appointed to Company B at Point Pleasant in August and September 1862, and August 1863. Other officers also enlisted men who went into Company B. Milton Stewart (commissioned Captain of Company B August 25th, 1862) enrolled at Point Pleasant in April, July, August and November of 1863; at Hurricane Bridge in March 1863; at Charleston in August 1863; at Barboursville in February 1864. Lieutenant Colonel James R. Hall enrolled at Point Pleasant in March and September 1863. Company B was mustered in at Point Pleasant on October 8th, 1862, with about 102 men. In all, 106 men served with Company B over the life of the Regiment.

Company C was in large part recruited by Lieutenant William E. Feazel, who seemed to be everywhere at once. Feazel enrolled volunteers at Charleston in July and August of 1862; at Point Pleasant in July, August and September of 1862; at the Forks of Coal River on July 24th, 1862 and at Barboursville in December of 1863. Van D. McDaniel, Co. C's first Captain, enlisted men for his command at Point Pleasant in January, March and August of 1863. Lieutenant Lemuel Harpold (a future Captain of Company C) enlisted recruits for the Company at Point Pleasant in December of 1862; at Coals Mouth in August and September 1863; at Barboursville in February, March and April of 1864; and at Point Pleasant in March of 1864. Circuit Court Justice of the Peace, Chief Justice and President of Mason Circuit Court Lewis Wetzel enrolled men for the Company at Point Pleasant in July and August of 1862. One "L.O. Hagans" enrolled for the Company at Wheeling on August 21st, 1862; John W. Neal (Lieut. J.W. Neal?) enrolled at Mason City on August 14th, 1862; Lieutenant J.H. Rosler, enrolled at Coals Mouth in August 1863; Lieutenant William N. Hawkins this Regiment, enrolled men on November 28th, 1863, Captain Milton Stewart commanding Company B, enrolled men in September and October 1863 at Barboursville; Lieutenant-Colonel James R. Hall enrolled at Coals Mouth in August 1863 and at Barboursville in November of 1863; and Captain J.A. Smith enlisted men who were assigned to Company C on February 18th, 1865, at Point Pleasant. Company C was mustered on October 8th, 1862, with about 83 men. In all, 112 men served in Company C over the life of the Regiment.

Company D was mustered into service on October 8th, 1862, with about 87 men. The recruits were mostly denizens of old Mason County. A number of them were miners who had come to this country from England, Scotland and Wales. Simon Williams, who became the Company's first captain, enlisted men at Point Pleasant in August and October of 1862; at Hartford City in August 1862; at Hurricane Bridge March 1863; at Barboursville September 1863; Murraysville November 1863; and at Barboursville in February and March 1864. Lieutenant J.W. Neal enrolled men who came to be assigned to Company D, at Point Pleasant in July and August of 1862; at Mason City in August 1862; at Hartford City in August of 1862; and at Murraysville or Morristown in August 1862. Lieutenant J.W. Harman enlisted men at Murraysville in November 1863. Lieutenant William N. Hawkins, Company E, enrolled men who were appointed to duty with Company D at Charleston in August of 1862, and at Point Pleasant in November of 1863. J.W. Hanna, 1st Lieutenant Company D, enrolled recruits at Coals Mouth in August and October of 1863; at Barboursville, Cabell County in November and December 1863, and January 1864; and at Murraysville in November 1863. George Snowden, 2nd Lieutenant Company D, enlisted recruits at Barboursville in August of 1863. Justice Lewis Wetzel enrolled recruits at Hartford City in August of 1862; and Lieutenant William E. Feazel enrolled men for Company D at Point Pleasant in August and September of 1862. A total of 108 names were entered on the rolls of Company D during its term of service.

Company E seems to have been largely recruited at Charleston, Kanawha County, Virginia on August 22nd, 1862, by Lieutenant William N. Hawkins. Hawkins recruited at Charleston in August 1862; at Tuppers Creek near Charleston, August 1862; at Point Pleasant and Charleston in March of 1863; at Charleston and Tupper's Creek in November and December 1863; and at the Mouth of Big Sandy on November 21st, 1863. The following officers also recruited men who were appointed to Company E: Lieutenant Theophilus Maher at Charleston in August 1862; one "T. Meeks" at Charleston in August 1862; Lieutenant John A. Martin at Point Pleasant September 15th, 1862; Lieutenant J.B. Bumgarner on August 9th, 1862, at Ceredo; Lieutenant John S. Cunningham at Charleston August 1863; John H. Rosler at Charleston August 1863; Captain John D. Carter, Company E, at Charleston August 1863; Captain Milton Stewart at Barboursville, Cabell County, October 1863; James C. Wheeler at Charleston in March 1864; and Captain J.A. Smith at Charleston October 1864. Men recruited by Lieutenant John A. Martin who were encouraged to enlist under the auspices of forming a company of sharp-shooters were mustered with Company E when it was mustered into the U.S. Service on October 9th, 1862, at Point Pleasant, Virginia, with about 82 men.

Lieutenant William E. Feazel recruited soldiers for the Regiment who were assigned to Company F at Point Pleasant in August and September 1862; Stephen Comstock, Lieutenant, enrolled soldiers at Point Pleasant in September 1862; Lieutenant William N. Hawkins recruited at Point Pleasant in September 1862; Justice Lewis Wetzel enrolled at Point Pleasant in September 1862; Colonel William R. Brown, this Regiment, enlisted for his command at Point Pleasant in September 1862; William I. Matthews, Lieutenant and later Adjutant for the 13th Regiment, enrolled men at Point Pleasant in September 1862; James R. Hall, Lieutenant-Colonel recruited at Point Pleasant in September and October of 1862, and in August of 1863; John A. Martin, Lieutenant recruited at Point Pleasant in August and September of 1862, up the Kanawha River at Brownstown in August 1862 and at U.S. Army Camp Piatt near Charleston in September 1862; Theophilus Maher, 2nd Lieutenant, Company A, enrolled recruits at Point Pleasant in October 1862; Timothy Russell, Lieutenant, Company F, recruited at Point Pleasant in April 1863 and at West Columbia in October of 1863; Albert F. McCown, future Captain commanding Company F, enlisted men at Point Pleasant in July and February of 1863, at Coals Mouth in August of 1863, at Barboursville in October, November and December of 1863, and at Guyandotte in March of 1864; John Cunningham, Adjutant this Regiment (formerly 11th Regiment Virginia Infantry Volunteers), recruited at Coals Mouth in September 1863; Milton Stewart, Captain, Company B, recruited at Point Pleasant in October 1863; James C. Wheeler recruited at Charleston in March 1864; and James Smith, Captain, recruited at Point Pleasant in February 1865. Company F was mustered in with about 85 men at Point Pleasant, Virginia, on October 9th, 1862. 109 soldiers served in Company F during its term of service.

Captain Allen C. Mason's Company G was a replacement, to fill the vacancy left when Captain John V. Young's Company G was returned to the 11th Regiment Virginia Volunteer Infantry late in 1863. Young's Company G, recruited at the start of the war, was first mustered in with the 11th Regiment Virginia/West Virginia Infantry Volunteers but serving detached, and driven back to Point Pleasant by the Confederate invasion of the Kanawha Valley in September 1862, at a time when the first companies of the 13th Regiment were being organized at the Point, Young's Company attached to and mustered in with the 13th Regiment when it was mustered in October 1862. Young wished to remain with the 13th Regiment and made appeal up the chain of command to that effect, but ultimately, Young and his Company were returned to the 11th Regiment. Allen C. Mason recruited men for replacement Company G at Point Pleasant in December 1863; at Guyandotte December 1863;

January, February, March and May 1864 at Guyandotte; at Barboursville December 1863; at West Columbia November and December 1863 and February 1864; at Hartford City December 1863 and January 1864; and at Cottageville in December 1863. Arthur W. Darnel, Lieutenant this Regiment, enrolled soldiers for Company G at Guyandotte in December 1863 and January 1864; and at Barboursville December 1863. Captain Allen C. Mason's Company (about 90 men) was mustered in February 28th, 1864, at Guyandotte, Virginia, by Lieutenant C.S. Roberts. Over the life of the company, the names of 112 men are carried on the rolls.

Company H was mustered into the United States Service on October 10th, 1862, at Point Pleasant, Virginia, with about 53 men. The following officers enrolled recruits who were appointed to Company H. Lieutenant J.B. Bumgardner enlisted men at Guyandotte, Cabell County, in July, August and September 1862; at Ceredo, Wayne County, in August, September and December 1862; and at Point Pleasant, Mason County, in July, August, September, October and December 1862; and January 1863. T.W. Hampton enrolled recruits in 1862 at Guyandotte, Cabell County; at Point Pleasant in September, October, November and December 1862 and at Kygersville in September 1862. William E. Feazel enlisted soldiers at Barboursville in August 1862; at Kygersville in September 1862 and at Point Pleasant in November 1862. O.W. Griswold enrolled recruits at Point Pleasant in September and November 1862; at Hurricane Bridge February and March 1863; at Barboursville in October, November and December 1863 and at Buffalo, Putnam County, in December 1863. J.A. Martin recruited in Kanawha and Mason Counties along the Elk River: in vicinity of Charleston at Camp Piatt, in August and September 1862; at Brownstown, near Charleston in August 1862; at Malden September 1862; and at Point Pleasant in September 1862. Albert F. McCown enlisted recruits at Point Pleasant in 1862. W.P. Mathers enlisted volunteers at Point Pleasant in August 1863. William Perdue, Lieutenant, Company H, enrolled recruits in February and March of 1864 at Barboursville, Cabell County. Over the life of the company, the names of 107 men are carried on the rolls.

Company I was mustered into Service by Lieutenant C.S. Roberts July 26th, 1863, at Charleston with about 45 men. The following recruiting officers enlisted men who were appointed to Company I. J.D. Young, Lieutenant, enlisted at Charleston in November and December 1862; at Charleston during the months of January and July 1863; and at Walton in December of 1863. Lieutenant William E. Feazel, who would command Company I, enlisted recruits at Charleston in November and December 1862; at Charleston January and June 1863; at Walton January 1863; at Point Pleasant March of 1863; at Guyandotte in October, November and December of 1863; at Barboursville November 1863; and at Charleston in September 1864. Peter Darnel, Sergeant, enlisted men at Charleston during March and August 1863;

at Guyandotte October 1863; and at Guyandotte in February 1864. William Shannon, Sergeant, then Lieutenant, recruited for Company I at Guyandotte October and November 1863; and at Guyandotte February 1864. John S. Cunningham, Adjutant, enrolled at Guyandotte September 1863; and at Charleston August and September 1863. William Mathews recruited at Point Pleasant in November 1862; and Milton Stewart, Captain, enlisted recruits who were mustered in to Company I at Barboursville in September 1863. J.M. (or J.N.) Butler enlisted recruits for Company I who joined at Point Pleasant in February and March 1863. James W. Hanna, Lieutenant, enrolled men for Company I at Coals Mouth in August of 1863. A total 100 men served in the rank and file over the life of the Company.

Company K was mustered by Lieutenant C.S. Roberts on October 3rd, 1863, at Charleston with about 36 men. Another 33 men were mustered at Barboursville November 25th, 1863, with smaller groups of recruits (under 20 men at a time in which a significant number of the male population surnamed "Hill" joined up) mustered in March and April 1864, at Charleston, in preparation for the opening of active campaigning that summer to end the war with strikes against both Confederate armies in the field and at Southern lines of communication and supply. The following recruiters enrolled men who were appointed to Company K. Henry Stump, who became Captain of the Company, enlisted recruits at Walton during the months of July, August, September, October, and December 1863 and January 1864; at Leon, Mason County, in November 1863; at Barboursville in September and December 1863; at Ripley in October 1863 and January 1864; and at Charleston in March 1864. T.C. Hill enlisted at Leon, Mason County, in October, November and December 1863 and January 1864; at Ripley in October 1863; at Barboursville December 1863. J. E. McCoy *re*-enlisted some of T.C. Hill's recruits so that there are double entries for the enrollment of some Company K soldiers in Regimental Books. Taking this into account, records preserve that McCoy enrolled soldiers at Leon in December of 1863 and January 1864; at Barboursville in December 1863 and February 1864; at Walton in January of 1864; and at Coals Mouth in February and March 1864. One "A. Fergason," who perhaps assisted McCoy, enlisted James S. Williams at Leon on January 1, 1864. Milton Stewart, Captain Company B this Regiment, enrolled recruits who mustered with Company K at Barboursville in September, October and in November 1863. Joseph Brumley, Lieutenant, enlisted men at Buffalo, in December 1863. A total of 106 were mustered in when Company K was organized and 119 men served in it over the life of the Company.

Soldiers

Abbot/Abbott, James (signed his name "James Abbot") Company H Private; enlisted August 22, 1862 at Guyandotte, mustered October 10, 1862 at Point Pleasant, age 44, born in Cabell County, Virginia/West Virginia, occupation: farmer.

Adkins/Atkins, John Company I Private; enlisted December 8, 1863 at Guyandotte, mustered February 29, 1864 at Guyandotte; age 20, born in Pike County, Kentucky, occupation: farmer.

Adkins, Spencer Company B Private; Corporal and Sergeant; enlisted August 9, 1862 at Point Pleasant, mustered October 8, 1862 at Point Pleasant, age 32, born in Kanawha County, Virginia/West Virginia, occupation: engineer; promoted to Corporal April 20, 1863, promoted to Sergeant November 10, 1864. Prior to enlistment in the Union Army, Spencer may have served as Private in Company A, 116ᵗʰ Regiment Virginia Militia ("Solger 63 Adkins, Spencer").

Adkins/Atkins, William S. Company G Private; enlisted January 4, 1864 at Buffalo, mustered February 28, 1864 at Guyandotte, age 32; born in Cabell County, Virginia/West Virginia, occupation: farmer.

Adkinson/Atkinson, George H. Company B Private; enlisted August 10, 1863 at Point Pleasant, or Coals Mouth, mustered October 6, 1863 at Barboursville, age 21, born in Mason County, Virginia/West Virginia, occupation: farmer.

Adkinson/Adkisson/Atkinson, John Company E Private; enlisted August 22, 1862 at Charleston, mustered October 9, 1862 at Point Pleasant, age 19, born in Kanawha County, Virginia/West Virginia, occupation: farmer.

Allen, Andrew J. Company H Private; enlisted September 12, 1862 at Camp Piatt, near Charleston, mustered October 10, 1862 at Point Pleasant, age 35; born in Franklin County, Virginia, occupation: farmer.

Andrews, Gustavus A. Company F Private; enlisted February 24, 1863 at Point Pleasant, mustered August 5, 1863 at Charleston, age 18, born in Laporte County, Indiana, occupation: shoemaker.

Arnold, George S. Company D Private; enlisted March 29, 1864 at Barboursville, mustered April 26, 1864 at Barboursville, age 18, born in Wood County, Virginia/West Virginia, occupation: blacksmith.

Arnold, Lewis A. Company D Private; enlisted March 29, 1864 at Barboursville, "assigned to Company D" "examined by Surgeon Abram D. Williams and certified 'free from all bodily and mental infirmity which would in any way disqualify him from performing the duties of a soldier,'" mustered April 26, 1864 at Barboursville, age 18, born in Wood County, Virginia/West Virginia, occupation: farmer; served as Private in the Jackson County Home Guards prior to enlistment.

Asberry/Asbery/Asbury, Abraham Company C Private; enlisted August 2, 1862 at Point Pleasant, received paid $30.00 Mason County Bounty and Premium, mustered October 8, 1862, age 44, born in Greenbrier County, Virginia/West Virginia, occupation: farmer.

Asbery/Asbury, Thomas (signed his name "Thomas Asbery") Company C Private; enlisted August 21/22, 1862 at Point Pleasant, received paid $30.00 Mason County Bounty and Premium, mustered October 8, 1862 at Point Pleasant; age 19, born in Mason County, Virginia/West Virginia, occupation: farmer.

Ascue, George Company E Private; enlisted August 22, 1862 at Charleston, mustered October 9, 1862 at Point Pleasant, age 34, born in Charleston, Virginia/West Virginia, occupation: farmer.

Ashby/Ashley, George Company K Private; enlisted September 1, 1863 at Walton, mustered October 3, 1863 at Charleston, age 17, born in Russell County, Virginia, occupation: farmer.

Ashley John R. Company I Private; enlisted July 1, 1863 at Charleston, mustered August 8, 1863 at Charleston, age 15/16 years, born in Clay County, Virginia/West Virginia, occupation: farmer.

Ashley, Thomas Company K Private enlisted July 25, 1863 at Walton, mustered October 3, 1863 at Charleston, age 34, born in Russell County, Virginia, occupation: farmer.

Bailey, David Company B Private; enlisted August 5, 1862 at Point Pleasant, received paid $30.00 Mason County Bounty and Premium, mustered October 8, 1862 at Point Pleasant, age 40, born in Philadelphia, Pennsylvania, occupation: farmer; detailed for Hospital Cook for the month of April 1863; killed May 28, 1863, by a citizen at Burdette Hardware store at Leon, in Mason County, Virginia/West Virginia.

Bailey/Bayly, John W. Company B Private, Bugler and Hospital Nurse, enlisted August 5, 1862 at Point Pleasant, received paid $30.00 Mason County Bounty and Premium, mustered October 8, 1862 at Point Pleasant, age 21, born in Alleghany County, Pennsylvania, occupation: farmer; detached as a Nurse in Army Hospital at Charleston, beginning July 1, 1864.

Ball, William Company B Private and Corporal; enlisted August 9, 1862 at Point Pleasant, appointed Fifth Corporal October 8, 1862, received paid $30.00 Mason

County Bounty and Premium, mustered October 8, 1862 at Point Pleasant, age 20, born at Point Pleasant, Mason County, Virginia/West Virginia; occupation: farmer.

Barbour/Barber, Francis M. (called "Frank") Company H Corporal; enlisted August 9, 1862 at Ceredo, mustered October 10, 1862 at Point Pleasant, age 19; born in Wayne County, Virginia/West Virginia, occupation: farmer; appointed 4th Corporal January 1, 1864.

Barkes, John (signed his name "John Be[?]ens") Company D 8th Corporal; enlisted August 18, 1862 at Hartford City, received paid $30.00 Mason County Bounty and Premium, mustered October 8, 1862 at Point. Pleasant, age 29; born in Jefferson County, Ohio, occupation: farmer.

Barnes/Barns, Lewis C. Company D Private; enlisted August 15, 1862 at Mason City, mustered October 8, 1862 at Point Pleasant, age 22, born in "Behuot" [Belmont?] County, Ohio, occupation: farmer.

Barnett, Christopher Columbus (called "Columbus") Company B Private; enlisted August 2, 1862 at Point Pleasant, received paid $30.00 Mason County Bounty and Premium, mustered October 8, 1862 at Point Pleasant, age 16, born in Mason County, Virginia/West Virginia, occupation: farmer.

Barnett, Fisher Company B Private; enlisted August 8, 1862 at Point Pleasant, received paid $30.00 Mason County Bounty and Premium, mustered October 8, 1862 at Point Pleasant, age 24, born in Mason County, Virginia/West Virginia, occupation: farmer.

Barnett, James Company B Private; enlisted September 7 or 22, 1862 at Point Pleasant, received paid $30.00 Mason County Bounty and Premium, mustered October 8, 1862 at Point Pleasant, age 18, born in Mason County, Virginia/West Virginia, occupation: farmer.

Barnett, Preston Company B Private; enlisted August 18, 1863 at Point Pleasant, mustered October 6, 1863 at Barboursville, age 20, "born in a log house at Rockcastle in 1843, Mason County, Virginia,"[709] occupation: farmer.

Barnett, Samuel Company B Private; enlisted August 8, 1862 at Point Pleasant, received paid $30.00 Mason County Bounty and Premium, mustered October 8, 1862 at Point Pleasant, age 29, born in Mason County, Virginia/West Virginia March 17, 1833, occupation: farmer. "Samuel Barnett the soldier took part in eleven battles and several skirmishes in which his regiment was engaged."[710]

Barnett, William Company B Private; enlisted August 13, 1862 at Point Pleasant, received paid $30.00 Mason County Bounty and Premium, mustered October 8, 1862 at Point Pleasant, age 33, born in Mason County, Virginia/West Virginia, occupation: farmer.

Barnet/Barnett/Barnette/Barnotte, Eliot/Elliot/Ellot Company K Private; enlisted December 12, 1863 at Leon, Mason County, mustered March 28, 1863 at Charleston, age 25, born in Mason County, Virginia/West Virginia, occupation: farmer.

Barnet/Barnett/Barrett, George W. Company C Private; enlisted August 14, 1862 at Point Pleasant, mustered October 8, 1862 at Point Pleasant, age 40, "born in Buckridge County, Virginia" (Rockbridge County, Virginia or Buck Ridge Rappahannock County, Virginia), occupation: farmer; detailed for Nurse in Army Hospital at Point Pleasant, October 16, 1862.

Barrett, Frank E. Company F Private; enlisted July 31, 1863 at Point Pleasant, mustered August 5, 1863 at Charleston, age 15 or 18, born in Cuyahoga County, Ohio, occupation: farmer.

Baxter, John W. Company A Corporal; enlisted August 14, 1862 at Charleston, appointed Corporal August 20, 1862, mustered October 7, 1862 at Point Pleasant, age 29, born in Kanawha County, Virginia/West Virginia, occupation: cooper.

Baxter, Michael Company A Private; August 12, 1862 at Charleston, mustered October 7, 1862 at Point Pleasant, age 22, born in Kanawha County, Virginia/West Virginia, occupation: farmer; died in Hospital at Charleston, Virginia/West Virginia or at his home near Charleston, of consumption on August 12, 1863.

Bench (also Bernch and Bemk), John L. Company H Private; enlisted August 8, 1862 at Ceredo, mustered October 10, 1862 at Point Pleasant, age 22, born in Wayne County, Virginia/West Virginia, occupation: farmer.

Berks, Jesse Company G Private; enlisted November 28, 1863 at Guyandotte, mustered February 28, 1864 at Guyandotte, age 24, born in Floyd County, Kentucky, occupation: farmer.

Birchfield/Burchfield, Nathaniel (or Nathan) Company D Private; enlisted August 15, 1862 at Hartford City, received paid $30.00 Mason County Bounty and Premium, mustered October 8, 1862 at Point Pleasant, age 34, born in Burke County, North Carolina, occupation: farmer.

Birchfield/Burchfield, William (signed his name "William Birchfield") Company D Private; enlisted August 15, 1862 at Mason City, received paid $30.00 Mason County Bounty and Premium, mustered October 8, 1862 at Point Pleasant, age 36, born in Burke County, North Carolina, occupation: farmer.

Bishop, John Company D Private and Sergeant; enlisted August 15, 1862 at Mason City, Mason County, mustered in October 8, 1862 at Point Pleasant, age 32, born 1830 in Pike County, Kentucky, occupation: cooper.

Blackburn, John F. Company D Private and Hospital Nurse; enlisted August 15, 1862 at Mason City, mustered October 8, 1862 at Point Pleasant, age 26, born in Jefferson County, Ohio, occupation: shoemaker. Blackburn had enrolled in two regiments: in the 13th and in the 11th Virginia Regiments (West Virginia Volunteer Infantry Regiments). On August 15, he enlisted in the 13th and on August 16, he enlisted in the 11th Virginia Infantry (Company K) at Murraysville, (West) Virginia, and was mustered into the 11th on August 31, 1862, at Ravenswood. Lieutenant J.W. Neal, who had enlisted Blackburn in the 13th at Mason City, reclaimed Blackburn and on October 8, 1862, he was mustered into the 13th at Point Pleasant. Blackburn suffered from what was suspected as tuberculosis, "was sickly" and perhaps for this reason, he was, on April 10, 1863, detailed on detached service from the Regiment as a hospital "nurse with the regimental field staff." He was discharged at U.S. General Hospital at Gallipolis, Ohio on October 16, 1863, "cause confirmed phthisis" (*i.e.,* tuberculosis).[711]

Blair, James C. Company H Private; enlisted August 9, 1862 at Ceredo, mustered October 10, 1862 at Point Pleasant, age 29, born in Russell County, Virginia, occupation: farmer; Blair may have been mustered into Company E but he seems not to have served with that Company nor been borne on the rolls of Company E, instead he served with Company H.

Blair, Joseph Company H Private; enlisted November 22, 1863 at Barboursville, mustered at Barboursville November 25, 1863, age 21, born in Russell County, Virginia, occupation: farmer.

Blake, Lewis A. Company C Private; enlisted August12, 1862 at Point Pleasant, received paid $30.00 Mason County Bounty and Premium, mustered October 8, 1862 at Point Pleasant, age 25, born in Mason County, Virginia/West Virginia, occupation: farmer.

Blessing, Calvin T. Company B Corporal and Sergeant; enlisted August 9, 1862 at Point Pleasant, received paid $30.00 Mason County Bounty and Premium, mustered October 8, 1862 appointed 8th Corporal October 8, 1862, age 18, born in Mason County, Virginia/West Virginia, occupation: farmer; promoted from Corporal to Sergeant February 10, 1865.

Bodkin/Bodkins, John Company E Private; enlisted August 14, 1862 at Charleston, mustered October 9, 1862 at Point Pleasant, age 26, born in Kanawha County, Virginia/West Virginia, occupation: farmer.

Boggess (also Boggass/Bogges), John A. (signed "Bo gess") Company K Private; enlisted September 28, 1863 at Barboursville, mustered November 25, 1863 at Barboursville, age 18, born in Mason County, Virginia/West Virginia, occupation: farmer.

Boggess/Booges, Benjamin S. (or F.) Company A Private; enlisted May 1, 1864 at Hurricane Bridge, mustered May 4, 1864 at Charleston, age 18, born in Monroe County, Virginia/ West Virginia, occupation: farmer.

Boggess, Christopher W. (Warren?) Company C 3rd Corporal; enlisted August 15, 1862 at Point Pleasant, received paid $30.00 Mason County Bounty and Premium mustered October 8, 1862 at Point Pleasant, age 19, born in Monroe County, Virginia/West Virginia, occupation: farmer.

Boggess, Robert O. (Osbourne?) Company B Sergeant and Company E 2nd Lieutenant; enlisted August 9, 1862 at Point Pleasant, received paid $30.00 Mason County Bounty and Premium, appointed Fifth Sergeant October 8, 1862, mustered October 8, 1862 at Point Pleasant, age 20; born in Mason County, Virginia/ West Virginia, occupation: farmer; promoted and commissioned 2nd Lieutenant Company E February 10, 1865.

Boles/Bowles, Alexander (signed his name "Alexandra Boles"; also "Alex Boles") Company F Private; enlisted August 20, 1863 at Coals Mouth, mustered October 6, 1863 at Barboursville, age 18, born in Washington County, Pennsylvania, occupation: farmer.

Booker, Albert/Alfred Company A Private; enlisted December 17, 1862 at Winfield, mustered December 17, 1862 at Winfield, age 16 or 18, born in Kanawha County, Virginia/West Virginia, occupation: farmer.

Boso (Boisseaux?), General L. Company D Private (Sergeant?); enlisted November 6, 1863 at Murraysville, Jackson County, on the Ohio River, mustered November 25, 1863 at Barboursville, age 20, born in Jackson County, Virginia/West Virginia, occupation: farmer; may have served as Private in the Jackson County Home Guards before enlistment.

Bostick, Alexander Company E Private; enlisted August 13, 1863 at Charleston, mustered October 6, 1863, age 18, born in Monroe County, Virginia/West Virginia, occupation: laborer.

Bostick (also Bostic), Alexander Company K Private; enlisted March 10, 1864 at Coals Mouth, mustered March 28, 1864 at Charleston, age 18, born in Kanawha County, Virginia/West Virginia, occupation: farmer.

Bostick, Austin (also known as Alderson Bostick) Company E Private; enlisted August 18, 1863 at Charleston, mustered October 9, 1863 at Charleston, age 16, born in Monroe County, Virginia/West Virginia, occupation: farmer.

Boswell, William S. Company K; Private; enlisted December 30, 1863 at Leon, mustered in March 28, 1864 at Charleston, age 30, born in Jackson County, Virginia/West Virginia, occupation: farmer.

Bowen, James H. Company I Private; enlisted December 28, 1863 at Guyandotte, mustered February 29, 1864 at Guyandotte, age 18, born in Lawrence County, Ohio, occupation: farmer.

Bowman (also Bouman), John Company C 5th Corporal; enlisted July 24, 1862 at Forks of Coal River, mustered October 8, 1862 at Point Pleasant, age 21, born in Kanawha County, Virginia/West Virginia, occupation: farmer.

Bowyer/Boyer, Sampson Company E Private; enlisted August 4, 1862 at Charleston, mustered October 9, 1862 at Point Pleasant, age 26, born in Kanawha County, Virginia/West Virginia, occupation: farmer; died of consumption in Army Hospital at Charleston June 1, 1863, "Sent Home".

Boyd, Ewell Company I Private; enlisted November 27, 1863 at Guyandotte, mustered February 29, 1864 at Guyandotte, age 26; occupation: laborer.

Boyd, William R. Company I Private; enlisted November 26, 1863 at Guyandotte, mustered February 29, 1864 at Guyandotte; age 18, born in Patrick County, Virginia, occupation: laborer.

Bradley/Bradly, William L. (signed his name "William L. Bradley") Company F 4th Corporal and Sergeant; enlisted September 9, 1862 at Point Pleasant, received paid $30.00 Mason County Bounty and Premium, mustered October 9, 1862 at Point Pleasant, age 27, born in Botetourt County, Virginia, occupation: farmer; promoted from Corporal to Sergeant May 1, 1864.

Brannon, Adam Justis Company G Private; enlisted December 9, 1863 at Barboursville, mustered February 28, 1864 at Guyandotte, age 18, born in Jackson County, Virginia/West Virginia, occupation: farmer.

Bridgeman, Emory J. Company F Private; enlisted October 7, 1862 at Point Pleasant, mustered October 9, 1862 at Point Pleasant, age 21, born in Meigs County, Ohio, occupation: clerk.

Brown, Amos C. Company A Sergeant; enlisted August 13, 1862 at Charleston, appointed Sergeant August 20, 1862, mustered October 7, 1862 at Point Pleasant, age 28, born in Shenandoah County, Virginia, occupation: boatman.

Brown, Andrew J. (called "Jackson" or "Jack") Company E Private; enlisted March 23, 1863 at Point Pleasant, mustered August 5, 1863 at Charleston, age 19, born in Kanawha County, Virginia/West Virginia, occupation: farmer.

Brown, Charles Company I Private; enlisted December 2, 1862 at Charleston, mustered July 26, 1863 at Charleston, age 18, born in Kanawha County, Virginia/West Virginia, occupation: farmer.

Brown, Elihu Company I Corporal; enlisted December 19, 1862 at Charleston, appointed Corporal September 1, 1863, mustered July 26, 1863 at Charleston, age 19, born in Nicholas County, Virginia/West Virginia, occupation: farmer.

Brown, George E. Company I Corporal; enlisted August 5, 1863 at Charleston, mustered September 16, 1863 at Charleston, age 18, born in Fayette County, Virginia/West Virginia, occupation: farmer; appointed Corporal December 30, 1863.

Brown, Henry Company D Private; enlisted February 26, 1864 at Barboursville, mustered February 27, 1864 at Barboursville, age 17, born in Wood County, Virginia/West Virginia, occupation: farmer.

Brown, Joseph (also called James?) Company I Corporal; enlisted August 5, 1863 at Charleston, mustered September 16, 1863 at Charleston, age 18, born in Nicholas County, Virginia/West Virginia, occupation: farmer; appointed Corporal June 5, 1864.

Brown, William Rufus Colonel commanding 13th Regiment Virginia/West Virginia Volunteer Infantry; age 38-39, born October 11, 1823 in Pennsylvania, occupation: machine shop foreman; commissioned Captain Company E 4th Virginia/West Virginia Volunteer Infantry Regiment July 22, 1861, honorably discharged August 31, 1862, commissioned Colonel 13th Virginia Regiment September 14/16, 1862, appointed Lieutenant-Colonel 13th Virginia/West Virginia Infantry October 10, 1862 as Regiment was of insufficient size to warrant a Colonel, promoted Colonel upon complete organization of the Regiment January 18, 1864, mustered as full Colonel February 28, 1864 at Barboursville, to date from January 18, 1864.

Brumaley/Brumley (also Bromley), Joseph (signed his name "Brumaley") Company F Lieutenant; enlisted September 9, 1862, commissioned 2nd Lieutenant Company F October 8, 1862 to rank October 1, 1862, received paid $30.00 Mason County Bounty and Premium, mustered October 9, 1862, aged 36 years, born in Virginia, occupation: farmer/farm superintendent; commissioned 1st Lieutenant December 14, 1864; may also have served as 1st Lieutenant Mason County 106th Militia, commissioned 1st Lieutenant December 10, 1861 to rank from November 20, 1861.

Buchannon, Thomas Company F Private; enlisted September 15, 1862 at Point Pleasant, mustered October 9, 1862 at Point Pleasant, age 35, born in Scotland, occupation: miner.

Bucknar/ Buckner, Obediah Company A Private; enlisted August 15, 1862 at Charleston, mustered October 7, 1862 at Point Pleasant, age 22, born in Clay County, Virginia/West Virginia, occupation: farmer.

Bumgardner/Bumgarner (also Baumgardner), John B. (also known as "Fatty") Company H 2nd Lieutenant and Recruiting officer for the Regiment, appointed 2nd Lieutenant Company H July 16, 1862 or December 5, 1862; born 1823 at Wytheville, Wythe County Virginia, resigned commission December 31, 1862.

Bumgardner/Bumgarner, Rezin (also Reazin) Company F 2nd Corporal; enlisted September 9, 1862 at Point Pleasant, received paid $30.00 Mason County Bounty and Premium, mustered October 9, 1862 at Point Pleasant age 42, born in Mason County, Virginia/West Virginia, occupation: farmer; detailed for duty as "Convalescent Nurse" at Charleston, U. S. A. Post Hospital at Martinsburg, Virginia/West Virginia.

Burditt (also Bartlett/Burded/Burdett/Burdith), James R. (signed his name "James Burditt") Company E Private; enlisted August 22, 1862 at Charleston, mustered October 9, 1862 at Point Pleasant, age 18, born in Kanawha County, Virginia/West Virginia, occupation: farmer.

Burnet/Burnett, James Company D Private; enlisted August 15, 1862 at Point Pleasant, received paid $30.00 Mason County Bounty and Premium, mustered October 8, 1862 at Point Pleasant, age 18, born in Mason County, Virginia/West Virginia, occupation: teamster.

Burns, Alexander Company E Private; enlisted November 16, 1863 at Charleston, mustered February 27, 1864 at Charleston, age 18, born in Kanawha County, Virginia/West Virginia, occupation: farmer.

Burns, Benjamin Company E Private; enlisted August 22, 1862 at Charleston, mustered October 9, 1862 at Point Pleasant, age 25, born in Monroe County, Virginia/West Virginia, occupation: farmer.

Burns, George Company A Private; enlisted March 10, 1864 at Hurricane Bridge, mustered April 26, 1864 at Hurricane Bridge, age 18, born in Cabell County, Virginia/West Virginia, occupation: farmer.

Burns, William W. Company I Private; enlisted December 13, 1862 at Charleston; mustered August 8, 1863 at Charleston, age 26; born in Monroe County, Virginia/West Virginia, occupation: farmer.

Burris, George Company C Private; enlisted August 22, 1862 at Point Pleasant, received paid $30.00 Mason County Bounty and Premium, mustered October 8, 1862, age 48, born in Shenandoah County, Virginia, occupation: farmer.

Burris/Burrus (also Burous/Burress/Burross/Burrows/Burus), James Perry (called "Perry") Company H Private; enlisted September 20, 1862 at Point Pleasant, mustered in October 11, 1862 at Point Pleasant, age 18, born in Kanawha County, Virginia/West Virginia, occupation: farmer.

Burris, John T. (signed his name "John T. Buris") Company C Private; enlisted August 3, 1863 at Point Pleasant, mustered in August 5 or 15, 1863 at Charleston, age 19, born in Mason County, Virginia/West Virginia, occupation: farmer. Prior to enlistment in the Union Army, Burris may have served as Private in Company A, 116th Regiment Virginia Militia ("Solger 65 Burris, John T.")

Burris, Samuel Company C Private; enlisted March 26, 1864 at Barboursville, mustered April 26, 1864 at Barboursville, age 18, born in Mason County, Virginia/West Virginia, occupation: farmer.

Burrows, David Company F Private; enlisted September 9, 1862 at Point Pleasant, mustered October 9, 1862 at Point Pleasant, age 21, born in Harrison County, Virginia/West Virginia, occupation: farmer. Burrows may or may not have been paid Mason County Bounty monies as for some unexplained reason, his name was lined through in the manuscript, as though he was at first thought eligible but then determined ineligible (*i.e., not* a Mason County resident claiming before expiration of the bounty).[712]

Butcher, John T. Company I Private; enlisted December 9, 1863 at Guyandotte, mustered February 29, 1864 at Guyandotte, age 21, born in Cabell County, Virginia/West Virginia, occupation: farmer.

Butcher, Lewis M. Company I Corporal; enlisted December 6, 1863 at Guyandotte, mustered February 29, 1864 at Guyandotte, age 23, born in Cabell County, Virginia/West Virginia, occupation: farmer; appointed Corporal December 17, 1864.

Butcher, William Company G Private; enlisted May 25, 1864 at Guyandotte, mustered April 26, 1864 at Barboursville, age 18, born in Gallia County, Ohio, occupation: miner.

Caldwell, Patrick H. Company B Corporal; enlisted August 4, 1862 at Point Pleasant, received paid $30.00 Mason County Bounty and Premium, mustered October 8, 1862, age 22, born in Gallia County, Ohio, occupation: farmer; appointed Corporal November 1, 1862; died in hospital at Hurricane Bridge, April 18, 1863 of "Typhoid Pneumonia."

Campbell, David Company G Private; enlisted December 20, 1863 at Barboursville, mustered February 28, 1864 at Guyandotte, age 18, born in Meigs County, Ohio, occupation: farmer.

Campbell, Thomas M. Company D Corporal and Sergeant; enrolled August 22, 1862 at Hartford City, received paid $30.00 Mason County Bounty and Premium, mustered October 8, 1862 at Point Pleasant, age 25, born in Northumberland County, England, occupation: miner; promoted to Sergeant in place of Henry C. Williamson promoted pursuant to Col. W.R. Brown, Gen. Order No. 1 (manu. dated Feb. 15, 1864) to rank as such from Feb. 10, 1864.

Canterbury, Joel F. Company H Private; enlisted August 17, 1862 at Ceredo, mustered October 10, 1862 at Point Pleasant, age 25, born in Wayne County, Virginia/West Virginia, occupation: farmer. Canterbury served with Wayne County Home Guards prior to enlistment in the 13ᵗʰ West Virginia Regiment.

Carlisle (also Carlile), Calvin Company C Private; enlisted August 27, 1862 at Point Pleasant, mustered October 8, 1862 at Point Pleasant, age 18, born in Monroe County, Virginia/West Virginia, occupation: farmer.

Carlin, James Company C Private; enlisted September 1 or 7, 1862 at Point Pleasant, received paid $30.00 Mason County Bounty and Premium, mustered October 8, 1862 at Point Pleasant, age 17, born in England, occupation: farmer.

Carlin, John Company C Private; enlisted August 19, 1863 at Coals Mouth, mustered August 19, 1863 at Barboursville, age 17, born in England; occupation: [illegible] possibly "miner" or "laborer".

Carney, Elvin Company K Private; enlisted March 30, 1864 at Charleston, mustered April 16, 1864 at Charleston, age 18, born Kanawha County, Virginia/West Virginia, occupation: farmer.

Carr, John Company D Private; enlisted August 15, 1862 at Hartford City, received paid $30.00 Mason County Bounty and Premium, mustered October 8, 1862 at Point Pleasant, age 37, born in Ireland, occupation: laborer.

Carrol (also Caral), Charles Company B Private; enlisted August 13, 1862 at Point Pleasant, received paid $30.00 Mason County Bounty and Premium, mustered October 8, 1862 at Point Pleasant, age 35, born in Richmond County, Virginia, occupation: farmer.

Carter, John Deriah Company E Captain; appointed Captain September 12, 1862, commissioned Captain Company E October 8, 1862, mustered October 9, 1862 at Point Pleasant, age 40, (occupation: machinist?).

Carter, William Company A Private; enlisted January 30, 1864 at Charleston, mustered in January 30/31, 1864 at Charleston, age 45, born in Monroe County or Marion County, Virginia/West Virginia, occupation: farmer.

Cartmill (also Cartmell/Cartnell), James Company H Private; enlisted March 28, 1864 at Barboursville, mustered April 26, 1864 at Barboursville, age 18 or 20, born in Wayne County, Virginia/West Virginia, occupation: farmer.

Cartmill, James A. Company D Corporal; enlisted August 15, 1862 at Hartford City, received paid $30.00 Mason County Bounty and Premium, mustered October 8, 1862 at Point Pleasant; age 18, born in Kanawha County, Virginia/West Virginia, occupation: cooper.

Casa, John W. Company I Private; enlisted November 24, 1862 at Charleston, mustered July 26, 1863 at Charleston, age 40, born in Russell County, Virginia, occupation: farmer.

Casdoph/Casdorph, Henry C. (signed his name "Casdoph") Company F Private; enlisted August 21, 1863 at Coals Mouth, mustered October 6, 1863 at Barboursville, age 18, born in Kanawha County, Virginia/West Virginia, occupation: farmer.

Casey, (also Caisey/Kasey), Edward Company C Private; enlisted August 15, 1862 at Point Pleasant, mustered October 8, 1862 at Point Pleasant, age 22, born in Mason County, Virginia/West Virginia, occupation: boatman.

Casey, Madison Company C Private; enlisted August 14, 1864 at Barboursville, mustered April 26, 1864 at Barboursville, age 18, born in Putnam County, Virginia/West Virginia, occupation: farmer.

Cason, John Company E Private; enlisted November 27, 1863 at Charleston, mustered February 27, 1864 at Charleston, age 17, born in Greenbrier County, Virginia/West Virginia, occupation: farmer.

Casto, David Company K Private; enlisted August 1, 1863 at Walton, mustered October 3, 1863 at Charleston, age 30, born in Jackson County, Virginia/West Virginia, occupation: farmer.

Casto, Edward Company K Private; enlisted September 1, 1863 at Walton, mustered October 3, 1863 at Charleston, age 24, born in Jackson County, Virginia/West Virginia, occupation: farmer.

Casto, Enoch Company B Private; enlisted August 5, 1863 at Charleston, mustered August 5, 1863 at Charleston, age 18, born in Jackson County, Virginia/West Virginia, occupation: farmer.

Casto, George, Jr. Company K Private and 4th Sergeant; enlisted September 1, 1863 at Walton, mustered October 3, 1863 at Charleston, age 41, born in Mason County, Virginia/West Virginia, occupation: farmer; may have served as Private in Captain Henry C. Hunter's Company of Jackson County Home Guards before enlistment in the 13th Regiment.

Casto, Isaac Alexander Company G Private; enlisted December 24, 1863 at Barboursville, mustered February 28, 1864 at Guyandotte, age 15, born in Mason County, Virginia/West Virginia, occupation: farmer.

Casto, Jacob ("Jake") Company G Private; enlisted December 24, 1863 at Buffalo, mustered February 28, 1864 at Guyandotte, age 18, born in Jackson County, Virginia/West Virginia, occupation: farmer, stonemason and bricklayer.

Casto, Job K. (seems to have signed his name "Job K. Casto", middle initial could also be "H." or "R.") Company K Private; enlisted September 1, 1863 at Walton, mustered October 3, 1863 at Charleston, age 18, born in Jackson County, Virginia/West Virginia, occupation: farmer.

Casto, Jonathan H. Company K Private; enlisted September 1, 1863 at Walton, mustered in October 3, 1863 at Charleston, age 25, born in Jackson County, Virginia/West Virginia, occupation: farmer; served with the Jackson County Home Guards before enlisting in the 13th Regiment.

Casto, Mason Company B Private; enlisted August 6, 1862 at Point Pleasant, received paid $30.00 Mason County Bounty and Premium, mustered October 8, 1862, age 19, born in Jackson County, Virginia/West Virginia, occupation: farmer.

Casto, Wilson C. Company K 3rd Corporal; enlisted September 1, 1863 at Walton, mustered October 3, 1863 at Charleston, age 18, born in Jackson County, Virginia/West Virginia, occupation: farmer; may have served with Jackson County Home Guards before enlistment.

Chandler (also Chanceller), Abraham E. (signed "Abraham E. Chandler") Company A Private and Corporal; enlisted August 10, 1863 at Coalsmouth, mustered October 6, 1863 at Barboursville, age 18, born in Kanawha County, Virginia/West Virginia, occupation: farmer; promoted to Corporal July 1, 1864.

Chancey/Chancy, John J. Company F Private; enlisted September 10, 1862 at Point Pleasant, mustered October 9, 1862 at Point Pleasant, age 32, born in Jackson County, Virginia/West Virginia, occupation: laborer.

Chapman, Oscar Company B Private; enlisted August 9, 1862 at Point Pleasant, received paid $30.00 Mason County Bounty and Premium, mustered October 8, 1862, age 18, born in Washington County, Ohio, occupation: farmer. Prior to enlistment in the Union Army, Chapman may have served as Private in Company A, 116th Regiment Virginia Militia ("Solger 66 Chapman, Oscar").

Cherry, Henry A. Company D Private and Independent Blazer Scout; enlisted August 18, 1862 at Hartford City, received paid $30.00 Mason County Bounty and Premium, mustered October 8, 1862 at Point Pleasant, age 24, born in Trumbull County, Ohio, occupation: laborer; on detached duty as Blazer Independent Scout in 1864.

Cherry, William B. Company D Private; enlisted November 5, 1863 at Point Pleasant, mustered February 27, 1864 at Barboursville; age 16, born in Meigs County, Ohio, occupation: farmer.

Cheuvront (also Cheveraint/Cheverald/Cheveront), Marshal/Marshel T. Company H Private; enlisted September 20, 1862 at Point Pleasant, mustered in December 11, 1862 at Point Pleasant, age 22, born in Lewis County, Virginia/West Virginia, occupation: farmer.

Childers/Childress, Charles W. Company F Private; enlisted September 9, 1862 at Point Pleasant, mustered October 9, 1862 at Point Pleasant, age 19, born in Putnam County, Virginia/West Virginia, occupation: farmer.

Childers, George W. Company H Corporal; enlisted August 12, 1862 at Barboursville, mustered October 10, 1862 at Point Pleasant, age 18, born in Cabell County, Virginia/West Virginia, occupation: farmer; appointed 2nd Corporal August 1, 1863.

Childers/Childress, Robert Company F Private; enlisted November 10, 1863 at Barboursville, mustered November 25, 1863 at Barboursville, age 18, born in Mason County, Virginia/West Virginia, occupation: farmer.

Childers/Childress, Daniel Company E Private; enlisted August 22, 1862 at Charleston, mustered October 9, 1862 at Point Pleasant, age 19, born in Kanawha County, Virginia/West Virginia, occupation: farmer; possibly "Daniel Childress" who served as an enlisted man in David Wilson's Company A Kanawha County Militia "enrolled April 10, 1862 at Davis Creek Kanawha County and mustered in June 10, 1862."[713]

Christian, George W. Company H Private; enlisted March 6, 1864 at Barboursville, deserted before being mustered, age 17, born in Wayne County, Virginia/West Virginia, occupation: farmer.

Christian, James A. Company H Private; enlisted August 15, 1862 at Ceredo, mustered October 10, 1862 at Point Pleasant, age 19, born in Wayne County, Virginia/West Virginia, occupation: farmer.

Clagg/Clogg, Loini (also Leomi/Leoni/Loany) (signed his name "Loini Clagg") Company F Private and Corporal; enlisted September 9, 1862 at Point Pleasant, received paid $30.00 Mason County Bounty and Premium, mustered in October 9, 1862 at Point Pleasant, age 27, born in Mason County, Virginia/West Virginia, occupation: farmer; promoted to Corporal March 15, 1862.

Clark/Clarke, Alexander Company E Private; enlisted August 22, 1862 at Charleston, mustered October 9, 1862 at Point Pleasant, age 30, born in Kanawha County, Virginia/West Virginia, occupation: farmer.

Clark, Owen B. Company E Private; enlisted August 22, 1862 at Charleston, mustered October 9, 1862, age 32, born in Kanawha County, Virginia/West Virginia, occupation: farmer; died of erysipelas at Point Pleasant February 25, 1863, "Sent Home."

Clark, Robert H. Company H Corporal and Sergeant; enlisted August 15, 1862 at Ceredo, appointed 5th Corporal August 15, 1862, mustered October 10, 1862 at Point Pleasant, age 21, born in Waldo (Waldo County?), Maine, occupation: farmer; appointed 1st Sergeant April 2, 1864.

Clark, Squire Company E Private; enlisted August 22, 1862 at Charleston, mustered October 9, 1862 at Point Pleasant, age 34, born in Kanawha County, Virginia/West Virginia, occupation: farmer.

Clark, William Company H Private; enlisted November. 8, 1863 at Barboursville, mustered November 25, 1863 at Point Pleasant or Barboursville, age 17, born in Cabell County, Virginia/West Virginia, occupation: farmer.

Clendenen/Clendennen, Strauther H. (also Strouther/Strawther. H.; signed his name "Strauther H. Clendenen") Company G Private; enlisted November 21, 1863 at West Columbia, mustered February 28, 1864 at Guyandotte, age 18, born in Mason County, Virginia/West Virginia, occupation: farmer.

Clinton, Charles B. Company E Private; enlisted August 22, 1862 at Charleston, mustered October 9, 1862 at Point Pleasant, age 17, born in Kanawha County, Virginia/West Virginia, occupation: farmer.

Clinton, George D. Company E Private and Corporal; enlisted March 23, 1863 at Point Pleasant, mustered August 5, 1863 at Charleston, age 18, born in Kanawha County, Virginia/West Virginia, occupation: farmer, promoted from Private to Corporal July 28, 1864.

Clonch/Clouch, Alexander Company C Private; enlisted August 8 or 9, 1862 at Point Pleasant, Virginia, received paid $30.00 Mason County Bounty and Premium, mustered October 8, 1862 at Point Pleasant, age 21, born in Kanawha County, Virginia/West Virginia, occupation: farmer.

Clonch, John A. (signed his name "Clonch") Company C Private; enlisted August 9, 1862 at Point Pleasant, received paid $30.00 Mason County Bounty and Premium, muster October. 8, 1862 at Point Pleasant, age 21, born in Mason County, Virginia/West Virginia, occupation: farmer.

Cobb, Allen S. Company I Private; enlisted December 13, 1862 at Charleston, mustered July 26, 1863 at Charleston, age 30, born in Kanawha County, Virginia/West Virginia, occupation: farmer.

Cobb, Andrew Jackson Company A Private; enlisted August 15, 1862 at Charleston, mustered October 7, 1862 at Point Pleasant, age 30, born in Roane County, Virginia/West Virginia, occupation: farmer.

Cobb, Francis M. Company A Private; enlisted August 14, 1862 at Charleston, mustered October 7, 1862 at Point Pleasant, age 22, born in Kanawha County, Virginia/West Virginia, occupation: farmer.

Cobb, Henry Company I Private; enlisted March 20, 1863 at Charleston, mustered July 26, 1863 at Charleston; aged 16 or 18 years, born in Nicholas County, Virginia/West Virginia, occupation: farmer.

Cobb, John M. Company I Private; enlisted December 13, 1862 at Charleston, mustered July 26, 1863 at Charleston, age 18, born in Kanawha County, Virginia/West Virginia, occupation: farmer.

Cobb, Joseph M. [Madison]. Company I Private; enlisted December 28, 1863 at Walton, mustered July 26, 1863 at Charleston, age 36, born in Kanawha County, Virginia/West Virginia, occupation: farmer.

Cobb, Lewis (Lewis S. or L.) Company E Corporal; enlisted August 22, 1862 at Charleston, appointed 2nd Corporal September 12, 1862, mustered October 9, 1862 at Point Pleasant, age 23, born in Kanawha County, Virginia/West Virginia, occupation: cooper.

Cobb, William Company I Private; enlisted August 1, 1863 at Charleston, mustered August 8, 1863 at Charleston, age 18, born in Clay County, Virginia/West Virginia, occupation: farmer.

Cobb, William Anderson Company A Private; enlisted August 15, 1862 at Charleston, mustered October 7, 1862 at Point Pleasant, age 28, born in Roane County, Virginia/West Virginia, occupation: farmer.

Cobb, William R. (signed his name "Robert Cobbs") Company E Private; enlisted August 13, 1863 at Charleston, mustered October 6, 1863 at Charleston, age 21, born in Kanawha County, Virginia/West Virginia, occupation: farmer. Detailed on March 10, 1864 for a body of Independent Scouts in compliance with General Orders No. 2 from "Head Quarters 3d Division Dept., W. Va." (dated "Charleston W.Va. February 16ᵗʰ 1864").

Cobbs, Fleming B. Company E Sergeant; enlisted August 22, 1862 at Charleston, appointed 3ʳᵈ Sergeant September 12, 1862, mustered October 9, 1862 at Point Pleasant, age 27, born in Kanawha County, Virginia/West Virginia, occupation: cooper.

Coleman, James Company A Private; enlisted December 15, 1863 at Barboursville, mustered February 27, 1864 at Barboursville, age 18, born in Kanawha County, Virginia/West Virginia, occupation: farmer.

Comer, Isaac Company E Private; enlisted December 30, 1863 at Tuppers Creek, mustered February 27, 1864 at Charleston, age 17, born in Kanawha County, Virginia/West Virginia, occupation: farmer.

Comer, John R. Company I Private; no date of enlistment or muster extant, just this record of death: "Mar[ch] 3, 1863: John R. Comer died in Reg[imen]t Hospital P[oin]t Pleasant."[714]

Compton, William P. Company A Private; enlisted August 14, 1862 at Charleston, mustered October 7, 1862 at Point Pleasant, age 42, born in Roanoke County, Virginia, occupation: farmer.

Comstock, Stephen 1st Lieutenant and Regimental Quarter Master; commissioned August 20, 1862, appointed 1st Lieutenant and Regimental Quarter Master August 21, 1862, age 42, owner-proprietor of Eagle Mills, located at Point Pleasant, Virginia, selling "lumber in the rough" and grinding corn, "custom wheat" etc. on Saturdays or any day he had "steam up" at his "new grist mill with French burrs."[715] Comstock served on Colonel Rutherford B. Hayes' staff (Hayes commanding 1st Brigade, 2nd Infantry Division Army of West Virginia) in August 1864; and may have served as Delegate from Mason County, to the 1st Wheeling Convention, which met May 13th, 1861 and served as appraiser for the county in 1862.[716]

Cook, Abner Company G Private; enlisted January 29, 1864 at Guyandotte, mustered February 28, 1864 at Guyandotte, age 25, born in Cabell County, Virginia/West Virginia, occupation: farmer.

Cook, Benjamin W. Company I Private; enlisted February 9, 1864 at Guyandotte, mustered in February 29, 1864 at Guyandotte, age 20, born in Cabell County, Virginia/West Virginia, occupation: farmer.

Cook, John Company E. Private; enlisted August 22, 1862 at Charleston, mustered October 9, 1862 at Point Pleasant, age 27, born in Kanawha County, Virginia/West Virginia, occupation: farmer.

Cooper, Wiley Company C Private; enlisted August 15, 1862, received paid $30.00 Mason County Bounty and Premium, mustered October 8, 1862 at Point Pleasant, Virginia, age 44, born in Franklin County, Virginia, occupation: farmer.

Copen, William Perry (called "Perry") Company A; Private and Corporal; enlisted August 14, 1862 at Charleston, mustered October 7, 1862 at Point Pleasant, age 27, born in Kanawha County, Virginia/West Virginia, occupation: farmer; appointed Corporal July 20, 1863.

Coughenour, Martin V. Company H Private; enlisted September 20, 1862 at Point Pleasant, mustered December 11, 1862 at Point Pleasant, age 22, born in Gallia County, Ohio, occupation: farmer.

Cowen (also Cowan), James (signed his name "James Cowen") Company I Private [Corporal?]; enlisted December 11, 1863 at Guyandotte, mustered February 29, 1864, age 21, born in Cabell County, Virginia/West Virginia, occupation: laborer.

Cox, James Company C Private, enlisted August 13, 1862 at Point Pleasant, Virginia, mustered October 8, 1862 at Point Pleasant, age 23, born in Putnam County, Virginia/West Virginia, occupation: farmer.

Craig, John Company A Private; enlisted October 1, 1863 at Barboursville, mustered October 6, 1863 at Barboursville, age 24, born in Kanawha County, Virginia/West Virginia, occupation: boatman.

Crane, George S. (or George V.?) Company E Private and Corporal; enlisted August 22, 1862 at Charleston, mustered October 9, 1862 at Point Pleasant, age 32, born in Kanawha County, Virginia/West Virginia, occupation: farmer; promoted to Corporal May 15, 1865.

Crawford, Abraham/Abram, W. Company I Private; enlisted September 14, 1863 at Guyandotte, mustered October 6, 1863 at Barboursville, age 18, born in Gallia County, Ohio, occupation: farmer.

Crawford (also Crafford), Wesley Company C Private; enlisted February 22, 1864 at Barboursville, mustered February 22, 1864 at Barboursville, age 18, born in Gallia County, Ohio, occupation: farmer.

Cremeans, William H. Company I Private; enlisted November 9, 1863 at Guyandotte, mustered November 25, 1863 at Guyandotte, age 15 or 18, born in Mason County, Virginia/West Virginia, occupation: farmer.

Crislip (also Creslip/Christlieb), Abraham R. Regimental Chaplain 13th West Virginia Volunteer Infantry Regiment; commissioned Chaplain April 5, 1865, mustered April 8, 1865 at Winchester, Virginia, age 40, born in Virginia, occupation: Reverend of the Methodist Episcopal Church.

Crofott (also Crofoot/Crowfoot), Francis M. (signed his name "Crofott") Company H Private; enlisted November 24, 1862 at Point Pleasant, mustered December 11, 1862 at Point Pleasant, age 17, born in Pomeroy, Ohio, occupation: farmer.

Crofott (also Crofoot/Crowfoot), Wesley W. (signed his name "Crofott") Company H Private and Corporal; enlisted September 20, 1862 at Point Pleasant, mustered December 11, 1862 at Point Pleasant, age 18, born in Pomeroy, Ohio, occupation: printer; appointed 4th Corporal November 30, 1864.

Crook, William Morrow (called "Morrow") Company H Corporal and 5th Sergeant; enlisted August 9, 1862 at Ceredo, appointed 4th Corporal August 9, 1862, mustered October 10, 1862 at Point Pleasant, age 18, born in Wayne County, Virginia/West Virginia, occupation: farmer; promoted 2nd Sergeant January 1, 1864.

Crump, James Company C Private; enlisted August 15, 1862 at Point Pleasant, received paid $30.00 Mason County Bounty and Premium, mustered October 8, 1862 at Point Pleasant, age 16 or 18, born in Mason County, Virginia/West Virginia, occupation: farmer.

Cruse, John T. Company I Private; enlisted March 13, 1863 at Point Pleasant, mustered July 26, 1863 at Charleston, age 24, born in Mason County, Virginia/West Virginia, occupation: farmer.

Cullins, Mathias (signed his name "Matthias") Company B Private; enlisted August 4, 1862 at Point Pleasant, received paid $30.00 Mason County Bounty and Premium, mustered October 8, 1862 at Point Pleasant, age 18, born at Pittsburg, Pennsylvania, occupation: farmer.

Cunningham, John S. Lieutenant and Adjutant; enrolled in Kanawha County 80th Militia, June 10, 1862 at St. Albans Virginia/West Virginia and commissioned Captain of 80th Militia by order of June 20, 1862 to rank from June 10, 1862; mustered into Company G 11th Virginia/West Virginia Volunteer Infantry Regiment; transferred from Company G and promoted 1st Lieutenant and Adjutant 13th West Virginia Infantry Regiment June 6, 1863, age about 35, born in New Jersey, occupation: civil engineer.

Cunningham, William P. Company K 1st Sergeant and 1st Lieutenant; enlisted August 1, 1863, mustered October 3, 1863 at Charleston; commissioned October 31, 1864, promoted from Orderly Sergeant to 1st Lieutenant November 10, 1864; age 32, born in Jackson County, Virginia/West Virginia, occupation: farmer; may have served as Private in Captain Henry C. Hunter's Company of Jackson County Home Guards before enlistment in the 13th Regiment.

Cyrus, William H. Company D Private; enlisted January 24, 1864 at Barboursville, mustered February 27, 1864 at Barboursville, age 22, born in Cabell County, Virginia/West Virginia; occupation: farmer. Before enlistment in the 13th Virginia/West Virginia Cyrus served with the 36th Virginia Infantry (Confederate States Army). Being transferred with the 13th West Virginia Regiment to the Shenandoah Valley, Virginia in July of 1864, Cyrus was very nearly captured there and fearful that if captured he would certainly be hung for desertion by his former Colonel, John McCausland commanding in the Shenandoah with Lieutenant General Jubal Early's army, Cyrus requested and was granted a transfer from the Shenandoah Valley theater of war. He was sent to Fort Ridgely, Department of the Northwest, an army outpost near the Dakota reservation in southwestern Minnesota. According to Cyrus, he was transferred "on account of having been in the Rebel army; transferred to Co. A., 1st U.S. Infantry."[717]

Dalrymple, Christian P. Company G Private; enlisted December 25, 1863 at Guyandotte, mustered February 28, 1864 at Guyandotte, age 18, born in Pennsylvania, occupation: farmer.

Dally (also Dalley), Charles D. Surgeon; commissioned Assistant Surgeon 5th Regiment Virginia/West Virginia Infantry September 4, 1862 and promoted to Surgeon 13th Regiment and joined 13th West Virginia Infantry Regiment as Surgeon February 6/16, 1864 at Point Pleasant, age 36, born in Pennsylvania, occupation: physician; absent in charge of Provisional Division Hospital Army of the Shenandoah from April 8, 1865 to June 6, 1865. Education: 1856 University of Pennsylvania under Preceptor: J.R. Crouch; 1878 Ohio State University Starling School of Medicine.

Daniel, Robert Company F Private; enlisted September 9, 1862 at Camp Piatt near Charleston, mustered October 9, 1862 at Point Pleasant, age 25, born in Carroll County, Virginia, occupation: farmer.

Daniel, William Company F Private; enlisted September 15, 1862 at Camp Piatt near Charleston, mustered October 9, 1862 at Point Pleasant, age 44 or 53, born in Carroll County, Virginia, occupation: farmer.

Daniel, William C. Company F Private; enlisted September 15, 1862 at Camp Piatt near Charleston, mustered October 9, 1862 at Point Pleasant, age 18, born in Raleigh County, Virginia/West Virginia, occupation: farmer.

Danner/Darmer, George Company A 1st Sergeant, 1st Lieutenant, and Captain Company A enlisted August 15, 1862 at Charleston, appointed Sergeant August 20, 1862, appointed 1st Sergeant September 27, 1862, mustered October 7, 1862 at Point Pleasant, age 36, born in Baden, Wuerttemberg, Germany or Baden Baden, Germany, occupation: farmer; promoted 1st Lieutenant July 20, 1863 and commissioned August 14/August 20, 1863; commissioned Captain October 30, 1864.

Darling, William H. Company G Private; enlisted December 31, 1863 at Guyandotte, mustered February 28, 1864 at Guyandotte, age 15 (born June 21, 1848), born in Lawrence County, Ohio, occupation: laborer.

Darnell, Arthur W. (called "Wick" Darnell) Companies D and G Sergeant, and 2nd Lieutenant; enlisted August 15, 1862 at Hartford City, received paid $30.00 Mason County Bounty and Premium, mustered as Sergeant Company D October 8/9, 1862 at Point Pleasant, aged 17 years, born in Kanawha County, Virginia/West Virginia, occupation: engineer; commissioned 2nd Lieutenant January 27, 1864 and transferred to Company G February 7, 1864.

Darnel/Darnell, Peter (signed "Darnell") Companies F and I Sergeant, 1st Lieutenant and Captain; enlisted September 9, 1862 at Point Pleasant, received paid $30.00 Mason County Bounty and Premium, mustered as Sergeant October 9, 1862 at Point Pleasant, age 45 years, born in Marshall County, Virginia/West Virginia October 11, 1816 (or born in Ohio County, Virginia/West Virginia), occupation: millwright; transferred from Company F and appointed 1st Lieutenant Company I November 1, 1863, commissioned 1st Lieutenant Company I December 18, 1863, mustered as 1st Lieutenant December 25, 1863 at Guyandotte; appointed Captain Company I by order January 7, 1865, mustered as Captain January 10, 1865 at Cumberland, Maryland.

Daugherty/ Dougherty, John Company F Private; enlisted December 24, 1863 at Barboursville, mustered February 27, 1864 at Barboursville, age 44, born in Augusta County, Virginia, occupation: engineer.

Davis, Andrew J. Company A Corporal; enlisted August 12, 1862 at Charleston, appointed Corporal August, 20, 1862, mustered October 7, 1862 at Point Pleasant, age 23, born in Braxton County, Virginia/West Virginia, occupation: farmer.

Davis, John H. Company I 1st Sergeant and 2nd Lieutenant; enlisted December 3, 1862 at Charleston, appointed 1st Sergeant May 1, 1863, mustered July 26, 1863 at Charleston, age 22, born in Kanawha County Virginia/West Virginia October 25, 1840, occupation: farmer; commissioned 2nd Lieutenant Company I January 7, 1865 and mustered January 10, 1865 at Cumberland, Maryland.

Davis, Robert H. Company A; Corporal, Sergeant, and 2nd Lieutenant; enlisted August 12 or 14, 1862 at Charleston, appointed Corporal August 20, 1862, mustered October 7, 1862 at Point Pleasant, aged 28 years, born in Nicholas County, Virginia/West Virginia, occupation: farmer; promoted Sergeant July 1st, 1863 (or July 20, 1863); discharged October 31, 1864 and promoted 2nd Lieutenant by order of Major General George Crook at Camp Russell, Virginia November 10, 1864.

Davis, Samuel H. Company I Private; (no enlistment information), mustered April 25, 1864 at Barboursville, age 44-45 years, born Lunenburg County, Virginia, occupation: farmer.

Davis, Thomas W. Company I Private; enlisted December 22, 1863 at Guyandotte, mustered February 29, 1864 at Guyandotte, age 18, born in Cabell County, Virginia/West Virginia, occupation: laborer.

Davis, Timothy Russell Company F Private; enlisted October 6, 1863 at West Columbia, mustered November 25, 1863 at Barboursville, age 18, born in Meigs County, Ohio, occupation: laborer.

Davis, William G. Company C Private and 7th Corporal; enlisted August 22, 1862 at Point Pleasant, received paid $30.00 Mason County Bounty and Premium, mustered October 8, 1862 at Point Pleasant, age 22, born in Belmont County, Ohio, occupation: farmer; appointed 7th Corporal January 8, 1863.

Davis, William G. Company I Private; enlisted November 7, 1863 at Guyandotte, mustered November 25, 1863 at Guyandotte, age 44, born in Cabell County, Virginia/West Virginia, occupation: farmer.

Davis, William M. Company A Corporal; enlisted August 15, 1862 at Charleston, mustered October 7, 1862 at Point Pleasant, age 30, born in Braxton County, Virginia/West Virginia, occupation: farmer; appointed Corporal June 1, 1864.

Denny (also Denney/Deny), James (signed his name "Deney") Company C Private; enlisted August 13 or 15, 1862 at Point Pleasant, received paid $30.00 Mason County Bounty and Premium, mustered October 8, 1862 at Point Pleasant, age 33, born in Springfield Township, Gallia County, Ohio occupation: farmer.

Dewese (also Dewees/Deweese), William T. (William Thomas Dewese?) Company B Private; enlisted August 8, 1862 at Point Pleasant, received paid $30.00 Mason County Bounty and Premium, mustered October 8, 1862, age 24, born in Jackson County, Virginia/West Virginia, occupation: farmer.

Dicken, James R. Company C Private; enlisted September 16, 1862 at Point Pleasant, mustered October 8, 1862 at Point Pleasant, age 17; born in Mason County, Virginia/West Virginia, occupation: farmer.

Dillion/Dillon, Charles Company G Private; enlisted January 17, 1864 at Guyandotte, mustered February 28, 1864 at Guyandotte, age 18, born Lawrence County, Ohio, occupation: laborer.

Dillion/Dillon, William J. (signed his name "William Dillon") Company G Private; enlisted December 25, 1863 at Guyandotte, mustered February 28, 1864 at Guyandotte, age 18, born in Lawrence County, Ohio, occupation: farmer.

Dillon/Dillion, George P. Company G Private; enlisted March 30, 1864 at Guyandotte, mustered April 26, 1864, age 22; born in Russell County, Virginia, occupation: farmer.

Dingey, Isaac Company D Private and Sergeant; enlisted August 22, 1862 at Hartford City, received paid $30.00 Mason County Bounty and Premium, mustered October 8, 1862 at Point Pleasant, age 31, born in Washington County, Ohio, occupation: cooper; Sergeant at time of discharge from the United States Service on February 16, 1865.

Dishman (also Dichmann/Dishmon/Dishmun), Samuel R. (signed "Dishman") Company H Private; enlisted August 14, 1862 at Ceredo, mustered October 10, 1862 at Point Pleasant, age 18, born in Wayne County, Virginia/West Virginia, occupation: farmer.

Dodson (also Dobson/Dotsin/Dotson), Charles G. Company C Private; enlisted August 15, 1862 at Point Pleasant, Virginia, received paid $30.00 Mason County Bounty and Premium, mustered October 8, 1862 at Point Pleasant, age 44; born in Rappahannock County, Virginia, occupation: farmer.

Donally (also Donnaley/Donnelly/Douneely), Peter (signed his name "Donally") Company F Private; enlisted September 21, 1862 at Point Pleasant, mustered October 9, 1862 at Point Pleasant, age 15, born in "Doun Co., Ireland" (County Down, Ireland), occupation: miner. Fifteen year old, native of Ireland, Private Peter Douneely (Donnelly) of Company F, deserted.[718]

Doolittle, David W. Company F Private; enlisted October 5, 1863 at West Columbia, mustered November 25, 1863 at Barboursville, age 35, born in Kanawha County, Virginia/West Virginia, occupation: miner.

Drake, James M. Company H Private and Corporal; enlisted October 23, 1862 at Guyandotte, mustered December 11, 1862 at Point Pleasant, age 27, born in Cabell County, Virginia/West Virginia, occupation: farmer; appointed 7th Corporal March 21, 1864.

Duke, John H. Company H; Corporal, Color Corporal and Sergeant; enlisted August 12, 1862 at Ceredo, Wayne County, appointed 7th Corporal August 12, 1862, mustered October 10, 1862 at Point Pleasant, age 24, born in Cabell County, Virginia/West Virginia, occupation: farmer; appointed 5th Sergeant March 21, 1865.

Duncan/Dunken/Dunkin, Benjamin A. Company C Private; enlisted August 15, 1862 at Point Pleasant, mustered October 8, 1862 at Point Pleasant, Virginia, age 21, born in Floyd County, Virginia, occupation: farmer.

Dunkle (also Dunkel or Duncan), Harvey Company H; 1st Sergeant and 2nd Lieutenant; enlisted July 22, 1862 at Ceredo, appointed 1st Sergeant July 22, 1862, mustered October 10, 1862 at Point Pleasant, aged 28 years, born in Wayne County, Virginia/West Virginia, occupation: farmer; appointed 2nd Lieutenant Company H and mustered April 2, 1864 at Cumberland, Maryland, commissioned 2nd Lieutenant Company H April 8, 1864.

Dunlap, Adam Company C Private; enlisted August 2, 1862 at Point Pleasant, received paid $30.00 Mason County Bounty and Premium, mustered October 8, 1862 at Point Pleasant, age 44, born in Jefferson County, Ohio, occupation: farmer; died in Regimental Hospital Point Pleasant February 1863 "of measles."

Dunlap, Israel Company C Private; enlisted March 21, 1864 at Barboursville, mustered April 26, 1864 at Barboursville, age 15 or 18; born in Hocking County, Ohio, occupation: farmer.

Dunlap, William Company C Private; enlisted August 15, 1862 at Point Pleasant, received paid $30.00 Mason County Bounty and Premium, mustered October 8, 1862 at Point Pleasant, age 19, born in Muskingum County, Ohio, occupation: farmer.

Eads, Charles Company C Private; enlisted September 10, 1862 at Point Pleasant, mustered October 8, 1862 at Point Pleasant, age 23, born in Mason County, Virginia/West Virginia, occupation: farmer; prior to enlistment in the Union Army, Eads may have served as Private in Company A, 116th Regiment Virginia Militia ("Solger 75 Eads, Charles").

Eads, David Company C Private; enlisted August 15, 1862 at Point Pleasant, received paid $30.00 Mason County Bounty and Premium, mustered October 8, 1862 at Point Pleasant, age 19, born in Mason County, Virginia/West Virginia, occupation: farmer.

Eads, William A. Company C Private; enlisted August 11, 1862 at Point Pleasant, received paid $30.00 Mason County Bounty and Premium, mustered October 8, 1862 at Point Pleasant, age 29, born in Mason County, Virginia/West Virginia, occupation: farmer.

Eaves/Eves, Alexander Company H Private; enlisted August 9, 1862 at Guyandotte, mustered January 6, 1863 at Point Pleasant, age 20, born in Cabell County, Virginia/West Virginia, occupation: farmer.

Eckard, Calvin J. Company B Sergeant; enlisted August 4, 1862 at Point Pleasant, received paid $30.00 Mason County Bounty and Premium, appointed Fourth Sergeant October 8, 1862, mustered October 8, 1862, age 19, born in Mason County, Virginia/West Virginia, occupation: farmer. Family lore preserves that Eckard served as militia before enlistment in the 13th Regiment ("C.J. Eckard volunteered for military duty May 14, 1861" in "Harry Lee Siders" submitted by Harry Lee Siders, David Siders and Don Lee Siders to *History of Mason County, W. Va. 1987,* p. 310.)

Eckard, Robert O. Company B Corporal; enlisted August 2, 1862 at Point Pleasant, received paid $30.00 Mason County Bounty and Premium, appointed 6th Corporal October 8, 1862, mustered October 8, 1862, age 21, born in Mason County, Virginia/West Virginia, occupation: farmer.

Eckard, William R. Company B Corporal; enlisted August 2, 1862 at Point Pleasant, received paid $30.00 Mason County Bounty and Premium, appointed 4th Corporal October 8, 1862, mustered October 8, 1862, age 21, born in Mason County, Virginia/West Virginia, occupation: farmer.

Edens, John Company A Private; enlisted October 22, 1863 at Barboursville, mustered November 25, 1863 at Barboursville, age 18, born in Tazewell County, Virginia, occupation: farmer.

Edens, John W. Company A Private; enlisted August 15, 1862 at Charleston, mustered October 7, 1862 at Point Pleasant, age 35, born in Botetourt County, Virginia, occupation: farmer.

Edens, Martin Van B. Company A Corporal; enlisted August 15, 1862 at Charleston, appointed Corporal September 23, 1862, mustered October 7, 1862 at Point Pleasant, age 28, born in Botetourt County, Virginia, occupation: cooper.

Edwards, Arthur Company F Teamster/Waggoner; enlisted September 9, 1862 at Point Pleasant, received paid $30.00 Mason County Bounty and Premium, mustered October 9, 1862 at Point Pleasant, age 42, born in Mason County, Virginia/West Virginia, occupation: farmer, Edwards entered on his duties as teamster in October 1862.

Edwards, Harrison Company F Private; enlisted March 31, 1864 at Guyandotte, mustered April 26, 1864 at Barboursville, age 21, born in Mason County, Virginia/West Virginia, occupation: farmer.

Edwards, James Company F Fifer and Corporal; enlisted September 9, 1862 at Point Pleasant, received paid $30.00 Mason County Bounty and Premium, mustered in October 9, 1862 at Point Pleasant, age 23, born in Mason County, Virginia/West Virginia, occupation: farmer.

Edwards, Lewis Company G Corporal; enlisted December 10, 1863 at West Columbia, age 31, born in Mason County, Virginia/West Virginia, occupation: farmer; promoted Corporal Feb. 15, 1864 pursuant to Col. W.R. Brown, Gen. Order No. 1 (manu. dated Feb. 15, 1864) to rank as such from Jan. 27, 1864, mustered February 28, 1864 at Guyandotte, promoted to Sergeant March 20, 1865.

Edwards, William Company B Private; enlisted August 4, 1862 at Point Pleasant, received paid $30.00 Mason County Bounty and Premium, mustered October 8, 1862, age 44, born in Washington, County, Ohio, occupation: farmer.

Elkins, Alexander Company H Private; enlisted December 27, 1863 at Barboursville, mustered February 27, 1864 at Barboursville, age 17, born in Wayne County, Virginia/West Virginia, occupation: farmer.

Elkins, Franklin Company G Private; enlisted December 29, 1863 at Guyandotte, mustered February 28, 1864 at Guyandotte, age 18, born in Lawrence County, Ohio, occupation: farmer.

Elkins, James P. Company H Corporal; enlisted August 11, 1862 at Ceredo, appointed 8th Corporal August 11, 1862, mustered October 10, 1862 at Point Pleasant, age 19, born in Wayne County, Virginia/West Virginia, occupation: farmer.

Ellis, Richard T. Company C Private; enlisted August 9 or 15, 1862 at Point Pleasant, received paid $30.00 Mason County Bounty and Premium, mustered October 8, 1862 at Point Pleasant, age 30, born in Monroe County, Virginia/West Virginia, occupation: farmer.

Embleton (also Embeltin), John (John G.?) Company D Private and Sergeant; enlisted August 15, 1862 at Mason City, received paid $30.00 Mason County Bounty and Premium, mustered October 8, 1862 at Point Pleasant, age 24, born in Durham County, England, occupation: miner; Sergeant at time of discharge from U.S. Service September 10, 1863 at Point Pleasant.

England, Julius G. Company I Private; enlisted November 26, 1862 at Charleston, mustered July 26, 1863 at Charleston, age 21, born in Kanawha County, Virginia/West Virginia, occupation: farmer.

England, William P. Company I Private; enlisted December 25, 1862 at Charleston, mustered July 26, 1863 at Charleston, age 30, born in Kanawha County, Virginia/West Virginia, occupation: farmer. Detailed on March 10, 1864 for a body of Independent Scouts in compliance with General Orders No. 2 from

"Head Quarters 3d Division Dept., W.Va." (dated "Charleston W.Va. February 16th 1864").

Entsminger, Isaac Company G Corporal; enlisted December 12, 1863 at Barboursville, promoted Corporal Feb. 15, 1864 pursuant to Col. W.R. Brown, Gen. Order No. 1 (manu. dated Feb. 15, 1864) to rank as such from Jan. 27, 1864, mustered February 28, 1864 at Guyandotte, age 40, born Gallia County, Ohio, occupation: miller.

Ewart, Lewis H. Company E Corporal; enlisted August 22, 1862 at Charleston, appointed 5th Corporal September 12, 1862, mustered October 9, 1862 at Point Pleasant, age 22, born in Kanawha County, Virginia/West Virginia, occupation: laborer.

Facemeirs/Facemier/ Facemire/Facemires/ Facemyers, Aaron V. Company A Private; enlisted August 15, 1862 at Charleston, mustered October 7, 1862 at Point Pleasant, age 20, born in Braxton County, Virginia/West Virginia, occupation: farmer.

Fadeldy/Fadeley, John Company I Sergeant, enlisted November 22, 1862 at Point Pleasant, appointed Sergeant May 1, 1863, mustered July 26, 1863 at Charleston, age 24, born in Shenandoah County, Virginia, occupation: farmer.

Farland/Farlin//Farling/Forrell, Burrell/Burwell (signed his name "Burel Farlin") Company E Private; enlisted December 30, 1863 at Charleston, mustered February 27, 1864 at Charleston, age 19, born in Wyoming County, Virginia/West Virginia, occupation: farmer.

Farley, George S. Company D Corporal and Sergeant; enlisted August 15 or 22, 1862 at Hartford City, received paid $30.00 Mason County Bounty and Premium, mustered in as Corporal October 8, 1862 at Point Pleasant, age 25, born in Northumberland County, England, occupation: miner; promoted to Sergeant, June 12, 1864.

Farley, Hazard Company F Private and Principal Musician (Drum Major); enlisted September 28, 1862 at Point Pleasant, mustered October 9, 1862 at Point Pleasant, age 43, born in Monroe County, Ohio, occupation: cooper, promoted to Drum Major September or October 28, 1862.

Fauber, George W. Company D Private; enlisted August 15 or 22, 1862 at Hartford City, received paid $30.00 Mason County Bounty and Premium, mustered October 8, 1862 at Point Pleasant, age 28, born in Kanawha County, Virginia/West Virginia, occupation: cooper. Prior to enlistment in the Union Army, Fauber may have served as Private in Company A, 116th Regiment Virginia Militia ("Solger 77 Farber, George").

Fauver, James M. Company B Private; enlisted August 4, 1862 at Point Pleasant, received paid $30.00 Mason County Bounty, mustered October 8, 1862, at Point Pleasant, age 18, born in Kanawha County, Virginia/West Virginia, occupation: farmer.

Fauver (also Farber/Fawver/Franver), Thomas D. Company G Private; enlisted December 7, 1863 at Barboursville, age 18, born in Kanawha County, Virginia, occupation: farmer. Prior to enlistment in the Union Army, Fauver may have served as Private in Company A, 116th Regiment Virginia Militia ("Solger 76 Farber, Thomas I").

Fawght/Fought, Thomas (signed his name "Fawght") Company H Private; enlisted August 7, 1863 at Point Pleasant, mustered October 6, 1863 at Charleston, age 29, born in Perry County, Ohio, occupation: farmer.

Feazel/Feazle, William E. Lieutenant and Captain; Lieutenant Company G 1st Virginia/West Virginia Volunteer Cavalry Regiment; 2nd Lieutenant and Recruiting Officer for 13th Infantry Regiment, mustered into the 13th Virginia/West Virginia Volunteer Infantry July 19, 1862, as 2nd Lieutenant and Recruiting Officer, aged 38 years, assigned to duty with Company C and commissioned 2nd Lieutenant Company C by order of September 12, 1862, mustered with Company C when the Company was mustered October 8/9, 1862 but then detached on recruiting service October 1862 by Special Order of Major General Robert H. Milroy, transferred to Company I October 6, 1863 and appointed 1st Lieutenant January 12 (or January 21), 1863, mustered May 1, 1863 at Charleston; appointed Captain Company I November 1, 1863 to fill vacancy, commissioned Captain December 18, 1863 and mustered in as Captain Company I December 24, 1863 at Guyandotte, resigned and discharged December 19, 1864.

Ferall, William P. Company K Private; enlisted July 25, 1863 at Walton, mustered October 3, 1863 at Charleston, age 32, born in Russell County, Virginia, occupation: farmer.

Ferguson, Anderson L. Company G Private; enlisted January 3, 1864 at Buffalo, mustered February 28, 1864 at Guyandotte, age 18, born in Putnam County, Virginia/West Virginia, occupation: farmer.

Ferguson, Andrew W. ("Andy") Company B Private; enlisted August 8, 1862 at Point Pleasant, received paid $30.00 Mason County Bounty and Premium, mustered October 8, 1862, age 37, born in Kanawha County, Virginia/West Virginia, occupation: carpenter.

Ferguson/Furgusson, James Company I Private; enlisted November 23, 1863 at Guyandotte, mustered November 25, 1863 at Guyandotte, age 44, born in Cabell County, Virginia/West Virginia, occupation: farmer.

Ferguson/Furgusson, Jesse Company I Private; enlisted November 23, 1863 at Guyandotte, mustered November 25, 1863 at Guyandotte, age 44, born in Cabell County, Virginia/West Virginia, occupation: farmer.

Ferguson, John H. Company B Private and Corporal; enlisted August 8, 1862, at Point Pleasant, received paid $30.00 Mason County Bounty and Premium, mustered October 8, 1862 at Point Pleasant, age 17, born 1845 in Putnam County, Virginia/West Virginia, occupation: farmer; appointed Corporal November 10, 1864.

Ferguson (also Fergesson), William Company G Private; enlisted December 12, 1863 at Barboursville, mustered February 28, 1864 at Guyandotte, age 18, born in Putnam County, Virginia/West Virginia, occupation: carpenter.

Fitswater/Fitzwater, George W. Company A Private; enlisted August 12, 1862 at Charleston, mustered in October 7, 1862 at Point Pleasant, age 18, born in Nicholas County, Virginia/West Virginia, occupation: farmer; died "of disease" in Army Hospital at Hurricane Bridge, Virginia/West Virginia April 2, 1863.

Field/Fields, Samuel Company A Private, enlisted December 15, 1863 at Barboursville, mustered February. 27, 1864 at Barboursville, age 16 (age given in official papers as 19), born in Bedford County, Virginia, occupation: farmer. The following order came down came down from division headquarters regarding Field's underage enlistment: "Samuel Field aged 17 next March and Edward Hammon aged 15 next February are claimed by their mothers to have been enlisted under military age without consent of parents. If you find this is so you will discharged them *unless they have been mustered into service by the mustering officer.*"[719]

Fife, Joseph W. Company G Private; enlisted December 27, 1863 at Guyandotte, mustered February 28, 1864 at Guyandotte, age 18, born in Gallia County, Ohio, occupation: farmer.

Fink, Harvey N. (or Harvey M. or W.) Company C Private; enlisted March 30, 1864 at Baboursville, mustered April 26, 1864 at Barboursville, age 18, born in Monroe County, Virginia/West Virginia, occupation: farmer.

Fisher, Andrew H. Company G Private; enlisted December 15, 1863 at West Columbia, mustered February 28, 1864 at Guyandotte, age 18, born in Mason County, Virginia/West Virginia, occupation: farmer.

Fisher, Daniel M. Company B Private; enlisted August 9, 1862 at Point Pleasant, received paid $30.00 Mason County Bounty and Premium, mustered October 8, 1862 at Point Pleasant, age 22, born in Mason County, Virginia/West Virginia, occupation: farmer.

Fisher, John H. Company B Private; enlisted September 2, 1862 at Point Pleasant, received paid $30.00 Mason County Bounty and Premium, mustered October 8, 1862 at Point Pleasant, age 24, born in Mason County, Virginia/West Virginia, occupation: farmer.

Fisher, John M. Company B Private; enlisted August 9, 1862 at Point Pleasant, received paid $30.00 Mason County Bounty and Premium, mustered into service October 8, 1862 at Point Pleasant, age 23, born in Rockingham County, Virginia, occupation: farmer.

Fisher, Thomas H. Company B Private, Corporal and Sergeant; enlisted September 4, 1862 at Point Pleasant, received paid $30.00 Mason County Bounty and Premium, mustered October 8, 1862 at Point Pleasant, age 22, born September 20, 1840 in Mason County, Virginia/West Virginia, occupation: farmer; appointed Corporal July 28, 1863, promoted to Sergeant November 10, 1864.

Flake (also Flack/Fluck), Samuel V. Company A Private; enlisted August 14, 1862 at Point Pleasant or August 15, 1862 at Charleston, noted as "Not mustered" on Roll dated October 9, 1862, also recorded as mustered into the U.S. Service December 17, 1862 at Winfield, age 18, born in Kanawha County, Virginia/West Virginia, occupation: farmer.

Flinn, Nelson C. (signed his name "Nelson C. Flinn") Company D Private/Corporal; enlisted August 15, 1863 at Coals Mouth, mustered October 6, 1863 at Barboursville, age 23, born in Wood County, Virginia/West Virginia, occupation: farmer; promoted Corporal pursuant to Col. W.R. Brown, Gen. Order No. 1 (manu. dated Feb. 15, 1864) to rank as such from Feb. 10, 1864.

Flowers, Thomas W[ilson] Company G Private; enlisted January 10, 1864 at Guyandotte, mustered February 28, 1864 at Guyandotte, age 16/17, born in Jackson County, Virginia/West Virginia, occupation: farmer.

Floyd, John H. Company G Corporal; enlisted December 3, 1863 at West Columbia, mustered February 28, 1864 at Guyandotte, age 18, born in Mason County, Virginia/West Virginia, occupation: farmer.

Fone/Fore/Four/Foure, Joel (signature appears to be "J. J. Fone") Company E Private; enlisted November 11, 1863 at Tuppers Creek, mustered February 27, 1864 at

Charleston, age 17, born in Kanawha County, Virginia/West Virginia, occupation: farmer.

Forbes (also Forbs), David L. Company F Sergeant; enlisted August 14, 1862 at Point Pleasant, received paid $30.00 Mason County Bounty and Premium, mustered October 9, 1862 at Point Pleasant,, age 20, born in Schuylkill County, Pennsylvania, occupation: blacksmith.

Forbush, James J. Company I Corporal; enlisted December 2, 1863 at Guyandotte, mustered February 29, 1864 at Guyandotte, age 32, born in Augusta County, Virginia, occupation: laborer.

Forrester (also Forester), Jerome B. Company C Private; enlisted August 7, 1862 at Point Pleasant, received paid $30.00 Mason County Bounty and Premium, mustered October 8, 1862 at Point Pleasant, age 18, born in Lancaster County, Ohio, occupation: farmer.

Frame, Christopher C. Company A Private and Corporal; enlisted August 15, 1862 at Charleston, mustered October 7, 1862 at Point Pleasant, age 21, born in Braxton County, Virginia/West Virginia, occupation: farmer; appointed Corporal July 1, 1864.

Frame/Frem, Frederick Company A Private; enlisted August 15, 1862 at Charleston, mustered October 7, 1862 at Point Pleasant, age 23, born in Nicholas County, Virginia/West Virginia, occupation farmer; died in Hospital at Winfield, Virginia/West Virginia, in the afternoon of November 29, 1862, of "Brain fever"/ died of "congestive fever after a severe illness of four days," body escorted home by brother C. C. Frame and Corporal John Baxter.

Frasier/Frazier, William T. Company C Private; enlisted February 18, 1865 at Point Pleasant, mustered February 18, 1865 at Point Pleasant, age 18, born in Mason County, Virginia/West Virginia, occupation: farmer.

Frost, Harrison Company B Private; enlisted August 9, 1862, at Point Pleasant, received paid $30.00 Mason County Bounty and Premium, mustered October 8, 1862 at Point Pleasant, age 39, born in Meigs County, Ohio, occupation: farmer.

Fry, John W. Company F Private and 5th Corporal; enlisted September 9, 1862 at Point Pleasant, received paid $30.00 Mason County Bounty and Premium, mustered October 9, 1862 at Point Pleasant, age 37, born in Mason County, Virginia/West Virginia, occupation: farmer.

Fry, Marion Company D Corporal and Sergeant; enlisted August 15, 1862 at Hartford City, received paid $30.00 Mason County Bounty and Premium, mustered

October 8, 1862 at Point Pleasant, age 21, born in Mason County, Virginia/West Virginia, occupation: farmer; detailed for cannonier on March 28, 1864 and promoted to Sergeant November 11, 1864.

Fry, Peter Company D Private; enlisted August 18, 1862 at Hartford City, received paid $30.00 Mason County Bounty and Premium, mustered October 8, 1862 at Point Pleasant, age 30, born in Mason County, Virginia/West Virginia, occupation: farmer.

Fuler/Fuller, Hiram (signed his name "Hiram Fuler") Company H Private; enlisted August 14, 1862 at Ceredo, mustered in October 10, 1862 at Point Pleasant, age 21, born in Pike County, (Company Descriptive Rolls indicate that Fuller was born in "Pike Co., Virginia", however there is no Virginia or West Virginia County by that name, likely States may however be Pike County, Kentucky and Pike Count, Ohio), occupation: farmer.

Fuller, James M. Company H Private; enlisted August. 12, 1862 at Ceredo, mustered in October 10, 1862 at Point Pleasant, age 18, born in Wayne County, Virginia/West Virginia, occupation: farmer.

Fuller, Stephen Company H Private; enlisted August 8, 1862 at Ceredo, mustered in October 10, 1862 at Point Pleasant, age 34, born in Russell County, Virginia, occupation: farmer.

Fuller, Stephen (or Stephen F. Fuller) Company H Private and Corporal; enlisted October 26, 1863 at Barboursville, mustered in November 25, 1863 at Barboursville, age 18, born in Russell County, Virginia, occupation: farmer.

Fulwiler (also Fullwiler), George W. Company H Private; enlisted August 8, 1862 at Ceredo, appointed 2nd Corporal August 8, 1862, mustered in October 10, 1862 at Point Pleasant, age 38, born in "Bartlett, Virginia" (Bartlett, Isle of Wight, Virginia?), occupation: farmer.

Gardner, Peter A. Company H Private; enlisted September 20, 1862 at Point Pleasant, mustered in December 11, 1862 at Point Pleasant, age 25, born in Mason County, Virginia/West Virginia, occupation: farmer.

Garton, Stephen Company G Private; enlisted January 3, 1864 at Buffalo, mustered February 28, 1864 at Guyandotte, age 19, born in Putnam County, Virginia/West Virginia, occupation: farmer.

Gaskins, Charles T. Company G Private; enlisted December 25, 1863 at West Columbia, promoted Corporal Feb. 15, 1864 pursuant to Col. W.R. Brown, Gen. Order No. 1 (manu. dated Feb. 15, 1864) to rank as such from Jan. 27, 1864, mustered

February 28, 1864 at Guyandotte, age 24, born in Mason County, Virginia/West Virginia, occupation: farmer.

Gaskins, James H. Company B Private; enlisted August 9, 1862 at Point Pleasant, received paid $30.00 Mason County Bounty and Premium, mustered October 8, 1862 at Point Pleasant, age 28, born in Mason County, Virginia/West Virginia, occupation: farmer. Prior to enlistment in regular forces, Gaskins may have served as an officer of militia. See James H. Gaskins 2nd Lieutenant of the Mason County 106th Militia West Virginia State Troops. Commissioned 2nd Lt. December 10, 1861 to rank from November 18, 1861. (Mason County 106th West Virginia State Troops, Militia West Virginia, microfilm.)

Gaskins, John R. Company B Private; enlisted July 15, 1863 at Point Pleasant, mustered August 3, 1863 at Charleston, age 22, born in Mason County, Virginia/West Virginia, occupation: farmer. Prior to enlistment in the Union Army, Gaskins may have served as Private in Company A, 116th Regiment Virginia Militia ("Solger 80 Gaskins, John"). He may also have served in Company A 4th Virginia Regiment as indicated in the *Annual Report of the Adjutant General of the State of West Virginia for the Year Ending December 31, 1865,* which records that John R. Gaskins (age 21) had been mustered into Company A 4th West Virginia Infantry Regiment on June 17, 1861 but had been discharged February 23, 1862.[720]

Gaskins, Samuel R. Company F Private; enlisted September 9, 1862 at Point Pleasant, received paid $30.00 Mason County Bounty and Premium, mustered October 9, 1862 at Point Pleasant, age 19, born in Mason County, Virginia/West Virginia, occupation: farmer.

Gatewood, Perry Company A Sergeant and Hospital Steward; enlisted August 14 or 15, 1862 at Charleston, appointed Sergeant August 20, 1862, mustered October 7, 1862 at Point Pleasant, age 41 or 42, born in Amherst County, Virginia, occupation: carpenter; "reduced to the file September 23, 1862 when appointed Hospital warden master." Transferred to non-commissioned staff as hospital steward March 1, 1864.

Geary (also Garry), Benjamin (signed his name "Benjamin Garry") Company D Private; enrolled at Hartford City August 15, 1862, received paid $30.00 Mason County Bounty and Premium, mustered October 8, 1862 at Point Pleasant, age 43, born in Luzerne County, Pennsylvania, occupation: cooper.

Geary, William B. Company D Private; enlisted August 15, 1862 at Hartford City, received paid $30.00 Mason County Bounty and Premium, mustered October

8, 1862 at Point Pleasant, age 16, born in Luzerne County, Pennsylvania, occupation: cooper.

George, Richard Company A Private; enlisted August 14, 1862 at Charleston, mustered October 7, 1862 at Point Pleasant, age 30, born in Darke County, Ohio, occupation: miner.

George, William Henry Company A Private and Corporal; enlisted August 14, 1862 at Charleston, mustered October 7, 1862 at Point Pleasant, age 20, born in Madison County, Virginia, occupation: farmer; appointed Corporal September 20, 1864.

Gibbs, Andrew J. Company D Private; enlisted August 19, 1862 at Hartford City, received paid $30.00 Mason County Bounty and Premium, mustered October 8, 1862 at Point Pleasant, age 18, born in Mason County, Virginia/West Virginia, occupation: farmer.

Gibbs, George W. Company D Private and Teamster; enlisted August 18, 1862 at Hartford City, received paid $30.00 Mason County Bounty and Premium, mustered October 8, 1862 at Point Pleasant, age 26, born in Mason County, Virginia/West Virginia, occupation: farmer.

Gibbs, John W. Company G Private; enlisted December 1, 1863 at Hartford City, mustered February 28, 1864 at Guyandotte, age 19, born in Mason County, Virginia/West Virginia, occupation: farmer.

Gibbs, Joseph F. Company F Private; enlisted October 28, 1863 at Barboursville, mustered November 25, 1863 at Barboursville, age 18, born in Mason County, Virginia/West Virginia, occupation: farmer.

Gibbs, Junius R. (also Junias R./Junous) Company D Private; enlisted August 19, 1862 at Hartford City, received paid $30.00 Mason County Bounty and Premium, mustered October 8, 1862 at Point Pleasant, age 18, born in Mason County, Virginia/West Virginia, occupation: farmer.

Gibbs, Sheldon Company D Private and Sergeant; enlisted August 18, 1862 at Hartford City, received paid $30.00 Mason County Bounty and Premium, mustered October 8, 1862 at Point Pleasant, age 28, born in Mason County, Virginia/West Virginia, occupation: farmer; had attained the rank of Sergeant at least by May 24, 1865, when he was discharged under General Orders No. 7, Adjutant General's Office, at Cumberland, Maryland.

Gibson, John A. Company E Private; enlisted August 22, 1862 at Charleston, mustered October 9, 1862 at Point Pleasant, age 20, born in Kanawha County, Virginia/West Virginia, occupation: farmer.

Gilaspie/Gillespie/Gillispie, Theophilus (also Theophilas/Theophalis) Company A Private; enlisted December 15, 1863 at Barboursville, mustered February 27, 1864 at Barboursville, age 22, born in Kanawha County, Virginia/West Virginia, occupation: farmer.

Gillaspie/Gillispie, John Company C Private; enlisted September 8, 1862 at Point Pleasant, mustered October 8, 1862 at Point Pleasant, age 18, born in Cabell County, Virginia/West Virginia, occupation: farmer.

Gillis, Roger Company G Private; discharged February 28, 1864, rejected recruit. See also Rodger Gillis below.

Gilpin, Joseph B. Company G Sergeant and 2nd Lieutenant; enlisted December 10, 1863 at Hartford City, promoted Sergeant Feb. 15, 1864 pursuant to Col. W.R. Brown, Gen. Order No. 1 (manu. dated Feb. 15, 1864) to rank as such from Jan. 27, 1864, mustered February 28, 1864 at Guyandotte, age 20, born in Jackson County, Virginia/West Virginia, occupation: farmer; promoted from Sergeant and commissioned 2nd Lieutenant Company G by order of March 18, 1865.

Glaze, Isaac M. Company K Private; enlisted September 7, 1863 at Walton, mustered October 3, 1863 at Charleston, age 21, born April 15, 1842 in Lewis County, Virginia/West Virginia, occupation: farmer.

Glenn, George Company G Private; enlisted December 20, 1863 at Cottageville, mustered February 28, 1864 at Guyandotte, age 18, born in Mason County, Virginia/West Virginia, occupation: farmer.

Glover, William Morton Company A Private; enlisted August 16, 1862 at Charleston, mustered October 7, 1862 at Point Pleasant, age 23, born in Kanawha County, Virginia/West Virginia, occupation: farmer. Prior to enlistment in the Union Army, Glover may have served as Private in Company A, 116th Regiment Virginia Militia ("Solger 78 Glover, William").

Goad/Good, James H. (seems to have signed his name "James H. Goad") Company I Corporal; enlisted December 5, 1862 at Charleston, appointed Corporal July 26, 1863, mustered July 26, 1863 at Charleston, age 19, born in Kanawha County, Virginia/West Virginia, occupation: farmer.

Good, John W. Company A Private, Corporal and Sergeant; enlisted August 12, 1862 at Charleston, mustered October 7, 1862 at Point Pleasant, age 21, born in

Jackson County, Virginia/West Virginia, occupation farmer; promoted Corporal March 1, 1864, promoted Sergeant from Corporal November 11, 1864.

Goodall, William T. Company E Private; enlisted September 15, 1862 at Point Pleasant, mustered October 9, 1862 at Point Pleasant, age 28, born in Kanawha County, Virginia/West Virginia, occupation: farmer.

Gorby, Alexander (signed his name "Gorbey") Company G Private; enlisted December 22, 1863 at Hartford City, mustered February 28, 1864 at Guyandotte, age 23, born in Tyler County, Virginia/West Virginia, occupation: farmer.

Gordon (also Gooden/Garden), Samuel Company H Private; enrolled September 20, 1862 at Point Pleasant, mustered December 11, 1862 at Point Pleasant, age 35, born in Rockbridge County, Virginia; occupation: farmer.

Gorman (also Garman), John Company C Private; enlisted August 22, 1862 at Point Pleasant, mustered October 8, 1862 at Point Pleasant, age 44, born in Northumberland County, Pennsylvania, occupation: carpenter.

Graham, Francis Company F Private; enlisted November 11, 1863 at Barboursville, mustered November 25, 1863 at Barboursville, age 35, born in Tyrone County, Ireland, occupation: tailor.

Graham, John M. or McGraham, John Company D Sergeant; enlisted August 22, 1862 at Hartford City, received paid $30.00 Mason County Bounty and Premium, mustered October 8, 1862 at Point Pleasant, age 32, born in Kanawha County, Virginia/West Virginia, occupation: cooper.

Graham, William Company D Private; enlisted August 4, 1862 at Hartford City, received paid $30.00 Mason County Bounty and Premium, mustered October. 8, 1862 at Point Pleasant, age 18, born in Allegheny County, Pennsylvania, occupation: farmer.

Gray, Parris Company K Private and Teamster; enlisted December 3, 1863 at Barboursville, mustered March 28, 1863 at Charleston, age 44, born in Delaware, occupation: farmer.

Gray/Grey, Robert Sheldon Company A Corporal; enlisted August 15, 1862 at Charleston, appointed Corporal August 20, 1862, mustered October 7, 1862 at Point Pleasant, age 24, born in Durham County, England (born in Durham, England, May 28, 1835), occupation: miner.

Gray, William Company A Private; enlisted August 15, 1862 at Charleston, mustered October 7, 1862 at Point Pleasant, age 32, born in Durham County, England, occupation: miner.

Greathouse, William H. Company H Private; enlisted August 12, 1862 at Ceredo, mustered October 10, 1862 at Point Pleasant, Virginia/West Virginia, age 44, occupation: farmer.

Green/Greer, Charles Company K Private; enlisted March 13, 1864 at Coals Mouth, mustered March 28, 1864 at Charleston, age 18, born in Jackson County, Virginia/West Virginia, occupation: farmer.

Green, George W. Company H Private; enlisted August 12, 1862 at Brownstown near Charleston mustered December 11, 1862 at Point Pleasant, age 24, born in Boone County, Virginia/West Virginia, occupation: farmer.

Green, John Company A Private, enlisted August 14, 1862 at Charleston, mustered October 7, 1862 at Point Pleasant, age 38, born in Kanawha County, Virginia/West Virginia, occupation: farmer.

Green, Leonard (signed his name "Lenard Green") Company K; Private; enlisted September 1, 1863 at Walton, mustered October 3, 1863 at Charleston, age 38, born in Jackson County, Virginia/West Virginia, occupation: farmer.

Green or Greer, Robert W. Company E Private; enlisted August 22, 1862 at Charleston, mustered October 9, 1862 at Point Pleasant, age 31, born in Braxton County, Virginia/West Virginia, occupation: farmer.

Greenlee, George A. Company G Private; enlisted February 11, 1865 at Point Pleasant, mustered February 14, 1865 at Point Pleasant, age 20, born in Mason County, Virginia/West Virginia, occupation: farmer.

Greenlee, George B. Company G Private; enlisted December 12, 1863 at Barboursville, mustered February 28, 1864 at Guyandotte, age 18, born in Mason County, Virginia/West Virginia, occupation: farmer.

Greenlee, Hezekiah Company G Private; enlisted and mustered February 14, 1865 at Point Pleasant, age 23, born in Mason County, Virginia/West Virginia, occupation: farmer.

Greenlee, John M. Company G Private; enlisted December 26, 1863 at Barboursville, mustered February 29, 1864 at Guyandotte, age 18, born in Mason County, Virginia/West Virginia, occupation: farmer.

Greenlee, Martin Company G Private; enlisted and mustered into service February 14, 1865 at Point Pleasant, age 21, born in Mason County, Virginia/West Virginia, occupation: farmer.

Greenlee, William C. Company B 1ˢᵗ Sergeant and Captain; enlisted August 8, 1862 and received paid $30.00 Mason County Bounty and Premium, mustered October 8, 1862, age 20, born in Mason County, Virginia/West Virginia, occupation: farmer; promoted from 1ˢᵗ Sergeant October 30, 1864; commissioned Captain Company B October 31, 1864, at age 22 claimed to be the "youngest captain" from the State of West Virginia.[721]

Greer, Hugh Jasper Company G Corporal and Sergeant; enlisted December 4, 1863 at Barboursville, promoted Corporal pursuant to Col. W.R. Brown, Gen. Order No. 1 (manu. dated Feb. 15, 1864) to rank as such from Jan. 27, 1864, mustered February 28, 1864 at Guyandotte, age 17-18, born in Jackson County, Virginia, occupation: farmer; promoted to 1ˢᵗ Sergeant April 28, 1865.

Greer, Oscar Newton Company G Private; enlisted and mustered February 14, 1865 at Point Pleasant, West Virginia, age 20, born in Jackson County, Virginia/West Virginia, occupation: farmer.

Greer, Newton W. Company K Private; enlisted February 20, 1864 at Coals Mouth, mustered March 11, 1864 at Charleston, age 18, born in Jackson County, Virginia/West Virginia, occupation: farmer.

Grinstead, Miletus (also Maletus) Company A Corporal and 1ˢᵗ Sergeant; enlisted August 15, 1862 at Charleston, appointed Corporal August 20, 1862, promoted Sergeant September 23, 1862, mustered October 7, 1862 at Point Pleasant, age 24, born in Jennings County, Indiana, occupation: coal digger/farmer; appointed 1ˢᵗ Sergeant July 20, 1863.

Griswold/Griswel, Oliver W. Company H 1ˢᵗ Lieutenant; enlisted July 22, 1862 at Ceredo, commissioned 1ˢᵗ Lieutenant September 12, 1862 to rank from September 1, 1862, mustered October 10, 1862 at Point Pleasant, aged 26 years, born in Suffolk County, New York, occupation: merchant.

Gunter, James H. Company E Private and Corporal; enlisted August 22, 1862 at Charleston, appointed 7ᵗʰ Corporal September 12, 1862, mustered October 9, 1862 at Point Pleasant, age 28, born in Kanawha County, Virginia/West Virginia, occupation: farmer. Prior to enlistment in the Union Army, Gunter may have served as Private in Company A, 116ᵗʰ Regiment Virginia Militia ("Solger 79 Gunter, James").

Hacker, John C. Company A Private and Blazer Scout/Independent Scout; enlisted Oct. 20, 1863 at Barboursville, mustered November 25, 1863 at Barboursville, age 18, born in Kanawha County, Virginia/West Virginia, occupation: farmer; detailed for Blazer Scouts in 1864.

Hacket/Hackett, Jasper N. Company H Private; enlisted September 20, 1862 at Point Pleasant, mustered December 11, 1862 at Point Pleasant, age 22, born in Cheshire, Gallia County, Ohio, occupation: farmer.

Hacket/Hackett, Thomas M. Company H Sergeant and Private, enlisted September 20, 1862 at Point Pleasant, appointed 2nd Sergeant September 20, 1862, mustered December 11, 1862 at Point Pleasant, age 21, born in Cheshire, Gallia County, Ohio, occupation: farmer.

Hackworth/ (also Hackwith), Jarret C./Jerret Company F Private; enlisted November 9, 1862 at Point Pleasant, mustered December 11 1862 at Point Pleasant, age 18, born in Lawrence County, Ohio, P.O. Box Racine, Ohio (J.C. Hackworth Private 13th. Memorandum from Prisoner of War Records, M508 Compiled Service Records, micro. Roll 205, NARA), occupation: farmer. There are a number of various spellings for this soldier's name in both Union and Confederate records (Jarret, Jaret, Jarred, J.C. and J.L. Hackworth and also Hackwith).

Hageley, Harrison Company I Private; enlisted September 24, 1863 at Barboursville, mustered November 25, 1863 at Guyandotte, age 22, born in Cabell County, Virginia/West Virginia, occupation: farmer.

Hageley, Joseph Company I Private; enlisted November 1, 1863 at Guyandotte, mustered November 25, 1863 at Guyandotte, age 20, born in Cabell County, Virginia/West Virginia, occupation: farmer.

Hagley, Peter Company G Private; discharged February. 28, 1864; a rejected recruit.

Hall, Henry Smith Company A Private; enlisted August 15, 1862 at Charleston, mustered October 7, 1862 at Point Pleasant, age 30, born in Franklin County, Virginia, occupation: farmer.

Hall, James Robert Captain, Major and Lieutenant Colonel commanding 13th Regiment Virginia/West Virginia Volunteer Infantry; commission Captain August 19, 1862 to rank from August 5, 1862, age 25, born in Mason County, Virginia/West Virginia, occupation clerk and deputy sheriff; commissioned Major August 20, 1862 at Point Pleasant, appointed Lieutenant-Colonel October 10, 1862, promoted to Lieutenant-Colonel January 18, 1864, mustered as Lieutenant Colonel February 28, 1864 at Barboursville, when the Regiment, at last at requisite strength, could be organized.

Hall, Jesse (Jesse D.?) (signed his name "Jesy Hall") Company E Private; enlisted August 22, 1862 at Charleston, mustered October 9, 1862 at Point Pleasant, age 17, born in Kanawha County, Virginia/West Virginia, occupation: farmer.

Hall, Job (also Jabe) Company A Private and Waggoner; enlisted August 15, 1862 at Charleston, mustered October 7, 1862 at Point Pleasant, age 19, born in Franklin County, Virginia, occupation: farmer.

Hall, Moses B. Company E Private, Corporal and Sergeant; enlisted August 22, 1862 at Charleston, mustered October 9, 1862 at Point Pleasant, age 25, born in Kanawha County, Virginia/West Virginia, occupation: farmer; promoted from Private to Corporal in 1864 and to Sergeant by order of Col. William Brown.

Hall, Woodson Bailey Company A Private; enlisted August 12, 1862 at Charleston, mustered October 7, 1862 at Point Pleasant, age 22, born in Franklin County, Virginia, occupation: farmer.

Hammonds, Edward Company A Private; enlisted December 15, 1863 at Barboursville, mustered February 27, 1864, at Barboursville, age 15 (age "18" given in official papers), born in Kanawha County, Virginia/West Virginia, occupation: farmer. The following order came down came down from division headquarters regarding Hammon's underage enlistment: "Samuel Field aged 17 next March and Edward Hammon aged 15 next February are claimed by their mothers to have been enlisted under military age without consent of parents. If you find this is so you will discharged them *unless they have been mustered into service by the mustering officer.*"[722]

Hampton, Taylor W. Company H Captain; enlisted September 20, 1862, at Point Pleasant, mustered October 10, 1862 at Point Pleasant, age 36 years, born in Trumbull County, Ohio, occupation: lawyer, commissioned Captain November 6, 1862 to rank from November 5, 1862, resigned March 10, 1863 to take command as Lieutenant-Colonel Ohio Volunteer Infantry (16ᵗʰ Ohio Infantry Regiment and/or 141ˢᵗ Ohio Infantry Regiment?).

Hampton, Thomas W. Company H Private; joined for duty and enrolled September 20, 1862 at Glenwood, mustered in December 11, 1862, age 37, (no additional information).[723]

Hanna, James William Company D 1ˢᵗ Lieutenant; enlisted August 15, 1862, received paid $30.00 Mason County Bounty and Premium, commissioned 1ˢᵗ Lieutenant by order of September 12, 1862 to date September 2, 1862, mustered October 8, 1862 at Point Pleasant, age 24 years, born in Kanawha County, Virginia/West Virginia, cooper (copper and barrel manufacturer).

Hannah (also Hanna), Job T. Company F 3ʳᵈ Sergeant/1ˢᵗ Sergeant; enlisted September 28, 1862 at Point Pleasant, mustered October 9, 1862 at Point Pleasant, age 20, born in Kanawha County, Virginia/West Virginia, occupation: cooper.

Hanna/Hannah, Mathew/Matthew Company F Private and Musician; enlisted September 28, 1862 at Point Pleasant, mustered October 9, 1862 at Point Pleasant, age 55, born in Washington County, Pennsylvania, occupation: cooper.

Hanna, Samuel D. Company D Private and Drum Major; enlisted August 13 or 15, 1862 at Hartford City, received paid $30.00 Mason County Bounty and Premium, mustered October 8, 1862 at Point Pleasant; age 18, born March 18, 1844, in Kanawha County, Virginia/West Virginia, occupation: cooper; promoted Principal Musician (Drum Major) and transferred to non-commissioned staff July 1, 1863.

Haptonstall/Hopingstall, Franklin L. (signed "F.L. Haptonstall") Company E Sergeant; enlisted August 13, 1862 at Charleston, appointed 4th Sergeant September 12, 1862, mustered October 9, 1862 at Point Pleasant, age 26, born in Greenbrier County, Virginia/West Virginia, occupation: plasterer.

Harden, John Company K 5th Sergeant and 1st Sergeant; enlisted October 1, 1863 at Walton, mustered in November 25, 1863 at Barboursville, age 34, born in Russell County, Virginia, occupation: farmer; promoted to 1st Sergeant November 10, 1864.

Harman, John P. (signed his name "Harmon") Company C Private; enlisted September 5, 1862 at Point Pleasant, Harden received paid $30.00 Mason County Bounty and Premium, muster October 8, 1862, age 32, born in Ohio County, Virginia/West Virginia, occupation: farmer; detailed for Nurse in Army Hospital at Point Pleasant, October 26, 1862.

Harper, Andrew J. Company K Private; enlisted July 25, 1863 at Walton, mustered in October 3, 1863 at Charleston, age 23, born in Kanawha County, Virginia/West Virginia, occupation: farmer.

Harper, David H. Company D Private; enlisted December 15, 1863 at Barboursville, mustered February 27, 1864 at Barboursville, age 17, born in Butler County, Pennsylvania, occupation: farmer.

Harper, Epperson Company K Private; enlisted August 1, 1863 at Walton, mustered November 25, 1863 at Barboursville, age 40, born in Russell County, Virginia, occupation: farmer.

Harper, Jordan Company K Private; enlisted August 1, 1863 at Walton, mustered October 3, 1863 at Charleston, age 26, born in Kanawha County, Virginia/West Virginia, occupation: farmer.

Harper, Joseph Company F Private; enlisted September 9, 1862 at Point Pleasant, mustered October 9, 1862 at Point Pleasant, age 36, born in County Down, Ireland, occupation: miner.

Harper, Robert Company K Private; enlisted September 1, 1863 at Walton, mustered October 3, 1863 at Charleston, age 18, born in Kanawha County, Virginia/West Virginia, occupation: farmer. Ordered by Col. W.R. Brown to serve as Independent Scout in "a body of scouts for this Regiment" on March 10, 1864 in compliance with General Orders No. 2 from "Head Quarters 3d Division Dept., W.Va." (dated "Charleston W.Va. February 16th 1864").

Harper, William Company F Private; enlisted September 9, 1862 at Point Pleasant, mustered October 9, 1862 at Point Pleasant, age 28, born in County Down, Ireland, occupation: miner.

Harper, William W[iley]. Company F Private and Sergeant-Major; Company K 2nd Lieutenant; and Regimental Chaplain; enlisted October 4, 1862 promoted Sergeant Major Company F and mustered into service October 4, 1862, age 41, born in Washington County, Pennsylvania, occupation: merchant; appointed 2nd Lieutenant Company K February 1st or 9th, 1864 by order of Brigadier General Benjamin F. Kelley (dated Cumberland, Maryland, March 10, 1864), commissioned Regimental Chaplain March 20, 1864, promoted Chaplain April 2, 1864. W.W. Harper seems also to have served as delegate from Mason County to the 1st Convention of Delegates held at Wheeling, May 13, 1861. A staunch supporter of the Union cause and correspondent to pro-Union newspapers from "Hartford City, Mason County." After enrolling for duty in the 13th Regiment, he stepped up to serve as a war correspondent to the home front outlining in some detail and with no small degree of feeling the fortunes of the Regiment and her soldiers.

Harpold, Lemuel Company C Lieutenant, Captain and Major; enlisted August 15, 1862, received paid $30.00 Mason County Bounty and Premium, commissioned 1st Lieutenant September 12, 1862, mustered October 8, 1862, age 36/38 years, born in Jackson County, Virginia/West Virginia, occupation: tanner; commissioned Captain Company C September 25, 1863; transferred from Company C and promoted Major March 10, 1865. Harpold may have served as Delegate from Mason County at the 1st Convention of Delegates held at Wheeling, Virginia/West Virginia May 13th, 1861.

Harris, Silas Company B Private; enlisted August 11, 1862 at Point Pleasant, received paid $30.00 Mason County Bounty and Premium, mustered October 8, 1862 at Point Pleasant, age 21, born in Mason County, Virginia/West Virginia, occupation: farmer. Prior to enlistment in the Union Army, Harris may have served as Private in Company A, 116th Regiment Virginia Militia ("Solger 83 Harris, Silas").

Harris, William L. Company B Private; enlisted at Barboursville, mustered February 26, 1864 at Barboursville, age 24, born in Mason County, Virginia/West Virginia, occupation: farmer. Prior to enlistment in the Union Army, may have served as Private in Company A, 116th Regiment Virginia Militia ("Solger 82 Harris, William"). See also "William Harris, 2nd Lieutenant Mason County 106th Militia West Virginia State Troops; commissioned by order of Dec[ember] 27, 1862 to rank from December 1, 1862. (WVSA) Detailed on March 10, 1864 for a body of Independent Scouts in compliance with General Orders No. 2 from "Head Quarters 3d Division Dept., W.Va." (dated "Charleston W.Va. February 16th 1864").

Harrison, David Company K Private; enlisted October 27, 1863 at Leon, mustered November 28, 1863 at Barboursville, age 36, born in Jackson County, Virginia/West Virginia, occupation: farmer.

Harrison, Jeremiah (called "Jerry") Company K 4th Corporal; enlisted January 6, 1864 at Leon, mustered March 11, 1864 at Charleston, age 28, born in Mason County, Virginia/West Virginia, occupation: farmer.

Harrison, John Company K Private; enlisted September 19, 1863 at Barboursville, mustered November 25, 1863 at Barboursville, age 19, born in Mason County, Virginia/West Virginia, occupation: farmer.

Harrison, John L. Company G Private; enlisted January 5, 1864 at Buffalo, mustered February 28, 1864 at Guyandotte, age 18, born in Putnam County, Virginia/West Virginia, occupation: farmer.

Harrison, Joseph Company K Private; enlisted December 28, 1863 at Leon, mustered March 28, 1864 at Charleston, age 26, born in Mason County, Virginia/West Virginia, occupation: farmer.

Harrison, Thomas Company K Private and Sergeant; enlisted November 4, 1863 at Leon, mustered November 25, 1863 at Barboursville, age 17, born in Mason County, Virginia/West Virginia, occupation: farmer.

Harshey, William T. (called "Thomas") Company D Private; enlisted August 20, 1863 at Coals Mouth, mustered October 6, 1863 at Barboursville, age 17, born in Jefferson County, Kentucky, occupation: blacksmith.

Hart, Jesse/Jessee Company B Private; enlisted August 9, 1862 at Point Pleasant, received paid $30.00 Mason County Bounty and Premium, mustered October 8,

1862 at Point Pleasant, age 18, born in Mason County, Virginia/West Virginia, occupation: farmer.

Hatcher, Julius H. Company D Sergeant; enlisted August 13 or 15, 1862 at Hartford City, received paid $30.00 Mason County Bounty and Premium, mustered in October 8, 1862 at Point Pleasant, age 24, born in Kanawha County, Virginia/West Virginia, occupation: farmer.

Hawkins, Benjamin F. Company K 1st Corporal and Sergeant; enlisted July 25, 1863 at Walton, mustered October 3, 1863 at Charleston, age 23, born in Fayette County, Virginia/West Virginia, occupation, farmer; promoted from 1st Corporal to 5th Sergeant November 10, 1864.

Hawkins, Peter Fielding Company G Corporal; enlisted December 3, 1863 at West Columbia, mustered February 28, 1863 at Guyandotte, age 42, born in Mason County, Virginia/West Virginia, occupation: farmer. Detailed for permanent duty as teamster with regimental quartermaster Lt. Stephen Comstock March 30, 1864.

Hawkins, William N. Company E Lieutenant; appointed 1st Lieutenant Company E September 12, 1862, commissioned 1st Lieutenant October 8, 1862, mustered October 9, 1862 at Point Pleasant, Virginia/West Virginia, aged 38 years, born in Virginia, resident of Charleston, Virginia/West Virginia, occupation: "Master Painter" (listed with an apprentice in 1860 Census for Kanawha County, Virginia).

Haynes, John R. Company E Private; enlisted August 16, 1862 at Tupper or Tupper's Creek, mustered October 9, 1862 at Point Pleasant, age 18, born in Kanawha County, Virginia/West Virginia, occupation: farmer.

Haynes, William M. Company E Private and Corporal; enlisted August 18, 1862 at Charleston, mustered October 9, 1862 at Point Pleasant, age 20, born in Kanawha County, Virginia/West Virginia, occupation: farmer; promoted to Corporal April 5, 1865.

Hays, George W. Company G Private; enlisted January 3, 1864 at Buffalo, mustered February 28, 1864 at Guyandotte, age 18, born in Putnam County, Virginia/West Virginia, occupation: farmer.

Hays/Hayes James Company B Private; enlisted August 12, 1862 at Point Pleasant, received paid $30.00 Mason County Bounty and Premium, mustered October 8, 1862 at Point Pleasant, age 34, born in Pocahontas County, Virginia/West Virginia, occupation: farmer.

Hays/Haze, Vincent A. Company E Sergeant; enlisted August 22, 1862 at Charleston, appointed 5th Sergeant September 12, 1862, mustered October 9, 1862 at Point Pleasant, age 25, born in Kanawha County, Virginia/West Virginia, occupation: farmer; was honored for having distinguished himself at the battle of Fisher's Hill, Virginia, fought September 22, 1864 where he was wounded in "capturing a color" from the enemy.

Hayse (also Hayes/Hays), Franklin Company F Private; enlisted September 2, 1862 at Point Pleasant, mustered October 9, 1862 at Point Pleasant, age 21, born in Kanawha County, Virginia/West Virginia, occupation: farmer; died of typhoid fever at Point Pleasant January 13 [or July 13], 1863 in Hospital.

Hayse (also Hayes/Hays), Henry W. Company F Private; enlisted September 15, 1862 at Point Pleasant, mustered October 9, 1862 at Point Pleasant, age 19, born in Kanawha County, Virginia/West Virginia, occupation: farmer; died of measles at Point Pleasant January 21, 1863 in Regimental Hospital.

Hayse (also Hayes), John Company F Private; enlisted September 15, 1862 at Point Pleasant, mustered October 9, 1862 at Point Pleasant, age 38, born in Kanawha County, Virginia/West Virginia, occupation: farmer.

Hayslett/Hazlett, John Company H Private; enlisted August 11, 1862 at Ceredo, mustered October 10, 1862 at Point Pleasant, age 20, born in Wayne County, Virginia/West Virginia, occupation: farmer. Hazlett served with Wayne County Home Guards prior to enlistment in the 13th West Virginia Regiment.

Helton/Hilton/Hylton, Ira (signed his name "Helton") Company C Private; enlisted August 29, 1862 at Point Pleasant, received paid $30.00 Mason County Bounty and Premium, mustered October 8, 1862 at Point Pleasant, age 23, born in Carroll County, Virginia/West Virginia, occupation: farmer.

Henkins/Herkins/Hurkins, William H. Company E Private; enlisted October 24, 1864 at Charleston, mustered October 24, 1864 at Charleston, age 18, born in Kanawha County, Virginia/West Virginia, occupation: farmer.

Hemmings/Hennings, Elijah/Elisha Company A Corporal and Sergeant; enlisted August 14, 1862 at Charleston, appointed Corporal August 20, 1862, mustered October 7, 1862 at Point Pleasant, age 25, born in Kanawha County, Virginia/West Virginia, occupation: farmer; appointed Sergeant July 20, 1863.

Hemmons/Hemmings/Hemmys/Hennings, Levi (signed his name "Hemmons") Company A Private and Drummer; enlisted August 14, 1862 at Charleston, mustered October 7, 1862 at Point Pleasant, age 18, born in Kanawha County, Virginia/West Virginia, occupation: farmer.

Henry, James M. Company H Sergeant; enlisted September 20, 1862 at Point Pleasant, appointed 4th Sergeant September 20, 1862, mustered December 11, 1862 at Point Pleasant, age 35, born in Columbiana County, Ohio, occupation: carpenter.

Henry, John W. Company C Private; enlisted August 11, 1862 at Point Pleasant, received paid $30.00 Mason County Bounty and Premium, mustered October 8, 1862, age 27, born in Mason County, Virginia/West Virginia, occupation: farmer.

Hensley/Hensly, Ephraim Company D Private; enlisted March 19, 1864 at Barboursville, mustered April 26, 1864 at Barboursville, age 18, born in Wayne County, Virginia/West Virginia, occupation: farmer.

Hess, John H. Company D Corporal; enlisted August 8 or 18, 1862 at Hartford City, received paid $30.00 Mason County Bounty and Premium, mustered October 8, 1862 at Point Pleasant, age 26, born in Fayette County, Virginia/West Virginia, occupation: farmer.

Hesson/Heson, John Company C Private; enlisted August 14, 1862 at Point Pleasant, received paid $30.00 Mason County Bounty and Premium, mustered October 8, 1862, age 18, born in Pennsylvania, occupation: farmer.

Hewison (also Heiston/Houston), Matthew (signed "Mathew Hewison") Company D Private; enlisted August 15, 1862 at Hartford City, received paid $30.00 Mason County Bounty and Premium, mustered October 8, 1862 at Point Pleasant, age 32, born in Durham County, England occupation: miner.

Hicks (also Hickes), George (signed his name "George Hicks") Company K Private; enlisted September 1, 1863 at Walton, mustered in October 3, 1863 at Charleston, age 18, born in Jackson County, Virginia/West Virginia, occupation: farmer.

Higginbotham (also Hickenggenbotham), James T. Company K Private; enlisted October 3, 1863 at Barboursville, mustered November 25, 1863 at Barboursville, age 18, born in Putnam County, Virginia/West Virginia, occupation: farmer.

High, Benjamin F. Company E Private; enlisted August 19, 1862 at Charleston, mustered October 9, 1862 at Point Pleasant, age 23, born in Kanawha County, Virginia/West Virginia, occupation: farmer; died at Point Pleasant November 27, 1862 of "congestion of the brain. Corpse sent home."

High, James Company E Private; enlisted August 22, 1862 at Charleston, mustered October 9, 1862 at Point Pleasant, age 21, born in Harrison County, Virginia/West Virginia, occupation: farmer.

Hill, Andrew C. (signed his name "Andrew C. Hill"; "C." may stand for "Clark") Company G Private; enlisted December 24, 1863 at Barboursville, mustered February 28, 1864 at Guyandotte, age 21, born in Mason County, Virginia/West Virginia, occupation: farmer.

Hill, Charles M. ("M." for "Melmont"?) Company K Private; enlisted September 14, 1863 at Barboursville, mustered November 25, 1863 at Barboursville, age 29, born in Mason County, Virginia/West Virginia, occupation: farmer.

Hill, Daniel Company K Private; enlisted December 31, 1863 at Leon, mustered March 28, 1864 at Charleston, age 31 or 32, born Mason County, Virginia/West Virginia; occupation: farmer.

Hill, David A. Company I Private; enlisted January 3, 1863 at Charleston, mustered July 26, 1863 at Charleston, age 25 (age 27? born July, 22, 1835), born in Kanawha County, Virginia/West Virginia, occupation: farmer.

Hill, Elijah Company K Private; enlisted September 21, 1863 at Barboursville, mustered November 25, 1863 at Barboursville, age 18, born in Mason County, Virginia/West Virginia, occupation: farmer.

Hill, Enoch Company K Private; enlisted February 1, 1864 at Barboursville, mustered March 11, 1864 at Charleston, age: officially noted down as "18" but likely closer to 16 years, born in Mason County, Virginia/West Virginia; occupation: farmer.

Hill, George A. Company K Private; enlisted September 20, 1863 at Barboursville, mustered October 3, 1863 at Charleston, age 17, born in Mason County, Virginia/West Virginia, occupation: farmer.

Hill, George W. Company Company K Private; enlisted October 20, 1863 at Guyandotte, mustered November 25, 1863 at Guyandotte, age 18; occupation: farmer.

Hill, George William Company G Private; enlisted December 24, 1863 at Barboursville, mustered February 28, 1864 at Guyandotte, age 18, born in Mason County, Virginia/West Virginia, occupation: farmer.

Hill, James A. Company K Private; enlisted September 19, 1863 at Barboursville, mustered November 25, 1863 at Barboursville, age 21, born in Mason County, Virginia/West Virginia; occupation: farmer.

Hill, Jasper M. or N. Company E Regimental Musician; enlisted October 12, 1863 at Barboursville, mustered October 13, 1863 at Charleston, age 16, born in Mason County, Virginia/West Virginia, occupation: farmer.

Hill, Jesse L. Company K Private; enlisted January 4, 1864 at Leon, mustered in March 11, 1864 at Charleston, age 18, born Mason County, Virginia/West Virginia, occupation: farmer.

Hill, John W. Company K Private; enlisted October 3, 1863 at Barboursville, mustered November 25, 1863 at Barboursville, age 18, born in Putnam County, Virginia/West Virginia, occupation: farmer.

Hill, Jonathan (also Johnson/John) Hill Company K Private; enlisted December 30, 1863 at Leon, mustered March 28, 1864 at Charleston, age 17/18, born in Mason County, Virginia/West Virginia, occupation: farmer.

Hill, William Riley Company B Private; enlisted August 15, 1863 Point Pleasant, mustered October 6, 1863 at Barboursville, age 19, born in Mason County, Virginia/West Virginia, occupation: farmer.

Hinds, Lehu Company I Private; enlisted October 15, 1863 at Guyandotte, mustered November 25, 1863 at Guyandotte, age 18, born in Wayne County, Virginia/West Virginia, occupation: farmer.

Hobbs, Winfield S. Company H Private; enlisted December 28, 1862 at Point Pleasant, mustered January 6, 1863 at Point Pleasant, age 17, born in Morgan County, Virginia/West Virginia, occupation: teamster.

Hodson/Hudson, John Company F Private; enlisted September 10, 1862 at Point Pleasant, mustered October 9, 1862 at Point Pleasant, age 18, born in Durham County, England, occupation: miner.

Hoffman, Elias Company D Private; enlisted August 15, 1862 at Hartford City, received paid $30.00 Mason County Bounty and Premium, mustered October 8, 1862 at Point Pleasant, age 22, born in Mason County, Virginia/West Virginia occupation: farmer; in Pioneer Corps from November 1864.

Hoffman, Henry Company D Private; enlisted August 15, 1862 at Hartford City, received paid $30.00 Mason County Bounty and Premium, mustered October 8, 1862 at Point Pleasant, age 19, born in Mason County Virginia/West Virginia, occupation: farmer.

Hoffman, Michael Company D Private; enlisted August 15, 1862 at Hartford City, received paid $30.00 Mason County Bounty and Premium, mustered in October

8, 1862 at Point Pleasant, age 22, born in Mason County, Virginia/West Virginia, occupation: farmer.

Hoffman, William H. G. (also William H. G. B.) Company A Private; enlisted August 15, 1862 at Charleston, mustered October 7, 1862 at Point Pleasant, age 29, born in Henry County, Virginia, occupation: farmer; appointed Corporal November 1, 1863, appointed Sergeant from Corporal July 1, 1864.

Hogg, John T., Jr., Company G Private; enlisted December 7, 1863 at Point Pleasant, mustered February 28, 1864 at Guyandotte, age 20, born in Mason County. Virginia/West Virginia, occupation: farmer.

Hogg, Taylor N. Company B Private; enlisted August 13, 1862 at Point Pleasant, received paid $30.00 Mason County Bounty and Premium, mustered October 8, 1862, age 20, born in Mason County, Virginia/West Virginia, occupation: farmer.

Holcomb (also Hocomb), James (signed his name "Holcomb") Company E Private, enlisted November 21, 1863 at the Mouth of Big Sandy, West Virginia, mustered February 27, 1864 at Charleston, age 23, born in Nicholas County, Virginia/ West Virginia, occupation: farmer.

Holly, Herman D. Company I Private; enlisted August 27, 1863 at Charleston, mustered October 6, 1863, age 18, born in Mason County, Virginia/West Virginia, occupation: farmer.

Holly (also Holley), Jeremiah (signed "Jery") Company E Private; enlisted December 10, 1863 at Charleston, mustered February 27, 1864 at Charleston, age 18, born in Kanawha County, Virginia/West Virginia, occupation: farmer.

Holly (also Holley), John Company E Private; enlisted November. 1, 1863 at Tuppers Creek, mustered February 27, 1864 at Charleston, age 18, born in Kanawha County, Virginia/West Virginia, occupation: farmer.

Holly (also Holley), Josiah (signed "Josiah T. Holley") Company I Private; enlisted August 27, 1863 at Charleston, mustered October 6, 1863, age 18, born in Mason County, Virginia/West Virginia, occupation: farmer.

Hooper, Stephen Company H Sergeant; enlisted September 20, 1862 at Point Pleasant, appointed 3rd Sergeant September 20, 1862, mustered December 11, 1862 at Point Pleasant, age 34, born in Harrison County, Ohio, occupation: cooper.

Hoscher, Andrew K. (signed "Andrew K. Husher") Company C Private; enlisted October 1, 1863 at Barboursville, mustered October 1, 1863 at Barboursville, age 18, born in Mason County, Virginia/West Virginia, occupation: farmer.

Hoscher, Elisha V. Company C Private; enlisted March 26, 1863 at Point Pleasant, mustered August 5, 1863 at Charleston, age 18, born in Mason County, Virginia/West Virginia, occupation: farmer.

Holt/Hoult, Rutter (signed "Holt") Company D Private; enlisted August 22, 1862 at Hartford City, received paid $30.00 Mason County Bounty and Premium, mustered October 8, 1862 at Point Pleasant, age 26, born in Durham County, England occupation: miner.

Hovey, William Marshall Company C Lieutenant, Captain; enlisted in Company E 4th Virginia/West Virginia Infantry Regiment on July 20, 1861, discharged from Company E 4th Virginia/West Virginia Volunteer Infantry Regiment to be promoted to 1st Lieutenant; commissioned 1st Lieutenant Company C 13th Virginia Regiment September 25, 1863 (or December 19, 1863), age 21 (born October 5, 1842), born in Meigs County, Ohio, occupation: clerk; promoted to Captain Company C February 18 (or March 13), 1865.

Howel/Howell, Milton (signed "Milton Howel") Company D Private; enlisted August 18, 1862 at Hartford City, received paid $30.00 Mason County Bounty and Premium, mustered October 8, 1862 at Point Pleasant, age 18, born in Marshall County, Virginia/West Virginia, occupation: farmer.

Howell, Elias Company C Private; enlisted August 24, 1863 at Coals Mouth, mustered August 24, 1863 at Barboursville, age 44, born in Lewis County, Virginia/West Virginia, occupation: farmer.

Hoy, Charles F. Company H Private; enlisted November 30, 1862 at Point Pleasant, age 65, born in Shenandoah County, Virginia, occupation: musician, discharged Dec. 11 or 12, 1862 for disability before being mustered into service.

Hudson, David Company E Private; enlisted August 22, 1862 at Charleston, mustered October 9, 1862 at Point Pleasant, age 18, born in Kanawha County, Virginia/West Virginia, occupation: farmer.

Hudson, Nelson Company E Private; enlisted August 22, 1862 at Charleston, mustered October 9, 1862, age 20, born in Kanawha County, Virginia/West Virginia, occupation: farmer.

Hudson, William Company C Private; joined for service and enrolled at Charleston August 31, 1862, mustered October 9, 1862 at Point Pleasant, age 18; occupation: musician, soldier's name appears on original muster in roll but he seems never to have served with the Regiment.

Huff, William C. Company I Private; enlisted November 27, 1863 at Guyandotte, mustered February 29, 1864 at Guyandotte, age 37, born in Montgomery County, Virginia, occupation: laborer.

Hughart, Henry Company G 1ˢᵗ Sergeant; enlisted November 20, 1863 at West Columbia, promoted 1ˢᵗ Sergeant pursuant to Col. W.R. Brown, Gen. Order No. 1 (manu. dated Feb. 15, 1864) to rank as such from Jan. 27, 1864, mustered February 28, 1864 at Guyandotte, age 24, born in Greenbrier County, Virginia/West Virginia, occupation: laborer.

Hughes, Thomas Jefferson Company A Private; enlisted August 12, 1862 at Charleston, mustered October 7, 1862 at Point Pleasant, age 34, born in Fayette County, Virginia/West Virginia, occupation: farmer, detailed for duty as wagoner from August 19, 1862 to October 21, 1862.

Humphrey, Lewis Duke Company A Private, age 29, enlisted August 13, 1862 at Charleston, mustered October 6, 1862, at Point Pleasant, born in Bedford County, Virginia, occupation: farmer.

Hunt, John M. Company K Private; enlisted January 1, 1864 at Walton, mustered March 11, 1864 at Charleston, age 18, born in Russell County, Virginia, occupation: farmer.

Hunt, Oliver B. Company K Private and 2ⁿᵈ Corporal; enlisted August 1, 1863 at Walton, mustered October 3, 1863 at Charleston, age 24, born in Russell County, Virginia, occupation: farmer.

Hunt, William M. Company K Private; enlisted August 1, 1863 at Walton, mustered October 3, 1863 at Charleston, age 18, born in Russell County, Virginia, occupation: farmer.

Hunter, Andrew J. "Jack" Company K; Private and 2ⁿᵈ Sergeant; enlisted September 1, 1863 at Walton, mustered October 3, 1863 at Charleston, age 18, born in Jackson County, Virginia/West Virginia, occupation: farmer.

Hunter, Henry C. Company K Private and 2ⁿᵈ Sergeant; enlisted September 1, 1863 at Walton, mustered October 3, 1863 at Charleston, age 45, born in Montgomery County, Virginia, occupation: farmer; Captain of Jackson County Home Guards before enlistment in 13ᵗʰ Virginia/West Virginia Infantry Regiment.

Hunter, John Company A Private and Corporal; enlisted August 15, 1862 at Charleston, mustered October 7, 1862 at Point Pleasant, age 36, born in Tyrone County, Ireland, occupation: farmer; appointed Corporal September 23, 1864.

Hurel, Irdell/Iredel Company A Private; enlisted August 15, 1862 at Charleston, mustered October 7, 1862 at Point Pleasant, age 35, born in Grayson County, Virginia, occupation: carpenter.

Hurel, William Company A Fifer and Corporal; enlisted March 1, 1863 at Hurricane Bridge, mustered July 9, 1863 at Charleston, age 18, born in Kanawha County, Virginia/West Virginia, occupation: farmer; appointed Corporal October 20, 1864.

Huchessen/Hutchinson, Peter D. (signed Peter D. Huchessen") Company H Private; enlisted August 11, 1862 at Ceredo, mustered in October 10, 1862 at Point Pleasant, age 21, born in Wayne County, Virginia/West Virginia, occupation: farmer.

Hutchinson (also Hutchessan), Joseph Company H Private; enlisted February 29, 1864 at Barboursville, mustered April 26, 1864 at Barboursville, age 18, born in Wayne County, Virginia/West Virginia, occupation: farmer.

Hyatt/Hyat, Emanuel Company B Private; enlisted August 8, 1862, at Point Pleasant, received paid $30.00 Mason County Bounty and Premium, mustered October 8, 1862, age 41, born in Muskingum County, Ohio, occupation: farmer.[724]

Hyatt (also Hayatt), William Company G Corporal; enlisted December 22, 1863 at Barboursville, mustered February 28, 1864 at Guyandotte, age 18, born in Muskingham County, Ohio, occupation: farmer.

Hyatte, Albert Company K Private; enlisted October 9, 1863 at Barboursville, mustered November 25, 1863 at Barboursville, age 15-16, born in Meigs County, Ohio, occupation: farmer.

Icenhower (also Icenhour), Allen A. Company F Private; enlisted September 20, 1862 at Point Pleasant, mustered October 9, 1862 at Point Pleasant, age 18, born in Rockbridge County, Virginia, occupation: laborer.

Icenhower (also Icenhour), Josephus Company F Private; enlisted September 20, 1862 at Point Pleasant, mustered October 9, 1862 at Point Pleasant, age 16, born 1847 at Kanawha Salines, six miles above Charleston on the Great Kanawha River, Kanawha County, Virginia/West Virginia, occupation: laborer.

Irby, George W. Company H Private; enlisted August 14, 1862 at Ceredo, mustered October 10, 1862 at Point Pleasant, age 31, born in Pittsylvania County, Virginia, occupation: farmer.

Jackson, Nathaniel Muncy (signed Nathaniel M. Jackson) Company I Corporal; enlisted December 24, 1862 at Charleston, appointed Corporal July 26, 1863, mustered July 26, 1863 at Charleston, age 23, born in Russell County, Virginia, occupation: farmer.

Jackson, William Company D Private; enlisted August 18, 1862 at Hartford City, received paid $30.00 Mason County Bounty and Premium, mustered October 8, 1862 at Point Pleasant, age 44, born in Scotland, occupation: miner.

James, Samuel Company E Private; enlisted September 15, 1862 at Point Pleasant, mustered October 9, 1862 at Point Pleasant, age 27, born in Kanawha County, Virginia/West Virginia, occupation: farmer.

Jamison/Jemison/Jannison, Albert C. Company H Private; enlisted September 20, 1862 at Point Pleasant or Kygerville, mustered in December 11, 1862 at Point Pleasant, age 15/16, born in Wellsville, Columbiana County, Ohio, occupation: musician; released by court order from the United States Service, Jamison being a minor, who had enlisted against the wishes of his father (Moses P. Jamison), and "being a boy of feeble constitution and delicate health, and unfit to endure the life of a soldier." (Kanawha Circuit Court Clerks Office, certified by John Slack, Clerk, June 10th, 1863.[725])

Jeffers/Jeffres/Jeffries, William H. (or William M.) (signed "Jeffers") Company C Private; enlisted August 12, 1862 at Point Pleasant, received paid $30.00 Mason County Bounty and Premium, mustered October 8, 1862 at Point Pleasant, age 18, born in Neville, Ohio (the entry in Regimental Descriptive Rolls reads: "Nevilleville, Ohio" which might also stand for Newville, Ohio, a ghost-town today), occupation: farmer.

Jeffres/Jeffries, Felix Company B Private; enlisted August 8, 1862 at Point Pleasant, received paid $30.00 Mason County Bounty and Premium, mustered October 8, 1862 at Point Pleasant, age 24, born in Mason County, Virginia/West Virginia: farmer.

Jeffres/Jeffries, James Company B Private; enlisted August 8, 1862 at Point Pleasant, received paid $30.00 Mason County Bounty and Premium, mustered October 8, 1862, age 24, born in Mason County, Virginia/West Virginia, occupation: farmer.

Jeffries, Eli Company B Private and Corporal; enlisted August 6, 1862 at Point Pleasant, mustered October 8, 1862 at Point Pleasant, age 30, born in Mason County, Virginia/West Virginia, occupation: cooper; appointed Corporal November 10, 1864.

Jeffries, Gideon Company B Private; enlisted August 8, 1862 at Point Pleasant, received paid $30.00 Mason County Bounty and Premium, mustered October 8,

1862 at Point Pleasant, age 22, born in Mason County, Virginia/West Virginia, occupation: farmer.

Jividen, Elias Company K 7ᵗʰ Private and Corporal; enlisted October 25, 1863 at Ripley, promoted to Corporal August 11, 1864, mustered November 25, 1863 at Barboursville, age 17, born in Jackson County, Virginia/West Virginia, occupation: farmer.

Jividen, Jonathan Company K; Private; enlisted October 9, 1863 at Barboursville, mustered November 25, 1863 at Barboursville, age 21, born in Jackson County, Virginia/West Virginia, occupation: farmer.

Jobling/Joblin, Jesse Company A Private; enlisted August 15, 1862 at Charleston, mustered October 7, 1862 at Point Pleasant, age 23, born in Kanawha County, Virginia/West Virginia, occupation: farmer.

Johnson, Abner F. Company F Corporal; enlisted April 2, 1863 at Point Pleasant, mustered in August 5, 1863 at Charleston, age 18, born in Washington County, Ohio, occupation: miller; promoted to Corporal September 1, 1864.

Johnson, Abraham/Abram (also Abner) Company B Private; enlisted August 4, 1862 at Point Pleasant, received paid $30.00 Mason County Bounty and Premium, mustered October 8, 1862, age 35, born in Monroe County, Ohio, occupation: farmer.

Johnson, Asa S. Company C Private; enlisted December 8, 1862 at Point Pleasant, mustered December 11, 1862 at Point Pleasant, age 22, born in Mason County, Virginia/West Virginia, occupation: farmer. Prior to enlistment in the Union Army, Johnson may have served as Private in Company A, 116ᵗʰ Regiment Virginia Militia ("Solger 85 Johnson, Asey").

Johnson, Charles A. Company H Private; enlisted November 22, 1863 at Barboursville, mustered November 25, 1863 at Barboursville, age 16, born in Morgan County, Virginia/West Virginia, occupation: farmer.

Johnson, David B. Company C 4ᵗʰ Corporal and Sergeant; enlisted August 15, 1862 at Point Pleasant, received paid $30.00 Mason County Bounty and Premium, mustered October 8, 1862 at Point Pleasant, age 40, born in Mason County, Virginia/West Virginia, occupation: farmer; promoted from Corporal to Sergeant March 1, 1865.

Johnson, Jeremiah Hamilton (called "Hamilton") Company F Corporal and 3ʳᵈ Sergeant; enlisted September 9, 1862 at Point Pleasant, paid $30.00 Mason County Bounty and Premium, mustered October 9, 1862, age 26, born February 25,

1836 in Frederick County, Virginia, occupation: farmer; appointed Company Commissary on Oct. 5, 1862[726] promoted Sergeant Feb. 15, 1864 to rank as such from Dec. 1, 1863 in place of Sergeant Peter Darnell discharged pursuant to Col. W.R. Brown, Gen. Order No. 1 (manu. dated Feb. 15, 1864); captured at the Battle Cedar Creek, Virginia October 19, 1864, sent to Andersonville Prison, Georgia returned to his Company May 15, 1865, promoted to 1st Sergeant May 18, 1865.

Johnson, James Company D Private, Corporal, Sergeant; enlisted August 10/11, 1862 at Hartford City, received paid $30.00 Mason County Bounty and Premium, mustered October 8, 1862 at Point Pleasant, age 24, born in Mason County, Virginia/West Virginia, occupation: farmer; possibly "Sergeant" at time of discharge May 24, 1865.

Johnson, James Company H Private; enlisted August 11, 1862 at Ceredo, mustered October 10, 1862 at Point Pleasant, age 18, born in Wayne County, Virginia/West Virginia, occupation: farmer. Johnson served with Wayne County Home Guards prior to enlistment in the 13th West Virginia Regiment.

Johnson, James Company I Private and Corporal; enlisted November 27, 1862 at Charleston, mustered July 26, 1863 at Charleston, age 16; born in England occupation: miner; appointed Corporal January 28, 1865.

Johnson, James W. Company A Captain; date of appointment August 19, 1862, commissioned Captain September 9, 1862, mustered October 7, 1862, age 25/26, born in Vermont, resident of Kanawha County, Virginia/West Virginia, occupation: lawyer; resigned July 20, 1863 having accepted an appointment in the U.S. Colored Troops, transferred to 3rd Regiment U.S. Colored Troops by War Department Order No. 335, issued July 20, 1863. The 3rd U.S.C.T. was organized near Philadelphia, Pennsylvania August 3-10 and ordered to the Department of the South. For mention of "James W. Johnson 13th Virginia, 1st Lieutenant Company C" 3rd U.S.C.T. see description of the moving out of the 3rd Regiment from Camp Chelton Hill in the *Army and Navy Official Gazette* Volume 1 1863-64 (Washington City: Office of John C. Rives), p. 104.

Johnson, Lewis C. Company D Private; enlisted August 15, 1862 at Hartford City, received paid $30.00 Mason County Bounty and Premium, mustered October 8, 1862 at Point Pleasant, age 17, born in Mason County, Virginia/West Virginia, occupation: farmer.

Johnson, William H. Company I Private; enlisted November 25, 1863 at Barboursville, mustered November 25, 1863 at Guyandotte, age 18, born in Cabell County, Virginia/West Virginia, occupation: farmer.

Jolley/Jolly, Andrew J. Company H Private; enlisted September 20, 1862 at Point Pleasant, mustered December 11, 1862 at Point Pleasant, age 42, born in Columbiana County, Ohio; occupation: farmer.

Jones, Alfred Company A Private and Corporal; enlisted August 12, 1862 at Charleston, mustered October 7, 1862 at Point Pleasant, age 20, born in Kanawha County, Virginia/West Virginia, occupation: farmer; appointed Corporal August 1, 1864.

Jones/Jaynes, Asa Company K Private; enlisted February 20, 1864 at Coals Mouth, mustered March 28, 1864 at Charleston, age 18, born in Jackson County, Virginia/West Virginia, occupation: farmer.

Jones, Elisha T. Company E Private; enlisted August 22, 1862 at Charleston, mustered October 9, 1862 at Point Pleasant, age 25, born in An[v?]a, Ohio (Anna, Ohio?), occupation: farmer; transferred to Veteran Reserve Corps (also called the Invalid Corps) at Gallispolis, Ohio, date not given.

Jones, Jesse L. (signed "Jesse L. Jones") Company F Private; enlisted September 9, 1862 at Point Pleasant, received paid $30.00 Mason County Bounty and Premium, mustered October 9, 1862 at Point Pleasant, age 35, born in Mason County, Virginia, occupation: caulker.

Jones, John Companies D and G 1ˢᵗ Sergeant Company D and 1ˢᵗ Lieutenant Company G; enlisted August 15, 1862 at Hartford City, received paid $30.00 Mason County Bounty and Premium, mustered in as Sergeant October 8, 1862 at Point Pleasant, age 22 /24, born in Jackson County, Virginia/West Virginia, occupation: "suryer" (sawyer or surveyor?); discharged from 1ˢᵗ Sergeant Company D and transferred promoted to 1ˢᵗ Lieutenant Company G on February 1/7, 1864 at organization of Company G by order of Brigadier General Benjamin. F. Kelly dated Cumberland, Maryland, March 10, 1864.

Jones, Marcus, L. Company C Private and Drummer; enlisted January 20, 1863 at Point Pleasant, mustered August 5, 1863 at Charleston, age 18, born in Meigs County, Ohio, occupation: farmer.

Jones, Newport Company G Private; enlisted December 25, 1863 at Hartford City, mustered February. 28, 1864 at Guyandotte, age 40, born in Jefferson County, Ohio, occupation: carpenter.

Jones, Samuel Company A Private; enlisted March 1, 1863 at Hurricane Bridge, mustered July 9, 1863 at Charleston, age 16/18, born in Kanawha County, Virginia/West Virginia, occupation: farmer.

Jones, William Company A Private; enlisted August 12, 1862 at Charleston, mustered October 7, 1862 at Point Pleasant, age 18, born in Kanawha County, Virginia/West Virginia, occupation: farmer. Jones was severely wounded in battle at Fisher's Hill, Virginia fought September 22, 1864, recovered sufficiently to be transferred to the 38th Company 2nd Battalion Veteran Reserve Corps.

Jones, Wilson Company A Private; enlisted December 29, 1863 at Charleston, mustered February 27, 1864 at Barboursville, age 17, born in Kanawha County, Virginia/West Virginia, occupation: farmer.

Jordan, William G. Company E Private; enlisted August 19, 1862 at Charleston, mustered October 9, 1862 at Point Pleasant, age 20, born in Kanawha County, Virginia/West Virginia, occupation: farmer.

Kearnes, William Company D Private; enlisted August 15, 1862 at Hartford City, received paid $30.00 Mason County Bounty and Premium, mustered October 8, 1862 at Point Pleasant, age 22, born in Mason County, Virginia/West Virginia, occupation: farmer; promoted to Corporal February 7, 1865.

Keefer, Daniel Company G Private; enlisted January 1 or 4, 1864 at Buffalo, mustered February 28, 1864 at Guyandotte, age 18-19, born Putnam County, Virginia/West Virginia, occupation: farmer.

Keith, Sylvester Company F Private and Blazer Scout/Independent Scout; enlisted September 9, 1862 at Point Pleasant, mustered October 9, 1862 at Point Pleasant, age 18, born in Washington County, Ohio, occupation: farmer.

Kelley, James S. Company C Sergeant; enlisted August 15, 1862 at Point Pleasant, received paid $30.00 Mason County Bounty and Premium, mustered October 8, 1862 at Point Pleasant, age 29; born in "County Unknown, Mishigan" [Michigan], occupation: farmer; appointed 4th Sergeant January 8, 9 or 3, 1863.

Kessell, Abraham Company K Private; enlisted December 1, 1863 at Barboursville, mustered March 28, 1864 at Charleston, age 18, born in Jackson County, Virginia/West Virginia, occupation: farmer and stonemason.

Kile/Kyle, Peter Company G Private; enlisted December 30, 1863 at Guyandotte, mustered February 28, 1864 at Guyandotte, age 22, born in Cabell County, Virginia/West Virginia, occupation: farmer.

Killingsworth, John Company D Private; enlisted August 18, 1862 at Hartford City, received paid $30.00 Mason County Bounty and Premium, mustered October 8, 1862 at Point Pleasant, age 36, born in Randolph County, Virginia, occupation: farmer.

Kimberlin/Kimberling, Benjamin F. Company H Private; enlisted January 5, 1863 at Point Pleasant, mustered January 11, 1863 at Point Pleasant, age 16, born in Mason County, Virginia/West Virginia, occupation: farmer.

Kimberlin/Kimberling, Joseph (signed "Kimberling") Company F Private; enlisted September 28, 1862 at Point Pleasant , mustered October 9, 1862 at Point Pleasant, age 18, born in Mason County, Virginia, occupation: farmer.

Kimes, John C. Company D Private; enlisted August 15, 1862 at Mason City, mustered October 8, 1862 at Point Pleasant, age 18, born in Jackson County, Virginia/West Virginia, occupation: blacksmith.

Kimes, Samuel R. Company D Private; enlisted August 15, 1862 at Mason City, mustered October 8, 1862 at Point Pleasant, age 20, born in Jackson County, Virginia/West Virginia, occupation: blacksmith.

Kimes, Winfield (signed "Winfield S. Kimes") Company D Private; enlisted October 17, 1863 at Coalsmouth, mustered November 25, 1863 at Barboursville, age 16, born in Jackson County, Virginia/West Virginia, occupation: blacksmith; may have served as Private in Jackson County Home Guards before enlisting in the 13th West Virginia Infantry Regiment.

Kincade, John W. Company C Private; enlisted July 25, 1862 at Charleston, mustered October 8, 1862 at Point Pleasant, age 18, born in Cabell County, Virginia/West Virginia, occupation: farmer.

King, George Washington Company A 1st Sergeant; enlisted August 12, 1862 at Charleston, appointed 1st Sergeant August 20, 1862, mustered October 7, 1862 at Point Pleasant, age 36, born in Kanawha County, Virginia/West Virginia, occupation: farmer.

King, Henry Company H Private; enlisted September 20, 1862 at Kygersville, age 24, born in Gallia County, Ohio, occupation: farmer, discharged by the Army Surgeon for disability before being mustered.

King, James Company F; Private and Drummer; enlisted August 15, 1862 at Point Pleasant, received paid $30.00 Mason County Bounty and Premium, mustered October 9, 1862 at Point Pleasant, age 18, born in Allegheny County, Pennsylvania, occupation: farmer.

King, Nathan/Nathaniel E. Company K Private; enrolled on and mustered February 23/25, 1865 at Charleston, (no age or place of birth indicated), occupation: farmer.

King, Rice Company H Private; enlisted September 15, 1862 at Malden, mustered October 10, 1862 at Point Pleasant, age 19, born in Monroe County, Virginia/West Virginia, occupation: farmer.

Kirby, Thomas Company I Private; enlisted November 25, 1862 at Charleston, mustered July 26, 1863 at Charleston, age 20, born in Kanawha County, Virginia/West Virginia, occupation: farmer.

Kleen (also Kileen), Patrick (signed "Patrick Kleen") Company D Private; enlisted August 22, 1862 at Hartford City, received paid $30.00 Mason County Bounty and Premium, mustered October 8, 1862 at Point Pleasant, age 35, born in Ireland, occupation: laborer.

Knapp, William Company B Private; enlisted August 4, 1862 at Point Pleasant, received paid $30.00 Mason County Bounty and Premium, mustered October 8, 1862 at Point Pleasant, age 33, born in Mason County, Virginia/West Virginia, occupation: farmer.

Knight, Samuel Nimrod (called "Nimrod") Company C Private; enlisted and mustered in at Barboursville, November 13, 1863, age 22, born in Cabell County, Virginia/West Virginia, occupation: farmer.

Krebs, Charles Company F Private and Corporal; enlisted September 9, 1862 at Point Pleasant, received paid $30.00 Mason County Bounty and Premium, mustered October 9, 1862 at Point Pleasant, age 29, born in Lancaster County, Pennsylvania, occupation: farmer; promoted to Corporal March 26, 1864.

Lacy, George W. Company E Private; enlisted August 22, 1862 at Charleston, mustered October 9, 1862 at Point Pleasant, age 18, born in Kanawha County, Virginia/West Virginia, occupation: farmer.

Lallance, Jacob Company E Private, Hospital Steward and Assistant Surgeon; enrolled as Head Hospital Steward October 3, 1862 at Point Pleasant, Virginia, mustered with Company E October 9, 1862 at Point Pleasant, aged 26 years, born in Meigs County, Ohio occupation: physician (allopath); promoted to Assistant Surgeon February 8, 1864.

Landers/Sanders, Meredith Company E Private; enlisted August 22, 1862 at Charleston, mustered October 9, 1862 at Point Pleasant, age 22, born in Kanawha County, Virginia/West Virginia, occupation: farmer.

Lanham, Abraham Company K Private; enlisted October 1, 1863 at Walton, mustered November 25, 1863 at Barboursville, age 25, born in Jackson County, Virginia/West Virginia, occupation: farmer.

Lanham/ Laniham, John W. Company F Private; enlisted December 25, 1863 at Barboursville, mustered February 27, 1864 at Barboursville, age 18, born in Kanawha County, Virginia/West Virginia, occupation: farmer.

Lanham, John W. Company K Private; enlisted October 1, 1863 at Walton, mustered in November 25, 1863 at Barboursville, age 18, born in Jackson County, Virginia/West Virginia, occupation: farmer.

Latham, Charles T[homas] Company B Lieutenant; entered the U.S. Service as Private July 26, 1862, appointed 2nd Lieutenant Company B August 23, 1862, commissioned Lieutenant September 12, 1862, mustered October 8, 1862 at Point Pleasant, age about 20, born in Pennsylvania, resident of the State of Virginia at the time of enlistment; occupation: shoemaker.

Lawrence also Lawrance and Lorenzo, Charles M. Company H Private; enlisted September 15, 1862 at Malden, mustered in October 10, 1862 at Point Pleasant, age 19, born in Monroe County, Virginia/West Virginia, occupation: farmer.

Lawrence, Preston C. Company H Private and Corporal; enlisted September 1, 1862 at Guyandotte, mustered October 10, 1862 at Point Pleasant, age 21, born in Fayette County, Virginia/West Virginia, occupation: farmer; appointed 2nd Corporal November 30, 1864.

Lawson, William Company B Private and Corporal; enlisted August 9, 1862 at Point Pleasant, received paid $30.00 Mason County Bounty and Premium, mustered October 8, 1862 at Point Pleasant, age 18, born in Mason County, Virginia/West Virginia, occupation: farmer; appointed Corporal November 10, 1864.

Lee, Felix M. Company G Private; enlisted and mustered into service February16, 1865 at Point Pleasant, age 44, born in Mason County, Virginia/West Virginia, occupation: farmer.

Lee, George S. Company G Private; enlisted and mustered into service February 16, 1865 at Point Pleasant, age 17, born Mason County, Virginia/West Virginia, occupation: farmer.

Lee, William Company B Private; enlisted August 13, 1862 at Point Pleasant, received paid $30.00 Mason County Bounty and Premium, mustered October 8, 1862, age 21, born in Mason County, Virginia/West Virginia, occupation: farmer.

Lee, William W. Company G Private; enlisted December 26, 1863 at Guyandotte, mustered February 28, 1864 at Guyandotte, age 18, born in Gallia County, Ohio; occupation: farmer.

Legg, James (also "Junius Logg") Company E Private, enlisted August 22, 1862 at Charleston, appointed 1ˢᵗ Corporal September 12, 1862, mustered October 9, 1862 at Point Pleasant, age 35, born in Monroe County, Virginia/West Virginia, occupation: cooper.

Lemaster (also Lamasters), George (signed "Lemaster") Company E Private and Blazer Scout/Independent Scout; enlisted August 9, 1862 at Ceredo, mustered October 9, 1862 at Point Pleasant, age 28, born in Wayne County, Virginia/West Virginia, occupation: farmer; detailed for duty with Blazer Scouts in 1864. Lemaster served in Wayne County Home Guards prior to enlistment in the 13ᵗʰ West Virginia Regiment.

Lenders (also Landers), William H. (signed "Lenders") Company D Private; enlisted August 18, 1862 at Hartford City, received paid $30.00 Mason County Bounty and Premium, mustered October 8, 1862 at Point Pleasant, age 30, born in Kanawha County, Virginia/West Virginia, occupation: boatman.

Lewis, Allen Company F Private and Corporal; enlisted March 31, 1864 at Guyandotte, mustered April 26, 1864 at Barboursville, age 30, born in Mason County (or Marion County) Virginia/West Virginia, occupation: farmer; promoted to Corporal (March 10, 1865?).

Lewis, Benjamin Company G Corporal; enlisted December 10, 1863 at West Columbia, mustered February 28, 1864 at Guyandotte, age 24, born in Mason County, Virginia/West Virginia, occupation: farmer.

Lewis, John Company F Private; enlisted September 10, 1862 at Point Pleasant, received paid $30.00 Mason County Bounty and Premium, mustered October 9, 1862 at Point Pleasant, age 45, born in Mason County, Virginia/West Virginia, occupation: farmer.

Lewis, Isaac A. Company G Private; enlisted February 1, 1864, at West Columbia, mustered February 28, 1864 at Guyandotte, age 20, born in Mason County, Virginia/West Virginia, occupation: farmer.

Lewis, Isaac I. (signed "Isaac I. Lewis") Company G Private; enlisted December 10, 1863 at West Columbia, mustered February 28, 1864 at Guyandotte, age 18, born in Mason County, Virginia/West Virginia, occupation: farmer.

Lewis, Robert Anderson Company G Corporal; enlisted December 1, 1863 at West Columbia, promoted Corporal Feb. 15, 1864 pursuant to Col. W.R. Brown, Gen. Order No. 1 (manu. dated Feb. 15, 1864) to rank as such from Jan. 27, 1864, mustered February 28, 1864 at Guyandotte, age 30, born in Mason County Virginia/West Virginia, occupation: farmer.

Lewis, William Company K Private; enlisted December 27, 1863 at Leon, mustered March 28, 1864 at Charleston, age 17, born in Kanawha County, Virginia/West Virginia, occupation: farmer.

Lewis, William Company K Private; enlisted February 25/ 26, 1864 at Coals Mouth, mustered March 28, 1864 at Charleston, age 18 and born in Jackson County, Virginia/West Virginia, farmer.

Light, James Company A Private; enlisted August 14, 1862 at Charleston, mustered October 7, 1862 at Point Pleasant, age 27, born in Randolph County, Virginia/West Virginia, occupation: farmer.

Light, Lorenzo M. Company G Private; enlisted December 7, 1863 at Barboursville, mustered February 28, 1864 at Guyandotte, age 20, born in Kanawha County, Virginia/West Virginia; occupation: farmer.

Linehan (also Lanihan/Lenihan/Linihan), James (signed "James Linehan") Company D Private or Corporal; enlisted August 21, 1862 at Point Pleasant, received paid $30.00 Mason County Bounty and Premium, mustered in October 8, 1862 at Point Pleasant, age 28, born in Ireland, occupation: laborer.

Lisle, David H. Company D Private; enlisted November 6, 1863 at Murraysville, mustered November 25, 1863 at Barboursville, age 16, born in Belmont County, Ohio, occupation: farmer.

Long, Andrew J. ("J" for "Jackson") Private Company G 60ᵗʰ Ohio Infantry Regiment and Private Company C 13ᵗʰ Virginia/West Virginia Regiment Infantry Volunteers and Blazer Scout; enlisted in the 13ᵗʰ Regiment March 23, 1863 at Point Pleasant, mustered in August 5, 1863 at Point Pleasant, age 19, born in Gallia County, Ohio, occupation: farmer. Detailed on March 10, 1864 for a body of Independent Scouts in compliance with General Orders No. 2 from "Head Quarters 3d Division Dept., W.Va." (dated "Charleston W.Va. February 16ᵗʰ 1864").

Long, James T. Company G 60ᵗʰ Ohio Regiment Infantry Volunteers and Private Company C 13ᵗʰ Virginia/West Virginia Regiment Infantry Volunteers; enlisted in the 13ᵗʰ Regiment August 15 or 17, 1863 at Coals Mouth, mustered August 17, 1863 at Barboursville, age 20, born in Gallia County, Ohio, occupation: farmer.

Love, Samuel C. Company B Private, Corporal and Sergeant; enlisted September 2nd or 4th, 1862 at Point Pleasant, received paid $30.00 Mason County Bounty and Premium, mustered October 8, 1862 at Point Pleasant, age 20, born in Mason County, Virginia/West Virginia, occupation: farmer; appointed Corporal December 15, 1862, promoted to Sergeant June 12, 1863, appointed 1st Sergeant February 10, 1865.

Lowe, Irvin Company I Private; enlisted January 11, 1863 at Walton, mustered in October 6, 1863 at Barboursville, age 31, born in Monroe County, Virginia/West Virginia, occupation: farmer.

Lowery/Lowry, David Company H Corporal and Sergeant; enlisted September 20, 1862 at Kygersville, appointed 6th Corporal September. 20, 1862, mustered December 11, 1862 at Point Pleasant, age 31, born in Beaver County, Pennsylvania, occupation: farmer; promoted to 4th Sergeant August 1, 1863.

Lunsford, James E. Company I Private; enlisted November 17, 1863 at Guyandotte, mustered November 25, 1863 at Guyandotte, age 15 or 18, born in Mason County, Virginia/West Virginia, occupation: laborer.

Lutton, Andrew J. Company C Private; enlisted November 28, 1863 at Point Pleasant, mustered November 23 or 28, 1863 at Barboursville, age 18, born in Moore Township, (Northampton, County?), Pennsylvania, occupation: farmer.

Lutton/Luton, Mathew Company C Private; enlisted August 21, 1862 at Point Pleasant, Virginia and received paid $30.00 Mason County Bounty and Premium, mustered October 8, 1862 at Point Pleasant, age 19, born in Alleghany County, Pennsylvania, occupation: farmer.

Maggi, George W. Company D Private and Corporal(?); enlisted August 15, 1862 at Morrisenville or Maysville, Virginia/West Virginia, mustered in October 8, 1862 at Point Pleasant, age 20, born in London, England, occupation: cooper.

Maher, Theophilus Company A 2nd Lieutenant and Recruiting Officer; appointed 2nd Lieutenant Company A July 28, 1862, commissioned 2nd Lieutenant Company A September 9, 1862 to rank from July 28, 1862, mustered October 7, 1862 at Point Pleasant, age *ca.*, 47 to 50, born in Virginia, occupation: superintendent of oil works; resigned commission February 1, 1863.

Mahan/Mahone, John P. (signed "J.P. Mahan") Company E Private and Corporal; enlisted August 22, 1862 at Charleston, mustered October 9, 1862 at Point Pleasant, age 17, born in Monroe County, Virginia/West Virginia, occupation: farmer, promoted from Private to Corporal July 28, 1864.

Mannan, George W. Company I Private; enlisted February 15, 1864 at Guyandotte, mustered February 29, 1864 at Guyandotte, age 21, born in Lawrence County, Ohio, occupation: laborer.

Marshall, Robert B. Company B Private; enlisted August 2, 1862 at Point Pleasant, received paid $30.00 Mason County Bounty and Premium, mustered October 8, 1862, age 30, born in Columbiana County, Ohio, occupation: steamboatman.

Martain/Martin, Moses/Mosis (signed "Moses Martain") Company K; Private; enlisted September 14, 1863 at Barboursville, mustered November 25, 1863 at Barboursville, age 18, born in Mason County, Virginia/West Virginia, occupation: farmer.

Martin, Alexander Company F Private and Corporal; enlisted September 9, 1862 at Point Pleasant, mustered October 9, 1862 at Point Pleasant, age 22, born in County Down, Ireland, occupation: miner.

Martin, Andrew Company I Private; enlisted December 13, 1862 at Charleston, mustered July 26, 1863 at Charleston, age 18, born in Kanawha County, Virginia/West Virginia, occupation: farmer.

Martin, John (signed "John Mortin") Company I Private and Corporal; enlisted June 1, 1863 at Charleston, mustered July 26, 1863 at Charleston, age 26, born in Kanawha County, Virginia/West Virginia, occupation: laborer; appointed Corporal September 1, 1863. Prior to enlistment in the 13th Regiment Volunteers, John Martin may have served in the Mason County Militia. See John Martin commissioned Second Lieutenant of the Mason County 106th Militia West Virginia State Troops by order November 24, 1862 to rank from November 19, 1862. (WVSA)

Mash/Marshe, William Company F Private; enlisted September 9, 1862 at Point Pleasant, received paid $30.00 Mason County Bounty and Premium, mustered October 9, 1862 at Point Pleasant, age 35, born in Rockingham County, Virginia, occupation: farmer.

Mason, Allen C. Company F and G 1st Sergeant Company F and Captain Company G; enlisted September 9, 1862, received paid $30.00 Mason County Bounty and Premium, mustered October 9, 1862 at Point Pleasant as 1st Sergeant, age 28, occupation: clerk, born in Jackson County, Virginia/West Virginia, discharged February 7th, 1864 to be promoted to Captain of Company G, commissioned Captain January 27, 1864 and promoted February 7, 1864 at organization of the Company.

Matheny, James A. (signed "James A. Matheny") Company E Private; enlisted November 5, 1863 at Point Pleasant, mustered February 27, 1864 at Charleston, age 17, born in Kanawha County, Virginia/West Virginia, occupation: farmer.

Matheny, Michael Company E Private; enlisted August 22, 1862 at Charleston, mustered October 9, 1862 at Point Pleasant, age 44, born in Adams County, Ohio, occupation: farmer.

Mathers, Samuel S. Company C and A Private and Lieutenant; enlisted August 21, 1862 at Wheeling, mustered as Private Company C on October 8/9, 1862, age 21, born in Washington County, Pennsylvania, occupation: merchant; promoted to 2nd Lieutenant and transferred to Company A February 1 or 4, 1863, commissioned 2nd Lieutenant February 4, 1863; promoted 1st Lieutenant Company A October 31 or November 10, 1864.

Matheny, Daniel B. Company G Private; enlisted December 25, 1863 at Buffalo, age 45, born in Preston County, Virginia/West Virginia, occupation: farmer.

Mathews/Matthews (also Mathers), William I. Company H; 1st Lieutenant and Adjutant 13th Regiment and Acting Assistant Adjutant General, Department of West Virginia; commissioned 1st Lieutenant and Adjutant July 23, 1862; mustered October 10, 1862 at Point Pleasant, age 25 years; appointed Captain Company H April 27, 1863. Matthews was assigned to duty at Department Head Quarters by Special Order No. 129 dated November 4, 1863. He remained absent from his company all of 1864 on duty as Department Head Quarters, promoted Major January/February 1865 to replace A.F. McCown resigned.

Mattox, Josiah Company B Private; enlisted August 9, 1862 at Point Pleasant, received paid $30.00 Mason County Bounty and Premium, age 29, born in Mason County, Virginia/West Virginia, occupation: farmer.

Mattox, Tobias L. (signed "Tobias L. Mattox") Company B 5th Corporal and Sergeant; enlisted August 4, 1862 at Point Pleasant, received paid $30.00 Mason County Bounty and Premium, appointed Fifth Corporal October 8, 1862, mustered October 8, 1862 at Point Pleasant, age 22, born in Mason County, Virginia/West Virginia, occupation: farmer; appointed Sergeant sometime before being killed in action at Cedar Creek, Virginia on October 19, 1864.

Maybee, James T. Company G Private; enlisted December 11, 1863 at Guyandotte, mustered February 28, 1864 at Guyandotte, age 18, born in Pennsylvania, occupation: farmer.

Maybee (also Magee), Munson W. Company G Private; enlisted December 22, 1863 at Guyandotte, mustered February 28, 1864 at Guyandotte, age 18, born in Pennsylvania, occupation: farmer.

Mays (also Mayo), John T. Company H Private; enlisted December 10, 1863 at Barboursville, mustered February 27, 1864 at Barboursville, age 24, born in Cabell County, Virginia/West Virginia, occupation: farmer.

Mays (also Mayo), Julius R. Company H Private; enlisted December 10, 1863 at Barboursville, mustered February 27, 1864 at Barboursville, age 28, born in Cabell County, Virginia/West Virginia, occupation: farmer.

Mays (also Mayes), Hezekiah Company D Private; enlisted November 22, 1863 at Barboursville, mustered November 25, 1863 at Barboursville, age 18, born in Cabell County, Virginia/West Virginia, occupation: farmer.

McCauley/McCauly, William B. Company C Corporal and Sergeant; enlisted August 22, 1862 at Point Pleasant, received paid $30.00 Mason County Bounty and Premium, mustered October 8, 1862 at Point Pleasant, age 26, born in Mason County, Virginia/West Virginia; occupation: carpenter; promoted 5th Sergeant from Corporal January 8 /9, 1863.

McClaskey, Floid/Floyd (signed "Floid McClaskey") Company I; Private; enlisted August 27, 1863 at Charleston, mustered October 6, 1863 at Barboursville, age 18, born in Mason County, Virginia/West Virginia, occupation: farmer; served in Mason County West Virginia State Guards prior to enlistment.

McCloud/McLoud, David/Daniel Company C Private; enlisted and mustered October 4, 1863 at Barboursville, age 18, born in Mason County, Virginia/West Virginia, occupation: farmer.

McCloud/McCloued, John Company C Private; enlisted August 12, 1862 and received paid $30.00 Mason County Bounty and Premium, mustered in October 8, 1862, age 18, born in "County unknown," Ohio, occupation: farmer.

McClure, Isaiah Company G Sergeant; enlisted December 29, 1863 at Point Pleasant, appointed Sergeant Feb. 15, 1864 pursuant to Col. W.R. Brown, Gen. Order No. 1 (manu. dated Feb. 15, 1864) to rank as such from Jan. 27, 1864, mustered February 28, 1864 at Guyandotte, age 26, born Morgan County, Ohio, occupation: teacher.

McCollister (also McColister), Jackson (signed "McCottister"?) Company I Private; enlisted February 28, 1863 at Point Pleasant, mustered July 26, 1863 at Charleston, age 18, born in Mason County, Virginia/West Virginia, occupation: farmer.

McCormack/McCormick, Samuel Company A Private; enlisted August 15, 1862 at Charleston, mustered October 7, 1862 at Point Pleasant, age 44, born in Kanawha County, Virginia/West Virginia, occupation: farmer.

McCown (also McCowen), Albert F. Company F Captain enlisted September 9, 1862, received paid $30.00 Mason County Bounty and Premium, commissioned Captain October 8, 1862 to rank October 1, 1862, mustered October 9, 1862 at Point Pleasant, age 30 to 32, born in Virginia, occupation: merchant; promoted Major December 13/14, 1864. Prior to enlistment in the 13th Virginia Regiment, McCown served as Captain of the Mason County 106th Militia West Virginia State Troops, commissioned May 27, 1862 to rank from April 19, 1862.

McCoy, Isaiah Company B Private; enlisted November 3, 1862 at Point Pleasant, mustered November 17, 1862 at Winfield, age 34, born in Mason County, Virginia/West Virginia, occupation: farmer.

McCoy, James Company B Private; enlisted August 4, 1862 at Point Pleasant, received paid $30.00 Mason County Bounty and Premium, mustered October 8, 1862, age 37, born in Mason County, Virginia/West Virginia, occupation: farmer.

McCoy, James R. Company F Private; enlisted November 10, 1863 at Barboursville, mustered November 25, 1863 at Barboursville, age 18, born in Mason County, Virginia/West Virginia, occupation: farmer.

McCoy, Joseph E. Sergeant Company G 9th Virginia/West Virginia Regiment Infantry Volunteers, 1st Lieutenant and Captain Company K 13th West Virginia Infantry Regiment, mustered into Company G 9th Virginia March 1, 1862 at Spencer, promoted from 3rd Sergeant Company G 9th Virginia, commissioned 1st Lieutenant Company K 13th West Virginia Volunteer Infantry Regiment October 31, 1864 or February 1, 1864 (no date of muster in available); promoted Captain Company K 13th Regiment West Virginia Infantry resigned November 10, 1864.

McCoy, Samuel E. (or A.) Company G Private; enlisted December 12, 1863 at Buffalo or West Columbia, mustered February 28, 1864 at Guyandotte, age 18, born in Putnam County, Virginia/West Virginia, occupation: blacksmith.

McCulock (also McColloch/McColough/McCulloch), John S[amuel] (signed "McCulock") Company C Private; enlisted August 14, 1862 at Point Pleasant, received paid $30.00 Mason County Bounty and Premium, mustered October 8, 1862, age 23, born in Mason County, Virginia/West Virginia, occupation: farmer. Prior to enlistment in the Union Army, McCullock may have served as Private in Company A, 116th Regiment Virginia Militia ("Private Cullough, John Mc."). Detailed for permanent duty as teamster with regimental quartermaster Lt. Stephen Comstock March 30, 1864 (Col. Brown Special Order No. 50, Order Book Co. C, NARA).

McDaniel, Alexander Company B Private; enlisted August 9, 1862 at Point Pleasant, received paid $30.00 Mason County Bounty and Premium, mustered October 8, 1862, age 18, born in Mason County, Virginia/West Virginia, occupation: farmer. Prior to enlistment in the Union Army, McDaniel may have served as Private in Company A, 116th Regiment Virginia Militia ("Solger 70 McDaniel, Ellick").

McDaniel, Augustus Company E Private; enlisted August 22, 1862 at Charleston, mustered October 9, 1862 at Point Pleasant, age 18, born in Kanawha County, Virginia/West Virginia, occupation: cooper.

McDaniel, George Company C Private; enlisted and mustered September 29, 1863 at Barboursville, age 18, born in Mason County, Virginia/West Virginia, occupation: farmer; Prior to enlistment in the Union Army, McDaniel may have served as Private in Company A, 116th Regiment Virginia Militia ("Solger 71 McDaniel, George").

McDaniel, John Company B Sergeant; enlisted August 5, 1862 at Point Pleasant, received paid $30.00 Mason County Bounty and Premium, appointed 3rd Sergeant October 8, 1862, mustered October 8, 1962, age 33, born in Mason County, Virginia/West Virginia, occupation: carpenter. McDaniel may have served with local militia prior to enlistment in 13th Regiment. See John McDaniel, Captain of the Mason County 106th Militia West Virginia State Troops. Commissioned Captain December 10, 1861 to rank from November 25, 1861. (WVSA)

McDaniel, Reuban/Reuben Company B Private; enlisted August 4/5, 1862 at Point Pleasant, received paid $30.00 Mason County Bounty and Premium, mustered October 8, 1862, age 21, born in Mason County, Virginia/West Virginia, occupation: farmer. Prior to enlistment in the Union Army, McDaniel may have served as Private in Company A, 116th Regiment Virginia Militia ("Solgers 72 McDaniel, Ruben").

McDaniel, Van D. Company C Captain; enlisted August 15, 1862, received paid $30.00 Mason County Bounty and Premium, appointed Captain of Company C September 1, 1862, commissioned Captain September 12, 1862, to rank from September 1, 1862, mustered October 8/9, 1862; age 26, born in Mason County, Virginia/West Virginia; occupation: farmer. Upon reorganization of Mason County Virginia Militia McDaniel had been elected Major of the Mason County 106th Militia West Virginia State Troops. He was commissioned Major February

26, 1862 to rank from February 22, 1862. He served as Major of the 106th until July, 1862, when the 13th Regiment Virginia Volunteers (Union Army) was being recruited. "Major McDaniel forsook his pleasant home, and raised from among his neighbors and acquaintances, a company of men, and was elected Captain."[727]

McDaniel, William (William C.?) Company C, Sergeant and 2nd Lieutenant; enlisted August 15, 1862 at Point Pleasant, received paid $30.00 Mason County Bounty and Premium, mustered in as Sergeant October 8, 1862, age 22, born in Mason County, Virginia/West Virginia, occupation: farmer; promoted from 3rd Orderly Sergeant to 2nd Sergeant January 6, 1863; commissioned 2nd Lieutenant Company C February 18, 1865 at Cumberland, Maryland, to rank from that date.

McDermitt/McDermot, James (signed "McDermit") Company B Private and Musician; enlisted August 9, 1862 at Point Pleasant, received paid $30.00 Mason County Bounty and Premium, mustered October 8, 1862, age 20, born in Mason County, Virginia/West Virginia, occupation: farmer.

McDermot (also McDearmit), George R. Company K Private; enlisted September 28, 1863 at Barboursville, mustered November 25, 1863 at Barboursville, age 18, born in Mason County, Virginia/West Virginia, occupation: farmer.

McDonald, Alexander (signed "A. G. McDonald") Company F Private; enlisted September 1, 1863 at Coals Mouth, mustered October 6, 1863 at Barboursville, age 35, born in Glasgow, Scotland, occupation: butcher.

McGlothlin (also McGlaughlin), John A. (signed "McGlothlin") Company E Private; enlisted December 20, 1863 at Charleston, mustered December 20, 1863 at Charleston, age 18, born in Greenbrier County, Virginia/West Virginia, occupation: farmer.

McGraw/McGrew, John M. or W. (signed "McGraw" also "McGrew") Company G Private; enlisted January 1, 1864 at Buffalo, mustered February 28, 1864 at Guyandotte, age 38, born in Fayette County, Virginia/West Virginia, occupation: farmer.

McGuire, Eli, S. Company K 6th Corporal; enlisted September 16, 1863 at Barboursville, mustered November 25, 1863 at Barboursville, age 40, born in Mason County, Virginia/West Virginia, occupation: farmer.

McGuire, John F. Company K Private; enlisted September 16, 1863 at Barboursville, mustered November 25, 1863 at Barboursville, age 16, born in Mason County, Virginia/West Virginia, occupation: farmer.

McGuire, William T. (called "Thomas") Company K; enlisted September 16, 1863 at Barboursville, mustered November 25, 1863 at Barboursville, age 18, born in Mason County, Virginia/West Virginia, occupation: farmer.

McKelley/McKelly, James Company H Private; enlisted August 8, 1862 at Ceredo, mustered October 10, 1862 at Point Pleasant, age 29, born in Russell County, Virginia, occupation: farmer.

McMaster, Thomas Company F Private; enlisted September 21, 1862 at Point Pleasant, mustered October 9, 1862 at Point Pleasant, age 32, born in County Down, Ireland, occupation: miner.

McMullen/ McMullin, William (signed "William A. McMullin") Company G Sergeant; enlisted December 10, 1863 at Barboursville, promoted to Sergeant pursuant to Col. W.R. Brown, Gen. Order No. 1 (manu. dated Feb. 15, 1864) to rank as such from Jan. 27, 1864, mustered February 28, 1864 at Guyandotte, age 19, born in Mason County, Virginia/West Virginia, occupation: farmer; appointed Sergeant January 15, 1864.

McSherry, John Company D Private; enlisted August 18, 1862 at Hartford City, mustered October 8, 1862 at Point Pleasant, received paid $30.00 Mason County Bounty and Premium, mustered October 8, 1862 at Point Pleasant, age 36, born in Scotland, occupation: miner.

Meadows, Peter H. (signed "Madors") Company C Private; enlisted August 11, 1862 at Point Pleasant, received paid $30.00 Mason County Bounty and Premium, mustered October 8/9, 1862 at Point Pleasant, age 22 or 18, born in Mason County, Virginia/West Virginia, occupation: farmer.

Means, James A. Company A Private and Corporal; enlisted August 14, 1862 at Charleston, mustered October 7, 1862 at Point Pleasant, age 29, born in Alleghany County, Virginia, occupation: farmer; appointed Corporal June 30, 1863.

Means, William A. Company A Private; enlisted August 22, 1862 at Charleston, mustered October 7, 1862, at Point Pleasant, age 19, born in Kanawha County, Virginia/West Virginia, occupation: farmer. Detailed on March 10, 1864 for a body of Independent Scouts in compliance with General Orders No. 2 from "Head Quarters 3d Division Dept., W.Va." (dated "Charleston W.Va. February 16ᵗʰ 1864").

Meek, Bazaliel (also Bazaleel/Bazallee) Company C Private; enlisted August 21, 1862 at Point Pleasant, Virginia, received paid $30.00 Mason County Bounty and Premium, mustered October 8, 1862 at Point Pleasant, age 30, born in "Alaganets, pensilvaie" [Allegheny County, Pennsylvania"], occupation: farmer. Prior to enlistment in the Union Army, Meek or Meeks, may have served as Private in Company A, 116th Regiment Virginia Militia ("Solger 91 Meeks, Bazel").

Meek, Henry A. Company B Private; enlisted August 4, 1862 at Point Pleasant, received paid $30.00 Mason County Bounty and Premium, mustered October 8, 1862, age 16/18, born in Allegheny County, Pennsylvania, occupation: farmer. Prior to enlistment in the Union Army, Meeks, may have served as Private in Company A, 116th Regiment Virginia Militia ("Solger 90 Meeks, Henry").

Meeks, Richard W. (also "Washington R. Meeks") Company D Corporal; enlisted August 15, 1862 at Hartford City, received paid $30.00 Mason County Bounty and Premium, mustered October 8, 1862 at Point Pleasant, born in Rockbridge County, Virginia, occupation: farmer.

Mesic/Messic/Messick, Jacob Company D Private; enlisted August 22, 1862 at Point Pleasant, received paid $30.00 Mason County Bounty and Premium, mustered October 8, 1862 at Point Pleasant, age 18, born in Rockingham County, Virginia, occupation: farmer.

Midkiff, Alexander Company C Private; enlisted August 1, 1863 at Coals Mouth, mustered August 1, 1863 at Barboursville, age 24, born in Kanawha County, Virginia/West Virginia, occupation: farmer.

Midkiff (also Medkiff), Levi Company C Private; enlisted August 8, 1862 at Point Pleasant, mustered October 8, 1862 at Point Pleasant, age 18, born in Kanawha County, Virginia/West Virginia, occupation: farmer.

Midkiff (also Medkiff), Lewis A. Company C Private; enlisted August 5, 1862 at Charleston, age 21, born in Kanawha County, Virginia/West Virginia, occupation: farmer. Recruit rejected. Midkiff was discovered to be a deserter from 8th Regiment Virginia/West Virginia Infantry and was returned to that regiment either after muster in (October 8/9, 1862 at Point Pleasant) or recruit was discovered to belong to the 8th Virginia at point of rendez-vous (that is, at Point Pleasant) and not mustered in with Company C.

Midkiff, Samuel Company A Corporal; enlisted August 13, 1862 at Charleston, mustered July 9, 1863 at Charleston, age 38, born in Kanawha County, Virginia/West Virginia, occupation; carpenter; appointed Corporal June 1, 1864.

Miller, George T. Company D Private and Corporal; enlisted August 11, 1862 at Hartford City, paid $30.00 Mason County Bounty and Premium, mustered October 8, 1862 at Point Pleasant, age 34, born in Kanawha County, Virginia/West Virginia, occupation: coppersmith. Detailed on March 10, 1864 for a body of Independent Scouts in compliance with General Orders No. 2 from "Head

Quarters 3d Division Dept., W.Va." (dated "Charleston W.Va. February 16ᵗʰ 1864").

Miller, Henry (signed "Henry C. Miller") Company E Private; enlisted November 11, 1863 at Tuppers Creek, mustered February 27, 1864 at Charleston, age 17, born in Kanawha County, Virginia/West Virginia, occupation: farmer.

Miller, Henry F. Company F Private; enlisted September 15, 1862 at Point Pleasant, mustered October 9, 1862 at Point Pleasant, age 30, born in Logan County, Virginia/West Virginia, occupation: farmer.

Miller, John Company E Private; enlisted August 16, 1862 at Tuppers Creek, mustered October 9, 1862 at Point Pleasant, age 27, born in Kanawha County, Virginia/West Virginia, occupation: farmer.

Miller, Harrison/Morrison Company E Private; enlisted August 16, 1862 at Tuppers Creek, mustered October 9, 1862 at Point Pleasant, age 18, born in Kanawha County, Virginia/West Virginia, occupation: farmer.

Miller, Peter Company H Private; enlisted August 12, 1862 at Ceredo, mustered October 10, 1862 at Point Pleasant, age 44, born in Logan County, Virginia/West Virginia; occupation: farmer.

Mills, Alexander H. Company D Private; enlisted August 15, 1862 at Mason City, mustered October 8, 1862 at Point Pleasant, age 18, born in Jackson County, Virginia/West Virginia, occupation: farmer.

Mills, Francis A. Company D Corporal; enlisted August 15, 1862 at Mason City, mustered October 8, 1862 at Point Pleasant, age 18, born in Jackson County, Virginia/West Virginia, occupation: farmer.

Mooney, James W. Company I Private; enlisted September 15, 1864 at Charleston, mustered September 15, 1864 at Charleston, age 18, born in Mercer County, Virginia, occupation: farmer.

Moore, Grandison/Grandissen B. Company E Corporal; enlisted August 22, 1862 at Charleston, , appointed 8ᵗʰ Corporal September 12, 1862, mustered October 9, 1862 at Charleston, age 42, born in Kanawha County, Virginia/West Virginia, occupation: farmer.

Moore, Henderson Company I Private; enlisted January 26, 1863 at Charleston, mustered July 26, 1863 at Charleston, age 18, born in Kanawha County, Virginia/West Virginia, occupation: farmer.

Moore, John G. Company A Private; enlisted August 15, 1862 at Charleston, mustered October 7, 1862 at Point Pleasant, age 20, born in Roane County, Virginia/West Virginia, occupation: farmer.

Moore, Thomas Company A Sergeant; enlisted August 15, 1862 at Charleston, appointed Sergeant August 20, 1862, mustered October 7, 1862 at Point Pleasant, age 26, born in New York City, New York, occupation: miner.

Moore, Wilson Company F Private; enlisted September 9 or 19, 1862 at Point Pleasant, received paid $30.00 Mason County Bounty and Premium, mustered October 9, 1862 at Point Pleasant, age 18, born in Stark County, Ohio, occupation: teamster.

Moore, Wilson Company K Private; enlisted October 1, 1863 at Walton, mustered November 25, 1863 at Barboursville, age 18, born in Kanawha County, Virginia/West Virginia, occupation: farmer.

Morgan, Silas Company E Sergeant and 2nd Lieutenant; enlisted August 22, 1862 at Charleston, appointed 2nd Sergeant September 12, 1862; mustered October 9, 1862 at Point Pleasant, age 25, born in "Princedown" (Prince Edward County?), Virginia, occupation: laborer; discharged for promotion to 2nd Lieutenant November 10th, 1864 by order of General George Crook at Camp Russell, near Kernstown, Virginia, promoted 2nd Lieutenant March 15, 1865.

Moriarty, John (signed "John Morarity") Company D Private; enlisted August 22, 1862 at Point Pleasant or Hartford City, received paid $30.00 Mason County Bounty and Premium, mustered October 8, 1862 at Point Pleasant, age 36, born in Ireland, occupation: laborer.

Moriston/Morriston, Alonzo T. (signed "A. T. Moriston") Company C Corporal; enlisted August 11 or 21, 1862 at Point Pleasant, received paid $30.00 Mason County Bounty and Premium, mustered October 8/9, 1862 at Point Pleasant, age 21, born in Mason County, Virginia/West Virginia, occupation: farmer.

Morris, Joab Company G Private; enlisted December 26, 1863 at Buffalo, mustered February 28, 1864 at Guyandotte, age 36, born in Green County, Pennsylvania, occupation: farmer.

Morrow (also Morow), Charles Company C Private; enlisted August 15, 1862 at Coals Mouth or Point Pleasant, received paid $30.00 Mason County Bounty and Premium, mustered October 8, 1862 at Point Pleasant, age 44, born in Washington, Ohio, occupation: farmer.

Mourning, Andrew J. Company C Private; enlisted August 20, 1863 at Coals Mouth, mustered August 20, 1863 at Barboursville, age 18, born in Mason County, Virginia/West Virginia, occupation: farmer. Prior to enlistment in the Union Army, Mourning may have served as Private in Company A, 116th Regiment Virginia Militia ("Solger 87 Mornen, Andy").

Mourning, George Company C Private; enlisted August 8, 1862 at Point Pleasant, received paid $30.00 Mason County Bounty and Premium, mustered October 8/9, 1862 at Point Pleasant, age 18, born in Mason County, Virginia/West Virginia, occupation: farmer. Prior to enlistment in the Union Army, Mourning may have served as Private in Company A, 116th Regiment Virginia Militia ("Solger 86 Mornen, George").

Mourning/Morning, William H. Company B Private; enlisted August 8, 1862 at Point Pleasant, mustered October 8, 1862 at Point Pleasant, age 18, born in Mason County, Virginia/West Virginia, occupation: farmer.

Mulford/Mulfred, William H. H. Company C Private/Corporal; enlisted July 25, 1862 or August 3, 1862 at Point Pleasant, should have been mustered in October 8/9, 1862 at Point Pleasant, age 18, born in Mason County, Virginia/West Virginia, occupation: farmer. Although clothing, payroll and federal bounty records exist for Mulford, he did not sign the muster roll, and consequently there was no evidence to indicate that he was ever mustered in. Carded Medical Records (RG94 Box 3849 NARA) contain a record for "William H. Mulford, Corporal Co. C" indicating that on July 31, 1864 he was admitted to Sandy Hook Field Hospital for exhaustion. "Age 28."

Munday (also Monday), John R. Company K Private; enlisted September 1, 1863 at Walton, mustered October 3, 1863 at Charleston, age 43, born in Mason County, Virginia/West Virginia, occupation: farmer.

Munday/Mundy, Marshal/Marshall T. Company E Corporal; enlisted August 16, 1862 at Tupper Creek, mustered October 9, 1862 at Point Pleasant, age 35, born in Kanawha County, Virginia/West Virginia, occupation: farmer.

Mundy (also Munday), Reuban/Rubin G. (signed "Ruben T. Mundy") Company E Private; enlisted August 5, 1863 at Charleston, mustered August 5, 1863 or October 6, 1863 at Charleston, age 44, born in Albemarle County, Virginia, occupation: farmer.

Munday/Mundy, William M. (or L.) Company E Private; enlisted August 16, 1862 at Tuppers Creek, mustered October 9, 1862 at Point Pleasant, age 26, born in Kanawha County, Virginia/West Virginia, occupation: farmer.

Murphy (also Murfey), James H. Company H Private; enlisted March 1, 1863 at Hurricane Bridge, mustered July 9, 1863 at Charleston, age 18, born in Wayne County, Virginia/West Virginia, occupation: farmer.

Nanley, Abner Company A Private; enlisted August 15, 1862 at Charleston, mustered October 7, 1862 at Point Pleasant, age 16, born in Kanawha County, Virginia/West Virginia, occupation: farmer.

Naylor (also Nailer/Nayler), John Miller Company A Private; enlisted August 13, 1862 at Charleston, mustered October 7, 1862 at Point Pleasant, age 40, born in Kanawha County, Virginia/West Virginia, occupation: farmer.

Nevill/Neville, Austin Company B Private; enlisted August 12, 1862 at Point Pleasant, received paid $30.00 Mason County Bounty and Premium, mustered October 8, 1862, age 21, born in Beaver County, Pennsylvania, occupation: farmer.

Neville, Hiram Company C Private; enlisted September 4, 1863 at Coals Mouth, mustered September 4, 1863 at Barboursville, age 18, born in Beaver County, Pennsylvania, occupation: farmer.

Neville (also Neviles), William T. Company B Private; enlisted April. 16, 1863 at Point Pleasant, mustered August 5, 1863 at Charleston, age 17, born in Mason County, Virginia/West Virginia, occupation: farmer.

Newcomb, Isaac B. Company H Private; enlisted August 8, 1862 at Ceredo, mustered October 10, 1862 at Point Pleasant, age 28; occupation: carpenter.

Newel/Newell, Preston Company B Private; enlisted August 8, 1862 at Point Pleasant, received paid $30.00 Mason County Bounty and Premium, mustered October 8, 1862, age 29, born in Mason County, Virginia/West Virginia, occupation: farmer.

Newell, Elijah Franklin Company A Private; enlisted August 21, 1862 at Point Pleasant, received paid Mason County Bounty and Premium, October 7, 1862 at Point Pleasant," age 41 or 38, born in Mason County, Virginia/West Virginia, occupation: farmer.

Newell (also Norvil), John T. Company A Private; enlisted August 21, 1862 at Point Pleasant, received paid Mason County Bounty and Premium, mustered October 7, 1862 at Point Pleasant," age 38/39, born in Mason County, Virginia/West Virginia, occupation: farmer.

Newhouse, John S. Company I Private; enlisted December 6, 1862 at Charleston, mustered July 26, 1863 at Charleston, age 20, born in Kanawha County, Virginia/West Virginia, occupation farmer.

Newman, Leroy Company H Private and Corporal; enlisted August 14, 1862 at Ceredo, appointed 1st Corporal August 14, 1862, mustered October 10, 1862 at Point Pleasant, age 26, born in Wayne County, Virginia/West Virginia, occupation: farmer.

Nichols, William T. Company B Private, enlisted March 26, 1863 at Point Pleasant, mustered August 5, 1863 at Charleston, age 18, born in Covington County, Kentucky, occupation: farmer.

Nicholson, Philip/Phillip W. Company F Sergeant; enlisted September 9, 1862 at Point Pleasant, mustered October 9, 1862 at Point Pleasant, age 33, born in Guernsey County, Ohio, occupation: carpenter. Detailed on March 10, 1864 for a body of Independent Scouts in compliance with General Orders No. 2 from "Head Quarters 3d Division Dept., W.Va." (dated "Charleston W.Va. February 16th 1864").

Noble, Anson Company G Private; enlisted November 1, 1863 at West Columbia, mustered February 28, 1864 at Guyandotte, age 18, born in Columbiana County, Ohio; occupation: farmer.

Noble, Marcus/Markes D. Company C 6th Corporal; enlisted August 15, 1862, received paid Mason County Bounty and Premium, mustered October 8/9, 1862 at Point Pleasant, age 25, born in Warren County, New York, occupation: farmer.

Null, Henry Company G Private; enlisted December 30, 1863 at Buffalo, mustered February 28, 1864 at Guyandotte, age 41, born in Putnam County, Virginia/West Virginia, occupation: laborer.

Null, James W. Company G Private; enlisted February 20, 1864 at Guyandotte, mustered February 28, 1864 at Guyandotte, age 29, born in Jackson County, Virginia/West Virginia, occupation: farmer.

O Bryne (also O'Brian/O'Brien/O'Brin/O'Brion), John (signed "O Bryne") Company C Private; enlisted August 6, 1862 at Charleston, mustered October 8/9, 1862 at Point Pleasant, age 30, born in New Bridge, County Kildare, Ireland, occupation: miner.

Ohlinger, Frederick Company D Private; enlisted November 28, 1863 at Point Pleasant, mustered February 27, 1864 at Barboursville, age 17, born in Mason County, Virginia/West Virginia, occupation: farmer.

Ohlinger/Olinger, Lorean (signed "Loreen Ohlinger") Company D Private; enlisted August 18, 1862 at Hartford City, received paid Mason County Bounty and Premium, mustered October 8, 1862 at Point Pleasant, age 22, born in Circleville, Ohio, occupation: farmer.

Oldakers, John T. Company B Private; enlisted September 20, 1862 at Point Pleasant, mustered October 8, 1862 at Point Pleasant, age 28, born in Putnam County, Virginia/West Virginia, occupation: farmer.

Oliver, John C. Company G Private; enlisted February 17, 1865 at Point Pleasant, mustered February 16/17 or 20, 1864 at Point Pleasant, age 17, born in Mason County, Virginia/West Virginia, occupation: farmer.

Oliver, Leonard (signed "Lenord Oliver") Company D Private; enlisted August 22, 1862 at Point Pleasant, received paid Mason County Bounty and Premium, mustered October 8, 1862 at Point Pleasant, age 44, born in Mason County, Virginia/West Virginia, occupation: farmer.

Oliver, Thomas Company D Private; enlisted October 30, 1862 at Point Pleasant, mustered December17, 1862 at Winfield, age 24, born in Mason County, Virginia/West Virginia, occupation: farmer.

Ong, Ernest M. (signed "Ernest M. Ong") Company I; Sergeant; enlisted October 1, 1863 at Guyandotte, appointed Sergeant October 1, 1863, mustered October 6, 1863 at Barboursville, age 18, born in Cabell County, Virginia/West Virginia, occupation: laborer.

Orth, John Company A Private; enlisted August 15, 1862 at Charleston, mustered October 7, 1862 at Point Pleasant, age 20, born in "Mering, Prussia" (Merseburg, County of Saxony, Prussia?), occupation: farmer.

Owens, Edmond/Edmund G. (signed "Edmond G. Owens") Company H Private; enlisted October 26, 1863 at Barboursville, mustered in November 25, 1863 at Barboursville, age 18, born in Cabell County, Virginia/West Virginia, occupation: farmer.

Owens, Henry T. Company H Corporal; enlisted August 14, 1862 at Ceredo, appointed 3rd Corporal August 14, 1862, mustered October 10, 1862 at Point Pleasant, age 27, born in Cabell County, Virginia/West Virginia, occupation: farmer.

Owens, James M. Company H Private; enlisted October 26, 1863 at Barboursville, mustered November 25, 1863, age 24, born in Cabell County, Virginia/West Virginia, occupation: farmer.

Page, Cornelius Company A Corporal; enlisted August 14, 1862 at Charleston, appointed Corporal August 20, 1862, mustered October 7, 1862 at Point Pleasant, age 54, born in Bedford County, Virginia, occupation: farmer.

Pantzle/Pantzler/Pontzler, Charles (signed "Charles Pontzle" or "Pantzle") Company K Private; enlisted September 26, 1863 at Barboursville, mustered November 25, 1863 at Barboursville, age 18, born in Alleghany County, Pennsylvania, occupation: farmer.

Parsons, James Company C Private; enlisted September 9, 1862 at Point Pleasant, received paid $30.00 Mason County Bounty and Premium, mustered October 8, 1862 at Point Pleasant, age 21, born in Charleston, occupation: farmer.

Patten/Patton, John B. Company C Private and Corporal; enlisted August 11, 1862 at Point Pleasant, received paid $30.00 Mason County Bounty and Premium, mustered October 8/9, 1862 at Point Pleasant, age 20, born in Lawrence County, Pennsylvania, occupation: farmer; promoted to 8th Corporal January 8/9, 1863.

Patterson, James W. Company B Private; enlisted August 9, 1862 at Point Pleasant, received paid $30.00 Mason County Bounty and Premium, mustered October 8, 1862 at Point Pleasant, age 24, born in Mason County, Virginia/West Virginia, occupation: farmer.

Patterson, John Ellsworth Alexander Company C Private; enlisted March 8/9, 1863 at Point Pleasant, mustered August 5, 1863 at Charleston, age 24, born in Cabell County or Mason County, Virginia/West Virginia; occupation: farmer.

Patterson, Hezekiah S. Company C Private; enlisted September 1,1863 at Coals Mouth, mustered in September 1, 1863 at Barboursville, age 18, born in Mason, County, Virginia/West Virginia, occupation: farmer.

Paul, John E. Company H Private; enlisted August 14, 1862 at Ceredo, mustered October 10, 1862 at Point Pleasant, age 45, born in Monroe County, Virginia/West Virginia, occupation: farmer.

Pauley, Cornelius (signed "Pauley") Company E Private and Corporal; enlisted August 2, 1862 at Charleston, mustered October 9, 1862 at Point Pleasant, age 25, born in Kanawha County, Virginia/West Virginia, occupation: farmer; appointed from Private to Corporal April 5, 1865.

Pauley/Polly, Enies/Ennis/Enos (signed "Enies Pauley") Company C Private; enlisted August 4, 1862 at Charleston, mustered October 8, 1862 at Point Pleasant, age 35/36, born in Logan County, Virginia/West Virginia, occupation: farmer.

Pauley, John Company E Private; enlisted August 22, 1862 at Charleston, mustered October 9, 1862 at Point Pleasant, age 18, born in Kanawha County, Virginia/West Virginia, occupation: farmer; died in hospital at Point Pleasant February 25, 1863 of "erysipelas", body "sent home."

Pauley, John F. Company E Private; enlisted August 22, 1862 at Charleston, mustered October 9, 1862 at Point Pleasant, age 27, born in Kanawha County, Virginia/West Virginia, occupation: farmer.

Pauley/Polly, Peter Company C Private; enlisted July 24, 1862 or August 20, 1862 at Charleston, mustered October 8/9, 1862 at Point Pleasant, age 33, born in Boone County, Virginia/West Virginia, occupation: cooper.

Pauley/Pauly, Ralph/Ref Company A Private; enlisted August 13, 1862, mustered July 9, 1863 at Charleston, age 30, born in Kanawha County, Virginia/West Virginia, occupation: farmer.

Payne/Payn, Thomas Company C Private; enlisted August 15, 1862 at Point Pleasant, Virginia, mustered October 8/9, 1862 at Point Pleasant, age 44, born in Rockingham County, Virginia, occupation: cooper.

Peyton, Catlette (also "Catler"), Company I Private; enlisted December 12, 1863 at Guyandotte, mustered February 29, 1864 at Guyandotte, age 18 born in Cabell County, Virginia/West Virginia, occupation: farmer. Detailed for daily duty as Artillerist.

Payton, John W. Company G Private; enlisted December 17, 1863 at Point Pleasant, mustered February 28, 1864 at Guyandotte, age 18, born in Mason County, Virginia/West Virginia, occupation: farmer.

Perdue, Levett/Lovett (also Lafayette) Company H Private; enlisted August 14, 1862 at Ceredo, mustered October 10, 1862 at Point Pleasant, age 18, born in Wayne County, Virginia/West Virginia; occupation: farmer. Detailed on March 10, 1864 for a body of Independent Scouts in compliance with General Orders No. 2 from "Head Quarters 3d Division Dept., W.Va." (dated "Charleston W.Va. February 16th 1864").

Perdue, Monterville Company H Private; enlisted August 14, 1862 at Ceredo, mustered October 10, 1862, at Point Pleasant, age 18, born in Wayne County, Virginia/West Virginia, occupation: farmer; died at Regimental Hospital at Point Pleasant November 28, 1862 "of disease."

Perdue, William Company H 2nd Lieutenant and 1st Lieutenant; enlisted July 18, 1862 at Ceredo, mustered October 10, 1862, age 29, born in Pittsylvania

County, Virginia/West Virginia, occupation: farmer; discharged for promotion to 2nd Lieutenant to rank from December 31, 1862, commissioned 2nd Lieutenant January 9, 1863; promoted 1st Lieutenant April 2/3, 1864.

Phelps, John Company D Private; enlisted August 13, 1862 at Point Pleasant, received paid $30.00 Mason County Bounty and Premium, mustered October 8, 1862 at Point Pleasant, age 45 or 42, born in Pennsylvania, occupation: farmer.

Phillips, Squire J. Company F 1st Corporal and Sergeant; enlisted September 9, 1862 at Point Pleasant, mustered October 9, 1862 at Point Pleasant, age 36 born September 1, 1827 in Kanawha County, Virginia/West Virginia, occupation: boatman; promoted from Corporal to Sergeant March 26, 1864.

Piatt, Andrew Company G Private; enlisted December 1, 1863 at Hartford City, mustered February 28, 1864 at Guyandotte, age 42, born in Augusta County, Virginia, occupation: farmer.

Piatt/Piatte, Benjamin Company I Private; enlisted October 1, 1863 at Guyandotte, mustered November 25, 1863 at Guyandotte, age 18, born in Rising Sun, Ohio County, Indiana, occupation: farmer.

Piatt/Piatte, John Company I Private; enlisted August 20, 1863 at Coals Mouth, mustered in October 6, 1863 at Barboursville, age 18, born in Madison County, Indiana; occupation: laborer.

Pickens, John Company D Private; enlisted August 22, 1862 at Hartford City, received paid $30.00 Mason County Bounty and Premium, mustered October 8, 1862 at Point Pleasant, age 40, born in Pennsylvania, occupation: farmer.

Pickens, Spencer Company B Private and Corporal; enlisted August 12/13, 1862 at Point Pleasant, received paid $30.00 Mason County Bounty and Premium, mustered October 8, 1862, age 30 (born January 15, 1832), born in Meigs County, Ohio, occupation: farmer; appointed Corporal July 6, 1864.

Pierce, Canaan/Canon Company E Private; enlisted August 22, 1862 at Charleston, mustered October 9, 1862 at Point Pleasant, age 35, born in Monroe County, Virginia/West Virginia, occupation: farmer.

Pierce, Indivan (called "Van") Company G Private; enlisted December 28, 1863 at Buffalo, mustered February 28, 1864 at Guyandotte, age 34, born Putnam County, Virginia/West Virginia, occupation: farmer.

Pillow, William J. Company B Private; enlisted August 9, 1862 at Point Pleasant, received paid $30.00 Mason County Bounty and Premium, mustered October 8, 1862, age 18, born in Carroll County, Virginia, occupation: farmer. Prior to enlistment in the Union Army, Pillow may have served as Private in Company A, 116th Regiment Virginia Militia ("Solger 94 Piller, William").

Pitchford/Pittsford, James M. Company K Private; enlisted March 25, 1864 at Coals Mouth, mustered March 11, 1864 at Charleston, age 18, born in Jackson County, Virginia/West Virginia, occupation: farmer.

Plants, Francis M. Company C Private; enlisted and mustered December 30, 1863 at Barboursville, age 18, born in Washington County, Pennsylvania, occupation: farmer.

Plants, George W. Company B Private; enlisted August 1, 1862 at Point Pleasant, received paid $30.00 Mason County Bounty and Premium, mustered October 8, 1862, age 23, born in Washington County, Pennsylvania, occupation: farmer.

Plants, John Company C Private and Sergeant; enlisted August 9, 1862 at Point Pleasant, received paid $30.00 Mason County Bounty and Premium, mustered October 8/9, 1862 at Point Pleasant, , age 32, born in Washington County, Pennsylvania, occupation: farmer, promoted to Sergeant August 1, 1863. Plants may have served with local militia prior to enlistment in 13th Regiment. See John Plants Captain of the Mason County 106th Militia West Virginia State Troops; commissioned Captain December 10, 1861 to rank from November 26, 1861. (WVSA)

Plybon, Jacob Company H 5th Sergeant, 1st Sergeant and 1st Lieutenant; enlisted August 9, 1862 at Ceredo, appointed 5th Sergeant August 9, 1862, mustered October 10, 1862 at Point Pleasant, age 24, born in Franklin County, Virginia, occupation: farmer; commissioned 1st Lieutenant Company H March 18, 1865.

Plybon, James C. Company H Private, enlisted August 14, 1862 at Ceredo, mustered October 10, 1862 at Point Pleasant, age 27, born in Franklin County, Virginia, occupation: farmer.

Porter, John Company I; Private; enlisted November 20, 1863 at Guyandotte, mustered November 25, 1863 at Guyandotte, age 31, born in Cabell County, Virginia/West Virginia, occupation: farmer.

Pounds, Joseph Company F; Private, Commissary Sergeant and 2nd Lieutenant; enlisted September 9, 1862 at Point Pleasant, paid the $30.00 Mason County Bounty and Premium, mustered October 9, 1862 at Point Pleasant, age 26, born in Monroe County, Ohio, occupation: teacher; promoted to Commissary Sergeant, May 10, 1864; promoted from Commissary Sergeant and commissioned 2nd Lieutenant Company F May 8, 1865.

Price, Thomas Company D Private; enlisted August 22, 1862 at Hartford City, received paid $30.00 Mason County Bounty and Premium, mustered October 8, 1862 at Point Pleasant, age 23, born in Lovette, Wales, occupation: miner.

Priestly, Zachariah (also Zacariah) Company C Private; enlisted July 24, 1862 at Forks of Coal River, mustered October 8/9, 1862 at Point Pleasant, age 21, born in Kanawha County, Virginia/West Virginia, occupation: farmer.

Prit/Pritt (also Pratt), Robert T. Company A Private; enlisted August 15, 1862 at Charleston, mustered October 7, 1862 at Point Pleasant, age 23, born in Monroe County, Virginia/West Virginia, occupation: farmer.

Proffit/Proffitt, Joseph B. Company G Corporal; enlisted December 19, 1863 at West Columbia, mustered February 28, 1864 at Guyandotte, age 37, born in Goochland County, Virginia, occupation: farmer; promoted Corporal Feb. 15, 1864 pursuant to Col. W.R. Brown, Gen. Order No. 1 (manu. dated Feb. 15, 1864) to rank as such from Jan. 27, 1864.

Profitt (also Proffit), Samuel N. (signed "Samuel N. Profitt") Company F Private; enlisted October 21, 1863 at Barboursville, mustered November 25, 1863 at Barboursville, age 18, born in Rockbridge County, Virginia, occupation: farmer.

Proor (also Prore), George Company D Private; enlisted November 6, 1863 at Murraysville, mustered November 25, 1863 at Barboursville, age 19, born in Wood County, Virginia/West Virginia, occupation: farmer.

Pullen/Pullins, James Company G Private; enlisted and mustered in February, 14, 1865 at Point Pleasant, age 24, born in Mason County, Virginia/West Virginia, occupation: farmer.

Putney, Robert W. Company K Private; enlisted October 23, 1863 at Leon, mustered November 25, 1863 at Barboursville, age 22, born in Buckingham County, Virginia/West Virginia, occupation: millwright.

Quigley, Charles (middle initial P. T. or R.) Company A Private; enlisted August 15, 1862 at Charleston, mustered October 7, 1862 at Point Pleasant, age 28, born in Botetourt County, Virginia, occupation: farmer.

Rader/Raider James (M.?) (signed "James Rader") Company E Private and Corporal; enlisted September 9, 1862 at Point Pleasant, mustered October 9, 1862 at Point Pleasant, age 19, born in Kanawha County, Virginia/West Virginia, occupation: farmer; promoted from Private to 4th Corporal July 28, 1864.

Rader/Raydor, John H. Company H Sergeant; enlisted September 15, 1862 at Point Pleasant, mustered October 10, 1862 at Point Pleasant, age 21, born in Jackson County, Virginia/West Virginia, occupation: farmer; appointed 2nd Sergeant April 1, 1863 and appointed 3rd Sergeant August 1, 1863.

Rader, Lewis A. Company I Corporal; enlisted March 20, 1863 at Charleston, mustered July 26, 1863 at Charleston, age 18, born in Kanawha County, Virginia/West Virginia, occupation: farmer; appointed Corporal September 1, 1863.

Raines/Rains, William Franklin ("Frank") Company E Private; enlisted August 22, 1862 at Charleston, mustered October 9, 1862 at Point Pleasant, age 18, born in Kanawha County, Virginia/West Virginia, occupation: farmer; died at Hospital Point Pleasant of "fever" January 20, 1863 and was buried at Point Pleasant.

Ramsey/Rumsy, George W. Company A Private; enrolled at Charleston August 13, 1862, mustered October 7, 1862 at Point Pleasant, age 20 (born June 11, 1852), born in Rockingham County, Virginia, occupation: farmer; detailed as Cook at Point Pleasant Hospital.

Ramsey/Ramsy, Ashar/Ashur Company A Corporal and Sergeant; enlisted August 13, 1862 at Charleston, appointed Corporal August 20, 1862, mustered October 7, 1862 at Point Pleasant; age 27, born in Rockingham County, Virginia, occupation: farmer; appointed Sergeant March 1, 1864.

Ramsey/Ramsy/Rumsy, George W. Company A Private; enlisted August 13, 1862 at Charleston and/or enlisted August 13 or 15, 1862 at Point Pleasant, mustered October 7, 1862 at Point Pleasant, age 39, born in Rockingham County, Virginia, occupation: farmer.

Randall/Randel/Randle/Rannells, Thomas E. Company C Private; enlisted July 24, 1862 at Charleston or enlisted September 12, 1862 at Point Pleasant, mustered October 8/9, 1862 at Point Pleasant, age 18, born in England, occupation: farmer.

Ranes (also Raines), Elmore Company K Private; enlisted October 1, 1863 at Walton, mustered November 25, 1863 at Barboursville, age 26, born in Lewis County, Virginia/West Virginia, occupation: farmer.

Ranes, Joseph M. (Marcellus?) Company K Private; enlisted September 1, 1863 at Walton mustered October 3, 1863 at Charleston, age 29; (born in Lewis County, Virginia/West Virginia?), occupation farmer.

Raney, George R. Company C Private; enlisted March 26, 1864 at Barboursville, mustered April 26, 1864 at Barboursville, age 18, born in Mason County, Virginia/West Virginia, occupation: farmer.

Rapp, John F. Company C Private; enlisted March 30, 1864 at Point Pleasant, mustered April 26, 1864 at Barboursville, age 18, born in Greene County, Virginia, occupation: farmer.

Ratliff, James M. Company G Private; enlisted January 20, 1864 at Guyandotte, mustered February 28, 1864 at Guyandotte, age 19, born in Lawrence County, Ohio, occupation: farmer. Detailed on March 10, 1864 for a body of Independent Scouts in compliance with General Orders No. 2 from "Head Quarters 3d Division Dept., W.Va." (dated "Charleston W.Va. February 16th 1864").

Ray, Albert Company H Private; enlisted August 15, 1862 at Ceredo, mustered October 10, 1862 at Point Pleasant, age 19, born in Cabell County, Virginia/West Virginia, occupation: farmer.

Rayburn (also Rayborn), Griffin Company K 5th Corporal; enlisted December 1, 1863 at Buffalo, mustered March 28, 1864 at Charleston, age 29, born in Mason County, Virginia/West Virginia, occupation: farmer.

Rayburn, James A. Company B Corporal; enlisted August 5, 1862 at Point Pleasant, received paid $30.00 Mason County Bounty and Premium, appointed Corporal (1st or 7th Corporal) October 8, 1862, mustered October 8, 1862, age 25, born in Gallia County, Ohio, occupation: farmer.

Rayburn, James R. (middle name Rayder ?) Company B Private; enlisted August 9, 1862 at Point Pleasant, received paid $30.00 Mason County Bounty and Premium, mustered October 8, 1862, age 19 (born July 4, 1843), born in Mason County, Virginia/West Virginia, occupation: farmer.

Rayburn (also Raborn), John A. Company B Private; enlisted August 7, 1862 at Point Pleasant, received paid $30.00 Mason County Bounty, mustered October 8, 1862 at Point Pleasant, age 19, born in Mason County, Virginia/West Virginia, occupation: farmer.

Rayburn, John R. Company B Private; enlisted September 4, 1863 at Point Pleasant, mustered November 25, 1863 at Barboursville, age 18, born in Mason County, Virginia/West Virginia, occupation: farmer.

Rayburn, Lovell C[antrell] Company B 2nd and 1st Lieutenant; enlisted August 8, 1862, appointed 1st Lieutenant Company B August 23, 1862, commissioned 1st Lieutenant by order of September 12, 1862, received paid $30.00 Mason County Bounty and Premium, mustered October 8, 1862 at Point Pleasant, age 22/23, resident of Virginia at time of enlistment. L. C. Rayburn may have served in Mason County 106th Regiment Virginia Militia as 1st Lieutenant before enlistment in the 13th Virginia Volunteers. See "L.C. Rayburn commissioned 1st Lieutenant December 10, 1861 to rank from November 16, 1861." (WVSA)

Rayburn, Mack Company G Private; enlisted December 4, 1863 at Barboursville, mustered February 28, 1864 at Guyandotte, age 18, born in Mason County, Virginia/West Virginia, occupation: farmer.

Reynolds (also Raynolds), William Company H Private; enlisted November 13, 1862 at Point Pleasant, discharged for disability before being mustered, age 26, born in Trumble County, Pennsylvania; occupation: farmer.

Reeves, William P. Company I Corporal; enlisted September 11, 1863 at Charleston, mustered October 6, 1863; age 18, born in Cincinnati, Ohio, occupation: farmer.

Rhoades/Rhode (also Rahoads), Joseph (signed "Rhode") Company K Private; enlisted August 1, 1863 at Walton, mustered October 3, 1863 at Charleston, age 45, born in Lee County, Virginia; occupation: farmer.

Rhoads/ Rhodes/Roads, Abijah/Abajaih Company B Private; enlisted August 13, 1862 at Point Pleasant, received paid $30.00 Mason County Bounty and Premium, mustered October 8, 1862, age 20, born in Mason County, Virginia/West Virginia, occupation: farmer.

Rhoades/Rhoads, Benjamin R. (signed "Rhodes") Company K Private; enlisted November 13, 1863 at Barboursville, mustered November 25, 1863 at Barboursville, age 29, born in Jackson County, Virginia/West Virginia, occupation: farmer.

Rhoads, Peter M. Company B Private; enlisted August 8, 1862 at Point Pleasant, received paid $30.00 Mason County Bounty and Premium, mustered October 8, 1862, age 25, born in Mason County, occupation: farmer.

Ribling, John Company I Private; enlisted December 29, 1863 at Guyandotte, mustered February 29, 1864 at Guyandotte, age 18, born in Mason County, Virginia/West Virginia, occupation: farmer.

Rice, Harrison Company B Private and Corporal; enlisted August 9, 1862 at Point Pleasant, received paid $30.00 Mason County Bounty and Premium, mustered October 8, 1862, age 18 (born November 16, 1844), born in Mason County, Virginia/West Virginia, occupation: farmer; appointed Corporal February 10, 1865.

Rice, Nelson O. Company B Private; enlisted August 8, 1862 at Point Pleasant, received paid $30.00 Mason County Bounty and Premium, mustered October 8,

1862, age 28, born in Bedford County, Virginia, occupation: farmer. Rice died of disease in U.S.A. General Army Hospital Point Pleasant, November 16, 1862.

Rice, Richard Company G Private; enlisted December 15, 1863 at Point Pleasant, mustered February 28, 1864 at Guyandotte, age 18, born in Mason County, Virginia/West Virginia, occupation: farmer.

Rice, Vincent D. Company B Private; enlisted August 9, 1862 at Point Pleasant, received paid $30.00 Mason County Bounty and Premium, mustered October 8, 1862, age 27, born in Mason County, Virginia/West Virginia, occupation: farmer; discharged at Point Pleasant "on account of disability" February 8 [or 28?], 1863 by order of Major General H. G. Wright, commanding Department of the Ohio.

Rickard, George Company G Private; enlisted December 10, 1863 [1864?] at West Columbia, mustered February 28, 1864 at Guyandotte, age 34, born in Mason County, Virginia/West Virginia, occupation: farmer.

Riffle, Charles Company F Private; enlisted September 9, 1862 at Point Pleasant, received paid $30.00 Mason County Bounty and Premium, mustered October 9, 1862 at Point Pleasant, age 25, born in Mason County, Virginia/West Virginia, occupation: farmer.

Riddle/ Ridley, John Company B Private; enlisted August 4, 1862 at Point Pleasant, received paid $30.00 Mason County Bounty and Premium, mustered October 8, 1862 at Point Pleasant, age 28, born in Ashland [County?], Ohio, occupation: farmer.

Riffle, John W. Company G Private; enlisted December 10, 1863 at Barboursville, mustered February 28, 1864 at Guyandotte, age 18, born in Mason County, Virginia/West Virginia, occupation: farmer.

Riffle, Lewis Company D Private; enlisted August 13, 1862 at Point Pleasant, received paid $30.00 Mason County Bounty and Premium, mustered October 8, 1862 at Point Pleasant, age 35, born in Vinton County, Ohio, occupation: farmer.

Riffle, Lewis E. Company F Private; enlisted September 9, 1862 at Point Pleasant, received paid $30.00 Mason County Bounty and Premium, mustered October. 9, 1862 at Point Pleasant, age 19, born in Mason County, Virginia/West Virginia, occupation: farmer; promoted to Corporal May 24, 1864.

Riffle, Robert Company G Private and Corporal; enlisted December 14, 1863 at Point Pleasant, mustered February 28, 1864 at Guyandotte, age 21, born in

Mason County, Virginia/West Virginia, occupation: farmer; promoted to Corporal February 20, 1865.

Riffle, Warren G. Company G Corporal and Sergeant; enlisted December 14, 1863 at Point Pleasant, mustered February 28, 1864 at Guyandotte, age 22, born in Mason County, Virginia/West Virginia, occupation: farmer; promoted from Corporal to Sergeant March 25, 1865.

Rigg/Riggs, Jarat Francis/Jarriott F./Jarrit F. (signed "Jarat"; called "Francis") Company H Private; enlisted August 11, 1862 at Ceredo, mustered October 10, 1862 at Point Pleasant, age 21, born in Wayne County, Virginia/West Virginia, occupation: farmer. Rigg served with Wayne County Home Guards prior to enlistment in the 13th West Virginia Regiment.

Riley, Elijah Edward Company I Private; enlisted December 22, 1862 at Charleston, mustered July 26, 1863 at Charleston; age 21, born in Kanawha County, Virginia/West Virginia, occupation: farmer; appointed Sergeant June 1, 1863.

Riley, John V. Company I Private; enlisted December 13, 1862 at Charleston, mustered July 26, 1863 at Charleston, age 18, born in Kanawha County, Virginia/West Virginia, occupation: farmer; appointed Corporal July 26, 1863.

Riley, William W. Company A Private; enlisted August 15, 1862 at Charleston, mustered October 7, 1862 at Point Pleasant, age 21, born in Kanawha County, Virginia/West Virginia, occupation: farmer.

Roberts, Adam W. Company B Private; enlisted March 14, 1863 at Hurricane Bridge, mustered August 5, 1863 at Charleston, age 20, born in Mason County, Virginia/West Virginia, occupation: carpenter.

Roberts, John Company I Private; enlisted November 18, 1863 at Guyandotte, mustered November 25, 1863 at Guyandotte, age 18, born in Cabell County, Virginia/West Virginia, occupation: farmer.

Roberts, Oliver P. Company F Private; enlisted July 15, 1863 at Point Pleasant, mustered August 4, 1863 at Charleston (or August 15, 1863 at Charleston) age 18, born in Mason County, Virginia/West Virginia, occupation: farmer. West Virginia State Archives preserve enlistment information for Oliver P. Roberts serving in Co. F of the 13th Va. Vols, that I append here as well. It is not known in which entry the error lies, perhaps both, or, as was often the case, there were two men (father/son; cousins etc.) who had the same names. West Virginia State Archives Charleston records that Oliver P. Roberts was a resident of or enrolled at Point Pleasant, his was age 35 and he was mustered into service October 9, 1862 at

Point Pleasant. (Co. F Enlisted Men, 13th Regiment Infantry, "Roster of the Regiment," micro., [p.32].)

Roberts, William T. Company F Private and 3rd Corporal enlisted September 10, 1862 at Point Pleasant, mustered October 9, 1862 at Point Pleasant, age 26, born in Henry County, Virginia, occupation: farmer.

Robinson, James Company D Private (Corporal); enlisted August 18, 1862 at Hartford City, received paid $30.00 Mason County Bounty and Premium, mustered October 8, 1862 at Point Pleasant, age 32, born in Durham County, England, occupation: miner.

Robinson, Joel G. Company E Corporal; enlisted August 22, 1862 at Charleston, appointed 6th Corporal September 12, 1862, mustered October 9, 1862 at Point Pleasant, age 25, born in Kanawha County, Virginia/West Virginia, occupation: farmer.

Robinson, Mark E. Company E Private; enlisted August 22, 1862 at Charleston, mustered October 9, 1862 at Point Pleasant, age 18, born in Kanawha County, Virginia/West Virginia, occupation: farmer.

Robinson, Samuel P. Company F Private and Teamster; enlisted September 21, 1862 at Point Pleasant, mustered October 9, 1862 at Point Pleasant, age 27, born in Kanawha County, Virginia/West Virginia, occupation: farmer; detailed October 26, 1862, to go to Charleston with John M. Young (Co. F) and Russell B. Shrewsberry (Co. F) all detailed teamsters on this date.

Rollins/Rollens, George F. Company C Corporal; enlisted August 26, 1862 at Point Pleasant, received paid $30.00 Mason County Bounty and Premium, mustered October 8/9, 1862 at Point Pleasant, age 18, born in Mason County, Virginia/West Virginia, occupation: farmer; promoted to Corporal July 11, 1865.

Roseberry (also Rosbery), Elijah M. Company C Private and Sergeant; enlisted August 9 or 15, 1862 at Point Pleasant, received paid $30.00 Mason County Bounty and Premium, mustered October 8/9, 1862 at Point Pleasant, age 32, born in Mason County, Virginia/West Virginia, occupation: farmer; promoted from Private to Sergeant October 15, 1863; Roseberry may have served with militia prior to enlistment in the 13th Virginia Volunteers. See Elijah M. Roseberry Captain of Mason County 106th Militia West Virginia State Troops; commissioned Captain May 27, 1862 to rank from April 29, 1862. (WVSA)

Roseberry Michael Company D Sergeant, 2nd and 1st Lieutenant; enlisted August 13 or 18, 1862 at Hartford City; mustered as Sergeant on October 8, 1862 at Point Pleasant, received paid $30.00 Mason County Bounty and Premium, mustered

October 8, 1862 at Point Pleasant, age 35, born in Mason County, Virginia/West Virginia, occupation: farmer (and teacher?); on Feb 12th 1864 Sergt. Rosberry was put in charge of the newly created regimental artillerist corps pursuant to Col. W.R. Brown's Special Order No. 21; Roseberry was promoted to 2nd Lieutenant October 31, 1864, commissioned 1st Lieutenant February 7, 1865.

Rosler, John Herman Company E 2nd Lieutenant and Captain; commissioned 2nd Lieutenant October 3/8/or 28, 1862 to rank from September 12, 1862, mustered October 9, 1862 at Point Pleasant, age 23, born in Wuerttemburg, Germany, occupation farm laborer/farmer; commissioned Captain October 31, 1864.

Roush, Jonas Company F Private; enlisted September 10, 1862 at Point Pleasant, received paid $30.00 Mason County Bounty and Premium, mustered October 9, 1862 at Point Pleasant, age 19, born in Mason County, Virginia/West Virginia, occupation: farmer.

Roush, Moses Company D Private; enlisted August 18, 1862 at Hartford City, received paid $30.00 Mason County Bounty and Premium, mustered October 8, 1862 at Point Pleasant, age 25, born in Mason County, Virginia/West Virginia, occupation: farmer.

Roush, Thomas Company F Private; enlisted August 3, 1863 at Point Pleasant, mustered August 5, 1863 at Charleston, age 19, born December 28, 1844 in Mason County, Virginia/West Virginia, occupation: farmer; died of typhoid fever in Regimental Hospital Barboursville, West Virginia, January 19, 1864.

Rowley, Emanuel Company F Private; enlisted September 9, 1862 at Point Pleasant, mustered October 9, 1862 at Point Pleasant, age 18, born in Kanawha County, Virginia/West Virginia, occupation: laborer.

Rucker, George Company E Private; enlisted September 15, 1862 at Point Pleasant, mustered October 9, 1862 at Point Pleasant "at the old Mason County Fair Ground,"[728] age 21, born in Kanawha County, Virginia/West Virginia, occupation: farmer.

Rucker, William Parkes Major 13th West Virginia Volunteer Infantry Regiment; appointed from civilian life and commissioned Major March 11, 1864, age 32, born in Virginia 1832, occupation: physician practicing in Lynchburg, Virginia (Jefferson Medical College class of 1855); served on General George Crook's staff, then was detailed to assist West Virginia Governor A. I. Boreman in organizing companies of Home Guards, in Colonel John H. Oley's "front and neighborhood." Oley's "front" being such interior counties as Monroe, Raleigh, Greenbrier. Fayette, Giles, Mercer.[729] Rucker resigned his commission November 23, 1864.

Rule, William H. Company G Corporal; enlisted December 20, 1863 at Cottageville, promoted Corporal Feb. 15, 1864 pursuant to Col. W.R. Brown, Gen. Order No. 1 (manu. dated Feb. 15, 1864) to rank as such from Jan. 27, 1864, mustered February 28, 1864 at Guyandotte, age 26, born in Rockbridge County, Virginia, occupation: carpenter.

Runnion, Elias L. Company G Private; enlisted December 23, 1863 at Barboursville, mustered February 28, 1864 at Guyandotte, age 18, born in Mason County, Virginia/West Virginia, occupation: farmer.

Russell, Alvin Company K; Private, 1st Corporal and 8th Sergeant; enlisted October 9, 1863 at Barboursville, mustered November 25, 1863, age 25, born in Meigs County, Ohio, occupation: farmer; promoted to Sergeant November 10, 1864.

Russell, Hiram/Hyram (signed "Hyram") Company F Private; enlisted September 9, 1862 at Point Pleasant, received paid $30.00 Mason County Bounty and Premium, mustered October 9, 1862 at Point Pleasant, age 25, born in Lewis County, Kentucky, occupation: laborer.

Russell, Napoleon B. Company F Private; enlisted October 25, 1863 at West Columbia, mustered November 25, 1863 at Barboursville, age 18, born in Mason County, Virginia/West Virginia, occupation: farmer.

Russell, Timothy Company F 1st Lieutenant; enlisted September 9, 1862, received paid $30.00 Mason County Bounty and Premium, commissioned 1st Lieutenant October 8, 1862 to rank from October 1, 1862, mustered October 9, 1862, aged 35 or 40 years, born in Ohio, lumberman and mill owner; commissioned Captain December 14, 1864. Russell may have served with Virginia Militia before enlistment in the 13th Regiment Volunteers. See Timothy Russell Captain of the Mason County 106th Militia West Virginia State Troops; commissioned Captain December 10, 1861 to rank from November 26, 1861. (WVSA)

Rutherford, Spencer Company H Private; enlisted August 8, 1862 at Ceredo, mustered October 10, 1862 at Point Pleasant, age 33, born in Wayne County, Virginia/West Virginia, occupation: farmer.

Samples, Agrippa Company A Private; enlisted August 12, 1862 at Charleston, mustered October 7, 1862 at Point Pleasant, age 23, born in Kanawha County, Virginia/West Virginia, occupation: farmer. Prior to enlistment in the Union Army, Samples may have served as Private in Company A, 116th Regiment Virginia Militia ("Solger 100 Griff Samples").

Samples, John Company I Private; enlisted December 1, 1863 at Guyandotte, mustered February 29, 1864 at Guyandotte; age 17 or 18, born in Kanawha County, Virginia/West Virginia, occupation: laborer.

Samples, Robert Company I Private, Corporal, and Sergeant; enlisted December 27, 1862 at Charleston, mustered July 26, 1863 at Charleston, age 28, born in Kanawha County, Virginia/West Virginia, occupation: farmer; appointed Corporal June 5, 1864, appointed Sergeant December 17, 1864.

Samuels, Caleb G. Company E Private; enlisted August 22, 1862 at Charleston, mustered October 9, 1862 at Point Pleasant, age 19, born in Kanawha County, Virginia/West Virginia, occupation: farmer.

Sands/Sans, George W. Company C Private; enrolled August 15, 1862 at Point Pleasant, received paid $30.00 Mason County Bounty and Premium, mustered October 8/9, 1862 at Point Pleasant or enlisted March 26, 1864 at Barboursville and mustered in April 26, 1864 at Barboursville, age 25, born in Amherst County, Virginia, occupation: farmer.

Sands/Sants, Henry Company A Private; enlisted August 12, 1862 at Charleston, mustered October 7, 1862 at Point Pleasant, age 26, born in Kanawha County, Virginia/West Virginia, occupation: lumberman.

Saunders (also Sanders), Clarington D. Company G Orderly Sergeant; enlisted December 28, 1863 at Buffalo, promoted Sergeant Feb. 15, 1864 pursuant to Col. W.R. Brown, Gen. Order No. 1 (manu. dated Feb. 15, 1864) to rank as such from Jan. 27, 1864, mustered February 28, 1864 at Guyandotte, age 43, born in Botetourt County, Virginia; occupation: laborer.

Sayr/Sayre, Mark Gillman/Gilman (signed "Sayr") Company C Private (Corporal?), enlisted August 29, 1862 at Point Pleasant, received paid $30.00 Mason County Bounty and Premium, mustered October 8, 1862 at Point Pleasant, age 32, born in Jackson County, Virginia/West Virginia, occupation: farmer; served as "2nd Lieutenant in Virginia Militia in 1861."[730]

Sayre, Hiram Company F Private; enlisted September 9, 1862 at Point Pleasant, received paid $30.00 Mason County Bounty and Premium, mustered October 9, 1862, age 20, born in Jackson County, Virginia/West Virginia, occupation: farmer.

Scantlin (also Scanlan/Scantling), Marcus. T. Cicero (signed AM.T.C. Scantlin") (called "Cicero" also "Marcus") Company F Private; enlisted September 9, 1862 at Point Pleasant, received paid $30.00 Mason County Bounty and Premium, mustered October 9, 1862 at Point Pleasant, age 23, born in Allegheny County, Pennsylvania, occupation: farmer.

Schlosser (also Schloser/Schlozer), Henry (signed "Shlosser") Company D Private; enlisted August 22, 1862 at Hartford City, received paid $30.00 Mason County Bounty and Premium, mustered October 8, 1862 at Point Pleasant, age 17, born in Germany, occupation: laborer.

Schools, Paul Oliver Company B Private; enlisted August 6, 1862 at Point Pleasant, mustered October 8, 1862 at Point Pleasant, age 24, born in County Derry, Ireland, arrived in America in 1842, settled in Wheeling but at age 18 moved to Mason County, occupation stonemason, plasterer and farmer. Schools served as Orderly to 13th Regimental Headquarters on "Daily Duty" starting sometime after June 30, 1864.[731] Prior to enlistment in the Union Army, Schools may have served as Private in Company A, 116th Regiment Virginia Militia ("Solger 101 Pal Schools") At the 8th Re-Union of the Army of West Virginia held at Wheeling August 29, 1907, Paul Schools was the only veteran of the 13th Regiment registered at Re-Union Head Quarters out of a total of 268 attendees (*Wheeling Intellingencer*).

Shmitter/Schmitter, Luke E. (signed "Luk Edward Shmitter") Company G Private; enlisted December 28, 1863 at Buffalo, mustered into service February 28, 1864 at Guyandotte, age 18, born in Switzerland, occupation: farmer; detailed for Blazer Independent Scouts.

Scott, Hezekiah (also Hezechaih) Company D Sergeant and 2nd Lieutenant; enlisted August 15 or 18, 1862 at Hartford City, received paid $30.00 Mason County Bounty and Premium, mustered as Sergeant, October 8, 1862 at Point Pleasant, age 20, born in Kanawha County, Virginia/West Virginia, occupation: cooper; promoted to 1st Sergeant pursuant to Col. W.R. Brown, Gen. Order No. 1 (manu. dated Feb. 15, 1864) to rank as such from Feb. 10, 1864, promoted from 1st Sergeant to 2nd Lieutenant February 7, 1865.

Scott, Joseph Company A Private; enlisted August 15, 1862 at Charleston, mustered October 7, 1862 at Point Pleasant, age 48, born in Kanawha County, Virginia/West Virginia, occupation: farmer.

Searles/Searls, Jacob H. Company K 3rd Corporal; enlisted October 3, 1863, mustered November 25, 1863, age 22, born in Meigs County, Ohio, occupation: blacksmith.

Searls (also Searles/Surrells), Gideon Company H Private; enlisted December 1, 1862 at Point Pleasant, mustered December 11, 1862 at Point Pleasant, age 19, born in Gallia County, Ohio, occupation: farmer.

Searls (also Searles), Levi Company H Private; enlisted and mustered February 21, 1865 at Point Pleasant, age 18, born in Kanawha County, Virginia/West Virginia, occupation: farmer.

See, William Company G Private; enlisted December 20, 1863 at Buffalo, mustered February 28, 1864 at Guyandotte, age 33, born in Mason County, Virginia/West Virginia, occupation: farmer.

Sela/Selay/Seley, John (signed "Sela") Company D Private; enlisted August 18, 1862 at Hartford City, received paid $30.00 Mason County Bounty and Premium, mustered October 8, 1862 at Point Pleasant, age 35, born in Wales, occupation: miner.

Shank/Shanks, Calvin C. or O. (signed "Shank") Company H Private and Drummer; enlisted December 11, 1863 at Buffalo, mustered February 27, 1864 at Barboursville, age 15, born in Putnam County, Virginia/West Virginia, occupation: farmer.

Shank, Edgar D. Company F Private; enlisted September 28, 1863 at West Columbia, mustered November 25, 1863 at Barboursville, age 18, born 1845 in Putnam County, Virginia/West Virginia, occupation: carpenter.

Shannon, William Company H and I Private; 3rd Sergeant, 2nd Lieutenant and 1st Lieutenant; enlisted July 22, 1862 at Ceredo, mustered October 9/10, 1862 at Point Pleasant, age 30 years; born in Wayne County Virginia/West Virginia, occupation: farmer; promoted from the ranks to 3rd Sergeant Company H June 2nd 1863, Company H Muster Roll for November and December 1863 shows 3rd Sergeant Shannon absent detached on recruiting service since October 16, 1863 by order of Colonel William R. Brown, commanding, Shannon discharged from Sergeant December 1, 1863 by order of Brigadier General B. F. Kelly at Barboursville for promotion to 2nd Lieutenant Company I upon organization of that Company, appointed 2nd Lieutenant November 1, 1863, commissioned 2nd Lieutenant Company I December 18, 1863 and mustered December 24, 1863 at Guyandotte, commissioned 1st Lieutenant Company I January 7, 1865 and mustered at Cumberland, Maryland. Shannon served in Wayne County Home Guards prior to enlistment in the 13th West Virginia Regiment.

Shaver (also Shaffer and Shaven), John Company K Private, enlisted October 1, 1863 at Walton, mustered November 25, 1863 at Barboursville, age 16, born July 4, 1847 in Kanawha County, Virginia/West Virginia, occupation: farmer.

Shaver, William T. Company H Private; enlisted December 23, 1862 at Point Pleasant, mustered January 6, 1863 at Point Pleasant, age 18, born in Gallia County, Ohio, occupation: musician.

Shaw, Samuel G. Regimental Surgeon; commissioned August 22, 1862, appointed Surgeon October 10, 1862, about 55 years of age, resident of Point Pleasant Virginia/West Virginia, occupation: allopathic physician (M.D. University of Pennsylvania; licensed in 1881) his practice and clinic were located on Main Street, Point Pleasant; resigned as Regimental Surgeon September 29, 1863; appointed "Examining Surgeon of the Board of Enrollment for the 3d Congressional District" February 1865.

Sheline, Michael Company C Private; joined for service and enrolled August 12, 1862 at Point Pleasant and received paid $30.00 Mason County Bounty and Premium upon muster in October 8/9, 1862 at Point Pleasant, or, Sheline enlisted March 31, 1864 at Point Pleasant and mustered April 26, 1864 at Barboursville, age 21, born in Virginia ("County not Known"), occupation: farmer. Prior to enlisting in the 13ᵗʰ Virginia Infantry Regiment Sheline may have served in Company B 4ᵗʰ Regiment Virginia/West Virginia Infantry Volunteers.

Sheline, William Company C Private; enlisted July 26, 1862 or August 22, 1862 at Point Pleasant, received paid $30.00 Mason County Bounty and Premium, mustered October 8, 1862 at Point Pleasant, age 44, born in Harrisburg, Pennsylvania, occupation: farmer.

Sheppard (also Shepherd/Sheopard), Andrew J. Company C Private; enlisted August 15/18, 1862 at Point Pleasant, received paid $30.00 Mason County Bounty and Premium, mustered October 8/9, 1862 at Point Pleasant, age 22, born in Montgomery County, Virginia, occupation: farmer.

Sherman/Sherimons, Harry F. (signed "Harry Sherman") Company D Private and Sergeant Major; enlisted August 15, 1862 at Mason City, mustered October 8, 1862 at Point Pleasant, age 22, born in Murrysville, Virginia/West Virginia, occupation: farmer; promoted to Sergeant pursuant to Col. W.R. Brown, Gen. Order No. 1 (manu. dated Feb. 15, 1864) to rank as such from Feb. 10, 1864, promoted to Sergeant Major February 6, 1865.

Sherwood, William W. Sutler 13th West Virginia Volunteer Infantry Regiment 1863 to 1865, age 30 (born September 1832), born in Ohio, resident of Point Pleasant close neighbors with the John Hall, Esq. family, occupation: wharf master.

Shinn, Nehemiah Company B Corporal; enlisted August 8, 1862 at Point Pleasant, received paid $30.00 Mason County Bounty and Premium, appointed Second Corporal October 8, 1862, mustered October 8, 1862, age 25, born in Jackson County, Virginia/West Virginia, occupation: farmer.

Shobe, Andrew B. Company C Corporal; enlisted August 14, 1862 at Mason City, received paid $30.00 Mason County Bounty and Premium, mustered October 8, 1862, age 19, born in Hardy County, Virginia/West Virginia, occupation: farmer.

Shoemaker (also Shomaker/Shumaker), Jacob Company H Private; enlisted November 14, 1862 at Point Pleasant or Kygerville, mustered December 11, 1862 at Point Pleasant, age 18, born in Cheshire, Gallia County, Ohio; occupation: farmer.

Shown, Samuel Company I Private; enlisted December 29, 1863 at Guyandotte, mustered February 29, 1864 at Guyandotte, age 18, born in Mason County, Virginia/West Virginia, occupation: farmer.

Shrewsberry/Shrewsbury, Columbus Sutler 13th West Virginia Volunteer Infantry Regiment; age about 32, born June 5, 1832 in Kanawha County, Virginia/West Virginia, carpenter, builder of salt furnaces, well borer in the Little Kanawha River Valley area in 1861 before volunteering for service in Company A 4th Virginia/West Virginia Infantry Regiment. Shrewsberry served in the 4th Regiment as Commissary Sergeant and 2nd Lieutenant. He was appointed Commissary Sergeant August 22 or 31, 1861, promoted 2nd Lieutenant December 5, 1862, commissioned 2nd Lieutenant Company A December 31, 1862, age 30 mustered as 2nd Lieutenant January 1, 1863, resigned from 4th Virginia on May 26, 1863 due to ill health; after discharge he went to Mason City where he took up boring wells again, beginning summer of 1863, he served as Sutler to 13th West Virginia Volunteer Infantry Regiment together with William W. Sherwood.

Shrewsberry/Shrewsbury, Russell B. Company F Private, Teamster (Corporal?); enlisted September 15, 1862 at Point Pleasant, mustered October 9, 1862 at Point Pleasant, age 34, born in Giles County, Virginia, occupation: farmer.

Shuler, Benjamin F. Company G Private; enlisted January 1, 1864 at Guyandotte, mustered February 28, 1864 at Guyandotte, age 18, born in Gallia County, Ohio, occupation: farmer.

Sigman, Joseph Company E Private; enlisted August 16, 1862 at Charleston, mustered October 9, 1862 at Point Pleasant, age 20, born in Franklin County, Virginia, occupation: farmer.

Sigman, Shields Company E Private; enlisted August 16, 1862 at Tuppers Creek, near Charleston, mustered October 9, 1862 at Point Pleasant, age 18, born in Franklin County, Virginia, occupation: farmer.

Sigman, William, Jr. Company E Private; enlisted March 17, 1863 at Point Pleasant, mustered August 5, 1863 at Charleston, age 18, born in Franklin County, Virginia, occupation: farmer.

Sigman/Sigmon, William Sr. (signed "Sigman" also "Sigmon") Company E Private; enlisted August 18, 1862 at Charleston, mustered October 9, 1862 at Point Pleasant, age 35, born in Franklin County, Virginia, occupation: farmer.

Simmons, Nathaniel Company H Private; enlisted December 18, 1863 at Barboursville, mustered February 27, 1864 at Barboursville, age 18, born in Cabell County, Virginia/West Virginia, occupation: farmer.

Simons (also Simmeons), Jacob Company F Private; enlisted September 9, 1862 at Point Pleasant, mustered October 9, 1862 at Point Pleasant, age 18, "born in Prussia", occupation: miner.

Sinclair/St. Clair, Alfred Company B Private; enlisted August 8, 1862 at Point Pleasant, received paid $30.00 Mason County Bounty and Premium, mustered October 8, 1862 at Point Pleasant, age 23, born in Meigs County, Ohio, occupation: farmer. Prior to enlistment in the Union Army, Sinclair may have served as Private in Company A, 116th Regiment Virginia Militia ("Solger 99 Sinclair, Alfred").

Sines, Henry J. Company B Private, Corporal and Sergeant; enlisted August 9, 1862 at Point Pleasant, received paid $30.00 Mason County Bounty and Premium, mustered October 8, 1862 at Point Pleasant, age 28, born in Muskingum County, Ohio, occupation: farmer; appointed Corporal September 22, 1863 and promoted to Sergeant November 10, 1864.

Sines, Jacob Company B Private; enlisted November 3, 1863 at Point Pleasant, mustered November 25, 1863 at Barboursville, age 19, born in Muskingum County, Ohio, occupation: farmer.

Sines, John Company B Private; enlisted July 7, 1863 at Point Pleasant, mustered August 5, 1863 at Charleston, age 18, born in Meigs County, Ohio, occupation: farmer.

Sisson, Francis W. ("Frank") Company C Quarter Master Sergeant and Company F 2nd Lieutenant, 1st Lieutenant and Adjutant; enlisted August 21, 1862 at Point Pleasant, transferred and mustered "Non-Commissioned Staff as Quarter Master Sergeant October 8/9, 1862 at Point Pleasant, age 27, born in Gallia County, Ohio, occupation: carpenter and businessman; promoted to 2nd Lieutenant Company F December 14, 1864, promoted, 1st Lieutenant and Adjutant January 20, 1865. Prior to enlistment in the 13th Regiment, Sisson may have served with militia. See Frank W. Sisson, 1st Lieutenant of the Mason County 106th Militia West Virginia State Troops, commissioned 1st Lieutenant of 106th Militia December 10, 1861 to rank from November 16, 1861. (WVSA)

Skidmore, Archibald (signed "A. I.; A. J.; or A. T. Skidmore") Company K Private; enlisted January 1, 1864 at unknown location or January 3 or 6, 1864 at Ripley, mustered in March 11, 1864 at Charleston, age 22, born in Jackson County, Virginia/West Virginia, occupation: farmer.

Slack, David K. Company F Corporal; enlisted October 2, 1862 at Point Pleasant, mustered October 9, 1862 at Point Pleasant, age 18, born in Kanawha County, Virginia/West Virginia, occupation: cooper.

Slack, Greenberry/Greenbury, Jr., Company A 1st Lieutenant and Captain; appointed 1st Lieutenant August 19, 1862, commissioned September 9, 1862, mustered October 7, 1862 at Point Pleasant, age about 24 (born October 1, 1836?), born in Kanawha County, Virginia/West Virginia, occupation: farm laborer; appointed Captain July 20, 1863, commission August 14, 1863. Prior to enlistment in the 13th Virginia Regiment, "Greenbury Slack Jr." was commissioned Captain of a Company in the 153rd Kanawha County Militia on May 14, 1862 to rank from April 30, 1862. (Kanawha County West Virginia State Troops mustered beginning June 10, 1862, at Charleston, WVSA.)

Slack, Samuel Company F Private; enlisted October 7, 1863 at Point Pleasant, mustered November 25, 1863 at Barboursville, age 18, born in Mason County, Virginia/West Virginia, occupation: farmer.

Slater, George Company E Private; enlisted August 22, 1862 at Charleston, mustered October 9, 1862 at Point Pleasant, age 19, born in Kanawha County, Virginia/West Virginia, occupation: farmer; died in hospital at Point Pleasant, of erysipelas January 24, 1863 and buried at Point Pleasant.

Slaughter, David S. Company K Private; enlisted October 29, 1863 at Ripley, mustered March 28, 1864 at Charleston, born in Lewis County, Virginia/West Virginia, age 18; occupation: farmer.

Slieth, James C. Company I Private; enlisted August 1, 1863 at Charleston, mustered August 8, 1863 at Charleston, age 20, born in Kanawha County, Virginia/West Virginia, occupation: farmer.

Slieth, John W. Company I Private; enlisted January 6, 1863 at Charleston, mustered July 26, 1863 at Charleston, age 18, born in Jackson County, Virginia/West Virginia; occupation: farmer.

Smalcomb/Smallcomb, George (signed "Smalcomb") Company D Private; enlisted August 18, 1862 at Hartford City, received paid $30.00 Mason County Bounty and Premium, mustered October 8, 1862 at Point Pleasant, age 29, born in Wales, occupation: miner.

Smith, Daniel Company G Private; enlisted March 26, 1864 at Guyandotte, mustered April 26, 1864 at Barboursville, age 18, born in Kanawha County, Virginia/West Virginia; occupation: farmer.

Smith, David Company A Private; enlisted August 15, 1862 at Charleston, mustered October 7, 1862 at Point Pleasant, age 16, born in Kanawha County, Virginia/West Virginia, occupation: farmer. Prior to enlistment in the 13th Virginia Smith may have served with militia. See David Smith enlisted man, Mason County 106th Militia West Virginia State Troops. 106th Militia reorganized November 1861. (WVSA)

Smith, George W. Company E Private; enlisted August 22, 1862 at Charleston, mustered October 9, 1862 at Point Pleasant, age 17, born in Kanawha County, Virginia, occupation: farmer; "promoted to Corporal 1864."

Smith, George W. Company K Private; enlisted January 1, 1864/January 3 or 6, 1864 at Leon, mustered March 11, 1864 at Charleston, age 26, born in Kanawha County, Virginia/West Virginia, occupation: farmer; may have previously served in Company F 16th Ohio Volunteer Infantry Regiment, mustered July, 1862 and mustered out April 1, 1863.

Smith, John Company F Private; enlisted September 15, 1862 at Point Pleasant, mustered October 9, 1862 at Point Pleasant, age 43, born in Russell County, Virginia, occupation: farmer.

Smith, John H. Company D Private; enlisted August 22, 1862 at Hartford City, received paid $30.00 Mason County Bounty and Premium, mustered October 8, 1862 at Point Pleasant, age 30, born in Rappahannock County, Virginia, occupation: farmer.

Smith, Josiah/Joseph Company I Private; enlisted December 9, 1863 at Guyandotte, mustered February 29, 1864 at Guyandotte, age 18, born in Lawrence County, Ohio occupation: farmer.

Smith, Luke S. Company D Private; enlisted December 26, 1863 at Barboursville, mustered February 27, 1864 at Barboursville, age 26, born in Logan County, Virginia/West Virginia, occupation: farmer.

Smith, Marshel (also Marshal/Marshall) (signed "Marshel Smith") Company D Private and Blazer Scout; enlisted August 22, 1862 at Hartford City, received paid $30.00 Mason County Bounty and Premium, mustered October 8, 1862 at Point Pleasant, age 24, born in Rappahannock County, Virginia, occupation: farmer; detached as Blazer Scout beginning May 30, 1864. Prior to enlistment in the 13th Virginia, Smith may have served with militia, see Marshall Smith. First Lieutenant of the Mason County 106th Militia West Virginia State Troops, commissioned 1st Lieutenant December 10, 1861 to rank from November 23, 1861. (WVSA)

Smith, Samuel Company B Private; enlisted August 8, 1862 at Point Pleasant, received paid $30.00 Mason County Bounty and Premium, mustered October 8, 1862 at Point Pleasant, age 26, born in Mason County, Virginia/West Virginia, occupation: farmer.

Smith, Thomas Jr. Company I Private; enlisted November 15, 1863 at Guyandotte, mustered November 25, 1863 at Guyandotte, age 18, born in Cabell County, Virginia/West Virginia, occupation: laborer.

Smith, William J. Company G Private; enlisted December 5, 1863 at Guyandotte, mustered February 28, 1864 at Guyandotte, age 38, born in England, occupation: cooper; "represented as a member of the 5th West Virginia Volunteer Infantry arrested and turned back to that Regiment."[732] Detailed on March 10, 1864 for a body of Independent Scouts in compliance with General Orders No 2 from "Head Quarters 3d Division Dept., W. Va." (dated "Charleston W. Va. February 16th 1864").

Smith, William Perry Company B Private; enlisted August 8, 1862 at Point Pleasant, received paid $30.00 Mason County Bounty and Premium, mustered in October 8, 1862 at Point Pleasant, age 20, born in Alleghany County, Pennsylvania, occupation: farmer.

Smoot, John Company B Private; enlisted August 9, 1862 at Point Pleasant, October 8, 1862 at Point Pleasant, age 18, born in Mason County, Virginia/West Virginia, occupation: painter (house painter; sign painter, etc.).

Sneed, John W. Company G Private; enlisted November 13, 1863 at Charleston, mustered February 28, 1864 at Guyandotte, age 18, born in Nicholas County, Virginia/West Virginia, occupation: farmer.

Snider, David M. Company I Private; enlisted December 1, 1863 at Guyandotte, mustered February 29, 1864 at Guyandotte, age 18, born in Nicholas County, Virginia/West Virginia, occupation: farmer.

Snider/Snyder, Hiram G. (signed "Snyder") Company I Private; enlisted November 24, 1862 at Charleston, mustered October 6, 1863 at Barboursville, age 40, born in Pendleton County, Virginia/West Virginia; occupation: geologist.

Snider, John E. Company H Private enlisted November 19, 1862 at Point Pleasant, mustered December 11, 1862 at Point Pleasant, age 19, born in Kanawha County, Virginia/West Virginia, occupation: farmer; (prior service with Company B 4ᵗʰ Virginia/West Virginia Infantry Regiment?).

Snyder/Snider, Milton Company E Private; enlisted September 15, 1862 at Point Pleasant, mustered October 9, 1862 at Point Pleasant, age 18, born in Kanawha County, Virginia/West Virginia, occupation: farmer.

Snodgrass, Andrew Company A Private; enlisted August 15, 1862 at Charleston, mustered October 7, 1862 at Point Pleasant, age 23, born in Kanawha County, Virginia/West Virginia, occupation: farmer.

Snodgrass, Daniel Henry Company A Private and Corporal; enlisted August 15, 1862 at Charleston, mustered October 7, 1862 at Point Pleasant, age 18, born in Kanawha County, Virginia/West Virginia, occupation: farmer; appointed Corporal November 11, 1864.

Snodgrass, Martin Company A Private; enlisted August 13, 1862 at Charleston, mustered October 7, 1862 at Point Pleasant, age 40, born in Kanawha County, Virginia/West Virginia, occupation: farmer.

Snodgrass, Nathan Company A Private; enlisted August 15, 1862 at Charleston, mustered October 7, 1862 at Point Pleasant, age 44, born in Kanawha County, Virginia/West Virginia, occupation: farmer.

Snodgrass, Robert H. Company A Private; enlisted August 15, 1862 at Charleston, mustered October 7, 1862 Point Pleasant, age 17, born in Kanawha County, Virginia/West Virginia, occupation: farmer.

Snodgrass, Samuel Company A Private; enlisted August 15, 1862 at Charleston, mustered October 7, 1862 at Point Pleasant, age 49, born in Botetourt County, Virginia, occupation: farmer.

Snowden, George Company D, 2nd Lieutenant; mustered October 8, 1862 at Point Pleasant, born in Durham County, England, age about 24 years, occupation: miner(?); commissioned 2nd Lieutenant Company D January 9, 1863 to rank from August 15, 1862. Prior to enlistment in the 13th Regiment Snowden may have served with Company E 4th Virginia/West Virginia Volunteer Infantry Regiment.

Snyder, Michael Company K Private; enlisted November 4, 1863 at Leon, mustered November 25, 1863, age 17, born in Mason County, Virginia/West Virginia, occupation: farmer.

Sowards (also Sourds), Isaac M. Company G Private; enlisted December 25, 1863 at Guyandotte, mustered February 28, 1864 at Guyandotte, age 17, born in Lawrence County, Ohio, occupation: farmer.

Sowards, William Company G Private; enlisted March 1, 1864 at Guyandotte, mustered April 26, 1864 at Barboursville, age 21, born in Lawrence County, Ohio, occupation: farmer.

Sowards, William W. Company G Private; enlisted December 20, 1863 at Barboursville, mustered February. 28, 1864 at Guyandotte, age 18, born in Lawrence County, Ohio, occupation: farmer.

Spencer, Alexander T. Company E Private; enlisted August 22, 1862 at Charleston, mustered October 9, 1862 at Point Pleasant, age 20, born in Kanawha County, Virginia/West Virginia, occupation: carpenter.

Spencer/Spenser, John Company C Waggoner; enlisted August 27, 1862 or September 12, 1862 at Point Pleasant, received paid $30.00 Mason County Bounty and Premium, mustered October 8, 1862 at Point Pleasant, age 24/25/26 or 34; born in Nicholas County, Virginia/West Virginia, occupation: farmer; detailed for teamster October 8, 1862 at Point Pleasant.

Spencer, Charles Company E Sergeant. See "Request For the Appointment of W. W. Harper to be Chaplain of the 13 Va. Vols." (manu. Uncat. 13th W.Va. Infantry Regiment Box WVSA)

Spradling, James Riley Company A Private; enlisted August 12, 1862 at Charleston, mustered October 7, 1862 at Point Pleasant, age 21, born in Kanawha County, Virginia/West Virginia, occupation: farmer.

Spurr, Charles E. Company E 1st Sergeant; enlisted August 22, 1862 at Charleston, appointed 1st Sergeant September 12, 1862, mustered October 9, 1862 at Point Pleasant, age 25, born in Frederick County, Virginia, occupation: carpenter.

Squires, Johnson Company E Corporal and Sergeant; enlisted August 22, 1862 at Charleston, appointed 4ᵗʰ Corporal then promoted from Corporal to 1ˢᵗ Sergeant by order of Colonel William R. Brown, commanding Regiment on September 12, 1862, mustered October 9, 1862 at Point Pleasant, age 25, born in Braxton County, Virginia/West Virginia, occupation: laborer.

St. John, Edward B. Company D Private, Hospital Steward Company D and 1ˢᵗ Lieutenant Company G; enlisted August 8, 1862 at Hartford City, received paid $30.00 Mason County Bounty and Premium, mustered October 8, 1862 at Point Pleasant, age 20, born in Jefferson County, Pennsylvania, occupation: clerk; transferred from Hospital Steward Company D by order and promoted to 1ˢᵗ Lieutenant Company G March 18, 1865.

Stanley, Enoch Company G Private; enlisted January 15, 1864 at Hartford City, mustered at Guyandotte, February 28, 1864, age 18, born in Jackson County, Virginia/West Virginia, occupation: farmer.

Staton (also Staten/Statton/ Staunton/Stratton), Marshal/Marshall (signed "Staton") Company D Private; enlisted March 12ᵗʰ, 1863 at Hurricane Bridge, mustered August 5, 1863 at Charleston, age 18, born in Buckingham County, Virginia/West Virginia, occupation: farmer.

Steed, John B. Company C Private; enlisted August 15, 1863 at Coals Mouth, mustered August 15, 1863 at Barboursville, age 44, born in Ohio County, Virginia/West Virginia, occupation: farmer.

Steel, Amos Company H Private; enlisted December 3, 1862 at Point Pleasant, mustered January 6, 1863 at Point Pleasant, age 22, born in Monroe County, Ohio, occupation: farmer.

Steel, Manassas/Manassay/Mannassa G. Company I Private; enlisted June 1, 1863 at Charleston, mustered July 26, 1863 at Charleston, age 29, born in Monroe County, Virginia/West Virginia, occupation: farmer.

Steel, Samuel Company I Private; enlisted Nov. 17, 1863 at Guyandotte, mustered in Nov. 25, 1863 at Guyandotte, age 22, born in Rockbridge Co., Virginia, occupation: laborer. Detailed for daily duty as artillerist April 1, 1864 (Col. W.R. Brown Spec. Order 51).

Stephens, Francis Company K 3ʳᵈ Sergeant. See "Request For the Appointment of W. W. Harper to be Chaplain of the 13 Va. Vols." (manu. Uncat. 13ᵗʰ W.Va. Infantry Regiment Box WVSA)

Stephenson/Stevenson, David Company F Private; enlisted August 12, 1862 at Brownstown, mustered October 9, 1862 at Point Pleasant, age 21, born in Kanawha County, Virginia/West Virginia, occupation: farmer.

Stephenson, John D. Company G Private; enlisted February 9, 1865 at Point Pleasant, mustered February 28, 1864 at Guyandotte, age 33, born in Mason County, Virginia/West Virginia, occupation: farmer.

Stevenson, Henry C. Company K Private; enlisted October 3, 1863 at Barboursville, mustered November 25, 1863 at Barboursville, age 30, born in Mason County, Virginia/West Virginia, occupation: farmer.

Stewart (also Steward), Adam (signed "Stewart") Company B Private; enlisted August 8, 1862 at Point Pleasant, received paid $30.00 Mason County Bounty and Premium, mustered October 8, 1862 at Point Pleasant, age 30, born in Jackson County, Virginia/West Virginia, occupation: farmer.

Stewart, Elisha, Jr. Company G Corporal; enlisted January 4, 1864 at Buffalo, mustered February 28, 1864, age 34, born in Jackson County, Virginia/West Virginia, occupation: farmer.

Stewart, Ephraim Company B Private; enlisted August 4, 1862 at Point Pleasant, received paid $30.00 Mason County Bounty and Premium, mustered October 8, 1862 at Point Pleasant, age 22, born in Jackson County, Virginia/West Virginia, occupation: farmer.

Stewart, George Company B Private and Corporal; enlisted August 8, 1862 at Point Pleasant, received paid $30.00 Mason County Bounty and Premium, mustered October 8, 1862 at Point Pleasant, age 33, born in Jackson County, Virginia/West Virginia, occupation: farmer; appointed Corporal June 12, 1863.

Stewart, Milton (Milton L.?) entered the U.S. Service on July 12, 1861 in the 4th Loyal Virginia Infantry Regiment as Private, at the time of enlistment was a resident of the State of Maryland, promoted Sergeant Company K 4th Virginia/West Virginia Infantry Regiment, commissioned Captain August 20, 1862 Company B 13th Virginia Regiment, then Lieutenant-Colonel and Inspector General; was in action first time at Romney, Virginia on September 24, 25 and 26, 1861, second time in action at Romney, Virginia on October 25, 1861, third time in action at Beach Creek, Logan County, Virginia on August 6, 1862, where he was taken prisoner near Logan Court House after a desperate struggle and held prisoner for a short time, was released to administer to two wounded officers (Maj. John Hall comdg. detachment of 4th Loyal Virginia Infantry and Captain William Straton/ Stratton of the 34th Battalion Confederate Cavalry). Stewart was again captured by a band of guerrillas, escaped and for gallantry in these encounters was promoted from Sergeant 4th Virginia/West Virginia Infantry to Captain Company B 13th Virginia/West Virginia Infantry Regiment, age 19 at date of appointment to Captain August 20, 1862, born in Somerset County, Pennsylvania, (occupation: printer?), commissioned Captain Company B August 25, 1862, mustered October 8, 1862 at Point Pleasant; commissioned Lieutenant-Colonel October 27, 1864, promoted to Lieutenant-Colonel October 30, 1864, [in January, 1865?] detailed Inspector General of the Army of West Virginia on Major-General George Crook's staff.

Stewart/Stuart, William Company H Private; enlisted August 12, 1862 at Ceredo, mustered October 10, 1862 at Point Pleasant, age 41, born in Wayne County, Virginia/West Virginia, occupation: farmer.

Still, George W. Company I Private; enrolled October 20, 1863 at Guyandotte, mustered November 25, 1863 at Guyandotte, age 18, born in Meigs County, Ohio, occupation: farmer.

Stindman/Stineman, Samuel Company E Private and Musician; enlisted August 22, 1862 at Point Pleasant, mustered October 9, 1862 at Point Pleasant, age 13 or 16, born in Westmoreland County, Pennsylvania, occupation: laborer.

Stone, Madison H. Company C Corporal; enlisted August 7, 1862 at Point Pleasant, mustered October 8/9, 1862 at Point Pleasant, age 40, born in Botetourt County, Virginia, occupation: carpenter; detached to Regimental Commissary department since enlistment, transferred and mustered on roll of non-commissioned staff as Quarter Master Sergeant January 24, 1865.

Stover, George W. Company K Private; enlisted December 24, 1863 at Barboursville, mustered March 28, 1864 at Charleston, age 19, born in Pendleton County, Virginia/West Virginia, occupation: farmer.

Strickland, David S. Company I Private; enlisted December 15, 1862 at Charleston, mustered July 26, 1863 at Charleston, age 19, born in Kanawha County, Virginia/West Virginia, occupation: farmer.

Strickland, John Company A Private; enlisted October 20/21, 1863 at Barboursville, mustered November 25, 1863 at Barboursville, age 18, born in Kanawha County, Virginia/West Virginia, occupation: farmer.

Strickland, Lewis M. Company I Private; enlisted December 26, 1863 at Guyandotte, mustered February 29, 1864 at Guyandotte, age 19, born in Kanawha County, Virginia/West Virginia, occupation: farmer.

Strickland, Sutton M. Company I Private; enlisted December 26, 1863 at Guyandotte, mustered February 29, 1864 at Guyandotte, age 18, born in Kanawha County, Virginia/West Virginia, occupation: laborer.

Strickland, William A. Company A Private; enlisted December 29, 1863 at Charleston, mustered February 27, 1864 at Barboursville, age 18, born in Kanawha County, Virginia/West Virginia, occupation: farmer.

Strickland, William L. Company I Private; enlisted December 17, 1862 at Charleston, mustered July 26, 1863 at Charleston, age 21, born in Kanawha County, Virginia/West Virginia, occupation: farmer.

Stump, Henry Company G 9th Virginia Infantry Regiment, 1st Lieutenant and Captain Company K 13th Virginia Infantry Regiment enlisted in Company G 9th Virginia Infantry and mustered into service March 1, 1862 at Spencer, Virginia, Private Stump received permission to recruit for Company I 13th West Virginia Volunteer Infantry which, as of summer 1863 was not yet full;[733] Stump promoted from Private to 1st Lieutenant September 30, 1863 and transferred to Company K 13th West Virginia Volunteer Infantry Regiment, aged about 43, born in Lewis County, Virginia/West Virginia, occupation: surveyor for Roane County, Virginia/West Virginia, promoted Captain Company K by order of February 9, 1864. According to family history, prior to enlistment in regular volunteer forces, Stump served as "Major of a Militia company which assembled and trained on fields at Walton and on the bottom at the mouth of Johnson Creek" in Roane County.[734]

Stump, Michael Company H Private; enlisted August 12, 1862 at Ceredo, mustered in October 10, 1862 at Point Pleasant, age 30, born in Tazewell County, Virginia, occupation: farmer. Appointed "Regimental Harness Maker and repairer" pursuant to Special Order No. 16 (Col. W.R. Brown dated "Feb 10th 1864").

Sulivan/Sullivan, Louis Company H Private; enlisted February 29, 1864 at Barboursville, mustered April 26, 1864 at Barboursville, age 32, born in Cabell County, Virginia/West Virginia, occupation: farmer.

Sullivan, Alfred T. Company B Private, Sergeant, 2nd and 1st Lieutenant; enlisted August 8, 1862 at Point Pleasant, received paid $30.00 Mason County Bounty and Premium, mustered October 8, 1862 at Point Pleasant, age 20, born March 20, 1843 near Leon, Mason County, Virginia/West Virginia, occupation: farmer; promoted from 2nd Sergeant October 31, 1864 to 1st Lieutenant, commissioned 1st Lieutenant November 10, 1864.

Sullivan, Daniel Company G Corporal and Sergeant; enlisted December 26, 1863 at Barboursville, promoted Corporal pursuant to Col. W.R. Brown, Gen. Order No. 1 (manu. dated Feb. 15, 1864) to rank as such from Jan. 27, 1864, mustered February 28, 1864 at Guyandotte, age 18, born in Cabell County, Virginia/West Virginia, occupation: farmer.

Summerfield, William Company I Private; enlisted December 7, 1862 at Charleston, mustered July 26, 1863 at Charleston, age 18, born in Kanawha County, Virginia/West Virginia, occupation: farmer.

Swain/Swann, James Company D Private (Sergeant?); enlisted September 20, 1863 at Barboursville, mustered October 6, 1863 at Barboursville, age 27, born in "Cleveland [Cleveland County ? Ohio?], V[irgini]a.," occupation: farmer. Prior to enlistment in the 13th Volunteers, Swain may have served in local militia. See James B. Swan 2nd Lieutenant Mason County 106th Militia West Virginia State Troops. Commissioned 2nd Lieutenant by order November 4, 1862 to rank from September 8, 1862. (WVSA)

Swain, Newman (Newman S.) Company D Private; enlisted September 4, 1862 at Point Pleasant, mustered October 8, 1862 at Point Pleasant, age 20, born in Jackson County, Virginia/West Virginia, occupation: farmer.

Swain/Swann, William Company D; Corporal; enlisted August 15, 1862 at Hartford City, mustered October 8, 1862 at Point Pleasant, age 32, born in Cleveland County, Ohio, occupation: farmer; promoted to Sergeant pursuant to Col. W.R. Brown, Gen. Order No. 1 (manu. dated Feb. 15, 1864) to rank as such from Feb. 10, 1864.

Swanson, John W. Company H Private; enlisted November 6, 1863 at Barboursville, mustered November 25, 1863 at Barboursville, age 18, born in Franklin County, Virginia, occupation: farmer.

Taylor, Andrew Company D Private; enlisted August 15, 1862 at Hartford City, mustered October 8, 1862 at Point Pleasant, age 18, born in Meigs County, Ohio, occupation: farmer.

Taylor, Charles A. (or Charles W.) Company H Private; enlisted September 20, 1862 at Point Pleasant, mustered December 11, 1862 at Point Pleasant, age 21, born in Gallia County, Ohio, occupation: farmer.

Taylor, Elmore Company K 5th Sergeant; enlisted July 25, 1863 at Walton, mustered October 3, 1863 at Charleston, age 21, born in Lewis County, Virginia/West Virginia, occupation: farmer.

Taylor, James A. Company K Private; enlisted September 1, 1863 at Walton, mustered October 3, 1863 at Charleston, age 18, born in Russell County, Virginia, occupation: farmer.

Taylor, James H. Company K Private; enlisted August 1, 1863 at Walton, mustered in October 3, 1863 at Charleston, age 19, born in Russell County, Virginia, occupation: farmer.

Taylor, James O. Company K Private; enlisted August 1, 1863 at Walton, mustered October 3, 1863 at Charleston, age 19, born in Craig County, Virginia; occupation: farmer.

Taylor, John Company D Private; enlisted August 15, 1862 at Hartford City, received paid $30.00 Mason County Bounty and Premium, mustered October 8, 1862 at Point Pleasant, age 16, born in Mason County, Virginia/West Virginia, occupation: farmer.

Taylor, John H. (signed "John H. [or M.] Taylor") Company I Private (Corporal?) enlisted March 13, 1863 at Point Pleasant, mustered July 26, 1863 at Charleston, age 18, occupation: farmer.

Taylor, Oliver Company H Private; enlisted November 12, 1862 at Point Pleasant, mustered December 11, 1862 at Point Pleasant, age 18, born in Cheshire, Gallia County, Ohio; occupation: farmer.

Taylor, William P. Company K Private; enlisted January 3 or 6, 1864 at Walton, mustered March 11, 1864 at Charleston, age 18, born in Russell County, Virginia, occupation: farmer.

Teel, Adam A. Company G Private; enlisted January 24, 1864 at Guyandotte, mustered February 28, 1864 at Guyandotte, age 18, born in Tazewell County, Virginia, occupation: farmer.

Teel, Jacob H. Company H Corporal; enlisted September 1, 1862 at Guyandotte, mustered October 10, 1862 at Point Pleasant, age 19, born in Rockbridge County, Virginia (or Breckenridge County, Kentucky), occupation: farmer; appointed 5th Corporal April 2, 1864.

Teel, John Franklin Company A Private; enlisted August 12, 1862 at Charleston, mustered October 7, 1862 at Point Pleasant, age 27, born in Rockbridge County, Virginia, occupation: farmer.

Teel, Samuel Company A Private; enlisted August 15, 1862 at Charleston, mustered October 7, 1862 at Point Pleasant, age 24, born in Kanawha County, Virginia/West Virginia, occupation: farmer.

Terly/Turley Andrew J. Company C 1st Corporal; enlisted July 24, 1862 at Forks of Coal, mustered in October 8/9, 1862, age 21, born in Kanawha County, Virginia/West Virginia, occupation: farmer.

Thacker, Harrison Company H Private; enlisted August17, 1862 at Ceredo, mustered October 10, 1862 at Point Pleasant, age 28, born in Cabell County, Virginia/West Virginia, occupation: farmer. Thacker served with Cabell County Home Guards prior to enlistment in the 13th West Virginia Regiment.

Thaxten/Thaxter/Thaxton/Thaxtor, William H. [William Henry?] Company E Private, enlisted March 14, 1863 at Charleston, mustered August 5, 1863 at Charleston, age 22, born in Kanawha County, Virginia/West Virginia, occupation: farmer.

Thomas, Joel P. Company E Corporal; enlisted August 22, 1862 at Charleston, appointed 3rd Corporal September 12, 1862, mustered October 9, 1862 at Point Pleasant, age 30, born in Bedford County, Virginia, occupation: farmer; discharged January 15, 1864 by Secretary of War in General Order No. 21 Series 1864, from the War Department, Washington City and transferred to Invalid Corps (also known as the Veteran Reserve Corps or V. R. C.).

Thomas, John Company A Private; enlisted August 12, 1862 at Charleston, mustered October 7, 1862 at Point Pleasant, age 51, born in Wythe County, Virginia, occupation: farmer.

Thomas, John A. Company E Private; enlisted August 22, 1862 at Charleston, mustered October 8, 1862 at Point Pleasant, age 27, born in Bedford County, Virginia, occupation: farmer.

Thomas, Marion Company G Private; enlisted December 26, 1863 at Guyandotte, mustered February 28, 1864 at Guyandotte, age 18, born in Meigs County, Ohio, occupation: farmer.

Thomas, Peter P. Company K Private; enlisted September 16, 1863 at Walton, mustered October 3, 1863 at Charleston, age 18, born in Kanawha County, Virginia/West Virginia, occupation: farmer. Thomas may have served as Private in Captain Henry C. Hunter's Company of Jackson County Home Guards sometime before enlisting in the 13th West Virginia Infantry Regiment.

Thomas, Rheuban (also Reuben/Rubin) (signed "Rheuban Thomas") Company H Private; enlisted September 20, 1862 at Point Pleasant, mustered December 11, 1862 at Point Pleasant, age 18, born in Gallia County, Ohio; occupation: farmer.

Thomas, William A. Company E Private and Corporal; enlisted August 22, 1862 at Charleston, mustered October 9, 1862 at Point Pleasant, age 18, born in Kanawha County, Virginia/West Virginia, occupation: farmer; appointed 3rd Corporal in 1864.

Thompson, John H. (signed "Thompson" and "Thomson") Company K Private; enlisted August 1, 1863 at Walton, mustered October 3, 1863 at Charleston, age 44, born in Pittsylvania County, Virginia, occupation: farmer.

Thompson, William H. Company C 2nd Corporal and Sergeant; enlisted September 1, 1862 at Point Pleasant, mustered in October 8, 1862 at Point Pleasant, age 22, born in Cabell County, Virginia/West Virginia, occupation: "Shemak" [shoemaker]; promoted from Corporal to Sergeant October 15, 1863, detailed on March 1, 1864 to recruit men for the 3rd West Virginia Cavalry Regiment, 17 men were recruited.[735]

Thornton, Francis Company B Private; enlisted August 8, 1862 at Point Pleasant, received paid $30.00 Mason County Bounty and Premium, mustered October 8, 1862 at Point Pleasant, age 24, born in Mason County, Virginia/West Virginia, occupation: farmer.

Thornton, John Company K Private; enlisted October 3, 1863 at Barboursville, mustered November 25, 1863 at Barboursville, age 23, born in Indiana, occupation: farmer.

Thornton, William Company K Private; enlisted October 1, 1863 at Barboursville, mustered November 25, 1863 at Barboursville, age 18, born in Putnam County, Virginia/West Virginia, occupation: farmer.

Tilden, Bradford N. Company F Private and Teamster; enlisted September 8, 1862 at Point Pleasant, mustered October 9, 1862 at Point Pleasant, age 22, born in Washington County, Vermont, occupation: clerk.

Tillis, Smith Company F Private; enlisted August 20, 1863 at Coals Mouth, mustered November 25, 1863 at Barboursville, age 18, born in Mason County, Virginia/West Virginia, occupation: farmer.

Tippin/Tipping, Henry (signed "Henry Tipping") Company F Private; enlisted September 10, 1862 at Point Pleasant, mustered October 9, 1862 at Point Pleasant, age 27 or 29, "born in Lynne County, Ireland" [Linn/Louth County, Ireland], occupation: miner.

Todd, Isaac N. Company K Private; enlisted March 3, 1864 at Coals Mouth, mustered March 11, 1864 at Charleston, age 18, 22 or 41, born in Augusta County, Virginia, occupation: farmer.

Tolbert, Archibald Company H Private; enlisted August 15, 1862 at Camp Piatt, near Charleston, mustered in October 10, 1862 at Point Pleasant, age 37, born in Monroe County, Virginia/West Virginia, occupation: farmer.

Toothman, James W. Company A Private; enlisted August 14, 1862 at Charleston, mustered October 7, 1862 at Point Pleasant, age 22, born in Greenbrier County, Virginia/West Virginia, occupation: farmer, "chosen Waggoner October 21, 1862 in place of Thom. T. Hughes, as more competent."

Townsend, Joseph Company I Private; enlisted June 10, 1863 at Charleston, mustered July 26, 1863 at Charleston, age 18, born in Carroll County, Ohio; occupation: laborer.

Triplet/Triplett, Eli Company E Private; enlisted August 22, 1862 at Charleston, mustered October 10, 1862 at Point Pleasant, age 18, born in Kanawha County, Virginia/West Virginia, occupation: laborer.

Truslow, James Company I Private; enlisted December 3, 1862 at Charleston, mustered July 26, 1863 at Charleston, age 15 or 18, born in Kanawha County, Virginia/West Virginia, occupation: farmer.

Tucker, Jacob W. Company D Private; enlisted July 28, 1862 at Point Pleasant, received paid $30.00 Mason County Bounty and Premium, mustered October 8, 1862 at Point Pleasant, age 40, born in Botetourt County, Virginia, occupation: carpenter.

Tulley/Turley, Floyd (signed "Floid Turley") Company I Private; enlisted December 15, 1863 at Guyandotte, mustered February 29, 1864 at Guyandotte, age 18, born in Cabell County, Virginia/West Virginia, occupation: farmer.

Tulley, Rezen P. (also Rezin) (signed "Rezen P. Tulley") Company I Private and Corporal; enlisted December 3, 1862 at Charleston, mustered July 26, 1863 at Charleston, age 44, born in Amherst County, Virginia, occupation: farmer; appointed Corporal June 1, 1864. Detailed for permanent duty as teamster with regimental quartermaster Lt. Stephen Comstock March 30, 1864. (Col. W.R. Brown Special Order No. 50)

Tully, Eli Company E Private; enlisted August 22, 1862 at Charleston, mustered October 9, 1862 at Point Pleasant, age 40, born in Amherst County, Virginia, occupation: farmer.

Tully, James H. Company A Musician and Corporal; enlisted August 14, 1862 at Charleston, chosen musician August 19, 1862, mustered October 7, 1862 at Point Pleasant, age 18, born in Kanawha County, Virginia/West Virginia, occupation: farmer; appointed Corporal June 30, 1863.

Tully, John Company A Private; enlisted August 14, 1862 at Charleston, mustered October 7, 1862 at Point Pleasant, age 25, born in Kanawha County, Virginia/West Virginia, occupation: farmer.

Tully, Sandy (signed "[S or T]andy Tully") Company I Private; enlisted December 6, 1862 at Charleston, mustered July. 26, 1863 at Charleston, age 16, born in Kanawha County, Virginia/West Virginia, occupation: farmer.

Tully, William Company E Private; enlisted August 22, 1862 at Charleston, mustered October 9, 1862 at Point Pleasant, age 38, born in Amherst County, Virginia, occupation: farmer.

Turner, George W. Company H Private; enlisted September 1, 1862 at Ceredo, mustered October 10, 1862 at Point Pleasant, age 18, born in Cabell County, Virginia/West Virginia, occupation: farmer.

Twaddle, John Company F Private and Teamster; enlisted September 10, 1862 at Point Pleasant, mustered October 9, 1862 at Point Pleasant, age 32, born in Jefferson County, Ohio, occupation: farmer.

Vance, Calvin Company A Private; enlisted August 14, 1862 at Charleston, mustered October 7, 1862 at Point Pleasant, age 20, born in Monroe County, Virginia/West Virginia, occupation: farmer.

Vance, George M. Company G Private; enlisted January 1, 1864 at Guyandotte, mustered February. 28, 1864 at Guyandotte, age 18, born in Gallia County, Ohio, occupation: farmer.

Vance, Martellus Company G Private; enlisted January 1, 1864 at Guyandotte, mustered February. 28, 1864 at Guyandotte, age 18, born in Gallia County, Ohio; occupation: farmer.

Vanmatre/Vanmeter, Francis M. Company F Private; enlisted September 10, 1862 at Point Pleasant, received paid $30.00 Mason County Bounty and Premium, mustered October 9, 1862 at Point Pleasant, age 21, born in Mason County, Virginia/West Virginia, occupation: farmer. Detailed for permanent duty as teamster with regimental quartermaster Lt. Stephen Comstock March 30, 1864. (Col. W.R. Brown Special Order No. 50)

Vanmatre/Vanmeter, Gwin (signed "Vanmatre") Company F Private; enlisted September 9, 1862 at Point Pleasant, received paid $30.00 Mason County Bounty and Premium, mustered October 9, 1862 at Point Pleasant, age 23, born in Mason County, Virginia/West Virginia, occupation: laborer.

Vanmatre/Vanmeter, Leonard Company F Private; enlisted October 2, 1862 at Point Pleasant, mustered October 9, 1862 at Point Pleasant, age 30, born in Mason County, Virginia/West Virginia, occupation: boatman.

Vanmatre/Vanmeter, William J. (signed "W. J. Vanmatre") Company F Private; enlisted September 9, 1862 at Point Pleasant, received paid $30.00 Mason County Bounty and Premium, mustered October 9, 1862 at Point Pleasant, age 28, born in Mason County, Virginia/West Virginia, occupation: farmer.

Vickers, Samuel C. Company E Private; enlisted March 24, 1864 at Charleston, mustered April 2, 1864 at Charleston, age 17, born in Mason County, Virginia/West Virginia, occupation: laborer.

Vincent (also Venson/Vinvent/Vivant), Henry L. Company D Private; enlisted August 15 or 18, 1862 at Hartford City, received paid $30.00 Mason County Bounty and Premium, mustered October 8, 1862 at Point Pleasant, age 15, born in Mason County, Virginia/West Virginia, occupation: farmer.

Vincent, Lewis F. Company D Private; enlisted August 15 or 18, 1862 at Hartford City, received paid $30.00 Mason County Bounty and Premium, mustered October 8, 1862 at Point Pleasant, age 25, born in Harrison County, Virginia/West Virginia, occupation: farmer.

Wakely/Wakly, Samuel Company G Private; enlisted December 15, 1863 at Guyandotte, mustered February 28, 1864 at Guyandotte, age 18, born in Athens County, Ohio, occupation: farmer.

Walker, Daniel L. (called Levi Walker?) (signed "Daniel L. Walker") Company K Private; enlisted August 1, 1863 at Walton, mustered October 3, 1863 at Charleston, age 18, born in Craig County, Virginia, occupation: farmer.

Walker, Daniel M. Company K Corporal; enlisted September 1, 1863 at Walton, mustered October 3, 1863 at Charleston, age 26, born in Monroe County, Virginia/West Virginia, occupation: farmer.

Walker, George W. Company K Private; enlisted August 1, 1863 at Walton, mustered October 3, 1863 at Charleston, age 18, born in Craig County, Virginia, at home in Roane Co., occupation: farmer.

Walker, James A. Company H Private; enlisted March 31, 1864 at Barboursville, mustered April. 26, 1864 at Barboursville, age 15, born in Rockbridge County, Virginia, occupation: farmer.

Walkup/Walkuss, James R. (signed "James R. Walkup") Company F 1st Sergeant; enlisted September 9, 1862 at Point Pleasant, received paid $30.00 Mason County Bounty and Premium, mustered October 9, 1862 at Point Pleasant, age 26, born in Lawrence County, Indiana, occupation: farmer.

Wallace, John Company F Private; enlisted October 25, 1863 at Barboursville, mustered November 25, 1863 at Barboursville, age 18, born in Kanawha County, Virginia/West Virginia, occupation: farmer.

Wallar, Anderson C. Company B Private and Corporal; enlisted August 9, 1862 at Point Pleasant, received paid $30.00 Mason County Bounty and Premium, mustered October 8, 1862 at Point Pleasant, age 18, born in Hocking County, Ohio, occupation: farmer; appointed Corporal July 28, 1863.

Wamsley, William J. (B. or S.) Company B Private; enlisted August 9, 1862 at Point Pleasant, received paid $30.00 Mason County Bounty and Premium, mustered October 8, 1862 at Point Pleasant, age 23, born in Mason County, Virginia/West Virginia, occupation: farmer.

Ward, Demarcus/Demarkes Company H Corporal; enlisted August 18, 1862 at Ceredo, mustered October 10, 1862 at Point Pleasant, age 17, born in Wayne County, occupation: farmer; appointed 1st Corporal April 2, 1864.

Ward, James William Company I Private; enlisted October 1, 1863 at Guyandotte, mustered October 6, 1863 at Barboursville, age 18, born in Cabell County, occupation: farmer.

Ward, Silas Company H, Private; enlisted November 29, 1862 at Barboursville, mustered December 11, 1862 at Point Pleasant, age 18, born in Franklin County, Virginia; occupation: farmer; died of typhoid fever in Regimental Hospital at Barboursville January 30, 1864.

Warner, Allen Company K Private; enlisted October 27, 1863 at Leon, mustered November 25, 1863 at Barboursville, age 36, born in Jackson County, Virginia/West Virginia, occupation: farmer.

Warner, Burwell S. Company K Private; enlisted October 4, 1863 at Barboursville, mustered November 25, 1863 at Barboursville, age 18, born in Mason County, Virginia/West Virginia, occupation: farmer.

Warner, George E. Company C Private and Musician; enlisted August 22, 1862 or September 5, 1862 at Point Pleasant, received paid $30.00 Mason County Bounty and Premium, mustered October 8/9, 1862, age 28, born in Mason County, Virginia/West Virginia, occupation: carpenter.

Warner, Thomas Company K Private; enlisted February 26, 1864 at Coals Mouth, mustered March 28, 1864 at Charleston, age 36, born in Mason County, Virginia/West Virginia, occupation: farmer.

Watkins, Benjamin Company D Private/Sergeant?; enlisted February 17, 1864 at Barboursville, mustered February 27, 1864 at Barboursville, age 18, born in Jackson County, Virginia/West Virginia, occupation: farmer.

Waugh, John Company B Private; enlisted August 13, 1862 at Point Pleasant, received paid $30.00 Mason County Bounty and Premium, mustered October 8, 1862 at Point Pleasant, age 44, born in Gallia County, Ohio, occupation: farmer.

Weaver, Samuel Company H Sergeant; enlisted September 15, 1862 at Point Pleasant, mustered October 10, 1862 at Point Pleasant, age 34, born in Augusta County, Virginia, occupation: farmer; appointed 6th Corporal August 1, 1863.

Webb, David J. Company D Private; enlisted December 26, 1863 at Barboursville, mustered February 27, 1864 at Barboursville, age 23, born in Ohio, occupation: farmer.

Webb, Edward (signed "Web") Company E Private; enlisted December 30, 1863 at Charleston, mustered February 27, 1864 at Charleston, age 19, born in Wyoming County, Virginia/West Virginia, occupation: farmer.

Webster, James Company G Private; resident of, or enrolled at Charleston, mustered June 2, 1864 at Charleston, age 18, born in Meigs County, Ohio, occupation: farmer.

Wells, William H. Company E Private; enlisted August 22, 1862 at Charleston, mustered October 9, 1862 at Point Pleasant, age 23, born in Kanawha County, Virginia/West Virginia, occupation: farmer; died at Point Pleasant of consumption January 24, 1863 and buried at Point Pleasant.

West, Isaac Company H Private; enlisted September 20, 1862 at Point Pleasant, mustered October 10, 1862 at Point Pleasant, age 18, born in Augusta County, Virginia, occupation: farmer.

Westfall, Clark Company K Private and Corporal (?); enlisted December 1, 1863 at Walton, mustered March 28, 1864 at Charleston, age 21, born in Jackson County, Virginia/West Virginia, occupation: farmer.

Westfall, Nathan Company K Private; enlisted September 1, 1863 at Walton, mustered October 3, 1863 at Charleston, age 26, born in Jackson County or Roane County, Virginia/West Virginia, occupation: farmer.

Whaley, Kellian Van Rensselaer Colonel and Recruiting Officer for the 13th Virginia Infantry Regiment, age about 41, born in Utica, New York in 1861, engaged in the lumber business at Point Pleasant, elected member of the House of Representatives from Virginia on the "Unconditional Unionist" platform in 1860, lost his seat when Virginia seceded from the Union and with the outbreak of hostilities became a Recruiting Officer for the Union Army, commissioned Major of the 9th Virginia Volunteers Infantry Regiment in 1861, captured November 10, 1861 when the town of Guyandotte was overrun, escaped his captors and upon his return was appointed Recruiting Officer and "Colonel" of the 13th Virginia Regiment.

White, Henderson Company I Private; enlisted August 5, 1863 at Charleston, mustered September 16, 1863 at Charleston, age 33, born in Logan County, Virginia/West Virginia, occupation: farmer.

White, John J. Company I Private and Corporal; enlisted December 15, 1862 at Charleston, appointed Corporal September 1, 1863, mustered July 26, 1863 at Charleston, age 18, born in Kanawha County, Virginia/West Virginia, occupation: farmer.

White, William P. Company F Private and Teamster; enlisted September 2, 1862 at Point Pleasant, mustered October 9, 1862 at Point Pleasant, age 20, born in Kanawha County, Virginia/West Virginia, occupation: farmer; promoted to Corporal May 18, 1865.

Whitehead, Jacob Company D Private; enlisted November 6, 1863 at Murraysville, mustered November 25, 1863 at Barboursville, age 44, born in Hardy County, Virginia/West Virginia, occupation: farmer.

Whitham, Philip/Phillip (signed "Phillip Whitham") Company I; enlisted March 3, 1863 at Point Pleasant, mustered July 26, 1863 at Charleston, age 18, born in Putnam County, Virginia/West Virginia, occupation: farmer.

Whittaker, William W. Company E Private; enlisted August 22, 1862 at Charleston, mustered October 9, 1862 at Point Pleasant, age 20, born in Kanawha County, Virginia/West Virginia, occupation: clerk; discharged by order of Major General H.G. Wright February 10, 1863, at Point Pleasant, because of disability.

Whittington, Albert Company E Private; enlisted August 28, 1862 at Charleston, mustered October 9, 1862 at Point Pleasant, age 26, born in Kanawha County, Virginia/West Virginia, occupation: farmer.

Whittington, James A. Company I Private; enlisted March 3, 1863 at Point Pleasant, mustered July 26, 1863 at Charleston, age 18, born in Putnam County, Virginia/West Virginia, occupation: farmer.

Whittington, John Allen Company I Private; enlisted March 3, 1863 at Point Pleasant, mustered July 26, 1863 at Charleston, age 19, born in Putnam County, Virginia/West Virginia, occupation: farmer.

Whittington, William H. (signed "William H. Whittington") Company I Private; enlisted March 3, 1863 at Point Pleasant, mustered July 26, 1863 at Charleston, age 18, born in Putnam County, Virginia/West Virginia, occupation: farmer.

Wiggand (also Weggand), Adam Company D Private and Corporal; enlisted August 13, 1862 at Point Pleasant, received paid $30.00 Mason County Bounty and Premium, mustered October 8, 1862 at Point Pleasant, age 24, born in Beaver County, Pennsylvania, occupation: farmer. Wiggand may have served with Mason County Militia prior to enlisting in the 13th Regiment. See Adam Wiggand Second Lieutenant of Mason County 106th Militia West Virginia State Troops. Commissioned 2d Lt. December 10, 1861 to rank from November 25, 1861 (WVSA); promoted to Corporal pursuant to Col. W.R. Brown, Gen. Order No. 1 (manu. dated Feb. 15, 1864) to rank as such from Feb. 10, 1864.

Wiley, Oren M. Company G Private; enlisted and mustered February 18, 1865 at Point Pleasant, for a term of one year, age 18, born in Washington County, Ohio, occupation: farmer.

Williams, Abram D. Assistant Surgeon; commissioned Assistant Surgeon May 6, 1863, joined for duty May 10, 1863 at Point Pleasant, age 23, born September 18, 1835 in Williams, Bedford County, Indiana or in Tennessee, occupation: doctor; 1863 graduate of Jefferson Medical College, Philadelphia, graduate studies in ophthalmology and otology under tutelage of his uncle Dr. Elkanah Williams. A. D. Williams resigned January 31, 1865, by "Special Order No. 24, dated Headquarters Dept of W Va." to go to Europe to complete his graduate studies.

Williams, Ira Company C Private; enlisted August 11 or 15, 1862 at Point Pleasant, and received paid $30.00 Mason County Bounty and Premium, muster October 8, 1862 at Point Pleasant, age 18, born in Mason County, Virginia/West Virginia, occupation: farmer.

Williams, James/James S./Jeremiah S. Company K Private and Corporal(?); enlisted about January 1, 1864 at Leon, mustered March 11, 1864 at Charleston, age 30, born in Kanawha County, Virginia/West Virginia, occupation: farmer.

Williams, John W. Company F Private; enlisted September 9, 1862 at Point Pleasant, received paid $30.00 Mason County Bounty and Premium, mustered October 9, 1862 at Point Pleasant, age 27, born in Mason County, Virginia/West Virginia, occupation: farmer.

Williams, Sanford Company I Private; enlisted December 11, 1862 at Charleston, mustered July 26, 1863 at Charleston, age 35, born in Franklin County, Virginia, occupation: farmer.

Williams, Simon Company D Captain and Mustering Officer, enlisted August 5, 1862, received paid $30.00 Mason County Bounty and Premium, commissioned Captain Company D September 12, 1862 to rank from September 2, 1862, mustered October 8, 1862, aged 34 years.

Williamson, Henry C. Company D Private and Sergeant Major; enlisted August 15, 1862 at Point Pleasant, mustered in October 8, 1862 at Point Pleasant, age 24, born in Wood County, Virginia/West Virginia, occupation: farmer; promoted to Sergeant, August 10, 1863, promoted Sergeant Major of the Regiment pursuant to Col. W.R. Brown, Gen. Order No. 1 (manu. dated Feb. 15, 1864) to rank as such from Feb. 10, 1864 and transferred to non-commissioned staff, promoted to 2nd Lieutenant December 14, 1864?; commissioned Captain Company D January 20, 1865.

Williamson, James Company D Private; enlisted August 12, 1863 at Coals Mouth, mustered November 25, 1863 at Barboursville, age 34, born in Ohio, occupation: farmer.

Williamson, Samuel B. Company D Private; enlisted February 18, 1864 at Barboursville, mustered February 27, 1864 at Barboursville, age 16, born in Jackson County, Virginia/West Virginia, occupation: farmer.

Williamson, Thomas Company F Private and Regimental Blacksmith; enlisted September 10, 1862 at Point Pleasant, mustered October 9, 1862 at Point Pleasant, age 45, born in Cumberland County, England, occupation: blacksmith, "detailed to go to Charleston as blacksmith on Oct[ober] 27, 1862".

Willis, Charles O. Company C Private; enlisted and mustered in October 4, 1863 at Barboursville, age 18, born in Meigs County, Ohio, occupation: farmer.

Willson/Wilson, Ezekiel H. (signed "Ezekiel H. Willson") Company B Private; enlisted August 12, 1862 at Point Pleasant, received paid $30.00 Mason County Bounty and Premium, mustered October 8, 1862 at Point Pleasant, age 33, born in Meigs County, Ohio, occupation: farmer.

Wilson, George Washington Company B Private; enlisted September 7, 1862 at Point Pleasant, received paid $30.00 Mason County Bounty and Premium, mustered October 8, 1862 at Point Pleasant, age 44, born in Lewis County, Virginia/West Virginia, occupation: farmer.

Wilson, James Company F Private; enlisted September 10, 1862 at Point Pleasant, mustered October 9, 1862 at Point Pleasant, age 40, born in Scotland, occupation: miner.

Two men named "**James Wilson:** from West Columbia answered the call and were mustered into Co. F on October 9th, 1862. One was James V. Wilson and the other James B. Wilson. They were both residents of Mason County. The elder James (aged about 40 years at the time of enrollment) was a miner and a native of Scotland, enlisted September 10th, 1862 at Point Pleasant, mustered in as Private. The younger James (about 31 years of age), an engineer, enlisted on September 9th, 1862 at Point Pleasant, promoted to Company Sergeant October 1st, 1862.

Wilson, James Company F and K Commissary Sergeant and 2nd Lieutenant; enlisted September 9, 1862 at Point Pleasant, received paid $30.00 Mason County Bounty and premium, mustered October 9, 1862 at Point Pleasant as Company Commissary Sergeant Company F, aged 31, born in Belmont County, Ohio, occupation: engineer; commissioned 2nd Lieutenant Company K April 29, 1864 and transferred to Company K May 4, 1864; resigned October 18, 1864.

Wilson, John A. Company F Private; enlisted September 21, 1862 at Point Pleasant, mustered October 9, 1862 at Point Pleasant, age 30, born in Antrim County, Ireland, occupation: miner.

Wilson, Milton Company A Private; enlisted August 12, 1862 at Charleston, mustered October 7, 1862 at Point Pleasant, age 36, born in "Williams Town Kentuckee" (Williamstown, Kentucky today in Grant and Pendleton Counties), occupation: farmer.

Windon, Francis Abney Company C 5th Orderly Sergeant; enlisted August 15, 1862 at Point Pleasant, received paid $30.00 Mason County Bounty and Premium, mustered as 5th Orderly Sergeant October 8, 1862 at Point Pleasant, age 22, born in Mason County, Virginia/West Virginia, occupation: farmer; promoted to 3rd Sergeant January 5, 1863.

Winebrener (also Winebreiner/Winebremn/Winebrenner), Alexander H. (signed "Winebrener") Company B Private; enlisted August 8, 1862 at Point Pleasant, received paid $30.00 Mason County Bounty and Premium, mustered October 8, 1862 at Point Pleasant, age 24, born in Monroe County, Virginia/West Virginia, occupation: blacksmith.

Winegar, James Company H Private; enlisted September 20, 1862 at Point Pleasant, mustered December 11, 1862 at Point Pleasant, age 33, born in Augusta County, Virginia, occupation: farmer.

Winkleblack, John A. Company F Private, Carpenter, Teamster and Commissary Sergeant; enlisted September 9, 1862 at Point Pleasant, mustered October 9, 1862 at Point Pleasant, age 43, born in Greenbrier County, Virginia/West Virginia, occupation: carpenter; detailed for Carpenter in the Regimental Quartermaster Department October 19, 1862, detailed Teamster together with Arthur Edwards; promoted May 14, 1865 to Commissary Sergeant.

Wintz, Baron D. Kalb Company A Private; enlisted August 15, 1862 at Charleston, mustered October 7, 1862 at Point Pleasant, age 18, born in Kanawha County, Virginia/West Virginia, occupation: farmer.

Wintz (also Wince), Philip (Jr.?) Company A Private; enlisted March 1, 1863 at Hurricane Bridge, mustered July 9, 1863 at Charleston, age 17/18, born in Kanawha County, Virginia/West Virginia, occupation: farmer.

Wise, Thomas W. Company G Private; enlisted December 20, 1863 at Cottageville, mustered February 28, 1864 at Guyandotte, age 19, born in Monroe County, Ohio, occupation: farmer; served as Private in the Jackson County Home Guards before enlisting in the United States Volunteer forces.

Withrew/Withrow, Thomas (Thomas A.?) Company A Private; enlisted August 5, 1863 at Coals Mouth or Charleston, mustered August 5, 1863 at Charleston, age 18, born in Putnam County, Virginia/West Virginia, occupation: farmer.

Withrew (also Wethrow/Witherall/Withrow), William Addisson Company A Private; enlisted August 15, 1862 at Charleston, mustered October 7, 1862 at Point Pleasant, age 19, born in Kanawha County, Virginia/West Virginia, occupation: farmer.

Wolf/Wolfe, Abraham/Abram Company K 2nd Corporal and 4th Sergeant; enlisted September 3, 1863 at Walton, mustered October 3, 1863 at Charleston, age 30, born in Jackson County, Virginia/West Virginia, occupation: farmer.

Wolf, Andrew Company F Private; enlisted February 14, 1865 at Point Pleasant to serve for a term of one year, mustered in February 14, 1865 at Point Pleasant, age 26, born in Smith County, Virginia, occupation: farmer.

Wolf, David Company B Private; enlisted August 12, 1862 at Point Pleasant, received paid $30.00 Mason County Bounty and Premium, mustered October 8, 1862 at Point Pleasant, age 25, born in Meigs County, Ohio, occupation: farmer. David Wolf transferred to Veteran Reserve Corps (66th Company 2nd Battalion V.R.C.?) January 1, 1865 "by order of War Dept."

Wolf, Harvey Company F Private; enlisted and mustered February 14, 1865 at Point Pleasant to serve for a term of one year, age 24, born in Wythe County, Virginia, occupation: farmer.

Wolf, James Company F Private; enlisted and mustered February 14, 1865 at Point Pleasant to serve for a term of one year, age 28, born in Wythe County, Virginia, occupation: farmer.

Wolf/Wolfe, William H. (signed his name "Woolf") Company D Private; enlisted August 15, 1862 at Point Pleasant, mustered October 8, 1862 at Point Pleasant, age 42 age given as 52 in Carded Medical Records (dated July 31, 1864), born in Frederick County, Virginia, occupation: farmer.

Wood, John P. Company C 1st Sergeant, 2nd Lieutenant and 1st Lieutenant; enlisted August 11, 1862 or August 27, 1862 at Point Pleasant, received paid $30.00 Mason County Bounty and Premium, muster in as 1st Sergeant October 8/9, 1862 at Point Pleasant, age 32, born in Albermarle County, Virginia, occupation: farmer; discharged from 1st Sergeant for promotion to 2nd Lieutenant September 25, 1863, mustered as 2nd Lieutenant October 6 or 7, 1863 at Barboursville, commissioned 1st Lieutenant February 18, 1865, mustered as 1st Lieutenant March 14, 1865, at Cumberland, Maryland.

Woodall, Robert (middle initial S. or V.) Company E Corporal, Hospital Steward (and 2nd Sergeant?); enlisted August 22, 1862 at Charleston, mustered October 9, 1862 at Point Pleasant, age 29, born in "Prince down, V[irgini]a" (Prince William County, Virginia; Prince George County, Virginia, Princeton, West Virginia?], occupation: cooper; appointed Corporal in 1864, promoted to Hospital Steward by order of Colonel William R. Brown (Special Order No. 21 April 1, 1865).

Woodrum, Archibald Company F Private; enlisted July 27, 1863 at Point Pleasant, mustered August 5, 1863 at Charleston, age 18, born in Monroe County, Virginia/West Virginia, occupation: laborer.

Woodrum, Richard "Dick" Company F 7th Corporal and Sergeant; enlisted September 9, 1862 at Point Pleasant, mustered October 9, 1862 at Point Pleasant, age 27, born in Monroe County, Virginia/West Virginia, occupation: engineer; promoted from Corporal to Sergeant May 18, 1865.

Woods, Alpheus/Alphius Company B Private and Corporal; enlisted August 9, 1862 at Point Pleasant, received paid $30.00 Mason County Bounty and Premium, mustered October 8, 1862 at Point Pleasant, age 19, born in Mason County, Virginia/West Virginia, occupation: farmer; appointed Corporal, July 6, 1864.

Woods, Charles P. (signed "Charles P. Woods") Company G Private; enlisted December 7, 1863 at Point Pleasant, mustered February 28, 1864 at Guyandotte, age 19, born in Mason County, Virginia/West Virginia, occupation: farmer.

Woods, George H. Company D Private; enlisted November 5, 1863, mustered November 25, 1863 at Barboursville, age 17, born in Cabell County, Virginia/West Virginia, occupation: farmer.

Woods, William F. Company C Private; enlisted August 11/12, 1862 at Point Pleasant, received paid $30.00 Mason County Bounty and Premium, mustered October 8/9, 1862 at Point Pleasant, age 24, born in Mason County, Virginia/West Virginia, occupation: farmer.

Woodyard, Isaac N. Company G Private; enlisted January 1, 1864 at Guyandotte, mustered February 28, 1864 at Guyandotte, age 18, born in Giles County, Virginia, occupation: laborer.

Woodyard, James L. Company C Private; enlisted August 12, 1862 or September 4, 1862 at Point Pleasant, received paid $30.00 Mason County Bounty and Premium, mustered October 8/9, 1862 at Point Pleasant, age 44, born in Adams or Athens County, Ohio, occupation: farmer.

Woodyard, Manly P. Company D Private; enlisted October 26, 1863 at Barboursville, mustered November 25, 1863 at Barboursville, age 35, born in Taylor County, Virginia/West Virginia, occupation: farmer.

Woodyard, Mathew E. Company G Private; enlisted January 5, 1864 at Guyandotte, mustered February 28, 1864 at Guyandotte, age 20, born in Giles County, Virginia, occupation: farmer.

Woolwine (also Wolwine), Henry Company H Private; enlisted August 15, 1862 at Camp Piatt near Charleston, mustered October 10, 1862 at Point Pleasant, age 18, born in Monroe County, Virginia/West Virginia, occupation: "wagon man" or "wagon maker."

Workman, Doliver Company H Private; enlisted December 1, 1862 at Ceredo, mustered December 11, 1862 at Point Pleasant, age 17, born in Cabell County, Virginia/West Virginia, occupation: farmer.

Wright, George M. Company F Private; enlisted September 10, 1862 at Point Pleasant, received paid $30.00 Mason County Bounty and Premium, mustered October 9, 1862 at Point Pleasant, age 19, born in Mason County, Virginia/West Virginia, occupation: farmer.

Wright, Kneely/Neely D. (signed "Kneely") Company F Private; enlisted September 10, 1862 at Point Pleasant, received paid $30.00 Mason County Bounty and Premium, mustered October 9, 1862 at Point Pleasant, age 18, born in Mason County, Virginia/West Virginia, occupation: farmer.

Yates, James A. Company C Private; enlisted August 20, 1862 at Point Pleasant, Virginia, received paid $30.00 Mason County Bounty and Premium, mustered October 8/9, 1862 at Point Pleasant, age 22, born in "County Not Known," Virginia, occupation: farmer.

Yeager, Nicholas Company G Private; enlisted December 7, 1863 at Point Pleasant, never mustered, died February 15, 1864 in 13th Regimental Hospital Barboursville, West Virginia "of Brain fever" while awaiting muster, age 18, born in Mason County, Virginia/West Virginia, occupation: farmer.

Yeager, Peter Company F Private, Butcher, Corporal; enlisted September 9, 1862 at Point Pleasant, received paid $30.00 Mason County Bounty and Premium, mustered October 9, 1862 at Point Pleasant, age 41, born in Mason County, Virginia/West Virginia, occupation: farmer; detailed for "Butcher" October 23, 1862, promoted to Corporal May 1, 1862. Yeager may have served with 106th Mason County Militia prior to enlistment in the 13th Volunteers. See Peter Yeager, Second Lieutenant of the Mason County 106th Militia West Virginia State Troops, Commissioned 2nd Lieutenant December 10, 1861 to rank from November 20, 1861. (WVSA)

Young, Charles W. (signed "Charls W. Young") Company E Private and Corporal; enlisted September 15, 1862 at Charleston, mustered October 9, 1862 at Point Pleasant, age 19, born in Kanawha County, Virginia/West Virginia, occupation: farmer; promoted from Private to Corporal by order of Colonel William R. Brown July 28, 1864.

Young, David R (or K.) Company I Private; enlisted December 20, 1862 at Charleston, mustered July 26, 1863 at Charleston, age 22, born in Kanawha County, Virginia/West Virginia, occupation: farmer.

Young, George W. Company E Private; enlisted August 22, 1862 at Charleston, mustered October 9, 1862 at Point Pleasant, age 25, born in Kanawha, County, Virginia/West Virginia, occupation: farmer.

Young, Henry Company E Private; enlisted August 22, 1862 at Charleston, mustered October 9, 1862 at Point Pleasant, age 37, born in Rockingham County, Virginia, occupation: cooper.

Young, John A./George A. Company I Corporal and Sergeant; enlisted December 9, 1862 at Charleston, appointed Corporal July 26, 1863, mustered July 26, 1863 at Charleston, age 28, born in Kanawha County, Virginia/West Virginia, occupation: farmer.

Young, John M. Company F Sergeant and 2nd Lieutenant; enlisted September 15, 1862 at Point Pleasant, mustered in as Sergeant October 9, 1862 at Point Pleasant mustered in as Sergeant Company F, aged 27, born in Kanawha County, Virginia/West Virginia, occupation: farmer; commissioned 2nd Lieutenant October 31, 1864 and transferred to Company K by order dated October 31, 1864, discharged at Camp Russell, Virginia to be promoted 2nd Lieutenant Company K November 10, 1864.

Young, Robert Company B Private; enlisted August 8, 1862 at Point Pleasant, received paid $30.00 Mason County Bounty and Premium, mustered October 8, 1862 at Point Pleasant, age 30, born in Allegheny County, Virginia, occupation: blacksmith.

Young, Robert L. Company I Sergeant; enlisted December 8, 1862 at Charleston, appointed Sergeant May 1, 1863, mustered July 26, 1863 at Charleston, age 22, born in Kanawha County, Virginia/West Virginia, occupation: farmer.

Young, Ultimus (Ultimus A. or K.?) Company B Private; enlisted August 2, 1862 at Point Pleasant, received paid $30.00 Mason County Bounty and Premium, mustered October 8, 1862 at Point Pleasant, age 18, born in Mason County, Virginia/West Virginia, occupation: farmer.

Zirckel, William Company G Private; enlisted December 11, 1863 at Hartford City, mustered February 28, 1864 at Guyandotte, age 18, born in Mason County, Virginia/West Virginia, occupation: farmer.

Zircle/ Zirckle/Zirkle, Jonathan (signed "Jonathan Zircle") Company D Private (Corporal?); enlisted August 15, 1862 at Hartford City, received paid $30.00 Mason County Bounty and Premium, mustered October 8, 1862 at Point Pleasant, age 18, born in Mason County, Virginia/West Virginia, occupation: farmer.

Image Gallery

RIPLEY, VIRGINIA,
July 6th, 1861.

To the true and loyal citizens of Western Virginia, and particularly those on the Ohio border, I would earnestly appeal to come to the defense of the Commonwealth, invaded and insulted as she is by a ruthless and unnatural enemy. None need be afraid that they will be held accountable for past opinions, votes, or acts under the delusions which have been practiced upon the Northwestern people, if they will now return to their patriotic duty and acknowledge their allegiance to Virginia and her Confederate States as their fine and lawful sovereign. You were Union men, so was I, and we had a right to be so until oppression and invasion and war drove us to the assertion of a second independence. The sovereign State proclaimed it by her Convention and by a majority of more than one hundred thousand votes at the polls. She has seceded from the old and formed a new Confederacy; she has commanded and we must obey her voice. I come to execute her commands, to hold out the olive branch to the true and peaceful citizens, to repel invasion from abroad and subdue treason only at home. Come to the call of the country which owes you protection as her native sons!

HENRY A. WISE,
Brig. Gen'l.

Broadside issued in the form of a letter, by Brigadier General, C.S.A., Henry A. Wise to the "true and loyal citizens of Western Virginia, and particularly those on the Ohio border." This letter, dated "Ripley, Virginia, July 6th, 1861," was published in wake of the Virginia legislature's vote to adopt the secession ordinance and to ally the fortunes of her citizens with that of the recently formed Confederate States of America without popular referendum. Brigadier General Wise, Governor of Virginia until 1860, was now in 1861, actively engaged in putting Virginia on a war-footing and raising troops to defend the new alliance. The people west of the Alleghenies, however, at least by half, would not just follow the rest of the State into the Confederacy and Wise knew it, thus this carefully worded appeal. Disaffection between citizens of the Northwestern counties from the State government at Richmond had long been festering. Their disaffection was due to implementation of policies, taxes and passage of laws which favored Eastern Virginia and which failed to provide equal protection of the laws and development of infrastructure in proportion to tax revenues paid by those living west of the Alleghenies. This rugged mountain range, naturally dividing the State in two, together with the lack of good roads by horse or train car which might have countered the divide created by terrain, only reinforced disaffection. A natural outcome of these causes and conditions was that citizens living in vicinity of the Ohio and it's tributary, the Kanawha, developed common bonds of interest with their more prosperous neighbors to the north: in Ohio, Indiana and Pennsylvania. Their markets and commerce, family and ideas for a better future lay with the Northern States, with the Union. Wise's language here, that all citizens were duty-bound to join the mother State in repelling the Northern "oppressors" and that they would be unconditionally forgiven their "delusion," failed to move and for his arrogance, may well have put steel in the hearts of those still undecided on the question of secession in 1861.

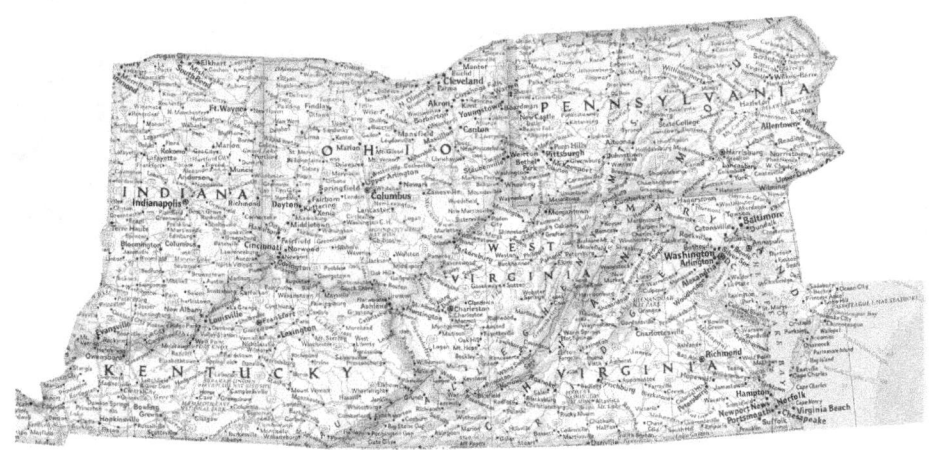

```
0    50   100  150 200  250 300
└────┴────┴────┴────┴────┴────┘
           SCALE IN MILES
```

Map of the border States: Kentucky, West Virginia, Virginia, Maryland, Indiana, Ohio and Pennsylvania

Map of the Northwestern counties

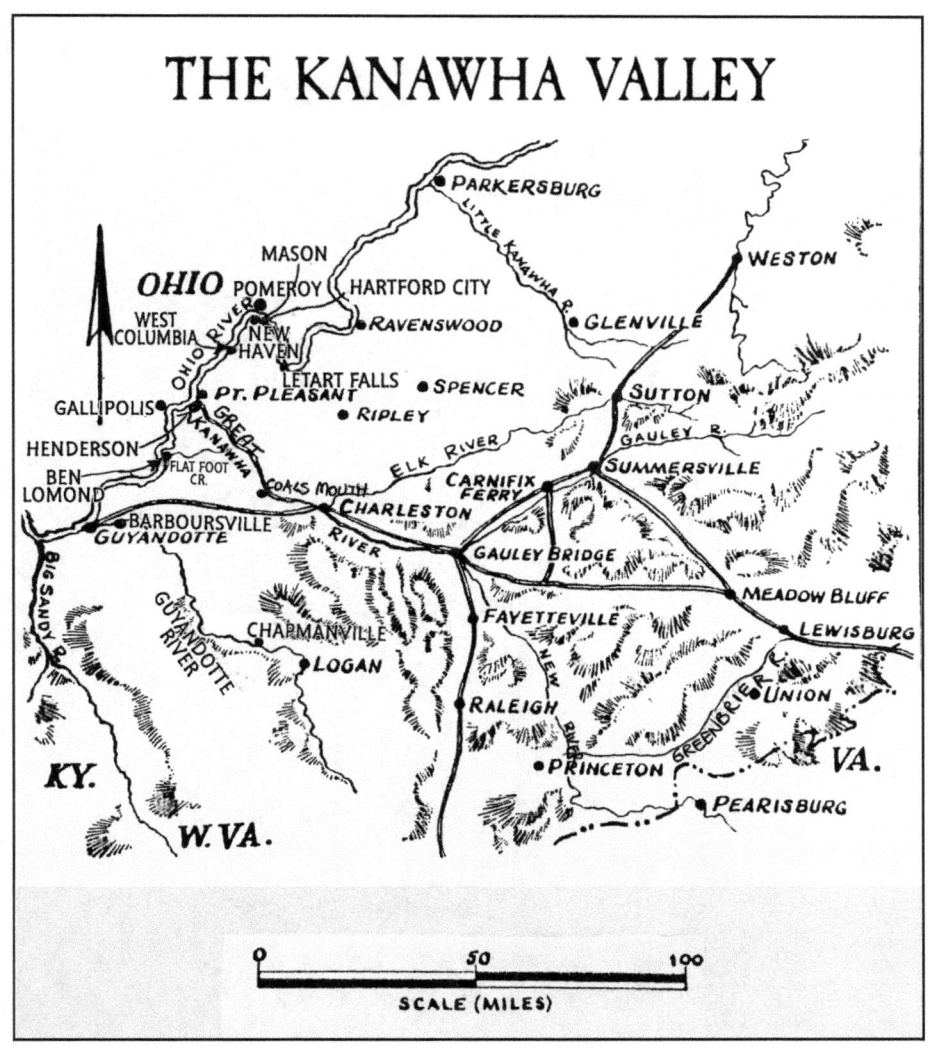

Map of the Kanawha Valley

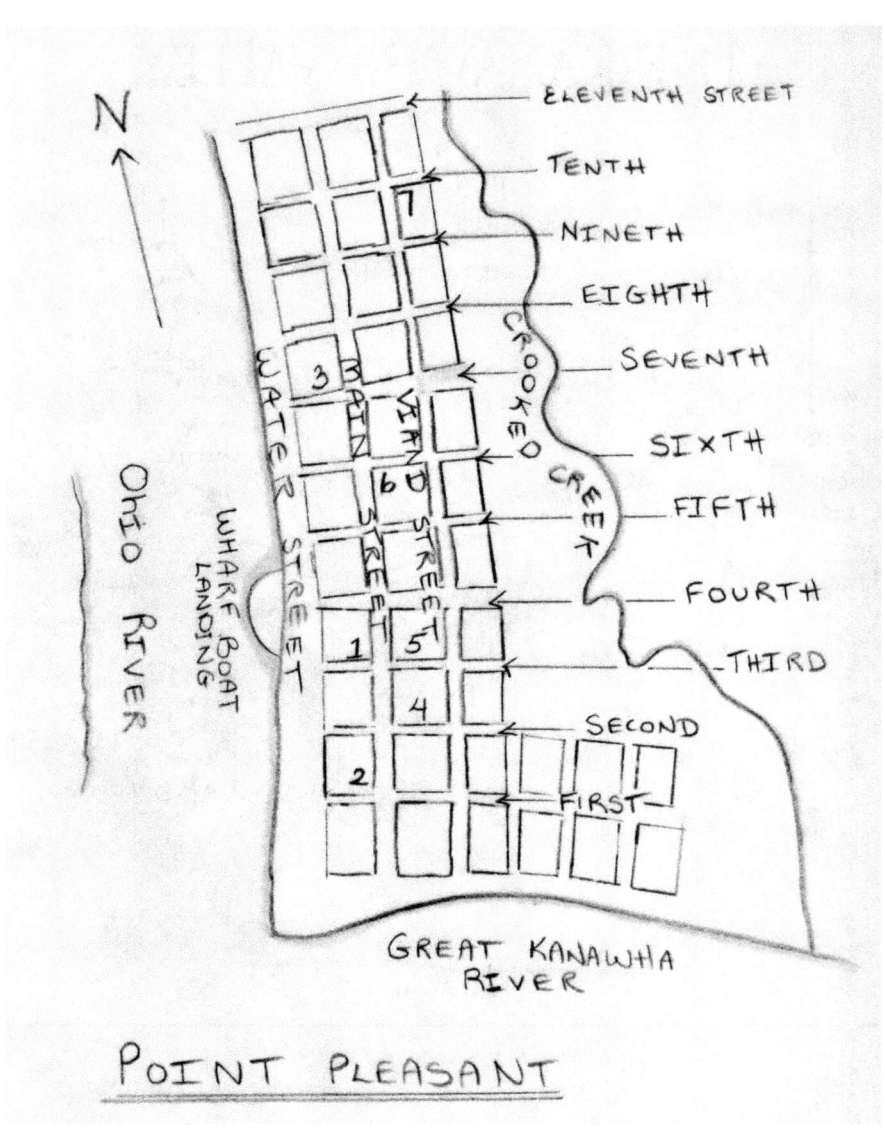

Map of Point Pleasant, Virginia (West Virginia) 1862, after two maps of the town dated 1832 and 1877-1878, provided courtesy of the Virginia State Library, Richmond. Points of interest: (1) Dr. Samuel G. Shaw's residence and office, Third and Main Streets. (2) Virginia House, First and Water Streets, a hotel owned and operated by J.P.R.B. Smith, Colonel commanding Mason County Militia (3) Presbyterian Church (South), Seventh and Main Streets (4) Southern Methodist Chruch South (5) Presbyterian Church (North) Third and Main Streets (6) Mason County Court House, Sixth Street between Main and

Viand Streets (7) Methodist Church (North and South), Tenth and Viand Streets. The first Methodist Church in Point Pleasant, at Tenth and Viand, may have been built as early as 1834. Then in 1844, there was a schism. Methodists separated into those who tolerated slavery (Methodist Church South) and those who did not (Methodist Church North). In 1858, the Methodist Church South separated from the original church and bought lots on the corner of Fifth and Viand and erected building(s). With the breaking out of the war, church services in the building(s) on South Viand were suspended. All churches in town, including the jail adjacent to the Court House were used as hospitals during 1862. Other landmarks not indicated by number on this map include the office of the Point Pleasant Weekly Register. *George W. Tippett, a native of Maryland and a Democrat by incli-nation, began publication of the* Register *on February 27, 1862 in the building on the corner of Third and Main Streets. Tippet had moved to Point Pleasant in 1855 and likely was in the printing business before launching the* Register, *a strictly pro-Union newspaper published every Thursday. A photo of Tippett posed in front of his office with family and others, is on exhibit at the Mansion House (1796), on "the Point". His original office inte-rior, equipments, presses and types was and perhaps still is on exhibit at the Point Pleasant historic village erected at the fairgrounds. The house of John Hall, Esq., father of James R. Hall, Lieutenant Colonel commanding the 13th West Virginia Infantry and John T. Hall, Major commanding 4th West Virginia Infantry, is located uptown on Main Street.*

The John and Olivia (Hogg) Hall house.

View from the railroad bridge over the Kanawha River facing southwest. In the middleground is the Kanawha River traffic bridge. In the foreground is part of the old militia muster grounds at Point Pleasant and across the river, on the heights at left are the old campgrounds used at times by the 13th West Virginia and other Union troops. In the far background at right is the Silver Bridge that connected Point Pleasant to Gallipolis, Ohio.

View looking south over the old muster grounds from the corner of Viand and Court Streets towards the Kanawha.

Linoleum Block Print Of The Mason County Court House, Point Pleasant, W. Va.

Old Mason County Court House, linoleum block print, from The Observer *(Point Pleasant, W. Va.), December 1933, p. 6. The old circuit court house pictured here was built in 1837. It was rebuilt in 1933.*

Sharp-Shooters.

We are pleased to notice from posted hand-bills, that our old friend Lieut. John A. Martin is raising a company of sharp-shooters, and that he has half his company already recruited. As this is by common consent the most desireable branch of the service, we advise all enterprising young men to avail themselves at once of this fine opportunity to join a "crack company." Remember you are relieved of all picket or menial duty, and are only expected to "pick off," from your distant stand-point, gunners and officers Let the company be immediately filled up.

"Sharpshooters" wanted for the 13th Virginia Infantry Regiment. Notice in the Point Pleasant Weekly Register *of October 2, 1862, p. 2.*

Guerillas.—It will be years before the outrages, persecutions, robberi s and mur 'ers committed by the rebel guerillas, or, as Jeff. Davis terms them, "partisan rangers," will all become known. Of the infamous character of the warfare which they carry on under the sanction of the rebel authorities at Richmond, we have the following testimony of Gen. Floyd ("the thief") in a letter to the Governor of Virginia:

"I have been aware of abuses and outrages of a most monstrous and shocking character, committed by those who I believe are organized as 'partisan rangers,' under authority of the Confederate officers--but so scrupulous have I been in abstaining from what might by the little and the ignorant be construed into unwarrantable interference, that I have forborne to issue any order to prevent what it was the duty of every Confederate officer, in the name of humanity, to put a stop to. The chief causes of the disaffection among the people of a large part of this community have arisen from the high-handed acts of robbery and rapine committed by many of the 'partisan rangers.' I know that a commission, if fairly executed, would disclose a lawlessness and monstrous abuse of authority and power which would be astonishing and shocking, and which would call for and i sure from the Secretary and the President prompt reform, and stern measures of redress against any repetition of them."

"Guerrillas" from Leslie's Illustrated Newspaper, *November 1, 1862, p. 83. "General Floyd" referred to here is John Buchanan Floyd, served as Governor of Virginia 1849-1852, as Secretary of War under President James Buchanan 1857-1860 and in 1861, was appointed Brigadier-General by President Jefferson Davis, C.S.A. Floyd's tenure as Secretary of War was tainted by corruption and when, in late 1860, President Buchanan learned that Floyd had issued orders that in effect syphoned arms and munitions from Northern to Southern arsenals in anticipation of civil war, Buchanan asked for Floyd's resignation December 23, 1860. Floyd was disliked by the Northern press and was very unpopular with loyal West Virginians, who loathed being set upon by such partisan rangers as Floyd was recruiting and inciting in 1861 and 1862.*

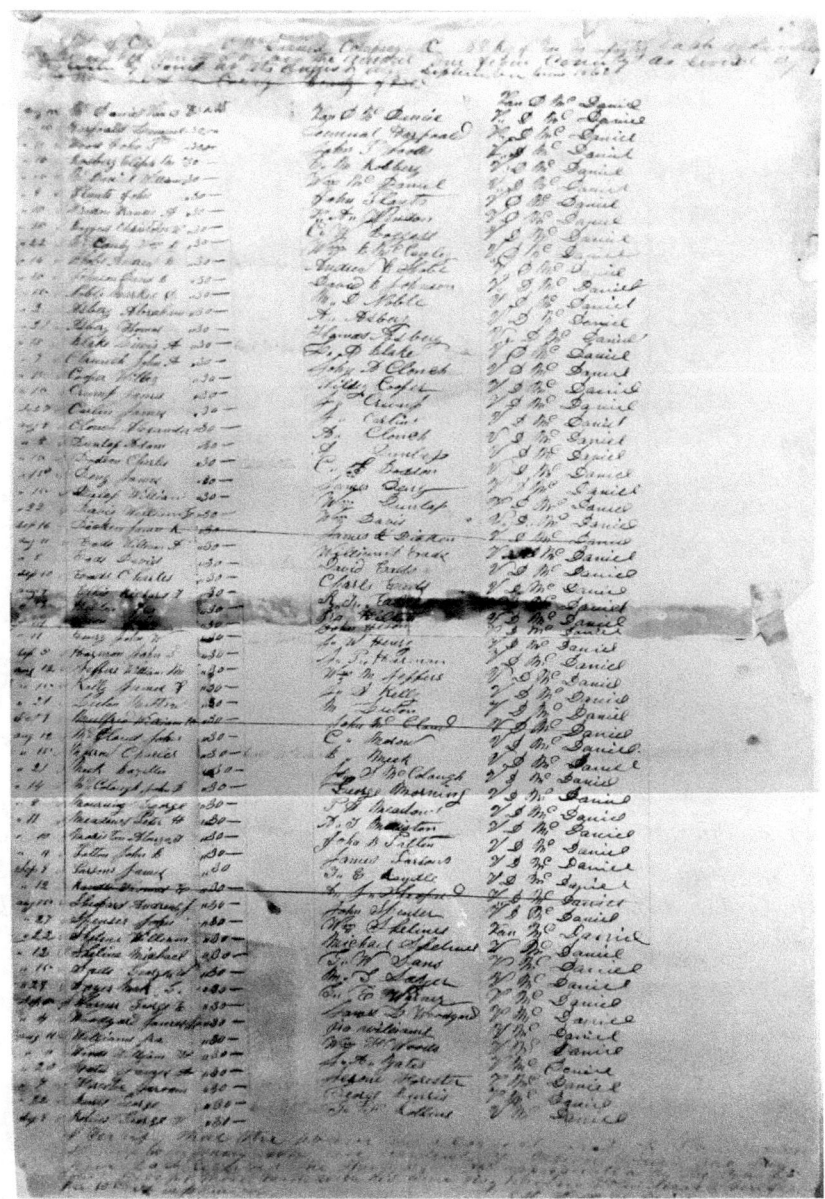

List of volunteers raised by Captain Van D. McDaniel in August and September 1862 (document dated "September 1862 Point Pleasant, Virginia, place of rendez-vous") and organized as Company C, 13th Regiment Virginia (West Virginia) Volunteer Infantry. Each named recruit on this list acknowledged receipt of the $30.00 Mason County bounty offered at this time. Courtesy of the West Virginia Regional History Library, Colson Hall, West Virginia University, Morgantown.

David Eads, Private Company C, clothing account. Eads had enlisted August 8th, 1862. Entries begin with clothing issued in the amount of $36.97 made on September 25th, 1862; and end with a final issue of clothing for $16.80 made on August 31st, 1864. Clothing Books Co. C, West Virginia State Archives, Charleston.

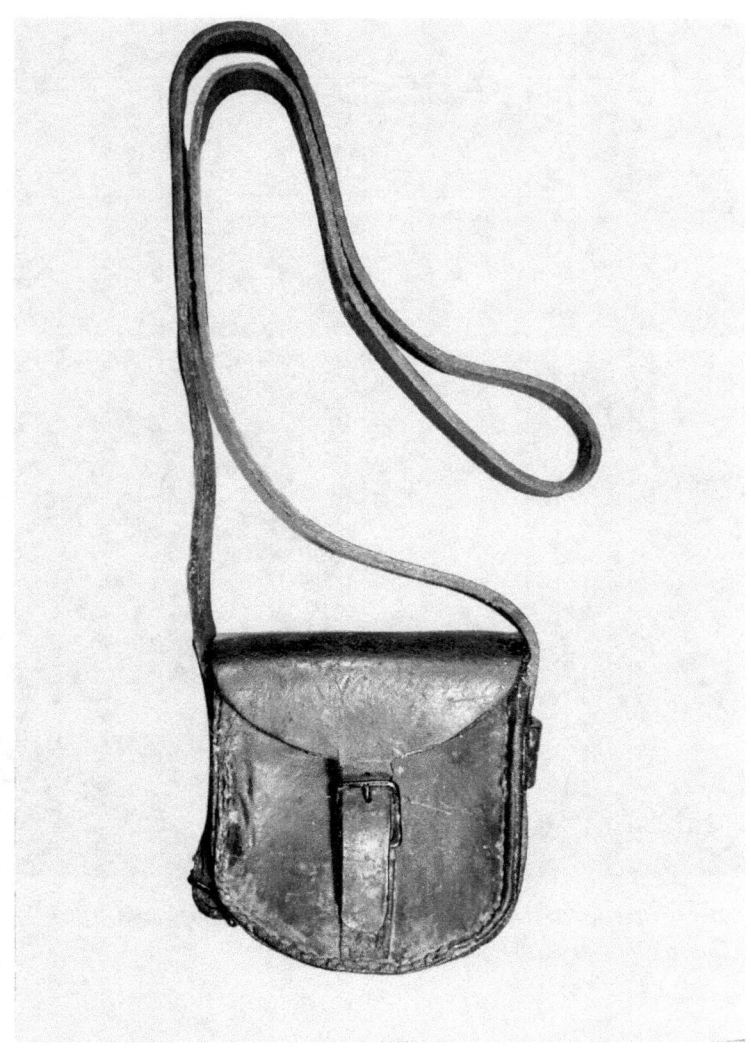

Civil War bullet bag. Courtesy of Gary E. Nebel.

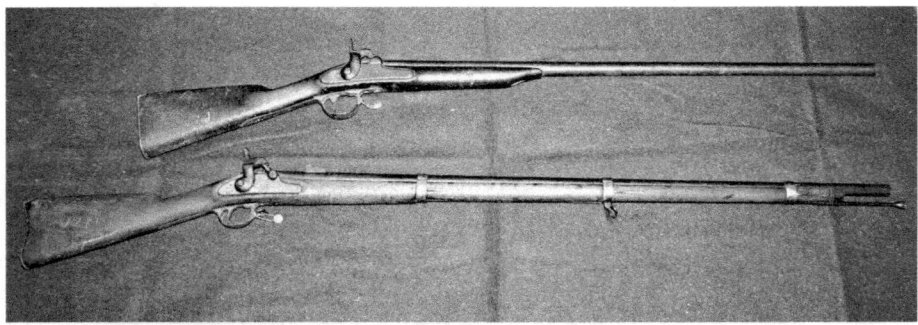

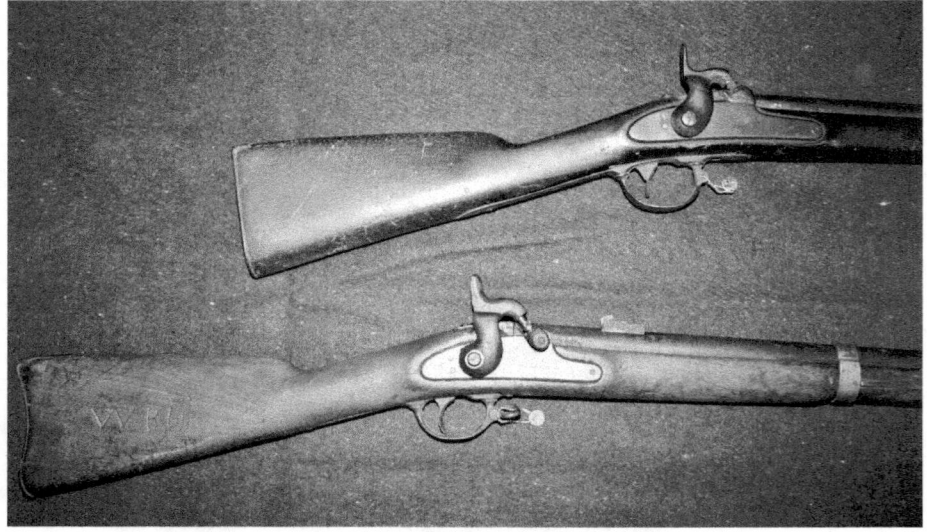

Detail of stocks and locks: 1847 Harper's Ferry musket (top) and 1861 Springfield (bottom). Courtesy of Gary E. Nebel.

J.B. Bumgardner (above) recruited many men for service in the 13ᵗʰ West Virginia Infantry Regiment in 1862. He also served in the unenviable post of tax collector for Cabell County beginning in March 1863.

William Rufus Brown, originally from Pennsylvania and later Pomeroy, Ohio, commanded the 13ᵗʰ Virginia (West Virginia) Regiment Infantry Volunteers as Colonel for the entire term of his service. Photograph published by the veterans' society of the Massachusetts Commandery Military Order of the Loyal Legion of the United States.

James Robert Hall, Lieutenant Colonel commanding 13ᵗʰ Regiment West Virginia Infantry Volunteers, portrait carte.

James R. Hall, Captain commanding 13th Virginia (West Virginia) Regiment, his signed oath to "support the Constitution of the United States and the laws made in pursuance there of [...] And [to] uphold and defend the government of Virginia as vindicated and restored by the Convention which assembled in Wheeling on the 11th day of June, 1861 [and] to perform the duty of his office of Captain in the 13th Regiment Virginia Volunteer Infantry to the best of [his] ability". Original in the West Virginia State Archives, Charleston.

Dr. Samuel G. Shaw, born <u>ca.</u> 1807, allopathic physician, M.D. University of Pennsylvania, commissioned August 22, 1862 and appointed Surgeon, 13th Virginia Volunteer Infantry Regiment October 10, 1862. From and original print in the Mansion House, Tu-Endie-Wei State Park, Point Pleasant, West Virginia.

Milton Stewart, Captain commanding Company B 13th West Virginia Regiment Infantry Volunteers. Image from ebay.com.

"*Dr. S.G. Shaw [advertisement]. Physician and Surgeon. Tenders his professional service to the public. Calls from the country promptly attended to. Office on Front Street and adjoining Virginia House. Feb. 27, 1862 – 1 y.*" *Advertisement appearing in the first edition of the Point Pleasant Weekly Register.*

HON. JOHN HALL
PRESIDENT OF THE FIRST CONSTITUTIONAL CONVENTION WHICH CONVENED
AT WHEELING NOVEMBER 26 1861
(From a photograph taken in the year 1867, and supplied for this work by his daughter
Mrs. Benj. J. Redmond, of Mason County, West Virginia

John Hall, Esquire. After a photograph taken in 1867.
Courtesy of William Matthews, Esq., a descendant.

John T. Hall, Major commanding 4th Virginia (West Virginia) Regiment Infantry Volunteers to his father, John Hall, Esq. regarding recruitment of the 13th Regiment. Letter dated [Charleston], August 1, 1862.

Major John T. Hall to his father, reverse side

Winfield Va Dec 28th 1862

Dear Mother

    I had expected to have
come Home between Christmas
+ New Year but it was abso-
-lutely impossible for me
to leave there is a good deal of
sickness in Camp here the
Men are Have the Typhoid
Phneumonia Measels & Mumps
— Robert Roggers has been quite
sick but is now better he has
the Arisepolis I think he will
be able to move to Pt Pleasant
in a day or two — There is no
news here — I will try and come
home about the 9th of Jany
Give my love to all

      Your affectionate son
      James R Hall
      Lt Col 13th Va Vol Infy

James R. Hall, Lieutenant Colonel commanding, 13th Virginia (West Virginia) Volunteer Infantry to his mother, Olivia Hall. Dated Winfield, Virginia December 28th, 1862.

Print of a posthumous double portrait of Lieutenant Colonel James R. on left and Major John T. on right. Commissioned after the war by their father, John Hall. Courtesy of William B. Matthews, a descendant of John and Olivia (Hogg) Hall.

Drawings illustrating Captain R. B. Wilson's series of letters to
The National Tribune detailing his service in the Kanawha Division.

An Infantryman.

A MARCH THROUGH THE RAIN.

Marching Through the Rain.

BROILING THEIR SALT PORK.

Broiling Their Salt Pork.

Gen. J. D. Cox.

General Jacob Dolson Cox

Gen. Crook.

General George Crook.

COLONEL

JUNIOR MAJOR .

MAJOR

LIEUTENANT
COLONEL   FIELD MUSICIANS

SERGEANT
MAJOR

ADJUTANT

COLORS,
NATIONAL AND REGIMENTAL

RIGHT GUIDE & FILE CLOSERS   LEFT GUIDE

or
SERGEANT   TWO RANKS OF RIFLEMEN

CAPTAIN

RIGHT
FLANK   REGIMENTAL LINE OF BATTLE

The formation of the regimental line of battle as taught in 1861-62 in the basic training of drill and tactics.

A drawing of a Civil War Infantry charge in line of battle

Endnotes

Before the War and Including 1862

1   Quotation and paraphrase of George Mason's "Virginia Declaration of Rights", ratified by the Virginia legislature June 12, 1776; essentially a restatement of John Locke's theory of natural rights, which ultimately was re-written by Thomas Jefferson to become the most famous predicating statement of the American Declaration of Independence, declared July 2, 1776.

2   It is ironic to note in this context that no two things hurt the Confederacy more in her struggle to survive the war than the fact that there was constant shortage of skilled labor and that her industrial capacity was concentrated in a relatively few areas. In Virginia, areas of concentration were in vicinity of Richmond near the James River.

3   The act also levied an onerous poll tax of $10.00 per head to support the Confederate war effort.

4   On June 6, 1861, Brigadier-General Henry A. Wise (C.S.A.) had been given command of some portion of the standing army of Virginia (militia) and advanced into the Kanawha Valley. By July 24, Wise and his army were on the retreat from the Kanawha.

5   Harper seems to refer to the derogatory "slave-ocracy" of the South. Since the beginning of the early confederation, the South had maneuvered for preferred status because of their slaves. The "Three-Fifths Compromise" (1787); the exclusion of slaves from the Bill of Rights (1789); and passage of the Fugitive Slave Act (1793) served to expand the privilege and power of the Southern slave-holding States over other States, creating what was called a "slave-ocracy", a separate aristocratic class of slave-owners, who lived a lifestyle of ease and privilege of a kind virtually unknown in much of Western Virginia and non-slave-holding States of the North.

6   W.W.H. (dated "Point Pleasant, Va., Feb. 7, '63."), "What Voting Against the New State Will Do !" Point Pleasant Weekly Register, March 4, 1863 [this date marked out by hand and "February 21" written in] No. 50, [p.1].) The open and actively pro-Union stance offered up by Mason County citizens beginning in 1861 resonated with other like-minded individuals laboring for the same ends in other parts of Virginia. Jacob Bird, Rev. M.E. Church was another highly outspoken Methodist preacher (called by secessionists "abolitionist preachers"), who at this time was laboring against secession wherever he might find audience across the State. To this end, in his travels, he sought to rally leaders of the Methodist and Baptist Churches solidly for the Union cause and in with approach of the general referendum on secession scheduled for May 23, 1861, advocated opposition to secession. Bird was originally from eastern Virginia. He had a home both east (near Monterey, Virginia) and west of the Alleghenies (Mason City, Mason County, Western Virginia) and in May 1861 he travelled together with his wife through towns and cities of Western Virginia distributing circulars opposing secession and determining who among his fellow preachers of the M.E. Church at Mason City, Parkersburg, Clarksburg, Buckhannon, Beverly and Cheat Mountain might be counted upon to resist secession and be enlisted to distribute circulars etc. to get the word of resistance out. Bird's adventures were published in Narrative of Two Perilous Adventures Recently Made into Dixie's Land.

Also an Account of Captain S.B. Phillips' Adventures in Western Virginia Since the Breaking Out of the War (Pittsburgh: W.S. Haven, Corner of Wood and Third Streets), 1862. Although Bird does not mention W.W. Harper by name in his Narrative it is likely the two men met at Mason City in 1861, when Bird spoke with civic leaders of Mason County previous to May 6 when he indicates that after a stay there, he left Mason City on the steamer Henry Logan for Clarksburg. Bird's meeting with "prominent citizens" of Mason County added further justification to his reasons for traveling the country at such a dangerous time: publishing word of the proposed time of the first Wheeling Convention and encouraging attendance; or as he put it: spreading word that "gentlemen" of Mason County desired "to hold a convention at the city of Wheeling on the 13th, of May, 1861 to "adopt measures to protect us from the threatened aggression of Eastern Virginia; and also to protest against the unconstitutional and traitorous act of the Richmond Convention in passing the ordinance of secession". At Clarksburg he writes that he "distributed some circulars, showing the position which Mason county had taken, or at least many of her most prominent citizens, in the troubles then menacing our State." (For the forgoing quotations see Bird's Narrative, p. 5.)

7   Barbara Holland, "Bang! Bang! Your Dead," Smithsonian, October, 1997 Volume 28 No. 7, p. 133.

8   "Virginia County Vote on the Secession Ordinance, May 23, 1861," Antebellum Historical Files. Grayson County Virginia Heritage Foundation, Inc., and New River Notes, 1998-2016, www.newrivernotes.com/index.htm.

9   Mason City, Mason County, in the 'Big Bend Area' of the Ohio River was a commercial hub, a bustling river town where manufacture and commerce provided employment for skilled and unskilled labor. Salt manufacturing was done at a plant, boat building and access to transport was readily at hand for river transport of products east and west on the Kanawha and north and south of the Ohio. Mason City had been a favorite gathering place before the war and during the conflict it was a lively forum: "Brass bands, flag raisings, and speeches for one side or the other were the order of the day". See Mildred Chapman Gibbs, Hartford, W.Va. Mason City, W.Va. The History of the Town and Its People (Middleport, Ohio: Quality Print Shop, 1978), p. 24. Many 13th West Virginia volunteers were recruited at stations opened in Mason City and the Bend Area.

10   Point Pleasant, Hartford City, West Columbia and Mason City—all river towns in Mason County were strong commercial centers and nuclei of Union sentiment.

11   South Carolina was first to ratify secession on December 20, 1860. She was closely followed by Mississippi, Florida, Alabama, Georgia, Louisiana, Texas and Virginia, on May 23, 1861.

12   Parson Brownlow was the penname under which William G. Brownlow published his pro-Union editorial column. Publication of his editorial essays began in the 1840s when he was editor of The Whig and continued throughout the Civil War. His writings were relentlessly pro-Union and were served up in a style very like that of Samuel Clemens ("Mark Twain"), rich in humor, hyperbole and full of colloquialisms. His articles enjoyed wide circulation, also in Western Virginia papers where they resonated with particular urgency. He was a Virginian by birth and had as a young man in the 1820s ridden circuit as a Methodist minister. After the war he became a politician from the State of Tennessee. Andrew Johnson was of course, President Lincoln's vice-president. He was born in North Carolina but moved to Tennessee in 1826. He grew up poor, did not attend school and as an adult worked as a tailor. He married in 1827 and it was his wife, Eliza McCardle, who taught him to read, write and mathematics. He was a compelling speaker, a Democrat and like Andrew Jackson, he regarded himself as a champion of the common man. He disliked the wealthy, favored populist policies and supported the States' rights argument (i.e., that under the principle of federalism, States can reserve to themselves passage, interpretation and execution of their own laws distinct from the Federal government). Johnson believed that the U.S. Constitution provided authority for individual ownership of slaves but when secession threatened to dismantle the national Union he became a pro-Union Democrat. He was the only Southern Senator to remain loyal to the Union. At about the same time as Dan Rice was on circuit speaking out against secession in Mason City, Senator Johnson was doing the same in Tennessee in anticipation of a third referendum to be taken in June 1861, as to whether the State of Tennessee would secede or remain with the Union. East Tennessee, like Western Virginia voted to stay in the Union (in all three votes taken in February, April and June 1861) but as in the case of Virginia, Tennessee overwhelmingly voted for secession. In 1862, Johnson resigned his Senate seat when appointed Vice-President by Lincoln.

13   Dan Rice, "Union Speech to the Volunteers and Citizens of Mason County" (dated "Mason City, Mason County, Virginia, May 1861"), from Maria Ward Brown, The Life of Dan Rice" (Long Beach, N.J.: published by the author, 1901),pp. 371-73 in "History of Mason County, W.Va." (Accession # 203668 Call # RL035.433H), Huntington Public Library, W.Va.

Seizing the Reins

14   See for example, William Fletcher's account as recorded by journalist, Whitelaw Reid. Fletcher, a son of Indianapolis banker, Dr. Calvin Fletcher, was serving as a Union spy in June and July 1861 when he passed through northcentral West Virginia long enough to draw a map of the Confederate training camp on Laurel Hill, Barbour County, then led by General Robert S. Garnet and to form an opinion of the condition of the local population of the country through which he passed. Fletcher was reported to have indicated that families had "nothing to eat but corn bread made of such meal as they could make by pounding corn on stones." Their "pork, flour and potatoes even" had been appropriated by the "Secession army." One man, (whom Fletcher found hiding in the woods) had tried to hide his pork in the woods by burying it, but the rebels found it and taking it, threatened to take him as well for attempting to conceal it. Fletcher traveled as secretly as possible, "avoid[ing] all roads and travel[ing] as far as possible through the woods beyond the byways." Everywhere he found poor farmers of the neighborhood in hiding in the woods to avoid conscription into the rebel army. "When he came to houses children fled at his approach and the women were so frightened that sometimes he could hardly procure intelligible answers to the simplest questions. The whole country was swept of horses and wagons, and the rebels were seizing without ceremony upon all grain and provisions far and wide that they could secure." See Whitelaw Reid quoting William Fletcher, who had just returned from a two days trip through the area around Laurel Hill, West Virginia in "West Virginians" (dated "1861, July 4 From Philippi") in James Smart, ed., A Radical View. The "Agate" Dispatches of Whitelaw Reid 1861-1865 Vol. 2 (Memphis: Memphis State University Press, 1976), pp. 25-27.

15   "For the Post. West Virginia—A Song," Morgantown Weekly Post (Monongalia County, Virginia/West Virginia), January 14, 1865, p. [1]. I have often wondered about the words to this song. Did the fact that James Buchanan had shown himself to be a weak President, together with John Brown's raid in October 1859 and Lincoln's election in 1860 move members of the slave-owning States such as Virginia, to quietly prepare for war by seizing and massing arms for the sake of convenience and military advantage? Almost certainly this was done. The 1860 Census indicates that in Virginia, more slaves were owned than in any other State (490,865), exceeding even Alabama and Mississippi in the Deep South by some 50,000 slaves. Valuation tables taking in account premiums paid for slaves who were artisans and otherwise skilled and reductions in value made for low productivity due to age, sex, or physical impairment such as being crippled or alcoholic or a runaway slave (for which a 60% reduction in value was made) and the average value of slave in 1860 was about $800.00. Moral questions aside, the multiplying of these numbers yields a whopping total value of slave property in Virginia at $392,692,000. In today's money (conservatively estimated $25.00—1.00 1860 dollar) that amounts to a moneyed interest in slave property in excess of 12 billion 400 million dollars in Virginia alone. That, was a vast moneyed interest and it is surprising that Union sympathizers did not anticipate the South's commitment to protecting that interest. There was certainly recent precedent for this in Virginia. Patrick Henry, then member of the House of Burgesses as an initial act of war formed a militia and seized Lord Dunsmore's arsenal.

16   Richmond had reportedly promised 50,000 men from Western counties to Confederate armies.

17   Paraphrase of Lee A. Wallace Jr., comp., A Guide to Virginia Military Organizations 1861-1865 (Richmond, Va.: Civil War Commission, 1964),pp. 261-62. The 106th Virginia Militia (Mason County) which provided a significant number of officers and men to the 13th Regiment was re-organized by November 1861. Other militia units which supplied men and officers to the 13th were the following. Putnam County militia re-organizing beginning November 15, 1861 (earliest commissions for officers date to that day); Capt. Joel Cunningham's Home Guards Roane County, mustered in June 1, 1861 at New Kentuck, Jackson County; re-organization of Kanawha County militia was well underway by June 1862 (Greenbury Slack Jr.'s commission as Captain cmdg. 153rd Kanawha County Militia, dates to May 14, 1862 to rank from April 30, 1862) and the 80th Kanawha Militia was enrolling men beginning June 1862. Cabell County Militia was re-organized by October 28, 1861 and

Wayne County 167th Militia was mustered in May 7, 1862.

18 See Annual Report of the Adjutant General of the State of West Virginia, for the year ending December 31, 1865 (Wheeling: John F, M'Dermot,, 1865-1866), p.8 describing the dilemma and daring of civilians here: "At the commencement of the war, whole regiments were organized and mustered into the United States service, from portions of the State at that time occupied by rebel troops, and recruiting for both armies going on in the same county; our border counties continually overrun by guerrillas, murders and thefts being daily occurrences [...] insomuch that it would seem, that it would require every loyal man to remain home for the protection of his family."

19 R.B. Wilson, [late Captain 12th Ohio Infantry Volunteers, Kanawha Division], 842 Lincoln Avenue, Toledo, O[hio], "Kanawha Division: Its Campaigns. [Part] I," The National Tribune (Washington, D. C.), February 11, 1897, pp. [1]-2. Joshua Horton and Solomon Teverbaugh with the 11th Ohio Infantry, which spent the winter of 1861-62 at Point Pleasant enjoyed the hospitality of the community but in describing duty in this rugged terrain wrote that "[t]here was poor chance for glory among the mountains of West Virginia, however much skill or bravery might be displayed." See Horton and Teverbaugh, compilers, A History of the Eleventh Regiment, (Ohio Volunteer Infantry,) containing the military record, so far as it possible to obtain it, of each officer and enlisted man of the command—a list of deaths—an account of the veterans—incidents of the field and camp—names of the three months' volunteers, etc. etc. (Dayton, Ohio: W.J. Shuey, Printer and Publisher, "Telescope" Office, 1866, p. 260.

20 "Frank H. Adjutant, 1st West Va. Vet." to the Wheeling Daily Intelligencer (dated "Head-Qr's of 1st W.Va. Vet's."), "The First West Virginia Veteran Regiment of Infantry," Daily Intelligencer, July 27, 1865, p. 1.

21 "Guerrilla Warfare," reprinted from the Wheeling Intelligencer in the Ironton Register, December 5, 1861, p. 2.

22 "SNAKE HUNTERS!," Ironton Register, Dec. 19, 1861, [n.p.]

23 This wholesale policy of a State advocating that guerrilla warfare be conducted against her own citizens as was the case here was not the norm in other border States. There was regular military policy in place providing that if Union people were not openly hostile to the Confederate government and went peacefully about their business, then they should be left in peace.

24 [Untitled,] Point Pleasant Weekly Register, April 17, 1862, [p.3]. It is of some interest that the names of Laidley, Parks, Summers and Hoge are mentioned in this context. All four men were members of the Virginia elite. John Laidley (1791-1863) was a lawyer; veteran of the war of 1812; delegate to the Virginia Constitutional Conventions of 1829 and 1830; a member of the Southern Methodist Church; opposed secession; founded Marshall Academy which became Marshall University, Huntington and served as prosecuting attorney for Cabell County until his death. The three younger men, Parks, Summers (Laidley's so-in-law) and Hoge were as many men of wealth and power at that time and place: hovering somewhere between being Unionist with Southern sympathies and Southerners with Union sympathies; shifting their posture to conform to the dramatic changes taking place in local politics and on the battlefield. Andrew Parks served as delegate from Kanawha to the Virginia Assembly in 1842 and seems to have been an ardent and out-spoken secessionist in 1861. George W. Summers (1804-1868) was admitted to the Virginia bar in 1827; served as delegate from Kanawha County to the Virginia Assembly on more than one occasion; owned slaves but favored gradual emancipation beginning in 1832; represented his district at the U.S. House of Representatives; was appointed circuit court judge for the 18th district in 1851 and voted against secession in 1861, thereafter he relinquished his seat at the Virginia Assembly, and retiring from public life (according to modern biographies) took no part in the new State movement as he was also against Western Virginia's secession from Virginia. James Hoge (1830-1882) also a lawyer; became commonwealth attorney in Putnam County in 1856; represented Putnam as delegate to the 1861 convention at Richmond, where he voted against secession on both April 4th and April 17th but then supported the Confederacy by serving as colonel of militia in the early calls for Virginia's militarization.

25 John Booth, Dr., Records (manuscript dated "May 9 — 10, 1862, Summerville, Va." MSS180 Box 2 Ohio Historical Society at Columbus), pp. 111-12.

The Partisan Acts. Intended and Unintended Consequences

26 Wallace Jr., Virginia Organizations, p. 227, referencing in fn. 1 Acts of the General Assembly of the State of Virginia, Passed At Extra Session, 1862, in the Eighty-Sixth Year of the Commonwealth, Richmond, 1862, pp. 5-7.

27 Ibid., referencing in fn. 3, Official Records of the War of the Rebellion Ser. I Vol. 51 Pt. 2, pp. 620-21.

28 Lewis Wetzel, "[Editorial,]" Point Pleasant Weekly Register, March 6, 1862, [n.p.] On the other hand, it must be recognized that this was no easy problem to maneuver. That is, dealing decisively with partisan raiders, local bushwhacker type terrorists, and Confederate forces and not just embittering local secessionists.

29 A letter from General John B. Floyd to Governor John Letcher (undated in reprint) was published in excerpt in the November 1, 1862 edition of Leslie's Illustrated Newspaper, p. 83. Floyd, recently appointed Major-General of Virginia Militia was at the time of this writing, himself recruiting partisans in Western Virginia. If the letter is authentic it provides interesting description from perspective of the former governor of Virginia, now Confederate officer and recruiter. Floyd informs the following: "I have been aware of abuses and outrages of a most monstrous and shocking character, committed by those who I believe are organized as 'partisan rangers,' under authority of the Confederate officers—but so scrupulous have I been in abstaining from what might by the little and the ignorant be construed into unwarrantable interference, that I have forborne to issue any order to prevent what it was the duty of every Confederate officer, in the name of humanity, to put a stop to. The chief causes of the disaffection among the people of a large part of this community have arisen from the high-handed acts of robbery and rapine committed by many of the 'partisan rangers.' I know that a commission, if fairly executed, would disclose a lawlessness and monstrous abuse of authority and power which would be astonishing and shocking, and which would call for and insure from the Secretary and the President prompt reform, and stern measures of redress against any repetition of them." (General [John B.] Floyd to the Governor of Virginia, [letter undated] reprinted in "Guerrillas," Leslie's Illustrated Newspaper, November 1, 1862, p. 83.

30 There seemed to be no lack of guerrillas in West Virginia at this, nor at any time during the conflict. Whenever Union troops were withdrawn for service in some other military theater and particularly when Confederate military fortunes were on the wane, rangers seemed to swarm making targets of citizens, property and any vulnerable military post. In Spring 1864, when West Virginia troops such as the 13th West Virginia were concentrated and withdrawn for use in the concerted movement against Confederate armies and lines of supply that became the Shenandoah Valley Campaign of 1864, bands of partisans filled the vacuum. Bands numbering from 12 to 15 to over 200 operated widely in Western Virginia. In Ceredo, Wayne County, for example, which had long been a hotbed for rebel activity, there was no longer any Federal military quartered in Ceredo—no regiment closer than Guyandotte, Cabell County (another hotbed requiring constant vigilance). By February 1865 things in Ceredo had so degenerated that in a history of the town published at that time was this: "Disloyalty has cropped out under drunkenness and personal hate, until one's life is endangered at any moment. Guerrillas and rebel sympathizers occupy the principal houses vacated by the owners. Not a public building stands untouched. The window and door frames, flooring and every sleeper of the Hotel have been torn out and burned up. The dismantling of the steam saw mill, and Match and Glass Factories, have long since been accomplished. Night is made hideous by the continued debaucheries of certain desperate characters, such as Jack Meddows and Pete Jeffers. There is not a loyal family left in Ceredo." ("Ceredo, West Virginia," reprinted from the Ironton Register in the Point Pleasant Weekly Register, Feb. 23, 1865 Vol. III No. 46, [n.p.])

31 A.J. Watterson to Adj. Gen. H.J. Samuels at Wheeling, Va. (dated "Mason County, Virginia, May 2, 1862"), Calendar of the Frances Harrison Pierpont Letters and Papers in W. Va. Depositories Prepared by the W. Va. Historical Records Survey Division of Professional and Service Projects, Works Projects Administration (Charleston, W.Va.: Historical Records Survey, October 1940), pp.109-10.

32 Bill Harper "perhaps the most notorious bushwhacker and outlaw in West Virginia" was said to have killed more men, absconded with more horses and destroyed more property "than any other man in the State." He was surrounded and killed in Pendleton County W.Va. but "did not give up his life" till shot "by 14 bullets." (Point Pleasant Weekly Register, February 25, 1864, [p.2].

33 On June 21, 1862 scouting parties from the 11th Virginia Infantry Volunteers, stationed at Spencer, Roane County, drove and routed Captain Downs and about twenty of his men in Roane.

34 Hurston/Herston and Burwell Spurlock together with M.J. and James Ferguson, among others are named as defendants in a suit of trespass on the case and attachment by plaintiff William O. Wright for wrongs and injuries done to person and property. See Point Pleasant Weekly Register, February 11, 1864, [p.3].

35 Albert G. Jenkins' command, the Border Rangers (later Company E, 8th Virginia Cavalry) had organized almost immediately after the Virginia legislature voted for secession. Jenkins representing Cabell County, had voted in favor of secession and upon his return from Richmond, met with his constituents at "Green Bottom," his plantation on the Ohio River. At this time, he informed them of the results of the vote and apparently invited them to his home for dinner. "Most of the men were armed with shotguns and after dinner each man provided himself with a piece of lead pipe of which Jenkins had a quantity." From there they "went to the old Green Bottom Church where they met a number of men from Mason County. The 101 men present, organized themselves into a company, and elected Jenkins Captain." See George Selden Wallace, Cabell County Annals & Families (Richmond: Garrett & Massie, Publishers, 1935), pp. 77 and 79; also Joe Geiger, Jr., The Civil War in Cabell Co., W. Va. 1861-1865, (Charleston, West Virginia: Pictorial Histories Publishing Co., 1991), p.10.

36 On May 15th, the State Line Act was passed by the Virginia General Assembly at Richmond to jumpstart enlistment for a new force with which to recover Western Virginia and her valuable Kanawha Valley salines. The Virginia State Line was to be strictly a volunteer force, not to be raised from those already obligated to serve under the new Confederate States Conscription law of April 16th, 1862 and the State line was not to exceed 10,000 in number (an optimistic number). Recruits were obligated to serve for just one year, long enough—it was supposed—for Federal forces to be driven from the West. Maj. Gen. John B. Floyd (elected Virginia Governor in 1848 and Secretary of War under President James Buchanan) was authorized to raise the volunteers. It was an uphill battle. The only pool from which Floyd could draw were those not liable for the draft, that was, those between age 35 and 45; and those under age eighteen. What Floyd soon found to his dismay was that the population of the Kanawha Valley and "the whole section" was largely disaffected from Virginia and the Southern cause and he could not raise volunteers. Floyd had to cast a wider net. To jumpstart Floyd's recruiting efforts, Governor John Letcher issued a proclamation on June 27th, (1862) in which he ordered the Virginia State Militia to report immediately to Floyd and enlist as volunteers in the State Line troops. This measure could scarcely have prompted much of a showing and is rather another indication of just how out of touch Richmond was with her Western citizens. Then to make matters worse, Floyd ran amuck of other recruiting officers enrolling recruits for the Confederate States Army. In the mountains near the Tennessee border, Brigadier-General Humphrey Marshall, C.S.A., stationed at Abingdon, Virginia complained that Floyd was recruiting from partisan ranger units and marching them off. This, stated Marshall was "exceedingly detrimental to the service of the Confederacy, and Governor Letcher ought to have it stopped." (H. Marshall to Hon. George W. Randolph, dated Abingdon, Va., August 19, 1862, O.R. Vol. XVI Part II, p. 765.) Floyd enlisted only about 4,000 men. These came from Virginia, Kentucky and Tennessee. February 28, 1863, the State Line was transferred to the Confederate States, by an act of the Virginia Assembly. (Wallace, Jr., Virginia Organizations, p. 236.)

37 Geiger, Jr., Civil War in Cabell County., pp. 52-53.

38 Sylvester Myers, Myer's History of West Virginia Vol. I (Wheeling, W. Va.: Wheeling News Lithograph Co., 1915), p. 471.

Major General John Fremont Stirs Things Up

39 The re-organization occurred together with President Lincoln's order that the Federal Armies commence a general advance against "Southerners in Rebellion."

40 Clarkson Fogg (an Ohioan serving in the 4th Regiment West Virginia Volunteer Infantry which had been recruited from southern Ohio and the northwestern counties of Virginia for instance, observed that Gen. Fremont's appointment to take over command of the department gave "general satisfaction here among officers and men, for the reason that it is believed he will pursue the policy indicated by his active movements while in command of the Department of the West. [...] All we ask is to be brought to face the Rebels and we will perform our duty to the satisfaction of those who looked to us to

conquer this rebellion [...] the majority of soldiers here as elsewhere, have lost confidence in McClellan [...] his inactivity [...] It is impossible to tell what disposition will be made of the West Virginia troops by Fremont." See Clarkson Fogg to his father (dated "Ceredo, March 29, [1862]"), "Letters of Corporal Clarkson Fogg," as published in excerpted transcription for sale in The Horse Soldier, Catalog 23 (Cashtown, Pennsylvania, [no date]), p. 45. Quartermaster of the 4th Regiment W.V.V.I. in his letter to the Register also approved, writing that "the appointment of Fremont as our leader, is generally well received by the 'boys.' Those who cannot agree with his politics, seem to have confidence in his ability and his willingness to 'do something or die young.' Which is the true spirit of young America, and will suit our boys to a T." See "Qr. Master, 4th Va. Reg. to Editor Register" (dated "Ceredo, Wayne County, Va., March 24th, 1862"), "Letter from the Fourth Virginia Regiment," Point Pleasant Weekly Register, March 20, 1862, [n.p.] Reader will notice that the later date of the 4th Va. correspondence and publication date of the paper suggest a misprint.

41   On August 30, 1861, Fremont was relieved of command by President Lincoln just as he was about to confiscate property from Missouran secessionists (that is, by emancipating their slaves). Lincoln feared that such measures might alienate other border States and drive them to the Confederacy. Lincoln's own Emancipation Proclamation of September 1862 to take effect January 1, 1863 was still another year away.

42   At Point Pleasant, there were nine Companies of the 11th Ohio Vol. Infantry (763 men); at "Buffalo Coals Mouth +c." eight Companies of 8th Virginia Vol. Infantry (806 men); at Charleston ten Companies 12th Ohio Vol. Infantry (989 men) and one Company 12th Ohio Vol. Cavalry (86 men); at Camp Piatt (12 miles above Charleston) ten Companies of 44th Ohio Vol. Infantry (951 men) and one Company 1st Virginia Vol. Cavalry (82 men); at "Clifton +c."(30 miles above Charleston) were ten Companies of the 37th Ohio Vol. Infantry (845 men); at Gauley Bridge were ten Companies of 28th Ohio Vol. Infantry (889 men) and one company 1st Illinois Volunteer Dragoons (88 men); entrenched at Gauley Mount ten Companies 47th Ohio Vol. Infantry (794 men) and one Company Ohio Vol. Artillery (107 men); at "Summerville + vicinity" were ten companies of the 36th Ohio Vol. Infantry (915 men); at Fayetteville were ten companies of 30th Ohio Vol. Infantry (670 men), five Companies of 23rd Ohio Vol. Infantry (377 men) and one company Ohio Vol.Artillery (98 men); at Beckley there were five companies of 23rd Ohio Vol. Infantry (377 men) and one company 2nd Virginia Vol. Cavalry (86 men); at Guyandotte were eleven companies of 2nd Virginia Vol. Cavalry (744 men) and six companies of 9th Virginia Vol. Infantry (566 men); at "Barboursville +vicinity" were ten companies of 34th Ohio Vol. Infantry (970 men); and at Ceredo (at the mouth of Twelve pole) were ten companies of the 4th Virginia Vol. Infantry (868 men). (W.I. Rosecrans to Brig. Gen. L. Thomas, Adj. Gen. U.S.A. at Washington. Report of the number and disposition of forces in the District Kanawha, which comprised "all the valleys of the Kanawha Guyandotte and mouth of Big Sandy, Brig. Genl. D. Cox Commanding" (manuscript dated "Hd. Qtrs Mountain Dept., Wheeling March 24, 1862" Letter 21 Registry # 393 Part I Mountain Department [No 16, 19MTN] Entry 3122 1 Volume Letters Sent National Archives and Records Administration at Washington D.C.), pp. 74-76.

43   Ibid., p. 76.

44   Fremont by Tracy, General Orders No. 11 (manu. dated "Head-Quarters, Mountain Department, Wheeling, Va., April 7, 1862" Miscellaneous West Virginia Papers NARA. At first, Fremont's tougher stance seemed to have had a quieting effect in at least one county. One Ohio soldier, E.H. Ever, (Co. F. 11th Ohio Vol. Infantry Regt.) stationed far to the interior at Raleigh, Mercer County indicated as much in his missive dated "Raleigh C[ourt] H[ouse], June 19, 1862" "No military news. All quiet in the mountains, and the tread of the bushwhacker is heard no more, since the proclamation of General Fremont ordering to take no more prisoners but substitute a leaden bullet." They don't like the Union bullets, and consequently they make themselves scarce." (Ever to "Friend Tippett," "Letter from the Eleventh Ohio Regiment," Point Pleasant Weekly Register, June 26, 1862, [p.1.])

45   "Public Meeting Last Monday," Point Pleasant Register, Thursday April 10, 1862, [p. 3].

46   Henry Jefferson Samuels (born 1825 in Barboursville, Cabell County) was a lawyer and one of the leading Union men in Northwestern Virginia. He attended Marshall Academy, a prescription school at Barboursville (later Marshall University); read law with an uncle and practiced law in his home county with such eminent attorneys as Elisha McComas and James H. Ferguson. Samuels was uncompromising and outspoken in his opposition to secession. With passage of the Secession Ordinance at Richmond on April 17th, 1861 and ratification of the ordinance in the general referendum of May

23rd, Samuels' prominence in the community and well-known stand against secession made of him a target and in June of 1861 he was forced to flee Cabell County. His fortunes had shifted by September 1861 when with restoration of the State government (the Provisional Government of Virginia) at Wheeling, Samuels was appointed West Virginia's first Adjutant General. He served the Union cause and his community prominently during the precarious days of the war, notably from 1863 to 1866 as Circuit Court Judge of Cabell County. (See Geiger, Jr., Civil War in Cabell County, p. 96.)

47   Captain of Militia, William Shannon, resident of Wayne County, Virginia was mustered in as Sergeant of Company H, 13th Regiment West Virginia Infantry Vols. on October 10, 1863 and immediately promoted to 2nd Lieutenant on November 1, 1863.

48   J.B. Baumgardner to H.J. Samuels, (manu. dated "Ceredo April 16, 1862"), Letters to Samuels and Pierpont Box 1 Folder 31, West Virginia State Archives, Charleston. Heretofore, business "ha[d] been almost entirely suspended in Ceredo" as residents of the town had "mostly left." With the coming of Spring, those remaining hoped to "revive business" but with the latest wave of raids, a local armed force was obviously a necessity not only to protect life and property but to provide some stability if business and trade were to resume. See Letter to Editors of the Press, (dated "Fourth Virginia, Ceredo, Va., March 22, 1862") reprinted from the Wheeling Daily Press in the Point Pleasant Weekly Register, April 10, 1862, [p.1].

49   Theodore F. Lang, Major 6th W.Va. Cavalry and Brevet Colonel, Loyal West Virginia From 1861 to 1865 (Baltimore, Md.: The Deutsch Publishing Co., 1895 reprinted Huntington, W. Va: Blue Acorn Press, 1998), p. 18.

50   Anna Starr to her Mother (manu. dated "Mason City [Virginia], May 5, 1862" SC1400), Civil War Files of William C. Starr, Indiana Historical Society, Indianapolis.

51   Maj. Gen. Fremont quoting Gov. F.H. Pierpont, in Orders to Colonel J.A.J. Lightburn, cmdg. at Charleston, by Albert Tracy, Col. & Assist. Adjt. Gen. (dated "Hdqtrs. Army in the Field, Petersburg, May 10, 1862"), reprinted in Melbourn C. Spaulding, "Records of Official Correspondence of the Federal and Confederate Armies in the Kanawha River Valley, 1861-1864" (1976), W.Va. State Archives, Charleston, as cited by Geiger, Jr., Civil War in Cabell County in Ch. 6 fn. 10, p. 138.

52   Ibid.

53   Bumgardner et. al. to Samuels, (dated May 14, 1862, Ceredo, Wayne County), Calendar of Pierpont Letters and Papers, p. 118.

54   There had been ten companies of Col. Joseph A. J. Lightburn's 4th Virginia Volunteer Infantry Regiment stationed here (about 868 men).

55   Tax collector

56   Baumgardner to Samuels, Adj. Gen. (manu. dated "Ceredo Wayne Co., Va. May 14, 1862") Letters to Samuels and Pierpont Box 1 Folder 31, W.Va. State Archives (hereinafter WVSA).

57   "Rebel Guerrillas in Western Virginia," reprinted from the New York Times in the Point Pleasant Weekly Register, May 1, 1862, [p. 3].

58   The terms jayhawk and jayhawking came into usage in Kansas, during the 'Bleeding Kansas' period of the 1850s, when the issue of permitting Kansas to enter the Union as a slave state of free, was bitterly contested by gangs of militia. The term is a combination of two aggressive birds living in Kansas: the sparrow hawk and the blue jay and jayhawking came to mean to make a sudden predatory attack, as a raid. The term seems to have been coined by pro-slavery groups in Missouri and Kansas but became adopted as a term of endearment by pro-Union groups in Kansas, Missouri and Western Virginia. A jayhawker was a pro-Union guerrilla or partisan fighter. Today it is the name for Kansans and is their State symbol.

Raising a Regiment: Mason County, Virginia. A Case Study

59   Quotations in this paragraph are taken from "Public Meeting Last Monday," Point Pleasant Weekly Register, April 10, 1862, [p. 3].

60   Chapter 190 "Offences Against the Sovereignty of the State," The Code of Virginia. Second Edition, Including Legislation To The Year 1860 (Richmond: Ritchie, Dunnavant & Co.), p. 783.

61   Ibid., "Public Meeting Last Monday," Weekly Register, April 10, 1862, [p. 3]. Formation of Committees for Public Safety

had been urged before. On August 20, 1861, Gen. W.I. Rosecrans, wrote from headquarters addressing loyal citizens of West Virginia urging that "each town and district choose five of its most reliable and energetic citizens as a committee of public safety, to act in concert with the civic and military authorities and be responsible for the preservation of peace and good order." See Brig.-Gen'l U. S. Army Commanding "To the Loyal Citizens of West Virginia," (dated Headquarters Army of Occupation, Clarksburg, W. Va., August 20, 1861), reprinted in Lang, Loyal West Virginia, p. 45. Language regarding what constituted "suspicious persons" was contained in Declaration of the People of Virginia of June 13, 1861 passed in the Ordinance of June 19, 1861 (the ordinance passed by the Wheeling Convention declaring independence and the reasons for severing ties with Virginia and authorizing re-organization of a new State government and appointment and election of officers upon a loyal basis) which broadly interpreted suspicious persons as those "requiring submission" to the "pretended edicts and decrees" of the State of Virginia; those seeking to enforce conscription into the Confederate armies for "offensive as well as defensive purposes" and those persons, who have instituted "a reign of terror intended to suppress the free expression of the will of the people, making election a mockery and a fraud" and those seizing and appropriating Government property; "organizing and mobilizing" for purposes of war against the national Union. See "Declaration of the People of Virginia Represented in Convention at Wheeling June 13, 1861" in W.S. Laidley, ed., "West Virginia Birthday," The West Virginia Historical Magazine Quarterly, Jan. 1901, Vol.1 No.1: p. 24.

62   John Hall, Sr. was a lawyer, an entrepreneur, politician, delegate to the Virginia legislature at Richmond before the war and major player in setting up the Provisional Government of West Virginia. He represented Mason County at the Wheeling Conventions, purchased arms upon his own note, secured loans to cover payment of bounties to new recruits and was instrumental in the recruitment of the 4th and 13th West Virginia Infantry Regiments in whom his sons, John, Jr. and James R. Hall served respectively, as officers.

63   "Public Meeting Last Monday," Weekly Register, April 10, 1862, [p. 3].

64   [Editorial], Point Pleasant Weekly Register, May 20, 1862, [n.p.]

65   Ibid., Weekly Register, May 20, 1862, [n.p.] "Secret meetings, not open to public view and free to every passerby" were perceived as "incendiary" by both Unionists and Secessionists. (Point Pleasant Weekly Register, June 5, 1862, [p.2].)

66   Lewis Wetzel was an accomplished and civic minded man in a long line of such men. It is claimed in Wetzel family history, that his namesake and grandfather was Lewis Wetzel (of Marshall County, Virginia/West Virginia) a famed scout and combatant in the American frontier conflicts of the 18th century. Lewis Wetzel, the editor, wore many hats. He served in the Virginia House of Delegates and as Mason County Justice; was an ardent supporter of the Union and instrumental in re-organization of the State and local government following Richmond's passage of the secession ordinance.

67   [Lewis Wetzel, ed.], "Guerrilla Warfare," Point Pleasant Weekly Register, May 22, 1862, [p. 2].

68   [No title], Point Pleasant Weekly Register, May 29, 1862, [p. 2].

69   G. Slack to F.H. Pierpont (manu. dated "Ka Charleston May 24th 186[2]"), Letters to Samuels and Pierpont Box 6 Folder 28, WVSA.

70   G. Slack to H.J. Samuels, (manu. dated "Charleston June 10th 1862"), Letters to Samuels and Pierpont Box 6 Folder 28, W.Va. State Archives. Correspondent is Greenbury Slack, Esquire or Greenbury Slack, Junior, his son, Captain 153rd Kanawha County Militia State Troops; commissioned 1st Lieutenant of Co. A 13th West Virginia Volunteer Infantry Regiment on Sept. 9, 1862 and promoted to Captain Co. A July 20, 1863.

71   G. Slack to H.J. Samuels (manuscript dated "Charleston June 10th 1862"), Letters to Samuels and Pierpont Box 6 Folder 28, WVSA.

72   "Mass Meeting in Kanawha," Point Pleasant Weekly Register, July 3, 1862 Vol. 1 No. 17, [p. 1].

73   D.R. King, cmdg., Orders (dated "Head Quarters Camp Ravenswood, June 7, 1862"), Point Pleasant Weekly Register, June 19, 1862, [p. 1].

74   Point Pleasant Weekly Register, July 3, 1862, [p. 2].

75   Those exempted were "all telegraph operators and maintenance personnel, engineers, artificiers, and workman employed in any public armory or arsenal, members of Congress, the Vice-President of the United States, customs officials, postal officers, and stage drivers, the merchant marine, and all persons exempted by the laws of the respective States

from military duty." See Francis Lord, They Fought for the Union, (Harrisonburg, Pennsylvania: The Stackpole Company, 1960), p. 4 and fn. 32 p. 18 citing for authority O.R. Third Series, Vol. 2, pp. 333-35. For the lighter side of exempted persons, see "Who Are Exempt from Draft" in "Appendix" at the end of this volume.

76   "The following orders have been issued by the War Department for the regulation of conscription," Ironton Register, August 21, 1862 Vol. 13 No. 6,[p. 2].

77   Point Pleasant Weekly Register, July 31, 1862 Vol. 1 No. 21, [p.2]. The extent of pro-Union sentiment can safely be gauged by the ratio of slaves to white population. Bearing in mind that by summer 1862, many slave holders were away in service in Confederate armies and assuming the following numbers are more-less a true accounting, consider that in June of 1862, Mason County was reported as having a total population of 9,138: 8,752 white with just 386 slaves. (Weekly Register, June 5, 1862, [p. 1].)

78   "Governor's Proclamation" (dated Executive Department, Wheeling, V[irgini]a. July 16, 1862), reprinted in the Point Pleasant Weekly Register, July 24, 1862 Vol. 1, No. 20, [p. 2].

79   Governor Francis H. Pierpont, "Message to the State Senate and House of Representatives," Point Pleasant Weekly Register, December 18, 1862, pp. 1 and 4.

80   "Governor's Proclamation" (dated "Executive Department, Wheeling, V[irgini]a. July 16, 1862"), Point Pleasant Weekly Register, July 24, 1862, Vol. 1, No. 20, [p. 2].

81   The foregoing list of men authorized to take names of volunteers is a short list of major players in securing the New State movement. Delegates to the 1st Wheeling Convention (May 13, 1861) were W.W. Branfield/Brumfield, John Hall, James F. Scott, George Leonard, and [E.T.] Graham/Grayham. Delegates to the 2nd Wheeling (June 11, 1861) were again Brumfield, Hall, Scott and Graham. John Hall also served as commissioner (together with Ephraim B. Hall of Marion Co., Peter Van Winkle of Wood Co., and Elbert H. Caldwell of Marshall Co. also appointed) to set before Congress Western Virginia's petition for statehood. The commissioners arrived at Washington on May 22, 1862; on May 29 the petition was presented; and on July 29, 1862 the U.S. Senate approved Western Virginia's admission to the Union pending ratification of an amendment to the State constitution providing for an immediate end to slavery (the Willey Amendment). Attorney Granville Parker of Cabell Co., an outspoken opponent of secession, who had been forced to flee the State in 1861 returned to join the Wheeling Conventions which met 1861-1863. Parker also went to Washington on his own account together with Lt. Gov. Daniel Polsley and Harrison Hagans to assist the May 1862 commission in securing statehood. Parker also wrote many newspaper articles informing the public about the progress of the new State movement which, in keeping the issue before the people boosted moral of both pro-Union citizens of that section and West Virginia soldiery. Parker's articles were collected published in 1881 under title, The Formation of West Virginia and Other Incidents in the Civil War.

82   For the forgoing quotations and paraphrase see "Governor's Proclamation," (dated Executive Department, Wheeling, V[irgini]a. July 16, 1862) and "To the Loyal Men of the 45th Senatorial District composed of the Counties of Mason, Wayne, Cabell, Jackson, Wirt and Part of Roane," both from the Point Pleasant Weekly Register, July 24, 1862, Vol. 1, No. 20, [p. 2]. The initial encampment of volunteers was typically located in the home community. This arrangement however, was typically temporary. Regimental life where instruction was administered usually took place in encampments removed from the home community. In the case of the 13th West Virginia they had little time to train as a regimental unit before they were divided to garrison, scout, guard and otherwise quiet and hold the country along and between the waterways.

83   "Annual Return of Alterations and Casualties incident to the Thirteenth Regt. of Va. Vol. Inf., Commanded by Col. Wm. R. Brown during the year 1862," Record Group 94 (RG94 Miscellaneous Unbound Regimental Papers Box 4838 13th W. Va. Inf. Vols. Annual Returns of Casualties 3 NARA).

The Point Pleasant *Weekly Register* and the 13ᵗʰ Regiment

84   "Meeting in Malden," Point Pleasant Weekly Register, June 19, 1862 Vol. 1, No. 15, [p. 2].

85   According to West Virginia's premier historian Virgil A. Lewis, in 1860 the only "American" weekly published in western Virginia was the Mason County Republican" it "had a circulation of 750" subscribers. See Lewis, First Biennial Report of the

Department of Archives and History of the State of West Virginia (Charleston: Tribune Printing Co., 1906), p.60.

86 "Great Mortality Among Newspapers in Western Virginia. From the Wellsburg Herald," Wheeling Daily Intelligencer, March 3, 1862, p. 2.

87 There is some evidence that recruiting stations once opened remained open during the conflict. John L. Mason recalling the state of affairs of West Columbia, Mason County during the war noted that "Occasionally, a confederate, worn out and starved would attempt to pass through town one way or the other and then the home guards, armed with shot guns, rifles or corn cutters would get out and capture the poor fellow who was either taken to Point Pleasant or Wheeling or Mason City where there was a recruiting station." (Mason, "A Reminiscence. West Columbia a Half Century Ago Letter 2," Point Pleasant State Gazette, June 24, 1909, [p.1].)

88 George W. Tippett was born January 31st, 1836. He moved to Point Pleasant in 1855 and purchased "a printing estab-lishment" shortly before February 10th, 1862, presumably with the intention of publishing a pro-Union newspaper. He was a pro-Union Democrat and made no bones about it. The Weekly Register office was located on the corner of Third and Main Street, in Point Pleasant. (George W. Tippett, ed., "The Twenty-Ninth Year of the Register," The Weekly Register, June 11, 1890, [p. 2].)

89 Henry J. Fisher was admitted to the bar in 1823 and practiced law until his death January 31st, 1883. As a young man he worked as a tinner and knew what it was to be poor. He was in every sense of the word a self-made man. He was said to have been "well-studied in American and English law," was very successful as a lawyer, accumulated a consid-erable fortune and amassed one of the largest libraries in the State. He was "considered by some the greatest lawyer of his time."(Robert H. Ferguson, History of Mason Co., W. Va., Point Pleasant, W. Va.: Col. Charles Lewis Chapter N.S.D.A.R., 1961, pp. 154-55.) Fisher was remembered in post-war years by one "Mr. Swallow" as a "venerable old lawyer". He was "in his prime" at the time of the Civil War and "[h]is spirited arguments with the men of the neighborhood [were] fresh in [Swallow's] memory. Mr. Fisher was one of the leading spirits of this section of the state and, in later years, became one of the warmest advocates of secession. He was one of the founders of the constitution of the Southern Confederacy and invested the bulk of his fortune in Confederate bonds, in aid of the cause he had espoused." ("Looking Backward Eighty Years. Reminiscences as Gleaned From Mr. Hiram H. Swallow and Others Who Remember the Past of this Locality," State Gazette, Thursday, July 29, 1909, Poffenbarger Papers Vol. 3, p. 24, Mason County Public Library at Point Pleasant.)

90 Horton and Teverbaugh, A History of the Eleventh Regiment, pp. 58-59.

91 The editors of the "Eleventh Ohio" were Charles H. Wright, H[iram] R. Howard and H. Lanbright. (Ibid., Horton and Teverbaugh, History of the Eleventh Regiment, p. 255.)

92 Wheeling Daily Intelligencer, March 3, 1862.

93 Roy Blessing, Former Reporter Remembers Early Register, a loose-leaf informational sheet accompanying the recon-structed Register office at the State Farm Museum, Point Pleasant, West Virginia, n.d.

94 George W. Tippett, "The Twenty-Ninth Year of the Register," The Weekly Register, June 11, 1890, [n.p.]

95 Ibid.

96 Ibid., Tippett, "The Twenty-Ninth Year of the Register," [n.p.] The printing office had had a series of proprietors, who had all failed for lack of patronage. By October 20th, 1864, however, the Register could boast that it had the "largest circulation of any paper published in this section of West Virginia" and that it was "the only one in this Congressional District that is published regularly." ("To Advertisers," Weekly Register, Oct. 20, 1864, [p. 3].) Point Pleasant was a town of commerce and re-shipping. Stocks of goods were bought by merchants from large commercial centers for resale here. They arrived by wagons, keel and flat boats. It became a big center for pork-packing and re-shipping. Setzser, Beale & Company, where Lewis Wetzel had a business interest, did big business pork packing. All pork from Gallia and Meigs Coun-ties was said to have been brought to Point Pleasant packing concerns for packing and re-shipment on the rivers. There were large warehouses and store-houses but as indicated by Tippett, few residences. The close of the Civil War found the town with too many inhabitants for accommodations and many moved away, unfortunately for the town, many of these were skilled labor looking for a better opportunity.

97 [Editorial], Weekly Register, October 10, 1862, [p. 2].

98 Livia Simpson-Poffenbarger, "Battle of Point Pleasant," Poffenbarger Papers, Vol. 9, pp. 17-18, Mason County Public Library, Point Pleasant.

99 Lewis Wetzel was shot to death in October 23rd, 1862, shortly after the 13th had been organized, by another Union man from the front lines—non-other than John Hall, Esquire, (father of Lt. Col. James R. Hall, of the 13th Volunteers). The vacant editorial chair of the Register was taken over on November 20th, 1862, by E.M. Fitzgerald (also written Fitz Gerald). E.M. was a local attorney. He practiced in Mason County and kept an office opposite the Mason County Courthouse. He also served as Secretary at the Mason and Putnam County Public Meetings held in 1862 and in 1863 served as a commissioner for the county committee in charge of securing county bounties for volunteers. (See Poffenbarger, "Battle of Point Pleasant," pp. 17-18 and Ferguson, History of Mason Co., W. Va., p. 117.)

100 Point Pleasant Weekly Register, Thursday October 16, 1862, Vol. 1 No. 30, [p. 2].

101 William W. Harper, Methodist Episcopal Minister at Point Pleasant, was sanctioned in 1862, to perform marriages and to take oaths of allegiance to the commonwealth. (Ferguson, History of Mason Co., W. Va., p. 125.) After the war, Harper did less preaching and instead became a teacher and entered political life. In 1866, he was elected Court Clerk of Mason County, West Virginia. See "First Edition. The $400 Story," Columbus, Ohio Dispatch, Friday August 25, 1876, [n.p.], in Comly Papers, microfilm Reel 2, p. 151, Rutherford B. Hayes Presidential Library, Fremont, Ohio.

102 Due to river access and to the quantities of coal found in Mason County, it became attractive to entrepreneurs from the New England States seeking to launch manufacturing: coal to fuel the endeavor and the Ohio River to serve as conveyance. The town of Hartford City came into being as a result of such a business venture. In 1853, capitalists from Connecticut, Morgan Buckley and William Healey started the Mason County Mining and Manufacturing Company and established the town of Hartford City (named for Hartford, the State capitol of Connecticut) on a portion of land on the Ohio River. Salt extraction was begun in 1856 and a post office opened in 1858. The company advertised for "all classes of workers" which included of course, the renting of slaves for labor. To what extent slaves were employed here, in a county where the Methodist Church North had a strong presence and what long-term effect employment of slaves might have had is beyond the scope of this study. Regimental descriptive rolls and military pension records suggest that it was white laborers that were drawn to enterprises from the Ohio Valley and farther afield. In the short-term, a brisk trade was done and boat traffic was lively. Hartford City became a boom town and other mines also came to be established, notably at New Haven (named for another Connecticut town). See, James T. Laing, "The Early Development of the Coal Industry in the Western Counties 1800-1865," West Virginia History, January 1966 Vol. 27 No. 2, pp. 144-55.

103 W.H.H., "To the Editor" (dated "September 22, 1863"), Point Pleasant Weekly Register, October 9, 1862, [p. 2].

104 The full quote is a follows: "It affords us much pleasure to announce that our esteemed friend W.W. Harper of Hartford City, has been appointed to this honorable position [Sergeant Major] in our new regiment—the 13th Va—He will bring to the discharge of his new and arduous duties, ready penmanship, a business tact, and also unexceptionable habits. We assure him of our best wishes in his new field of labor for the glorious old Union so dear to him." ("Sergeant Major," Weekly Register, October 9, 1862, [p. 2].)

105 Committees of Safety served as official boards before whom local residents were brought to determine where their loyalties lay. Usually the signing of an oath of allegiance satisfied committee members and the arrested person was released.

106 MAC [pseud.], "From Western Virginia," letter to the Cincinnati Commercial (dated "Gallipolis, [Ohio], Sept[ember] 18, 1862"), reprinted in the Point Pleasant Weekly Register, September 18, 1862, [p. 1].

107 "The Weather," Point Pleasant Weekly Register, Oct. 9, 1862, [p. 2].

108 An article entitled "Who are Entitled to Pensions" (Point Pleasant Weekly Register of April 30, 1863 Vol. II, [n.p.]) explained the new entitlements passed by Congress. The act granted pensions to the following: disabled or invalid soldiers, who had served in the Union army since March 4th, 1861; old widows; children (under age 16); as well as mothers and sisters of soldiers killed in battle, or who died of wounds received or disease contracted in the line of duty. The new provisions were more liberal than the old pension laws for the War of 1812. Non-commissioned officers, musicians and privates received $3.00/month; 2nd Lieutenants received $15.00/month; 1st Lieutenants received $17.00/month; Captains received

$20.00/month; Majors received $25.00/month and all officers of high rank received $30.00/month. For those veterans, who were only partially disabled, the amount of pension was rated according to their disability (one fourth, one half etc.). The proportion was discretionary and was assigned typically by an examining physician as a fraction, that is the degree to which the wound or disease contracted in the line of service actually disabled a man from obtaining a livelihood.

June and July 1862:
"Will we be driven out of the Kanawha Valley?"

109 See James M. McCann, Army of Northern Virginia for his description of scouts who served as mail carriers between Confederate soldiers at the front and their families at home in Western Virginia. They travelled only at night on unfrequented paths carrying as much as one hundred letters or more at a time, with about six days rations, blankets and heavy arms. They rested by day often at the home of some devoted Southerner in any number of ingenious hiding places described by McCann (tunneled out straw ricks; false floor boards, etc.). The scout also gathered intelligence as to numbers and troop movements and also recruited for the Confederate army. He might remain in hostile territory for months and finally march out into the night with as many as a hundred men. ("Scouting in West Virginia," Confederate Veteran, July 1894 No. 2, pp. 214-15).

110 Paraphrase of Tim McKinney, The Civil War in Fayette County West Virginia (Charleston, West Virginia: Pictorial Histories Publishing Co., 1988), p. 23.

111 J.B. McGinnis to H.J. Samuels, (dated Mason County, Virginia, June 27, 1862), Calendar of Pierpont Letters and Papers, p. 135.

112 J.B. McGinnis to H.J. Samuels (manu. dated "Mason County, Virginia, June 27, 1862"), Letters to Samuels and Pierpont Box 4 Folder 39, WVSA.

113 "What is the Prospect?," Gallipolis Journal, July 31, 1862, p. 3.

114 "S.P.C.," a soldier correspondent to the Cincinnati, Ohio Gazette (dated Meadow Bluff, Va. June 18, 1862), reprinted from the Gazette of June 28, 1862 as "Designs of the Rebels," in the Point Pleasant Weekly Register, July 3, 1862, [p. 3].

115 [Lewis Wetzel], [Editorial], Point Pleasant Weekly Register, July 31, 1862 Vol. 1 No. 21, [p.2].

116 President Abraham Lincoln to Governor F. H. Pierpont, (telegraph dated Washington, July 28, 1862), Calendar of Pierpont Letters and Papers, p. 151.

117 Cabell County boom towns of Guyandotte, Barboursville and smaller centers along the Ohio such as Mud Bridge and Howell's Mill had long been well connected by road and boat to Eastern Virginia and the South and with the outbreak of hostilities, all became centers for Confederate activity. Guyandotte and Barboursville were important commercial hubs on the Ohio River. They were connected to Richmond by the James River and Kanawha Turnpike (extended to Guyandotte in the 1830s) and by tributary roads such as the Charleston-Point Pleasant turnpike completed 1838; the Fayette-Kanawha pike completed 1848 and the Gauley Bridge pike completed 1850. More than this, Cabell County citizens made provision for road maintenance by setting up tollgates at 4 mile intervals for collection of revenue. In 1854, John Laidley, Peter Buffington and others from Guyandotte had a suspension bridge (initially a toll bridge) built across the Guyandotte River near town. Such improvements promoted commerce, prosperity and strengthened ties to markets and other interests in Eastern Virginia and with the South. Skilled labor such as tanners, tailors, shoemakers, and blacksmiths were attracted to the area, hotels, livery stables, department stores and other amenities were added. Guyandotte became one of the largest shipping ports on the Ohio River. Cash crops such as grain, pork and lumber from fertile bottom lands adjacent were prepared and packed here for conveyance. With expansion of business, oak bottoms for steamboats were cut at the lumber mill of Miller & Moore and Buffington Mill became one of the largest mills in that stretch of the Ohio River (that is, between Cincinnati and Pittsburg). Neighboring Barboursville became known for its manufacture of brick, furniture, wagons, buggies, harnesses, barges; steamboat bottoms, and attire such as hats. Commerce and prosperity established by routes overland and by water on the Ohio and Mississippi Rivers for over 30 years thus closely connected Cabell County citizens with Eastern Virginia and markets in the South in a way that did not happen with neighboring towns upriver, which

had not enjoyed the benefits of such public improvements. See Charles H. Ambler, A History of West Virginia, (New York: Prentice Hall Inc., 1933), pp. 242-43 and Geiger, Jr., Civil War in Cabell County, p.2.

118 "State of West Virginia," Point Pleasant Weekly Register, July 21, 1864, [p. 2].

119 John Alford to H.J. Samuels, (manu. dated "Barboursville, Cabell Co., Va. July 10, 1862"), Letters to Samuels and Pierpont Box 1, Folder 7, WVSA.

120 Samuel A. Childers to H.J. Samuels, (manu. dated "Barboursville July 12, 1862"), Letters to Samuels and Pierpont Box 1 Folder 120, W.Va. State Archives.

121 John Alford to H. J. Samuels, (manu. dated "Barboursville, Cabell County Court House July 18, 1862"), Letters to Samuels and Pierpont Box 1 Folder 7, WVSA.

122 A.C. Mason to William E. Wetzel, Marshall of Mason County, John Hall to H.J. Samuels in postscript (manu. dated "West Columbia, Virginia, July 21, 1862"), Letters to Samuels and Pierpont Box 4 Folder 59, WVSA. Gallipolis had long served as a depot of supplies for the Kanawha Valley. With the commencement of hostilities, many Federal troops passed through Gallipolis, great warehouses were built near the river to contain government stores and supply the army and a sprawling army hospital capable of accommodating 4,000 patients had been built on the Barlow Farm at the upper end of town near the river.

123 R.C.M. Lovell to Adj. Gen. H.J. Samuels, at Wheeling (telegraph dated "Mason City, Mason County, V[irgini]a, Feb[ruary] 31, 1862"), Calendar of Pierpont Letters and Papers, p. 91. Old State muskets were in use in 1861 when they could be obtained. At best, they were suitable for hunting small game but they were not up to the mark as a weapons of war.

124 Gallipolis Journal, July 31, 1862, p. 3.

125 See Dr. Nare to Col. J.A.J. Lightburn (dated Buffalo, July 27 [1862] and forwarded to Gen. J.D. Cox), reprinted in Geiger, Jr., Civil War in Cabell County, p. 70, Geiger citing in fn. 11, p. 138, Spaulding, "Records of Official Correspondence of the Federal and Confederate Armies in the Kanawha River Valley, 1861-1864," WVSA.

126 Buffalo, wrote a correspondent to the Point Pleasant Register was a town famous for "mud, dog-fennel and contraband whiskey." ("By Peg," "Buffalo Items," Point Pleasant Weekly Register, July 24, 1862 Vol. 1, No. 20, [p. 2].)

127 J.A.J. Lightburn, Col. Comdg. Brig[ade]., Special Order No. 33, (dated "Hd. Qtrs. 4th Brig. Charleston. Aug. 1, 1862" Registry # 393 Pt. 2 Entry 1219 Press Copies of Letters Sent and Special Orders May — Sept. 1862 National Archives and Records Administration, Wash. D. C.), p. [91].

Recruitment in the Valley

128 Hewitt's paraphrase of the Surgeon's remarks. William Hewitt, History of the 12th West Virginia. Volunteer Infantry. The Part It took in the War of the Rebellion 1861-1865, 12th W.Va. Infantry Association, [1892], p. 5.

129 Moses Martin to his Father (manu. dated "Camp Simmons Charlestewn Va June 7th/62"), Moses E. Martin Military Pension file, NARA.

130 William Shannon, Captain to H.J. Samuels (manu. dated "June 24, 1862, Wayne County, Virginia"), Letters to Samuels and Pierpont Box 6 Folder 11, WVSA.

Organization of the Regiment Moves Forward

131 W.I. Mathews, 1st Lieut. and Adj. 13th Regt. Va. Vol. Infantry to Adj. Gen. H.J. Samuels (manu. dated "Ravenswood, Virginia July 29, 1862"), Letters to Samuels and Pierpont Box 4 Folder 60, WVSA and Calendar of Pierpont Letters and Papers, p. 151.

132 William I. Mathews, 1st Lieutenant and Adjutant 13th Regt. Va. Vol. Infantry to H.J. Samuels, Adjutant General of the State of Virginia (manu. dated "Point Pleasant, August 19, 1862"), Letters to Samuels and Pierpont Box 4 Folder 60, WVSA.

133 Gist was married to Polsley's daughter Ada. Daniel Polsley (born 1803 in Palatine, Marion County, West Virginia) had been a lawyer since 1827 and an editor publisher (of the Western Transcript a Whig newspaper) beginning 1833. In 1845

he sold out his law practice and closed his printing office and took up agricultural pursuits on a 1,200 acre farm in Mason County, along the Ohio River opposite Racine, Ohio. Here he lived quietly until 1861, when he was elected to represent Mason County at the Wheeling Conventions of that year. During the process of setting up of the Provisional State Government, he was appointed Lieutenant-Governor under Gov. Francis H. Pierpont. In 1862 he was made judge of the 7th West Virginia Circuit Court, in which capacity he served until 1866, when he was elected as a Republican to the 40th U.S. Congress. He served for one term only and upon his return removed to Point Pleasant where he died in 1877. See George W. Atkinson, L.L.B and L.L.D, Bench and Bar of West Virginia, Charleston, W. Va.: Virginian Law Book Co., p.30.

134 George W. Gist, 2nd Lieutenant to H.J. Samuels (manu. dated "Letart Mason County, Virginia August 30, 1862"), Letters to Samuels and Pierpont Box 2 Folder 98, WVSA.

135 The Slack family were early settlers in Kanawha County. John and Greenbury Slack were prominent in business and civic affairs of the county. The family was Methodist Episcopal. (George W. Atkinson, A.M., History of Kanawha County, Charleston: Printed at Office of the West Virginia Journal, 1876.) Greenbury Slack, Esquire was elected State Senator in the November elections of 1864.

136 T. Maher to H.J. Samuels, (manu. dated "Point Pleasant, Mason County, Virginia, September 1, 1862") Uncatalogued 13th W. Va. Box, WVSA.

137 RG94 Miscellaneous Records (List of Commissioned Officers of Co. A 13th Regt. W.V.V.I. NARA), [p 1] and 13th Regiment Infantry, "Roster of the Regiment," WVSA, p. [4].

138 Kanawha County State troops were mustered beginning June 10, 1862, at Charleston. (Militia West Virginia on micro. WVSA).

Appointment of Officers and Recruitment of the 13th Continues

139 For the foregoing quotations, see "Papers concerning the examination of Lt. H. Atkinson 13 Va. Vols regarding his fitness for the Colonelcy of the 13th," M508 Compiled Military Service Records of Volunteers 13th Regiment Infantry Union (Personal Papers arranged by organization microfilm roll 260 NARA).

140 Whaley died in 1876 and was buried in Lone Oak Cemetery, Point Pleasant, West Virginia. See Sandy Leuthold, "Whaley Family of Mason County, W.Va.," History of Mason County, W. Va., 1987 2nd ed. (Waynesville, N.C.: Walsworth Publishing Co., 1991), p. 373.

141 "How Many Soldiers Have We Got!," Weekly Register, March 20, 1862, [p. 2].

142 "Certificate of Disability for Discharge" (RG 94: Records of the Adjutant General's Office Compiled Military Service Records 27th Pennsylvania Regiment Infantry Vols. NARA, Washington D.C.), courtesy of Mike Musick,.

143 K.V. Whaley to Gov. Pierpont at Wheeling, Va., (manu. dated "Washington City D.C. 7th January 1862"), Uncatalogued 13th West Virginia Infantry Regiment Box, WVSA.

144 Charles R. Doran, Colonel, Staff and Field Officers 13th Regiment, Uncat. 13th W.Va. Inftry. Regt. Box, WVSA.

145 Cowan to Pierpont, (manu. dated "Washington Jan. 13. 1862"), Uncat. 13th W.Va. Box, WVSA.

146 Dorone to Pierpont, (manu. dated "Head Quarters 13th Regiment Company A, Eastern Virginia Brigade, Philadelphia, Pennsylvania, Feb. 18, 1862, No. 344 and 347, North 3rd Street"), Letters to Samuels and Pierpont Box 2 Folder 35, WVSA.

147 Underwood to Pierpoint, (manu. dated "Fifth Auditors Office Feby 10, 1862"), Letters to Samuels and Pierpont Box 6 Folder 98, WVSA.

148 Underwood to H.J. Samuels, at Wheeling, (manu. dated "Fifth Auditors Office Feby 28, 1862"), Letters to Samuels and Pierpont Box 6, Folder 98, WVSA.

149 Charles R. Doron, Col. 13th Regt. Va. Vols. to General Lorenzo W. Thomas, Adjutant Genl. U. S. Army, (manu. dated "Head-quarters 13th Regiment Virginia Volunteers, No. 344, & 347 North 3rd St., Philadelphia, Feb. July 19th 1862" RG 94 Letters Received Volunteer Service Branch File D 108 V.S. 1862 NARA), courtesy of Mike Musick.

150 Ibid.

151 Colonel Charles R. Doron, commanding 13th Regiment Virginia Volunteers to Governor Frances H. Pierpont, at Wheel-

ing, (telegraph dated "Washington, February 27, 1862), Calendar of Pierpont Letters and Papers, p. 90.

152 Underwood to [Gov. F.H. Pierpont], (dated Fifth Auditor's Office at Washington, February 28, 1862), Calendar of Pierpont Letters and Papers, pp. 90-91.

153 Whaley to Pierpont, at Wheeling, (telegraph dated Washington, March 1, 1862), Calendar of Pierpont Letters and Papers, p. 91.

154 Doron to Hon. Edwin M. Stanton, Secretary of War, (manu. dated "Philadelphia, Penna., July 10th 1862" RG 94. Letters Received Volunteer Service Branch File D 458 V.S.1862, NARA), courtesy of M. Musick.

155 Ibid.

156 Charles R. Doron, Late Col. 13th Regt. Va. Vols. to Abraham Lincoln, President of the United States, (manu. dated "Philadelphia, Penna., July 19th 1862" RG 94 Letters. Received Volunteer Service Branch File D 656 V.S. 1862 NARA), courtesy of M. Musick.

157 Gen. A.J. Williams et al to Sec. Edwin M. Stanton, (manu. dated "Hd. Qtrs. 3 Brigade Genl Banks Div Hancock, Md. Feb. 26, 1862"), Uncat. 13th W.Va. Inftry. Regt. Box, WVSA.

158 Grafflin, Christopher L., Staff and Field Officers 13th W.V.V.I. Regiment, Uncat. 13th W.Va. Inftry. Regt. Box, WVSA, [n.p.].

159 Lewis Wetzel, W.H. Tomlinson. Charles B. Waggoner, James H. Holloway and W.E. Wetzel to Adjutant General H.J. Samuels at Wheeling, Virginia (dated Point Pleasant, Virginia, August 2nd, 1862), Calendar of Pierpont Letters and Papers, p. 154.

160 13th Regiment Infantry, "Roster of the Regiment," WVSA, p. [4].

161 See a rather cryptic letter written by a superior officer [Rosecrans ?] to one "Col. H" of the 1st Virginia Cavalry from "Hd. Qtrs Department of Western Va., [at] Wheeling," in which the writer informs "Col. H." that "H." "had no authority to recall Lt. W.E. Feazil of the 1st Va. Cav from recruiting service as he was detailed for a tour of 6 months and could not be recalled except by superior authority." See [Rosecrans ?] to Col. H, cmdg. 1st Virginia Cavalry (manu. dated "Hd. Qtrs. Dept. of Western Va., Wheeling, Jan. 24, 1862" Registry # 393 Part I Volume 1 Mountain Department [No 16, 19MTN] Letters Sent [Letter 38] Entry 3122 NARA), p. 16

162 Pierpont to Samuels, (manu. dated "Wheeling, July 19, 1862"), Letters to Samuels and Pierpont Box 6 Folder 3, WVSA.

163 RG94 Miscellaneous Records (List of Commissioned Officers of Co. C 13th Regt. W.V.V.I. NARA),[n.p]. Feazel was transferred from Co. C and commissioned 1st Lieutenant Co. I, 13th Virginia on January 21st, 1863 and mustered in with that company as 1st Lieut. on May 1st, 1863. He was promoted to Captain of Co. I on December 18th, 1863 to fill an original vacancy and mustered in as captain of this company on December 24th, 1863. Capt. Feazel resigned and was discharged from the U.S. Service on December 19th, 1864. See Lang, Loyal West Virginia, p. 287; Co. I Commissioned Officers, "13th Regiment Infantry Roster of the Regiment," WVSA, p. [43] and "Thirteenth Regiment Infantry, Roster of the Field, Staff and Company Officers from the date of original organization to the date of muster out, on 22d day of June, 1865, Compiled from muster-out rolls," Francis P. Pierpont, Adjutant General State of W. Va., Annual Report of the Adjutant General of the State of West Virginia for the Year Ending December 31, 1865 (Wheeling: John Frew, Public Printer, 1866), p. 55.

164 Manu., Uncat. 13th W.Va. Inftry. Regt. Box, WVSA, [n.p.]

165 Ibid.

166 R.C.M. Lovell to H.J. Samuels, (manu. dated "Mason City, [Virginia], July 22, 1862"), Uncat. 13th W.Va. Inftry. Regt. Box, WVSA, [n.p.]

167 Van D. McDaniel had served as Surveyor for Mason County Road District No. 34 before his military service. (Mason County Court Records November Term 1862, p. 326.)

168 Lewis Wetzel et.al. to F.H. Pierpont, Gov. of Va., (manu. dated "Point Pleasant, Va., July 23rd, 1862") Box of 14th West Va. Infantry Regt., Adjutant General Papers, WVSA, courtesy of Terry Lowry.

169 Letter to Pierpont (manu. dated "July 21, 1862"), Uncat. 13th W.Va. Inf. Regt. Box, WVSA.

170 Greenberry Slack to H.J. Samuels, (manu. dated "Charleston, [Virginia], July 24, 1862"), Uncat. 13th W.Va. Inf.. Regt. Box, WVSA.

171 Calendar of Pierpont Letters and Papers, p. 150.

172 All the foregoing men are named in papers contained in Uncat. 13th W.Va. Inf. Regt. Box, WVSA.

173 George W. Story, 4th W.Va. Vol. Infantry, to F.H. Pierpont, (manu. dated "Charleston, Kanawha County, Virginia, August 1, 1862"), Letters to Samuels and Pierpont Box 6 Folder 60, WVSA.

174 Calendar of Pierpont Letters and Papers, pp. 153-54.

175 John Hall, Major 4th Virginia Infantry to John Hall, Sr., (dated "Charleston, [Va.], August 1, 1862"), from the private papers of William Matthews of Huntington, a descendent of John Hall, Sr. Just days after writing this letter, Maj. Hall died of mortal wounds received in action on August 6th, (1862) at the Kennedy farm on Beech Fork, near Chapmansville. Hall and his command, a detachment of 4th V.V.I., which included Milton Stewart, (future Capt. Co. B 13th V.V.I.), who stayed with Hall until he expired, were attacked by guerrillas under "Colonel Stratton, Major Witcher and Captain Herndon". (Calendar of Pierpont Letters and Papers, pp. 166-67.)

176 James R. Hall to H.J. Samuels, (manu. dated "Head Qtrs 13th Regt Va Vol Pt. Pleasant Aug. 28, 1862"), Uncat. 13th W.Va. Inftry. Regt. Box, WVSA.

177 James R. Hall to H.J. Samuels, (manu., dated "Head Qtrs 13th Regt Va Vol Pt. Pleasant Aug. 28, 1862"), Uncat. 13th W.Va. Inftry. Regt. Box, WVSA.

Mason County Provides for Its Volunteers

178 "Putnam," "Letter for the Register" (dated "Putnam county, Aug. 5, 1862"), Point Pleasant Weekly Register, August 7, 1862, [p.2].

179 Point Pleasant Weekly Register, July 31, 1862 Vol. 1 No. 21, [p. 2].

180 Ibid.

181 Point Pleasant Weekly Register, August 7, 1862,Vol. 1 No. 22, [p. 2]. The September 10th terminus may have been extended at least once more. The $25.00 city bounty would be available to recruits who enlisted before September 20th, 1862; any recruit enlisting after Sept. 20th being ineligible. (Point Pleasant Weekly Register, September 4, 1862, [n.p.])

182 Lieut. William E. Feazel to Adj. Gen. H.J. Samuels at Wheeling, (dated Point Pleasant, Virginia, August 5th, 1862), Calendar of Pierpont Letters and Papers, p. 156.

183 Geiger, Jr., Civil War in Cabell County, p. 77.

184 In the early days of the war, Richard Bush held clandestine Union meetings in the dead of night, at his home on Redmond Ridge, in vicinity of the Kanawha in Clendenin District, Mason County. His residence and farm were located across the Kanawha and upriver from Point Pleasant. Such meetings were termed "incendiary" and "Abolition meetings" by secessionists and if discovered, repercussions could be expected. Besides his duties as Justice of the Peace, and other roles of civic duty which he assumed, he was a rather well-to-do farmer. He had married Mary Ann Eads in 1832 and they raised a large family of fourteen children. Richard's nephews: William A. Eads; David Eads and Charles H. Eads would all enlist in the 13th Virginia Infantry Volunteers this summer.

185 James H. Holloway, Clerk of the Mason County Court, [Untitled], Point Pleasant Weekly Register, August 7, 1862, p. 2 and John Hall, "Bounty Commissioners," Mason County Journal, June 19, 1867, [p.2].

186 Ibid., "Bounty Commissioners."

187 Ibid.

188 Point Pleasant Weekly Register, September 4, 1862. The September 10th terminus may have been extended at least once more. September 20th was also publicized as a cut-off date for recruits to receive the local bounty; any recruit enlisting after Sept. 20th being ineligible. About a year later, a notice appeared in the Weekly Register, informing Mason County volunteer soldiers that the county court had decided to pay to every volunteer in Mason county, the $30.00 extra bounty originally promised only to the first one hundred and twenty-five men, who had enlisted. ("Entitled To Volunteers," Weekly Register, September 4, 1863 Vol. 1 No. 26, [n.p.])

189 Mason County Court Records, Copy Teste W.W. Harper in John Hall, "Bounty Commissioners," Mason County Journal June 19, 1867, [p.2].

190 A.I. Boreman to Gov. Pierpont recommending Fulton (manu. dated "Parkersburg, Va., Aug. 4, 1862"), Uncat. 13th W.Va.

Inf. Regt. Box, WVSA.

191 J.B. Bumgardner to H.J. Samuels (manu. dated "August 3, 1862"), Letters to Pierpont and Samuels Box 1 Folder 31, WVSA.

192 Manu. (dated "Aug. 4, 1862"), Uncat. 13th W.Va. Inf. Regt. Box, WVSA.

193 Calendar of Pierpont Letters and Papers, p. 154.

194 James P. Elkins, 2nd Lieutenant to Adjt. Gen. H. J. Samuels, at Wheeling (dated Coalsmouth, Kanawha, Co., V[irgini]a, August 5th , 1862), Calendar of Pierpont Letters and Papers in W.Va. Depositories, p. 156.

195 John S. Cunningham to H.J. Samuels (manu. dated "Coalsmouth August 28, 1862"), Letters to Samuels and Pierpont Box 2 Folder 11, WVSA. Two days later, on September 30th, Capt. of Co. G, John V. Young, in camp with the 13th at Point Pleasant reported to Gov. Pierpont, that he had 86 men present for duty in his Company and that he had 97 men present and absent. See Young, Capt. cmdg. Co. G, 11th Regt. Virginia Vol. Inftry., to F.H. Pierpont, Governor of Virginia (manu. dated "Point Pleasant, Mason County, Virginia September 30th, 1862"), Letters to Pierpont and Samuels, WVSA. John S. Cunningham, was transferred from 11th Infantry Volunteers and promoted to 1st Lieutenant and Adjutant of the 13th W.Va. Regiment on June 6, 1863. See 13th Regiment Infantry, Roster of the Regiment, WVSA, [p. 1].

196 Protocol for this was established early on by General Orders issued by the War Department on May 25th, 1861. These orders directed governors of States to appoint a surgeon and assistant surgeon for each regiment.

197 S.S. Slack to Gov. Francis H. Pierpont, at Wheeling (telegraph dated Charleston, Virginia, August 20th, 1862), Calendar of Pierpont Letters and Papers, pp.171-72.

James R. Hall Recruits a Company

198 John Hall to H.J. Samuels (manu. dated "Point Pleasant, July 25, 1862"), Letters to Samuels and Pierpont Box 3, Folder 5, WVSA.

199 John Hall to J.H Samuels, Adj. Gen. Wheeling, Va. (manu. dated "Point Pleasant Oct. 31, 1861"), Adjutant General Correspondence 1861-65 Miscellaneous, WVSA, courtesy of Terry Lowery. Student records at Virginia Military Institute indicate that James R. remained a student there for one year and two months.

200 A private soldier's actual pay was considerably less than $200 per year. Monthly pay amounted to $13.00. Perhaps Hall added all bounties together with estimates for clothing, food and medical, added this to $156.00 per year (a private's total pay for a year) and divided by three years obligation to arrive at the $200.00 per year amount.

201 "Volunteers Wanted," Point Pleasant Weekly Register, Thursday July 31, 1862 Vol. 1 No. 21, [p.2]. Hall probably made arrangements with local private citizens to subsist and quarter his recruits. Union citizens, such as M. Westmoreland, of Hartford City, Mason County, subsisted "State Militiamen and 13th recruits in 1862, before they were mustered into service." (M. Westmoreland to "Adjutant General State of W.V." (manu. dated "Hartford City, Mason County, W. V., 1865"), Uncat. 13th W.Va. Inf. Regt. Box, WVSA. Hall reportedly "recruited a company within a week, and was elected Captain." ("Death of Lieut.-Colonel James R. Hall," Point Pleasant Weekly Register, October 27, 1864, [p. 2].)

202 [No title], Point Pleasant Weekly Register, July 31, 1862 Vol. 1 No. 21, [p.2].

203 "Get Substitutes," Weekly Register, July 31, 1862, Vol. 1 No. 21, [p.2].

204 Ibid.

205 Paraphrase of "Volunteering and Drafting," Point Pleasant Weekly Register, July 31, 1862 Vol. 1 No. 21, [p.2].

206 Quotes and paraphrase of "The Draft," Point Pleasant Weekly Register, August. 21, 1862 Vol. 1 No. 24, [p. 2].

207 John Hall to H.J. Samuels (manu. dated "Point Pleasant, July 30, 1862"), Letters to Samuels and Pierpont Box 3 Folder 5, WVSA. James was busy serving process before the county court convened on August 4th. When court did convene it was a busy few days at Point Pleasant.

208 Hall to Samuels (manu. dated "Point Pleasant, Virginia August 4, 1862"), Letters to Samuels and Pierpont, WVSA.

209 John Hall to Adj. Gen. H.J. Samuels (manu. dated "Point Pleasant August 17, 1862"), Letters to Samuels and Pierpont Box 2, WVSA.

210 Theodore Lang provides numbers, writing that Maj. John T. Hall's force numbered just 48 men. They were attacked

(continued Lang) by "200 Confederate mounted infantry" under command of "Colonel Stratton and Major Witcher, at Beech Creek, near Logan Court House. (See Lang, Loyal West Virginia, p. 246.)

211 Hall to Samuels (manu. dated "Point Pleasant August 17, 1862"), Letters to Samuels and Pierpont Box 2, WVSA.

212 Sergeant Milton Stewart, Co. K, 4th Virginia (West) Volunteer Infantry, "Murder of Major Hall," Gallipolis Journal, August 21, 1862, p. 2.

213 "Death of Lieutenant -Colonel James R. Hall," Point Pleasant Weekly Register October 27, 1864, [p. 2] and James R. Hall, Muster out Card, Uncat. 13th W.Va. Inf. Regt. Box, WVSA.

214 In addition to the advantage of having one of the finest military educations, Crook was a gifted military tactician in his own right. He was revered and respected by his men. It was said that he had his headquarters on the skirmish line and led his troops by example from the front. He was, to quote one of his subordinate officers "a notably keen, resolute and clearheaded man, genial, low speaking and inclined to reticence, whose equanimity was never disturbed or ruffled under the most trying circumstances." See Henry A. DuPont, "Battle of Fisher's Hill" (WS 31768 dated 9-26-[19]21), Hagley Museum and Library, Wilmington, Delaware, trans., p. 5.

215 Point Pleasant Weekly Register, July 31, 1862, [p. 1].

216 War Department, "Order" (dated "August 8, 1862"), Point Pleasant Weekly Register, August 14, 1862, [n.p.]

217 Point Pleasant Weekly Register, August 14th, 1862, [p.2].

218 Ibid. The States and military districts took it upon themselves to deal with captured guerrillas, inasmuch as the Federal Government could not make up its mind what to do with them. One of the reasons for this was that when it was decided to put guerrillas to death, the Confederate government let it be known that they would also put to death an equal number of Federal prisoners held by them, and the issue stalled.

219 Point Pleasant Weekly Register, August 7, 1862, [p. 2].

220 William E. Feazel, 2nd Lieutenant 13th Regiment Virginia Volunteer Infantry to H.J. Samuels, Adj. Gen. of Virginia (manu. dated "Head Quarters 13th Va. Vol. Inf[an]t[ry] Recruiting Station, Point Pleasant, V[irgini], August 11, 1862"), Letters to Samuels Folder #188, WVSA.

221 Brigadier General W.I. Rosecrans to Gov. Pierpont, at Wheeling (telegraph dated Clarksburg, Virginia, Aug. 12th, 1862), Calendar of Pierpont Letters and Papers, p. 164.

222 J.P.R.B. Smith (John Peter Roman Bureau—named for a distinguished French emigrant to Gallipolis), nicknamed "Alphabet Smith," was born in Point Pleasant March 17th, 1838 to Nathan Smith and Ann (Roseberry) Smith. Smith had been a collector of revenue and then was appointed Colonel of Militia by Governor Henry A. Wise of Virginia. When the Civil War broke out, then Virginia Governor, John Letcher commissioned Smith Colonel of the 106th Regiment Virginia Militia. The 106th became part of the loyal West Virginia Home Guard. As head of the Home Guards, he prevented the shipment of contraband goods through the Kanawha Valley, supported regular army units as might be required and otherwise used his guards as a peace-keeping force. When Jenkins raided Point Pleasant on March 30th, 1863, Smith cooperated with Captain John D. Carter, commanding Co. E of the 13th, to protect the town. On July 28th, 1864, he was appointed to the U.S. Volunteer Army with the rank and pay of major. He was assigned to the Department of West Virginia and ordered to Wheeling.

Smith was also an enterprising businessman. Described as a "polite young man of popular manners" he became in summer of 1862, the proprietor of the Virginia House, a once popular hotel, which had fallen on hard times as had much of business at that time. Smith reopened the hotel for customers on August 11th, 1862. After the war, on May 10th, 1865, he married Maria L. Thomas. He was appointed delegate to the Senatorial Convention (as was Peter Darnell, late Captain formerly of Co. I of the 13th). Smith was a candidate for county recorder in 1868 and was unanimously elected by delegates to the County Convention for that year. By 1894, Smith was serving his third term (6 years to the term) as Mason County Clerk. He died in Mason County on October 20th, 1911. See "Point Pleasant, West Va," *Illustrated Industrial Edition. The State Gazette Supplement,* Thursday, February 2, 1905, p. 9; "Col. J.P.R.B. Smith Dead," *Poffenbarger Papers,* Vol. 5, p. 66, Mason County Public Lib., Point Pleasant, W.Va.; "Virginia House," Point Pleasant *Weekly Register,* August 14, 1862, [p.2]; *The Mason County Journal,* August 21, 1867; "Township Meetings," the *Mason County Journal,* September 2, 1868, [n.p.] and "Democratic and Conservative County Convention," *The Mason County Journal*, September 9, 1868, [n.p.]

223 Brigadier General George C. Bowyer, commanding 22d Brigade Virginia Militia to Col. J.P.R.B. Smith, (dated "Winfield, Virginia, August 4, 1862"), as cited by Smith "Commander of the 106th" in "Notice of Regimental Muster" to the officers and privates of the 106th in "ATTENTION MILITIA," Point Pleasant Weekly Register August 7, 1862, [p. 2].

224 H.J. Samuels to F.H. Pierpont (manu. dated "Wheeling, Va., Jan. 3, 1861"), Letters to Samuels and Pierpont Box 6, Folder 3, WVSA.

225 Announcement that the re-organization of the Mason County Militia was "entirely completed" was made in "County Militia," Point Pleasant Weekly Register, March 6, 1862, Vol. 1 No. 1, [p. 3].

226 Ibid. Smith's intentions would seem to have placed the militia on sterner footing. Consider remarks made by State Adj. Gen. Pierpont in his annual report for 1865, that before the Civil War, militia was required to assemble 4 times annually and that these musters were "always [...] a burlesque on military organizations." (Pierpont, Annual Report of the Adjutant General of the State of West Virginia, p. 19.)

227 "County Militia," Point Pleasant Weekly Register, March 6, 1862 Vol. 1 No. 1, [p. 3]. "Muster day" had in previous years also been an occasion for some socializing and "imbibing" as evidenced by the following. One "Mr. Swallow," a former resident of Mason County born May 1823, visited Mason Co. from Minneapolis, Kansas, in his 87th year and recalled memories from when he was about 6 years old. He said: "at that time, every store sold liquor and that a bar in connection with a hotel was a matter of course. There was no revenue on whiskey and it was consequently cheap. There was little drunkenness, the most being evident on Saturday, when the weeks work was done, or at the conclusion of 'Muster Day.' Before the men departed for their homes, they all imbibed." See "Looking Backward Eighty Years. Reminiscences As Gleaned from Mr. Hiram H. Swallow and others Who Remember the Best of this Locality Article II," The State Gazette (Point Pleasant, W.Va.), July 29, 1909, in History of Mason County, W.Va. (Accession # 203668, Call # RL 975.433H), Huntington Public Library, [p. 1].

228 "106th Regiment Mason County," West Virginia State Troops Artillery and Militia (micro.), WVSA.

229 Ibid.

230 [Captain John T. Greer], "Original Muster Roll of Company A, 116th Regiment West Virginia Militia" (manu. dated "March 10, 1861" "Torn from an old ledger," owned by Greer and in 1889, given by him to Livia Simpson-Poffenbarger, publisher of the Point Pleasant State Gazette, who donated the original to the Department of Archives and History, Charleston W. Va., December 15, 1929), copy of orig. manu. in Poffenbarger Papers, Vol. 9 pp 1-2 and trans. pub. in the State Gazette in Poffenbarger Papers Vol. 5, pp. 54-58 and Vol. 9, pp. 3-7, Mason County Public Library, Point Pleasant, W.Va.

231 [Greer], "Muster Roll of Company A, 116th Regiment West Virginia Militia" and RG 94. Miscellaneous Records (Descriptive Books Company A, B and C NARA), [n.p.]

232 G. Slack to F.H. Pierpont (manu. dated "Ka Charleston May 24th 186[2]"), Letters to Samuels and Pierpont Box 6 Folder 28, WVSA.

233 G. Slack to the Governor [F.H. Pierpont] (manu. dated "Charleston March 20th 1862"), Letters of Samuels and Pierpont Box 6 Folder 28, WVSA.

234 See for the foregoing "Kanawha County," West Virginia State Troops Artillery and Militia (micro.), WVSA.

235 Jackson Countians in America's Wars, 1775-1918 (Jackson County Historical Society of W.Va. Ripley, W.Va., 1978), p. 2.

236 "Cabell County" and "Wayne County Home Guards, Scouts and Militia" West Virginia State Troops Artillery and Militia (micro.), WVSA.

Volunteers from "the Bend"

237 Gibbs, Mason City, p. 33.

238 Mason, "A Reminiscence. West Columbia. First Letter," The State Gazette, June 17, 1909, [p.1].

239 Mason, "A Reminiscence. West Columbia. Fourth Letter," The State Gazette, July 8, 1909, [p. 1].

240 Mason, "A Reminiscence. West Columbia. Third Letter," The State Gazette, July 1, 1909.[p. 2].

241 The paper was begun in summer of 1857. D.S. Vanmatre was editor and publisher. It was "a family newspaper devoted

to polite literature, general intelligence, agriculture, amusement, etc." See Mason, "A Reminiscence. West Columbia. First Letter," The State Gazette, June 17, 1909, [n.p.]

242 Ibid., [p.2].

243 John L. Mason noted that on March 4th, 1861, Allen C. Mason was teaching school, in the first floor or basement of the United Brethren Church at West Columbia. The first floor basement had been converted and set up for "school purposes, the second floor was for religious services and the third floor contained a large hall." (Ibid.).

244 Mason, "A Reminiscence. West Columbia. Second Letter," The State Gazette, June 24, 1909, [p.1].

245 Mason, "A Reminiscence. First Letter," The State Gazette, June 17, 1909, [n.p.]

246 Rezin may or may not have served in the 13th Val. V.I. John L. Mason is the authority claiming that that Rezin served with his sons in the regiment. See for more about this colorful old Dutch family Virgil A. Lewis, "Pioneer Families of Mason County—Their Ancestors and Descendants [No. 11] The Van Matres," Point Pleasant Weekly Register, April 14th, 1886, [p.1] and Samuel Kercheval, A History of the Shenandoah Valley orig. pub. Winchester, Virginia, 1833. The Van Matres came to New York as colonists of the Dutch East India Company. In 1664, the East India Company gave over control of the New York colony to the English. Many Dutch colonists embraced this change, among them was John Van Matres ancestor of the Van Matres of Mason County, who was among the first to set out for country to the south.

August 1862

247 W.H.H. Russell, Lieut.-Col. 4th V.V.I., comdg. post at Guyadotte to ACol. Parker, Mr. Wilgus, and others" (dated "Hdqtrs, Camp Guyandotte, Va., Aug. 11, 1862"), Ironton Register, August 14, 1862, [n.p.]

248 The foregoing quotations from the Point Pleasant Weekly Register, August 14, 1862, p.3.

249 Ibid., [p. 2].

250 [Lewis Wetzel], "General Muster," Point Pleasant Weekly Register August 21, 1862 Vol. 1 No. 24, [p. 2].

251 [Resolutions were passed by the "Regimental Muster], "Tribute of Respect," Point Pleasant Weekly Register, August. 21, 1862, [p. 2].

252 "Mason County," Point Pleasant Weekly Register, August 14, 1862, [p. 2].

253 West Virginia Clothing Books Companies A and B 13th Infantry (manu. WVSA), [n.p.] The infantryman was allowed $42.00 in clothing for the space of one year. His clothing issue consisted typically of underwear, socks, shirts, trousers, blouse, overcoat, perhaps a dress coat, and a forage cap or hat, shoes, wool and rubber blanket. There was no "summer wardrobe." All clothing was woolen and warm. Unfortunately the years allotment of clothing was not sufficient to last the year through. When the soldier's deshabille became acute, wives, mothers and sisters, sewed shirts and sent them to their soldier but if the soldier had to have the quartermaster issue him a duplicate item during the year it was charged against his salary.

254 William I. Mathews, "1st Lieutenant and Adjutant 13th Regiment," to Adj. Gen. H.J. Samuels (manu. dated "Ravenswood, Virginia August 15, 1862"), Letters to Samuels and Pierpont Box 4 Folder 60, WVSA.

255 Lewis Wetzel to "Gen. H.J. Samuels" (manu. dated "Point Pleasant, Virginia August 16th, 1862"), Letters of Samuels and Pierpont Box 7 Folder 25, WVSA.

256 William Rufus Brown was born June 1823 in Pennsylvania. He may have lost his family, as sources indicate that from the time he was a boy, he had earned his own living. "He was in every sense of the word a self-made man, and possessed all those sterling virtues which characterize a man, who from his boyhood wins his way to fame and fortune by hard licks." When the war broke out he was living in Ohio and worked as foreman in one of the large machine shops at Pomeroy. He desired to raise a company but the Ohio State quota was full, so "he took a company of men from the shops and went over into West Virginia and enlisted." He was made captain of the company and was assigned to the 4th Virginia Volunteer Infantry, which was being raised by Lieutenant William Russell, Colonel J. A. J. Lightburn and John Hall Sr. He was mustered in as Captain of Co. E, 4th Virginia Infantry Regiment on July 22nd, 1861. He was honorably discharged on August 31st, 1862 to be promoted Colonel of the 13th Virginia Infantry. He commanded the 13th during its entire term of service

and was promoted to the rank of Brevet Brigadier General of Volunteers on March 13th, 1865 "for gallantry and meritorious service during the war". After the war, he moved with his family to South Kansas, where he farmed and served as county commissioner, probate judge and at the time of his death, as a member of the board of education. He died at his residence in Independence, Kansas, during the evening of March 24th, 1891 "from a severe attack of pneumonia. [He was] aged sixty five years and nine months." Paraphrase and quotations are from [Obituary of General William R. Brown] in Star and Kansan, Friday, March 27, 1891, [n.p.] and "Mustered Out. Brigadier-General, W.R. Brown, Entered into Rest," South Kansan Tribune, Wednesday, March 25, 1891, [n.p], courtesy of Roger D. Hunt.

257 John Hall to "General H.J. Samuels, at Wheeling" (manu. dated "Point Pleasant August 17, 1862"), Letters to Samuels and Pierpont Box 2, WVSA.

258 John Hall, to Gov. Francis H. Pierpont (telegraph dated "Point Pleasant, Virginia August 19, 1862"), Calendar of Pierpont Letters and Papers, p. 170.

259 George M. Gist to Adj. Gen. H.J. Samuels at Wheeling, Virginia (dated "Letart, Mason County, Virginia, August 30, 1862"), Calendar of Pierpont Letters and Papers, p. 176.

260 Hall to Pierpont (telegraph dated "Point Pleasant, Virginia August 19, 1862"), Calendar, p. 170.

261 Gist to Samuels (dated "Letart, Mason County, Virginia, August 30, 1862"), Calendar, p. 176.

262 Mathews to Pierpont (dated "August 19, 1862"), Calendar, p. 170.

263 James R. Hall, "Oath of Office of Captain in the 13th Regiment Virginia Volunteer Infantry," Uncat. 13th W.Va. Inf. Reg. Box, WVSA. The Convention which convened on February 13, 1861, is also called the Secession Convention. Virginia was slow to join the Southern Confederacy of seceded States but after raging for months over the issue of whether or not to adopt the Secession Ordinance, a majority of Virginia delegates voted to secede. From this time forward, Virginia's sufferings became legion. She became the main stay of the Confederacy and for four long years served as the main theater of war. The largest armies would fight the bloodiest battles of the war here. Indeed, more battles large and small were fought here by far than in any other State.

264 W.N. Hawkins, Adjutant U.S.A. to Governor Pierpont (telegraph dated "Charleston, Virginia, Aug. 21, 1862"), Calendar of Pierpont Letters and Papers, p. 172.

265 The foregoing quotes taken from the Point Pleasant Weekly Register, August 21, 1862, Vol. 1 No. 24, p. 2.

266 Adj. Gen. H. J. Samuels to "Commandant of U. S. Forces in Eastern Virginia" (manu. dated "August, 21, 1862"), Letters to Samuels and Pierpont Box 6 Folder 3, WVSA.

267 See for example J.P.R.B. Smith, "Affidavit" (dated "Sept. 10, 1879") and affidavits of Schools and Cinclair (dated August 1877) in which it is stated that J.P.R.B. Smith took money home from Private John Smoot and gave it to his father or someone of his family. (John Smoot Military Pension File NARA.)

268 J.A.J Lightburn, Col. Commanding District Kanawha, at Gauley, V[irgini]a to Gov. Pierpont, at Wheeling (telegraph dated "Gauley, Virginia, August 22, 1862"), Calendar of Pierpont Letters and Papers, p. 173.

269 James R. Hall to Adj. Gen. H.J. Samuels (telegraph dated "Point Pleasant, Virginia, August 24, 1862") and W.I. Mathews to Adj. Gen. H.J. Samuels (manu. dated "Hd Qtrs 13th Regt Va Vol Inf Pt Pleasant Sept 3, 1862"), both documents from Uncat. 13th W.Va. Inf. Regt. Box, WVSA.

270 Col. J.A.J. Lightburn to Capt. C.W. Moulton (manu. dated "August 26, 1862"), Uncat. 13th W.Va. Inf. Regt. Box, WVSA.

271 Gallispolis Journal, August 28, 1862, p. 2.

272 Cunningham to Samuels (dated "Coalsmouth, Virginia, Aug. 28, 1862"), Calendar of Pierpont Letters and Papers, p. 175.

273 H.J. Samuels to Lt. Col. J.R. Hall (manu. dated "Wheeling, August 29, 1862"), Letters of Samuels and Pierpont Box 6, Folder 3, WVSA. The steamer Science, was one of the steamboats which from early in the war had transported Federal troops on the Kanawha and Ohio Rivers.

274 The Confederacy exerted itself repeatedly that the Kanawha Valley (navigable from Point Pleasant to the Falls of Kanawha) might be wrested from the Union and held. The all-important salt industry critical for food preservation, access to the Ohio River and its tributaries which flowed through the Valley, fertile farmland adjacent, and access to the B&O Railroad (the Grafton to Parkersburg branch) made this Valley especially valuable to Northern military authorities. The

Kanawha was one of two valleys in the northwest with tributaries flowing roughly parallel to one another into the Ohio. The other was the Guyandotte Valley, which was permitted to become "fastened in the meshes of secession". Northern military authorities grew keen to control the Kanawha River Valley and finally did. This was not the case with the Guyandotte Valley, according one writer (R.L. Stewart), where "50,000" people lived and where a lot of bad trouble of a local nature went on, often against Union military and civilians. Robert L. Stewart questioned the wisdom of neglecting the Guyandotte River Valley in his letter to the Cincinnati Commercial (dated "Ironton, Ohio Nov. 18, [1861]") in which he criticized the Federal military for their slow undirected response in coming to the support of Unionists fighting all out guerrilla war in the Northwestern border counties. Referencing both Kanawha and Guyandotte river valleys Stewart complained bitterly about the state of affairs in Cabell and Wayne Counties both adjacent to the Guyandotte River: that "indifference and imbecility" controlled military affairs in all the region on the western border between the Kanawha and Big Sandy river;" that Guyandotte town had given a majority of votes for secession—the only town in the entire region to do so; that "just enough had been done" that summer "to antagonize but not subdue secessionists, to make Union men of Wayne, and Cabell tremble for their lives." (Reprinted in the Ironton Register, Thursday, November 28, 1861, p.1.)

275 Roush's book was based upon on a series of letters written by Burrows to his wife, Lovina, and upon his own research. See Herbert L. Roush, Sr., If Thou Wilt Remember, Revised Edition (Lowell, Michigan: Modern Printing, Copyright 1995 Herbert L. Roush Sr.), pp. 13-17.

276 [Untitled], Point Pleasant Weekly Register, September 4, 1862, [p. 2].

277 Roush, If Thou Wilt Remember, pp. 13-15.

Alarms become real: invasion of the Kanawha Valley

278 Gallipolis Journal, August 28, 1862, p. 2.

279 Milton W. Humphreys, Bryan's Battery, King's Artillery, C.S.A., Military Operations 1861-1863 Fayetteville West Virginia (Fayetteville, W.Va.: Charles A. Goddard,1926), pp. 12-13.

280 Lang, Loyal West Virginia, pp. 247-48; Mary Kincade, "Fayetteville, West Virginia, During the Civil War," West Virginia History Vol. XIV No. 4 (1953), pp. 351-52 and Humphreys, Military Operations 1861-1863 Fayetteville, pp. 12-13. The 2nd Virginia Cavalry were recruited largely from southern Ohio.

281 Indiana was at the time of the Civil War and even today in its southern part, more of a Southern state than a Northern one. The state legislature was fairly copperhead and there were instances of civil insurrection in response to the national drafts. Governor Oliver P. Morton, to quote from editorial remarks in the Wheeling Daily Intelligencer (July 24, 1864, [p.2]) did indeed run his state government "on his own responsibility."

282 From the Pomeroy Telegraph, reprinted in the Ironton Register, August 28, 1862 Vol. 13 No. 5, [p.2].

283 Gen. Loring was a feather in the cap of the Confederate military machine. He had distinguished himself in the Mexican War as major with a regiment of mounted riflemen. He had lost his left arm at the battle of Chapultepec (1847) and been promoted for his bravery. As Milton Humphreys pointed out: Loring had distinguished himself with the rank of Major in a war in which Robert E. Lee served as a captain and Thomas J. Jackson as lieutenant and "the army was elated at his assignment" to the Department of Western Virginia. (Humphreys, Military Operations 1861-1863 Fayetteville, p. 12.)

284 Ibid., Humphreys, pp. 12-13.

285 The Charleston saltworks were not in the town of Charleston proper but were scattered along the road for a distance of 12 miles between Charleston and Camp Piatt. The owners of the saltworks were by and large secessionist. Almost all labor at the salines was performed by African Americans.

286 Dr. John Booth's notes on the Kanawha Valley 1862 (MSS180 Box 2 Pad #3 OHS), pp. 128-29.

287 Col. J.A.J. Lightburn, cmdg. at Gauley, Virginia to Gov. F.H. Pierpont at Wheeling (telegraph dated "September 6, 1862"), Calendar of Pierpont Letters and Papers, p. 181.

288 Kincade, "Fayetteville, West Virginia, During the Civil War," p. 352 and McKinney, Civil War in Fayette County, pp. 147-48.

289 "The Notorious Rebel Colonel Jenkins" reprinted from the Washington, Ohio Register, September 1, [1862] in the Cin-

cinnati Daily Enquirer, September 13, 1862, p. 1.

290 Daniel Frost, Col. 11th Virginia to Gov. F.H. Pierpont at Wheeling (telegraph dated "Parkersburg, Va. September 5, 1862"), Calendar of Pierpont Letters and Papers, p.180. It was the building housing Daniel Frost's printing office (home to the Virginia Chronicle, a Union paper edited by Frost) that was burned. Frost was much hated by the Rebels for his paper, his opposition to secession and his part in the re-organization of the Virginia State government at Wheeling.

291 D. Frost at Parkersburg, Va. to Gov. Pierpont at Wheeling (telegraph dated "September 5, 1862"), Calendar of Pierpont Letters and Papers, p.180. Another account says Jenkins crossed into Ohio on September 3rd at Buffington Island. See "Summary of Jenkins' Raid," Ironton Register, September 18, 1862, p. 2.

292 "Summary of Jenkins' Raid," Ironton Register, September 18, 1862, p. 2.

293 [Untitled], reprinted from the "Pomeroy Telegraph" in the Point Pleasant Weekly Register of September 18, 1862, [p. 2].

294 McKinney, Civil War in Fayette County, pp. 147-48.

295 Lewis Wetzel to Adj. Gen. H.J. Samuels, at Wheeling (dated "Point Pleasant, Mason County, Virginia, September 9, 1862"), Calendar of Pierpont Letters and Papers, p. 183.

296 [Editorial], Point Pleasant Weekly Register, September 18, 1862, [p. 2].

297 There is however, no official record to document either of these statements (i.e., that Butler was a recruiting officer for the 13th or that he was enrolled in the 13th Regiment.)

298 Austin D. Butler, Butler Generation in America (undated manu. loaned to me by Terry Lowery), pp. 6-7.

299 It is not entirely clear which Point Pleasant road is referred to. Roads connecting Charleston and Point Pleasant lay on both sides of the Kanawha.

300 "The Notorious Rebel Colonel Jenkins," reprint Daily Enquirer, Sept. 13, 1862, p. 1.

301 Horton and Teverbaugh, A History of the Eleventh Regiment, pp. 77-78. Other historians have noted that on their retreat, the Confederates met Charles B. Waggoner, a staunch Union man and member of the Wheeling Convention, whom they took prisoner. Thirty political prisoners had to be released by the Governor of Ohio to secure Waggoner's safe return.

302 William E. Feazel, 2nd Lieut., 13th Virginia Regiment to Adj. Gen. H.J. Samuels at Wheeling, Virginia (manu. dated "Head Quarters 13th Regiment Va. Inf[an]t[r]y Point Pleasant V[irgini]a Sept[ember] 7th 1862"), Letters to Samuels and Pierpont #188, WVSA.

303 McKinney, Civil War in Fayette County, pp. 147-48; and Geiger, Civil War in Cabell County, p. 72.

304 John Hall to Gov. F.H. Pierpont (dated "Gauley Bridge, September 10, 1862"), Calendar of Pierpont Letters and Papers, p. 183.

305 Jenkins "captured 300 prisoners, 5,000 stand of arms and many army stores, [and] destroyed many official records." (Roy Bird Cook, "Albert Gallatin Jenkins .. a Confederate Portrait," The West Virginia Review, May (1934) Vol. 11, p. 226.

306 The Point Pleasant Weekly Register reported for example, that on September 4th, W.J. Kenny, the "notorious alien-secessionist" was again seen at his house in Mason county. On the evening of his return "rebels of all grades could be seen entering his house their purpose unknown." ([Untitled], Point Pleasant Weekly Register, September 4, 1862, [p. 2].)

Pressure from without and within

307 Lt.-Col. James R. Hall to H.J. Samuels (dated "Point Pleasant, August 30, 1862"), Calendar of Pierpont Letters and Papers, pp. 176-77.

308 "Mason County," Point Pleasant Weekly Register, September 4, 1862, [p. 2].

309 Charles B. Waggener, W.H. Tomlinson, John Hoits, C.C. Miller, James H. Holloway, Lewis Wetzel, J.P.R.B. Smith and S.M. Campbell to H.J. Samuels Adjutant General (manu. dated "Point Pleasant Va Sept 1st 1862"), Letters to Samuels and Pierpont Box 6 Folder 86, WVSA.

310 W.H. Tomlinson to H.J. Samuels (manu. dated "Point Pleasant, Va., Sept. 1, 1862"), Letters to Samuels and Pierpont Box 6, Folder 86, WVSA. The outcome of all this was that the colonelcy went to William R. Brown (Captain of Company E, 4th

Virginia Infantry Regiment) of Pomeroy, and a handful of officers hailed from Ohio but the large majority of officers were Virginians.

311 W.I. Mathews to H.J. Samuels (manu. dated "Hd Qtrs 13th Regt Va Vol Inf Pt Pleasant Sept 3, 1862"), Uncat 13th West Virginia Infantry Regiment Box, WVSA.

312 Ibid.

313 William E. Feazel, 2nd Lieut., 13th Va. Regiment to Adj. Gen. H.J. Samuels at Wheeling, Virginia (manu. dated "Head Quarters 13th Regiment Va. Inf[an]t[r]y Point Pleasant V[irgini]a Sept[ember] 7th 1862"), Letters to Samuels and Pierpont #188, WVSA.

314 Francis H. Pierpont, Governor of [Western] Virginia, by Henry J. Samuels, Adj. Gen., "Proclamation to the People" (dated "Wheeling, Virginia, September 9, 1862), reprinted as "PROCLAMATION BY THE GOVERNOR," Point Pleasant Weekly Register, September 18, 1862, [n.p.]

315 McCown's recruitment of a company for the 13th was noted by another correspondent. On September 28th, Susan J. Phelps wrote from Mason City to Mrs. Anna Starr that "Albert McCown has raised a company in the 13th Va. Regiment." Susan J. Phelps to Mrs. Anna Starr (manu. dated "Mason City, [Virginia], September 28, 1862" SC1400 Civil War Files of William C. Starr), Manuscript Collection Indiana State Historical Society, Indianapolis.

316 Lewis Wetzel to Adj. General H.J. Samuels (dated "Point Pleasant Va Sept 9th 1862"), Letters to Samuels and Pierpont Box 7 Folder 25, WVSA and Wetzel to Samuels, at Wheeling, Virginia (dated "Point Pleasant, September 9, 1862"), Calendar of Pierpont Letters and Papers, p. 183.

317 Pierpont, "Proclamation to the People" (dated Wheeling, Virginia, September 9, 1862), reprinted as "PROCLAMATION," Point Pleasant Weekly Register, September 18, 1862, [n.p.]

318 Lieut. J.R. Hall and Adj. [W.I] Mathews to Gov. F.H. Pierpont at Wheeling, Va. (telegram dated "Point Pleasant, Virginia September 11, 1862"), Calendar of Pierpont Letters and Papers, p. 185.

Meanwhile, General William W. Loring ...

319 Dr. John. P. Hale, History of the Great Kanawha Valley; with Family History and Biographical Sketches Vol. 2 (Madison, Wis.: Brant, Fuller 7 Co., 189), p. 269. Loring's force has been variously estimated. Theodore F. Lang estimated Loring's force at between "8,000 and 10,000" (Lang, Loyal West Virginia, p. 248). Confederate officer and historian Milton Humphreys stated that Loring invaded the Kanawha Valley with 5,000 men and sixteen pieces of artillery to drive the Federals from the region. (Humphreys, Military Operations 1861-1863 Fayetteville, p. 12.)

320 Col. J.A.J. Lightburn to Gen. H.W. Halleck (dated Gauley Bridge, Virginia, September 9, 1862), O.R. XIX, Part II, Washington: Government Printing Office, 1887, p. 232.

321 Col. J.A.J. Lightburn to "J.R. Hall, commanding 13th at Buffalow" (manu. dated "Head Qtrs. District of Kanawha. Gauley, Sept. 9, 1862"), Uncat. 13th W.Va. Inf. Reg. Box, WVSA.

322 John Hall to Gov. Pierpont (dated "Gauley Bridge, September 10, 1862"), Calendar of Pierpont Letters and Papers, p. 183.

323 John L Vance, Lieutenant-Colonel, "The Retreat of the Union Forces from the Kanawha Valley in 1862" (dated December 7, 1892) in Sketches of War History 1861-1865 Papers presented to the Commandery of the State of Ohio, Military Order of the Loyal Legion of the United States 1890-1896 (MOLLUS) Vol. IV, W.H. Chamberlin, ed. (Cincinnati, The Robert Clarke Company, 1896, Reprint Broadfoot Publishing Company: Wilmington, North Carolina), p. 129.

324 See Col. J.A.J. Lightburn, comdg. at Camp Piatt, Va. to Gov. F.H. Pierpont at Wheeling, Va. (telegram dated "Camp Piatt, September 12, 1862"), Calendar of Pierpont Letters and Papers, pp. 185-86.

325 The hunt for Jenkins' men was taken over by the 2nd Virginia cavalry. Jenkins thus occupied with the 2nd was prevented from harassing Lightburn's retreat from Charleston. Jenkins was it seems, limited to bushwhacking in the area, in rear of Lightburn's army. (See "Summary of Jenkins' Raid," Ironton Register, September 18, 1862, p. 2.)

326 Col. J.P.R.B. Smith, Col. commanding the 106th Va. Militia, "PROCLAMATION!" (dated "Sept. 13, 1862"), Point Pleasant Weekly Register, September 18, 1862, [p.2].

327 Col. Samuel B. Burnett, 19th Regt. Virginia State Militia, Weston, Va. (telegraph dated "Sept. 15, 1862"), Calendar of Pierpont Letters and Papers, p. 188.

Abandoning the Kanawha

328 Lang, Loyal West Virginia, p. 248. Charleston is roughly 58 to 60 miles from Point Pleasant.

329 "From the Kanawha Valley—Destruction of Charleston—The Retreat of Col. Lightburn," Wheeling Daily Intelligencer, Friday Morning, Sept. 19, 1862. Contemporary accounts vary in their estimates of the number of wagons in Lightburn's train. Estimates of six hundred, seven hundred and even eleven hundred wagons were reported.

330 "E", officer in 34th Ohio Vol. Infantry (letter dated "Sept. 15, 1862 General U.S.A. Hospital, Gallipolis, Ohio"), "The Retreat from the Kanawha Valley," The Guerrilla. Devoted to Southern Rights and Institutions, September 29, 1862 Vol. 1 No. 2, p. 2.

331 Bicentennial Committee of Alpha Delta Chapter of Delta Kappa Gamma Society International, compiler, Early History of Pioneer Days in Jackson County, (orig. pub. 1976 reprinted by the Jackson County Public Library, 1981), p. 131.

332 "Official Report of Lieutenant Col. Russell, Commanding 4th Regiment V.V.I. U. S. A." (dated "Headquarters 4th Reg. V.V.I., Point Pleasant, Va., Sept. 20, 1862"), Point Pleasant Weekly Register, October 9, 1862, [p. 1].

333 "From the Kanawha Valley—Destruction of Charleston—The Retreat of Col. Lightburn," Wheeling Daily Intelligencer, Friday Morning, September 19, 1862, [n.p.]

334 On September 14th the 91st Ohio Volunteer Infantry reached Point Pleasant. They would remain there until September 26th. See Whitelaw Reid, Ohio In The War: Her Statesmen, Her Generals, And Soldiers Vol. II, (Publishers: Moore, Wilstach & Baldwin, Cincinnati, Ohio, 1868), p. 506. On the 14th, Colonel Jonathan Craynor, at Catlettsburg, Kentucky, was ordered by Gen. H.G. Wright to hurry with his command to Gallipolis, to take post there or at Point Pleasant. Tennessee troops (belonging to Brigadier-General George W. Morgan's command) were also ordered to West Virginia. This caused considerable controversy to say the least. The Tennessee troops in Morgan's command consisted of the First; Second; Third; Fourth; Fifth and Sixth Tennessee Infantry Regiments, and a detachment of Tennessee cavalry—not equipped—in all about 3,437 men. These were ordered away from the Cumberland Gap, on the Kentucky-Tennessee border, to aid Western Virginia. This order took the men away from protecting their home neighborhoods and families, at a time when Confederates were overrunning that country and making Union families to suffer. Not that the East Tennesseans were dead to feeling sympathy for the Western Virginians. Quite the reverse, if it were known. East Tennesseans and loyal West Virginians could have commiserated and wondered at the commonality of their experience thus far into hostilities. In both areas, there were few slaves and agricultural and mechanical labor was performed chiefly by whites. Likewise, men of both States had been compelled to leave their fields and businesses to band together to resist Southern attempts to secure supremacy and both groups had joined the U.S. service under the most hazardous circumstances. See Brig.-Gen. George W. Morgan to Maj.-Gen. Wright at Cincinnati (dated Portland, Oct. 12, 1862), O.R. Ser. I, Vol. XVI Part II (Washington: Government Printing Office, 1886), p. 609. Unfortunately, it was not just the matter of timing, in being ordered away from protecting their own hearth and home in time of crisis but to make matters worse, Morgan's Tennesseans detested campaigning in Western Virginia, where their "army was frozen and starved out last winter." See Horace Maynard to Gen. H.W. Halleck quoting from a letter of one of Morgan's field officers (dated Westborough [Ky. or Tenn.] Oct. 22, 1862), O.R. Vol. XVI Part II, p. 635. They preferred to campaign in Kentucky (Morgan to Wright dated Portland, Oct. 12, 1862, O.R. XVI Part II, p. 609) and Wright also was loath to send them to reinforce Lightburn when he himself had so few veteran troops. Morgan's whole division was probably in no condition to be thrown into Western Virginia either, as, to quote Brig.-Gen. Morgan, "[e]xcessive toil endured for a long time" had somewhat demoralized his troops (Morgan to Wright dated "Portland called Oak Hill, October 9, 1862, O.R. Vol. XVI, p. 600) and others reported Morgan's division as being "literally naked and barefooted and without equipage" and owed 6 months back pay (Maynard to Halleck, p. 635). In any event, by October 9th, the crisis in the Kanawha was winding down. Morgan's troops were ordered from Portland, Ohio into Western Virginia but only as far as Point Pleasant. On October 13th, Wright wrote reassuringly to Morgan that he hoped to have Morgan's command "out of Western Virginia and in Kentucky in 30 days." (Wright to Morgan dated Oct. 13, 1862, O.R. XVI Part II, p. 614).

335 Sarah Frances Young, Diary 1861-1862 (Young Civil War Papers Roy Bird Cook Coll. Vol. 31 Box 10 WVU), p. 8.

336 "E.," "The Retreat from the Kanawha Valley," The Guerrilla, September 29, 1862 Vol. 1, No. 2, p. 2 and Hale, History of the Great Kanawha Valley Vol. 1, p. 270.

337 "From Point Pleasant," Wheeling Daily Intelligencer, Saturday Morning, September 27, 1862, [n.p.]

338 "MAC," "From Western Virginia" (letter to the Cincinnati Commercial dated "Gallipolis, [Ohio], Sept[ember] 18, 1862"), reprinted in the Point Pleasant Weekly Register, September 18, 1862, [p. 1].

339 Col. J.A.J. Lightburn, cmdg. at Point Pleasant, Virginia to F.H. Pierpont (telegraph dated September 18, 1862), Calendar of Pierpont Letters and Papers, p. 191.

340 "TO ARMS!! TO ARMS!!," Point Pleasant Weekly Register September 18, 1862, [p. 2.]

341 Quoted in Dean W. Moore, Washington's Woods. A History of Ravenswood and Jackson County, West Va. (Parsons, W.Va.: McClain Printing Co., 1971), pp. 121-22.

342 "The Retreat of Col. Lightburn—Scenes at Pomeroy," reprinted from the Pomeroy Telegraph in the Wheeling Daily Intelligencer, Thursday Morning, September 25, 1862, p. 1.

343 "Exodus From the Kanawha," reprint of accounts from the Cincinnati Commercial in The Guerrilla, September 29, 1862, Vol. 1, No. 2, p. 1.

344 Meigs County, Ohio, Hardesty's Historical and Geographical Encyclopedia (orig. pub. 1883), reprinted Defiance Ohio: The Hubbard Company, 1982, p. 275.

345 Gen. W.W. Loring to Sec. of War Geo. W. Randolph (dated HdQtrs. Dept. of Western Va. Charleston, W. Va., Sept. 19, 1862), O.R. XIX Part II (Washington: Government Printing Office, 1887), pp. 611-12.

346 Humphreys, Military Operations 1861-1863 Fayetteville, p. 17.

347 Governor Francis H. Pierpont, "Message to the State Senate and House of Representatives," Point Pleasant Weekly Register, December 18, 1862, [pp. 1 and 4]. Estimates of how much salt Confederates conveyed away varied of course. A Gallipolis correspondent for example, reported that "fully 200,000 bushels of salt—a supply fully adequate for the demands of the Confederacy for some time to come" had been transported away. See "Letter From Gallipolis" (dated "Gallipolis, Ohio Oct. 19, [1862]"), Ironton Register, [n.p.].

348 F.H. Pierpont, Governor of Western Virginia to H.W. Halleck, General-In-Chief (dated Wheeling, Va. Sept. 18, 1862), O.R. Ser. I. Vol. XIX Part II, p. 328.

349 F.H. Pierpont to Gen. Halleck (dated Wheeling, Va., Sept. 12, 1862), O.R. XIX Part II, p. 279 and Halleck to Pierpont (dated War Dept. Wash., Sept. 13, 1862), ibid., p. 288.

350 Authorized by Paragraph II, Gen. Orders No. 135, War Department, Adj. General's Office, Sept. 19, 1862.

351 Halleck to Pierpont (dated Washington Sept. 19, 1862), O.R. XIX Part II, p. 334.

352 "A Convalescent" to the Editor of the Point Pleasant Weekly Register (dated "U.S. Gen. Hospital, Sept 21, [1862]"), "The Meeting," Weekly Register, September 24, 1863,[n.p.]

353 Clement Vallandigham was a graduate of Jefferson College, Pennsylvania, a lawyer and politician, an Ohio Unionist, a Democrat and leader of the Ohio Copperhead movement. The much reviled Vallandigham was no intellectual lightweight and his words against the war and against the abandonment of States' Rights have an ominous ring today as we observe the excesses of a Federal government grown out of all proportion, out of touch with their constituents, out of control and unashamed to flaunt its hubris and corruption in the public eye. Though personally unsympathetic to the practice of slavery, he believed that the Federal government had no standing, to regulate it. He supported the idea that any State had the right to secede and that military coercion by the Federal government to force a States membership in the Union had no constitutional leg to stand on. He was a supporter of the United States Constitution and the Union and expressed his posture in the Copperhead slogan coined by him (in May 1862): "To maintain the Constitution as it is, and restore the Union as it was." When the North won the Civil War, it broke the back of the "States' Rights" argument, but this was not all. In the macrocosm, because the argument had been used to permit the practice and propagation of slavery it was no longer a respectable argument and there is undeniable justice in that. However, in the grand scheme of things, the emasculation of the States' Rights argument opened the door to another evil, even as it closed the door on American slavery and it was this:

the Federal government was (to quote one astute constitutional scholar, namely my husband, Bruce) "no longer a creature of the States. The States were now subjects of the Federal government" and it is inescapably apparent today where that has left the individual citizen. We have come full circle.

354 "A Convalescent" to the Editor (dated "U.S. Gen. Hospital, Sept 21, [1862]"), "The Meeting," Point Pleasant Weekly Register, September 24, 1863.

355 "From Point Pleasant," Wheeling Daily Intelligencer, Saturday Morning, Sept. 27, 1862, [n.p.]

356 See Geiger, Civil War in Cabell County, p. 77.

357 Col. J.A.J. Lightburn to Maj.-Gen. H.G. Wright (telegraph dated Hd. Qtrs. Dist. of Kanawha, Sept. 23, 1862, 8:20 p.m.), O.R. Vol. XVI Part II, p. 542.

358 Maj. Gen. Loring to George W. Randolph, Sec. of War, Letter (dated Headquarters Department, Sept. 22, 1862), O.R. XIX Part II, p. 617.

359 Lightburn to Pierpont (dated "Point Pleasant, Sept. 22, 1862"), Calendar of Pierpont Letters and Papers, p. 193.

360 Col. J.A.J. Lightburn to Gov. F.H. Pierpont (telegraph dated "Point Pleasant, Virginia, September 21, 1862"), Calendar of Pierpont Letters and Papers, p. 193.

361 J.A.J. Lightburn, Col. comdg. by B.D. Boswell, Lt. and A.A.A. G., General Order No. 10 (manu. dated "Head Quarters District of Kanawha, Point Pleasant, Va., Sept. 20, 1862" RG94 Box 4838 Miscellaneous unbound regimental papers 13th West Virginia Special Orders and General Orders NARA).

362 Lightburn, Col. comdg. District by Boswell, General Order No. 12 (manu. dated "Head Quarters District of Kanawha, Point Pleasant, Va., Sept. 20, 1862" RG94 Box 4838 Misc. unbound regimental papers).

363 Lightburn, Col. Comdg. by Boswell, Gen. Order No. 13 (manu. dated "Head Quarters District of Kanawha, Point Pleasant, Sept. 20, 1862" RG94 Box 4838 Misc. unbound regimental papers).

364 Lightburn, Col. Comdg., District of Kanawha by Boswell, General Order No. 14 (manu. dated "Head Quarters District of Kanawha, Point Pleasant [Virginia], Sept. 21, 1862" RG94 Box 4838 Misc. unbound regimental papers).

365 Lightburn, Col. Comdg. District of Kanawha, by Boswell, Gen. Order No. 15 (manu. dated "Head Quarters District of Kanawha, Point Pleasant, Va., Sept. 21, 1862" RG94 Box 4838 Misc. unbound regimental papers).

366 "Sharp Shooters," Point Pleasant Weekly Register, Oct. 2, 1862, [p. 2].

367 Letters are respectively: John A. Martin to D. Polsey (dated "Charleston, Virginia, July 14, 1862") and J.A.J. Lightburn to H.J. Samuels (dated "Head Quarters 4 Brigade Charleston, July 25, 1862") both manu. from Uncat. 13th W.Va. Inf. Reg. Box, WVSA.

368 John A. Martin, "Oath of Office of 2nd Lieutenant to Recruit for the 13th Virginia Regiment Volunteers, manu. Uncat. 13th W.Va. Inf. Reg. Box, WVSA. Martin's unfinished company of sharpshooters was absorbed into other 13th Va. companies.

369 George Rucker (manu. MS 94-95), Rucker Family, WVSA. Camp Sherman was probably on the Virginia side opposite the "Point".

370 Major-General John E. Wool (b. 1784) was a much regarded military man. He had fought in the War of 1812, the Mexican-American War; and now at the tender age of about 78 years was serving in the Civil War. He was considered an officer with an outstanding talent for organization, a piece of trivia which in the context here may bring a smile.

371 The Point Pleasant Weekly Register, October 16, 1862, [p. 2].

372 Halleck to Wright (dated War Dept. Wash., Sept. 20, 1862), O.R. XVI Part II, pp. 530-31.

373 Abolitionism in the 10 to 15 years before the war was seen as the sum of all evil. The label came to be the catch-all for all that was perceived as degenerate and deleterious in politics, society and in morals. "Socialism, free love, negro equality, slave insurrection and general spoliation of women and property, were attributed to designing abolitionists." (Lang, Loyal West Virginia, p. 129.)

374 Gov. Francis H. Pierpont, "Message to the State Senate and House of Representatives" Point Pleasant Weekly Register, December 18, 1862, pp. 1 and 4.

375 John A. Turley, Col. comdg. 3d Brigade by J.W. Longhbon, Adjt. to Col. Brown, Comdg 13th Va. Vol. Infty. (manu. dated "Head Quarters 3d Brigade Dist[rict] of Ka[nawha], Pt. Pleasant Va. Sept. 23d, 1862" RG94 Miscellaneous Unbound Regtl

Papers Box 4839 13th W. Va. Letters Office of the Adjutant General Muster Rolls, Returns Regimental Papers NARA.) Notation below is: "30 [+]16['][Total] 46"

376 William Starr to Anna Starr (manu. dated "Point Pleasant, Virginia, September 25, 1862" SC1400 Civil War Files of William C. Starr), IHS.

377 2nd Lieut. William E. Feazel was detached on recruiting service by Special Order [no Order number given] from General Robert H. Milroy. (RG94 Regimental Books 13th W.V.V.I. "List of Commissioned Officers" NARA.)

378 James R. Hall to Adj. Gen. H.J. Samuels (manu. dated "Point Pleasant, Virginia, September 25th, 1862"), File 234, WVSA.

379 West Virginia Clothing Books Companies A, B and C 13th W.V.V.Infantry. These were blank books printed at R & P Office and records entered by hand as clothing was issued, WVSA.

380 Assist. Adj.-Gen. N.H. McClean, Chief of Staff of the Dept. of the Ohio to Gov. David Tod (dated HdQtrs. Dept. of the Ohio Cincinnati, Sept. 25, 1862), O.R. XVI Part II, p. 546.

381 Special Orders. No. 261 (dated HdQtrs. Of the Army, Adj. Gen'ls Office, Wash., Sept. 25, 1862), O.R. XVI Part II, p. 546.

382 Halleck to Wright (dated War Department, Sept. 26, 1862), O.R. XIX Part II, p. 362.

383 Col. John A. Turley cmdg. 91st Ohio Regiment, "Report of John Turley, Ninety-First Ohio Infantry" (dated Hdqrs. Ninety-First Regt. Ohio Infantry, Point Pleasant, Va., September 28, 1862), O.R. XIX Part II, p. 6. Loring apparently also referred to this engagement in his report to Secretary Randolph stating that Jenkins had an affair with the Nationals 22 miles east of Point Pleasant on September 27th, in an effort to get at military supplies kept at the mouth of the Kanawha River. Loring reported that Jenkins was successful and drove the enemy back. See Maj. Gen. W.W. Loring to Geo. W. Randolph, Sec. of War (dated HdQtrs. Dept. of Western Va., Charleston, Sept. 28, 1862), O.R. XIX Part II, p. 635.

384 For the foregoing quotations regarding seized horses see Col. William R. Brown, 13th Va. Vol[unteer]s to Gov. F.H. Pierpont at Wheeling, Va. (telegraph dated "Point Pleasant, Virginia September 27, 1862"), Calendar of Pierpont Letters and Papers, p. 197.

October 1862

385 RG94 Regimental Books (manu. "Remarks for the Month of October 1862" following Morning Reports of Captain A.F. McCown's Company F of the 13th Regiment of Virginia Volunteers Army of the United States, Colonel William R. Brown for the Month of October 1862 NARA), [n.p.]

386 Manu., Uncat. 13th West Virginia Infantry Regiment Box, WVSA.

387 RG94 Regimental Books ("Remarks for the Month of October 1862" following Morning Reports of McCown's Co. F 13th Regiment of Virginia Vols. Army of the U.S. NARA), [n.p.]

388 Lang, Loyal West Virginia, p. [105].

389 George K. Jenvy to the Marietta, Ohio Register, "Letter from the 2nd Virginia Cavalry" (dated "Point Pleasant, Oct. 5, 1862").

390 Brig. Gen. Q.A. Gilmore at Point Pleasant, Va. to Gov. F.H. Pierpont (telegraph dated "October 3, 1862"), Calendar of Pierpont Letters and Papers, p. 199.

391 Cumberland Division commanded by George W. Morgan was comprised of First Brigade, James G. Spears; Third Brigade, Samuel P. Carter; and Fourth Brigade, John F. De Courcy.

392 See correspondences between Wright and Halleck all dated October 4, 1862 in O.R. Vol. XVI Part II, pp. 573-74.

393 H.G. Wright to Maj. Gen to H.W. Halleck (dated Cincinnati, Ohio, Oct. 1, 1862), O.R. XVI Part II, p. 562.

394 News of Loring's poor luck in recruiting troops filtered west where it was remarked upon in the Point Pleasant Register. The newspaper claimed that to make up for this shortfall, the Rebels were taking every able-bodied man in the Kanawha Valley in enforcement of the Conscription Act. In addition, it was reported, that there were no surgeons with Loring's troops, to examine whether or not men were fit to serve. (Point Pleasant Weekly Register, October 16, 1862, [n.p.])

395 R.E. Lee, however (despite his own failure to retain the Kanawha Valley in 1861) believed that Loring could and should retain possession of the Kanawha Valley and salt works and keep Federals out of that country even without reinforce-

ments, as reinforcements sent to Federal forces in Western Virginia, wrote Lee to Loring, did not constitute a strong reinforcement. See Lee to Loring (dated Hd. Qtrs., Army of Northern Va. Near Winchester, Va., Oct. 11, 1862), O.R. XIX Part II, pp. 661 and 666.

396 Maj. Gen. W.W. Loring to Geo. W. Randolph, Sec. of War (dated HdQtrs. Dept. of Western Va., Charleston, Sept. 28, 1862), O.R. XIX Part II, p. 635.

Muster-in of the 13ᵗʰ Virginia Volunteer Infantry Regiment

397 "The Weather," Point Pleasant Weekly Register, October 9, 1862, [p. 2].

398 RG94 Regimental Books ("Remarks for the Month of October 1862" following Morning Reports of McCown's Co. F 13th Regiment of Virginia Vols. Army of the U.S. NARA), [n.p.]

399 Jenvy, "Letter to the Marietta Register" (dated "Point Pleasant Oct. 5th, 1862").

400 Ibid.

401 John T. Toland, Col. cmdg. Brigade, by E.W. Clark, Lt.+A.A.A.G, General Orders No. 4 (manu. dated "Head Quarters 1st Provisional Brigade, Div. of Kanawha, Point Pleasant, Va., Oct. 6, 1862" RG 94 Box 4838 Misc. unbound regimental papers 13th W.Va. Special Orders and General Orders NARA).

402 Brig. Gen. Q. H. Gillmore, by W.L.M. Qurger, Capt. and Asst. Adjt. Gen., Special Order No. 6 (manu. dated "Head Quarters Dist. of West Virginia, Point Pleasant, Va. Oct. 6, 1862" RG 94 Box 4838 Misc. unbound regimental papers 13th W.Va. Special Orders and General Orders NARA).

403 J.A.J. Lightburn, Col. comdg., by B.D. Boswell, Lt. and A.A.A.G., General Orders No. 4 (manu. dated "Head Quarters Div. of the Kanawha Point Pleasant, Va., Oct. 6, 1862" RG 94 Box 4838 Misc. unbound regimental papers 13th W.Va. Spec. Orders and Gen. Orders NARA).

404 Camp Toland (named for Colonel John T. Toland, comdg. 1st Brigade) was located on the land of one "Mrs. Smith" on the Virginia side of the Ohio and south bank of the Kanawha river opposite Point Pleasant. Cavalry as well as infantry encamped here.

405 [Editorial], Point Pleasant Weekly Register, October 9, 1862, [p.2.]

406 "Record of Events Field and Staff," Muster Roll Co. A 13th Va. Vol. Infantry to October 31, 1862 (microfilm # 594 Roll 196 NARA) and Supp. O.R. Vol. 74, pp. 554-55.

407 $25.00 plus $2.00. RG94 Regimental Books 13th W.V.V.I. (manu. "Remarks for the Month of October 1862" following Morning Reports of Co. A 13th Regiment of Virginia Vols. Army of the U.S. NARA), [n.p.]

408 Col. J.T. Toland, comdg. Brigade, by E.W. Clark, Lt. and A.A.A.G, General Orders No. 6 (manu.. dated "Head Quarters 1st Provisional Brig. 1st Kanawha, Point Pleasant, Va., Oct. 7, 1862" RG94 Box 4838 Misc. unbound regimental papers 13th W.Va. Special Orders and General Orders NARA).

409 RG94 Regimental Books 13th W.V.V.I. (manuscripts Morning Reports of Company B and Captain Simon Williams Company D 13th Reg. of Va. Vols. Army of the U.S. NARA), [n.p.]

410 The town of Leon was located at the mouth of Thirteen Mile Creek, a tributary of the Kanawha in Mason County. It was founded sometime between 1835 and 1840.

411 Janice C. Veazy, "David Bailey," History of Mason County, W.Va. 1987 2nd ed., p. 10.

412 "Record of Events Field and Staff," Muster Roll Co. C 13th Va. Vol. Infantry to October 31, 1862 (microfilm # 594 Roll 196 NARA).

413 Return of Captain Lemuel Harpold's Co C December 10, 1864 (manu. Uncat. 13th W.Va. Inf. Reg. Box WVSA).

414 R.R. Crawford, 2nd Lieutenant and Mustering Officer, notation appended to Muster-in Roll of Captain Van D. McDaniel's Co. C (manu. Uncat. 13th W.Va. Inf. Reg. Box WVSA).

415 RG94 Regimental Books (manu. Morning Reports of October 1862 of Captain Van D. McDaniel's Company Co. C 13th Regiment of Va. Vols. Army of the U.S. NARA), [n.p.]

416 Supp. O.R. Vol. 74, p. 560.

417 These camps were within easy reach of one another and also in contact with the military post at Gallipolis, Ohio across the Ohio River from Point Pleasant. See Clarkson Fogg (4th West Virginia Volunteer Infantry Regiment) writing from Camp Lightburn (of date Nov. 19, 1861) in which he informed that two days previous "a submarine telegraph wire" had been stretched across the river bed of the Ohio from Camp Lightburn providing communication connection "with Ohio and Clarksburg, Virginia and intermediate points". (Letters of Corporal Clarkson Fogg" as published in excerpted transcription for sale in The Horse Soldier Catalog 23, Imprint: Cashtown, Pennsylvania, [n.d.], p. 45.

418 "Record of Events Field and Staff" Muster Roll Co. D 13th Va. Vol. Infantry to October 31, 1862 (microfilm # 594 Roll 196 NARA).

419 RG94 Regimental Books (manu. Morning Reports of October 1862 Captain Simon Williams' Company D NARA), [n.p.]

420 William Starr to his wife, Anna (manu. dated "Headquarters 9th Reg. V.V. Inf. Camp Lightburn Pt. Pleasant, Oct. 8, 1862" SC1400 Civil War Files of William C. Starr IHS).

421 RG94 Regimental Books (manu. "Remarks for the Month of October 1862" following Morning Reports of Company A 13th Regiment of Virginia Volunteers Army of the U.S. NARA), [n.p.].

422 "Record of Events Field and Staff," Muster Roll Co. E 13th Va. Vol. Infantry to October 31, 1862 (microfilm # 594 Roll 196 NARA) and Supp. O.R. Vol. 74, p. 563.

423 West Virginia Clothing Books Companies E, F and G 13th Infantry (manu. WVSA), [n.p.]

424 "Record of Events Field and Staff," Muster Roll Co. F 13th Va. Vol. Inf. to October 31, 1862 (microfilm # 594 Roll 196 NARA).

425 RG94 Regimental Books (manu. "Remarks for the Month of October 1862" following Morning Reports of McCown's Co. F 13th Regiment of Va. Vols. Army of the U.S. NARA), [n.p.]; "Record of Events Field and Staff," Muster Roll Co. F to October 31, 1862 and Supp. O.R. Vol. 74, p. 565.

426 John V. Young, Capt. Co. G, to F.H. Pierpont (manu. "dated Head Quarters Co G, 13th Regiment V.V.I., Camp Defiance, August 12, 1863" Uncat. 13th W.Va. Inf. Regt. Box WVSA).

427 Captain Blundon, 8th Virginia Volunteer Infantry and Rev. A.Q.W. Gregg went down to Coals Mouth and upon their return told Young's family that he had " a noble Company." See Sarah Frances Young, Diary 1861-1862 (manu. diary entry for "March 11, 1862" Young Civil War Papers Vol. 31 Box 10 WVU), p.3.

428 Col. J.A.J. Lightburn, to F.H. Pierpont (telegraph dated "Point Pleasant, Virginia Sept. 19, 1862"), Calendar of Pierpont Letters and Papers, p. 191.

429 John V. Young, Captain cmdg. Co. G, 11th Regiment Virginia Vol. Inf. to F.H. Pierpont, Governor of Virginia (manu. dated "Point Pleasant, Mason County, Virginia September 30th, 1862" Letters to Pierpont and Samuels WVSA).

430 E.B. Linch, Second Auditor, Treasury Department, [probably of Provisional Government at Wheeling] to J.V. Young, Captain 13th Regiment West Virginia Infantry (manu. dated "Treasury Department, Second Auditor's Office, October 20, 1862"), Civil War Scrapbook (Accession #859) Regional History Library, Colson Hall, WVU.

431 13th Regiment Infantry (Roster of the Regiment WVSA), p. [1].

Captain Young

432 Sarah Frances Young, Diary 1861-1862 (manu. diary entry for "February 11, 1861" Young Civil War Papers Vol. 31, Box 10 WVU), p.3.

433 John V. Young to Adj. Gen. H.J. Samuels at Wheeling (dated "May 24, 1862, Coalsmouth, Kanawha County, Va.") Calendar of Pierpont Letters and Papers, pp. 124-25.

434 See H.J. Samuels to Greenly [Greenbury ?] Slack (manu. dated "Wheeling, Va., Nov. 15, 1861") and John V. Young, Captain 11th Regiment Infantry to Adj. Gen. H.J. Samuels (manu. dated "Coalsmouth May 24, 1862") and John V. Young, Capt. Co G, 11th Regt. Va. Vol. to Gen. J.D. Cox (manu. dated "Coals Mouth Kanawha Co Va June 17th 1862"), all in Letter to Samuels and Pierpont Papers Box 6 Folder 3, WVSA.

435 Young to Cox (manu. dated "Coals Mouth Kanawha Co Va June 17th 1862"), Letters to Pierpont and Samuels, WVSA.

436 Ibid.

437 Young may be referring here to Morris Kirtley of Cabell County, who served with Company G of the 10th Virginia Cavalry.

438 John V. Young, Capt. 11th Reg. Inf. to Adj. Gen. H.J. Samuels (manu. dated "Coalsmouth May 24, 1862"), Letters to Pierpont and Samuels, WVSA.

439 Peg," "Buffalo Items," Point Pleasant Weekly Register, July 3, 1862 Vol. 1, No. 17, [p. 3].

440 Robert Brooks to H.J. Samuels (manu. dated "Coles Mouth May 20 1862"), Letters to Samuels and Pierpont, WVSA.

441 R[obert] Brooks to "Governor of Virginia F.H. Peirpont" (manu. dated "Coles Mouth Kanawha County Va May 24, [18]62"), Letters to Samuels and Pierpont, WVSA.

442 Clark E. Elkins, A.J. Bicholas, P. Elkins, Isaac Taylor, W.Y. McDonill, Selas Davis and F.G. Hensley to Gov. Pierpont, at Wheeling (dated "May 24, 1862, Coalsmouth, Kanawha County"), Calendar of Pierpont Letters and Papers, p. 125.

443 "Record of Events Field and Staff," Muster Roll Co. G 11th and 13th Va. Vol. Inf. (micro. #594 Roll 196 NARA).

444 "Record of Events Field and Staff," Muster Roll Co. H 13th Va. Vol. Inf. (microfilm # 594 Roll 196 NARA).

445 RG94 Regimental Books (manu. Morning Reports of Captain J.W. Hampton's Co. H 13th Regiment of Virginia Volunteers Army of the U.S. for the month of October 1862 NARA), [n.p.]

446 Supp. O.R. Vol. 74, p. 569.

447 RG94 Regimental Books (manu. Morning Reports of Hampton's Co. H 13th Reg. of Va. Vols. for the month of October 1862 NARA), [n.p.]

448 The oath of allegiance as reproduced by Francis Lord in his book They Fought for the Union (Harrisonburg, Pennsylvania: The Stackpole Company, 1960) is as follows: I [first name and surname] do solemnly swear [or affirm] that I will bear true allegiance to the United States of America, and that I will serve them honestly and faithfully against all their enemies or opposers whatsoever, and observe and obey the orders of the President of the United States, and the orders of the officers appointed over me, according to the rules and articles for the government of the armies of the United States. (Lord, pp. 14-15, citing the United States War Department, Revised Regulations for the Army of the United States 1861, Section 935, p. 131). The oath of allegiance to the government was not required of non-citizen volunteers as the perception was that it conflicted with the duty owed by them to their own country and sovereigns.

449 "The 13th Regiment V.V.I.," Point Pleasant Weekly Register, Oct. 9, 1862 Vol. I No. 29, [p.2.]

450 Maj.-Gen. Wright to Maj. Gen. Jacob D. Cox, at Gallipolis, Ohio (dated Headquarters Department of the Ohio, Cincinnati, Ohio, October 23, 1862—10 p.m.), O.R. XIX Part II, pp. 475-76.

Confederate Occupation of the Kanawha Valley Is Concluded

451 Gallipolis Journal, October 9, 1862, p. 2.

452 "Sergeant-Major," Point Pleasant Weekly Register, Oct. 9, 1862, [p. 2].

453 Maj. Gen. McClellan, Special Order 271 (manu. dated "Head Quarters Army of the Potomac, Camp Near Sharpsburg, Oct. 4, 1862" General's Papers), RG 94, Adj. General's Office 1870-1917 (Box 10 Entry 159), NARA.

454 Brig. Gen. Jacob D. Cox to Gov. Francis H. Pierpont (dated "Washington, October 6, 1862"), Calendar of Pierpont Letters and Papers in W.Va. Depositories, p. 203.

455 Wright to Halleck (dated HdQtrs. Dept. of the Ohio, Cincinnati, Ohio, Oct. 13, 1862), O.R. Vol. XVI Part II, p. 614.

456 "Record of Events Field and Staff Oct. to Dec. 31, 1862 Station Point Pleasant" (micro. #594 Roll 196 NARA) and Supp. O.R. Vol. 74, pp. 544-49.

457 William R. Brown, M508 Compiled Military Service Records (micro. Roll 204 NARA).

458 "Regimental Return 13th Va. Vol. Infantry for October 1862" (micro. # 594 Roll 196 NARA).

459 November 27, 1863, Col. Brown wrote to Capt. Th. Melvin requesting that he and Lt. Col. Hall be mustered in according to the Commissions held by them (i.e., Colonel and Lieutenant Colonel) adding in justification: "This Regiment was mustered into the U.S. service on the 10th day of Oct 1862. At that time it consisted of 8 companies making an aggregate of 657 men.." See William R. Brown, Col. comdg to Th. Melvin, Capt.+A.A.G. (manu. dated "Head Quarters 13th Regt V.V.I. Barboursville, Nov. 27, 1863" RG 94 Box 4839 Misc. unbound regimental papers 13th W.Va. Letters Adj. General's Office NARA).

460 Point Pleasant would serve as the regiment's station until February 28, 1863. In March 1863, the regiment was transferred to the Middle Military Department. See Frederick H. Dyer, Compendium of the War of the Rebellion, (Des Moines: Iowa, Dyer Publishing Co., 1908), p. 1665.)

461 RG94 Regimental Books (manu. "Remarks" following Morning Reports of Co. A 13th Regiment of Virginia Vols Army of the U.S. for the month of October 1862 NARA), [n.p.]

462 "Personal," Point Pleasant Weekly Register, Thursday October 16, 1862 Vol. 1 No. 30, [p. 2].

463 Point Pleasant Weekly Register, Thursday October 16, 1862 and transcription of John V. Young to his "Wife and Children" (dated "Point Pleasant, October 6, [1862]" WVU), p. 189.

464 The scouting party seems to have been the one sent out by Col. John H. Oley (commanding 8th Virginia Infantry Regiment) from Point Pleasant on or about October 12th pursuant to Gen. J.D. Cox's orders. At this time, Oley sent out a scout of 75 men from camp "with orders to go as far as Charleston if possible." By the time of Oley's writing to H.J. Samuels on October 16th, the scouts had been gone 4 days and were probably "near Charleston" but Oley had not yet "heard anything from them." See John H. Oley to Adj. Gen. H.J. Samuels at Wheeling (dated "Point Pleasant, V[irgini]a, Oct. 16, 1862"), Calendar of Pierpont Letters and Papers, pp. 205 -06.

465 Maj. Gen. J.D. Cox to Maj. N.H. McClean, Asst. Adj. Gen. (dated Gallipolis, October 15, 1862), O.R. XIX Part II, pp. 432-33.

Government Issue

466 Quartermaster M.C. Meigs to Maj. Gen. G.B. McClellen (dated Quarter Master Generals Office, Washington City, October 7, 1862), O.R. XIX Part II, p. 396.

467 Virgil A. Lewis, First Biennial Report of the Department of Archives and History of the State of West Virginia (Charleston, W.Va.: Tribune Printing Co. 1906), p.62.

468 Ibid., p.71.

469 Gen. H.W. Halleck to Gov. F.H. Pierpont (telegraph dated "October 10, 1862"), Calendar of Pierpont Letters and Papers, p. 204.

470 Western Virginia's lack of overland transportation had long been one of its most critical and costly problems. What in peacetime had been a cause of concern for Western inhabitants trying to get their surplus agricultural products to markets was now and for the duration of the war, a huge logistical problem for the armies that sought to occupy this country.

471 Letter of Col. John H. Oley, provided to me courtesy of Terry Lowery in a correspondence dated 2.7.2002.

472 See illustrations L5Ba andL5Bb in David E. Schenkman, Civil War Sutler Tokens and Cardboard Scrip (Post Office Box 155 Bryans Road, Maryland 20616: Jade House Publications), p. 74.

473 "Thirteenth Virginia Regiment," Point Pleasant Weekly Register, October 16, 1862, [p. 2].

474 The first set of Commissioners had been appointed by the Mason County Court on August 4, 1862. This group included John Hall, J.D. Thompson and Lewis Wetzel, deceased.

475 Copy Teste: D.W. Polsley, Clerk. The foregoing synopsis of the proceedings of the Meeting of the Mason County Board of Supervisors is a paraphrase of John Hall's letter to Editor Howard, "Bounty Commissioners," Mason County Journal, June 19, 1867, [p. 2].

476 At a later time the Mason County Board of Supervisors appointed additional commissioners, John Mason and E.M. Fitz Gerald to pay local bounties to volunteers. Bounties offered later in the war were much higher for obvious reasons. Mason and Fitz Gerald paid a bounty of $300 to each of 26 men ($7,800 total cost to the county); bounties of $200 to each of 23 men ($4,600 total cost to the county) and to one man a bounty of $20, making altogether 50 men that were paid by these two commissioners. E.M. Fitz Gerald was paid a compensation of $155.55 and John Mason $50. (Hall, "Bounty Commissioners," Mason County Journal June 19, 1867, [p.2].)

477 Ibid., Hall, "Bounty Commissioners," Mason County Journal, June 19, 1867 [p.2]. Hall's purchase of rifles was a generous stop gap measure inasmuch as it seems that Western Virginia was not appointed a regular ordnance officer until October 1862. See Gen. H.W. Halleck to Gov. F.H. Pierpont, at Wheeling, dated "October 10, 1862;" Halleck writing from Washington

that "[a] regular ordnance officer will be assigned for duty in western Virginia." (Calendar of Pierpont Letters and Papers, p. 91.)

478 Lang, Loyal West Virginia, 289-90.

479 J.T. Tolan[d], Col. comdg. Brigade, by J[ohn] L. Mallernee [4th V.V.I], Lt. A.D.C. to Col. Brown, Comdg. 13th (manu. dated "Hd.Qtrs.1st Prov. Brig., Point Pleasant Va., Oct. 10, 1864" RG 94 Box 4839 Misc. unbound regimental papers 13th W.Va. Letters Adj. General's Office NARA).

480 RG94 Regimental Books (manu. "Remarks" Morning Reports Co. A 13th Regiment of Virginia Vols. Army of the U.S. for the month of October 1862 NARA), [n.p.]

481 Soldier reported "deserted on "October 11". RG94 Regimental Books (manu. "Remarks for the Month of October 1862" following Morning Reports of McCown's Co. F 13th Regiment of Virginia Vols. Army of the U.S. NARA), [n.p.]

482 "Military Inspection," Point Pleasant Weekly Register, Thursday October, 16, 1862 Vol. 1 No. 30, [p. 2].

483 Virginia place names at that time were generally approximate, loose and varied designations. Bearing this in mind, it seems that the location of Mrs. Smith's land, variously described as 'on the Va. side of the Ohio' and on the 'south side of the Kanawha opposite Point Pleasant,' seems to describe what was also termed 'the point.' The point was located on what was also known as the 'Major Smith Farm,' owned by Major Smith and his wife, Elizabeth. The point overlooked both the Ohio and Kanawha rivers, the town of Point Pleasant, military camps, supply depot and hospital, and the surrounding countryside, offering am important vantage point for observation. General John McCausland, who resided inland on the Kanawha in Mason County after the war, was buried here upon his death , on the high ground "on the point," overlooking the Ohio river, on the "Major Smith farm".

484 Gallipolis Journal, October 16, 1862, p. 2.

485 John L. Toland, Col. cmdg. Brigade by John L. Mallanee [Mallernee, 4th V.V.I.], Lt. and A.A.G. to Col. Wm. R. Brown, comdg. 13th Regt. V.V.I., 1st Prov[isional]. Brig[ade] (manu. dated "Head Quarters 1st Prov. Brigade, Point Pleasant, Va., Oct. 12, 1862") RG 94 Box 4838 Misc. unbound regimental papers 13th W.Va. Spec. Orders and Gen. Orders NARA).

486 Brig. Gen. Milroy by Henry C. Flesher, A.A.A.G. to Col. Wm. R. Brown, comdg. 13th Regt. V.V.I. Special Orders No. 19 (manu. dated "Head Quarters Army Kanawha, Point Pleasant, Va., Oct. 14, 1862" RG 94 Box 4838 Misc. unbound regimental papers 13th W.Va. Spec. Orders and Gen. Orders NARA).

487 RG94 Regimental Books (manu. "Remarks" following Morning Reports Co. A 13th Reg. of Va. Vols. Army of the U.S. for the month of October 1862 NARA), [n.p.]

488 Ibid.

489 RG94 Regimental Books (manu. "Remarks" following Morning Reports Co. C 13th of Va. Vols. Army of the U.S. for the month of October 1862 NARA), [n.p.]

490 Wright to Cox (dated Headquarters Dept. of the Ohio, Cincinnati, Ohio, Oct. 16, 1862), O.R. XIX Part II, p. 438.

491 "Army Medical Intelligence," American Medical Times, October 18, 1862, Vol. 1-5 July 1860-December 27, 1862, pp. 223-24.

492 W.W. Harper, "Sword Presentation," Point Pleasant Weekly Register, October 16, 1862, [p.3].

493 Point Pleasant Weekly Register, Oct. 16, 1862, [n.p.]

494 RG94 Regimental Books (manu. "Remarks" following Morning Reports Co A 13th Regiment Va. Vols. Army of the U.S. for the month of October 1862 NARA), [n.p.]

495 A note should inserted at this point that Tu-Endie-Wei Park with its broad open space and grand view up and down the Ohio and Kanawha Rivers did not exist at the time of the Civil War. This land was instead built over with "the old buildings many of which were dilapidated" even at that time. See "Mr. John Dasher visits his old home and details many valuable and Interesting Recollections," State Gazette, Thursday, Sept. 30, 1909, in Poffenbarger Papers Vol. 3, p. 35, Mason Co. Pub. Lib., Point Pleasant.

496 "Col. G.B. Thomas," The State Gazette, February 2, 1905, Supp., p. 23.

497 "Re Union of the 13th and 4th W. Va. Regiments," Point Pleasant Register, October 26, 1886, [n.p.], courtesy of Terry Lowery.

498 "Mr. John Dasher visits his old home [...] Interesting Recollections," State Gazette, Sept. 30, 1909, Poffenbarger Papers Vol. 3, p. 35.

499 The location of the Point Pleasant army hospital and later complaints that the hospital was treating patients with highly contagious and dangerous diseases (thus exposing the town's residents) also supports the idea that the whole of Point Pleasant was embraced in the military encampment. Army hospitals were usually located (1) as close to the army as possible and (2) as close to transportation (in this case the rivers) as possible. It is known that the Point Pleasant General Army Hospital (also called the 13th Regimental Hospital) was located in the two Methodist Churches in town. The first church building was a wood and log structure, built in 1834 on Second and Main Streets, Point Pleasant. Later it was replaced by a brick church. In 1844 there was separation in the church at large over the slavery issue (whether or not Methodists would be "North or South of God") and in 1858 the Methodist Episcopal Church (anti-slavery) bought lots on the corner of 5th and Viand (in rear of the courthouse) and built another church. The first church on South Main became the Southern Methodist Church (tolerant of slavery). Sources suggest that both churches were used as a hospital as services had been suspended. Dr. Samuel G. Shaw had his offices and clinic at Third and Main in the next block up from the Southern Methodist Church and the Northern Methodist Church building (and parsonage building ?) was adjacent to the military depot, stables etc. Both locations were easily accessible from the wharf fronting on the Ohio.

500 "West Virginia" to the "Editors of the Wheeling Intelligencer" (dated "Point Pleasant, Va. Oct. 17, 1862"), Wheeling Intelligencer, October 22, 1862, p. 2.

501 Col. W.R. Brown, by W.I. Mathews, Adjutant General. Orders No. 1 (manu. dated "Head Quarters 13th Regiment Virginia Volunteer Infantry, Point Pleasant, Virginia, October 18th, 1862" RG94 Order Book Co. C Regimental Books 13th Regiment Infantry Volunteers NARA), [n.p.]

502 RG94 Regimental Books (manu. "Remarks" following Morning Reports of Co. F 13th Regiment of Va. Vols. Army of the U.S. for the month of October 1862 NARA), [n.p.]

503 "D.," correspondence to the Wheeling Daily Intelligencer (dated "Point Pleasant, Va., Oct. 18, 1862"), "Late News from the Kanawha Valley—The Operations of the Rebels and their Retreat," Daily Intelligencer, October. 22, 1862, p. 2.

504 While the War Department in Washington was trying to make up its mind as to what to do with captured guerrillas, individual military districts, not having the luxury of time, implemented their own measures to deal with the situation. Some districts such as Kentucky shot guerrillas on sight as a matter of policy. Others such as Tennessee concentrated on the support system (i.e., the citizenry, who aided and abetted guerrillas) threatening imprisonment, property forfeiture and confiscation, should a person or persons be caught. In Western Virginia the policy was to administer the oath of allegiance. It was administered en masse, and not just to captured guerrillas.

505 [Parole of A.M. McCausland] (dated "Head Quarters Div of Kanawha Pt Pleasant, Oct. 18, 1862" RG 94 Box 4839 Misc. unbound regimental papers 13th W.Va. Letters Adj. General's Office NARA).

506 G.W. Randolph, Sec. of War to John Echols, Brig. Gen. (dated War Dept., Richmond, Va., Oct. 15, 1862), O.R. XIX Part II, pp. 666-67.

507 Maj.-Gen. J.D. Cox to Maj. N.H. McClean, Assist. Adj. Gen., Cincinnati (dated Gallipolis, October 18, 1862), O.R. XIX Part II, pp. 448-49.

508 Ibid.

509 Maj.-Gen. J.D Cox to Gen. B.F. Kelley (dated Gallipolis, October 18, 1862), O.R. XIX Part II, p. 449.

510 Wright to Cra[y]nor at Guyandotte (dated HdQtrs. Dept. of the Ohio, Cincinnati, Ohio, October 19, 1862), O.R. Vol. XVI Part II, p. 632.

511 John S. Witcher, of Cabell County to Adj. Gen. H.J. Samuels (dated "Proctorville, Ohio, October 19, 1862"), Calendar of Pierpont Letters and Papers, p.206.

512 J.D. Cox, Maj.-Gen., cmdg. District of Western Virginia to Maj. N.H. McClean, Asst. Adjt.-Gen., at Cincinnati (dated Gallipolis, October 20, 1862), O.R. XIX Part II, pp. 458-59.

513 RG94 Regimental Books (manu. "Remarks for the Month of October 1862" following Morning Reports of Co. A 13th Regt. Va. Vols. Army of the U.S. NARA), [n.p.]

514 RG94 Regimental Books (manu. "Remarks for the Month of October 1862" following Morning Reports of Co. F 13th Regt. Va. Vols. Army of the U.S. NARA), [n.p.]

515 Maj. Gen. J.D. Cox "to Generals Milroy and Crook at Clarksburg" (dated Gallipolis, Ohio, Oct. 20, 1862) O.R. XIX Part II, p. 456 and G.M. Bascom, Maj. and Asst. Adj. Gen. to Col. J.A.J. Lightburn, cmdg. Division at Buffalo (dated Gallipolis, Ohio, Oct. 22, 1862), O.R. XIX Part II, p. 469.

516 "MILES" (probably a soldier serving with the 91st Ohio Volunteer Infantry "the Zouaves" dated "October 19 to October 22, 1862"), Gallipolis Journal, November 6, 1862, p. 4.

517 "WEST VIRGINIA," pseud., (letter to the Intelligencer from Point Pleasant, from someone who owned a boarding house near or within sight of the military post there, J.P.R.B. Smith, perhaps, Col. of the 106th Mason County Militia in 1862, who owned the Virginia House located on Water Street, Point Pleasant), Wheeling Daily Intelligencer, November 13, 1862, p.1.

518 RG94 Regimental Books (manu. "Remarks for the Month of October 1862" Morning Reports of Co. A 13th Regt. Va. Vols. Army of the U.S. NARA), [n.p.]

519 RG94 Regimental Books (manu. "Remarks for the Month of October 1862" Morning Reports of Co. F 13th Regt. Va. Vols. Army of the U.S. NARA), [n.p.]

520 Special Order No. 16 (manu. dated "Head-Quarters Dist. of Western Va. Gallipolis, Ohio, Oct. 20th, 1862" RG 94 Box 4838 Misc. unbound regimental papers 13th W.Va. Spec, Orders and Gen. Orders NARA).

"... the greatest political feud in [Mason] County."

521 Correspondent to the Cincinnati Gazette (dated "Gallipolis Oct. 26th"), reprinted in the Point Pleasant Weekly Register, October. 30, 1862, [p. 2].

522 Ibid.

523 Mason County Court Records (November Term 1862), pp. 325-26.

524 T.B.A. David to Gov. F.H. Pierpont, at Wheeling (telegraph dated "Point Pleasant, October 23, 1862"), Calendar of Pierpont Letters and Papers, p. 208.

525 Correspondence to the Cincinnati Gazette (dated "Gallipolis Oct. 26th"), reprinted in the Point Pleasant Weekly Register, October. 30, 1862, [p. 2].

526 Ibid.

527 "The Killing of Lewis Wetzel," Wheeling Daily Intelligencer, October 25, 1862, [n.p.]

528 Certainly falling out over a newspaper article was nothing new in 19th century Virginia or in the country at large, for that matter. Fueled by the passions of the War, many a newspaper editor, particularly in the Virginias it seems, was in the thick of some politically related conflict, requiring a challenge. The notion we have today, about journalistic impartiality in reporting was utterly unknown at that time and editors put their pistols on when they dressed in the morning and kept loaded weapons in their press rooms. According to Barbara Holland, in her well-researched and delightfully irreverent article ("Bang! Bang! You're Dead") she observes that "Virginia editors had a particularly short life. The two brothers who edited the Richmond Examiner in the early 19th century both died in duels. Edgar Allan Poe challenged one of the paper's later editors but showed up too drunk to shoot. Before the Civil War, O. Jennings Wise, editor of the Richmond Enquirer, fought eight duels in only two years. John Daniel of the Examiner disagreed with Edward Johnston of the Whig over the esthetic merits of a particular statue. In the inevitable duel they both missed." Of course Hall and Wetzel did not fight a duel and oddly enough of course, Wetzel and Hall were on the same side of the larger conflict. Theirs seems to have been a conflict within a conflict, Hall perhaps regarding the so-called political affront offered by Wetzel in his editorials as a challenge that undermined not only the Union cause and New State movement but his own, perhaps even his sons' future ability to be 'useful,' (i.e., politically influential) as such things were then delicately termed. See for a rollicking good read, Barbara Holland, "Bang! Bang! Your Dead," Smithsonian, October 1997, Vol. 28, No, 7: pp. 132-33.

529 Correspondence to the Cincinnati Gazette (dated "Gallipolis Oct. 26th"), reprinted in the Point Pleasant Weekly Register, October. 30, 1862, [p. 2].

530 For the foregoing see Mason County Court Records (November Term 1862), pp. 325-26.

531 The Commonwealth vs. William R. Brown, Mason County Court Records (November Term 1862), p. 329.

532 Mason County Court Records (November Term 1862), reproduced as "Copy of Entries Made Concerning Case of State vs. John Hall" in Poffenbarger Papers Vol. 10, pp. 23-24, Mason Co. Pub. Lib.

533 Ibid., p. 25. On April 21st 1863 another motion to grant bail was made and granted (for $35,000). The list of sureties reads like an 1862 Who's Who of Mason County. Sureties were John Hall, James R. Hall, Benjamin J. Redmond, John Sebrill, James Hoge, John P.R.B. Smith, Adison McCulloch, Marcus Kimberling, Thomas Fowler, Alexander McCausland, Thomas Davis, and Thomas G. Hogg. (Ibid., p. 27.)

534 George W. Tippett to Jeff C. Samuels, Adj. Gen. (manu. dated "Register Office, Point Pleasant, Va., Jan. 30th, 1863"), Letters to Samuels and Pierpont, WVSA.

535 Mason County Court Records (March Term 1864), p. 54.

General Cox Retakes the Kanawha Valley

536 Maj. Gen. J.D. Cox to Maj. N.H. McClean, Asst. Adj. Gen. (dated Gallipolis, October 15, 1862), O.R. XIX Part II, pp. 432 – 33.

537 This date comes from "an old steamboat Captain", who was quoted in the Ironton (Ohio) Register, saying: "The Ohio River is as low now, [lower] than it has been since the summer of 1838." ("From the Mountains," Ironton Register, October 30, 1862, p. 1.)

538 J.D. Cox, Maj. Gen., cmdg. District of Western Virginia to Maj. N.H. McClean, Asst. Adjt.-Gen., at Cincinnati (dated Gallipolis, October 20, 1862), O.R. XIX Part II, pp. 458-59.

539 Maj. Gen. Wright to Maj. Gen. Jacob D. Cox, at Gallipolis, Ohio (dated Headquarters Department of the Ohio, Cincinnati, Ohio, October 23, 1862—10 p.m.), O.R. XIX Part II, pp. 475-76.

540 J.D. Cox to Maj. N.H. McClean, Asst. Adj. Gen. Head Quarters Cincinnati (dated Gallipolis, Oct. 23, 1862), O.R. XIX Part II, pp. 474-75.

541 Gen. J.D. Cox to Col Jonathan Cranor, cmdg. a brigade at Guyandotte (dated Headquarters District of Western Virginia, Gallipolis, October 24, 1862), O.R. XIX Part II, p. 481.

542 Cox to Milroy and Crook (both dated Gallipolis, October 24, 1862), O.R. XIX Part II, pp. 481-82.

543 Col. John Dils, Jr., 39th Kentucky Vols., to Maj. Gen. Wright (dated Catlettsburg, Ky. Oct. 25, 1862), O.R. Vol. XVI Part II, p. 644.

544 Clarkson Fogg, Corporal 4th W.Va. Inftry. (dated Charleston Oct[ober] 30, 1862), "Letters & Documents," The Horse Soldier Catalogue #23, p. 47.

545 Gen. John Echols to Gen. S. Cooper (dated HdQtrs. Dept. of Western Va. Buster's Five miles from the Falls of the Kanawha, W.Va. Oct. 28, 1862), O.R. XIX Part II, p. 685.

546 Vance, "Retreat from the Kanawha Valley in 1862," MOLLUS Vol. IV, pp. 118-32.

547 Maj. Gen. J.D. Cox to Maj. N.H. McLean (dated Charleston, Oct. 31, 1862), O.R. XIX Part II, p. 520. Camp Piatt was located on the Kanawha River opposite a place called Brownstown. Brownstown is a historical town and does not exist under this name today. Camp Piatt was down below the saltworks just to the northwest of Witcher Creek.. William H. Powell commanding the 2nd Virginia Cavalry noted in his post-war writings that Camp Piatt was located "about 12 miles above Charleston". (Maj.-Gen. W.H. Powell, "Sinking Creek Valley Raid. In the Mountains of Va.," The American Tribune (Indianapolis, Ind.), Friday, Jan. 9, 1891 Vol. X, p.3.)

548 Cox to N.H. McLean (dated Headquarters District of Western Virginia, Charleston, November 1, 1862), O.R. XIX Part II, p. 531.

549 Halleck to Wright (dated November 1, 1862), O.R. Ser. I Vol. XX Part II, p. 4.

550 Crook would remain commander-in-chief of the Kanawha Division (as division commander, then as corps commander) until early 1865 when he was transferred to the cavalry corps of the Army of the Potomac. In the words of Crook's subordinate officer Rutherford B. Hayes, Crook was a "model commander" "a favorite" with his officers and men.

"The volunteers in the ranks, the plain men who carried the musket, believed in him, trusted him, and knew him to be their friend. He appreciated their character and the motives that led them to enlist in the army. To General Crook the private soldier was not only a part of a machine, but a fellow man, intrinsically the equal in intellect and worth of the officer who commanded him. Without lowering or loosening the reins of discipline, he treated his subordinates according to this high and enlightened estimate of them. His officers and men soon found that to the advantages of his West Point education, and to his ten years service in the regular army, he added energy, courage, promptness, enterprise, an instinctive and marvelous knowledge of the condition and designs of the enemy, and a military common sense which mark the natural born soldier." (General Hayes Speech" in *Proceedings of the 8th Annual Reunion of the Society of the Army of West Virginia held at Cumberland, Md. Sept. 2,3,4, 1884*, pp. 28-29.)

551 Uncat. 13th W.Va. Inftry. Regiment Box, WVSA.

In camp with the 13th

552 For the foregoing, RG94 Regimental Books (manu. "Remarks for the Month of October 1862" following Morning Reports of McCown's Co. F and Morning Reports of McDaniel's Co. C for the Month of October 1862), [n. pp.]

553 Ibid., Morning Reports Co. A.

554 G. Slack to Gov. F.H. Pierpoint (manu. dated "Pt Pleasant Octr 27th 1862"), Samuels – Pierpont Papers Box 6 Folder 28, WVSA.

555 WEST VIRGINIA, pseud., correspondence to the Daily Intelligencer from a boarding house in Point Pleasant, near the military post there [J.P.R.B. Smith, who owned the Virginia House on Water Street?], Wheeling Daily Intelligencer, Nov. 13, 1862, p.1.

556 RG94 Regimental Books (manu. "Remarks for the Month of October 1862" following Morning Reports Co. A 13th Regt. Inf. Vols.), [n.p.]

557 Lt. Col. James R. Hall to Col. Wm. R. Brown (manu. dated "Point Pleasant, V[irgini]a, Nov[ember] 2d, 1862" RG94 Misc. Dept. of W.Va. Papers Box NARA).

558 J.V. Young to his wife, Paulina (manu. dated "Point Pleasant Oct. 28 [1862]" Young Civil War Papers Vol. 31, Box 10 WVU), trans., pp. 139-40.

November and December 1862

559 Young's Company was mustered in as Company G, 13th Regiment Virginia Vols. at Point Pleasant, although he had already been counted with the 11th Virginia.

560 Young to his daughters Sallie and Emma (dated "Point Pleasant, October 29, 1862" Young Civil War Papers Vol. 31, Box 10 WVU), trans., p. 54.

561 Sarah Frances Young (manu. diary entry for "October 31, 1862" Diary 1861-1862 Vol. 31 Box 10 WVU), p. 11.

562 RG94 Regimental Books (manu. Morning Reports of Co. A 13th Regt. of Va. Vols. Army of the U.S. and "Remarks" for the month of October 1862 NARA), [n.p.]

563 "Record of Events Field and Staff," Company Muster Rolls to Oct. 31, 1862 for Companies A, D and H, Microfilm #594 Roll 196, NARA and Supp. O.R. Vol. 74, p. 558 and 563.

564 William R. Brown, Colonel 13th Virginia Volunteers Infantry to H.J. Samuels, Adjutant General of Virginia (manu. dated "Point Pleasant, Virginia, October 31, 1862"), Letters to Samuels and Pierpont, WVSA.

565 D. Hallsty to Gov. F.H. Pierpoint" (telegraph dated "Point Pleasant, Virginia, October 31, 1862"), Calendar of Pierpont Letters and Papers, p. 214.

566 Return for the Department of the Ohio, Maj. Gen. Horatio G. Wright, U.S. Army, cmdg. (dated October 31, 1862), O.R. Vol. XVI Part II, p. 658.

567 The 5th (West) Virginia Infantry Regiment was organized in the first wave of recruitment (officially organized at Ceredo, October 18, 1861). Many Wayne County men enrolled in the 13th when it was organized the following year. The 5th and 13th were sister regiments in terms of nature of service performed and in brigade. They stood shoulder to shoulder for nearly the entire war.

568 "Troops of the District of Western Virginia serving in West Virginia, October 31, 1862 Extract from the monthly returns of the Department of the Ohio, Maj. Gen. Horatio G. Wright, U.S. Army, cmdg., for October 31, 1862," O.R. XIX Part II, pp. 522-23.

569 Gen. J.D. Cox to Maj. N.H. McClean at Cincinnati, Ohio (dated Charleston, Va., Nov. 2, 1862), O.R. XIX Part II, pp. 535-37.

570 Hall to Samuels (manu. dated "Point Pleasant, Virginia, November 1, 1862" File # 234), WVSA.

571 Regimental Return 13th Va. Vol. Infantry for November 1862; "Record of Events Field and Staff," Company Muster Rolls Nov. and Dec.1862 for Cos. C, F and H, micro. #594 Roll 196, NARA and Supp. O.R. Vol. 74, p. 563.

572 Sarah Frances Young, Diary 1861-1862 (manu. diary entry for "Nov. 2, 1862," Young Civil War Papers Vol. 31, Box 10), p.11.

573 Gen. J.D. Cox to Col. Jonathan Cranor, cmdg. Brigade at Guyandotte (dated HdQtrs. District of Western Va., Charleston, Nov. 2, 1862), O.R. XIX Part II, pp. 534-35.

574 John Bowyer [Sheriff of Putnam County, Virginia ?] to Capt. John V. Young (manu. dated "Putnam C H, Va., Nov. 4th, 1862" Young Civil War Papers Vol. 31, Box 10 WVU), [n.p.]

575 Brig. Genl. E.P. Scammon, by James L. Botsford, Lt.+A.A.A.G to Col. Brown (manu. dated "November 4, 1862" RG 94 Box 4839 Misc. unbound regimental papers 13th W.Va. Letters Adj. General's Office NARA).

576 Maj.Gen. H.G. Wright, by W.P. Anderson, Asst. Adj. Gen. to Co. of 13th W. Vols., Point Pleasant, Va. (manu. dated "Hd. Qtrs., Dept. of the Ohio" RG 94 Box 4839 Misc. unbound regimental papers 13th W.Va. Letters Adj. General's Office NARA).

577 RG94 Regimental Books (manu. "Remarks" following Morning Reports of Co. A 13th Regt. of Va. Vols. for the month of November 1862 NARA), [n.p.]

578 [Editorial], Point Pleasant Weekly Register, November 6, 1862 Vol. 1 No. 33, [p. 2].

579 "A Proclamation By the Governor," Point Pleasant Weekly Register, Nov. 20, 1862, [p. 2]. President Abraham Lincoln followed suit in 1863 proclaiming the national holiday of Thanksgiving.

580 Field History of the 13th Regiment West Virginia Infantry (manu. Uncatalogued 13th West Virginia Infantry Regiment Box WVSA), [n.p.]

581 "Chaplain 13th Regiment," Point Pleasant Weekly Register, November 13, 1862 Vol. 1 No. 34, [p. 2] and J. Drummond, S.R. Brokmer, L. Barnes, R.S. Woodyard, and James L. Clark to Gov. F.H. Pierpont (dated "November 13, 1862"), Calendar of Pierpont Letters and Papers, p. 217.

Jackson's Movements Have Repercussions in the West

582 Gen. J.D. Cox to Maj. N.H. McLean, Chief of Staff, Head Quarters Department of the Ohio (dated Charleston, Nov. 17, 1862), O.R. XXI, p. 768.

583 Cox to Wright probably (dated probably Charleston, Nov. 15 or 16, 1862 and quoted by Wright to Halleck in his dispatch dated HdQtrs. Cincinnati, Nov. 16, 1862—3.10 p.m.), O.R. XXI, p. 763.

584 Maj. Gen. H.G. Wright to Maj. Gen. J.D. Cox (dated Cincinnati, Nov. 15, 1862), O.R. XXI, p. 759.

585 Maj. Gen. Cox to Gen. Robert H. Milroy (dated Charleston, Nov. 21, 1862), O.R. XXI, p. 786-87.

586 Gen. B.F. Kelley to Maj. G.M. Bascom, Assist. Adj.-Gen., at Charleston (dated Cumberland, Nov. 19, 1862, 10.50 p.m.), O.R. XXI, p. 775.

587 [Editorial], Point Pleasant Weekly Register, November 13, 1862 Vol. 1 No. 34, [p. 2].

588 F.H. Pierpont to Col. Brown + Lt. Col. Hall of the 13 Va Regt U. S. Vol Inf. (dated "The Commonwealth of Virginia. Executive Department, Wheeling Nov. 6, 1862" RG 94 Box 4839 Misc. unbound regimental papers 13th W.Va. Letters Adj. General's Office NARA).

589 Maj. Gen. Cox, by G.M. Bascom, Major and A.A.G., Special Orders No. 41 (dated "Head Quarters District of West Va.,

Charleston, Va. 14 Nov[em]b[e]r, 1862" RG 94 Box 4838 Misc. unbound regimental papers 13th W.Va. Spec. Orders and Gen. Orders NARA).

590 Edward Siber, Col. comd. By C.A. Shepard, Lt. + A.A.A.G. to Col. W.R. Brown, "comd 13 R. Va., Vols., Pt. Pleasant, Va." (dated "Head Quarters 2 Brigade, Charleston, Va., Nov. 14, 1862"), RG 94 Box 4839 Misc. unbound regimental papers 13th W.Va. Letters Adj. General's Office, NARA.

591 Brig. Gen. George Crook, General Orders No. 1 (dated "Head Quarters 1st Kanawha Division, Charleston, Va., Nov. 15, 1862" RG 94 Box 4838 Misc. unbound regimental papers 13th W.Va. Spec. Orders and Gen. Orders NARA). Two copies of this order are preserved in this Record Group file. One copy directs that "one half of 13th at Red. House and etc." and the other saying "5 Cos. at Red. House and 5 Cos. at Point Pleasant."

592 "Attention Militia," Point Pleasant Weekly Register, November 19, 1862, [n.p.]

593 J.V. Young, Capt. Co G 13th V.V.I. to Col. J.R. Hall (dated "Hd Qrs on the Middle Fork of Mud River Two miles below Griffith-ville, Saturday Ev[eni]ng, Nov. 15, 1862" RG 94 Box 4839 Misc. unbound regimental papers 13th W.Va. Letters Adj. General's Office NARA). Jayhawkers were Union people, who used irregular warfare tactics against enemy combatants.

594 Brig. Genl. Crook, by R.P. Kennedy, Capt. and A.A.G, General Orders No. 3 (dated "Head Quarters 1st Kanawha Div., Charleston, Va., Nov. 23, 1862" RG 94 Box 4838 Misc. unbound regimental papers 13th W.Va. Spec. Orders and Gen. Orders NARA).

595 R.B. Wilson, 842 Lincoln Avenue, Toledo, O[hio], "Kanawha Division: Its Campaigns. [Part] I," The National Tribune (Washington, D.C.), February 11, 1897, p. 2.

596 Col. W.R. Brown, by W.I. Mathews, Adjutant, General Order No. 2 (dated "Head Quarters 13th Regt. Virginia Volunteer Infantry, Point Pleasant, Virginia, Nov. 24th, 1862" RG94 Order Book Co. C Regimental Books 13th Reg. Inf. Vols. NARA), [n.p.]

597 James R. Hall, Lieutenant-Colonel Commanding Detachment 13th Virginia Regiment, by E.J. B[rid]dgeman, Acting Adjt."General Order No. 2 (dated "Head Quarters Detachment 13th Va. Vols. Winfield Va Nov. 25, 1862" Civil War Scrapbook Accession # 859), Regional History Library, Colson Hall, WVU, Morgantown. Hall's order in its entirety is: "Whereas His Excellency F.H. Pierpont Governor of Virginia having issued a Proclamation recommending and setting aside Thursday the 27th instant as a day of Thanksgiving and prayer to Almighty God for his many blessings, and that this unholy Rebellion may be brought to a speedy close, and that peace and prosperity may again be restored to our once happy country — And having also enjoined it upon all the Troops constituting the Virginia Regiments to strictly observe that day — Therefore it is ordered that all duty except Guard duty be suspended that the day be in every respect duly reverenced + all the soldiers attend divine service."

598 RG94 Regimental Books (manu. "Remarks" Morning Reports Co. A 13th Reg. of Va. Vols. Army of the U.S. for the month of November 1862 NARA), [n.p.]

599 "Record of Events Field and Staff," Company Muster Rolls dated Dec. 31, 1862, micro. #594 Roll 196, NARA.

600 RG94 Regimental Books (manu. Morning Reports Co. A of the 13th Reg. of Va. Vols. Army of the U.S. for the Month of November 1862), [n.p.]

601 Col. P.P. Lane, 11th Ohio Regt. Cmdg. post at Somerville to Gen. Crook (dated Nov. 22, 1862), O.R. XXI, p. 791.

602 RG94 Regimental Books (manu. Misc. Records Descriptive Roll Co. E. 13th Regiment V.V.V.I. "Register of Deaths" NARA), [n.p.]

603 RG94 Regimental Books (manu. Morning Reports Co. A 13th Reg. of Va. Vols. Army of the U.S. and "Remarks" for the month of November 1862 NARA), [n.p.] and "Record of Events Field and Staff," Muster Roll Co. A 13th Va. Vol. Infantry (dated Dec. 31, 1862 micro. #594 Roll 196) all sources at NARA, Washington D.C.

604 Army physicals at this time were performed by a local physician and consisted of the volunteer stripping down to the skin and being examined for general physical strength and soundness. Eyesight was checked and the man asked to perform basic movements such as kicking, jumping, bending, etc.

605 For all proceeding sections describing sickness in Co. A in November 1862 see RG94 Regimental Books (manu. Morning Reports of Co. A 13th Regiment of Virginia Vols. Army of the U.S. for the month of November 1862 and "Remarks" NARA), [n.p.]

606 RG94 Regimental Books (manu. Morning Reports of Co. B 13th Reg. of Va Vols. Army of the U.S. for the month of November 1862 and "Remarks" NARA), [n.p.]
607 RG94 Regimental Books (manu. Morning Reports of Co. C 13th Reg of Va. Vols. Army of the U.S. for the month of November 1862 NARA), [n.p.]
608 RG94 Regimental Books (manu. Morning Reports of Co. D 13th Regiment of Virginia Vols. Army of the U.S. for the month of November 1862 NARA), [n.p.]
609 RG94 Regimental Books (manu. Morning Reports Co. F 13th Reg. of Va. Vols. Army of the U.S. for the month of November 1862 and "Remarks" NARA), [n.p.]
610 RG94 Regimental Books (manu. Morning Reports Co. H 13th Reg. of Va. Vols. Army of the U.S. for the month of November 1862 and "Remarks" NARA), [n.p.]

Rumors of Rebels in Logan County

611 All quotations in this paragraph from Maj.-Gen. John B. Floyd to Governor of Virginia John Letcher (dated "Hd. Qtrs. Va. State Line. Camp Clarkson, Tazewell County, Va., Dec. 17, 1862"), O.R. XXI, pp. 1065-66.
612 Maj. Gen. Cox, by G.M. Bascom Major and Asst. Adj. General to Gen. Crook, at Gauley (dated Hd. Qtrs. Charleston Nov. 28, 1862), O.R. XXI, p. 808.
613 Brig.-Gen. George Crook, by R.P. Kennedy, Captain and Assist. Adjt.-Gen. to Lieut. Col. J.R. Hall, Thirteenth Virginia, Red House (dated "Charleston, Va. November 28, 1862"), O.R. Ser. 1 Vol. LI Part I, Supp., p. 951.
614 Maj. and Asst. Adj. Gen. G.M. Bascom to Col. J.L. Zeigler (dated Charleston, Nov. 28, 1862), O.R. XXI, p. 809.
615 Patrick H. Caldwell to his father, Robert Caldwell (manu. dated "Winfield Putnam County Va November the 29th 1862"), Patrick H. Caldwell Military Pension file, NARA.
616 William E. Feazel to Adj. Gen. of Va., H.J. Samuels (manu dated "Point Pleasant, V[irgini]a, Nov[ember] 30th 1862" WVSA).
617 Wm E Feazel, 2nd Lieut., 13th Va Vol Inftry to H.J. Samuels (manu. dated "Dec. 7, 1862 WVSA).
618 Lt. Col J.R. Hall to Gov. F.H. Pierpont, at Wheeling (telegraph dated "13th Virginia, Camp Piatt, V[irgini]a, Dec[ember] 16, 1862"), Calendar of Pierpont Letters and Papers, p. 226.

December 1862

619 E.P. Scammon was a native of Maine. He graduated 9th in West Point class of 1837 and remained at West Point for a year after graduation serving as Assistant Professor of Mathematics. Due to his ranking and talent, he was selected as one of the original set of officers appointed to the newly created U.S. Army Corps of Topographic Engineers (created in 1838). He served in Seminole Wars and Mexican American War. In 1856, however, he was dismissed from the service for using bad language and disobeying an order. Thereafter, he moved to Ohio and became Professor of Mathematics at Mount Saint Mary's College; then President and Professor of Mathematics at the Polytechnic College of the Catholic Institute at Cincinnati. At the outbreak of the Civil War, he offered his services to Ohio Governor, William Dennison and was appointed Colonel of the 23rd Ohio Volunteer Infantry Regiment. He commanded the 1st Brigade Kanawha Division during the Maryland Campaign of 1862 and fought at Antietam. For his services he was promoted to brigadier general of volunteers in October 1862. Scammon was considered a spit-and-polish kind of officer—extreme in terms of discipline and with a large ego. Not the kind of personality that endeared him to a command made up largely of farmers and day laborers with some smattering of professional men. Scammon was captured by partisan guerrillas on the night of February 3rd, 1864, from off the B.C. Levi, a steamer docked for the night at Red House Shoals and after being exchanged, did not return to West Virginia.
620 J.D. Cox, Maj.-Gen., cmdg. to Gov. Francis H Pierpont (dated Hd. Qtrs. District of Western Va, Marietta, Ohio, Dec. 15, 1862), O.R. XXI, pp. 857-58.

621 Maj. Gen. Cox, by G.M. Bascom, Maj. and A.A.G., General Order No.7 (manu.dated "Head Quarters District of Western Va., Marietta, Ohio, Dec. 11th, [18]62" RG 94 Box 4838 Misc. unbound regimental papers 13th W.Va. Special Orders and General Orders NARA).

622 [Untitled], reprint from the Gallipolis Journal in the Point Pleasant Weekly Register, December 25, 1862, [p. 1].

623 Governor Francis H. Pierpont, "Message to the State Senate and House of Representatives," Point Pleasant Weekly Register, December 18, 1862, [pp. 1 and 4].

624 "Record of Events Field and Staff," Co. A Muster Roll (dated Dec. 31, 1862), micro. #594 Roll 196, NARA.

625 "Seldom," pseud., writing in praise of the Home Guards or State Troops, in the Kanawha region, particularly in support of those under command of Capt. Rucker "operating in the frontier of Putnam and Mason counties." ("Seldom," "Home Guards," Wheeling Daily Intelligencer reprinted in the Point Pleasant Weekly Register, September 24, 1863, [n.p.])

626 "Terrible Death and Horrible Outrage" reprinted from the Wheeling Daily Intelligencer in the Point Pleasant Weekly Register, December 11, 1862, [n.p.]

627 "Mark Time," pseud., Gallipolis Journal, December 4, 1862, p. 3.

628 For the foregoing quotations as to the lamentable state of affairs in Cabell County, F.H. Pierpont to Gen. Cox, at Kanawha C.H. Virginia (manu. dated "The Commonwealth of Virginia, Executive Department, Wheeling Dec[embe]r. 5 1862" RG 94 Box 4839 Misc. unbound regimental papers 13th W.Va. Letters Adj. General's Office NARA).

629 Ibid.

630 [Untitled backpage newsbrief], Point Pleasant Weekly Register, December 18, 1862 Vol. 1 No. 39, [p. 4].

631 Thomas Hayslip, Postal worker at Guyandotte, Cabell County, Va. to Adt. Gen. H.J. Samuels, at Wheeling (dated "December 19, 1862"), Calendar of Pierpont Letters and Papers, p. 228.

632 Horton and Teverbaugh, A History of the Eleventh Regiment, p. 262.

633 J.Q. Howard, The Life Public Services and Select Speeches of Rutherford B. Hayes (Cincinnati: Robert Clark & Co, 1876), p. 37.

634 Ibid., Horton & Teverbaugh, 1866, p. 262.

635 James R. Hall, Lt. Col. 13th Va. Vol. Infty to Col. W[illia]m R. Brown, comdg 13th Va Vols. (manu. dated "Head Quarters Detachment 13th Va. V. Winfield Va Dec. 11, 1862" RG 94 Box 4839 Misc. unbound regimental papers 13th W.Va. Letters Adj. General's Office NARA).

636 Ibid.

637 Reprinted from the Gallipolis Journal in the Point Pleasant Weekly Register, December 25, 1862, [p. 1].

638 F.H. Pierpont to Gen. Cox, at Charleston, Virginia (manu. dated "The Commonwealth of Virginia. Executive Department, Wheeling. Dec[embe]r. 4 1862." RG94 Miscellaneous Department of W.Va. Papers NARA). The court house as well as the churches of the town and vacant store rooms had been used by the military for quarters, etc., since the first year of the war.

639 Brig. Gen. George Crook to [Gen. Cox?] (manu. dated "Head Quarters 1st Kanawha Division, Charleston, Virginia, December 19, 1862" RG 94 Box 4839 Misc. unbound regimental papers 13th W.Va. Letters Adj. General's Office NARA).

Morning Reports submitted for the 13th Virginia Volunteers for December 1862

640 There is some discrepancy in regimental records. The Descriptive Roll for Co. B records that Vincent Rice was discharged at Point Pleasant, on February 8th, 1863 by order of Maj. Gen. H.G. Wright. See RG94 Regimental Books (manu. Misc. Records Descriptive Roll Co. B. 13th Regiment V.V.V.I. NARA), [n.p.]

641 West Virginia Clothing Books Companies E, F, G 13th Infantry (manu. WVSA), [n.p.].

642 Albert Ray Military Pension file, NARA. The soldier was diagnosed had orchitis. This occurs in about a quarter of men, who contract mumps after puberty. Dr. Samuel G. Shaw, who treated Ray, was regimental surgeon for the 13th Virginia; his commission as surgeon dated to August 22, 1862. Shaw was by no means a young man, being born in the first decade of the 19th century; likely not fit for duty in the field and he resigned his commission on September 29, 1863. He had his

residence, private hospital and apothecary near the Point (the confluence of the Ohio and Kanawha) on Main Street, Point Pleasant. Dr. Shaw, recalled one denizen, "resided in a brick house that stood for many years, where the A.F. Kiser residence is now built. He first had his office and conducted a drug store on Front street [as in Waterfront, facing the Ohio], between 1st and 2nd, and later built a frame office at the corner of 3rd and Main Streets, which gave place later to the Kiser Jewelry store." ("Looking Backward Eighty Years. Reminiscences As Gleaned from Mr. Hiram H. Swallow and others Who Remembers the Best of this Locality Article I," The State Gazette, Point Pleasant, W. Va., July 29, 1909, in History of Mason County, W. Va. Accession # 203668, Call # RL 975.433H, Huntington Public Library, [p. 3].) In support of Tippett's start-up of the Weekly Register, Shaw bought a year's advertisement which carried the following information: "Dr. S.G. Shaw. Physician and Surgeon, Tenders his professional services to the public. Calls from the country promptly attended to. Office on Front Street adjoining the "Virginia House. Feb. 27, 1862 – 1 y." (Point Pleasant Weekly Register, Thursday Morning, April 16, 1863 Vol. II No. 5, [p.1]). In the last year of the war "Dr. Samuel Shaw, of this place [Point Pleasant], [wa] s commissioned by the Secretary of War, as Examining Surgeon of the Board of Enrollment for this (3d) Congressional District. The appointment is a good one[…]." ("A Good Appointment," Point Pleasant Weekly Register, February 9, 1865, [p. 2].) In Adams' Doctors in Blue, Shaw was listed as an "allopath," who practiced in West Virginia. In 1881 when West Virginia started licensing its doctors, Shaw was licensed. See George Worthington Adams, Doctors in Blue. The Medical History of the Union Army in the Civil War (Baton Rouge and London: Louisiana State Univ. Press, 1952), p. 1398.

643 West Virginia Clothing Books Cos. H and I 13th Infantry (manu. WVSA), [n.p.]

644 Brig. Gen. George Crook, by Major G. M. Bascam, A.A. General to unknown addressee (manu. dated "Head Quarters 1st Kanawha Division, Charleston, Virginia, December 6th, 1862" RG94 Misc. Dept. of W.Va. Papers Box NARA).

645 "Muster-In Roll of a Detachment of Recruits for the 13th Regiment of Virginia Infantry Volunteers commanded by Colonel William R. Brown called into the service of the United States by the President from the 11th day of December 1862—date of this muster—for the term of Three Years unless sooner discharged," Uncat. 13th W.Va. Inf. Reg. Box, WVSA.

646 Col. W.R. Brown, by W.I. Mathews, Adj., General Order No. 3 (manu. dated "Head Quarters 13th Regiment Virginia Volunteer Infantry, Point Pleasant, December 8th, 186[2]" RG94 Order Book Co. C Regimental Books 13th Va. Reg. Inf. Vols. NARA), [n.p.]

647 See for this assignment, in multiple volumes of pretty stiff reading: United States Infantry Tactics for the Instruction, Exercise, and Manoevres of the United States Infantry Including Infantry of the line, Light Infantry, and Riflemen. Prepared under Direction of the War Department and Authorized and Adopted by the Secretary of War May, 1, 1861.

648 Maj. Gen. Cox, by G.M. Bascam, Maj. and A.A.A.G, Special Orders No. 162 (manu. dated "Head Quarters District of Western Va., Marietta Ohio, Dec. 16, 1862" RG 94 Box 4838 Misc. unbound regimental papers 13th W.Va. Spec. Orders and Gen. Orders NARA).

649 Ernst Schach, Major and Provost Marshal to Col. W.R. Brown (manu. dated "Office of Provost Marshal, Charleston, Va., Dec. 19, [18]62" RG 94 Box 4838 13th W.Va. Receipts Prisoners of War in Misc. unbound regimental papers 13th W.Va. Spec. Orders and Gen. Orders NARA).

650 Capt. F. Smith, comdg "Ind[e]p[enden]t Ohio Vol Cav Comp." (manu. dated "Head Quarters Dist. of West Va, Marietta O[hio], Dec. 25, 1862" RG 94 Box 4838 13th W.Va. Receipts Prisoners of War in Misc. unbound regimental papers 13th W.Va. Spec. Orders and Gen. Orders NARA).

651 Point Pleasant Weekly Register, December 25, 1862 and "T.," "Served Him Right," Point Pleasant Weekly Register, January 1, 1863 Vol. I, No. 41, [p. 1].

652 Point Pleasant Weekly Registers of December 25, 1862 and January 1, 1863 Vol. I No. 41, [p. 1].

653 G.S. Guthrie to H.J. Samuels (manu. dated "Pomeroy Dec. 22, 1862"), Letters to Samuels and Pierpont Box 2 Folder 11, WVSA.

654 Lt. Col. James R. Hall to his Mother (manu. dated "Winfield, Virginia, December 28, 1862"), courtesy of William B. Matthews of Huntington, W.Va., attorney and descendant of John Hall, Sr., through one of his daughters.)

655 Brig. Genl Crook to Col. Brown (manu. dated "Hd Qtrs. 1st Kanawha Div., Charleston, Va., Dec. 30, 1862" RG 94 Box 4839 Misc. unbound regimental papers 13th W.Va. Letters Adj. General's Office NARA).

656 Point Pleasant Register, Dec. 4, 1862, [n.p.]

657 Point Pleasant Weekly Register. Dec. 11, 1862, [p. 2].

658 Point Pleasant Register, Dec. 4, 1862, [n.p.]

659 "Important to Volunteers," Point Pleasant Weekly Register, December 11, 1862, Vol. 1 No. 38, [p. 2].

660 Governor Francis H. Pierpont, "Message to the State Senate and House of Representatives," Point Pleasant Weekly Register, December 18, 1862, [pp. 1 and 4].

661 Cox to Maj. N.H. McLean, Chief of Staff (dated Marietta, Dec. 13, 1862), O.R. XXI, p. 849.

662 Wright to Halleck (dated Cincinnati, Dec. 13, 1862), O.R. XXI, p. 849.

663 Cox to Maj. N.H. McLean, Chief of Staff (dated Marietta, Dec. 13, 1862), O.R. XXI, p. 849.

664 Brig.-Gen. Crook to Maj.-Gen. Cox (dated Charleston, [W. Va.] Dec. 13, 1862), O.R. XXI, pp. 852-53.

665 Wright to Halleck (dated Cincinnati, Dec. 13, 1862), O.R. XXI, p. 849.

666 Halleck to Wright (dated Dec. 14, 1862), O.R. XXI, p. 854.

667 J.D. Cox, Maj.-Gen.l, cmdg to Gov. Francis H Pierpont (dated Hd. Qtrs. District of Western Va, Marietta, Ohio, Dec. 15, 1862), O.R. XXI, p. 857-58.

668 Cox to Pierpont (dated Hd. Qtrs. Distict of Western Va, Marietta, Ohio, Dec. 15, 1862), O.R. XXI, pp. 857-58.

669 Cox to Leonard (dated Hd. Qtrs. District of Western Va., Marietta, Ohio, Dec. 23, 1862), O.R. XXI, pp. 880 – 81.

670 Ibid.

671 Col. Baubauk, by And. C Kemper A.A.G., Special Orders, No. 61 (manu. dated "Head Quarters Military Command Cincinnati, Ohio, Cincinnati Dec. 27, 1862" RG 94 Box 4838 Misc. unbound regimental papers 13th W.Va. Spec. Orders and Gen. Orders NARA).

672 William R. Brown, Col. comdg. to R.P. Kennedy, Capt. and A.A.G. (manu. dated "Head Quarters 13th Regt Va., Point Pleasant, Va., Dec. 27, 1862) RG 94 Box 4839 Misc. unbound regimental papers 13th W.Va. Letters Adj. General's Office NARA).

673 William M. Crook, Co. H, 13th [West] Virginia Infantry Regiment.

674 Orig. manuscripts in Demarcus Ward Military Pension file, NARA.

675 "Abstract from return of the Department of the Ohio, Maj. Gen. H. G. Wright commanding, for the month of December, 1862; headquarters Cincinnati, Ohio," O.R. Vol. XX, Part II, pp. 287 and 289.

676 One wonders if included in this tally of artillery pieces were the two Napoleon guns which had been in position at Point Pleasant. Charles Cameron Lewis's father had been in charge of them and in 1861, had them shipped to Charleston, to be forwarded to Richmond, before Federal forces crossed over to Point Pleasant. See The State Gazette in Poffenbarger Papers, Vol. 4, p. 71, Mason Co. Pub. Lib.

677 "Abstract from return of the District of West Virginia, Maj. Gen. Jacob D. Cox, U.S. Army, cmdg., for December 31, 1862, Headquarters at Marietta, Ohio," O.R. XXI, p. 940.

678 "Annual Return of Alterations and Casualties incident to the Thirteenth Regt. of Va. Vol. Inf., Commanded by Col. Wm. R. Brown during the year 1862" (manu. RG 94 Box 4838 Annual Returns of Casualties 3 Misc. unbound regimental papers 13th W.Va.,NARA).

679 Brig.-Gen. George Crook to Maj. Gen Cox (dated Hd. Qtrs. First Kanawha Division, Charleston, W. Va., Dec. 29, 1862), O.R. XXI, p. 899.

680 R.B. Wilson, "Kanawha Division: Its Campaigns. [Part] I-continued," The National Tribune (Washington, D.C.), February 18, 1897, pp. [1]-2.

681 Evelyn Abraham Benson, comp., "The Dark and Fruitless Winter of '62-3," With the Army of West Virginia. Reminiscences & Letters of Lt. James Abraham Pennsylvania Dragoons Company A First Regiment, Virginia Cavalry (Publication No. 1 of the Abraham Archives, Evelyn A. Benson, Lancaster, Pa., 1974), [n.p.]

682 H[arrison] G[ray] O[tis], editor, "Personal Recollections of the War—No. III," Santa Barbara Daily Press, Saturday Evening, October 28, 1876, courtesy of Darl Stephenson.

Appendix
"Who Are Exempt From the Draft"

683 "Looking Backward Eighty Years. Reminiscences As Gleaned from Mr. Hiram H. Swallow and others Who Remembers the Past of this Locality. Article II," The State Gazette (Point Pleasant, W.Va.), August 5, 1909, preserved in History of Mason County, W.Va., Huntington Public Library.

684 Ibid.

685 His condition was at this point in time much improved and he and his family entertained the hope that a cure had been effected. (James R. Hall to Col. F.H. Smith, Superintendent of the Virginia Military Institute (manu. dated "Point Pleasant, Virginia March 13th, 1861") VMI Archives, Lexington, Va.

686 Although it had long been desired, it was only after severance from Virginia was completed with admission into the Union as the 35th State that West Virginia could provide by law to have free or public schools. The act authorizing public funds to pay for free schools was passed in November 1863. In Mason County for one, by early August, 1864, the fund was in place to pay a teacher's salary till the end of 1864 or later, when the "remaining expenses can be canceled when the State funds are distributed, April 1st." ("Free Schools," Point Pleasant Weekly Register Sept. 1, 1864, Vol. III No. 21.) In Cologne Township (late Lemaster Township), the Board of Education in meeting held Saturday, Aug. 27, 1864, resolved to levy a tax of "five cents on the hundred dollars taxable value on all property in the township for the erection of a school and also to levy 5 cents on the hundred dollars for a school fund" as allowed by law of the November 1863 Act. (Point Pleasant Weekly Register, Sept. 8, 1864 Vol. III No. 22.)

687 "Synopsis of the Course of Studies at the Va. Mil. Institute" (School year 1856 VMI Archives Lexington), p. 14.

688 John Hall to Col. F. Smith (manu. dated "Point Pleasant, May 15th, 1856" VMI Archives).

689 Hall to Smith (manu. dated "Point Pleasant, October 24th, 1856" VMI Archives).

690 Hall to Smith (manu. dated "Point Pleasant, May 15th, 1856" VMI Archives).

691 Hall, James Robert, "Card," VMI Archives.

692 Hall to Smith (manu. dated "Point Pleasant, Va., Tuesday July 12th, 1859" Letter 342 VMI Archives).

693 Hall, John Taylor, "Card," VMI Archives.

694 Edward A. Miller, Jr., made a tally and noted that the Halls were two out of a meager 8 per cent who had both worn the V.M.I. cadet uniform and Union blue. An impressive 92% of cadets wore Confederate grey. The Hall brothers were two out of just 13 V.M.I. students that certainly joined Federal service. See Miller, "VMI Men Who Wore Yankee Blue, 1861-1865," VMI Alumni Review, Spring 1996, p. 2.

695 Colonel R.B. Hayes to Honorable John Hall (dated "Headqtrs 2d Div. Army of W.V., Cedar Creek, Va., Oct. 22, 1864"), published as "A High Tribute To The Late Lieut. Col. James R. Hall" in the Point Pleasant Weekly Register, November 10, 1864, [p. 3]; the Mason County Journal Nov. 25, 1864; and as "A High Tribute to the Late Lieut. Col. James R. Hall" in The Ironton Register Dec. 29, 1864, [p. 1].

13th Regiment Infantry Volunteers Officers and Men

696 This seems not to have been unusual. If one accepts Virgil A. Lewis' numbers that very roughly speaking that West Virginia furnished upwards of 30,000 soldiers to the Union (Lewis, Soldiery of West Virginia, Baltimore reprint, 1972, p. 206) compare with Annual Report of the Adjutant General of the State of West Virginia, for the year ending December 31, 1865 (Wheeling: John Frew, Public Printer, 1866, p. 10) which indicates that since the start of the war "only two hundred and fifty-seven men" had been drafted and just "seventy-three substitutes ha[d] been furnished" making the percent of draftees and substitutes to total number of volunteers only about one percent.

697 See Kenneth W. Munden, and Henry Putney Beers, Guide to Federal Archives Relating to the Civil War (Washington: The National Archives and Records Service General Services Administration, 1962), p. 253-.

698 William R. Brown, cmdg, 13th Regiment Virginia Volunteer Infantry to Th. Melvin,

Captain and A[ssistant] A[djutant] G[eneral] (dated "Head Quarters 13th Regt. V.V.I. Barboursville Nov 27th 1863"), NARA, Washington D. C.

699 Some counties were too poor, too sparsely populated and too far interior to have been in position to raise bounties for volunteers who went into the 13th or if they did raise bounties for their volunteers pursuant to Lincoln's latest call, they submitted no statements informing the newly restored State Government at Wheeling. This seems to have been the case for Wayne and Putnam Counties. For a comparison of bounties raised by West Virginia counties see Virgil A. Lewis, *Third Biennial Report Of the Department of Archives and History of the State of West Virginia* (Charleston: The News-Mail Company, 1911), p. 207.

700 In August 1864, there was talk of again offering a county bounty as Mason Countians who enlisted with regiments raised in other counties under the War Department's various calls for volunteers were credited to that county and not to Mason. See the editorial column of the Point Pleasant Weekly Register under title "Bounty" (August 18, 1864, Vol. III No. 19, [n.p.]) in which complaint is made that when Mason County men enlisted in other counties those counties received credit for Mason's volunteers against that county's obligation to supply a certain quota or be subject to conscription (draft). The editor suggested that the Chairman of the Board of Supervisors call the Board together for a meeting "to provide such bounty as will induce Mason county volunteers, to enlist in this county instead of elsewhere."

701 Point Pleasant Weekly Register July 28, 1864, Vol. III No. 17, [n.p.]

702 Fragment of a telegraph message sent to Hd. Qtrs. 13th Regt. W.V.I. dated probably 1864 in RG 94 Box 4838 Miscellaneous unbound regimental papers 13th West Virginia Telegrams, NARA.

703 Point Pleasant Weekly Register, Apr. 21, 1864, Vol. III No. 4, [n. p.]

704 John L. Mason, "A Reminiscence. West Columbia of a Half Century Ago Contrasted With the West Columbia of Today. Second Letter to the State Gazette, Point Pleasant, W.Va., June 24, 1909," in History of Mason County, W.Va. (Accession # 203668 Call # RL035.433H.). Cabell County Public Library, Huntington.

705 At the start of the war each regiment had its own brass band but by July 1862, when the 13th Virginia was being recruited, the War Department had done away with the regimental band in volunteer units with General Order No. 91. One can only imagine the cacophony that might have prompted this change. Instead, one band, limited to not more than 16 players was allowed per brigade. Union army regulations, however, permitted each infantry company to have two field musicians, i.e., a drummer and fifer. Company drummers and fifers in turn, made up the drum corps of the regiment. This latter seems to have been the model in the 13th, where "musicians" were either drummers or fifers led by a Drum Major (Hazard Farley beginning September 1862 and Samuel D. Hanna in July 1863). See Robert Garofalo and Mark Elrod, A Pictorial History of Civil War Era Musical Instruments and Military Bands (Charleston, W.Va.: Pictorial Histories Publishing Co.), p. 56.

706 Orville J. Victor, ed., Incidents and Anecdotes of the War (New York: James D. Torrey, 1862), p. 389 and Edmund C. Stedman and Ellen M. Hutchinson, eds., A Library of American Literature (New York: Charles L. Webster & Co.), 1891.

707 See a transcription of this document in Poffenbarger Papers Vol. 5, p. 56, Mason County Public Library, Point Pleasant, West Virginia.

708 Munden, Kenneth W. and Henry Putney Beers. Guide to Federal Archives Relating to the Civil War. Washington: The National Archives and Records Service General Services Administration, 1962, p. 344.

709 Raymond L. Barnette, "Preston Barnett," Jackson County West Virginia Past and Present (Waynesville, NC: Don Mills, Inc., 1990), p. 109.

710 "Mason County Cologne District. Samuel Barnett", H.H. Hardesty, Hardesty's Historical and Geographical Encyclopedia [...] containing a special history of the Virginias, outline of maps and histories of Mason and Putnam Counties, West Virginia Vol. 5 (Chicago: H. H. Hardesty, 1883), pp. 125-126.

711 RG94 Miscellaneous Records Descriptive Roll Co. D, 13th Regt. W.V.V.I., NARA, [n. p.] and email from John Dawson, referencing soldier's military pension file (correspondence dated April 26, 1998).

712 See Muster Roll Co. F (recording date of enlistment, receipt or non-receipt of Mason Co. Bounty), Records of Mason County Soldiers #1541 (unpub. manu. W.Va. Regional History Library and Archives at Colson Hall, WVU, Morgantown.

713 Kanawha County West Virginia State Troops, Militia West Virginia (micro.), West Va. State Archives, Charleston.

714 RG94 Morning Reports of Captain William Feazle's Company I of the 13th Regiment of Virginia Volunteers Army of the United States, Colonel William R. Brown for the Month of March 1863, NARA.

715 [S. Comstock advertisement for Eagle Mills], Point Pleasant Weekly Register, March 6, 1862 Vol.1 No. 1, [p.1].

716 See a three week advertisement taken out March 24, 1862, to reclaim a large flat boat found adrift in the Kanawha River. "We, Stephen Comstock, John W. Deem and Wm. E. Wetzel, three free holders of said County [Mason], do hereby certify on our oaths, reviewed and appraised a flat boat one hundred and thirty-two feet four inches long and twenty-one feet wide with poplar gunwales and poplar bottom [...] supposed to be about one year old." Point Pleasant Weekly Register, March 27, 1862, [p.3].

717 William H. Cyrus to Adjutant General of State of West Virginia (dated "July 10, 1865, Fort Ridgeby, Missota"), Uncata-logued 13th West Virginia Infantry Box, WVSA.

718 Soldier reported "deserted on "October 11" in RG94 Regimental Books (manu. "Remarks for the Month of October 1862" Morning Reports of McCown's Co. F 13th Regiment of Virginia Vols. Army of the U.S. NARA), [n.p.]

719 R.B. Hayes, Col. Comdg to Col. W.R. Brown, 13th Va. Vols. (manu. dated "Hd Qtrs. 1st Brigade, 3d Div., 8th Army Corps, Dec. 24, 1863" RG 94 Box 4839 Misc. unbound regimental papers 13th W.Va. Letters Adjutant General's Office NARA).

720 F. Pierpont, Adjutant General State of W. Va., Annual Report of the Adjutant General of the State of West Virginia for the Year Ending December 31, 1865, p. 109.

721 Hardesty's Vol. 5 "W.C. Greenlee", p. 127.

722 R.B. Hayes, Col. Comdg to Col. W.R. Brown, 13th Va. Vols. (manu. dated "Hd Qtrs. 1st Brigade, 3d Div., 8th Army Corps, Dec. 24, 1863" RG 94 Box 4839 Misc. unbound regimental papers 13th W.Va. Letters Adjutant General's Office NARA).

723 Muster-In Roll of "Detachment of Recruits for the 13th Regiment of Virginia Infantry Volunteers commanded by Colonel William R. Brown called into the service of the United States by the President from the 11th day of December 1862, (date of this muster,) for the term of three years unless sooner discharged" Uncat. 13th W.Va. Infantry Box, WVSA.

724 Family histories contained in History of Mason Co., W. Va. 1987 record that Hyatt the 13th Va. soldier was born Novem-ber 18, 1819 in Washington County, Ohio, see pp. 164-165.

725 Case of Albert C. Jamison on Writ of Habeas Corpus, transcription in RG94 Regimental Books 13th Regiment of Virginia Volunteers Order Book Company C, NARA, [n.p.]

726 RG94 Morning Reports of McCown's Company F 13th Regiment of Virginia Volunteers Army of the U.S. for the month of October 1862, NARA), [n.p.]

727 Obituary, "Capt. V. [D]. McDaniel," Point Pleasant Weekly Register, October 1, 1863, [p. 2].

728 George Rucker, manu. MS 94-45 Rucker Family, WVSA.

729 Oley to Pierpont (manu. dated "Hd. Qtrs. Kanawha Valley forces Charleston W. Va. July 14, 1864") and Special Order No. 21 (manu. dated "Hd. Qtrs. Army of the Kanawha, July 9, 1864") both in Uncat. 13th W. Va. Box, WVSA.

730 Herbert D. Sayre and Audrey Sayre Hartley, "J. J. and Ella M. Cozant Sayre," Jackson County West Virginia Past and Present (Waynesville, NC: Don Mills, Inc., 1990), p. 413.

731 Paul Schools, "Affidavit" in John W. Gibbs Company G 13th Regiment W.V.V.I. Military Pension file, NARA.

732 Co. G Enlisted Men. 13th Regiment Infantry, "Roster of the Regiment" (micro. WVSA), [p. 38] and "Thirteenth Regiment Infantry; and List of deaths, discharges, and desertions in the Thirteenth Regiment West Va Inf Vols, from the date of original organization to the date of muster out, on 22d day of June, 1865. Compiled from muster-out rolls" in F. Peirpoint, Adj. Gen. State of W.Va., Annual Report of the Adjutant General of the State of West Virginia for the Year Ending December 31, 1865, p. 206.

733 "J.T B.," letter of authority (manu. dated "June 27, 1863"), Uncat. 13th W.Va. Infantry Box, WVSA.

734 William H. Bishop, Roane County, West Virginia Families (Baltimore, Maryland: Genealogical Publishing Co., 1995), pp. 673-675.

735 James P. Matthew, Lieutenant and Acting Regimental Quarter Master for the 3rd Virginia Cavalry to Governor Arthur I. Boreman (manu. dated "Point Pleasant, [Virginia] April 29, 1864"), Papers of Governor A.I. Boreman, WVSA.

Index